The Course of
Modern Jewish History

Updated and Expanded Edition

HOWARD MORLEY SACHAR

The Course of
Modern Jewish History

Updated and Expanded Edition

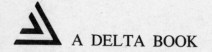 A DELTA BOOK

A DELTA BOOK

Published by
DELL PUBLISHING CO., INC.
1 Dag Hammarskjold Plaza
New York, New York 10017

Dell books are available at discounts in quantity lots for sales
promotion, industrial or fund raising use. Special books can also
be created by Dell for the specific needs of any business.

For details contact the Special Marketing Division, Dell Publishing
Co., Inc., 1 Dag Hammarskjold Plaza, New York, N.Y. 10017

Contents

Contents

Contents

Contents

Contents

Contents

Contents

Contents

MAPS

Preface

Fortunately for the modernist, the task of writing a history of the Jews since the French Revolution has been greatly facilitated by the enormous quantities of detailed historical studies published during the past thirty years. Those studies have included many hundreds of books, among them exhaustive and authoritative multivolume histories by Dubnow in Poland, Elbogen in Germany, Klausner in Israel, and Baron in the United States. They have embraced thousands, even tens of thousands, of monographs, in a wide variety of scholarly journals in Europe, Israel, and the United States. One need only glance, as an example, through the pages of one American-Jewish periodical, *Jewish Social Studies,* to appreciate the scrupulous and imaginative research that has characterized the majority of these writings. Indeed, if there is any single difficulty the reader encounters as he turns to the study of modern Jewish history, it arises not from a paucity of material, but rather from an *embarras des richesses*. And it is this factor, the sheer quantity of monographic information, which has suggested the possible usefulness of a one-volume work, a distillation of some of the basic research of the last few decades. In preparing this brief survey, I have attempted primarily to synthesize and, whenever possible, to place in perspective for the general reader the basic information accumulated by modern scholarship. For those who would probe further into the many forces and issues that have animated Jewish life in modern times, a bibliography has been prepared which should adequately cover their needs.

It is hardly necessary to add that Jewish history cannot be understood without an evaluation of the influence of non-Jewish factors. This is true of every phase of Jewish civilization; but nowhere, surely, is it more transparently evident than of the modern period. For the very existence of a genuinely modern Jewish civilization is due, almost entirely, to the impact of non-Jewish political, economic, and cultural influences. It is well known, for example, that until the eighteenth century Jews still lived very much as they had lived in medieval days: locked off in a hermetic and backward ghetto world. Modern European capitalism, mercantilism, and rationalism were

19

directly responsible for battering down the walls of that ghetto, emancipating the Jews physically, politically, and intellectually, and enabling them to move into the bright sunlight of nineteenth-century civilization. The growth of industrialism and romanticism wrested back and consolidated Jewish freedom in the decades following the Congress of Vienna, and effected, as well, significant changes in Jewish religious beliefs and practices. The triumph of the European nation-state was of the most fundamental importance in awakening Jewish nationalism; while European diplomatic considerations were crucial in implementing the vision of the Jewish National Home. Of course, the process worked both ways. The historic circumstances of Jewish life—Jewish internationalism, Jewish financial experience, the Jewish intellectual tradition—were no less important in influencing the direction of European economic and cultural activity. They were also the circumstances that accounted for the peculiar interrelationship between anti-Semitism and modern totalitarianism.

If this book possesses any interpretive value, it will be found, I think, in the effort I have made to demonstrate the interaction between these Jewish and non-Jewish factors. Virtually all the research of recent decades has illuminated this interaction. But it has been my opportunity, as it has been the opportunity of others who are now writing in this area, to be able to discuss it from a natural chronological vantage point: a decade after the decimation of European Jewry, the "coming of age" of American Jewry, and the rise of the State of Israel. These developments are of such watershed importance in modern Jewish history that their use as a frame of reference seems to me both logical and inescapable.

In the preparation of this volume I have indebted myself to a number of authorities who were kind enough to offer suggestions in the areas of their specialization. My thanks go to Professor Eli Sobel of the University of California at Los Angeles for his helpful comments on the German-Jewish literary tradition; to Mr. Marvin Lowenthal of Brandeis University for his most learned and detailed criticisms of the chapters on Western Europe. I am grateful to Professors Nahum Glatzer and Joseph Cheskis of Brandeis University for their patient evaluation of the chapters on Eastern Europe; and to Professor Paul Alexander, also of Brandeis University, for his comments on the Nazi epoch. Professor William Haber of the University of Michigan gave most generously of his time to discuss the chapters on Jewish economic life; while Dr. James S. Grotstein of the Medical School of the University of California at Los Angeles offered many valued suggestions on the psychology of totalitarianism.

My thanks to Dr. Abram Vossen Goodman of Temple Sinai, Lawrence, Long Island, for his penetrating comments on the chapters dealing with America. Mr. Harry Lang, formerly Labor Editor of the *Jewish Daily Forward,* and his wife, Lucy Robbins Lang, offered many vital insights into the American-Jewish labor movement. Lt. Col. Netanel Lorch, formerly Chief Historian of the Army of Israel, and Professor Marie Syrkin of Brandeis University were exceptionally helpful in evaluating the chapters on Zionism, Palestine, and Israel.

I am indebted to Miss Esther Euler, Director of the Office of Inter-Library Loans at the University of California at Los Angeles, for her willing assistance in securing volumes from libraries throughout the country. I am equally grateful to Mr. Herbert Zaffren, Administrator of the Library of the Hebrew Union College-Jewish Institute of Religion; to Rabbi Rudolf Lupo of the Los Angeles Jewish Community Council Library, and to his associate, Mr. S. Brisman, for their many kindnesses on my behalf. Those thanks are extended, too, to Rabbi William Kramer, Temple Israel, Los Angeles, for his generosity—and trustfulness—in lending me volumes from his extensive private library. My brother, David B. Sachar, rendered invaluable assistance in the preparation of the bibliography; while my secretary, Mrs. Violet Waldman, gave to the long and arduous task of transcription a devotion which was above and beyond the call of duty.

My gratitude is greatest of all to Dr. Abram Leon Sachar for his detailed and patient evaluation of the entire manuscript; there is not a chapter in this work which has not benefited from his wisdom as a scholar, his experience as a leader in Jewish life, and his endless devotion as a father.

For the uses to which this accumulated data has been put I alone, of course, am responsible.

H. M. S.

Haifa
October 28, 1957

The Course of
Modern Jewish History

Updated and Expanded Edition

I

The Jew as Non-European

In the eighteenth century a majestic silhouette of spires and battlements greeted the traveler who made his way down the valley of the lower Main River in southwestern Germany. It was the silhouette of Frankfurt, one of the four remaining free cities of the Holy Roman Empire, and one of Germany's most important commercial entrepôts. Frankfurt's cobblestoned streets teemed with activity—shouting hucksters, bawling cattle driven in for slaughter, rattling vegetable barrows pushed along to market, paunchy burghers and weather-lined farmers arguing the cost and quality of merchandise and produce. No one could fail to be impressed by the well-being, the air of good-fellowship that seemed, for the most part, to characterize Frankfurt's citizenry. But as the traveler continued down the long business thoroughfare, turning from time to time to sample the wares in crooked little side streets, he found his way barred by what appeared to be yet another small city within the larger urban area, a dwarfed, walled-off collection of alleys and creaking ancient buildings, its ugliness and loneliness in marked contrast to the warmth and charm of greater Frankfurt. The solitary gate guarded by an armed warden gave our traveler the palpable impression that a prison community was locked within. He was not far wrong. This little encincture— a hideous anomaly in one of Europe's most dynamic market communities— was the *Judengasse,* the ghetto of the Jews.

The ghetto walls in Frankfurt, and in hundreds of other cities and towns in Germany and elsewhere, provided telling physical evidence of a basic fact of Jewish life in the era before the French Revolution. That fact was the isolation of the Jews from their European neighbors, their indeterminate status as non-Europeans. It is fair to ask, then, if the Jews were actually foreigners or interlopers. Were they, for example, voluntary immigrants, newly arrived from other lands or continents? Or had they perhaps been imported into Europe as captives, much as African Negroes had been imported to America in the seventeenth and eighteenth centuries? In truth, these Jews were not

25

"foreigners" in the usual sense of the word. Nor were they newcomers to Europe. Most of them were descended from Jews who had lived on European soil for many centuries, often antedating many of the settlements of the non-Jewish populations of Europe. Sizable Jewish communities had existed in Europe long before the rise of Christianity. Yet it was the very rise of Christianity, the emergence of Europe's Christian dynasties between the fourth and fifteenth centuries, that destroyed the equality of Jewish status and the economic and political basis of Jewish security. The Jews were isolated, in fact, not because they were suspect as newcomers, but rather because they were feared as Christ-killers and, perhaps (as we shall see in Chapter XI), resented as Christ-givers.

The *Judengasse* signified more than Jewish isolation, however. It also signified Jewish autonomy. Corporativism, the division of society into separate and frequently autonomous corporations, was one of the central characteristics of European life under the *ancien régime:* the free city of Frankfurt, the separate little Jewish city within Frankfurt were merely additional evidences of this fact. Society under the *ancien régime* was not composed primarily of individuals, but rather of corporate groups of individuals, each group with its own carefully delimited rights and responsibilities. The result was a vast agglomeration of chartered freedoms, ranging from the aristocrat's right to receive tolls at a bridge to the peasant's right to pasture a cow in a common field. Corporativism was a relic of a feudal technique that developed in the eighth and ninth centuries, in the years of the Norman and Saracen invasions. It was a technique by which the ruler decentralized responsibilities and rights, in the hope that barons and townships would perform functions for him that he, the king, could not afford, or did not have the strength, to perform himself. The need for such a corporate division of society had long since vanished. But, like so many other relics of the medieval feudal world, it persisted into the eighteenth century. The result was a welter of small autonomous local units: manors, parishes, towns, guilds, universities and academies, commercial and financial companies.

It is not surprising, therefore, that the four hundred thousand Jews of Western Europe in the eighteenth century should also have been organized on the basis of corporate autonomy. Yet, as we have seen, they could hardly be permitted entrance into feudal society, or even into the guilds of municipal corporations. As infidels, they were incapable of pronouncing the required Christian oaths of fealty and loyalty. Where, then, could they go? They could not be dealt with as individuals; individualism was unknown in the *ancien régime.* They had to "belong" somewhere; they had to be reached by duke, baron, or bishop for fiscal purposes. It was to solve this problem that Christian rulers permitted the Jews to enroll in their own autonomous corporations. In a decentralized society they had the right—indeed, the responsibility—of governing themselves, of caring for social services that duke or baron declined to perform. The Jews, therefore, were obliged to provide their own educational, religious, administrative, social, medical, and penal services. So long as the Jewish communities paid their collective taxes or assizes, the ruler had no objection to their ghetto sovereignty.

Like most of the other corporate groups, the Jews did not resent their autonomous status. It provided the leaders of the Jewish community with the opportunity of maintaining the Jewish religion and all that this religion embraced in the way of educational processes, judicial action, and social welfare. Thus, the synagogue remained the center of Jewish life, its activities unimpeded by the government. The Jews administered their own laws, based on their own Talmudical precepts. Virtually all legal disputes were resolved within the Jewish community, in Jewish courts before Jewish judges. Jewish police enforced Jewish judgments, clapped lawbreakers into Jewish-controlled jails; while the most dreaded punishment of all was the one reserved for incorrigible offenders—the *herem,* the awesome rabbinical ban of excommunication. It was Jews, too, who built the ghetto's conduits, supervised Jewish hospitals and old folks' homes, guarded Jewish gates, cleaned Jewish streets, assessed and collected Jewish taxes.

Inevitably this complex schedule of activities required a Jewish government. Such a government existed in each major Jewish community. Technically, it was based on a full assembly of all male Jews who were the heads of families. But the Jews were children of their times. Even as Christian society was usually divided into three estates, so, too, the Jewish community was divided—although by wealth—into classes. In practice, only the more affluent voted on matters of communal policy, and elected the lay elders who administered Jewish public affairs. The elders, in turn, possessed far-reaching and rather autocratic appointive powers; for example, they appointed the tax assessors and auditors, the judges, and the rabbis of the leading synagogues. Occasionally, to be sure, the rabbis would seek to modify the harsh realities of communal politics; but the prestige of the rabbinate had declined drastically as early as the seventeenth century—just as the power of bishops and priests had declined in Christian society. For all practical purposes the Jewish community was a closed world dominated by wealthy Jewish laymen and politicians.

One of the factors that made the control of these lay elders so oppressive was the financial structure of the *Judengasse.* The Jews were obliged, in the first place, to pay heavy revenues to cover the costs of Jewish communal life; in addition, they were required to pay substantial assizes and yearly taxes to the royal, baronial, and ecclesiastical treasuries. As a rule, the responsibility for assessing and collecting all these taxes was left to Jewish communal officials. Few of these officials evidenced any strong feelings of *noblesse oblige;* on the contrary, most of them were quite rapacious. For in early modern times the wealthy Jewish controlling oligarchy made every effort to shunt the burden of taxation onto the impoverished Jewish masses. Taxes were far-reaching and ingenious, and once they were assessed, there could be little evasion. This financial burden, not only doubly heavy but inequitably distributed, was becoming virtually insupportable by the late eighteenth century. On the eve of the Emancipation era, while most Jewish communities still managed to maintain the integrity of their religious, educational, and judicial systems, they were, nevertheless, on the verge of bankruptcy and open class warfare.

THE PRICE OF JEWISH EXISTENCE IN THE WEST

The reader may wonder that the Jews, who were closed out of Christian life, were permitted to remain in Western lands at all. There was no squeamishness about expulsions or expropriations, even as there were no twinges of conscience about tortures, executions, or disgrace. Caprice ruled as often as custom. Why, then, should hundreds of thousands of Jews have been tolerated on the Christian soil of Europe?

Certainly, if the Church had had its way, the "infidels" would not have been permitted to "contaminate" Christian communities. In fact, the Catholic hierarchy, and later the Protestant clergy, continually besought the sovereigns of Europe to exile their Jewish populations altogether. But the Jews were not to be dispensed with so quickly. Driven from agriculture and the normal avenues of commercial activity, they had been compelled to specialize in petty trade and in usury. Infidels or no, they did manage to accumulate liquid wealth; and the rulers who needed money for mercenary armies were willing to protect their Jews if only to tax that liquid wealth away. Was it not carrying Christianity too far to expect princes to overlook such a convenient source of revenue—especially if there was an occasional overflow that could be shared for the greater glory of God?

The rulers managed to appease the Church, however, by hedging Jewish life with innumerable and humiliating restrictions designed to preserve the barrier between Christian and Jew. Even the celebrated Enlightened Despot, Frederick II of Prussia, did not hesitate to manipulate his Jews in the most arbitrary and capricious fashion in order to fulfill the economic functions he had in mind for them. Whenever a Jew entered a town, he was subject to the degrading *Leibzoll,* a body or head tax, which had to be paid at the town gate for entry. The duties levied by the customs officials of Mainz, for example, were classified under the following headings: Honey, Hops, Wood, Jews, Chalk, Cheese, Charcoal. A Jew was compelled to pay three gulden to enter Munich and forty kreutzer a day to remain there. At the Leipzig fair the Jews were required to wear yellow "wheels," or badges, of medieval vintage to mark their race, and were obliged to set up their booths in the *Brühl,* a pestilent, swampy marsh. Moreover, they were permitted to engage only in the most peripheral kind of secondhand retailing.

Closed off from agriculture, from "respectable" commerce, subject to heavy taxes and even more onerous travel restrictions, most of the 300,000 Jews of Germany in the eighteenth century were quite poor, eking out their existence on the barest margin of survival. Of course, economic conditions varied. There were occasional wealthy Jews to be found in Frankfurt, Berlin, or Hamburg; there were Jews of affluence who were under the special protection of the royal or ducal palaces in Germany. In France, the Sephardic Jews of Guyenne were rather prosperous, enjoying the same ancient trading privileges as their French neighbors. But these were the exceptions. Whatever a few fortunate Jews managed to accumulate was often relentlessly taxed away. There were many dangerous occupations in the Europe of those days.

Surely not least among them was the Jew's effort to preserve life and limb and to salvage his precarious estate.

Yet we must not forget that most Christian Europeans were also impoverished and insecure: that the farmer in his village hut was fortunate to have meat in his cooking pot more than once a week; that the typical city dweller was a confused, transplanted rustic for whom hunger was a familiar bedfellow. Nor were the Jews the only group to suffer from galling restrictions. The French and German peasantries of the eighteenth century were encumbered by a wide variety of burdensome tailles, tithes, decimes, and quitrents, were obliged to pay innumerable tolls and dues at bridges and fairs, to work on roads, to serve in the militia, and to buy their goods from royal monopolies. While Jewish disabilities in the early modern era were the severest in Western Europe, they were not incalculably more burdensome than those suffered by millions of other Europeans. The prayers of Christians and Jews were incomprehensible to one another, perhaps even to themselves. But all hearts were united in a common longing for the better day, with its release from the servitudes of poverty and indignity.

There were really only a few restrictions on Jewish life that were excessively difficult to bear. Of all the humiliations suffered by the Jews, the ghetto, the *Judengasse* to which we referred briefly at the opening of this chapter, was perhaps the most degrading of all. There were, of course, masses of German Jews scattered throughout many small towns in which walled ghettos did not exist, in which Jewish living quarters were simply restricted to specific areas of settlement. But this was ghettoization, too, if, as was nearly always the case, the Jews were quarantined from all social contact with Christians.

It is rather ironical that the first Spanish and Sicilian ghettos of the early medieval era were actually requested by the Jews themselves as a tangible physical symbol of their corporate autonomy. Beyond business hours, after all, what need or desire could they possibly have for contact with the Christian world? Who could have imagined in those early medieval days, when populations were small and plague-decimated, that in time the ghetto would become dangerously overcrowded? In the late Middle Ages perhaps some Jews perceived the encroaching danger. But it was too late by then, for in the sixteenth century the ghetto was imposed forcibly from above as a kind of demographic strait jacket, and not merely as a convenient reflection of Jewish capitulatory autonomy. During the bitter doctrinal strife of the Counter Reformation the Church became most frantically conscious of the need to put nonbelievers beyond the pale of society. In the case of the Jews, who absorbed much of the punishment well-armed Protestant populations were able to escape, the grotesquerie of a badge, a gaberdine, a peaked hat was apparently no longer enough to warn Christians off: quarantine was deemed necessary. To set an example, Pope Paul IV created the first "official" ghetto in Rome in 1555. Other Catholic sovereigns followed Paul's example; and then the German Protestant duchies, craving their own religious uniformity, issued the fiats that ghettoized the Jewries of northern Europe. Thus, the legal, government-authorized ghetto emerged as the unique creation of the sixteenth century. It was destined to be the last relic of Jewish disabilities to be abrogated, more than two centuries later.

Almost invariably the ghetto was deliberately assigned to the most squalid section of the city. For example, Pope Paul IV ordered the Roman ghetto to be located on the malarial left bank of the Tiber, near the *giotto,* the gun factory, whence the institution of ghetto probably derived its name. As late as the nineteenth century this congested area was described by an Italian writer as, "a formless heap of hovels and dirty cottages, ill-kept, in which a population of nearly four thousand souls vegetates, when half that number could with difficulty live there. The conglomeration of human beings, wretched for the most part, render this hideous dwelling place nauseous and deadly." So were they all. Fire periodically gutted the ghettos of Frankfurt and Nikolsburg. There were no facilities for the disposal of sewage, and plagues and epidemics not infrequently ravaged the isolated Jewish populations. Jewish children were usually drawn and sallow from bad drinking water and insufficient exercise. Because, too, the Jews were denied the necessary space in which to construct new dwellings, they were obliged to enlarge the older buildings, occasionally even to the height of ten stories— winning the dubious distinction of Europe's first skyscrapers. Jewish tenement dwellers reached their rooms either by panting up narrow circular stairways or by lifting themselves from the streets by means of pulleys and ropes. Under the circumstances, fatal accidents were far from uncommon. Yet, except for the express purposes of business, Jews were forbidden to leave the ghetto. After nightfall, on Sundays, and on Christian holidays, the gates, wherever they existed, were locked, and the Jews were shut off from the outside world altogether.

What was particularly galling to Western Jewry behind their ghetto walls in the cities or in their slum neighborhoods in the towns were the arbitrary and unnatural restrictions on family life. Frederick II of Prussia, for example, in 1750 divided his Jewry into various classes: the specially privileged, who were given temporary travel and domicile rights; and the generally privileged, a small group of industrialists temporarily valuable to him, who were assigned full rights of residence and occupation. Even generally privileged Jews, however, were strictly limited in the number of children they were permitted to settle with them. "In order that in the future all fraud, cheating and secret and forbidden increase of the number of families may be more carefully avoided," the charter declared, "no Jew shall be allowed to marry, nor will he receive permission to settle in further numbers, nor will he be believed, until a careful investigation has been made by the War and Domains Offices." In 1710 the free port of Hamburg issued an ordinance by which Jews were forbidden to build a synagogue, to attend private services in greater numbers than ten families, to marry or hold commerce with Christian women, to pass across church grounds during Christian services, to live elsewhere than in the Neustadt, the slum area, to exhibit any ostentation in dress, to appear in public on any occasion at which crowds of people assembled. The Jews, in sum, were enjoined to live quietly and unobtrusively —"*still und ruhig leben.*"

It was not a pleasant life by any stretch of the imagination; indeed, it became increasingly intolerable in the eighteenth century by reason of its very anachronism. When American Negroes in the ante-bellum South sang folk songs, their lyrics alluded to green pastures, to golden slippers, to spirits of departed ancestors promenading in heaven in robes that were white, always white. The Jews who were locked off in ghettos reacted similarly. They, too, compensated for their alienation from pastoral surroundings by idealizing nature's charms and allurements. Witness Marvin Lowenthal's suggestive description of a seventeenth-century German synagogue that he encountered in Bechhoffen during a tour of Germany in the 1930's:

> A shewbread table is the center of attention on the north wall, and a lighted menorah on the south. The ark is richly carved and the wall about it sown with inscriptions, foliage, and symbolic lions, trees, trumpets, and harvest fruits. The timbers of the barrel vault are alive with birds and beasts—unicorn, horse, lion, hare, fox, elephant, and squirrel—the One Hundred and Fourth Psalm set to line and color. Two trumpeting lions flanked by Jerusalem and again the harvest fruits share the drum of the west wall; and beneath are the panelled inscriptions, among them, appropriately near the doorway, the saying from the Talmud: "Since Jerusalem has fallen, closed are all the gates of heaven save one, the gate of tears."

JEWISH SELF-GOVERNMENT IN EASTERN EUROPE

If our eighteenth-century traveler had been transplanted from Germany to Poland, he would have encountered strikingly different external surroundings. Wandering through the flat, mud-caked Polish plain, our traveler would have noted few bustling municipalities such as Frankfurt; primitive ramshackle Slavic villages were the rule here. And if there were few cities to be found in this sprawling hinterland, similarly there were few ghettos. There were, on the other hand, towns and hamlets whose populations were almost entirely Jewish: Jews who were tradesmen and innkeepers, lumbermen and even farmers, apparently moving in and out of the village limits at their own discretion.

But the superficial externals had little relationship to established practice. Simply because there were no ghettos in the Western sense, our traveler-friend would have erred in assuming that Jewish isolation was any less complete in Poland than it was in Germany or Italy. Actually, isolation from the Christian world was even more fundamental a fact of Jewish existence east of the Vistula than it was in Central and Western Europe. As far as the primitive and devoutly Catholic Polish peasant was concerned, the strange, Oriental people of Israel, denying Christ and repudiating the Holy Ghost, practicing bizarre and mysterious rites, praying in a terrifying gibberish undoubtedly a code of the Devil—what could they be but cursed anti-Christs incarnate? Did not the parish priest make this abundantly clear at Easter time in flaming sermons on the Crucifixion? The less one had to do with these denizens of darkness, the safer one was from contamination.

The popular suspicion and revulsion of the Poles were matched by the conscious retreat into self-sufficiency of the Jews. The Jews welcomed the opportunity to cultivate autonomy. Jewish self-government in Poland was as far-reaching as in the West—indeed, more far-reaching. For even in the period of its maximum strength in the sixteenth and seventeenth centuries, the Polish monarchy had been obliged to delegate administrative responsibilities on a corporative basis. Since the early modern era, therefore, the Jews of Poland had been permitted—in fact, obliged—to direct their own financial and communal affairs.

Polish Jewry had a name for this self-government. They called it a *kahal,* an all-inclusive Jewish community authority. The *kahal* embraced nearly every phase of Jewish public life: religion, education, law, hygiene, social welfare. The Polish monarchy had no intention of interfering with this authority, so long as the Jews paid their taxes to the royal treasury. And by the middle of the eighteenth century those taxes comprised an increasingly large proportion of the king's revenue. If, for example, the ruler needed funds to pay off his hired mercenaries, to cover the salaries of his expanding bureaucracy, or even to ransom Polish nobles who happened to fall into the hands of the Turks, the Jews could always be depended upon to pay quietly. But however uncomplainingly they may have paid, the Jews found those expenses increasingly burdensome. For the levies were not merely superimposed upon the cost of maintaining a completely autonomous Jewish community; they were also assessed and collected in an arbitrary and inequitable manner.

In truth, the Polish-Jewish *kahal* was in every respect as autocratic as the Jewish government of the West. Property qualifications determined the franchise here, too. The principal officers of the *kahal,* with their immense power to influence the courts and the excise commissions, were very often wealthy tyrants who shifted the burden of taxation onto their disfranchised and impoverished brethren. And, as we have seen, taxation never ended. Thus, by the seventeenth century, the *kahals* frequently were obliged to resort to loans to meet the demands of the Polish government and of their own communal officials. A century later the borrowing was further compounded to meet the interest on earlier, outstanding debts. Eventually most of the *kahals* of the larger Polish-Jewish communities faced not only the sullen disaffection of their citizens, but also the imminent prospect of bankruptcy.

In these respects, Polish-Jewish self-government did not differ appreciably from its counterpart in the West. Yet there was one important distinction between the *kahals* and the Jewish corporations of Germany or Italy. The Eastern Jewish communities were organized into a great national federation. This federation was the *Kahal* of "Four Lands"—Great Poland, Little Poland, Volhynia, and Lithuania, the four major provinces of the Kingdom of Poland. This nation-wide apparatus of government guarded Jewish civil interests in Poland by acting as the intermediary between the Jews and the Polish diet and court. It apportioned the taxes due the state among the various district *kahals* and collected them. It attempted, too, with rather less success, to govern the inner life of Polish Jewry by regulating the economic, religious, judicial, cultural, and administrative activities of the individual *kahals*. The *Kahal* of Four Lands never really reached maximum efficiency, and its role as a supreme Jewish government in Poland was at all times more of an ideal than a reality. Nevertheless, it did perform useful functions as spokesman and defender of Jewish rights before the Polish court and as guardian of Jewish honor when attempts were made to assail it. Inadequate as the *kahal* system was, it might have survived, with some modifications, had Poland itself not been on the verge of political and economic collapse.

THE DECLINING WORLD OF THE EAST

In the sixteenth century the Kingdom of Poland was the second largest state in Europe and one of the most powerful. Two centuries later it had become one of the weakest and most vulnerable. By the eighteenth century, although neither its government nor its citizens recognized the fact, Poland was slated for an early death. An enervated and incompetent Saxon dynasty had allowed the reins of government to slip from its hands. The country had drifted steadily into political chaos, its diet controlled by a rapacious nobility, its economy virtually bankrupt, its army underpaid and ill-trained.

Similarly, the Jews of Poland had once been the elect of world Jewry: a vigorous and wealthy commercial nation within a powerful state. But now the fortunes of this strategically placed Jewish population, which may have numbered a million by 1772, declined as rapidly as the strength and efficiency of the Polish state itself. Tens of thousands of Jews—and Poles—had been slain in the middle of the seventeenth century by the insurrectionist Ukrainian armies of Bogdan Chmielnicki. No sooner had the survivors begun to reconstruct their lives than the disastrous rule of the Saxon kings began. Deprived of the protection of a firm and respected dynasty, the Jews were delivered into the hands of the powerful *szlachta,* the magnates. These brutal and licentious nobles, claiming the ownership, toil, and rents of their serfs, laid equal claim to the labor and earnings of the Jewish businessmen and stewards who for centuries had collected the feudal rents and had sold the baronial liquor. The nobility exercised complete jurisdiction over their Jewish *arendars* (stewards) and provisioners, over all the middlemen who had formerly been independent businessmen or paid representatives—as well as over all other Jewish residents of the great feudal estates. And when social unrest among the Polish peasantry became a factor to be reckoned with, the *szlachta* shrewdly plied the peasant leaders with liquor and encouraged them to vent their wrath on the "Christ-killers."

In their assaults on Jewish security, the nobles relied upon an important ally: the most powerful Catholic Church in Europe, a Church almost completely dominated by the Jesuit Order. In the West, the rise of absolute monarchies resulted in a corresponding decline in the power of the Church. In the East, conversely, the collapse of Poland's monarchy permitted an increase of clerical power to an extent unknown until then in Polish history.

The enactments of the Catholic synods, carrying unqualified authority, were invariably permeated with malign hatred of the Jews. All the old restrictions of the early Middle Ages were revived, and they embittered every area of Jewish life. The eighteenth century, too, witnessed a frenzy of blood accusations openly stimulated by the Polish clerics and directed equally at the Jews and at the Greek Orthodox. The resulting atrocities bore a familiar medieval stamp. On a trumped-up charge of "tampering with holy oil" the Reizes brothers of Lwów had their tongues torn from their throats. Other Jews were occasionally lynched for "blasphemous" remarks uttered in "the vicinity of churchgoers." A quotation from the diary of an eighteenth-century Polish nobleman tells of imprisoning a Jew for debt:

> Yesterday, I ordered to bind him with chains and to confine him in the pigsty; however, I allowed his wife and sons to remain in the inn. Only his youngest son, Leizer, did I take to my home and ordered to teach him the principles of our faith as well as our prayers. The boy possesses very remarkable potentialities. I intend to have him baptized, and have already written about it to the bishop; he has promised to be present at the baptism and to prepare the soul of the boy. At first Leizer refused to cross himself and to repeat our prayers; but Strilitzki flogged him, and today he has already eaten swine's flesh. The priest of our church, Bonia-fiati, a member of the Order *Minorum de Observantia,* worked with the sweat of his brow to overcome the boy's stubbornness and to bring him into our faith.

Yet all these horrors notwithstanding, we must not forget that, even as in Western Europe, the Jews were not the only victims of harsh political and economic conditions. The misery was fully shared by the typical Polish serf. As late as the eighteenth century, he was not permitted to commute his rents, a privilege long since extended to French and German farmers. His obligations to his lord were far more onerous than those of any other European peasant. He was fortunate, in fact, to be left with a third of the grain he harvested; the rest went into the *Pan's* granary. Except for Sunday Mass, he was not permitted to leave his strip of land. Under the law he possessed no rights whatever, and he could not appeal to the courts even to protest his lord's cruelest, most unreasonable acts. If, by chance, his daughter was comely, she was at the lord's mercy the moment she reached adolescence. The Polish peasant, perhaps the most miserable in all Christendom, was invariably ill-fed, ill-clothed, ill-housed. He lived in squalor and died in misery.

Perhaps the Jew should have found a modicum of comfort in the contrast. For all the cruelty of Church and *szlachta,* the collapse of political and economic security, the oppression of *ḳahal* taxation, the typical Polish Jew still managed to live better than the typical Polish Christian. The Jew was literate; as a petty trader in town or village he usually had a little money left in his pocket. In fact, unlike the Jews of Western Europe, the Polish Jew still enjoyed a fair degree of freedom of movement—far more, certainly, than the Polish serf. What made the Jew's life particularly oppressive in eighteenth-century Poland was the knowledge that, as time passed, the margin of difference between himself and his Christian neighbor was steadily vanishing. As he stared into the slack-jawed face of the Polish *khlop*, he recognized with horror that he was gazing at the brutalized image of himself. Each passing year was driving him closer to this kind of cloddishness. Once the margin of physical and intellectual separation vanished altogether, the Jew's status as "infidel"—despised, reviled, tortured—would become completely intolerable.

CONCLUSION

It is a sorely tried Polish Jewry we encounter on the eve of *Rozbier,* the partitions of Poland, and in the West, at the threshold of the French Revolution. In Poland and the Ukraine there were a million impoverished and humiliated souls, driven frantic by the autocracy of noble and *kahal* alike, by cruel flogging and murderous taxation. In Germany the ghetto Jews eked out only a slightly better living and were no less pariahs in the eyes of their Christian neighbors. The essential difference, therefore, between Polish Jewry and Western European Jewry was not to be found in their political status; both communities were quarantined as non-Europeans. Nor was it to be found in their economic status; both groups survived on the narrow edge of peddlery and petty trade. Both groups, too, for that matter, were governed by Jewish communal organizations whose officials were frequently as autocratic and rapacious as any in the Christian world. In all these respects, there was little to choose between East and West. Rather the basic difference between the Jews of Poland and the Jews of Western Europe was this: in the East, the circumstances of Jewish life were steadily worsening; in the West, there were tentative indications that better times were on the way.

Notes

Page 31. Quotation from Marvin Lowenthal, *A World Passed By,* pp. 307-8.

Page 34. Quotation from S. M. Dubnow, *Toldot ha-Hasidut,* Tel Aviv, 1930, as quoted and translated in Israel Kazis, *Hasidism,* pp. 10-11.

II

The Glimmering of Dawn in the West

During the seventeenth and eighteenth centuries a significant and far-reaching revolution occurred in European life. It was a commercial revolution, precipitated when the feudal and agricultural economy of Europe was inundated by vast new supplies of money. The mines of Mexico and Peru provided gold and silver ingots for the Old World in quantities heretofore undreamed of. The more this currency poured into Europe's veins, the more Europe became dependent upon it for a rising standard of living. Money provided luxuries in food and dress for the city dweller. For the peasant in the field money meant an opportunity to pay off feudal obligations and to own a plot of soil free and clear. For the king, above all, money represented hired armies and bureaucrats, and independence of a jealous and covetous nobility. In the seventeenth and eighteenth centuries, money was indispensable to the purposes of such monarchs as Frederick William, the Great Elector of Brandenburg, and Louis XIV, the Sun King of France—men for whom absolutist authority in their realms was hardly less than an obsession.

Moreover the typical monarch of the Baroque Age viewed money as a commodity which could not be shared with his dynastic neighbors but which had, rather, to be hoarded. It was important, therefore, that the balance of trade be kept favorable, in order that more industrial and agricultural produce be exported than imported. Each ruler sought now to monopolize the trade and wealth of Europe, to build up a reservoir of industries, markets, and raw materials. Many a bloody battle of the early modern era was fought for remote and pestilent islands that were endowed with spices or mineral resources. This process of gouging out unshared empires of trade at the expense of one's neighbors was called mercantilism. By the opening of the eighteenth century the typical mercantilist, preoccupied with accumulating money, was little concerned with matters of religion or religious heresy; for in the world of mercantilism the issues of morality and religion were

36

irrelevant nuisances. Certainly no self-respecting mercantilist state could countenance religious persecution; after all, the suppression or eviction of any one religious group might well throw an entire economy out of gear. The mercantilist age was, an age of comparative religious toleration because such toleration usually proved more profitable. The divisions of theology were less compelling now than the multiplication of revenues.

Because money was the great equalizer, it was inevitable that Christian Europe should begin to view its Jews in a completely new light. Here was a people who understood commerce, a people uninhibited by feudal ties of ecclesiastical traditions. Never having been bound to an agrarian economy, the Jews have been compelled, as a result, to pioneer in business and finance. The practical monarchs of Western Europe were aware of this fact; they recognized the usefulness of an experienced mercantile people, a footloose urban people with international connections, avid, even desperate, to exploit opportunity wherever it might be found. Hence the age of mercantilism, which was also the age of absolutism, coincided with the transfer of the Jewish problem from the religious to the political sphere. Viewed as an additional source of national power, certain classes of Jews were extended grudging toleration by the rulers of the Netherlands, England, even later of France and Brandenburg-Prussia. Of course the new toleration was not granted to all Jews, or even to most of them. The great majority still was involved in peddling, and was confined to the slum or ghetto neighborhoods of Europe's cities. But the growth of a class of "exception Jews" revealed the dichotomy of attitude of many European monarchs.

Frederick II of Prussia was an example of this kind of ambivalence. He was perhaps the most brilliant of the Enlightened Despots, a man who created a strikingly taut and efficient cameralist administration, who fancied himself the patron saint of European rationalism. But Frederick personally despised the Jews. In his *Political Testament* of 1752 he described them as the most dangerous of all sects, "avaricious, superstitious, backward," a group that stood in the way of the general progress of mankind. We have seen (in Chapter I) the degrading disabilities he imposed on his captive Jewish population. Nevertheless, Frederick was perfectly capable of sublimating his prejudices in order to make effective use of the Jews in the mechanism of his state. This sense of dynastic responsibility explained his determination to prohibit Jews from engaging in some branches of trade, and his willingness, on the other hand, to permit them into other branches. It explained the fact that he made life miserable for them by the most cunning variety of restrictions and, at the same time, singled out individual Jews for bounties, concessions, and special privileges, appointed them as court purveyors, entrusted factories and companies to them, and used them as the intermediaries in his export trade. For Frederick was first and foremost a mercantilist; he was willing to exploit any group capable of contributing to a wealthy Prussian state and an efficient Prussian bureaucracy. When, in 1763, therefore, Frederick grudgingly permitted younger children of Jews to join their older brothers or sisters beyond the ghetto walls, he demanded in return that the parents either establish factories or "promote the marketing of home products outside the countryside." Because agrarian Poland was a source of raw materials and a natural market for Prussian manufactured goods, the king resolved to use his Jews, long familiar with the Polish commercial world, as his principal intermediaries.

The policy of Frederick the Great was paralleled by many monarchs and princes in the early modern era. Despite a cruel grillwork of prohibitions and tax burdens, selected Jews of one German state after another were granted privileged status, rights of domicile outside the ghetto, rights of exemption from Jew-taxes—if in return they created valuable industries and trade connections for their rulers. Of course, only small groups of Jews were equipped to meet these standards; but their numbers were growing. In the group of Westphalian communities known as Paderborn, for example, Jews had long been limited to trade in pawned articles and gold and jewels. These restrictions had resulted from the pressure of Christian guild merchants and artisans. But by the early eighteenth century the guilds had largely atrophied, for they had been unable to meet the economic demands of a growing population. The Jews ventured tentatively into the vacuum. They moved from pawnbroking to peddling, from peddling to retailing. Some Jews eventually became fairly prosperous exporters and importers. Viewing with pleased surprise the wealth that these Jewish merchants provided for Westphalia, the dukes began to rescind many of the remaining restrictions upon Jewish activity. As a result, some Jews entered the fur trade, the trade in agricultural products, the traffic in linen and yarns. Groups of especially favored Jewish merchants were allowed to remain outside the ghetto for longer intervals to trade in Westphalian fairs without the usual disabilities, and could raise their children in comparatively decent surroundings.

The improvement in Jewish economic status is most graphically described in the diary entries of an eighteenth-century German Jewess, Glückel of Hameln. During the early years of Glückel's life in Hanover, her husband and brothers earn their livelihood as petty traders, trudging from door to door in Hamburg, buying old gold and selling it to jewelers or merchants. The wife of one of Glückel's neighbors sells feminine knickknacks, *Galanteriewaren*, at the Kiel fair, while other Jewish neighbors deal in ribbons, hardware, and cutlery, in small loans and secondhand jewelry. Gradually Glückel's relatives and friends enter the retail trade in cattle and old clothes. Near the end of her life some of them even begin to buy goods from Amsterdam, Danzig, and Poland, and sell them in the leading German fairs. They undertake contracts for delivering silver to government mints; they sell cash and bills of exchange on a scale that approaches banking.

Of course, the majority of Jewish disabilities remained. As a rule, Jews still were confined to ghettoized areas, subjected to oppressive and degrading taxes. Most of them were quite poor. But increasing numbers of Jews were beginning to edge into the world beyond the ghetto. Taking advantage of the growing indifference to theological and religious matters that characterized eighteenth-century life, they began, at least in small measure, to share the profits of the new commercial order. The economic security won by a minority of Jewish entrepreneurs provided a material basis for the political, social, and cultural emancipation that was to follow.

THE JEWS AND THE RISE OF CAPITALISM

Thus far we have discussed the confluence of economic conditions that affected Jewish status in modern Europe. But the process worked the other way as well. Indeed, so closely has Jewish economic activity been intertwined with the history of capitalism that many historians have forgotten that the Jews were its putty as well as its molders. Jews helped to shape the destiny of capitalism, but capitalism also shaped the destiny of the Jews. The eminent German economic historian, Werner Sombart, for example, turned his attention to the Jews in a celebrated volume, published in 1911, entitled *Die Juden und das Wirtschaftsleben,* "The Jews and Economic Life," later published in England under the title, *The Jews and Modern Capitalism.* Sombart solemnly identified the spirit of Judaism with the spirit of capitalism. Judaism for him was characterized by "the close relationship between religion and business, the arithmetical concept of sin, and above all the rationalization of life." Added to these factors, Sombart suggested, was Jewry's "racial" instinct for nomadry, as well as Jewry's hostile and opportunistic attitude toward Christians. The combination of these racial and religious characteristics caused "Israel to move like the sun across Europe." The notion was in some ways rather flattering, but of course it was thoroughly specious. Judaism's major emphasis, like Christianity's, was upon good works and the moral life. Jewish tradition viewed business as a necessary chore, while the study of Torah and Talmud were the revered avocations for the believing Jew. Sombart's "racial" views were a truer summary of the prevailing prejudices of imperial Germany than of Jewish mores and motivations.

But one need not accept Sombart's misconceptions and exaggerations to recognize that the Jews did play a significant role in the development of early capitalism. There were circumstances peculiar to Jewish life which, as we have suggested, catapulted the Jews into business and finance. These included their detachment from the soil, their urban concentration, the insecurity of their legal status, their international connections, their experience in dealing with money, the speculative thinking that circumstances (not religion or race) had made necessary. Even if they did not actually originate capitalism, as Sombart suggested, the Jews were often the yeast in the capitalist fermentation. It was primarily Jews, for example, who took the initiative in developing a vital interurban trade; for their connections in cities and countries throughout Europe could not be matched by any other people or any other economic group. Itinerant Jewish hawkers were present in disproportionately large numbers at the great fairs of Central and Eastern Europe, especially those held at Leipzig and Lwów. By the end of the eighteenth century, in fact, nearly a third of the traders at these world-famous market places were Jews from all corners of Europe.

In England, Austria, and Poland, Jewish textile firms sent hundreds of agents into villages to purchase wool; later, Jewish manufacturers converted the wool into cloth. The participation of Jews in textile production was especially noteworthy in Prussia, where the cotton-goods industry was largely their creation, as were the silk and velvet industries. Jews, after all, had been secondhand dealers in dry goods for centuries; they needed only to expand the scale of their operations. As exporters and importers, as moneylenders and brokers, as factors and textile manufacturers, the Jews fulfilled Frederick the Great's ambition and justified his cynical tolerance. Their role was crucial in transforming an agrarian and backward state, poor in credit and resources, into a rather important European economic Power.

In the Netherlands and England, Sephardic (Spanish-Jewish) bankers were integrally involved in the import-export trade. The Sephardic names of Caceres, Carvajal, Conegliano, and Henriques figured prominently among the flourishing banking houses of Amsterdam and London. By supplying credit for initial tonnage, these Sephardic bankers assisted measurably in the development of a large-scale colonial trade in sugar and indigo. In London, the Carvajal family alone imported vast sums of bullion every year, perhaps as much as one twelfth of England's national income in the late seventeenth century. Nor was banking confined to Sephardic Jews. By the middle of the eighteenth century Jewish financiers and bankers appeared in large numbers in Central Europe. Even before the French Revolution, Frankfurt, which had become the center of German banking, enjoyed much of its pre-eminence because of Jewish enterprise. By 1823 the Bavarian government owed no less than 21 per cent of its public debt to Jews. The story of Jewish international banking, however, the influential role played by Jewish bankers in supporting most of the dynasties of Western Europe, is a saga in itself.

THE COURT JEWS

The kings and dukes of the early modern era, continually engaged in bitter dynastic wars, were in equally continual need of supplies and munitions from all parts of Europe. The purveyors and factors who provided those supplies were almost invariably Jews, the only people capable of mobilizing Jewish peddlers throughout Europe to act as their purchasing agents. The Jews were imaginative, mobile, and trained in exploiting the opportunities of purchase, in appraising values, in buying up war surplus. Many a Jewish businessman in the seventeenth century laid the foundation for his modest fortune by his swift purchase and disposal of the debris left on the battlefields of the Thirty Years' War. Of course, foraging for one's duke behind enemy lines, or even within one's own lines, was dangerous work, and not infrequently Jews were caught and executed as spies. But risky as it was (far too much so for provincial Christian businessmen), the Jews were willing to chance it; for, as a rule, the reward transcended the perquisites of financial profit. It was common for a duke to grant his Jewish purveyor the right to live outside the ghetto on a permanent basis, the right to live at court and share the privileges of Christian courtiers. These were incentives of the most dazzling attractiveness, and the Jews found them irresistible. Then, too, between the prince of the Baroque Age and the daring Jewish purveyor of that period there often existed a close communion, even affection, which had nothing to do with services and rewards. Despite their differences in background and opportunity, the prince was lonely and isolated because of his omnipotence and inaccessibility; the Jew because of his birth and religion. They understood each other and worked together well.

The Jewish purveyors and bankers of the seventeenth and eighteenth centuries were a strange breed of adventurous, ambitious men. Samuel Oppenheimer of Heidelberg, for example, served as contractor for Elector Karl Ludwig of the Palatinate, and this relationship opened many other royal doors to him. At the end of the seventeenth century, when Louis XIV of France was the most dreaded predator in Western Europe, Emperor Leopold I of Austria, a fanatical Catholic, was obliged to turn to Oppenheimer for help; he recognized that Oppenheimer was the one person who could provide the Hapsburg armies with food, fodder, and munitions. The Austrian emperor's confidence was not misplaced. Oppenheimer's agents, his widely placed business friends and relatives provided him with the necessary supplies. Moreover, the supplies were turned over to Leopold on credit; while Oppenheimer himself borrowed from his fellow Jewish purveyors, from Aron Beer of Frankfurt, from Loew Sinzheim, the Court Purveyor of Mainz, from Moyses Isaac, the Court Jew of Bamberg, and others. When Oppenheimer died in 1703, the Court of Vienna faced virtual bankruptcy, for Austrian finances were integrally tied in with Oppenheimer's. The Hapsburgs recouped, however, by turning to yet other Jewish purveyors.

European history in the Baroque Age is studded with the names of these resourceful Jewish agents: men such as Israel Aaron, the first Jew to be admitted to East Prussia, who served as army supplier to Frederick William, the Great Elector, during all of Frederick William's European wars; the banker Elias Gumperts of Cleves, who also was of use to the Great Elector in furnishing stone, wood, palisades, uniforms, munitions, food, and money for fortresses along the Rhine; Abraham Isaak Auerbach of Crefeld, who delivered supplies to the Bishop of Münster. During the War of the Austrian Succession and the Seven Years' War in the eighteenth century, we find Jewish purveyors aligned with a Bavarian army that at one moment fought with, and the next moment against, the Prussians. In the majority of instances Jewish loyalty was extended to a dynastic employer and rarely to anyone else. In contrast to the non-Jewish bourgeoisie, the Jews sensed that they were under the special protection of the state, and that their economic fate depended on the political interests of their sovereigns.

Many Jews provided their rulers not merely with munitions and foodstuffs, but also with supplies of money. In the early modern era the courts of Europe were almost completely dependent upon private bankers for short-term loans. It happened that most of the money trade in those days, for reasons we have described, was in the hands of experienced Jewish dealers in gems and precious metals. The identical circumstances that produced the Jewish merchant and purveyor produced the Jewish banker: his connection with the Netherlands, the banking center of Europe, through his

Sephardic brethren; his international contacts in all the mercantile centers of Europe; above all, his long experience in dealing with precious metals and the currencies of the Continent. Again, the return for these short-term loans transcended mere interest-payment. As in the case of the Jewish purveyors, compensation frequently included the alleviation of Jewish disabilities, occasionally the right to live at court—often with a title.

One of the most colorful of these court bankers was Joseph Süss-Oppenheimer, nephew of Samuel Oppenheimer of Heidelberg. The origins of "the Jew Süss" are shrouded in mystery. Ostensibly, he was the son of a wandering Jewish actor; but the rumor persisted that he was actually the illegitimate son of Georg Eberhard von Heidersdorf, Imperial Deputy-Generalissimo and Knight of the Teutonic Order. Süss was raised by his wealthy uncle, and was trained by him in the art of banking. Before he was eighteen he was already delighting the cupidity of the landgrave of Hesse-Darmstadt whom he served as private banker. Süss had a highly refined instinct for ruthless and adventurous speculation; and he was blessed, as well, with an attractive appearance and a suave manner which he employed to good advantage in his career. After becoming purveyor, factor, gem-collector, and banker to Prince Karl Alexander of Württemberg, Süss exploited his opportunities with such acumen that he obtained virtually complete control of the financial administration of the duchy.

Württemberg was a sovereignty of no small importance; and Süss, with his grip on the state economy, managed to become a major influence in Central Europe—at a time when most of Europe's Jews were locked off within ghettos. Unfortunately Süss could not restrain his innate piracy. He did not hesitate, for example, to pocket large sums in bribes from industries that had been assigned government contracts. The Christian officials at court, wincing at the sight of this favored Jewish parvenu, lost no opportunity to attack his integrity. While Prince Karl Alexander was not unaware of what was going on, he was well satisfied with Süss's personal loyalty and zeal and with the profits that they produced. When the prince died, however, Süss was left without a protector. In 1737 a jury of nobles convicted him of fraud and embezzlement. He died on the gallows, contemptuously refusing to embrace the Christianity that might have saved his life.

It must be remembered that the *Hofjuden,* the Court Jews, were only a handful of individuals, notable because they had won release from the confinements of the somber ghetto world. Their position was at all times as precarious as the whim of their patrons; and they were determined, therefore, to enjoy their moment of glory to the hilt. The *Hofjuden* emulated Christian courtiers in fondness for ceremony and formality, for ostentation and display, for costly buildings and elaborate dress, for titles and the simulacra of authority. Which of them knew when the brief moment of glory might end? It was not uncommon, after all, for a duke, a margrave, or a bishop to renege on his debts, leaving his Jewish creditors penniless. Except for their dealings with the ruler, none of these elegant "exception Jews" possessed any valid connection whatever with the Christian world. Although they made important contributions to the nation-state and modern capitalism, they were never involved as integrally in the mainstream of Europe's business activity as the armies of Jewish peddlers and retailers who continued to live under the bans and restraints of the ghetto.

In view of the opportunism that characterized many of these court purveyors and bankers, it would have been natural for them to sever connections with their less privileged coreligionists. The fact was, however, that most of these *Hofjuden* remained remarkably loyal and exerted themselves to the utmost in behalf of their fellow Jews. As a consequence of their exalted position they were the *shtadtlanim,* the intercessors, through whom Jewish petitions were presented to the ruler. It was through *shtadtlanim,* for example, that the cities of Dresden, Leipzig, Kassel, Brunswick, and Breslau were opened to Jewish settlement. Most Jewish communities paid dearly for this paternal care, for Jewish bankers and purveyors made their influence felt in the ghetto by exercising control over Jewish corporate life. This pattern of obsequious Jewish dependence upon a few wealthy intercessors was destined to endure in Jewish life long after political emancipation. But in an age of ghettos and Jewish disabilities the wealthy *shtadtlan* was the only available life line to physical security and economic opportunity. The Jewish masses may have resented the brazenness and the the ostentation of the Oppenheimers, Sinzheims, Beers, and the others, but they were grateful for the welcome words spoken with timeliness in the right places.

As for the ruler, the internal structure of the Jewish community was a matter of complete indifference. He was quite willing to be persuaded that the gradual and selective emancipation of Jews could have useful consequences for the state. To him Jewish financiers were the one truly dependable source of funds for bureaucratic purposes. He could not rely upon Christian entrepreneurs, who bore little love for the courtier-ridden administrations of the *ancien régime,* and who stolidly concentrated on their own private business ventures.

This canny willingness to unlock Jewish funds for state needs was inherited by the later bourgeois administrations, and was as important a factor in raising the status of Jewish life as the middle-class egalitarianism that burgeoned up from below. Of course, there were other circumstances, too, that were responsible for eventual Jewish emancipation. The splinterization of the state into a welter of inefficient corporate groups, including the Corporation of the Jews, was an absurd and expensive anachronism that eventually had to be dispensed with. As we shall see, it was society's gradual recognition of these factors—the genius of the Jewish financier, the obsolescence of corporativism—which, together with the growth of rational humanitarianism, laid the groundwork for the political liberation of the Jewish people at the end of the eighteenth century.

THE ERA OF ENLIGHTENMENT

Even before 1789 little islands of hospitality began to open to the Jews on a collective basis, where there was no distinction between Jewish bankers and Jewish peddlers. England, for example, had locked its doors to Jews since the thirteenth century—although a few families continued to live on clandestinely in London. But, as we have seen, the tenor of the times had changed since the early medieval era. In the mid-seventeenth century a group of Sephardic refugees, living in temporary asylum in Holland, were emboldened to petition the authorities of England for admission. It happened that the English government in the 1650's was largely concentrated in the hands of the austere and iron-willed Oliver Cromwell, the Lord Protector. Cromwell considered the Jewish petition carefully. The more he pondered the matter, the more he was inclined to grant entry to the Jews. It was probably a combination of hardheaded mercantilist reasoning and the typically Puritan brand of Old Testament sentimentality that made up Cromwell's mind. Over the opposition of his council and without bothering to pass a law on the matter, he let it be known that Jewish immigration would not be blocked.

By 1660 there were thirty-five Sephardic families in London. Their numbers slowly increased. They were treated tolerantly, and managed to work themselves fully into England's economic life. In the eighteenth century their right of domicile was recognized officially when they were permitted to use the courts for the recovery of their debts. By then the religious passions that had flared up during the Civil War were largely spent. Jews began to prosper. The most prominent among them, the financiers and merchants, were "accepted" into the upper echelons of English society. Several Jews were now directors of the East India Company and of Lloyd's of London. They were active, as well, in medical and cultural life. The portraits of these eighteenth-century English Jews reveal velveteened dandies, the image of their Christian neighbors.

In the seventeenth century the Netherlands, too, debated the question of extending asylum and protection to the Jews who petitioned for entrance. The Dutch government asked the country's most respected jurist, Hugo Grotius, to preside over a commission to study the Jewish petition. After a fortnight of consultations, Grotius and his colleagues decided in favor of admission. The citizens of the powerful little Dutch province had firsthand knowledge, after all, of the rigors of persecution; they were themselves in the process of struggling loose from the Spanish Inquisition. But the Dutch were less motivated by sympathy than by a desire to promote their trade; they recognized the potential value of Jewish mercantile experience. The Jews, it must be said, soon fulfilled the fondest expectations of their hosts, for their economic activity in the Netherlands was extensive and productive. In brokerage, credit, and speculation Jewish participation was far out of proportion to their numbers. So prominent, indeed, was the role played by Jews on the Amsterdam Stock Exchange that when a committee was appointed to draw up new rules of stock trading, thirty-seven of the committee's forty-one members were Jews. A quarter of the Dutch East India Company's stockholders were Jews, and about the same proportion of Jews owned stock in the Dutch West India Company. Free from ghetto confinement, equal before the law, Jews found ample opportunity to demonstrate their talent and business acumen in the Netherlands.

By the late seventeenth and early eighteenth centuries, moreover, the spirit of rationalism made its appearance in Europe, and proved as corrosive as the spirit of capitalism in its effect on the *ancien régime*. Isaac Newton and John Locke had proved that human reason could explain, even predict, the workings of natural phenomena and human affairs. The *philosophes* of France popularized the virtues of reason among the wealthy and literate bourgeoisie of Europe. The middle class, in turn, swiftly transformed rationalism into a weapon with which to attack the institutions they detested most. Thus, they branded as unreasonable the monopoly of government by dessicated courtiers, the otherworldly pratings of priests and bishops, the callous and bigoted treatment of minorities. And if Beccaria could expose Europe's prison system as cruel and unreasonable, it was not difficult for others to apply the same criticism to the prison system of Jewish disabilities. Here and there devotees of the fashionable new religion of reason wondered what function was served by indiscriminately maintaining ancient persecutions and archaic ghettos.

At first, to be sure, many of Europe's leading rationalists approached the Jewish question rather cautiously. On the level of Enlightened Despotism, for example, acts of religious toleration were few and far between. Joseph II of Austria abrogated a number of Jewish disabilities; but upon his death they were restored by his brother Leopold. It was characteristic of most of the royal advocates of the new secular faith that they did little more than scratch the surface of existing intolerance. Moreover, several of the French *philosophes* believed that rational consistency required them to regard the Jews as an obscurantist people, superstitious, backward, perhaps even less enlightened than the Catholic peasantry. Baron d'Holbach, in his essay, "The Spirit of Judaism," insisted that the Jewish religion was permeated with avarice and self-interest; while Diderot, in an article written for the *Encyclopédie,* described the Jews as a nation of bigoted obscurantists. Even the mighty Voltaire, the mordant wit who laid bare the foibles of the *ancien régime* more trenchantly and ruthlessly than any other writer of the eighteenth century, so detested the Jews as relics of primitive Semitism that he felt compelled to observe: "You will find in them only an ignorant and barbarous people who have long exercised the most sordid avarice and detestable superstition, and an insurmountable hate for all peoples who have tolerated and enriched them." For the Jews, after all, were pietists, and the *philosophes* were rationalists; the Jews were clannish, and the *philosophes* were cosmopolitan. Conversely, the *philosophes* were anti-Christian, and Christianity had sprung from Judaism.

When, therefore, a few vanguard spokesmen for the Enlightenment contemplated the alleviation of Jewish disabilities, they were careful to avoid generalizations about the Jews. Even the most ardent philo-Semites preferred to treat their friendships as selective, singling out individual Jews. It gave them satisfaction to dote on a few wealthy and cultured "exception

Jews" as proof that there was an enlightenment which did not indiscriminately keep all members of a hapless people behind ghetto walls; and as proof, too, of the potentialities that might eventually be discovered and released in the larger Jewish population. One of those most deeply moved by the humanitarian ideals of the Age of Reason was Christian Wilhelm von Dohm, a Prussian historian. Dohm's celebrated pro-Jewish tract, *Uber die Bürgerliche Verbesserung der Juden,* "On the Civil Improvement of the Jews," stemmed largely from his admiration for a cultivated and lovable "exception Jew," Moses Mendelssohn.

Perhaps the most notable of the German philo-Semites was the philosopher and *littérateur,* Gotthold Ephraim Lessing. Lessing had favored the cause of "worthy" Jews from the very outset of his literary career. His play, *Die Juden,* written in 1749, was the first creative literary effort in modern times— by a Christian—to portray a Jew in sympathetic terms, as a cultured individual of refined and elevated sensibilities. Later, when Lessing came to know Moses Mendelssohn, he was so profoundly affected by the beauty of Mendelssohn's character that he immortalized him in a celebrated drama, *Nathan der Weise,* "Nathan the Wise." Nathan, the protagonist, was made the very apotheosis of wisdom, kindness, and nobility—a living challenge to Christian intolerance. "Nathan, Nathan," cried the Friar in the play, "you are a Christian! By God, you are a Christian! There never was a better Christian!" The success of the play was phenomenal; indeed, it was a landmark in modern German history, a significant commentary on the self-consciousness of the German Enlightenment during its crucial gestation period. The willingness of some rationalists to recognize, however cautiously, or even reluctantly, that there were occasional Jews who deserved emancipation, was an important augery of hope for the Jewish community. Measured by twentieth-century standards, these occasional gestures of Christian solicitude may not appear particularly impressive. But viewed against the dark and melancholy backdrop of medieval or even early modern European obscurantism, they were regarded as the rays of a rising sun. And, as we shall see (in Chapter III), in France the enlightened bourgeois would soon be compelled to extend the boundaries of his fellowship to include the Jews not only *en détail,* but also *en général.*

MOSES MENDELSSOHN AND JEWISH ENLIGHTENMENT

We may wonder if the Western Enlightenment, which was beginning to reshape the *Weltanschauung* of the Christian world, also exercised an influence on the intellectual outlook of Western Jewry. Clearly emancipation could not effectively have been extended as an act of grace from above unless the Jewish community was prepared intellectually and emotionally for entrance into the West. Without doubt the great majority of Western Jews, still living in a shadowed world of parochialism and Talmudic dialectic, was quite unaware of the currents of humanism that swirled through Western society and lapped at the very walls of the ghetto. The Jewish world was a dreary one, with few cultural compensations for its eighteenth-century inhabitants.

And yet tiny sunbursts of humanistic activity were beginning to make their appearance in Western Jewish life as early as the fifteenth or sixteenth centuries, when the Italian Renaissance became the center of interest for isolated groups of Jewish intellectuals. Spanish rationalism demonstrably influenced the thinking of such seventeenth-century Sephardic Jews as Baruch Spinoza and Uriel da Costa. The beauties of nature were captured in the classically elegant Hebrew poetry of Moses Chaim Luzzatto, a Jewish pietist who lived in eighteenth-century Italy. Luzzatto, in fact, wrote countless plays and poems on philosophical and secular as well as on religious themes, and he wrote them in the most limpid Hebrew style since the poets of the Spanish Golden Age. Then, too, from the end of the seventeenth century to the French Revolution several hundred Jews managed to attend German universities, as well as a large variety of secondary schools. Participation in secular culture was not entirely without precedent, therefore, even before Moses Mendelssohn appeared on the scene of modern history.

But it was Moses Mendelssohn who is properly associated with the first significant flowering of Jewish Enlightenment. The biography of this homely, humpbacked German Jew is truly one of the romances of modern times. His career bridged the worlds of the Yiddish and the German languages, the worlds of the ghetto and the celebrated European salons. Neither a great philosopher nor a penetrating theologian, nor even a Jewish spokesman of exceptional courage, Moses Mendelssohn nevertheless emerges as the key personality of Western European Jewry in the early modern era.

Born of a poor ghetto family of Dessau, in 1729, Mendelssohn spent his earliest years in typical Orthodox Jewish surroundings. Later, as an adolescent, he came under the influence of a brilliant intellect, Rabbi David Hirschel Frankel of Dessau. Frankel was as much at home in Plato as in the Talmud, and it was with loving pride that he transmitted the essence of both traditions to his exceptionally avid protégé. When Frankel left for Berlin to become Chief Rabbi of the Jewish community there, Moses Mendelssohn, a mere fourteen years of age, followed him on foot to the Prussian capital. Berlin's Jewish population was comparatively prosperous, and several of its members were not unversed in secular literature. Young Mendelssohn, who lived in the garret of a Jewish merchant and eked out a precarious living copying letters for his landlord, soon found that there were other brains to be picked than Frankel's. Several influential "privileged Jews" provided Mendelssohn with German books; others, as much impressed by his diligence as by his amazingly retentive memory, helped him to master German and Latin, and the intricacies of philosophy and metaphysics. When a particularly wealthy Berlin "privileged Jew" offered Mendelssohn a position as tutor to his children, the young man found himself at last with the security and the comparative leisure necessary for his philosophic studies.

Physically, Mendelssohn was hardly prepossessing. His early years of poverty had left him with thin, delicate bones and a badly humped back caused by rickets. Yet his personal disposition was so gentle, his mastery of German literature so complete, his usage of German style so fastidious, that he exercised a magnetic fascination upon all who met him. It was during the course of a chess game at a friend's home one afternoon that he made the acquaintance of Gotthold Lessing. Later, as the two engaged in a lively discussion on philosophical matters, Lessing began to sense the true dimensions of Mendelssohn's talent. He took the young Jew under his wing, encouraged him in his writing, and introduced him to the German literary world. It was Lessing who ensured the publication of Mendelssohn's first treatise, *Philosophical Dialogues,* a subtle critique of Spinoza's metaphysics, which established Mendelssohn's reputation as a thinker of clarity and originality. When at the age of thirty-two he wooed and won Fromet Guggenheim for his wife, Mendelssohn's happiness was complete. At personal peace with himself, comfortably married, financially secure, he settled into the most creative period of his life. Essays and pamphlets, volumes of philosophy, poured rapidly, uninterruptedly from his pen. In 1763 one of his philosophic essays won the prize of the Berlin Academy (Immanuel Kant was one of the competitors that year). Four years later he produced his most original work, *Phädon,* a defense of the immortality of the soul and of the existence of God. The German reading public was startled by the lucidity of Mendelssohn's thought and the elegance of his style. In the salons of Germany's major cities he was referred to increasingly as "the Jewish Socrates."

And yet European intellectual circles were by no means prepared to extend to other Jews the friendship and admiration they felt for Moses Mendelssohn. He was never lionized as a representative of the Jewish people, but rather as an exotic "exception Jew," indeed, the "exception Jew" par excellence. German society much preferred to single out Mendelssohn for glorification as evidence of their own ability to appreciate the occasional freaks produced by a "backward" people. To paraphrase a well-worn historic reference, if there had been no Mendelssohn, the rationalists would probably have found it necessary to invent him. He complimented their fastidiousness even if he left no enduring mark on their thinking.

Mendelssohn's main impact was upon his own people. Well-meaning Christians frequently asked him how he found it possible, as an intellectual of taste and discrimination, to remain a professing Jew, a member of "the most obscurantist" of religious groups. He rarely took offense at these queries; rather it was his practice, patiently and calmly to defend Judaism as a rational humane theology, and the Jews themselves as sensitive, enlightened bearers of a noble tradition. Yet the more Mendelssohn brooded about the circumstances of ghetto life, the backward Jewish educational system, the intellectual inbreeding, the more he recognized that the charge of obscurantism was not entirely unjustified. Why, he wondered, should Jews be restricted to the use of the Yiddish patois? Why should they be ignorant of the German language and the German culture? Something surely had to be done to prod the Jewish community into an increased awareness of the secular world about them. Ultimately Mendelssohn himself decided to take the initiative in providing his people with a key to its treasures.

With the aid of a devoted disciple, Napthali Hirz Wessely, Mendelssohn undertook to translate the Torah, the Five Books of Moses, into German. It was an exceptionally time-consuming and complicated undertaking, for it involved an ingenious combination of Hebrew characters with up-to-date German phonetics—as distinguished from the sixteenth-century German phonetics that passed for Yiddish. The translation was not completed until 1783, after five years of meticulous, frequently exhaustive labor. Yet the task was well worth the effort, for the success of the translation exceeded Mendelssohn's fondest expectations. In the sixteenth century, Martin Luther translated the Latin Bible into German, a translation that stimulated the German people into acquiring a reading knowledge of their own language. Mendelssohn's translation performed basically the same function for the Jews of Germany. Within a generation the Mendelssohn Bible had found its way to the bookshelves of nearly every literate Jewish home in Central Europe. Soon thereafter a few secular schools were established in the ghettos of the larger German cities, as Jews in growing numbers sought to understand more of the non-Jewish civilization about them. The passion for exploration would probably have grown without Mendelssohn; but the speed of this integrating development was largely the result of his patient pioneering.

What is Mendelssohn's place in history? He was not a profound philosopher or critic. His works cannot compare with the writings of his contemporaries, Kant and Lessing; indeed, Mendelssohn's philosophical discourses are hardly read today. Neither was Mendelssohn a forerunner of reform within Judaism. Although he was a deist by philosophic conviction, in response to Christian critics he preferred to defend Orthodox Judaism as "Revealed Legislation." It was a sophistry that spoke well for Mendelssohn's devotion to his people but poorly for his intellectual honesty. He was not a crusader for Jewish rights; in fact, he was rather timid when it came to the hard in-fighting required for political emancipation. His faith in militant propaganda was limited, for he was frankly fearful of arousing the anger of Christian authorities. Mendelssohn's role in history therefore was that of the awakener of secular interests among his own people. He devoutly believed that his translation of the Torah would touch off a quiet revolution in Jewish cultural life. He was right. Within two decades after his death, the Jews of Germany had mastered German culture and the German genre at least as thoroughly as their non-Jewish neighbors. It was a mastery that immeasurably enriched German as well as Jewish civilization.

MENDELSSOHN'S DISCIPLES AND JEWISH SECULARISM

For a few years after Mendelssohn's death in 1786, secular information was transmitted to the Jewish world through the medium of the Hebrew language. This was the technique Mendelssohn's disciples employed to destroy the hybrid vernacular of Yiddish. But once interest in secular matters had been stimulated Hebrew was discarded, and the German language completely superseded it. Jewish secularism was no less "Mendelssohnian," however, no less secular, for the fact that its temporary vehicle for several years remained the Hebrew language. Unhappily Mendelssohn's disciples—Wessely, Isaac Euchel, Mendel Breslau, Shalom Hacohen—were not of the same mold as the great pioneer himself. Their Hebrew-language magazine, *Ha-meassef*, "The Collector," polemicized the virtues of secularism to the point of monotony. Certainly none of the *Measseffim*, as the contributors to the journal were called, considered themselves disloyal Jews; but the more they immersed themselves in German civilization, the more many of them felt compelled to compromise, even to abandon, the values and traditions of Jewish life. Ultimately, in fact, the impact of a rich and attractive culture unbalanced Mendelssohn's disciples as it had never unbalanced Mendelssohn himself.

The career of Solomon Maimon provides a dramatic, if extreme, example of this kind of ambivalence. If any man could have surpassed Mendelssohn in intellectual capacity, if not in practical intelligence, Solomon Maimon was that man. He was born Solomon ben Joshua in Nieśwież, Lithuania, in 1754. As a child, he was able to thread his way through the labyrinths of the Talmud with such phenomenal ease that the incredulous rabbis of his province offered to ordain him as a rabbi at the age of eleven. When he refused the honor he was married off, as an alternate reward, to a well-born daughter of the town. At the age of fourteen Maimon became a father. The responsibilities of fatherhood however provided him neither with maturity nor common sense.

When he was twenty-five Maimon suddenly abandoned his wife and son, and trekked his way to the Prussian city of Königsberg, where he hoped to study medicine. Virtually penniless, he sought aid from a few wealthy Jewish families; but his uncouth beard and coarse Lithuanian accent did not ingratiate him with the "exception Jews" of the community, and he was rebuffed. Moreover, Maimon was something of an iconoclast; he was forever criticizing the Talmud or Orthodox Jewish practice for irrationality. When he moved to Berlin and continued to publicize his heretical opinions, he was summarily expelled by the Orthodox Jewish authorities. In Posen Maimon got himself hired as a tutor and was fired shortly thereafter as a freethinker. Later, disenchanted with the hostility that he seemed to encounter everywhere among his own people, Maimon flirted briefly with the idea of conversion. But if he was too much of a freethinker for the Jews he was hardly less so for Christians. His cynical and frankly opportunistic overtures were rejected by the Protestant clergy. Utterly despondent, on the verge of starvation, rejected by Christian and Jew alike, Maimon made a bungling attempt to drown himself. He was found with half his body hanging over the water, his feet refusing to follow; it was a position rather symbolic of his wretched predicament as a confused European Jew, at home neither among the educated nor the uneducated, the Christians nor the Jews.

Maimon returned to Berlin. And here, at last, his career took a turn for the better. His first book, *Essay on the Transcendental Philosophy,* was published in 1790, and was widely praised by Kant. Lectures and tutoring followed; for a while, Maimon even began to eat regularly. He hurled himself into writing, and soon other volumes followed: *Philosophical Dictionary; Commentary on the "More Nebuchim" of Maimonides;* various other works of philosophy; and a dubiously truthful autobiography. In these volumes, remarkably enough, Maimon finally achieved a synthesis of rationalism and Judaism; the two, he agreed, were not necessarily contradictory. In this regard his works possess much greater philosophic value than Mendelssohn's rather labored defenses of "revealed legislation." Of course there is no doubt that in his own day Mendelssohn's reputation far overshadowed Maimon's. Mendelssohn was a more lucid advocate of Jewish-Christian friendship; he was able to win legions of followers in both the Christian and Jewish worlds through the sheer force of his personality. As a consequence of his Torah translation, Mendelssohn's intellectual and social influence on German Jewry far transcended the influence of the uncouth Lithuanian, whose rarest talent was for making himself hated.

Yet it was Maimon's career not Mendelssohn's that provided an omen of German-Jewish intellectualism in the generation to follow. In renouncing allegiance to the Jewish tradition, and in failing to win—even rejecting—Christian respectability, Maimon staked out the path that a succession of creative and famous Jews were to follow (see Chapter XIX). All too many became intellectual vagabonds who lived outside the limits of the Jewish community but could not bring themselves to become members of any other well-defined society. Moses Hadas has put it well in suggesting that Maimon, who was buried in a pauper's grave, was the first modern Jew (as Heinrich Heine was probably the best-known) to prophesy correctly that neither Mass nor kaddish, the Jewish mourners' prayer, would be recited at his death.

CONCLUSION

What, then, can be said of the four hundred thousand Jews of Western Europe on the eve of the French Revolution? For the great majority of these people both the physical and the intellectual gates to Western life remained closed. Most Jews still were confined to filthy slum areas, forbidden access to Western cultural circles, denied the right of free movement. Their lives were still dominated by peddling and Talmudic argumentation.

But powerful new movements were undermining the foundations of the *ancien régime*: mercantilism, capitalism, rationalism. Cracks, too, began to appear in the walls of the ghettos; hundreds, perhaps even thousands, of Jews were beginning to see a hopeful future. The flamboyant *Hofjuden* were followed by a retinue of increasingly prosperous Jewish brokers and traders. Luzzatto, Mendelssohn, and Maimon led the way for scores of Jewish intellectuals, who became progressively aware of the reservoir of secular wonders untapped on the other side of the ghetto. In the latter part of the eighteenth century, the vanguard were still "exception Jews." But their numbers were growing. Economically and intellectually, on the eve of 1789, the Jews were not entirely unprepared for membership in Western society. And economically and intellectually, the Western world was not entirely unprepared to receive them.

Notes

Page 38. An excellent summary of Glückel of Hameln's life in Hanover may be found in the introduction to the Marvin Lowenthal translation of *Memoirs of Glückel of Hameln.*

Page 51. For an interpretation of Maimon's career, see the introduction to the Moses Hadas translation of *Solomon Maimon: An Autobiography.*

III

Emancipation in the West

In 1789 King Louis XVI of France faced bankruptcy. In search of financial advice, the distraught monarch summoned an Estates-General on May 5 of that year. Louis received more advice than he bargained for, however; for the Estates-General summarily converted itself into the National Assembly, and set about writing a constitution for France. In the prefix to the Constitution, the Declaration of the Rights of Man, the legislators began by proclaiming the equality of men, the right of all men, regardless of their station or birth, to participate directly or indirectly in the affairs of government. They implemented this manifesto by transforming the government of France into a balanced constitutional monarchy, and by eliminating those medieval anachronisms—economic feudalism, oppressive and inequitable taxation, social stratification—that could not withstand the scrutiny of Reason. Simultaneously they attacked the chaos of bailiwicks and senechalities that passed for a system of national administration. In their place the Assembly substituted a clear-cut, "businesslike" system of departments, districts, cantons, and municipalities.

And then, with long suppressed impatience, the gathering of bourgeois lawyers and businessmen turned to the grossest anachronism of all: corporativism. The old estates were abolished, as were guilds and municipal corporations. The structure of the Catholic Church was radically altered; its lands were confiscated, its priests and bishops transformed into salaried servants of the state. Protestants were enfranchised. The old enclaves of corporate sovereignty disappeared forever; the resources of every group and every individual were now to be brought into direct relationship with the state, and the tiresome and expensive process of negotiating with intermediaries was to be put to an end. The time had also come, therefore, for a readjustment of Jewish corporate status.

On the eve of the Revolution there were about forty thousand Jews in France. A few thousand Jews were scattered in Bordeaux and Bayonne, in the Comtat Venaissin in and around Avignon, and in a few cities of Provence. But the largest group, some thirty thousand, were German-speaking Jews who resided in the border provinces of Alsace and Lorraine. Life was far from intolerable for any of these people. Nowhere were they subjected to physical persecution. They were permitted to worship as they pleased and to build synagogues for that worship. But it was not until a law was passed in 1787 that the Jews of Alsace were allowed to participate freely in commerce, in the arts and crafts; while in Landes and Gironde Jews were even permitted to participate in municipal government. For the majority of Jews, however, the adversities of second-class citizenship still remained. In Paris, for example, Jews enjoyed no legally recognized status whatever; it was only by sufferance of police bribery that the city's eight hundred Sephardic Jews managed to remain. In Strasbourg, the capital of Alsace, Jews were denied rights of domicile altogether; each night Jewish peddlers were hustled out of town to the blasts of a warden's trumpet. In the smaller communities of Alsace and Lorraine most Jews lived either in physical ghettos or in the slum areas of town. Having but recently been permitted to participate in normal commerce, thousands of Alsatian Jews, still unfamiliar with "respectable" livelihoods, continued to peddle, to engage in pawnbroking and moneylending. And they were as a result quite poor. In some cities "Jew-taxes" still remained, while in others Jewish testimony was not admitted in litigation against Christians. These disabilities were not unbearable, but they were humiliating.

During the eighteenth century, as we have seen, the degradations of Jewish life were beginning to elicit the sympathy of important spokesmen in the intellectual world. The rational humanitarianism of France, not all of which was limited to the bourgeoisie, stood out, during this period, in marked contrast to the medieval obscurantism of most of the German states. In 1777 a visiting Egyptian rabbi noted with wonderment that he was treated with great respect by the Christian thinkers of Paris. One of his diary entries stated:

> The evening before, Tuesday, the Marquis de Thomé, a Christian savant, came to see me with great demonstrations of respect, as well as another Christian of mark and an "Italian abbé." They stayed nearly two hours, and I answered their questions. At the end the Marquis asked me to bless him: I blessed him, as well as the other Christians—it is strange!

The most celebrated of the French *philosophes,* Voltaire and Diderot, may have regarded the devoutly religious Jews with a measure of contempt. But even Diderot recognized their value as instruments of communication between the nations of Europe. "They are," he wrote, "like the cogs and nails needed in a great building in order to join and hold together all other parts." Montesquieu, shrewdly sensing the benefits to be obtained from a liberation of Jewish credit, urged an end to unnatural Jewish disabilities. There were others, too, who were "rational" enough to recognize that Jewish obscurantism and the predilection of Jews for usury were the results of Christian intolerance, and not the other way around. At a meeting of the Metz Royal Academy of Sciences in 1785, Pierre Louis Roederer, the Academy's most distinguished member, posed the question of Jewish emancipation. He was warmly applauded for his suggestion that Jewish "avarice" was the logical consequence of Christian persecution.

It was a view stated with particular cogency by the Count de Mirabeau. In 1787 this distinguished rationalist published a tract entitled *On Moses Mendelssohn and Political Reform of the Jews*—one of many such Mendelssohn testimonials to appear in the late eighteenth century. While recognizing that the "sage of Dessau" was an "exception Jew," Mirabeau ventured to predict that Mendelssohn was merely a particularly brilliant example of the untapped reservoir of Jewish talent in the ghetto world. "Do you want to make the Jews better men, useful citizens?" he wrote. "Banish from society all debasing distinctions against them: open to them all avenues of subsistence and livelihood." Mirabeau's sentiments were echoed by a liberal cleric, Abbé Henri Grégoire, in an essay entitled *On the Physical, Moral and Political Regeneration of the Jews*. "If the Jew has faults," the abbé suggested, "it is Christian society which is responsible. . . . In their place would we not be worse?" He returned to the subject repeatedly as the most persistent philo-Semite in the National Assembly. The Jews followed the remarks of Mirabeau and Abbé Grégoire with intense gratitude, and with equally intense impatience. For once the Revolution began, the Jews wanted action.

JEWISH EMANCIPATION, 1789-1791

By the late summer of 1789, equality of status had become a matter of particular urgency to the Jewish population of France. During the General Assembly's tumultuous summer sessions corporate autonomy had been abolished for the Jewish community and for all other religious, social, economic, and political groups. It was, in fact, precisely because the Jews were so swiftly stripped of these rights of self-government that they were convinced that equivalent political enfranchisement would inevitably follow. Lippman Cerf-Berr, an exceptionally favored Jew of Strasbourg, who had once been court purveyor to Louis XVI, presented the petitions of his people to Mirabeau and the abbé Grégoire, and then waited expectantly for the Jews to share in the blessings of the Revolution. The two philo-Semites spoke eloquently and often on behalf of religious equality, invoking all the appropriate rationalist deities. But emancipation was not to come so easily; the deputies from Alsace and Lorraine despised the Jews as usurers, and made every effort to block their enfranchisement. It appeared for a moment, in August of 1789, as if the Declaration of the Rights of Man, which prefaced the French Constitution, would be applied specifically to religious disabilities; but after a rather turbulent debate on the subject, the Assembly limited itself to a mild assurance that no one must be "disturbed" for his religious beliefs. Four months later, on December 24, 1789, the delegates granted civil and political rights to non-Catholics. But—significantly—this emancipation was at first limited to Protestants. The Alsatian deputies would not budge on the issue of the Jews.

It is worth noting that the Jews themselves were not immune to the factious class snobberies of their neighbors. Sensing that the Alsatians could not abide the Ashkenazic (mid-European) Jews who had settled in the border provinces, a handful of Sephardic-Jewish communities in southern France decided to dissociate themselves from their "low-born" brethren to the east. "We are French," they explained to the Assembly, "having been naturalized as such by letters patent of 1550, renewed in each reign, notably in 1776." Surely, suggested these descendants of Spanish "aristocrats," the Alsatians could have no objection to *their* enfranchisement? The stolid middle-class burghers of Alsace, who were uncomfortable about rupturing the doctrinal consistency of the Revolution, reluctantly acquiesced. On January 27, 1790, "active" citizenship was extended to the "well-born," the "productive" Sephardic Jews of southern France, who now declared themselves satisfied, and bowed out of the struggle for emancipation.

This Sephardic "treason" infuriated Cerf-Berr and his adherents; but when they turned once again to Mirabeau and the abbé Grégoire for support these good friends were frankly at a loss. At this moment, unexpected counsel came from another quarter, from the brilliant lawyer and delegate, Godard. It was Godard who called the attention of the Jews to the subtle shiftings of political balance in France, to the mounting strength of the *petit-bourgeoisie* of Paris. The Commune of Paris was the center of Jacobin political power, and was exerting a growing influence over the decisions of the General Assembly. At the suggestion of Godard, therefore, the Jews of Paris appeared before the Commune in January of 1791, dressed in their uniforms as National Guardsmen, and bearing certificates of "good behavior" from the Christian citizens of Paris. Godard himself pleaded the Jewish cause, and pleaded it eloquently and effectively. Deeply moved, the members of the Commune sent word to the Jacobin delegates in the General Assembly that the "General Will" required Jewish emancipation.

In the summer of 1791 the General Assembly finally remitted all "Jew-taxes." Still the advocates of the Jews pressed on. By September the Alsatian bloc, heavily infiltrated now by Jacobins, abandoned efforts to stem the egalitarian tide; on September 28, 1791, they joined with the other members of the Assembly in admitting all Jews, Ashkenazic and Sephardic alike, to full rights of French citizenship. Actually, the delegates could not have evaded the issue of Jewish emancipation much longer. They were hardly secure enough in their political triumph to risk inconsistency in the application of liberal ideals. And they were well aware that limitations on Jewish freedom were neither national nor—in those days of revolutionary camaraderie—particularly fraternal. Most of the delegates, too, were either merchants or lawyers with well-developed business instincts; as practical men they were by no means oblivious to the role that Jewish wealth could play in a capitalist economy. Any one of these factors alone might not have determined the issue of Jewish emancipation; together they were irresistible.

Cerf-Berr, who wept uncontrollably when he learned the news of Emancipation, sat down on the evening of September 29 to dispatch a letter of congratulations to his coreligionists in Alsace. "God chose the noble French nation to reinstate us in our privileges," he wrote, "and bring us to a new birth, just as in former days He selected Antiochus and Pompey to degrade and oppress us. . . . This nation asks no thanks, except that we show ourselves worthy citizens." French Jewry fulfilled these expectations with passionate eagerness. They hurled themselves into the mainstream of French life, joining the National Guard by the thousands, serving with gallantry in the French army, making generous financial contributions —even to the extent of donating their plate—to the Revolutionary armies. Jews occupied public office and became lieutenants of the gendarmerie. They began tentatively, and then in increasing numbers, to send their children to the public schools. By 1810 Jewish integration into French life was so much a matter of public notice that the Metz Town Council, in special session, proclaimed that "many followers of the law of Moses each day make laudable efforts to draw closer to our customs, usages, our civilization, our special practices, to escape at last from the state of abjection to which our old laws and perhaps our prejudices condemned them." This rapid acculturation did not, on the other hand, result in abandonment of loyalty to the ancestral religion. Even the Robespierre Terror of 1793-94, which locked and shuttered churches and synagogues alike, left no permanent imprint on the Jews. They found it entirely possible to live their lives as practising Jews and patriotic Frenchmen.

One of the ways, certainly, in which Jews drew closer to French customs and usages was by taking advantage of the opportunity to diversify their economic activity. In central and southern France, Jewish entrance into the respected professions, into wholesaling and retailing, was particularly notable. It was only in Alsace, on the periphery of integral France, that the Jews abandoned their historic connection with moneylending more slowly. During the early days of the Revolution, when the General Assembly confiscated and auctioned off the estates of *émigré* aristocrats, the peasants of Alsace were frequently able to participate in the bidding by borrowing funds from Jewish moneylenders. By the end of the eighteenth century, as a result, some 400,000 peasants, landowners now, were up to their ears in debt to a few thousand Jews. Later, when Napoleon came to power, one of his first acts was to retire the worthless assignat currency, which had originally been issued by the National Assembly. Unfortunately for the Alsatians, payment in the new hard currency proved to be virtually impossible, especially when many of the breadwinners were off with Napoleon's armies. Thus, between 1802 and 1804 the courts were obliged to issue thousands of foreclosure judgments on behalf of Jewish creditors. The consequence of these foreclosures was an almost immediate revival of Alsace's endemic Jew-hatred—which manifested itself in general rioting and the pillage of Jewish homes and shops.

It happened that these anti-Jewish demonstrations coincided exactly with the emergent political reaction in France. By 1794 the Revolution had overreached itself; Robespierre and his *petit-bourgeois* followers had terrorized the moderates beyond endurance. When the middle class finally struck back Robespierre himself was decapitated by the same guillotine to which he had sent so many of his enemies. For the next five years, from 1795 to 1799, the country was governed by the rather corrupt Directoire, composed of bourgeois profiteers; in 1799, as the pendulum continued to move to the right, this group, too, was overthrown by a Man on Horseback, Napoleon Bonaparte. Napoleon preserved the spirit of fraternity, of nationalism, even the priceless revolutionary gain of equality before the law; in fact, as we shall see, he extended equality before the law to the rest of Europe. But he scrapped political liberty, and set about ruling France with a heavy authoritarian hand. Viewing these developments, conservative and Royalist elements in France took heart. They intensified their propaganda campaign against the Revolution; and—with a shrewd glance at the embittered debtors of Alsace—they were not slow to identify the Revolution with Jewish emancipation. It was a technique to be employed repeatedly and with equal absence of scruple during the entire course of the nineteenth century.

The Royalists circulated ominous warnings throughout France that Jews and Protestants were buying up the countryside and desecrating the holy places. One news item in a Catholic journal warned that a *"société de capitalistes juifs"* was offering 800,000 francs for the Chartreux church in Paris, and planned to substitute the Old for the New Testament. The Royalist journals, *La Mercure de France* and *La Décade philosophique,* dealt with the Jews in articles that were as vindictive as they were extensive. Louis Gabriel de Bonald, "the philosopher of Royalism," took the lead in this campaign; he was joined by Chateaubriand and other Royalist ideologists, who trotted out the old pre-Revolutionary canards: *viz.,* that the Jews were a nation within a nation, an alien and unassimilable body. The Achilles' heel of the Jewish position was, of course, the disproportionate Jewish involvement in Alsatian moneylending, and the Royalists made the most of it. Did not the Jewish religion, Bonald asked, require Jews to view all Christians with hostility? Was not Mosaic law hostile to the law of Jesus? Were not the Jews incapable of carrying out their civic duties? Other charges were even more shocking and scurrilous. Few Jews were seriously concerned about the reaction of the typical Frenchman to this demagogic propaganda. The overriding question was: how much attention was the Emperor Napoleon paying to it?

NAPOLEON BONAPARTE AND THE JEWS

Actually, Napolenon had given very little consideration to the "Jewish question" until his return from the victory at Austerlitz. Then, stopping off at Strasbourg in January of 1806, he was inundated with anti-Jewish grievances, with accounts of the "ruination" of the peasantry by Jewish moneylenders. The petitioners begged the Emperor to take special measures against Jewish foreclosures. General François Etienne Kellermann, who had himself made a fortune in land, proposed that the Jews of Alsace and Lorraine be expelled without mercy. Napoleon was genuinely impressed by these tearful appeals; he had long held a jaundiced opinion of merchants and financiers as a class, and was particularly unsympathetic to usurers. Accordingly he promised the Alsatians that something would be done immediately to put the matter "in good order."

Upon returning to Paris, Napoleon gave increasing attention, as well, to the mounting Royalist campaign against the Jews. Perhaps, he reasoned, it would be possible to take the wind out of the Catholic-Bourbon sails, and at the same time "correct" Jewish behavior, by declaring a moratorium on all debts due Jewish moneylenders. When, however, Napoleon broached the idea before his Council of State, he found opinion sharply divided. One councilor, fiery young Count Louis Mathieu Molé, whose hatred for the Jews was compounded by a persistent false rumor that his, Molé's, great-grandmother had been Jewish, supported the Emperor's proposal enthusiastically, and even urged an outright rescission of Jewish emancipation. But there were other councilors who pointed out that the success of the Emperor's administration was largely due to its support of the Revolution's most priceless ideal, equality before the law. At first Napoleon was prepared to discount this critical reluctance—until another idea occurred to him. On May 30, 1806, he declared a moratorium of one year on all Jewish judgments for debt against the farmers of the eastern departments—i.e., Alsace and Lorraine. By itself, to be sure, this measure appeared to override his more cautious advisors. But the Emperor had no intention of merely hurling the Jews back into limbo; he was far too astute a statesman to hobble his regime by reducing the Jews to a sullen and un-co-operative enclave.

Napoleon's instinct for ingratiating himself with the religious factions of his country had always been sure and timely. He had shrewdly converted Catholic hostility into friendship by arranging a concordat with the Papacy in 1801. In return for restoring Roman Catholicism as the Established Church of France, Napoleon assumed control over all Church appointments. "You will see," he said to Louis Antoine de Bourrienne, "what a party I shall know how to make of the priests." Similarly, Napoleon had granted a "constitution" to French Protestants, extending recognition to them as an "official" religious group. In exchange, of course, he assured himself of Protestant loyalty, as well as control over all Protestant pastoral appointments. The wily and cynical Emperor had few scruples even about flirting with Islam during his early campaign in Egypt. He solemnly mouthed quotations from the Koran, sported a fez, socialized with the muftis—and managed in this fashion to win a futwa of approval for his campaign against the British and the Turks. Nor did Napoleon hesitate, in that same abortive Egyptian campaign, to promise the Jews of Asia and Africa a homeland in Palestine, if they would but rally to the French standard. Here, to be sure, Bonaparte failed. The handful of Jews in Palestine remained loyal to the Turks. But an occasional setback did not shake Napoleon's determination to placate all religious sects. "My policy," Napoleon told the Council of State in August 1801, "is to govern men as the great majority of them wish to be governed. That, I believe, is the way to recognize the sovereignty of the people. It was as a Catholic that I won the war in the Vendée, as a Moslem that I established myself in Egypt, and as an Ultramontane that I won the confidence of the Italians. If I were governing Jews, I should rebuild the temple of Solomon."

And now, in fact, Napoleon did determine to govern the Jews, "to revive among the Jews . . . the sentiments of civic morality that unfortunately have been moribund among too large a number of them by a state of abasement in which they have long languished." Napoleon felt that he could manipulate this minority for his own purposes if he worked as carefully and as adroitly as he had worked with the Catholics and the Protestants. He must insure unequivocal Jewish loyalty to the state; he must stimulate vocational reform among the Jews. Of course, all guarantees and changes must appear to come voluntarily from the Jews themselves. To that end, Napoleon summoned an Assembly of Jewish Notables, a gathering of 112 outstanding businessmen, financiers, rabbis, and scholars —all hand-picked by the prefects of the departments of France and of the puppet kingdom of Italy. Napoleon knew how to stage an impressive production. When the Jews arrived in Paris on July 29, 1806, they were received at the Hôtel de Ville by an honor guard beating a drum tattoo.

The opening moments, however, were ominous. Count Molé, who represented the Emperor at the historic gathering, greeted the Notables with a coldly insulting speech of welcome. They had been charged, Molé pointed out, with being usurers. The charges were well-founded, he insisted; nevertheless the Emperor, in his wisdom and goodness, would offer the Jews an opportunity to remedy these practices themselves. In fact, the Emperor would preserve for the Jews the totality of their rights as Frenchmen— providing that they proved themselves worthy of these rights. What was expected, Molé went on, was that the Assembly should define their attitude toward their country by satisfactorily answering twelve specific questions. Then, as the Jewish Notables waited in grim silence, Molé began to enumerate the questions. 1. Are the Jews permitted to have more than one wife? 2. Does Judaism permit divorce? 3. Can Jews and Christians marry? (The delegates began to squirm and stare at each other incredulously.) 4. In the eyes of the Jews are the French brothers or strangers? 5. What behavior does Jewish law prescribe toward French Christians? 6. Do Jews born in France consider France their country? Are they willing to defend it and obey its laws? 7. Who names the rabbis? 8. What police jurisdiction do the rabbis exercise over the Jews? 9. Are Jewish electoral forms and police jurisdictions prescribed by Jewish law or merely by custom? 10. Does Jewish law prohibit the Jews from entering the professions? 11. Does Jewish law encourage Jews to practise usury among their own community? 12. Among the Christians? Molé finished, folded his paper, and stared at the Notables. The Jews sat in stunned silence for several moments. Then Abraham Furtado, a suave and eloquent Sephardic financier whom the Assembly had chosen for its president, arose and gravely thanked the Government for its many kindnesses; he assured Molé and the other Commissioners that the Jews welcomed the opportunity of proving their devotion to their country. They would, he informed the officials, answer the questions forthwith. Molé nodded curtly, and led the Commissioners from the room.

The Assembly knew that it would have to work fast. At Furtado's suggestion therefore the questions were turned over to a committee of rabbis and laymen. Within a few weeks this committee prepared a series of skillful and dignified answers that was approved almost immediately by the Assembly as a whole. Few of the questions posed any real difficulty. Of course the Jews considered France their country and Frenchmen their brothers. Of course they were willing to defend France—"to the death." Of course the rabbis exercised no police jurisdiction; their authority was purely spiritual. Of course the Jews were monogamous. The question of mixed marriages was somewhat more complicated, however, for the rabbis were in conscience bound to oppose weddings outside the faith. But the laymen who predominated in the Assembly managed to come up with a compromise answer. The Bible, the Notables declared, forbade marriage with heathen peoples in ancient times; yet inasmuch as French Christians were manifestly not heathens, the prohibition did not apply to contemporary France. As far as usury was concerned, while moneylending was not forbidden in the Talmud, Jewish law was equally explicit that only a fair rate of interest might be charged.

When the Assembly presented its answers to the Government, Molé was struck by what appeared to him to be evasive references: now to Moses, now to the Talmud, now to practical Jewish usage. He was particularly suspicious of the answer on usury. Thus, in his report to the Emperor, his commentary on the replies was cynical, even hostile. Napoleon, on the other hand, declared himself satisfied; he had received the professions of loyalty that he demanded. He was determined now to create an instrument which would endow such professions with a kind of "religious" prestige. Besides, Napoleon had long awaited an opportune moment to dazzle the Jews of France with his benevolence and, as a consequence, to win their undying loyalty for his cause. The time had come to show his hand. On September 3, 1806, he issued a summons for a Sanhedrin.

THE SANHEDRIN—AND ITS PRICE

The Sanhedrin, the Supreme Court of the Jews during the ancient days of the Jewish Commonwealth, had not been activated after the destruction of the Temple and had remained a moribund institution for the eighteen hundred years of the Diaspora. When therefore Molé announced to the Assembly of Jewish Notables that this traditional symbol of Jewish sovereignty was to be revived, the Jews at first were speechless with amazement. The Emperor, Molé informed the gathering, felt it necessary that the answers of the Assembly of Notables be transformed into official Jewish law, into canon law, as it were; and presumably a Sanhedrin alone had the authority to perform this function. The Jews could not have been ignorant of the political motives behind Napoleon's decisions; but the solemn tribute to their historic tradition moved them to tears. Furtado's reply to Molé expressed the Assembly's deep gratitude that there was official concern for Jewish sensibilities; the Jews would be worthy of the great honor that had been accorded them. Brushing all misgivings aside, the Assembly endorsed the Emperor's call. The news quickly swept through Europe. Hosannas of joy were intoned in Jewish synagogues throughout France and Italy, even, as we shall see, as far east as Russia. With one brilliant gesture, Napoleon had transformed himself into the great "white eagle" of Jewish folklore.

On February 4, 1807, what purported to be a revived Sanhedrin gathered in Paris: a gathering of eighty delegates, forty-six of them rabbis. Their chairman, David Sinzheim, Rabbi of Strasbourg, was a man of known patriotism and wide Jewish erudition; he presided over the subsequent sessions with quiet and effective authority. Napoleon was determined to press this group into firmer commitments than he had received from its predecessor. He informed the Commissioners that he expected specific answers to the twelve questions, and he insisted that the responses exert nothing less than Talmudical authority in Jewish society. The Emperor also expected the Sanhedrin to condemn the behavior of the Alsatian-Jewish moneylenders in the most solemn of "religious" terms; to prohibit Jews from moneylending altogether—unless the "usurers" themselves owned land and, as a result, had a stake in the welfare of France. Napoleon's ulterior motives were now quite apparent. The Sanhedrin was a flattering sop to Jewish pride. In return he expected the Jews to use their own agencies to "Gallicize" all elements within their own community, to transform them into "first-class" citizens in terms of civic responsibility.

Napoleon was not disappointed. On nearly every issue the Sanhedrin endorsed the answers of the earlier body. Once again it was affirmed that the laws of Moses and of the rabbis were exclusively religious in their application; that France alone could claim the political allegiance of French Jewry. The decisions of civil tribunals were declared to have priority over those of religious tribunals. This priority was made the basis for the answer on intermarriage, for the rabbis disdained this time to give theological justification for mixed marriages. The delegates reaffirmed the "love" they bore their fellow Frenchmen. They encouraged Jewish participation in all vocations and professions. They publicly condemned moneylending at high rates of interest. In general terms, clearly, Napoleon had secured "spiritual" endorsement for Jewish political loyalty. Should the Sanhedrin now be obliged to go into the matter of usury in detail? Napoleon consulted his Council, and the Councilors agreed that the Emperor had already obtained the basic pledges he needed. It would be better, they suggested, not to overtax the rabbis. Thus, in April of 1807, the Sanhedrin was adjourned.

Napoleon was a devious man. Each of his major decisions was usually the result of a complex skein of motivations. If he had reasons of self-interest in summoning the Sanhedrin, those reasons were more far-reaching than might have been apparent to the Jews of France. For one thing, the Emperor certainly did intend that the leading representatives of the Jews should take an unequivocal position on the issue of citizenship. He wanted specific assurances, formalized in religious terms, that rabbinical jurisdiction in civil and judicial matters was a thing of the past, that the Jews had turned their backs forever on their separate nationhood, on their corporative status, on their traditional hope for a return to Palestine. All these assurances Napoleon received. The members of the Assembly and of the Sanhedrin were unquestionably sincere in linking their future, for good and always, with the future of France. "We no longer form a nation within a nation," Abraham Furtado declared, approving the answers of the Sanhedrin. "France is our country. Jews, such today is your status: your obligations are outlined, your happiness is waiting."

As we shall see, Furtado's rather florid announcement was more than mere rhetoric. The Sanhedrin's solemn renunciation of separate Jewish nationhood was truly of watershed importance in Jewish history. It set the tone of Western Jewish life for over a century to come. When Portalis *fils,* one of Napoleon's Commissioners, wrote later that "the Jews ceased to be a people and remained only a religion," he perceived the Sanhedrin's true significance perhaps even more accurately than did the Jews themselves. While the Notables may have meant merely to reject the canard of dual political loyalties, Jews in later generations—Jews in America as well as in Western Europe—would reinterpret the Sanhedrin's solemn assurances in such a way as to divest Jewish identification of all but its narrowest religious connotation. The Twelve Answers provided a rationale for "salon Jews" and *Kaiserjuden*; for Germans, Frenchmen, and Americans of the "Israelitish" or "Mosaic" persuasion; for Jews in a hurry to assume the protective coloration of their Christian neighbors. The ultimate significance of the Paris Sanhedrin, therefore, was not its rejection of corporate Jewish autonomy, but rather the sanction it provided for some Western Jews to reject Jewish civilization in its wider ethnic and cultural implications. It was more than Napoleon could have hoped for.

The Emperor had yet other purposes in mind when he summoned the Sanhedrin. By September of 1806 French armies had reached the shores of the Vistula. Joachim Murat and his cavalry, Louis Nicholas Davout and his infantry were installed in Warsaw. This vast soldiery had no means of subsistence, however; the Russians had destroyed or carried away all staples. All the boats had been sunk, and the Vistula was now impassable. It was at this juncture that it occurred to Napoleon, as it had occurred to so many of his predecessors in earlier centuries, that those dependable middlemen, the Jews, could be of value. The Jews were numerous in Poland; with their business experience and international connections, they were in a position to provide grain, oats, and barley for the *grande armée.* In summoning the Sanhedrin, Napoleon probably believed that he could assure himself not merely of the loyalty of French Jewry, but of Polish Jewry as well. It was this factor that accounted for the care with which the Emperor, even deep in Poland, followed the deliberations of the Sanhedrin, soliciting from his Commissioners the most minute details of the proceedings, directing negotiations through a chain of couriers. Napoleon's ruse was not without success. Polish Jewry knew nothing of Napoleon's motivations. They knew only that he treated his Jews—in Poland as well as in France—like human beings; while Prussian and Austrian authorities treated them like dogs. Jewish contractors and peddlers by the hundreds willingly undertook the responsibility of provisioning the French army in the Duchy of Warsaw. As far as the typical Polish-Jewish family was concerned, Napoleon was a hero, a liberator, a modern-day Cyrus. Indeed, a legendary Napoleon emerged, benign and understanding, who became a permanent part of the folklore of Eastern Europe's Yiddish-speaking Jews.

Finally, Napoleon summoned the Sanhedrin, to divert attention from his plan to rescind some of the gains of Jewish emancipation. In an "Organic Regulation on the Mosaic Religion," issued in March of 1808, Napoleon declared Judaism to be an "official" religion of France. The salaries of rabbis were set by the state, but paid by "consistories," departmental associations of Jewish laymen. While the rabbis of each consistory were obliged to supervise Jewish religious life, they also became the agents of Napoleon's policy, charged with the responsibility of preaching loyalty to France and obedience to French laws. The consistory's officials, lay and spiritual, were obliged to reprimand those Jews who were lapsing back into usury; they were obliged also to insure that all able-bodied Jewish youths made themselves available for conscription. Eventually, the consistorial system became a kind of police force over Jewish morals, under the cold and unsympathetic supervision of the Ministry of Religion.

In a second measure, issued simultaneously with the Organic Regulation, Napoleon tightly regulated the commercial activity of French Jewry. A number of arbitrary and crippling restrictions were imposed on Jewish moneylenders—restrictions that were not applied to Christians. With a view to reducing the Jewish population of Alsace, Napoleon forbade those Jews who had temporarily left the border provinces to return to their former homes. Even in the interior of France, Jews were not permitted to change their domicile, unless they first purchased rural property and promised to devote themselves exclusively to agriculture. This regulation very appropriately was identified in Jewish history as the "Infamous Decree." Its infamy was not merely that, in discriminating in this fashion against Jews, it struck at Jewish equality before the law—in short, at Emancipation. It was also cunningly contrived to do so at the moment when the Jews were still dazzled by the afterglow of the Sanhedrin.

The Infamous Decree probably hastened the decline of moneylending, peddling, and old-clothes dealing as major fields of Jewish enterprise; by 1810 and 1811 Jews were moving rapidly into retailing, crafts, the mechanical arts, and the professions. But this readjustment undoubtedly would have taken place without Napoleon's gratuitous and insulting discrimination. Nor, indeed, were the consistories necessary to remind the Jews of their civic duties. Long before the establishment of this moral police system,

Jews had been enlisting in the French army. Before and after 1808, Jews fought, were decorated, and died on all the battlefields of Europe. At Waterloo alone fifty-two Jews were killed in action. Yet it is ironic that in Napoleon's lifetime and afterward, the Jews of France preferred to overlook the Emperor's rather devious mixture of kicks and kindnesses. Exactly as Napoleon had intended, it was the Sanhedrin which continued to loom largest in their minds. For decades there were French Jews who sang dithyrambically of "the incomparable eagle," "the great liberator." The eagle's liberation however was extended primarily to other nation's Jews, those who lived beyond the boundaries of France, conveniently far from home.

THE GHETTOS FALL IN EUROPE

Having consolidated his power in France after the concordat with the Papacy in 1801, Napoleon turned to the task of devouring his European neighbors. No army or combination of armies could stand in the Emperor's way, for his strategic genius was combined with the fervor of the Revolution, and the immense physical and military resources of the largest state in Western Europe. At Marengo, Ulm, Austerlitz, and Jena his troops, systematically blasted to bits the coalition of Prussian, Austrian, and Russian armies. By 1807, Napoleon has become master of the Continent, from the English Channel to the banks of the Vistula, from the Baltic Sea to the Straits of Messina. Belgium, the Netherlands, Italy, all were in French hands. The old Holy Roman Empire no longer existed. Germany was now divided into three neatly truncated political divisions: Austria, which retained its territorial integrity but forsook its imperial overlordship in Germany; Prussia, less than half its former size, its eastern provinces incorporated into the Duchy of Warsaw; and the rest of Germany—the area that had encompassed some three hundred principalities—now transformed into a Confederation of the Rhine, under the presidency of the French emperor. Napoleon was determined, too, that the puppet states of the Confederation should be made over in the image of France. Thus, in each of the states, he inaugurated a formal constitution on the French model, granting to the incredulous German inhabitants equality before the law and a wide variety of civil liberties.

The Jews of Germany, too, were ultimate beneficiaries of these French reforms. Taking courage from the emancipation of their coreligionists to the West, leading Jewish spokesmen in the various kingdoms and duchies of the Holy Roman Empire began, as early as 1792, to petition their monarchs for a semblance of judicial equality, for equal rights of domicile and travel, and for equality of vocational status. The typical German duke, however, was as unwilling to emancipate his Jews as he was reluctant to emancipate his serfs. In the case of the Jews, moreover, a hostile public opinion remained as an obstacle to civil equality. For medievalism in both its intellectual and economic forms lingered on in the German world. The *Mittelstand,* the middle class, which alone of Europe's economic groups maintained a vested interest in Enlightenment, was dwarfed and stunted in Germany, still struggling to fight its way back to life and influence after the Armageddon of the Thirty Years' War. Whenever Jews petitioned for rights, therefore, counterpetitions were produced by leading German citizens, urging the authorities to keep the Jews in their ghettos. "The only way I see by which civil rights can be given to them [the Jews]," wrote Johann Fichte, in a famous phrase, "is to cut off their heads in one night, and to set new ones on their shoulders, which should contain not a single Jewish idea." Even the greathearted Johann Gottfried von Herder, who frequently expressed his admiration for the Israel of antiquity, felt such an aversion to the Jews of his own day that it was an effort for him to treat the incomparable Moses Mendelssohn in a friendly manner. The prospect of Jewish emancipation genuinely frightened most Germans, who viewed their Jews as cheap peddlers and obscurantists, as aliens with little understanding of Germany's Christian romantic traditions. Now with the rise of Napoleon, with French armies humiliating German pride in one battle after another, a vindictive chauvinism swept through Central Europe and fastened upon the Jews as foreigners, potential traitors, and Francophiles.

Much as they were embittered by Christian intolerance, the Jews of Germany, and particularly of Prussia, refused to be provoked into acts of treason against their dynasties during the Napoleonic Wars. In the case of the wretched ghettoized Jewries of Mainz and other Rhine cities, it was probably fear of reprisal that prevented them from committing any overt deeds of disloyalty. Berlin Jews, on the other hand, were under the Mendelssohnian influence and honestly believed themselves to be Prussian; their loyalty was dictated by patriotism, and by a sincere conviction that the Jewish problem would soon be solved within the framework of Prussian politics. The French were more amused than provoked. "Caged birds," observed one French commander, "whistle the tunes that are played to them." But as the French besieged one German state after another, as they gradually rewrote and liberalized German law and administration on the French model, they gave German Jewry a different "song to sing."

For in each of these occupied duchies French engineers quite literally burned and battered down the walls of the ghettos, often to the accompaniment of music and fireworks, and the cheering of the troops. French officers personally escorted the confused and frightened denizens of the ghetto through gaping holes in the walls into bright sunlight. Throughout French-occupied territory, Jewish equality before the law, as indeed legal equality for all inhabitants, was constitutionalized. In Westphalia, for example, a decree issued in January 1808, by Napoleon's brother Jerome, placed the Jews on a footing of absolute equality with other subjects. Jews were free at last to move into public office and the professions—and they did so in disproportionately large numbers. Many Jews enlisted in the army, and a number rose to be captains and quartermasters. Liberation spread from Westphalia to the duchies of Baden, Hesse-Nassau, Mecklenburg, and to a majority of the member states of the Confederation of the Rhine. The most significant exception was the Kingdom of Bavaria, where Napoleon, preoccupied with other matters, never quite found time to press the issue of Jewish emancipation to its conclusion.

The situation in Prussia was rather more complicated however. The Prussians may have been defeated and demoralized, but the country was not occupied by French soldiers; French bayonets could not thrust home emancipation here as they had in the Confederation of the Rhine. As early as 1801, therefore, when news of Jewish emancipation in French-occupied territory reached Prussia, a new series of regulations was clamped upon the Jewish community, giving the police discretionary powers of punishment in the event of "suspicious" Jewish behavior. King Frederick William III admitted a certain harshness in the new legislation, but insisted that it was justified because the Jews "constituted as it were a state within a state"; the Jews, he added, must first prove themselves "worthy of citizenship."

And then the disaster of Jena annihilated the Prussian army, reduced Prussian territory by half, and thrust upon the Government in Berlin the desperate and urgent need for reform. To be sure, French soldiers did not occupy the remnant kingdom, but who knew when they might? Prussia could not be defended unless it became as efficient an organism as triumphant France. Thus, under the direction of Barons Stein and Hardenberg, crucial, and, in some instances, far-reaching changes were effected: serfdom was abolished; a decentralized administration was transformed into a tight unitary bureaucracy; a free, compulsory school system was created; conscription was inaugurated. Virtually all these reforms were imposed from above and were designed to strengthen, not weaken, royal authority. But whatever the motivations, the results could only be an improvement over the older kind of dynastic cameralism.

In the midst of the Stein and Hardenberg "clean sweep," attention was once again drawn to the petitions of the Jews. The basic cause for Prussian reform was the desire to create an efficient military state, to eradicate, or at least to modify, the expensive anachronism of corporativism. If guilds, feudal prerogatives, and municipal corporations were abolished, then, too, Jewish autonomy had to be dispensed with, and the Jews brought into direct relationship with the government. It could not have escaped Stein's attention, moreover, that if the Jews were emancipated, Jewish credit also would be unlocked for state purposes. Nor was the prospect of Jewish equality as frightening as it had been before the battle of Jena. The Treaty of Tilsit had shorn Prussia of those eastern provinces which contained the largest and poorest Jewish population, the tradition-bound, Polish-Jewish masses of Posen. If emancipation was to be granted, it would be extended to a remnant Jewry, a rather well-to-do group, not entirely unacquainted with German culture. What more would this mean, Hardenberg argued, than a continuation of the prevailing fashion of favoring individual "exception Jews"?

Yet the liberation of Prussian Jewry was not a simple project for Hardenberg to broach to the king. In fact, it was ironic that in Prussia the same nationalistic impulse for regeneration should have been the occasion for a wild

Jew-hatred, part of that emergent Teutomania which was destined in the next century to be the horror and despair of Western civilization. But, for the time being at least, statist considerations prevailed. On March 11, 1812, on the eve of Prussia's War of Liberation, the Jews of Prussia received the grant of Emancipation. It was still only a partial grant. Although the Jews were delivered from their former disabilities—from the obligation of paying special taxes, of living in slum neighborhoods, of paying special tolls in their travels—they were still denied the right to occupy state positions. In this sense, therefore, Emancipation was still tinctured by suspicion of Jewish disloyalty. It hardly mattered that Jews took part in the military struggle against the French, many of them dying in the battles of Leipzig and Waterloo; that a rather large number distinguished themselves for heroism and were awarded the Iron Cross. They continued, nevertheless, to live under a cloud of distrust for generations to come, with consequences no less tragic for the Jewish psyche than for the German.

Of all the states of Central and Western Europe only the Hapsburg Empire, the citadel of European Catholicism, managed to stave off reform for a few more generations. The Jews of Austria as a result continued to live on as "non-Europeans," enduring the unrelieved burden of medieval disabilities. In Vienna a few "tolerated" Jewish families were given priviliged status, although even they were still required to pay special taxes. All other Jews found themselves locked in on every side, without legal rights, denied access to respectable trades and professions, and subject to expulsion at a moment's notice. In neighboring Bohemia and Moravia, restrictions on Jewish residence rights were maintained even more rigidly than in Austria; as late as 1815 only fourteen thousand Jewish families lived in the two crown lands—most of them in the city of Prague. The seventy-five thousand Jews of Hungary were tolerated only in the smaller towns and villages of the southeast, and itinerant Jewish merchants were hustled out of the free cities as soon as they had transacted their business. Only in the former Polish province of Galicia, where there lived some 250,000 Jews—the principal reservoir of the Jewish population of the Hapsburg Empire—were domicile restrictions rather slight. Even here, however, Jews were forbidden to own or lease land except for personal farming, a restriction that was tantamount to exclusion from the countryside. In the entire Hapsburg Empire, in fact, there was not a single province where free domicile for Jews was extended as a fundamental right. But of course Jewish self-government continued to operate. Corporativism too endured on all levels of Hapsburg society, a symptom of that unregenerate traditionalism which was destined ultimately to disintegrate the Austrian dynasty.

In all other areas of Europe where French soldiers marched, Jewish emancipation followed. In the Netherlands, for example, Jews had been living in comparative security and comfort for many years. But they still remained subject to several significant disabilities; they were debarred from public office, as well as from all crucial trade guilds; they were obliged to pay taxes for the support of the Established Church. While the Dutch bore the Jews little enmity, they were cautious about extending complete equality to fifty thousand people—who represented, after all, a sizable minority in a country of only two million. And then in 1796, even before Napoleon appeared on the scene, a French Revolutionary army overran the Netherlands and established the Batavian Republic. Almost immediately Noel, the French ambassador, who was in reality the Protector, installed the full apparatus of Revolutionary innovations: equality before the law, administrative centralization, freedom for all minorities. In September 1796, a few tactful reminders from Noel were sufficient to prod the Dutch National Assembly to proclaim complete Jewish equality. As an indication of this measure's effect on the status of Dutch Jewry, it is sufficient to note that two years later, in 1798, a Jewish member, Isaac da Costa Atias, was elected president of the National Assembly.

French occupation of Italy, in 1797, antedated the Napoleonic Empire. Later the peninsula was further divided and redivided under Bonapartist hegemony, but the precedents of equality before the law and freedom of economic opportunity, which had already been effectively established by the Revolutionary armies, were not altered by Napoleon or by the relatives whom he elevated to the various Italian thrones. No group in Italy welcomed these innovations with more ecstatic approval than the Jews, who had lived for centuries under the most fanatic and malevolent Catholic dynasties in Western Europe. Italian Jewry numbered perhaps thirty thousand at the end of the eighteenth century, and was divided fairly evenly between Rome, on the one hand, and the cities of Florence, Venice, Verona, and Ancona, on the other. Their ghettos were the most squalid in all Europe. But now, at last, the gates of these ugly prisons were battered down. Within a month of the arrival of the French armies in 1797, the Jews were granted complete civil equality. Unquestionably, most of the Italian Jews were desperately poor people, the poorest and most backward in Western Europe. In the brief interval of their emancipation few of them moved beyond the periphery of their old ghetto neighborhoods, or made more than a tentative effort to abandon the traditional livelihoods of peddlery and secondhand trade. Yet there was a small minority of Jews who participated fully, and often with great distinction, in the municipal governments of northern Italy. There were others, a somewhat larger group, who enrolled in the National Guard, and fought with Napoleon's armies on the battlefields of Europe. And in 1806 and 1807 twenty Italian Jews participated in the sessions of the Assembly of Jewish Notables and the Sanhedrin in Paris. It was perhaps the most cherished moment of Italian Jewry's brief but exhilarating interlude of freedom.

Finally, during the twenty-six years that elapsed between the beginning of the French Revolution and Napoleon's defeat at Waterloo, thirty thousand English Jews, the majority living in London, continued quietly to enjoy and consolidate their liberties. Like other Englishmen, they participated fully in the war effort against Napoleon; and—again like other Englishmen—they profited from the growing wave of war prosperity. In the early years of the nineteeth century Jewish peddlers and old-clothes dealers were gradually transformed into thriving and respectable tradesmen; in this period, too, the great banking fortunes of Rothschild and Goldsmid were established, while countless other Jews moved into the world of finance and large-scale commerce, into retailing and the professions. Gradually, steadily, an effective combination of middle-class utilitarianism and Anglican evangelicalism whittled away at the few nominal Jewish disabilities that remained. Jews were now accepted for commissions in the army and navy, admitted to the bar, and, as we shall see, finally naturalized, in 1826, as full-fledged citizens. The right to sit in Parliament or to serve as officials of the Crown still was denied them; but few Jews doubted that these rights would soon be attained. In contrast to developments on the Continent, perhaps in favorable contrast, Jewish emancipation in England was not the result of military action or clamorous Parliamentary debate. The phlegmatic calm and gradualism with which it was achieved was typically British.

CONCLUSION

Why, then, were the Jews emancipated? One reason, certainly, was the rationalist ideology of the times; no flaws or inconsistencies dared be permitted in the shining new theory of equality before the law. Another, perhaps even more important factor was honest Jacobinism, that full-hearted fraternalism which rushed through France with truly Messianic fervor, and which swept before it all ancient cruelties and anachronisms. It was this sentiment, one suspects, that animated the revolutionary troops whose battering-rams cracked open the walls of the German and Italian ghettos.

At least as decisive as these rationalist and romantic motivations, however, was the need felt by European legislators and bureaucrats, especially in France and Prussia, to create taut and efficient governments, to complete the process of state unification first embarked upon by the Enlightened Despots of the eighteenth century. This meant, first of all, that all relics of corporativism had to be dispensed with, including the ghettoized autonomy of the Jews. It meant, too, that the reservoir of Jewish credit could no longer be unlocked capriciously and arbitrarily, in fits and starts, through Court Jews and "exception Jews." The main dam gate itself had to be swung open, and the full potentialities of Jewish wealth and enterprise released once and for all.

For the Jews themselves, Emancipation meant an end not only to archaic disabilities, but also to the rights and privileges of self-government. As the nineteenth century progressed, the solemn decision of the Sanhedrin took on ever deeper significance. For better or worse the Jews had made their entrance into Western society, and had cast their lot with the nations that had granted them citizenship. With the passage of the years the memory of their ghetto sovereignty would fade steadily into the haze of folklore. If they had forsworn their sovereign rights as Jews, they were determined henceforth that they would tenaciously defend their sovereign rights as French or German citizens.

Notes

Page 54. The quotation from the Egyptian rabbi, Haim David Azular, is taken from *Jewish Travellers,* Elkan Adler, editor, pp. 357-58.

IV

Incarceration:

The Jews of Eastern Europe

Had our traveler friend of the first chapter visited the Court of Poland in the 1770's, the Court of King Stanislaus II, he would have encountered there most of the simulacra of the Western Enlightenment: peruked courtiers, quoting the most fashionable pronouncements of Voltaire and Montesquieu; learned scientists and scholars, dining and wining under royal patronage; hard-working legislators, concentrating increasingly on the problems of political reform. All this activity, however, was little more than Poland's death agony, the last blaze of a nation's instinct for life before it guttered out. The truth was that Poland had waited too long to reform itself: the country's economy and political processes were paralyzed; mighty Russia had taken Poland's non-Catholic minority peoples under her "protection," and was even now preparing to swallow Poland altogether. It was to anticipate this move, in fact, that the rulers of Prussia and Austria decided to lure the Russian czarina into a collective partition of Poland. The ruse succeeded, and in 1772 preliminary surgery was performed on the hapless Polish State: Austria carved out Galicia, Prussia seized Posen, and Russia occupied the Polish province of White Russia.

Even the most obtuse Polish courtier recognized now that it was merely a matter of time before Russia returned to finish the job. It was this awareness which spurred Poland's political leaders into a desperate race with the calendar. After several years of preliminary study and negotiation, the Polish Diet finally managed to formulate a new constitution for the country, the May Constitution of 1791. It was not by any means a democratic document: the country was still divided into estates; voting was still determined by property qualifications. But ministerial responsibility was established; the *Liberum Veto,* the right of single-dissent veto which had virtually paralyzed legislative action, was abolished; other important administrative reforms were inaugurated. For a moment it appeared as if Poland had saved itself. But it was an illusion. Prussian and Russian troops moved swiftly in 1792; the country was again occupied, and again parceled out. Prussia annexed Great Poland and completed its seizure of Posen; Russia annexed the most important territories of Lithuania and the Ukraine. There was little of Poland left now to defend. The great Polish warrior Thaddeus Kosciusko, inspired by the example of the American and French Revolutions, led a brief, desperate effort to win back the lost provinces; but his army was quickly crushed. The defeat of Kosciusko removed the last obstacle to a third and final partition. It came in 1795: Russia swallowed up the rest of Lithuania and the Ukraine, while Prussia seized Warsaw and its environs.

If, however, Austria and Prussia believed that they had permanently enlarged their holdings as a result of their effortless spoliation of Poland, they were soon to be disenchanted. Napoleon Bonaparte seized their Polish acquisitions from them, and converted the territories into a puppet Duchy of Warsaw. Later, near the end of the Napoleonic Wars, Russian troops marched into the Duchy of Warsaw—and stayed there. At the Congress of Vienna, Czar Alexander was persuaded to return small portions of Posen and Galicia to Prussia and Austria; but the bulk of the Duchy of Warsaw was transformed into a satellite Kingdom of Poland and annexed to Russia. The greater part of the original Polish Kingdom was destined now to remain in the grip of the Russian Bear until 1918. And so, too, was the inherited swarming reservoir of Polish Jewry.

The Jews, as we recall, were treated badly during the last half-century of Polish independence. The paralysis of the Polish government destroyed Jewish security; Jews were driven out of the countryside, out of the mercantile guilds, and into a life of peddling and hawking. They were systematically reduced to the status of pariahs at a juncture in history when Western Jews were beginning to emerge from this kind of degraded existence. Thus it was a matter of some urgency to Polish Jewry that the constitutional reforms of 1791 be extended to them. For a moment it actually seemed as if their hopes might be fulfilled. While the constitution was being prepared, a group of Polish legislators investigated the Jewish community and, on the basis of their study, suggested an alleviation of anti-Jewish disabilities. But nothing was done. The May Constitution, with all the important changes it effected in Poland's life, did not touch on matters of minority status. The Jews were completely cut off in this last will of dying Poland.

It was rather surprising, as a result, that the Jews should have felt much concern one way or the other about Poland's impending demise. Nevertheless, a rather large number of Jews participated in Kosciusko's abortive uprising of 1794. Thousands of Jews contributed food, clothing, and money to the insurgent forces. Under the direction of Berek Joselevitch, the Jewish estate manager of a Catholic bishop, a Jewish legion was organized to to fight at the ramparts of Warsaw. Like Joselevitch, most of the Jewish volunteers were under the influence of French revolutionary ideas, and were convinced that national liberty was one of the indispensable prerequisites for Jewish emancipation. Nearly every member of this Jewish legion was cut down by the Russian cavalry. Joselevitch himself survived the assault;

but later, as a member of a Polish uhlan regiment, he was killed in battle by the Austrians. Coming as it did after the disappointment of the May Constitution, this last, virually inexplicable example of Jewish loyalty rather touched the Poles. Joselevitch became the hero of Polish songs and fables; during the nineteenth century his name was enshrined in Polish folklore as the man who "resuscitated the image of those men of valor over whom in days gone by wept the daughters of Zion." But when the efforts of Kosciusko and Joselevitch failed, the Jews were obliged to abandon their hopes of winning emancipation from a "grateful" Polish government. For the bulk of Polish Jewry, together with Poland itself, was now to be turned over to the less than tender mercies of Czarina Catherine II of Russia.

HASIDISM: POLISH JEWRY'S SPIRITUAL ANCHOR

During the latter half of the eighteenth century, as the Jews of Poland sensed the imminent collapse of their political and economic security, they turned instinctively to their ancestral religion for courage and consolation. But like many other distraught peoples of the early modern era—English workingmen, German and Czech peasants, Russian serfs—they were not always able to find the spiritual comfort they needed in traditional theologies or liturgies. To a rather alarming extent, Judaism had formalized, grown cold. The formalization of religion was in fact a Europe-wide characteristic of the Age of Reason. The cool classicism of the seventeenth and eighteenth centuries, the rise of rationalist philosophy, exerted a corrosive influence on doctrinal beliefs. In place of the burning religious passions of the sixteenth century, a kind of utilitarian ethic was now making its appearance, an emphasis upon natural religion. It was during this period, for example, that the nonemotional dogmas of Deism and Unitarianism arose, the blandly "sensible" preachments of the Cambridge Platonists and the North German Lutheran pastorate, as well as a variety of other formalistic and rationalist dogmas.

In the case of Judaism, however, this formalization was more the result of physical isolation than of the impact of rationalism. Locked off in their own ghettoized world for centuries, unexposed to the winds of European humanism, Jewish religious education—study of the Talmud had always been synonymous with pietism in the Jewish tradition—became increasingly the province of a limited group of scholars. By the eighteenth century this scholarship had largely divorced itself from the realities of contemporary life and from the emotional needs of the heart. It was characterized by *pilpul,* a dialectical technique of reconciling apparently contradictory concepts in the Talmudic text, often by straining original meanings through the needle's eye. This kind of intellectual exercise, which at one time may have had the value of sharpening the mind, degenerated now into little more than sophistry, and largely obscured the rich moral and ethical significance of the fundamental Talmudic teachings. Moreover it failed lamentably to provide spiritual consolation for the anguished and demoralized Jewish population of Eastern Europe.

Within both the Christian and Jewish worlds important groups were prepared to protest this religious formalism, the widening chasm between the mind and the heart. In seventeenth-century Germany the agony of the Thirty Years' War had literally pulverized the German peasantry into a race of hysterical, grass-eating mystics. Classical, formal Lutheranism failed to assuage the emotional terrors of these wretches; a gust of warm German pietism came much closer to providing a measure of solace. In southern Germany, largely Catholic, the Jansenist conception of Catholicism also represented a reaction against the Scholastic supremacy of Reason; it left room for the expression of longings that were at the core of the simple man. In eighteenth-century England the sudden shock of agricultural enclosures, the squalor and insecurity of the early industrial slums created the background for George Whitefield's and John Wesley's revivalist revolt against Anglican "sensibility." Throughout Europe, even as far away as Russia, little sects of evangelicals—Shakers, Baptists, Dunkers, innumerable varieties of Slavic millennialists—made their appearance, and emphasized a number of common factors: new birth, illumination, animation, song, intense emotionalism. It was an inward religion. It spoke to the heart. This evangelical pietism also appeared among the Jews of Eastern Europe in the eighteenth century. It was called Hasidism.

There was probably no causal connection between Christian evangelicalism and Hasidism. Jewish life in Poland in the eighteenth century was too highly insulated for the penetration of prolonged cultural influence from Western Europe. But the circumstances that produced Christian evangelicalism were largely duplicated in Jewish life: religion had become arid and formal, life was harsh and uncertain, and its cruelty was deepening in the frightful era of *Rozbier,* the partitions of Poland. There were other factors too that accounted for the rise of the Hasidic movement. It was also a social revolt of impoverished Jewish workers against the more affluent Jewish merchants. For middle-class Jews had managed to transform their superior Talmudic education into a symbol of social aristocracy. The uneducated Jewish laboring men of Galicia and the Ukraine, bitterly resenting the social stigma attached to illiteracy, had long been waiting for an opportunity to strike back at the Talmudists.

There were precedents in Polish-Jewish history for anti-intellectual movements. The crudest was the pseudo-Messianism of the seventeenth century. In the period immediately following the Chmielnicki massacres countless thousands of Polish Jews had been deranged into a kind of prayerful expectancy that a Messiah would arise to lead them back to the Holy Land. Charlatans were not lacking to capitalize on this hysteria. Sabbatai Zevi, for example, a Jew of Smyrna, and Jacob Frank, a Podolian Jew, made bombastic claims to the "Messiahship," building up a formidable response among distraught Polish Jews by promising to lead a mass return to Palestine. Although these men dissipated their followings by opportunistically accepting conversion—to Islam, in the case of Sabbatai Zevi, to Christianity, in the case of Frank—the frenzied apocalypticism did not die so easily. Within the framework of authentic Judaism a "respectable" mysticism was making its appearance, the mysticism of the Practical Cabala. It bore little relationship to the older Cabala, the mystery literature of the sixteenth century. Indeed, the Cabalistic emphasis upon juggling of letters and symbols, as a short cut to divine communion, was hardly more than a Jewish version of medieval superstition. Toward the end of the sixteenth century, however, an eccentric Jewish mystic, Rabbi Isaac Luria, seized upon the concepts of the transmigration of souls and the reincarnation of man through asceticism, and combined them with the meticulous observance of daily ritual required by the Talmud. Out of this fusion of mysticism and ritualism emerged the Practical Cabala. Its principal exponents were itinerant lay preachers, who traveled from town to town in Eastern Europe emphasizing the importance of fasting and penitence, threatening a demon-filled hell for the impure, and a physical heaven for the properly penitent.

These, then, were the factors that laid the groundwork for the rise of Hasidism in the eighteenth and early nineteenth centuries: the disintegration of the Polish world; the aridity of the Talmudic educational system, the growing separation of the learned from the unlearned; the pseudo-Messianism of the seventeeth and eighteenth centuries; and the semi-respectable mysticism of the Practical Cabala. As yet, however, a *force majeure* was lacking to build a dynamic movement on the foundations of Polish-Jewish unrest. Such a *force majeure* finally appeared in the person of the Baal Shem-Tob—the "Master of the Good Name."

Israel ben Eliezer of Miedzyboz was born and raised in Podolia, spent the better part of his career in Podolia, and died there in 1760. Although seven decisive years of this strange man's life were spent meditating in the Carpathian Mountains of Moldavia, the Podolian background was very probably the crucial influence of his life. The Practical Cabala was a major force in this province, and of prime significance in the life of Israel ben Eliezer, who at first lived by its principles and then later rejected its asceticism. Shortly after his marriage at the age of fifteen, the pock-marked and ungainly youth traveled to the Carpathian Mountains, where he earned his livelihood as a ditchdigger. His work was frequently interrupted however by visions and long spells of mystical introspection. Eventually he decided that his true calling was faith healing. He shared this calling with many other Jews, each of whom called himself a Baal Shem-Tob, that is, a divinely endorsed intermediary with God. For a while faith healing became Israel's principal vocation: when he was not laying on hands, he spent his time praying in a solitary hut in the woods, while his wife went about the business of earning their bread.

Convinced of the importance of his "revelations," Israel, the Baal Shem-Tob—as his followers now also called him—returned at last to Podolia, where he began to preach a simple and unsophisticated brand of religious fundamentalism. He borrowed liberally from Cabalistic mysticism; but the parables in which he spoke, the "legends of the Baal Shem," were almost entirely his own, and they were expounded with passion and transparent integrity. Through these simple folk tales and homilies the Baal Shem emphasized the importance of worshiping God through prayer rather than study, through joy and ecstatic flights of the soul. The prayers of the poor and illiterate were of enduring value, too, he pointed out, if they were deeply felt and sincerely expressed.

Because the circumstances of Jewish life were particularly opportune for this kind of evangelicalism, the Baal Shem's message swept with torrential speed and power through the densely populated Jewish communities of Poland. People came by the thousands to hear him, to listen to his message, to receive is blessing, to join him in his frenzied and foot-stomping prayer sessions. After the Baal Shem died in 1760, his disciples traveled to all corners of Poland to preach Hasidism, and to gain new recruits for the movement. Much as the rabbis, the defenders of traditional Judaism, protested against this revivalist "heresy"—even persuading the *Kahal* of Four Lands to issue a *herem* against it in 1772—Hasidism continued to draw hundreds of thousands of new followers each year. The movement grew even more rapidly during the partitions of Poland, for it served then as a kind of emotional escape from mysterious and frightening political developments. By 1815, fifty-five years after the death of the strange and hypnotic Baal Shem-Tob, Hasidism had been accepted by the majority of Jewish communities of Eastern Europe.

It is fruitless to attempt an analysis of the theology of Hasidism, for it was not so much a theology as an exceptionally appealing way of life. Hasidism preserved the Baal Shem's emphasis on the value of prayer and personal devotion, and his contempt for mere study and Talmudic erudition. Only in the world of the spirit, its adherents agreed, could one find fulfillment; there all men, rich and poor, literate and illiterate, were equal. While Hasidism accepted the mysticism of the Practical Cabala, it rejected the emphasis on self-mortification. The Hasidim were unalterably convinced that every deed of a man's life, no matter how prosaic or mundane, could be rendered sacred if it were performed with joy; the Baal Shem-Tob had urged his followers not to rebel against their desires, but rather "to seize them and bind them to God." There was a good deal of the painfully superstitious in Hasidic thinking: its insistence that a divine power was locked away in the letters of God's name; its faith in the coming of a physical Messiah; its emphasis on angels and angelology. There was much, too, that was primitive and crude: the fiercely joyous revivalist prayer meetings, the noise, the wild dancing, the unrestrained drinking. One sees these people today, not only in the occasional Hasidic prayer rooms of Williamsburg in Brooklyn, but also in the fundamentalist camp meetings of the American Bible Belt.

But if some elements in Hasidism were superstitious, primitive, and crude, others were quite beautiful and meaningful. For example, there existed among the Hasidim a warm and wholesome camaraderie that was not limited to the festive hours of common prayer and the common meal. It shone through all the hours of every day. In moments of happiness—and when was a true Hasid not happy?—they drank to one another, sang and danced together; in the frequent moments of common danger they gladly risked their lives for each other. Every act in the life of a true Hasid mirrored his unshakable belief, as Martin Buber puts it, that "in spite of intolerable suffering man must endure, the heart-beat of life is holy joy, and that always and everywhere, one can force a way through to that joy—provided one devotes oneself entirely to his deed." To the typical illiterate porter or dray-man, Hasidism offered something no less important than security and joy: it offered him a sense of equality with his fellow Jews, a belief that he, too, in his naive love and enthusiasm, could and would be heard by God.

THE DECLINE OF HASIDISM

Had our traveler friend entered a Polish village at the end of the eighteenth century, he might well have encountered a crowd of Jews waiting attendance on an exotically attired man, an apparition seemingly from another world. The man wore a broad-brimmed beaver hat, a huge billowing cassock; his face was ornamented by sideburns descending in long, twisting curlicues. This strange creature was a zaddik, a "true believer," a full-time Hasidic prayer leader and faith healer. The first zaddikim were the Baal Shem's original followers: Dov Baer, "the Great *Maggid*," Rabbi Pinkas of Koretz, Schneuer Zalman of Liozna, Menahem Mendel of Vitebsk, Jacob Joseph Cohen, and seven or eight others who were the Baal Shem's protégés during his lifetime. After the Baal Shem's death, however, the number of zaddikim multiplied. According to Hasidic tradition, the Great *Maggid* alone had three hundred disciples. Soon, indeed, "dynasties" of zaddikim developed, as men passed the calling to their sons or sons-in-law.

The true zaddik—the personal follower of the Baal Shem, for example—interpreted his role with simplicity and humility. He sought to make communion with God easier for the common folk by strengthening them in their hour of sorrow, developing their capacity for prayer, joining his own prayer to theirs. He never pretended to miraculous powers. But often in spite of himself the zaddik became a hero to these unfortunate people. More often than not, he was considered a living incarnation of true piety, a wonder-worker who penetrated the inner core of God's language, who stood on the same level as Moses and the Prophets, who not only spoke with the authority of the Torah, but who could even change and abrogate the Torah. Of course, then, he had to be freed from the worries of earning a livelihood, that he might "cleave unto the Lord." No doubt many of these zaddikim were honest and pious men who took no undue advantage of such hero worship. The lovable "Reb" Levi Isaac of Berdichev was genuinely devoted to his followers, and there was no showmanship or histrionics when he hurled himself into ecstasies of prayer in order to reach God on their behalf. "Reb" Schneuer Zalman lived among the poor, and sternly rejected all opportunities for personal enrichment as he ministered to their spiritual needs.

Nevertheless, there were charlatans aplenty who exploited the blind trust placed in them by their followers; in fact their numbers were on the increase by the opening of the nineteenth century. The Baal Shem's own grandson, Baruch of Miedzyboz, was typical of this breed of opportunists.

Maintaining his grandfather's "dynasty" in Podolia, Baruch lived in the grand manner of a Polish noble. The wealth he acquired from his "saintly" activities permitted him to hold court in his mansion for the multitudes of Hasidic pilgrims who came to receive his blessing, and in return to shower him with their painfully earned gifts. If Baruch of Miedzyboz sponsored lavish parties for his friends it was done, he insisted, for the sake of "bringing men nearer to God through the joy of living." This crudely materialistic concept of joy became increasingly typical of the zaddikim of the nineteenth century. Many of them did not hesitate to consolidate their power by becoming "business consultants," or in the modern idiom, "influence peddlers." It was the frequent transformation of the saintly prayer leader into the avaricious self-seeker that accounted, in large measure, for the ultimate decline of the Hasidic movement. Even if most of them had been scrupulously honest, which they most certainly were not, their acquired functions were Christological, not Jewish. No man could speak for God as if he were part of the Godhead, according to Jewish tradition. From the days of Jesus through all the bloody travail of the Catholic saints in the centuries that followed, Jews had suffered and died because they rejected this principle. They could not accept it now and call this acceptance Judaism.

The most effective weapon against Hasidism was not only the movement's own doctrinal aberrations, the acrobatics of its clamorous prayer meetings, the wild gyrations and gesticulations that were often sexual in origin. The most effective weapon was the reformation of the Talmudic tradition itself. This reform began in Lithuania, the citadel of Talmudic learning. Lithuania had been spared the disintegration of Jewish morale consequent upon the Chmielnicki uprisings—which took place in the Ukraine—and was further removed from the semi-Oriental mysticism that suffused southern Poland. In Lithuania, too, flourished the great Talmudic academies, the pride and glory of East European Jewry. And Vilna, the capital of Lithuania, produced the most massive Jewish intellect since Baruch Spinoza.

Elijah of Vilna, born in 1720, lived for seventy-seven years. His life encompassed the great ideological struggle between the Talmudic and the Hasidic traditions. Elijah's erudition was truly phenomenal—so phenomenal that even as a young man he was popularly known as the Vilna *Gaon,* the genius of Vilna. His learning was not confined to Judaic lore; he spoke at least ten languages, and was at home in mathematics and science. Neither was the *Gaon* a mere prodigy. His philosophic and religious views were usually as practical as they were profound, mellowed with the well-considered wisdom of human experience. While he did not hesitate to anathematize Hasidism, the *Gaon* was sufficiently far-visioned to recognize that the entire structure of Talmudic learning had to be revamped. He admitted openly that the Lithuanian Talmudists, even the best of the lot, were the slaves of *pilpul.* Accordingly, he encouraged his followers to study secular science, to purge the Jewish educational system of the kind of vacuous sophistry that was threatening traditional Judaism with downfall. He himself set about writing Hebrew books that dealt not merely with the Talmud, but with algebra, geometry, astronomy, and grammar. The *Gaon* did not single-handedly destroy *pilpul* in his own lifetime. But he made major inroads on its domination. After his death his disciples succeeded gradually in leavening and modernizing Talmudic studies.

Compromise came from the Hasidic side, too. In their later years, the Baal Shem's principal disciples, Dov Baer, Jacob Joseph Cohen, Schneuer Zalman, Mendel of Vitebsk, recognized that the anti-intellectualism of the Hasidic pietists was moving to untenable extremes. Dov Baer, Cohen, and the others had envisaged Hasidism essentially as a corrective movement that would pour warmth and joy back into life and religion. Now, therefore, they sought to find a proper equilibrium. Together with a number of their followers, they managed to work out a modified doctrine which became known as "rational Hasidism." It was a doctrine that purged Jewish evangelicalism of numerous vulgar superstitions, eliminated its childlike naïveté, encouraged its adherents to recognize that learning was not to be shunned, but was rather to be placed in its proper context. This effort for inner reform was carried into the second quarter of the nineteenth century.

By the 1840's, the schism between Hasidism and Talmudism had been narrowed considerably. Because of the work of the Vilna *Gaon* Talmudic Judaism was no longer to be equated with *pilpul*. There was fairer appreciation of the worth of the poor and ignorant Jew whose prayers were expressed with honest emotion. With Hasidism no longer the monopoly of the overbearing zaddikim, "civil war" between the two groups was arrested. Each faction had now reached the point at which it no longer viewed the other as the major threat to its existence. There could be only one common danger now: the vindictive and fanatical Greek Orthodox clergy, the advance guard of the new Russian captor.

THE RUSSIAN CAPTOR—AND ITS SCHIZOID MONARCHS

Eighteenth-century Russia extended from the banks of the Vistula to the steppes of Siberia, from the Baltic to the Black Sea; geographically, it was the largest empire in the world. And yet the Byzantine cupolas of Russia's cities, the primitive thatched huts of its countryside, the bearded, illiterate peasants who slept on the same mud floors with their animals, the lethargy, the timelessness of its daily life—all suggested the central truth of Russian history: that the Empire of the Czars was a semi-Oriental nation, that its people were still semibarbarous. The all-engulfing, atavistic kind of religiosity that had declined in Western Europe some two centuries earlier, endured in Russia with all its obscurantist consequences. To the devoutly Greek Orthodox Russian, therefore, the Jew was not a cheap peddler, not a contemptible old-clothes dealer: the Jew was an infidel, the poisoner of the true faith, the killer of Christ. Had the Jews not lured into their sect an entire kingdom of Khazars in the seventh century? Had they not converted to Judaism important members of the Greek Orthodox clergy in the sixteenth century? The memory of these "Judaizing heresies" still throbbed like an old wound in the minds of the clergy and the autocracy. After the reign of Ivan IV the Jews had not been permitted to live in Russia. By this exclusion, it was hoped, the simple, devout Russian people would never again be "contaminated" by the devious race of Israel.

During the eighteenth century, the Imperial Russian Court at St. Petersburg sternly denied the petitions of Polish-Jewish merchants who sought the right of temporary domicile in Russia. Even that inspired barbarian, Peter I, who imported thousands of non-Russian nationals for the sake of modernizing his empire, refused to admit Jews. "I prefer," he said, "to see in our midst nations professing Islam and paganism rather than Jews. . . . It is my endeavor to eradicate evil, not to multiply it." A full century and a half later, Czarina Catherine II expressed the same hostility in denying entrance to a group of Jewish tradesmen. "From the enemies of Christ," she explained to the mercantilists in her Council, "I desire neither gain nor profit." In that same year, 1762, Catherine permitted all foreigners to travel and settle in Russia—"*kromye Zhydov*"—"except the Jews"; it was a phrase that would reappear continually in subsequent ukases and statutes. Then, only a decade later, the country which had feared a few thousand Jews and opposed any contact with them, suddenly inherited hundreds of thousands of them as a legacy of the first Polish partition. Before the century ended in fact Russia found itself with nearly a million Polish Jews on its hands.

In view of Catherine's prejudices, she might have been expected to deal harshly with these newcomers. But court policy was not quite so clear-cut. One of the basic characteristics of modern Russian history was the rather erratic effort made by the country's rulers and intelligentsia to ape the customs and manners of the West. Particularly in their attempt to prod the sluggish Russian masses into the faster tempo of Western life, the czars borrowed freely from Western political and intellectual terminology. Catherine, a German princess by birth, in continual contact with the enlightened courts of Prussia and Austria, was willing to pay lip service to the ideal of modernization. She quoted from the *philosophes*; she established schools, newspapers, and printing houses; she made vague promises of administrative reform. Insisting that she had an open mind on the matter of religious nonconformity, she published a Charter of Religious Toleration for her Moslem subjects, and expressed a willingness to allow "schismatics" within her empire. The truth was, however, that Catherine's promises were mere empty verbalization. Far from reforming the government on the lines of Western absolutism, the czarina decentralized her administration by turning over vast areas of land to the nobility—without demanding state service in return. The apparatus of Russian government remained disjointed and hopelessly inefficient, and legal procedures continued to be arbitrary and capricious. It was a strange combination of intellectual progressivism and bureaucratic ineptitude. It was this chaos of cross-purposes in fact which accounted for Catherine's ambivalent attitude toward her Jews.

In 1772, in her posture as Enlightened Despot, the czarina promised her new Jewish subjects all the liberties that they had enjoyed in Poland. Within the next two decades however, as additional hundreds of thousands of Jews were added to Russia by the second and third Polish partitions, Catherine decided to reconsider that promise. It was at this time, too, that the French Revolution began setting dangerous examples of political and religious liberalism. It was not long before Catherine abandoned her façade of toleration. In 1794 she issued a ukase that was destined, in the century to come, to have far-reaching and momentous consequences for Russian-Jewish life. The ukase confined Jews to a "Pale of Settlement," an area delimited by the boundaries of the former Polish kingdom. No Jew henceforth dared venture beyond this tightly quarantined territory. It is doubtful if any decree in history, even the Spanish expulsion edict of 1492 or the establishment of the Western ghetto in the sixteenth century, imposed a more burdensome political, economic, or intellectual strait jacket on an entire people.

But Catherine had yet other penalties in mind for her Jews. Each economic estate in Russia was obliged to pay collective, corporative taxes. Those taxes were doubled when they were applied to the Jews (with the exception of Karaite—schismatic—Jews). The disabilities of corporativism were therefore preserved; but not the rights of corporativism. Although the *kahals* (see Chapter I) were allowed to function for religious and administrative purposes, an edict of 1796 deprived these institutions of their former judicial powers. Jews were now expected to have recourse to Russian courts for the settlement of their legal disputes. If Catherine's approach to the Jewish problem was confused and contradictory, it was hardly more so than her other policies: the facile promise of freedom and modernization, and the even more facile sabotage of civil rights and administrative efficiency. This capriciousness was not to end with Catherine. She transmitted it to her descendants.

The czarina died in 1796, unmourned by those who, only a few decades earlier, had welcomed the advent of her reign. For five years her distraught and incompetent son, Paul I, sat on the throne of Russia. Then in 1801 Paul was murdered in a palace revolution and was succeeded by his son, Alexander I. Alexander was an impressive man, tall, handsome, gravely courteous and dignified in bearing. Much was expected of him by Russia's intelligentsia, for he enjoyed a vague reputation for progressivism. Indeed he was trained for progressivism; at his grandmother's insistence, his tutor had been Frédéric de La Harpe, the eminent Swiss rationalist. His closest friend during the early years of his reign was Mikhail Speranski, the Polish liberal. But it soon became apparent that all the confusions, the contrariness, the hesitations and dissimulations of his predecessors were concentrated in abundant measure in this young man. Alexander started off well, dabbling with the ideas of Enlightenment, encouraging the use of rationalist jargon in court and administrative circles. Like his grandmother, he, too, toyed with the notion of reforming his bureaucracy. But, again like Catherine, he stopped short—in this case at Speranski's audacious suggestion of a limited monarchy. Actually Alexander was never quite sure what he really believed; profoundly emotional, he was given to introspection, to long, dreamy moods which he identified with mysticism, but which cynics interpreted as laziness.

During the Napoleonic Wars, Alexander scrapped his plans for reform altogether. He recognized, for one thing, that egalitarianism was becoming a dangerous weapon in the hands of Napoleon. He was also the first European monarch to be influenced by the religious obscurantism that heralded the coming European reaction. At the Congress of Vienna the czar was frequently to be found on his knees, sobbing before a crucifix in the presence of Baroness Julie von Krüdener, a psychotic German Pietist. Rapidly losing his stomach for godless liberalism, Alexander turned increasingly to conservatives as his friends and associates—until he fell permanently under the spell of the sadistic and dissolute arch-reactionary, Count Aleksei Arakcheev. During the last years of the czar's life there was little progress of any kind in Russia, neither political, economic, nor intellectual; he had determined to impose the silence of the churchyard on his people, to return to the womb of Byzantine medievalism. It was this split personality who sought to deal with the Jewish problem.

THE CONSTITUTION OF THE JEWS

Undoubtedly the Jews did present a problem. When Alexander first ascended the throne he found that he had inherited a Jewish population of nearly a million. Fourteen years later, in 1815, with the annexation of the puppet Kingdom of Poland, some two hundred thousand more Jews were to be added to his realm. Here was a compact, apparently unassimilable mass of human beings, living, for the most part, in cities or towns, zealously preserving their religious distinctiveness, their national customs of diet and dress, their communal autonomy, their predilection for commerce. How were these people to be absorbed? How were they to be made loyal and useful Russian citizens? How, in the words of the senator-poet, Gabriel Dzyerzharin, would "the stubborn and cunning tribe of Hebrews be properly set to rights?"

In 1802 Alexander appointed a committee to study the Jewish problem. Wearing his cap of progressivism, the czar maneuvered the composition of the committee in such a way that liberals outnumbered Dzyerzharin and his fellow reactionaries. As the czar had planned, the liberal members gradually took matters in hand, insisting that "it is more desirable and safe to lead the Jews to self-improvement by opening to them the roads that will lead them to happiness. . . . A minimum of restrictions, a maximum of liberties." When delegates from the *kahals* were actually called in to present the case for the Jews, rumors began to circulate through the Pale of Settlement that better times were coming, that Alexander, the Little Father, was preparing to open his arms to his Jewish stepchildren. In 1804 the committee presented its report to the czar. Its recommendations presumably were friendly, but with characteristic captiousness, Alexander ignored the recommendations. The Statute Concerning the Organization of the Jews, issued by the czar that same year, was a stunningly reactionary document.

The statute, known thereafter as the Constitution of the Jews, was typically Romanov in its mixture of liberties and disabilities. On the one hand, the *kahals* were deprived of much of their corporative authority. They were denied the right to impose their own taxes on the Jewish communities, and were obliged to confine themselves to the collection of state taxes. Similarly much of the spiritual authority of the *kahals* was stripped away through the elimination of the *herem,* the rabbinical ban of excommunication. The Constitution further sought to encourage more "wholesome" agricultural pursuits among the Jews. It offered five years of tax exemption to those Jewish families who would settle in the new territories of southeastern Russia and farm the land there. In addition, the Constitution granted the Jews free access to all public schools and universities in Russia. Of course, this provision was a blind for conversion; the Minister of Education, Golitzin, was the most notorious Pietist in the country, and he made sure that public education in Russia, however rudimentary, was suffused with the "Christian'" spirit. But at least on the face of the measure, it appeared as if another obstacle was removed from the path of Jewish "amalgamation."

But then the entire point of the Constitution was vitiated by its key provision. The Jews were to be denied the right to hold leases on land or to operate taverns; they were to be expelled from all villages and hamlets and sent back into the larger towns and cities. In short, the Jews were to be impacted even more tightly than before into a restricted Pale of Settlement. With one stroke the statute would have eliminated the livelihood of half the Jewish population of Russia. The logical consequences of the planned expulsion would have been an even more complete isolation of Jews from their Russian neighbors, an even more thoroughgoing Jewish urbanization. These were the very consequences, presumably, that Alexander hoped to avoid. The provision was scheduled to go into effect in 1808.

None of Alexander's objectives were attained. For one thing, the Jews repudiated those provisions in the Constitution that were openly directed at "amalgamation." Having little faith in the tender mercies of Russian justice, most Jews still consulted their rabbinical courts, and observed their religious and cultural traditions as strictly as if the *herem* were still in force. Similarly agriculture held little if any attraction for them; by the end of Alexander's reign this precarious and unfamiliar livelihood had attracted a mere 2,294 Jews into the farming areas of New Russia. As for the thinly disguised conversionary mechanism of Russian education, of eighty thousand pupils attending Russian primary and secondary schools as late as 1840, only forty-eight were Jews. In truth, even the threat of expulsion from the countryside could not have driven the Jews into apostasy. The brutish life of the illiterate and superstitious Russian *muzhik* exercised no attraction whatever for the literate, devoutly religious Russian Jew. Virtually any hardship could be borne more easily than entrance into the bucolic and primitive Slavic world. Here, then, was the central tragedy of Alexander's Jewish policy: it was fraught with contradictions, with gratuitous and self-defeating cruelties. Because it was destined to be preserved, with only minor variations, for nearly half a century, the Constitution marked the true beginning of the long nightmare of Russian-Jewish life.

It was quite apparent to Jewish leaders in the Pale that if the expulsion were systematically carried out, tens of thousands, perhaps hundreds of thousands of Jews would be driven to the brink of starvation. A flood of petitions poured in on the czar: they came not only from the *kahals,* but from the Russian squirearchy as well. What would happen to the economy of the countryside, these boyars asked, if half a million Jewish middlemen were removed from the scene? Alexander remained unmoved; in 1807 he reaffirmed his intention to proceed with the expulsion. It was at this moment, however, that Napoleon Bonaparte convened the Sanhedrin in Paris. For a brief instant it appeared to the desolated Jewish community of the Pale as if a new deliverer had arisen in the West. The czar, too, sensed the implications of the Sanhedrin almost immediately. He had only recently been at war with France, and had great respect for Napoleon's military prowess; if he could help it he would not provide the French emperor with new allies—especially when such allies lived on Russian soil. On the very eve of the expulsion therefore Alexander decided to announce a temporary suspension of his plan. The continual danger of renewed war with Napoleon, and finally the actual outbreak of war in 1812, prevented Alexander from going back to his plan. After the war the czar was preoccupied with other matters.

The Jews had every reason in the world to co-operate with the invading French armies. They had little feeling of nationalist loyalty to Mother Russia; whatever mother they had was Polish; Russia was their captor, and a cruel one at that. It is ironical, however, that the pattern of German-Jewish behavior during the Napoleonic invasion was largely repeated in Russia; for the most part, the Jews in the Pale avoided any disloyalty to the czarist regime. It is not likely that they were influenced by Alexander's transparently opportunistic promise of future emancipation. The habit of docile obedience, inbred by centuries of insecurity, probably had much more to do with their coldness to the blandishments of Napoleon. So, too, did Orthodox Jewry's suspicion of French religious liberalism influence the inaction of the Jews. With the exception of the Jewish community of Lithuania, the citizens of the Pale were not obliged to commit themselves until the war was won. Within less than a year the armies of France, decimated by illness and starvation, staggered out of Russia.

But if Russian Jewry had not expected much in the way of reward for what was after all halfhearted loyalty, neither, on the other hand, did they expect an intensification of governmental hostility toward them. The decade following 1813 was the period of Alexander's most inflexible conservatism. The czar was determined to support the Metternichian system to the limit in Europe and to brook no reformist nonsense at home. Jews were forbidden access to the Caucasus, and were evicted from the border areas of Volhynia, and the rural areas in the governments of Mogilev and Vitebsk. The full-fledged expulsion scheme of 1804 was discarded as unworkable, but restrictions on Jewish rights of domicile mounted steadily.

And yet, oppressive as these circumstances were, most Jews could count themselves less unfortunate than their Russian neighbors. The typical Russian peasant was bound in serfdom to his soil. Diseased, ignorant, hopelessly superstitious, he lived in a rude hut, slept in his clothes, and fed his fire with animal dung. He, too, had reason—indeed, greater reason—to strive for an improvement in his lot, for some liberalization of court policy. But the idea that he might join hands with his Jewish neighbors was inconceivable. The Jews were an alien race; they were anti-Christs who worshiped and blasphemed in a foreign language. When the *muzhik* heard the Jews chanting in distant synagogues, he crossed himself in fear of a strange Oriental people.

NICHOLAS I: GOVERNMENT BY BARRACKS MASTER

In 1825 Alexander died. He was succeeded by a brother, Nicholas I, so murderously reactionary that by contrast the years preceding 1825 eventually seemed quite mild. Nicholas I's character presented none of the complexities that have baffled Alexander's biographers. A stocky, muscular man with hard eyes and a thin slit of a mouth, Nicholas was a czar who knew what he wanted. He was a military man, with the clear and narrow mind of the professional soldier. He believed passionately in the principles of autocracy and divine right; he was prepared, if necessary, to defend them not only in Russia but in the rest of Europe. The moment he ascended the throne he set about enlarging and strengthening the army, and tightening Russia's administration along Prussian cameralist lines. When, in 1830, the Kingdom of Poland revolted against Russian rule, Nicholas crushed the uprising with a savagery that boded ill not only for the Poles, but also for the rest of his factious subject peoples. In fact, the czar detested the minority nationalities of his empire precisely because he was convinced of their intrinsic disloyalty. They must, he insisted, be absorbed into Russian life with all possible speed. Nor was there to be any squeamishness about destroying their religious traditions if it meant that amalgamation could be accomplished more rapidly.

Although the Jews had hardly expected emancipation at the new czar's hands, they were quite unprepared for his ruthlessly vindictive anti-Jewish campaign. From the outset of his reign, Nicholas made it clear that he regarded the Jews as an alien people, a people which must adapt itself rapidly to the Slavic Greek-Orthodox majority or suffer frightful consequences. In August 1827, Nicholas issued a ukase that numbed the hearts of Russian Jewry. It was a reinterpretation of Russia's Conscription Law. The draft had been in effect in Russia for several decades; Russian youths of eighteen were subject to military service for the incredible duration of twenty-five years. Now, by the new ukase of August 26, conscription was applied to the Jews with certain refinements that were truly exquisite in their cruelty. Jewish children were to be drafted at the age of twelve; they were to spend six years of preliminary "cantonment" before the "normal" period of twenty-five-year service began. In other words, Jewish children were to be impressed into military service for a period of thirty-one years. At its best the Russian conscription system was a form of life sentence at hard labor. But in the case of the Jews it became perfectly clear that conscription was a technique of forced conversion to Christianity.

One of the most devilish aspects of this ukase was its requirement that the *kahals* themselves furnish the Jewish recruits. No measure could have more swiftly discredited Jewish self-government in the eyes of its people. It was not uncommon, for example, for wealthy families to bribe the *kahal* authorities into recruiting from poorer neighborhoods. The bitterness of the Jewish poor toward the Jewish "rich," evidenced earlier in the Hasidic revolt, reached its greatest intensity during the conscription era.

> Rich Mr. Rockover has seven sons,
> Not a one a uniform dons;
> But poor widow Leah has an only child
> And they hunt him down as if he were wild.
>
> It is right to draft the hard-working masses;
> Shopmakers or tailors—they're only asses!
> But the children of the idle rich
> Must carry on, without a hitch.

The folklore of the period abounded in tragic memoirs: stories of the *khappers,* the predatory recruiting agents of the *kahal,* roaming the streets at night, waiting for an opportune moment to burst open the door of a home and seize an unsuspecting Jewish child; of mothers shrieking in agony as their offspring were torn from them; of fathers who maimed their sons deliberately in order to spare them from conscription; of hundreds of Jewish boys hiding in the woods when news of the arrival of a team of *khappers* reached the community. Almost invariably, however, these youngsters were caught and carted off to the barracks. Alexander Herzen, the distinguished Russian journalist, recalled his shock at witnessing wagonloads of these Jewish children, blue with exposure and terror, being led off to camp.

Once its children were conscripted, no Jewish family ever expected to see them again. Either they would die, or they would be converted. Whatever their fate, they were presumed to be lost to their people, and the kaddish, the mourners' prayer, was usually intoned for them upon their departure. After the children reached the camp the conversionary purpose of their conscription was soon revealed to them. Few tortures were too brutal for the barracks masters to apply. The children were beaten, starved, doused with water, driven by whips to church services—where the battalion priests co-operated fully in the missionary endeavor. Not infrequently Jewish recruits preferred suicide to baptism. One account of the period tells of Czar Nicholas's inspection of the military headquarters at Kazan. Arrangements were made to have groups of cantoned Jewish children baptized in the czar's presence. The children were brought to the banks of the Volga River. At the czar's command the children were submerged—and did not come up. The history of Jewish conscription during Nicholas's reign is studded with descriptions of similar horrors.

Conscription however was not the end of Jewish disabilities. The arbitrary expulsion of Jews from cities and governments within the Pale continued. In 1835 a new ukase, the so-called "Charter of Disabilities," drove the Jews from the countryside of the province of Kiev and out of the capital city of Kiev itself. Although the generalized scheme of expulsion was not revived, the area of Jewish domicile was drastically reduced by the end of Nicholas's reign. By 1855 the Pale of Settlement consisted of Lithuania, Little Russia, New Russia, and certain cities of the Ukraine; it was a territory much smaller than the Jewish-inhabited area of the original Kingdom of Poland. In addition, the Jews were prohibited from employing Christian domestics, or from marrying before the age of eighteen. They were forbidden to use the Yiddish language in any of their public documents.

Nor did Nicholas abandon the efforts made by his predecessor to "amalgamate" his Jews through agriculture. In 1835, at the suggestion of Egor Kankrin, the Minister of Finance, the government opened the wastelands of Siberia to Jewish colonization, and promised not to conscript the children of Jewish farm families. This was no small incentive for agricultural settlement, and at first it seemed to be effective; several thousand Jewish families migrated eastward to Siberia. But even these plans of the czar were defeated by mismanagement. The few Jews who survived the long trek found the Siberian soil frozen and barren. The tools, equipment, and seed, which had been promised to them, had been confiscated or sold by corrupt officials. Of the thirteen or fourteen thousand Jews who reached Siberia, the majority either died or returned to the Pale in rags, ill and destitute. In 1837 Nicholas decided to call a halt to the agricultural program, in order "to protect the native population of Siberia [which was composed of Uzbeks and Kalmuks] from the Jews."

Meantime in 1836 the czar attempted in still another way to crush the "perversity" out of his Jewish subjects. He placed their spiritual life under strict surveillance. The censorship that was universal throughout Russia was now applied to Jewish religious literature. Jewish printing presses and private libraries were subjected to continual and heavy-handed ransacking. Thousands of Hebrew and Yiddish books, containing passages "at variance with imperial edicts," were burned publicly. It is worth noting that the Russians understood very little of what they were destroying. In 1844, for example, the Minister of the Interior sent a report to the czar containing a rather ominous piece of "information": apparently a secret Jewish volume entitled "Rambam" required Jews to kidnap Christian children, murder them, and drink their blood. In actuality "Rambam" was the familiar Hebrew name for the Jewish philosopher, Moses Maimonides, one of the most rational and humane minds of the Middle Ages. In another report, however, that the Minister of Education submitted to Nicholas in 1850, "Rambam" was recommended as a textbook in morality for Jewish youth. If conscription failed to "amalgamate" the Jews, if harsh taxes, expulsion decrees, and other systematic abuses merely drove the Jews into a more adamant resistance, it was hardly surprising that the brutal and clumsy censorship campaign should also have proved fruitless.

NICHOLAS CHANGES HIS TACTICS

From coronation to death, Nicholas continued to regard his Jewish subjects with unqualified loathing. Nevertheless, he was finally persuaded in the 1840's that naked cruelty, pure Byzantine disregard of human values, would not solve the problem of Jewish "amalgamation." In spite of every conceivable repressive measure, the Jews remained a cohesive mass, devoutly traditional in religion and occupation, a separate nation sticking like a bone in Russia's throat. The more they were abused, the more stubborn they became, more of a threat to that dream of Russian homogeneity which Nicholas dearly cherished. Somehow a more "scientific" approach would have to be devised.

In 1840 the czar asked his minister of state, Count P. D. Kiselev, to convene a committee capable of producing new and original ideas for solving the Jewish problem. Kiselev was not a blind reactionary by any means, nor were the men who were selected for his committee. But as dependents of the czar, whose prejudices they knew well, they were not prepared to state flatly that emancipation was perhaps the only logical key to Jewish "amalgamation." Kiselev and his colleagues found it expedient, rather, to come up with a somewhat less radical alternative. Their report suggested that the root of the problem lay in Jewish "religious fanaticism and separatism"; that the inspiration for Jewish exclusiveness was the Talmud, which fostered in the Jews "utmost contempt towards the nations of other faiths," and implanted in them the desire "to rule over the rest of the world." Under the influence of the "seditious" teachings of the Talmud, "the Jews cannot but regard their presence in any other land except Palestine as a sojourn in captivity." This addiction to the Talmud explained Jewish loyalty to their own institutions of self-government and to their own school system. It was apparent, the report of the Kiselev Committee concluded, that the only solution was to abolish Jewish autonomy altogether, and to effect major changes in Jewish educational and cultural life. Nicholas read the report with satisfaction; he noted his complete agreement in the margin. This, he observed, was getting to the heart of the matter at last.

It will be recalled that as early as Catherine II and Alexander I the *kahals* were deprived of much of their authority, stripped of all but their fiscal and quasi-administrative functions. The Kiselev Committee now suggested that even these functions were superfluous and ought to be abolished. The czar's solution was even simpler. In 1844 he summarily ordered the liquidation of the *kahals* altogether. In this fashion Jewish self-government was abruptly terminated, and the Jewish community was placed under general Russian administration. In truth, this was a measure that had long been overdue. Obviously if Russia were ever to create a modern and efficient bureaucracy on the Western model, all vestiges of corporativism would have to be discarded. From the Jewish point of view the authority of the *kahals* had long been declining—the Kiselev report notwithstanding. Indeed, that authority had disappeared almost entirely after 1827, when the *kahals* began sending out agents to round up Jewish conscripts. Autocratic and unrepresentative, the *kahals* had been living on borrowed time for decades.

In the West, as we have seen, the destruction of corporativism was followed by the extension of the full rights of citizenship to the Jews. But this was hardly to be the case in backward Russia. Here the Jews were left in limbo, without access to Russian governmental services, without Russian funds for municipal needs, without even the assurance that honest justice would be dispensed by Russian courts. But the czar had not reckoned on Jewish community discipline. Nicholas could suppress the *kahals,* but he could not do away with voluntary self-help associations. These associations—*hevras,* as they were called—were destined to become the true guardians of Jewish communal life. They answered an extraordinarily wide variety of occupational, educational, religious, and philanthropic needs. There was a *hevra* devoted to undertaking and burial; and a *hevra* which maintained orphanages and homes for the aged. There was a *hevra* supported by each major craft—cobbling, carpentry, masonry, and others—which provided for family needs in the event that a member became destitute. There was a *hevra* which provided free education for the children of indigent families. There was even a *hevra* which warned the community if *khappers* were in the vicinity.

All these *hevras* were voluntary; but rare indeed was the Jewish town or village in which a network of *hevras* did not regulate the major areas of Jewish public life. Voluntary, too, was litigation brought before Jewish courts of arbitration—but no less common. Russian judicial processes were traditionally ignored, as were Russian administrative services whenever they were provided. What was true of czarist conscription, expulsion, and censorship was no less true of czarist "unification." By failing to extend emancipation, Nicholas insured the continued cohesion of the Jewish community, the cohesion he wished to destroy.

UVAROV ESTABLISHES A SCHOOL SYSTEM

Nicholas resorted finally to the most cunning weapon of all in his implacable campaign against Jewish separatism. It was the weapon of education. Russian schools had been open to Jewish children since the early days of Alexander's reign. There were very few Jewish families, however, willing to expose their children to Russian teachers whose manifest task it was to train devout and docile Christians. Even after 1840 the government's goal did not change; education still meant indoctrination in Greek Orthodoxy, and Greek Orthodoxy still remained an essential pillar of autocracy. But by 1840, at least, it was apparent that greater ingenuity was needed in applying these czarist educational ideals to the Jews.

It happened that the Russian Minister of Public Education, Count Sergei S. Uvarov, was endowed with this kind of ingenuity. A man of refinement and intellect, he had been something of a liberal in his early years. His immense personal ambition, however, led him into political conservatism, and into a brilliant bureaucratic career under Nicholas I. Indeed it was Uvarov who formulated the accepted *raison d'être* of the regime: Orthodoxy, Autocracy, Nationalism. His assumption of the intellectual leadership of Russian nationalism was rather ironic in a way, for he used nothing but French and German in his own writings, and hardly ever read a Russian book. Yet he had little difficulty in convincing both himself and the czar that a policy of inflexible conservatism was "the last anchor of salvation and the best guarantee of Russia's strength and greatness." It was Uvarov's theory of education, for example, that students ought to be discouraged from pursuing studies beyond the status of their social origin; and to that end he devised a school curriculum which was an ingenious blend of classicism and Greek Orthodoxy. One way or another, he was determined to preserve the intellectual climate of *quieta non movere*.

When Uvarov turned his attention to the Jewish question he must have recalled a visit he made to Prussia in the late 1830's. Walking through the streets of Berlin, he had been astonished at the sight of great numbers of thoroughly Westernized, thoroughly "assimilated" Jews. He learned that these were Jews who had been brought most directly into contact with Western culture, and who had abandoned their preoccupation with the Talmud. This, it now occurred to Uvarov, was the clue to Jewish re-education for which he had been searching. The Jews must be introduced to a curriculum of secular studies. It was not Uvarov's intention to create a nation of Jewish secularists, by any means, but rather to wean Jews away from the Talmud, the citadel of Jewish separatism. Once this was accomplished, the Jews could be exposed increasingly to Christian principles. In a memorandum of 1840, Uvarov suggested to the czar that the conversionary purpose of Jewish re-education be carefully disguised. In fact, he added, secular education could be made much more palatable to the Jews if it were conducted not through Russian schools, but rather through an entirely separate Jewish school system. In these Jewish schools children would be taught the Russian language, secular sciences, Hebrew, and "religion according to the Holy Writ." The teachers in the elementary schools would be recruited from *melamdim* "who could be depended upon," while those in the secondary schools would be chosen from among the "modernized" Jews of Russia and Germany.

The Kiselev Committee and the czar were impressed with Uvarov's scheme. They pointed out, however, that the Jewish masses could best be persuaded to accept the idea if a Jewish educator were placed in charge of the new school system, and took the initiative in acquainting the "obstreperous nation with the benevolent intentions of the Government." The Jews were not to suspect either the motives behind the education plan or that plan's integral relationship with the galaxy of horrors unveiled, at strategic intervals, by the bureaucracy at St. Petersburg. Uvarov's first objective therefore was to find a competent Jewish educator willing to implement the Government's program. The educator would have to be a "modern" Jew, so obsessed, indeed, with the importance of enlightenment that he would not scrutinize the Government's ulterior motives too closely. Eventually, reliable information reached Uvarov that such a man was to be found in the north, in the great Jewish community of Riga.

The choice had fallen upon Max Lilienthal, a young German Jew who had been educated at the University of Munich, and who was a Doctor of Philosophy as well as a rabbi. Lilienthal had been called to Riga early in 1840 to create a modern secular school for the children of the more prosperous Jews of that community. Within less than a year he had succeeded brilliantly in introducing the children under his care to the glories of humanism. Lilienthal was personally quite attractive, broad-shouldered and tall, with dark, piercing eyes and a fine lofty brow; his voice was deep and resonant, and his use of German, Hebrew, and—when necessary—Yiddish, was ornate and literary. When Uvarov summoned him to St. Petersburg early in 1841, Lilienthal was only twenty-five, and in the full vigor and enthusiasm of youth.

Uvarov asked his visitor point-blank to create a secular Jewish school system for the entire Pale of Settlement. Lilienthal was flattered but suspicious. Why should a special effort be made to educate a comparatively literate people like the Jews—and not the vast illiterate masses of Russian people? Uvarov blandly assured the young man that secular education was a necessary preliminary for Jewish emancipation. Lilienthal then asked for time to communicate with his friends, and Uvarov agreed. A brief but intensive correspondence followed between Lilienthal and the leading enlightened Jews of the West—Ludwig Philippson, Abraham Geiger, Adolphe Crémieux, Sir Moses Montefiore (see Chapter VII). To a man, they urged him not to be overly concerned with Uvarov's motivations: secular education could only be a blessing for the deeply pious but obscurantist Jews of Eastern Europe. Lilienthal was convinced. In the autumn of 1841 he arrived in St. Petersburg to begin making arrangements for the new project.

Lilienthal was not unaware of the extraordinary complexity of his task. The Government had but recently intensified its anti-Jewish program; large settlements of Jews were being expelled from border areas; onerous new taxes were imposed upon various "useless" categories of Jews, categories that included the bulk of Jewish peddlers and petty tradesmen. Against the background of these new disabilities, the leaders of the Pale had every reason to be suspicious of a new educational scheme. In order to win support and co-operation for the projected school system, therefore, Lilienthal decided to travel through the Pale's great belt of Jewish communities, and to meet personally with the various Jewish communal authorities. By 1842, after many months of negotiations with Government officials, he was ready to leave. On the very eve of his tour, Lilienthal issued an address to Russian Jewry which he entitled *Maggid Yeshuah,* "The Announcer of Salvation." In this celebrated document he explained the Government's plan for a new Jewish school system, and humbly begged the co-operation of his fellow Jews. He pointed out that if they failed to take advantage of this opportunity, their enemies could justly attribute the wretched conditions of Jewish life to Jewish ignorance. Convinced that he had laid the groundwork for his journey, Lilienthal thereupon began his travels through the Pale.

Nearly everywhere he went he encountered the most disheartening apprehension and distrust. In his memoirs Lilienthal recalled his initial contact with the Jewish community of Vilna:

> The elders sat there absorbed in deep contemplation. Some of them, leaning on their silver-adorned staffs or smoothing their long beards, seemed as if agitated by earnest thoughts and justifiable suspicions; others were engaged in a lively but quiet discussion on the principles involved; some put to me the ominous question: "Doctor, are you fully acquainted with the leading principles of our Government? You are a stranger; do you know what you are undertaking? The course pursued against all denominations but the Greek [Orthodox] proves clearly that the Government intends to have but one Church in the whole Empire; that it has in view only its future strength and greatness and not our own future prosperity. We are sorry to state that we have no confidence in the new measures proposed by the ministerial council, and that we look with gloomy foreboding into the future."

Some communities, in fact, were not willing to give Lilienthal the courtesy of a hearing. In Minsk he was jostled and insulted by crowds in the street. Bands of young Hasidic Jews followed him, shouting derisively: "Get thee gone, shaven one; get thee gone." Later when he attempted to address a mass meeting, the audience became so unruly that it was necessary to summon the Minsk fire department to break up the meeting.

But Lilienthal won important support from the minority of humanistic Jews of the Pale who called themselves *maskilim*—enlightened ones. He also persuaded Uvarov to make a tactical gesture that alleviated his task considerably. In the summer of 1842 the Government summoned to St. Petersburg a commission of four leading Jews. Sitting on the commission were the distinguished rabbis Isaac of Voloshin and Mendel Schneuerson—the former the leader of the Talmudists, the latter the spokesman for the Hasidim. The other two members were Michael Heilprin, banker of Berdichev, and Bezalel Stern, superintendent of the Jewish School of Odessa. After a series of long and courteous interviews, Uvarov and Lilienthal succeeded in persuading these men that the proposed educational reforms would most emphatically not be directed against the Jewish religion. It was not, however, until the end of 1843 that the members of the commission were willing to sign their names to a report approving the forthcoming school system. It took herculean patience and tact on Lilienthal's part; he was forever cajoling, reassuring, flattering. Nor did he hesitate to plead the cause of his brethren with the Government, demanding for them civil emancipation, wider economic opportunities, rock-bound assurances that the educational program was not a scheme for proselytization. These exhausting and delicate negotiations were no small accomplishment for a Western Jew, not yet thirty years of age.

By 1844 Uvarov felt that the foundations had been prepared. The Government thereupon issued an Imperial Rescript establishing the long-awaited system of Jewish Crown schools. The institutions of *heder* (primary school) and *Talmud Torah* (secondary school) were not abolished. But Jewish attendance at the new Crown schools was encouraged by giving Crown students exemption from military conscription. It was a powerful inducement. A program of secular studies was inaugurated, including the Russian language—although, as a sop to Jewish sensibilities, Hebrew remained on the curriculum. And then, behind the protective façade of Lilienthal's reputation, the Government began to appoint a staff for the school system. In nearly every instance the principals of both elementary and secondary schools were Christians. Most of them were the dregs of the country schools. What was worse they had the right to appoint the *melamdim,* the Jewish teachers. The *melamdim,* in turn, were hardly an improvement over the principals. While they possessed some understanding of the Russian language, their familiarity with Jewish lore was negligible—which, of course, was precisely the reason for their appointment. The majority of Jewish families avoided these men like the plague. Parents sent their children to the Crown schools for general instruction, but they retained their own family *melamdim* for tutoring in Jewish subjects.

Parental misgivings notwithstanding, it is not impossible that, given time and co-operation, the Crown school system would have made some progress in acquainting Jewish children with Russian culture. Before this could happen, however, an ominous piece of information leaked out. In 1844 as Nicholas I signed the Imperial Rescript setting up the new schools, he sent a confidential memorandum to Uvarov. The memorandum reaffirmed the czar's intention that "the aim pursued in the training of the Jews is that of bringing them nearer to the Christian population and of eradicating the prejudices fostered in them by the study of the Talmud." Uvarov answered this with a pious memorandum of his own, assuring the czar that as the new system of Jewish education became widely established, the "Jewish" courses would be minimized, and eventually displaced altogether by instruction in the catechism. It was not easy to keep secrets in a corrupt and backward government. Rumors of this correspondence began to circulate among the Jewish communities. The rumors could not be authenticated; but the kind of ignoramuses who were appointed as teachers in the Crown schools appeared to confirm the worst of Jewish suspicions.

Attendance at the Crown schools, which had never been significant, began to fall off. By 1852, the city of Shklov, with a Jewish population of ten thousand, had a registration of twenty-seven pupils in its Crown school. Vitebsk, with a Jewish population even larger than that of Shklov, sent nineteen students to the Crown school that same year. In 1857, hardly more than a decade after the establishment of the project, the total number of Jewish pupils in the Crown schools was 3,293. It was apparent that the scheme had reached a dead end; that the Jews, who certainly were in no hurry to make their children available for conscription, saw through Uvarov's motives with deadly clarity. In 1848 Uvarov decided to resign his portfolio in the Government; the patent failure of his experiment had made his position untenable.

And what of Lilienthal during all this time? He had long since left the scene. In December 1844, he had written his fiancée, Fraülein Pepi Nettre of Munich, asking her to make ready for their marriage in the following May, and to bring her heavy furs to Russia with her. Shortly after writing this letter Lilienthal suddenly left Russia. The explanation for his departure was rather simple. Already in serious doubt about the honesty of Uvarov's intentions, Lilienthal was confronted one day by a high official in the Russian Ministry of Education. Now that Lilienthal had "Christianized" the staff of the Crown schools, the official suggested, would it not be advisable for the good doctor to give serious thought to embracing the holy Russian Orthodox religion? The full realization of how he had been duped suddenly dawned on Lilienthal. Nearly ill from chagrin and humiliation, he rushed back to Munich, married his fiancée, and swiftly departed for America with his bride. Three years later he himself admitted publicly, in an article he wrote for Philippson's *Allgemeine Zeitung des Judentums,* that "only when the Jew will bow down to the Greek cross will the Tsar be satisfied, irrespective of whether the converts be good or bad people." Lilienthal lived until 1882, and occupied distinguished pulpits in New York and Cincinnati. The memory of his heroic effort on behalf of his people, and of his heroic naïveté, must have haunted him until his death.

CONCLUSION

The failure of Uvarov's education scheme represented a kind of watershed in Russian-Jewish history. Since the partitions of Poland, three Russian rulers—Catherine II, Alexander I, and Nicholas I—had made serious attempts to cope with a vast Jewish nation within their borders, to "amalgamate" that nation with the Russian population. Two of these monarchs hopelessly entangled themselves in cross-purposes: Catherine and Alexander sought to lure Jews into Russian schools and into agriculture; and then quarantined them within a Pale of Settlement. This inconsistency was characteristic of rulers who "tightened" their autocracies by handing over vast acreages of land and attendant governmental perquisites to their nobles, who brought "enlightenment" to their land by sternly banning the importation of "noxious" Western books and journals.

But Nicholas I at least moved closer to consistency. Inheriting a Jewish policy that was a mixture of abuse and benevolence, Nicholas abandoned the pretext of benevolence. Gentleness and kindness, after all, were alien to the nature of the "policeman of Europe," the ruthless suppressor of the Polish and Hungarian insurrections. Nicholas was not inclined to emancipate his Jews, to alleviate Jewish disabilities, to open the Pale, to offer Jews any significant encouragement to "Russianize" themselves. By destroying Jewish self-government, by dragging Jewish children to the baptismal font via the barracks, Nicholas simply presented Russian Jewry with the alternative of apostasy or slow death. Given the opportunity to secularize the Jews through education, Nicholas chose instead to use the school system as a conversionary mechanism.

None of these approaches succeeded. Uvarov's education scheme was the last desperate device of the proponents of homogeneity through force. The Jews remained Jews: stubborn, devout, clannish. There was only one approach possible now; and it would require a fundamental modernization of Russian political thinking. That approach was Emancipation.

Notes

Page 76. A superb analysis of the social background of the Hasidic movement is provided in Israel Kazis, *Hasidism*.

Page 87. The doggerel is taken from Isaac Levitats, *The Jewish Community in Russia, 1772-1844*, p. 65.

V

The Triumph of Liberalism

In September of 1814 the citizens of Vienna lined their city's greatest avenue, the *Landstrasse,* to view an awesome procession of visiting dignitaries. The visitors were the monarchs and ministers of state of nearly every nation in Europe, together with their elobarate retinues of retainers and mistresses. Their arrival for an international congress was Vienna's and Europe's most dazzling social event since the conclave at Westphalia nearly two centuries earlier. In spite of the minuets and the pageants, however, the champagne and the *affaires,* the visitors at Vienna devoted themselves primarily to serious business: to the reconstruction of a continent, which Napoleon had left unrecognizable. Alexander I of Russia was there, magnificently uniformed and bemedaled, spouting mystical and rather unctuous platitudes about the "Christian, fraternal" solidarity of monarchs. Prince Karl von Hardenberg and Baron Alexander von Humboldt of Prussia were there, the former notoriously garrulous, the latter notoriously taciturn, and both determined to preserve Prussia's territorial integrity at all costs. Castlereagh and Wellington of England were there, tall, lean, pinch-faced men, whose ramrod backs suggested an inflexible diplomatic position: England must have a balance of power in Europe, and Russia must not upset that balance. Talleyrand of France was there, a subtle mind, shrewdly insisting upon that principle of legitimacy which would ultimately save the boundaries of his country. And Metternich was there, the foppish and timorous Rhinelander who guided the destinies of the Hapsburg monarchy, and who convinced his colleagues, if they needed convincing, that Europe wanted peace and quiet, not reform.

Virtually all the statesmen at Vienna were agreed, for that matter, that in the Europe of their lifetimes security and stability must prevail. It was not that they were all archreactionaries. Most of them recognized that the clock could not be turned back altogether, that the Holy Roman Empire, for example, could not be reconstituted, nor the majority of petty German princelings restored to their thrones. But if Europe could not be restored to its eighteenth-century "normalcy," some workable compromise would have to be arranged between the old and the new which would avoid the dangers of revolutionary anarchy. The desire to return to peace and quiet was shared by most of the nations of Europe, by people who were exhausted and bled white by the Napoleonic wars. Conservatism was the mood of the generation of Vienna, the prevailing mood not only in politics but also in religion, philosophy, art, and literature. Conservatism in the period following Waterloo represented nostalgia for the past, for the massive weight of tradition, for the respected wisdom of ages gone by. De Maistre and Chateaubriand in France, Savigny and Schleiermacher and Herder in Germany, all shrank from that bold and blasphemous doctrine of the Enlightenment which presumed to suggest that human reason was infallible. Had not the Jacobins of France operated on this basis—and with calamitous results for all of Europe? The time had come to dispense with dangerous innovations: with representative government, social democracy, secularism, and Jewish emancipation.

It is noteworthy, however, that this conservatism was least severe in France, the nation whose population had suffered most from Napoleon's adventures. Part of the reason lay in the astute leadership of Prince Talleyrand. By dissociating his country from the adventures of the Corsican usurper, Talleyrand persuaded the statesmen at Vienna that France's territorial integrity ought not to be severely tampered with. If tact and moderation had spared his country's boundaries, Talleyrand was determined that the same tact and moderation should be applied to domestic matters. Of course, it was imperative that the Bourbon dynasty be restored; and Louis XVIII, the corpulent scion of that line, was not a particularly popular man. But both Talleyrand and Louis recognized a basic fact: egalitarianism had not been imposed upon France as it had been imposed upon the states of Central Europe. Egalitarianism, in fact, had sprouted and bloomed in France, had emerged from French history and economic circumstances; it could not be legislated away so easily. Thus, Louis XVIII was persuaded to grant a charter that provided for a reasonable and moderate constitutional monarchy. The basic economic and legal gains of the Revolution were preserved. So, too, was Jewish equality before the law.

After 1815, the Jews of France were permitted not merely to enjoy the gains of the Revolutionary epoch; they were liberated, as well, from many of the Napoleonic disabilities. For example, the Infamous Decree of 1808, which had imposed gratuitous restrictions upon Jewish economic activity, was not renewed when it expired in 1818. The detested and insulting *More Judaico,* an elaborate Jewish oath that Jews were obliged to take if they wished to testify in court, gradually fell into disuse during the early years of the Restoration. When the country took a turn to the left in 1830 and dropped its Bourbon dynasty, the problem of minorities was viewed even more liberally by the new Orleanist regime. As a result, the system of Jewish consistories was radically revamped. Consistorial committees of rabbis and laymen continued to supervise all the religious activities of French Jewry;

but the degrading scrutiny of Jewish business behavior, Jewish "patriotism," Jewish participation in military conscription was dropped.

In the years that followed, Jews enjoyed increasingly wider opportunities of attending universities, winning promotion in the army, obtaining complete legal protection in all their business activities. Nowhere on the continent of Europe, save perhaps in the little Kingdom of the Netherlands, was Jewish emancipation reasserted so early, so bloodlessly, so undramatically. When, in 1834, the rather pedestrian Jewish banker, Benoît Fould, was elected to the Chamber of Deputies from the district of St. Quentin, Heinrich Heine could observe aptly: "Emancipation is complete, now that a Jew without brains, talent, ability, or any endowment save that of wealth can, like any Christian similarly endowed, be elected to the highest legislative Chamber." The struggle for Jewish emancipation shifted eastward now, across the Rhine, below the Swiss Alps, and along the Danube Valley. Here were the battlefields upon which the issues of Jewish status and freedom would finally be resolved.

In Italy, for example, the conservatism of which we have spoken came much closer to naked reaction. At the Congress of Vienna, few European statesmen found it possible to take seriously the concept of a single Italian nation. The peninsula had been divided into separate political units ever since the Lombard conquest in the sixth century; there seemed little reason, therefore, to consolidate it into a united country in 1815. Accordingly the diplomats at Vienna proceeded to parcel out eighteen million Italians much as trustees of an estate might distribute farms and tenants. Lombardy and Venetia were joined into a puppet kingdom governed from Vienna. Modena, Parma, and Lucca were allocated to Hapsburg "viceroys"; the Papal States were restored to the "bishop of Rome"; and the Bourbons were returned to the throne in Naples-Sicily. The one truly sovereign Italian buffer state, Sardinia-Piedmont, was quite insecure, dependent upon the Allies for its very life. The hungry legatees into whose hands Italy was delivered were only too willing to hark back to medievalism for their administrative rationale; it was a rationale, after all, that had operated without challenge up to the very moment of French conquest. Virtually all vestiges of the Napoleonic period were obliterated: equality before the law, religious toleration, political rights—and Jewish emancipation.

In 1815, as in 1789, the thirty-five thousand Jews of Italy were divided fairly equally between Piedmont, Lombardy-Venetia, Tuscany, and the Papal States. They watched helplessly now as their rulers brought back from exile many of the archaic prejudices and institutions of the pre-Napoleonic period. Not that all the old disabilities could be restored; pariahdom could not be re-established with a mere stroke of the pen. The Austrians, for example, recognized that the Jews could be of service to the state if used properly; and thus the Viceroy of Lombardy-Venetia contented himself with excluding Jews from public office, denying them the right to own real estate and to participate in the professions. These restrictions were far from unbearable. In Tuscany too the Jews were spared a reimposition of onerous taxes and ghetto domicile.

Unfortunately, these states covered a relatively small area of Italy. Elsewhere reaction triumphed much more completely. In Sardinia-Piedmont, for example, the entire grillwork of Jewish restrictions was once again enforced under the supervision of a powerful Jesuit Order: as in pre-Revolutionary days, Jews were confined to ghettos, excluded from all educational institutions, and forbidden to engage in the professions. All the old degrading Jew-taxes were reintroduced. In the duchy of Modena, the Jews were obliged once again to pay an annual tribute as the price of their toleration. The circumstances of Jewish life were perhaps most oppressive of all in the Papal States, where Pius VII returned from his long exile determined to re-establish the ecclesiastical regime of the eighteenth century down to its last detail. The Inquisition was actually reinstated. Jews were herded back into their ghettos, required to wear their medieval Jew-badges, to attend conversionary sermons once a month. Pope Leo XII, who succeeded Pius VII in 1823, was even more blindly vindictive than his predecessor; indeed, he went to the lengths of encouraging forced baptisms, and tolerated without protest the occasional kidnaping of Jewish children. Jews began to emigrate to France in droves. It was apparent that the pendulum of reaction had swung to its furthest extreme in the Italian peninsula.

THE CONGRESS OF VIENNA AND GERMANY

At Vienna, Germany, too, was dismembered with the same cynicism that had characterized the Italian partition. Of course, there was no question of reviving the moribund Holy Roman Empire; indeed, some seventy-two princes and dukes were sent into permanent retirement, and forty-two free cities were deprived of their autonomy. But the statesmen at the Winter Palace nevertheless flatly rejected the anguished appeal of German liberals for a truly united Germany. What they produced instead was a ramshackle confederation hardly more cohesive than the old empire. There was no German king, no German flag or army, no German currency—in short, no German fatherland. This was exactly the way Metternich wanted it; it was the technique by which the patchwork Hapsburg Empire could continue to dominate German affairs. "Poor faithful German nation," wrote the poet Ernst Arndt, "thou art to have no national Emperor. Thy princes wish to play the Emperor. Instead of one lord thou art to have two dozen who will never be able to agree upon German questions."

It was apparent that if the German diplomats at Vienna were determined to eradicate all vestiges of Napoleon's legislation, one of the most likely casualties would be Jewish emancipation. Nevertheless, the wealthy Jewish bankers of Berlin, Frankfurt, and Vienna were determined to salvage as much of that emancipation as possible. They recognized, too, that there would never be a better opportunity for a concerted effort than the winter of 1814-15. Accordingly the salons of the Rothschilds, the von Herzs, the Itzigs, and the von Arnsteins, were thrown open to the visiting statesmen. Metternich, Humboldt, Hardenberg, the princes and dukes of the smaller German states were overwhelmed with favors and attentions, magnificent banquets and lavish gifts of jewelry. In a letter to his wife, Humboldt described one old Jewish gentleman who paid him a visit—"an old man from Prague, whose demeanor pleased me quite well, as he was not among the new fashioned Jews . . ."—and offered him three diamond rings as a present or the alternative of four thousand ducats credit. It did not take the Jewish bankers long to single out Hardenberg and Humboldt of Prussia as their most likely champions. These were the only statesmen in Germany, after all, who had taken the lead in voluntarily emancipating their own Jews (Stein was now living in Russia). Humboldt was particularly friendly to the cause of Jewish emancipation. He wrote his wife again on January 17, 1815: "Arnsteins have again given wax-figures. I did not attend. I am working with all my might to give the Jews all civil rights, so that it will no longer be necessary, out of generosity, to go to Jewish houses."

In February Humboldt and Hardenberg sought to incorporate Jewish emancipation into the emergent Constitution of the German Confederation. Because the measure met with strenuous resistance, version after version was drafted, revised, discarded. At last, however, it appeared as if the Prussian delegates had worked out a satisfactory compromise: the projected statement, Article XVI of the Treaty of Vienna, assured the Jews of all "rights heretofore accorded to them in the several states." And then, at the last moment before acceptance, in a session of June 8, 1815, a Hanseatic delegate cunningly changed the meaning of the clause by substituting the word "by" for "in." The clause thus worded extended to the Jews the civil "rights heretofore accorded to them *by* the several states." The consequences of this substitution were quite drastic. With the exception of Prussia, none of the German states had voluntarily accorded the Jews civil rights during the Napoleonic period; rather, they had been prodded into Jewish emancipation by French bayonets. Nowhere, in other words, had the Jews been granted civil rights *by* the states. The clause as it was written gave the Jews precisely nothing. For a number of weeks after the measure's ratification the Jews of Germany exulted in their "victory." Only gradually did it begin to dawn on them that they had been swindled out of emancipation by a preposition.

Yet the tragic failure of Emancipation at Vienna did not entirely vitiate the affirmative significance of the Congress. After all, the subject of Jewish rights had been discussed at an international conference for the first time in history. An important precedent thus had been established in dealing with humanitarian issues, issues formerly regarded as of purely domestic concern. Some of the greatest statesmen of Europe had publicly espoused the principle of Jewish emancipation. Most Jews were convinced as a result, that it was only a matter of time before the gains of the Napoleonic period would be permanently consolidated.

It did not quite happen that way. Bound to the bedrock of conservatism, the rulers of the German states were unwilling to restore voluntarily even the smallest fragment of the liberal apparatus. This was particularly true in the Hapsburg Empire, which had not felt obliged to reform itself even after the disaster of Austerlitz. Metternich and his colleagues were passionately addicted to the *status quo*; it was a passion fed by one of the most obscurantist Catholic hierarchies in Europe. Only in later decades, when the non-German races within the Hapsburg Empire began to stir with disaffection, did Metternich grudgingly admit to the need for some kind of decentralization. By then however he was overshadowed in the administration by the autocratic Kolowrat, Minister of the Interior; and Kolowrat was not constrained to budge.

In the Hapsburg Empire, therefore, all nationalities suffered from Vienna's vindictive administrative strait jacket. The 325,000 Jews of Austria, Hungary, and Galicia were no exception—except that they suffered more. Ironically, Metternich was willing to intervene vigorously, at the instigation of the Rothschilds, on behalf of the Jews in other lands; but within Austria he hesitated to alleviate even the harshest injustice, lest the flood tide of revolution be released. In the case of the Jews, of course, it was not merely a matter of national rights, but of civil rights, as well. The old Jew-streets, the restrictions on occupation were preserved intact. In Bohemia and Moravia Jews still were excluded from the rural areas; while in Prague Jews were confined to the most squalid section of the city. Only a few hundred "tolerated" Jews were permitted to reside in Vienna; until the second half of the nineteenth century it was not uncommon for officials to awaken Jews in the middle of the night, or search the passing omnibuses, or descend upon synagogues, or force the Jews to show their residence permits. Jews were obliged to take separate and humiliating oaths in law courts, to pay special taxes for residence and business rights. There were occasional critics of this kind of obscurantism. Even crusty old Field Marshal Joseph Radetzky declared it a patriotic duty "to win over the class which, by reason of its intelligence and wealth, exerts so great an influence." But Metternich held firm. Little wonder that many young Jews moved secretely into the revolutionary movements that were festering beneath the surface of Hapsburg political life.

Oppression was felt even more keenly in the other states of Germany, for there it came as retribution for the brief egalitarian period of Napoleonic domination. As material prosperity declined with the tapering-off of war expenditures, the harassed German *Mittelstand* relapsed briefly—but significantly—into impotence. The nationalist secret societies, the *Burschenschaften*, the *Tugenbund*, struggled fitfully for a while, and then were throttled to death by the Carlsbad Decrees of 1819. Constitutionalism vanished like a wraith, while romantic conservatism burgeoned forth in the works of political theorists, artists, musicians, and writers, who harked back to the dear dead days of Gothic medievalism, and who endowed very tangible feudal and class interests with the magic of an ideology. Immanuel Fichte and Georg Hegel deduced from the past that the welfare of the State-Leviathan took precedence over the happiness of individuals. The theologian Schleiermacher sanctified the state on the level of theology. German prose and poetry conjured up the past in fairy tales, legends, epics; music was rewoven about the themes of minnesingers. Law, too, was visualized by Savigny as the result of inexorable historic circumstances. The sustained emphasis upon tradition, the past, and the state augured ill for the liberals, the reformers, the emancipators—and especially for the Jews.

For during this period between 1815 and about 1840 romantic nationalism, linked as it was to political reaction, intensified popular anti-Jewish sentiment. Now, in fact, Jew-hatred was endowed by the romantic theorists with an intellectual rationale. Friedrich Rühs of the University of Berlin and Wilhelm Ries of the University of Heidelberg viewed the Jewish minority as a "state within a state," as a "menace . . . to the welfare and character of the Germans." One Hartwig Hundt, in a terrifying volume entitled *Mirror of the Jews*, went so far as to urge castration of Jewish males, and the sale of Jewish children to West Indian plantations. Crowds in the streets of Würzburg, Bamberg, Karlsruhe, Heidelberg, Mannheim, Frankfurt, and Hamburg assaulted their Jews physically, broke windows in Jewish homes and looted Jewish stores.

Most of the old Jewish disabilities were revived. In the Hanseatic cities, in Bavaria, Saxony, and Saxe-Weimar, the Jews were confined once again to ghetto neighborhoods. Jewish participation in the guilds was prohibited in nearly every state in Germany. Even in Prussia, which had reformed itself after Jena, many of the old curbs upon opportunity were restored. Of course the reforms of Stein and Hardenberg had never been applied to the Prussian provinces that were reconquered from France; but even in central Prussian territory an arbitrary interpretation of the 1812 Emancipation edict cut Jews off from civil appointments, from many crucial livelihoods, and from all school privileges. Jews were warned not to bear Christian names, to employ Christian domestics, or to march in public parades. While the revival of ancient disabilities was particularly galling to the enlightened Jewish community of Berlin, all German Jews, whether of Prussia or of the former Confederation of the Rhine, found the restrictions of 1815 less endurable than those they had known in the days before Napoleon. They had tasted Emancipation, and they gagged on a less appetizing diet.

LIBERALISM AND THE JEWS

The Jews were not alone, of course, in mourning the demise of liberalism. They found a powerful ally in the emergent middle class. The hardheaded businessmen, the youthful idealists of Central and Western Europe, were deeply committed to the ideals of political and economic freedom. They were convinced, too, of the invincibility of their cause; for their principal weapon was the driving power of the Industrial Revolution, that great clattering giant which thrust men of means and ambition ever more directly into the center of human affairs. Liberty was no platitude to these people; it had already brought enrichment to their lives, and like the Jews, they were prepared to fight to win it back. Once they obtained control of their governments, they were determined to weld their petty duchies into united nations with efficient administrations and unrestricted markets.

The liberals had no intention, therefore, of allowing the conservatives to monopolize the issue of romantic nationalism. After all, romanticism worked both ways; it was as much an expression of the "General Will" as it was of medieval quietism. This kind of liberal nationalism simmered slowly throughout Europe, out of sight of censor and secret police, only occasionally making its appearance at a mass rally or in a spate of printed circulars. By the fourth decade of the nineteenth century, however, conservatism, that had operated virtually without interference after the Congress of Vienna, was put increasingly on the defensive. The passionate idealism of Giuseppe Mazzini in Italy, Johann Bluntschli in Prussia, Louis Kossuth in Hungary, Alphonse Lamartine in France, attracted larger and more devoted numbers of adherents. Moreover, the liberal constitutionalists and nationalists were far less hesitant about joining hands with the Jews than they had been during the uncertain, suspicious days of the French Revolution. For the Jews were no longer strangers; during the Napoleonic period they had proved themselves good citizens and valuable allies. Equality of race and creed was no longer a dangerous abstraction. It had worked. If the Jews were willing, they would be welcomed with open arms into liberal ranks.

The Jews were more than willing. They understood that their security in Europe was linked to the success of liberalism with the certainty of a mathematical law. In the Italian peninsula, for example, Jews took a particularly active part in the nationalist movement. Thousands of young Jews joined Mazzini's "Young Italy," and bore arms in the abortive uprisings of the early 1830's. Jews were among the people closest to Mazzini, the "soul" of Italian nationalism. In northern Italy Giuseppe Vitalevi was Mazzini's principal lieutenant. Mazzini's expedition into Savoy, in April 1833, was financed by the wealthy Jewish banking firm of Todros in Turin. Mazzini could count on Jewish support outside of Italy, as well; during his long exile in London, his most devoted British friends were the Rossellis, Jewish merchants of Italian origin, while the London home of Sara Levi Nathan was the center of Italian political activity in exile for many years after Mazzini's death. Fortunately for the Jews, Mazzini's successors in Italy were no less closely wed to liberal ideals. Count Camillo di Cavour, the brilliant Piedmontese aristocrat who became the "pen" of the Italian *Risorgimento,* was an ardent advocate of Jewish civil rights. As a warmhearted humanitarian, the very concept of second-class citizens offended his sensibilities; while as a trained economist, he was certainly not unwilling to liberate Jewish credit. In 1847 in the midst of his reformist program in Sardinia-Piedmont, Cavour initiated a petition demanding Jewish emancipation, and was joined by hundreds of distinguished Piedmontese citizenship including the celebrated painter and novelist, Massimo d'Azeglio. In no country in Europe was the alliance between the Jews and the liberals more fundamental than in Italy, and in no country did that alliance reap richer rewards.

In Germany, too, Jews were among the most active participants in the constitutional movement. Perhaps the three outstanding representatives of German-Jewish liberalism in the period before 1848 were Gabriel Riesser, Ludwig Börne, and Heinrich Heine. Riesser, a Prussian Jew, was in the forefront of the liberal cause for nearly twenty years. In 1848, in fact, he was destined to play an important role in the Frankfurt Parliament. Riesser was perhaps the classic example of the modern enlightened Jew; a Heidelberg graduate, a Doctor of Laws, a Reform Jew, he devoted his lifetime to the vindication of the thesis that Jews were entirely capable of full-hearted German citizenship. When Heinrich Paulus, a spokesman for the *status quo,* stigmatized the Jews as aliens who were fundamentally incapable of understanding the German "soul," Riesser delivered an impassioned response in the authentic spirit of the 1807 Sanhedrin: "Where is the other state," he cried, "to which we owe loyalty? What other fatherland calls us to its defense? We have not emigrated to Germany, we were born here, and either we are Germans or we are men without a country. There is only one baptism that can consecrate a man to a nationality: that is the baptism of blood shed in a common battle for freedom and fatherland." Those who were willing to listen to Riesser ignored the florid rhetoric: his words made sense in the nineteenth century. Riesser was indefatigable as a champion of Jewish rights: urging the Jews of Baden to reject any religious concessions as the price of citizenship; savagely, and at great personal peril, attacking the obscurantist xenophobia of King Frederick William IV of Prussia; asserting, in pamphlet after pamphlet, the sense of kinship Jews felt for their Christian neighbors. In the career of no other man were the affirmations of the Sanhedrin more clearly exemplified.

In far-ranging influence on German liberal ideas, however, Riesser was superseded by Börne and Heine. Although they were both compelled to do their most effective writing in exile in Paris, they were probably nineteenth-century Germany's most articulate champions of freedom and constitutionalism. Börne, who was born Loeb Baruch in the Frankfurt *Judengasse* only three years before the French Revolution, lived to become one of Europe's prime masters of incendiary journalism. A lean, sunken-cheeked man, cold and forbidding in appearance, Börne was blunt to the point of tactlessness. But he insisted that in such times integrity was more urgent than amenities. His "Letters from Paris" were biting, savage indictments of the reactionary monarchies of contemporary Germany. Steadfastly republican in his political outlook, Börne was a founder of "Young Germany," the one truly egalitarian political force in the German-speaking world of his day. Although he was converted to Protestantism in his youth, Börne refused to dissociate himself from his Jewish forebears. In a letter from Paris in 1832, he wrote:

> I would indeed not be worthy to enjoy the light of the sun if I paid with scornful grumbling for the great act of grace that God has shown me of letting me be both a German and a Jew. . . . Because I was a bondsman, I therefore love liberty more than you. . . . Yes, because I was born without a fatherland my desire for a fatherland is more passionate than yours. . . .

Here spoke a man without a government, Jewish or German, in limbo, seeking, Hamletlike, for a father, for a fatherland.

Heine, the details of whose dramatic life we shall discuss in a subsequent chapter (Chapter VII), was perhaps the most colorful of these three Jewish liberals. Born and raised in Düsseldorf, educated as a lawyer at the universities of Bonn and Göttingen, fully acquainted with the German vernacular and with virtually every facet of German culture, Heine was well qualified to pass judgment on the problems of contemporary German life. Thin, highstrung, notoriously bohemian in conduct, he was the rare combination of sensitive poet and hardfisted political journalist. His first published political tract was a seemingly harmless collection of travel pictures, which described a leisurely junket through Germany. But the pictures turned out instead to be incisive exposés of German political conditions. So incisive were they, in fact, that Heine, like Börne, was compelled to seek refuge in Paris. There he lived for twenty years, surviving on an allowance provided by a wealthy uncle.

Because Heine was merciless in his political criticism, he spent the most creative years of his life in a frustrating, energy-consuming feud with the German censors. Enough of his work managed to get through, however, to make the effort worth his while. When he described his country's vested interests, he was unsparing. The German aristocracy was for him "a handful of common nobles who have learned nothing beyond horse-trading, card-sharping, drinking feats, and similar stupid and rascally accomplishments. . . . They are indeed like thieves who pick one another's pockets while they are being led to the gallows . . ." But when he dwelt on the German people, as a people, he mellowed satire with enough banter to end up almost on a note of affection.

> An Englishman [he wrote] loves liberty like his lawfully wedded wife. She is a possession; he may not treat her with much tenderness, but he knows how to defend her. A Frenchman loves liberty like his mistress, and he will do a thousand follies for her sake. A German loves liberty like his old grandmother. And yet, after all, no one can tell how things will turn out. The grumpy Englishman, in an ill temper with his wife, is capable of dragging her by a rope to Smithfield. The inconstant Frenchman may become unfaithful to his adored and be off flirting round the Palais Royal with another. But the German will never quite desert his old grandmother; he will always keep for her a nook near the chimney-corner where she can tell fairy-tales to the listening children.

He called himself the first internationalist, and believed that as a Jew (like Börne, he was a converted Jew) he could play the middleman between France and Germany. Heine was indeed one of the pioneers of the romantic, Mazzinilike nationalism that envisaged a Europe of self-realized free peoples living in mutual amity.

> And what is the great task of our day? [he asked.] It is emancipation. Not simply the emancipation of the Irish, the Greeks, Frankfort Jews, West Indian blacks, and all such oppressed peoples, but the emancipation of the whole world, and especially of Europe, which has now come of age, and is tearing itself loose from the apron-strings of the privileged

classes, the aristocracy. Though certain philosophical renegades of freedom may force chains of the finest syllogisms to prove to us that millions of men were merely created to serve as beasts of burden for a few thousand privileged knights—yet they cannot convince us, until they can prove to us, as Voltaire said, that the former came into the world with saddles on their backs, and the latter with spurs on their feet.

Heine came to be deeply admired by the literate German *Mittelstand,* who hung on his every word and repeated his epigrams and barbs with delight. Few Germans, Jew or Christian, exercised so powerful an influence on the liberal thought of the early nineteenth century. His views were echoed with equal persistence, if not always with equal eloquence, by Moses Hess, Jacob Jacoby, Andreas Gottschalk, Jacob de Jonge, and many other dedicated German Jews. In their careers they prophetically blended the quest for Jewish security with the mission of European liberalism. The fusion became particularly significant in 1848 and after.

1848: THE WATERSHED

Early in 1848 the citizens of Paris lost patience with their pathetic "umbrella king," the Orleanist, Louis Philippe. Louis Philippe was certainly no tyrant. He was in fact a rather kindly man, well-disposed toward constitutionalism. But his foreign policy had been a failure and his domestic policy had been a bore. The mobs that converged on the Hôtel de Ville in 1848 decided that the time had come to substitute a solid republic for a rather vapid constitutional monarchy. Perhaps the changeover was not of momentous significance in France itself. But the pattern that it set for other lands was revolutionary. In Italy, for example, the overthrow of Louis Philippe was precisely the spark needed to ignite a chain reaction of insurrections throughout the length and breadth of the peninsula. From Venice to Sicily Italian mobs stampeded through the streets of their kingdoms and marched on the palaces of their rulers. Charles Albert in Turin, Ferdinand II in Naples, Pius IX in Rome, the Grand Duke of Tuscany in Florence, all were terrified into granting constitutions and sovereign political rights to their peoples. Austrian garrisons were routed from their barracks and sent fleeing back across the Alps. There was little that Austria could do, for at that moment the Hapsburg bureaucracy was beset by other revolts in Vienna, Prague, and Budapest.

The leading spirit in the Venetian Revolution was Daniele Manin, a man of Jewish blood, the grandson of baptized grandparents. Perhaps it was no coincidence therefore that the first act of the Venetian Republic, after its establishment in March of 1848, was to proclaim complete civil and political equality for all inhabitants, whatever their race or creed. Gratefully, the Jews took an active part in the affairs of the short-lived republic. Several Jews, including several rabbis, sat in the Venetian National Assembly; Leone Picherel became Minister of Agriculture, and Isaaco Pesaro became Minister of Finance. In the Papal States, too, where the flamboyant warrior-democrat Giuseppe Garibaldi defied Pope Pius IX himself, the new Roman Republic announced the end of ghetto domicile, together with all other humiliating anti-Jewish restrictions. The political developments of Venetia and Rome were repeated in Lombardy, Naples-Sicily, and the smaller states of the peninsula. Everywhere Jews were ardent partisans of the new constitutional regimes and willing members of the armies that supported them. When King Charles Albert of Sardinia took it upon himself to assume the leadership in uniting Italy under the House of Savoy, Jews by the thousands flocked to his banner. It appeared for a moment as if Emancipation had been permanently restored.

Germany, too, was affected by the revolutionary fever. In one German duchy after another rioting crowds of students and workers intimidated the sovereign authorities into promises of constitutional reform. In Prussia and Saxony, basic civil rights were recognized and given the authority of law. The rulers of Baden, Württemberg, Hanover, and nearly all other German states felt constrained to provide their subjects with liberal constitutions. Exultant students, businessmen, and intellectuals of Germany hailed the arrival of the "golden era." Because moreover the time seemed ripe for welding the factious agglomeration of states into a united Germany, the leading liberals of each of the German duchies and kingdoms hurried to Frankfurt to draft a national constitution. Unhappily the delegates—most of them lawyers and professors—turned out to be windy idealists, and soon lost themselves in abstract argumentation and points of technical procedure. Yet, until the moment when the imperial crown of the "new" Germany was rejected by Frederick William IV of Prussia in March of 1849, it seemed as if the ancient dream of one all-embracing German political unit was about to become a reality.

Recognizing that the hour of liberation had struck for them, the Jews of Germany hurled themselves passionately into the revolutionary movements. Jews figured prominently among the liberals who fought on the barricades during the March uprising in Berlin, and several scores of them died in the street riots. The Prussian National Assembly, which met in May of 1848 to draw up the new Prussian constitution, included a number of Jewish deputies; one of them, Dr. Raphael Kosch, was elected as the Assembly's vice-president. The Prussian Constitution of 1848 fulfilled the fondest hopes of its Jewish supporters: complete equality before the law was recognized for all citizens of Prussia, regardless of class or birth—and this applied to the tens of thousands of Polish Jews in Prussian Posen as well. Nor did the other German states, newly "constitutionalized," fail to emancipate their Jewries. In Baden a constitutional convention formulated a truly liberal set of fundamental guarantees for Jews and Christians alike. The King of Bavaria willingly emancipated his Jews when the burgomasters of Munich, Nuremberg, and Würtzburg convinced him that Jewish credit was needed for state purposes. In Brunswick, Anhalt-Dessau, Saxony, Hamburg, and Lübeck, Jewish delegates sat in the constituent assemblies to insure the final approval of Jewish rights.

The Jews were determined, too, that Jewish freedom should be secured on a truly national basis in the Frankfurt parliament. No less than seven Jews sat in this body as tangible evidence of the strikingly large Jewish participation in the liberal movement. One of the delegates, Gabriel Riesser, served as vice-president of the parliament; and near the end of the gathering's sessions, Eduard von Simson, a baptized Jew, succeeded Heinrich von Gagern as the parliament's president. Again Jewish confidence in the breadth of liberal egalitarianism was not misplaced. One of the parliament's first projects was to draft a statement on the "Fundamental Rights of the German People," which provided that "enjoyment of civic and citizen rights will not be conditioned or limited by religious faith." When, however, the delegates considered a proposal to make "the peculiar conditions of the Israelitish race" the object of special legislation—a gesture made as a warmhearted act of deference to the Jews—it was the Jew, Gabriel Riesser, who leaped to his feet in protest. The Jews were neither a separate race nor a nation, he insisted heatedly; they were "Germans of the Jewish faith," and therefore ought to be "subjected" to no more than a general statement of equal rights. The other delegates, who hardly knew what to make of Riesser's splenetic reaction, hastily agreed.

How apparent it was, in this illuminating little sidelight on the constitutional struggle, that the ideals of the Sanhedrin had anchored themselves firmly in the hearts of German-Jewish liberals! They were determined to secure their civil and religious rights as Germans, not as Jews. After all, Riesser, and his counterparts in the liberal camps of other Western European lands, had made great personal sacrifices in order to identify themselves as loyal and reliable "nationals"; it was hardly surprising, as a result, that they were almost belligerent on this issue. The moment Jewish liberals were singled out, even by their friends, as German Jews, or members of the Israelitish "race," rather than as Germans of the Jewish "faith" or "persuasion," they bristled as if they had been mortally insulted. Their passion for unqualified group identification led large numbers of German Jews, even courageous individualists like Riesser, instinctively to minimize the points of difference between themselves and their non-Jewish neighbors. This self-consciousness, born in the post-Mendelssohnian era, nurtured (as we shall see in Chapter VII) in the Prussian salons, exacerbated by the alternating fortunes of political emancipation, was now well on its way to becoming the distinctive cultural malaise of German Jewry.

Perhaps in no other period of European history was Jewish involvement in the liberal cause more integral than in this dramatic interlude of 1848. It was one of those fleeting moments when ancient enmities and suspicions were forgotten; when, in the exultation of a common goal, Jew and Christian locked arms with each other. In the various congresses, mass meetings, political clubs, and demonstrations of the time Jews were everywhere welcome, everywhere active. Dr. Sigismund Stern was president of Berlin's constitutional club. Julius Friedländer signed the appeal for a congress of Prussian militias in November 1848. In Breslau, Moses Schreiber was cofounder of the German People's Union. In Mainz, Ludwig Bamberger was the founder of the Democratic Party. Rabbi Abraham Adler of Worms founded that city's radical democratic newspaper, *Die Neue Zeit*. In later years, as we shall see, Jewish disabilities were alleviated with equal thoroughness—if rather less spectacularly. But in the entire modern period of German-Jewish life, 1848 was the one moment in which Jew and German came closest to fundamental comradeship.

The revolutionary upswing of Central Germany was largely duplicated in the Austrian Empire. No European dynasty was more firmly wedded to conservative principles than the House of Hapsburg. And yet, despite all Metternich's precautions, or perhaps because of them, the revolutionary fever of 1848 spread to the Austrian capital, as well as the capitals of the dependent provinces of the empire. An uprising in Vienna forced the aging chancellor into permanent exile; while the feeble and harebrained emperor, Ferdinand I, was intimidated into promises of reform. In Bohemia, too, the Czechs overpowered their Austrian garrisons, insisting upon their right to autonomy. So, indeed, did the Magyars, who were prepared to establish an independent regime of their own. All the new governments demanded, and received, recognition from the paralyzed ministry at Vienna; and all adopted liberal programs, guaranteeing their peasants relief from feudal dues, the middle class freedom of speech and press, and all citizens the benefit of representative government.

Jews participated fully in the chain reaction of uprisings. In Vienna at the first clash between students and the military, Jews fell side by side with Christians; all were buried in a common grave, while the mourners were addressed by Jewish and Christian clerics in a joint service. Ludwig August Frankl wrote *Die Universitat*—the anthem of the Viennese uprising. Adolf Fischhof was sent as the Viennese delegate to the diet, which formulated the Austrian constitution. Rabbis Mannheimer and Meisels of Cracow represented Galicia at the Constitutional Convention in Vienna, treating the other delegates to the spectacle of skullcaps and caftans in the august halls of the parliament. All of these Jewish delegates, whether Westernized Viennese or bearded Galicians, must have experienced the same exhilaration when the diet constitutionalized Jewish equality before the law.

The revolutionary upswing was repeated in Hungary, a land in which nearly one hundred thousand Jews had suffered for years under a bitterly reactionary *Landtag* and an even more reactionary Catholic Church. To enlist the support of Hungarian Jewry, Louis Kossuth, the leader of the Hungarian revolt, appeared personally in the synagogue of Grosswardein to solicit Jewish forgiveness for past persecutions, and to pledge himself to work diligently for the equality of all citizens. The Jews trusted Kossuth; some twenty thousand of them enlisted in the Hungarian National Army. Distinguished Jewish public figures, Rabbi Loeb Schwab and his son-in-law Leopold Löw, conducted public prayer meetings on behalf of the revolutionary cause. Kossuth's egalitarian instincts however were not yet shared by his people. As passionate nationalists, the Hungarians craved homogeneity as much as they craved freedom; exactly because they feared a minority problem of their own they hesitated to emancipate the Slovenes, Croats, and Jews who lived in Hungary. Action came only when the disaffected Slav minority, under the leadership of Joseph Jelačić, launched an attack upon the Hungarian revolutionary government. At that point the Hungarian diet in Szeged hesitated no longer, and equal civil and political rights were extended to all minorities within the Magyar kingdom.

In Bohemia and Slovakia contact between the Jews and the nationalist movements was made even more difficult than in Hungary. The Slavic majorities of these lands were not among the most culturally advanced of Europe's peoples. The Jews of Bohemia and Moravia, in contrast with the Slavic peasantry among whom they lived, were devotees of German culture—and as such, they were subjected to fiercely anti-Jewish riots the moment the Czech, Moravian, and Slovakian uprisings began in March of 1848. Here there was none of the camaraderie that characterized Jewish-Christian relations in other countries during this period.

Unfortunately for liberals, nationalists, and Jews alike, the forces of conservatism were not to be summarily dislodged. The brave hopes of 1848 turned into a midsummer night's dream. In Italy, for example, Charles Albert's forces were destroyed at Custoza in the summer of 1848 by a resurgent Austrian army. Faced with the threat of Austrian intervention, the constitutional regimes in each of the Italian states toppled like tenpins; and in Rome, where republican forces appeared solidly entrenched, a French army appeared to restore the Pope to his pontifical throne. Everywhere, too, Jews were subjected to the old disabilities; in Rome they were even herded back into ghettos. The revolution guttered out in Germany as well. The *Mittelstand* was not yet shored up by the power of a far-reaching industrial revolution; industrial change was coming in Germany, but too late to save the revolutionary cause of 1848. Ultimately, Frederick William's household cannon succeeded in dispersing the crowds that had dictated his policy for so many months from the streets of Berlin. In Bavaria, too, royalist forces regained control of the apparatus of government. Meanwhile the delegates to the Frankfurt parliament, faced with King Frederick William's refusal to accept the imperial crown, had already begun to disperse in confusion when Austrian armies threatened to intervene. It was at this juncture, in 1849, that the abortive attempt at unification was abandoned by the liberals—to be reattempted later by the conservatives. As the pendulum swung back to the right, one German sovereign after another betrayed his promise of constitutionalism and returned to autocratic rule. In such a climate there was little hope for Jewish emancipation. Exhausted, having shot their bolt, many thousands of German liberals and German Jews left their native lands forever, convinced that constitutionalism was destined to remain a dead issue in Germany—at least for their lifetimes.

Finally, in Austria, Bohemia, and Hungary, the imperial armies managed to trample the revolutionary forces underfoot. The endemic rivalry between Germans and Czechs in Bohemia enabled Prince Alfred Windisch-Graetz to recapture Prague. This victory in turn released enough Austrian troops to crush the revolts both in Italy and in Austria proper. After the occupation of Vienna in October 1848, Emperor Ferdinand was persuaded to abdicate in favor of his nephew, Franz Josef I. The new emperor abruptly dismissed the revolutionary assembly, discarded the newly completed constitution, and issued an appeal to Nicholas I of Russia for help in suppressing the Hungarian insurrection. The "policeman of Europe" was only too happy to set an example for his own factious minorities; his Cossack shock troops marched into Hungary and swiftly battered the Magyars into submission. With the return of the gibbet and the firing squad, silence reigned once more throughout Central Europe.

As far as the Jews were concerned, it was the same melancholy story of restored disabilities. Once again they were denied the franchise, the protection of equality before the law, the right to own land, the right to choose their professions as they liked. And yet, it was an epoch not without ultimate value to the Jews of Europe. The year 1848 was the great testing ground for Jewish political activity. Between 1789 and 1815 the Jews had secured their emancipation primarily as passive beneficiaries of the Revolution and of Napoleon, its heir. This time, in the second phase of Jewish emancipation, the Jews themselves labored for their freedom, and did so by battling for constitutionalism in its largest framework. "First comes the man," declared Rabbi Mannheimer of Cracow in a sermon to his flock, "then the citizen, and only then the Jew. No one must be able to accuse us of always thinking of ourselves first." After 1848 it would be difficult to make such an accusation again.

EMANCIPATION IS COMPLETED: 1848-1871

The eventual triumph of European liberalism, and of Jewish emancipation, came quietly, almost anticlimactically. Within two decades after the 1848 uprisings, grudging concessions on the part of the conservatives, and important diplomatic coups on the part of liberal leaders, achieved the seemingly impossible: a united Italy, a united Germany, an autonomous Hungary —and moderately constitutional regimes in all those lands. Cavour, the far-visioned Piedmontese prime minister, was willing to make compromises in means in order to achieve the end of a united peninsula under Savoyard sovereignty. He shrewdly courted Napoleon III of France into an alliance in 1859, and then launched a calculated attack upon the Austrians that same year. This time outnumbered, the Austrians were compelled to give in. Within eighteen months the banner of the House of Savoy fluttered over an Italian kingdom united, save for the city of Rome; and in 1870 Rome, too, was incorporated into the state. The Piedmontese *Statuto* became the law of the land. Civil rights and political enfranchisement were extended to all inhabitants of Italy, Jews and Christians alike.

Cavour had his reasons to be grateful to the Jews—not only for the support of Jewish liberals, but for the important financial aid of Jewish bankers, the Rothschilds, the Bendi, the brothers Tedesco. In 1860 he appointed Sansone d'Ancona, a Jew, as director of finances and public works for Tuscany. The learned Hebrew scholar, Giacomo Dina of Piedmont, became the leading editorial writer of *Opinione,* Cavour's official political organ. Isacco Artom became Cavour's confidential secretary, and in later life undersecretary of foreign affairs. In 1848 there had been no European country save Spain where the restrictions placed upon Jews were more galling and more humiliating than in Italy. After 1860 there was no country on the continent of Europe where conditions were better for Jews. Since that date a cordial relationship developed between Italians and Jews which, even during the brief Mussolini aberration, was never seriously questioned.

The loss of the Italian provinces had a profound psychological impact upon the bureacracy in Vienna. For the first time even the most obtuse and traditionalist Hapsburg official could recognize that major reforms would have to be made—if the ramshackle empire was to survive at all. Even as the court at Vienna began to contemplate possible administrative reforms, Prussia suddenly crushed the Austrian army at Sadowa in 1866, and permanently ended the Hapsburg influence in German politics. Franz Josef procrastinated no longer. He still possessed Bohemia, Moravia, Slovakia, Hungary, and Galicia, and he was determined to keep them loyal at all costs. In 1867 the emperor issued a remarkable constitution which literally divided the empire into two parts; the Magyars, the largest of the non-German races, were now granted complete autonomy in their internal affairs. Moreover, basic rights of citizenship were extended to all the subject peoples of the Hapsburg Empire, including equality before the law for Christian, Jew, and Moslem. All limitations on domicile, officeholding, and occupation were abolished, even in backward Galicia. Thus did Emancipation come quietly and completely for half a million Hapsburg Jews. Franz Josef's friendship was gratefully reciprocated by his Jewish subjects; in the few decades remaining to the Hapsburg regime, no other national group was more loyal, or made more important economic and cultural contributions to Austrian and Hungarian life.

In Central and Western Germany, too, progress was rapid in the second half of the nineteenth century. In 1850, King Frederick William IV of Prussia grudgingly decided to reform his regime, if only for the sake of counterbalancing the power of his hated rival, the Hapsburg dynasty. With great reluctance, the Prussian monarch issued a constitution that was moderate, even reasonably liberal for its time. The franchise was extended to the Prussian population on a property qualification basis. The Reichstag was given rather more than consultative powers. And the Jews, too, were granted important rights: the right to vote, the right to own land, the right to enter the professions. Only the right of holding office under the Crown was denied them. It was a giant step toward Emancipation. It was also a giant step toward Prussian prosperity, as restrictions against full-orbed Jewish economic activity were now abrogated.

While the political revolutions of 1848 may have failed in most of Germany, the Industrial Revolution had not been interrupted. In the 1850's and 1860's there was extraordinary progress throughout the German world; and in state after German state the old order was compelled to compromise with the needs and aspirations of a dynamic middle class. Absolutism and feudal privileges were everywhere fundamentally modified, as business efficiency became the leitmotiv of the new Germany. It was as an integral part of the

Mittelstand that the Jews began to achieve a more secure status in Germany, even before that country's unification under Bismarck. In Bavaria and in the Thuringian states, most of the remaining restrictions on Jewish economic activity were abolished.

Then in 1866 "the Iron Chancellor," Otto von Bismarck, propelled Prussia into the leadership of the German world. Albrecht von Roon and Helmuth von Moltke broke the back of the Austrian army in the brief war that finally evicted the Hapsburg Empire from German affairs. Prussia incorporated Hanover and Hesse-Cassel into its territory, and assumed the official leadership of a North German Confederation of States. Four years later, after a victorious war against France, Bismarck was able to transform his Prussian monarch into the Imperial Kaiser of a united German Empire. That same year the constitution of the North German Confederation was adapted to the larger unit, and its civil rights provisions were applied to the empire as a whole. The franchise was extended to all male citizens; the Reichstag was given veto power over legislation; equality before the law became the right of every German inhabitant, Junker and businessman, Christian and Jew.

The new imperial government was far from liberal: there was no ministerial responsibility; a Bundesrat of hereditary princes exercised coequal power with a democratic Reichstag. It was, in fact, one of the fundamental tragedies of modern European history that Germany should have been united by "blood and iron" under authoritarian auspices, rather than through the initiative of a liberal middle class. But so deep-rooted was the desire for a single, all-embracing German state that even German liberals, entrenched in the National Liberal Party, were willing to make compromises. They were prepared to surrender pure constitutionalism for the opportunities of a huge, unrestricted market, personal freedom, and equal civil and political rights. The leading German-Jewish liberals—Moritz Lazarus, Eduard Lasker, Ludwig Bamberger—were no less willing to accept such a compromise on behalf of their own people. The Jews, to be sure, were still ineligible to become judges or crown ministers or even full professors in the universities; but in all other respects their freedom was constitutionalized. They walked the streets as free men. No longer would urchins jeer the Jew in the street with the old eighteenth-century taunt: *"Mach Mores, Jude,"* "your manners, Jew!"

Progress in England more than kept pace with developments on the Continent. By the end of the Napoleonic wars, as we have seen, Jews had won acceptance on all levels of English society. They were settled freely throughout the kingdom, and engaged in virtually any business of their choice. They purchased land at their own discretion, were assured of complete legal protection, and even voted in parliamentary elections. As late as mid-nineteenth century however public life was entirely barred to Jews. No Jew was permitted to sit in Parliament or in a muncipal council; no Jew could hold any office under the Crown. The obstructive oath still remained; loyalty had to be sworn "on the true faith of a Christian." When two Acts of Parliament early in the nineteenth century granted Catholics and Nonconformists the right to sit in Parliament the Jews were pointedly excluded.

But middle-class toleration, even fraternalism, anticipated "official" emancipation. In 1847 the City of London, the very nerve center of Britain's business life, elected Lionel Rothschild on the Whig ticket as its Member of Parliament. When Parliament refused to seat the distinguished Jewish banker after he refused to pronounce the oath, the City of London promptly re-elected him, and continued to re-elect him on and off for ten years. After each election Rothschild engaged in an embarrassing little pantomime: he approached his seat in Commons, paused, sighed audibly, and walked out. The "gratuitous" action of the voters of the City of London utterly mystified the Tories. As respectable a politician as Henry Drummond could find no better explanation of Rothschild's re-election in 1857 than that "the rabble of London, partly out of love of mischief, partly from contempt of the House of Commons, and partly from a desire to give a slap in the face to Christianity, elected a Jew." Actually the Whig constituency of London expected that Rothschild's re-election would persuade Parliament to rescind the oath— indeed, the House of Commons had already expressed its willingness to do so—and thus vindicate the triumph of middle-class egalitarianism.

It was no accident that the coalition of aristocrats, squires, and Anglican bishops resisted Jewish emancipation so adamantly. They correctly viewed Jewish participation in the government as the one final, conclusive symbol of the triumph of the middle class. The more vigorously such eminent Whigs as Joseph Hume, Daniel O'Connell, Thomas Babington Macaulay, and Lord John Russell espoused the cause of Jewish emancipation, the more stubbornly the Tories in the House of Lords held firm. "What can the Jew care about the cause for which 'Hampden bled on the field and Sidney on the scaffold?' " asked the conservative London *Times* in an editorial in 1830; "the names of Somers, Locke, of Holt and Russell, at the sound of which every English-man's heart leaps with sympathy, must to him be a 'mere sounding brass and tinkling cymbal.' " Macaulay provided the liberal response three years later in his maiden speech in Parliament, speaking in typically Benthamite terminology: "Every man has a right to all that may conduce to his pleasure, if it does not inflict pain on anyone else. This is one of the broadest maxims of human nature." Here, in fact, was the basic ideological conflict of English political life in the early nineteenth century, perfectly crystallized on the issue of Jewish emancipation.

Eventually both sides wearied of the struggle. In 1858 the Tory prime minister, Edward Stanley, Lord Derby, persuaded his colleagues that the retention of Jewish disabilities was becoming a public embarrassment to the party. Reluctantly the Lords agreed. An Act was passed in 1858 that allowed each house of Parliament to establish its own rules of oath-taking; and Lionel Rothschild was seated in the Commons that year. Two years later another Act of Parliament resolved that any Jew duly elected to the Commons might swear the oath in the fashion most acceptable to him. An identical ruling was applied to Crown offices. In 1871 Lionel Rothschild, the old war horse of Jewish emancipation, lived to see his son Nathan elevated to the peerage as Baron Nathan Rothschild. That same year, too, Parliament authorized Oxford and Cambridge to award degrees to Jews and Nonconformists, thereby lifting from the Jews their last remaining disability. It was also the year in which Sir George Jessel was appointed solicitor general, the first Jew to become a minister of the Crown. The list of Jewish nobility and Crown officers, of Jewish members of Parliament and Privy Council, rapidly increased in succeeding decades. By the turn of the century few eyebrows were raised when King Edward VII attended the wedding of a Jewish friend in London's great West End Synagogue. The Jews of England may not have been freer than—as an example—the Jews of Italy. But in no other land had they so demonstrably "arrived."

CONCLUSION

The factors responsible for Jewish emancipation between 1815 and 1870 were an extension of the rationale that had been championed ever since the French Revolution by businessmen and intellectuals to justify their assumption of governmental authority. That rationale had to be invulnerable; it had to be seamlessly welded. It could not be right for one and wrong for another. In short, it was necessary for the philosophy of liberalism to operate with complete consistency, for the popular and the unpopular, the Christian and the Jew. No less important, however, in the struggle for Jewish rights was the desire of the expanding state to acquire vital new sources of revenue. The state was vastly more efficient now that the dross and irrationalities of the preindustrial era had been stripped away. But by mid-nineteenth century its expenses, too, were multiplied a hundredfold. Entirely apart from abstract philosophical principles, it was sound administration to liberate Jewish enterprise and wealth for public purposes.

There was, perhaps, one additional factor responsible for Jewish emancipation during the middle part of the nineteenth century, a factor that was not present in the earlier Napoleonic period. It was familiarity. Jews were no longer strangers behind ghetto walls, abstract creatures to be pitied and indulged because of a doctrinaire humanitarianism. They were comrades in arms, flesh-and-blood people, who had fought the good liberal fight for several decades at the side of their Christian colleagues—the pugnacious Riesser; the radical Jewish Forty-Eighters; the fervent Lasker and Bamberger; the brave Jewish soldiers of the Austrian and Franco-Prussian wars and the *Risorgimento;* the men who had bled and died on the barricades of Paris. These were not textbook heroes. They were people who had clearly and demonstrably risked everything—their funds, their honor, their lives—to be accepted as citizens of their emergent nations. By 1870 the middle class had largely taken over the management of affairs in Europe, even in Bismarck's Germany. It was much easier now for most of these business-minded Europeans to open their doors to the Jews. For they were neighbors who were known to be trustworthy.

VI

Jewish Economic Life and the

Frankfurt Tradition

THE IMPACT OF THE INDUSTRIAL REVOLUTION

If our amiable tourist friend of the first chapter could miraculously have been transported from the Germany of 1770 to the Germany of a century later, he would hardly have been able to recognize the countryside. The fields that had once been so peaceful and verdant now were blackened by the smoke of blast furnaces. A domestic economy of handicrafts and artisanry had given way to an economy based on coal and iron. Great steam engines propelled looms, wheels, and ships, and provided the motor equivalent of hundreds of pairs of hands. The new technology had originated in England. But by mid-nineteenth century steam engines and power looms were not uncommon on the Continent, nor even in the Germanic world, the principal abode of Western Jewry. "I found in Berlin," declared a British witness in 1841 before the Royal Commission on the Extent of Machinery, "the most enterprising and systematic exertions made on the part of the government to obtain a command of the manufacture of machinery. I found no expense spared for the purpose and the exertions quite astonished me." Coal and iron were systematically exploited. Factories and railroads were built. About the centers of industrial production great complexes of secondary industries burgeoned to supply the factories. About these, in turn, tertiary industries in the outermost reaches of petty retailing sprang up to supply the families of workers. These were the populous urban areas of Europe, exercising sudden and magnetic fascination for overcrowded and hungry rural communities.

One of the factors which made the Industrial Revolution possible was the growth of a labor reservoir; it was a reservoir that was fed systematically by rivulets of migration from rural areas. For a thousand years the population of Europe had grown slowly, imperceptibly. Then, in the eighteenth century, the old stable balance of population began suddenly to collapse under the impact of improvements in technology and hygiene. Between 1750 and 1850 the population of the Continent jumped from one hundred forty million to two hundred sixty million; by 1914 to nearly half a billion. Where one man stood in 1750, two men stood a century later—and then three men sixty-five years after that. The pressure of millions of new people placed unendurable new strains upon village and family life. On the farms young men and women helplessly watched the steady shrinkage of their inheritances and dowries. Thus began the great city-directed migration of rustics, choking the slums and backwashes of the industrial cities, peopling the cadres of factory labor. With the departing peasants went the collection of dependents—the smiths, millers, priests, and innkeepers—who had formed the fabric of rural society. What need was there for them now? What need, moreover, for the petty trade of Jews?

Taking advantage of that freedom of movement which was one of the choicest blessings of the Emancipation, the Jews, too, began to move out of the rural areas to join the march cityward. The Jews, after all, had few emotional attachments to the demeaning livelihoods of peddling and hawking that had been forced upon them in earlier centuries. Long before renewed persecutions hurled tens of thousands of Jewish families to the four corners of the earth, overpopulation and the lure of city life set the Western Jewish community in motion. Beginning in the 1820's and continuing until well after the mid-nineteenth century, Jewish migrants were familiar figures on the highways of Europe—little groups of tired men and women, with their children, raising puffs of dust from the dry summer roads.

The bustling urban centers of Western Europe lured thousands of Jews from the towns and villages. So, too, did Vienna and Berlin on the eastern fringes of the non-Slavic world. Between 1850 and 1864 the Jewish population of Paris rose from 20,000 to 30,000. The Jewish population of Berlin rose from 6,450 in 1840 to 35,000 by 1871, as the backward agricultural province of Posen emptied the majority of its Jewish families into Western Prussia. In the eight years between 1846 and 1854 the Jewish population of Vienna jumped from 3,739 to 14,000, then to five times that number by the end of the century. The smaller communities from which Vienna drew, such as Pressburg or Prossnitz, were not emptied; rather they recruited their populations in turn from the smaller villages in their own hinterland. In 1849 Budapest was the home for 19,000 Jews. In 1880 the same city supported about 72,000 Jews and gave every indication of further expansion ("Juda-pest," it was dubbed by the cynical Magyars). Much of this, of course, was natural increase, and was shared in common with the general population. But the days in which the very continued existence of the Jewish people hung in the balance evidently had passed; the precariousness of minority life in a world dominated by plagues and pogroms was apparently resolved. In 1800 the Jews numbered, throughout the world, approximately two and a half million. By 1825 this number reached three and a quarter million. By 1850 there were nearly five million Jews; by 1880 some seven and a half million, and by 1900 over ten million.

A significant result of this population "explosion" was a shift in the geographic center of Jewish life. In 1825 Africa and Asia were the habitats for some half million Jews. While this number did not alter appreciably in

1850 or even in 1900, the Jewish population of Europe alone shot up from approximately 2,750,000 in 1825 to 8,700,000 in 1900—and this in spite of massive overseas migrations from the European reservoir. The dark-skinned Asian and Moroccan Jewries, who counted so significantly in the story of Jewish life until the advent of the modern era, now declined in numerical importance and in economic and intellectual creativity. Indeed, they became a "world passed by."

Unlike most of the migrants from rural to urban areas in Western Europe, the Jews were not apprehensive about adjustment to city life; they knew that sizable numbers of their coreligionists awaited them. They knew, too, that rabbis and ritual slaughterers were to be found in the cities; that synagogues and charitable associations had been organized centuries before in the ghettos of Vienna and Berlin. Now, therefore, the dust-grimed Jewish families who made their way into the city gates and were greeted by friends and relatives, found no reason to be terrified by the prospect of urbanization; no violence would be done their religious or cultural traditions. They recognized, as well, that the old-time Jewish city dwellers possessed experience and connections with which to facilitate their adjustment to the maelstrom of the urban market place. The Jews therefore accustomed themselves to the swift-moving pace of industrial and commercial life rather more rapidly than their Christian neighbors.

The climate of the industrial age was favorable to the Jews. In the West, Jew-hatred was rapidly being abandoned as a state policy. Because the industrial order was secular and cosmopolitan in its outlook, the businessman, the trader assumed more worth and recognition than he had enjoyed even a century earlier. It was as a result of these circumstances that the Jews, the oldest urbanized people in the world, a foot-loose, mobile people, unbound by ecclesiastical tradition or feudal ties, now found themselves pressed into the strategic and advantageous positions of the new evolving order as merchants, exporters, importers, and industrialists.

At the beginning of the nineteenth century, for example, as the effects of the Industrial Revolution made themselves felt, the Board of Governors of the Berlin Stock Exchange no longer found it feasible to discriminate against Jews. For that matter, Jews had been permitted to act as brokers in the London Stock Exchange as early as the turn of the century. It was vitally important for the constitutional and quasi-constitutional governments of nineteenth-century Europe to iron out the inequalities of the *ancien régime* as quickly and completely as possible for the sake of doctrinal consistency. But in the case of the Jews another factor operated as well. Emancipation was, as we have seen, the culmination of a gradual extension of specific Jewish privileges, granted originally to individuals only, the *Hofjuden,* then through them to a larger number of wealthy Jews. Only when this limited group proved itself unable to accommodate the burgeoning demands of state business were special and general privileges finally extended to the whole of Western and Central European Jewry. Now, therefore, the confluence of secularism and the Industrial Revolution opened up undreamed-of possibilities of employment for Jews and Christians alike.

At first, in the period following the Congress of Vienna, when both state law and Jewish vocational habits had not achieved the easy flexibility that was characteristic of the mid-nineteenth-century thaw, the Jewish economic pattern did not differ significantly from its contours of fifty years earlier. In Prussia, for example, in the year 1813, only 2 per cent of the Jews of the country were engaged in the more remunerative livelihoods of banking, manufacturing, or large-scale trade; and a mere 8 per cent were traders beyond the retail level. Some 40 per cent of Prussian Jewry, on the other hand, were petty traders, limited to the peddling or small shopkeeping that had been the vocational traditions of their families for centuries. Most of these people were loathe to venture into the uncharted speculations that required large-scale capital. By 1852, however, the inroads of the new order began to make themselves felt. The total percentage of Jews in crafts and industries had risen to nearly 20 per cent; while the pack peddlers, who had composed a fifth of the Jewish community at the beginning of the century, declined to an insignificant 6 per cent. By 1900 even this number was to shrink to less than 1 per cent.

The moment restrictions were removed, the Jews made a noticeable effort to adjust themselves to the vocational structure of Western life. The melancholy cry of "old clothes" resounded less frequently now in the dingy side streets of Europe's cities. The shuffling, obsequious peddler, with his Yiddish accent and hangdog expression, was rapidly becoming a vanishing phenomenon. Jewish store-owners and businessmen, immaculate in modern dress, erect and dignified in bearing, presided at desks and behind counters. Jewish carpenters fashioned furniture for Christian drawing rooms. Jewish physicians examined Christian patients. Jewish apothecaries prepared medicines that Christians did not fear to swallow. Jewish advocates defended the rights and liberties of Christians in the European courtrooms. And, from time to time, Christian children learned their own language and literature from Jewish schoolteachers.

Emancipation notwithstanding, the disproportionately large Jewish involvement in trade remained. There were reasons for this: the professions were not commonly opened to Jews in the states of Germany until after the mid-century, and the old bureaucracy, strongly entrenched, silently sabotaged the efforts of Jews to enter state service. It was safer, too, for Jews to remain in business for themselves, free from the lingering whims and prejudices of Christian employers. Retailing, particularly, was a safe vocation for an insecure people, for money remained liquid and conveniently portable. It was hardly surprising, then, that the number of Jews engaged in trade, far from declining by mid-century, actually increased. But "Jewish" trade was no longer primarily limited to peddling. The larger fortunes to be made from genteel storekeeping, in which business experience and liquidity of capital were still operating factors, attracted well over half of Prussian Jewry in 1861. During the same period, only 8 or 9 per cent of the non-Prussians were thus occupied. Modest little shops with Jewish names on the windows abounded on the boulevards of German and Austrian cities. Most of the

Jewish businessmen were well within the middle-income levels—bourgeoisie par excellence.

These respectable Jewish shopkeepers rarely broke completely with their family callings. They simply expanded the scale of their activities. Because the Jews had acted as middlemen between country and city—buying up the grain and mash of peasants and selling them to the inns, buying up flax, wool, and cattle and marketing them in the village squares—they were able now to use their experience and priority of contacts in these fields to assume leading positions in the large-scale trade of wool, grain, hides, and metals. Because, for example, they had originally been compelled by law to deal primarily in old clothes, the Jews now found themselves increasingly active in all branches of the clothing industry, from the purchase and processing of raw material to the distribution of the finished product. Free from the restrictions and traditions of the depleted guilds, many of these Jewish textile entrepreneurs were able swiftly and imaginatively to develop new techniques of production and distribution, to profit from the revolution in European clothing styles. What, then, was Jewish business? It encompassed the small clothing shop, boasting the unheard-of innovation of ready-made suits; the jewelry store, promising reasonable terms of credit; the furrier's salon, with discreet announcements calling especial attention to imported Russian sables; the embryonic department store, advertising the most exotic diversification in town; the junkyard's appraiser, casting an experienced eye into and around stables, up and down alleyways. These, more often than not, were the symbols of Jewish economic life in Western Europe during the second half of the nineteenth century.

The mid-nineteenth century presented a kind of *mélange,* as economic and social patterns conflicted and commingled. The life of the Jew, also, was twisted and remolded between the vocational habits of the old world and the economic demands of the new. He, too, found it necessary to divest himself of the desperation-rooted business aggressiveness of the ghetto in order to survive in the modern metropolitan market. Together with his Christian neighbors, the Jew was obliged to make his peace with the cacophony of modern urban civilization. Israel Zangwill, the gifted British-Jewish novelist, captured this spirit as he described Petticoat Lane, the teeming Jewish market area in London's East End:

[Petticoat] Lane was always the great market-place, and every insalu-brious street and alley abutting on it was covered with the overflowings of its commerce and its mud. Wentworth Street and Gouldston Street were the chief branches, and in festival times the latter was a pande-monium of caged poultry, clucking and quacking and screaming. Fowls and geese and ducks were bought alive, and taken to have their throats cut for a fee by the official slaughterer. At Purim a gaiety, as of the Roman carnival, enlivened the swampy Wentworth Street, and brought a smile into the unwashed face of the pavement. The confectioners' shops, crammed with "stuffed monkeys" and "bolas," were besieged by hilarious crowds of handsome girls and their young men, fat women and their children, all washing down the luscious spicy compounds with cups of chocolate; temporarily erected swinging cradles bore a vociferous, many-colored burden to the skies; cardboard noses, grotesque in their departure from truth, abounded. . . . It was only gradually that the community was Anglicized. Under the sway of centrifugal impulses, the wealthier members began to form new colonies, moulting their old feathers and replacing them by finer, and flying ever further from the center. Men of organizing ability founded unrivalled philanthropic and educational institutions on British lines; millionaires fought for political emancipation; brokers brazenly foisted themselves on the "Change"; very slowly the conventional Anglican tradition was established; and on that human palimpsest which has borne the inscription of all languages and all epochs, was writ large the sign-manuel of England.

Feverish energy, healthy energy, uncircumscribed at last by the bounds of ghetto or statute!

THE JEWS AND THE RISE OF INVESTMENT CAPITALISM

During the first half of the nineteenth century the world of European high finance was deeply influenced by a small but immensely imaginative group of Jewish investment bankers. In truth, the growth of international Jewish banking has long been one of the most intriguing phenomena of modern European history. These financiers were only a handful of men, in no way typical of the great mass of West European Jewry. But the impact of their careers was far out of proportion to their numbers. They vitally affected—if, indeed, they did not dominate—the economic policies of the Western state system. And their reputations, the rumors and legends that accumulated about their names, were of profound consequence for the destiny of all the Jews of Europe.

Today when one thinks of a bank one has in mind our private commercial institution of deposit, which has traditionally issued loans for industrial or mercantile purposes. But this bank of deposit historically had little to do with supplying credit to governments or underwriting state bonds; it was rather the more specialized investment banking house that fulfilled such functions. During the early nineteenth century, the investment bank granted no commercial credit, issued no notes, and received no deposits. Its money came almost exclusively from private family fortunes. The investment bank performed the service either of extending direct loans to governments or of issuing new securities, primarily government securities, and selling them to investors. Usually these staid old houses underwrote government loans at a profitable discount, and then proceeded to find purchasers for the bonds at par or above par value. If governments wished to float loans, therefore, their convenient, their indispensable intermediary was the investment bank, which alone could supply the funds on short notice.

The investment bank fulfilled a particularly important function for the impoverished German states of the early nineteenth century. The German economy remained virtually prostrate from Waterloo until the late 1830's. Farms had gone to seed; industry lay stillborn amid rotting hand looms in cottage kitchens. And government tax revenues, as a result, were proportionately small. Credit for reconstruction, for government operation was urgently needed. Yet in the entire Kingdom of Prussia before 1866 the number of persons employed in banking and stockbrokerage amounted to less than two thousand. The Berlin Stock Exchange was hardly more imposing than a good-sized auction house, its system of security capitalism fraught with too much risk for conservative Prussian financiers.

What had all this to do with the Jews? A great deal. For there were Jews who were willing to supply credit to the state, and to float its loans. These Jewish financiers, many of them direct descendants of the *Hofjuden* who had financed governments since the eighteenth century, were endowed with long experience in dealing with portable funds, and frequently coveted the special protection and marks of prestige that a government could confer for services rendered. Most of them, moreover, possessed the funded capital of several generations. We recall (from Chapter II) that as early as the seventeenth and eighteenth centuries many German Jews were able to accumulate substantial fortunes as a result of their international connections, their freedom from feudal restraints, and, above all, their experience in dealing with liquid capital. These fortunes even then were frequently invested in government loans, and soon constituted the most accessible supply of public credit in Germany in those days. In 1725 seventeen out of 563 Jewish taxpayers in Hamburg possessed fortunes valued at more than 100,000 florins each, an unprecedented sum for one small municipality. And in 1800 in Frankfurt am Main, with its Jewish population of six hundred families, most of them living in the squalid *Judengasse,* 43 per cent of the entire Jewish capital was owned by sixty families, who in turn controlled the twelve largest investment firms in the city. Indeed, Frankfurt may well be termed the cradle of Jewish finance in Europe.

The story of the city of Frankfurt is a rather dramatic one. As far back as the sixteenth century this municipality achieved international importance as a financial center. Located in the sunny, fertile Rhineland, Frankfurt was only a few miles away from the crowded avenue of commerce that connected wealthy Holland, by way of the St. Gotthard pass, with the ancient trade emporium of Venice; this was, in fact, the most heavily trafficked highway in Europe. Frankfurt's reputation as a major European crossroads soon established it as the logical seat of the Federal Diet, and the political focus of Germany after the Westphalia settlement. The Frankfurt Stock Exchange, when compared to the exchanges in other German cities, already occupied a prominent position as early as the eighteenth century. The period of its most remarkable efflorescence, however, took place during the decade following Waterloo. The enormous expense of the Napoleonic wars had drained the Continent. Thus, the Frankfurt exchange, while a mere parvenu beside the great exchanges of London and Amsterdam, now found itself with virtually a monopoly of German financial activity—such as it was.

For half a century Frankfurt was destined to remain the most influential money power in Germany. The bulk of the city's wealth was concentrated in the hands of Jewish investment bankers. The foremost Jewish firms—the Seligmans, Oppenheimers, Rothschilds, and others—achieved so wide a dominance in Europe that the very word "Frankfurt" came to mean much more than a physical city. The House of Haber, for example, which had become prominent during the Napoleonic wars, was by 1820 among the most respected financial institutions of Germany and perhaps of Europe. Typically, the Haber family inherited its funds from several generations of privileged court bankers of the duchies of Württemberg and Baden. The family preserved and multiplied its holdings during the ensuing decades, acquiring a fortune of such magnitude that by 1853 Samuel von Haber the younger became a founder of the mighty Darmstaedter Bank, one of the three largest in Central Europe.

The Speyer Bank, which was created late in the eighteenth century, was a vital link between Germany and the American market. Like the Rothschild firm, this house maintained important family branches throughout Europe. In 1800, in fact, the Speyer Bank was many times more powerful than the emergent House of Rothschild, and remained exceptionally influential throughout the course of the nineteenth century. The Frankfurt bank of the brothers Bethmann, which had succeeded in salvaging Hapsburg finances in the eighteenth century, was perhaps the first to carry on an active underwriting business for Central Europe. Under the imaginative direction of Simon Moritz von Bethmann, this firm for a while outstripped all others in Frankfurt, and contributed significantly to the city's reputation throughout the world.

There were other dominant banks that spread through Europe: the Warburgs in Hamburg; the Mendelssohns and the Bleichröders in Berlin; the Oppenheimers of Cologne and Vienna; the houses of Eskeles and Arnstein in Vienna; the firms of Montagu, Goldsmid, Hambro, and Sassoon in London. But because so many of these families originated or rose to high position in Frankfurt, the imaginative inception of Jewish investment banking may, for the sake of simplicity, be called the "Frankfurt tradition."

THE HOUSE OF ROTHSCHILD

Perhaps the spectacular rise of the Frankfurt tradition is best illustrated in the career of the Rothschilds. Like many of the other Jewish banking houses, the Rothschilds originated in the Frankfurt *Judengasse*. Theirs was a typical lower-middle-class Jewish family, engaged in the pettiest varieties of retail trade. In 1743 Meyer Amschel Rothschild was born. Twelve years later he was orphaned and placed in the care of relatives. He was intended for a rabbinical career, and for a number of years immersed himself in the intricacies of the Talmud at the academy in Fürth. But Meyer Amschel's mind was too practical to content itself for long with dialectic and *pilpul*; he left the academy and entered a Frankfurt banking firm. Within a few years he managed to win control of the firm.

Oddly enough, it was Meyer Amschel's passion for collecting old coins that laid the basis for his rise to wealth and power. For numismatics was also the hobby of William, the landgrave, later elector, of Hesse-Cassel. The meeting of these two young men had epoch-making consequences for European history. A fortuitous acquaintance broadened into mutual affection. Gradually young Rothschild was drawn into the landgrave's brokerage business. William of Hesse-Cassel was that rarity among European royalty, an astute businessman. When Napoleon Bonaparte hurled his armies across the borders of Europe, William made his own ample fortune available for discounting the loans of his fellow sovereigns. He decided, too, to employ Rothschild as his agent. Rothschild was not unprepared for the responsibility. He had long since married and, in good Jewish tradition, raised a large family. He had the strategic foresight to place his five sons in the capitals of Europe, where they could act as the family's trusted agents. When, therefore, the armies of France entered Hesse-Cassel and sent William packing, the elector made an inspired choice: he entrusted all his bullion and notes for safekeeping and investment to Rothschild.

Meyer Amschel hid William's fortune in underground chambers in Frankfurt, catacombs originally constructed by Jews as sanctuary from hostile mobs. All the threats and bullying of Napoleon's invading army could not intimidate Meyer Amschel, now a middle-aged man, into revealing the whereabouts of the bullion. But the money, although hidden, was far from sterilized. With Rothschilds in London, Paris, Naples, Vienna, and Frankfurt, the reserve funds could be listed as assets in any one of five countries—and invested in whichever part of Europe the opportunities for profit appeared good. Such opportunities appeared best in England, where highly advantageous discount terms persuaded Nathan Rothschild, on behalf of the family, to underwrite the British national bond issue. Later other loans were successfully extended to Denmark and several German states. All this was done on behalf of Elector William of Hesse-Cassel. Soon the original sum doubled, trebled, and then quadrupled. Eventually, with the discount and commission rates the Rothschilds had obtained in their capacity as William's agents, there was a fortune too for Meyer Amschel's family. With equal imagination and profit, the Rothschilds began to apply their own capital to government loans. Henceforth, until Waterloo, the fate of both estates was intertwined.

In 1812 old Meyer Amschel died. No man had ever been better equipped to make the most of historic opportunities, for his business acumen had been a combination of audacity and profound moral courage. During his lifetime his coarse Yiddish accent and habitual green skullcap were recognized and caricatured throughout Europe. He was not an unattractive man physically, his nose and chin strong, his complexion ivory, his goatee elegant. He was known and admired, too, for his philanthropy and devoted family attachments; and he remained until the end of his life an unassuming and devoutly Orthodox Jew.

Meyer Amschel's fortune and business sagacity were passed on to his five sons. Each of them held a 20 per cent interest in the firm, and they guided the destinies of their house, as well as the fortune of William of Hesse-Cassel, from their various vantage points in Europe. A historic pyramiding of a family empire was about to get under way. For the year of old Rothschild's death was the year in which Wellesley began his Peninsular campaign against the French armies in Spain. Nathan Rothschild in London guaranteed the payment of bullion to Wellesley's troops—for a discount, of course. It was a monumental gamble; if the British lost the campaign, Wellesley's notes, anchored to the hope of Spanish taxes, would swiftly enough become worthless. But Wellington did not lose. Napoleon's brother Joseph was driven from his Spanish throne by the Iron Duke's forces: Spanish guerrillas harassed the last French soldier back across the Pyrenees; the notes were paid off in full. During the next two years the Rothschild personal fortune was associated increasingly with the British government and the German members of the allied coalition. It was a fantastically profitable association. By 1815, the year of Napoleon's final defeat at Waterloo, the Rothschild family had not only reaped enormous profits from the allied state loans they had floated, from the bullion payments they had made, but they also had won the confidence and friendship of the legitimate rulers of Europe. When Elector William of Hesse-Cassel returned from exile in Prague, the Rothschilds were able to return to him a vastly aggrandized personal fortune. But they also decided to strike out on their own, for they had accumulated enough funds to launch their own banking house.

Under the leadership of Nathan in London, who was the astutest of the brothers, the House of Rothschild entered its period of most dramatic financial success. The thirty-three years between 1815 and 1848 were the truly phenomenal years of Rothschild influence. It was a period in which loans, totaling many millions of florins (and pounds, francs, and marks), were floated for most of the important governments of Europe, in which few significant public works' projects were undertaken without assurance of Rothschild support. During this period, when the five brothers literally presidered over the solvency and prestige of governments, no one considered grandiloquent the sobriquet which legend attached to this firm: "the sixth dynasty of Europe."

After the revolutions of 1848, however, the House of Rothschild began increasingly to channel its loans into private industry; it had been chastened by the evident precariousness of the governments with which it had intertwined its fate. By mid-century the firm diverted larger amounts of its assets into European railroads. It was the House of Rothschild that largely financed the magnificent Austrian railroad, the *Kaiser Ferdinand Nordbahn;* that sponsored the Paris-St. Germain railroad, the massive French Northern trunk route, and a large radiating complex of Belgian roads. Although the Rothschilds were loathe to be known as supporters of private industry, these investments made them, willy-nilly, the most influential railroad pioneers on the Continent. As the years passed, and as the original five brothers passed on, their children continued to commingle Rothschild investment capital among various private and commercial undertakings. The House of Rothschild did not entirely abandon its eminent position as Europe's court bank.

But after the 1870's and 1880's, what remained of the old connections were principally sentimental memories and colorful legends of an era in which one Jewish family could make autocrats tremble.

THE FRANKFURT TRADITION: INTERNATIONALIZATION

Today the international scope of the stock market is an accepted fact. One hardly gives a second thought to the complex mechanism brought into play with the purchase and sale of foreign securities. People, however, were hardly as sophisticated about financial matters in the early nineteenth century. Investment in the bonds of foreign governments, the rapid-order sale of these bonds, the issuance of dividends in native currency—all this was beyond the ken of most provincial European investors. Jewish financiers now broadened their horizons. As a consequence of the uniquely international network of Rothschilds and other Jewish banking families, and the example of their extraordinary profits, the public gradually became accustomed to investing its capital in foreign holdings. Writers of the early nineteenth century described it as a marvelous thing that "every holder of Government stock . . . can receive his dividends in various places at his convenience without any difficulty. The Rothschilds in Frankfort pay interest for many Governments; the Paris House pays the dividends on the Austrian *Métalliques;* the Neopolitan *Rentes,* the Anglo-Neopolitan Loan either in London, Naples, or Paris." By 1820, in the London Exchange, for example, it was a daily routine for hundreds of top-hatted, normally phlegmatic Englishmen to stand before the board listing foreign securities, jostling one another impatiently in their haste to understand the latest convolution of European politics, in their eagerness to purchase or sell, to "make a killing."

The financial advantages of Jewish international banking connections were so apparent that the Rothschilds themselves consciously exaggerated their supranational characteristics. This involved more merely than the strategic location of five sons throughout Europe. Meyer Amschel Rothschild established connections with the princely House of Thurn, which was hereditary postmaster of the old Holy Roman Empire, in order to secure the use of its courier service for his own firm. The brothers Rothschild managed as well to obtain consular positions for themselves in the capitals of their respective countries, and instantly shared their information with each other for quick use on the Exchange.

From time to time the contacts among these Jewish financiers resulted in celebrated coups. The late 1860's and early 1870's, for example, was a time when few officials of the British Board of Trade were interested in the projected canal across the Isthmus of Suez. The slower Cape route to India seemed sufficient for British shipping; besides, it was strategically safer. When the Suez Canal was built, therefore, the British lethargically stood by as the company's four hundred thousand shares were snapped up by the Ottoman Government, the khedive of Egypt, and French financiers. A few years later, vital information leaked to the Rothschilds: the French shareholders were collecting vast and unanticipated profits, principally from British shipping in the Canal. As an investment alone the Canal would be of immense value to Great Britain. This information was conveyed to Prime Minister Benjamin Disraeli by the Rothschilds of England via the Rothschilds of France. Disraeli was grateful for the crucial intelligence. In fact he had long since recognized the strategic value of a shorter life line to India; but he saw no way of obtaining a controlling share in the company without engaging in disastrously expensive competitive bidding.

Shortly thereafter, however, Henry Oppenheim, a Jewish publisher, who possessed large financial interests in Egypt, made a further discovery. The khedive of Egypt, whose expensive and irresponsible debaucheries had brought him to the verge of bankruptcy, was anxious to sell his controlling shares in the company. He would dispose of the shares, if necessary, for as paltry a sum as four million pounds sterling. This information was at once communicated to Disraeli, who exulted at the prospect of a major strategic coup for his country. Unfortunately, Parliament was not in session to vote the necessary funds. Cognizant of the danger of delay, Disraeli did some fast thinking; he asked his "kinsman," Lionel Nathan Rothschild for the necessary loan. Rothschild nearly choked. Suppose, asked the banker, Parliament should refuse to repurchase the stock? Disraeli discounted this possibility. After ten more minutes of conversation Rothschild agreed, and "Dizzy" dispatched to Victoria the famous note: "It is just settled: you have it, Madame." When Parliament reconvened it vindicated the faith of Disraeli and Rothschild by repurchasing the stock for the Government. International connections! How crucial they were! Even the *petit-bourgeoisie* sensed it.

> My mother [Heinrich Heine had once written] now began to dream of a splendid future for me along another road. The House of Rothschild, with whose head my father was on friendly terms, had already begun its amazing period of success. Other titans of finance and industry had similarly arisen in our neighborhood, and my mother maintained that the time had now come when a shrewd head could do the most wonderful things in the mercantile branches and could attain the highest position. She finally decided that I should become a financial power, and now I had to study foreign languages. . . .

International banking connections were planned and maintained as carefully as the dynastic alliances of the era; and the network was often equally elaborate—viz.: the founder of the immensely powerful House of Bischoffscheim was Raphael, who died in 1815. Raphael's eldest son, Louis Raphael, founded a branch of the firm in Antwerp and married Amalia Goldschmidt, a sister of Benedict Goldschmidt, the wealthy and highly respected Frankfurt banker. In his Europe-wide financial transactions, Louis Raphael Bischoffscheim received vital support from his wife's family, from his nephew by marriage, Ludwig Bamberger, of the famous German-Jewish firm of Bamberger and Company—who was the future co-founder of both the Reichsbank and the Deutsche Bank. When in 1830 Belgium won its independence from the House of Orange, Jonathan, second son of Raphael, left Antwerp and settled in Brussels, marrying there into the opulent Hirsch family. Together with these related houses and associated banks on both sides of his family, Jonathan carried through strategic railway flotations in Italy, France, and the Balkans. The reader may amuse himself further by contemplating other networks: Benedict Goldschmidt, of Bischoffscheim and Goldschmidt, sired ten children. One child, Leopold Benedict H., married Regina, a daughter of Jonathan Bischoffscheim; another, Maximilian, married Minka Carolina, the daughter of Baron Wilhelm von Rothschild. Of the daughters of old Raphael Bischoffscheim, Amalia married the banker August Bamberger of Mainz, whose son, Heinrich, married the sister of Baron de Hirsch. A second daughter of Raphael Bischoffscheim, Clara, was the wife of L. Cahen d'Anvers, one of the promoters of the *Crédit Mobilier*. The celebrated Montefiores, too, were intermarried with the Rothschild family.

As for the Rothschilds themselves, there was something of the comic opera in the diplomatic solemnity with which they planned the marriages among their various branches. Among the more important unions: the son of Karl von Rothschild, Meyer Karl of Naples, married Louise, the youngest daughter of Nathan Meyer Rothschild of New Court—his cousin. Of the seven daughters of the marriage, Adele became the wife of Salomon, a son of the Paris James; Emma married the first Lord Rothschild; Theresa married James Edward, a son of the London Nathan and grandson of Nathan Meyer. The marriages between cousins, second cousins, nieces and nephews rivaled, in nearly every respect, the alliances among Bourbons and Hapsburgs. By the latter part of the nineteenth century there were no less than fifty-eight marriages among Rothschild cousins of various degrees!

In a sense the deliberate internationalization of these Jewish firms was a reaction to the Sanhedrin's National Affirmation of 1807 (see Chapter III). For all its advantages to the Jewish bourgeoisie, because this affirmation was beginning to nationalize the Jewries of Europe, it threatened to destroy the inter-European advantages on which the position of these financial wizards rested. The exclusive position that the Rothschilds, particularly, occupied in the Jewish world supplemented the old religious and spiritual cohesion of the Jews—a cohesion which was disintegrating now under the impact of Western culture. As far as Christian Europe was concerned, this one family— let alone the many other Jewish bankers whose children intermarried—was proof of Jewish internationalism. The distinguished historian, Hannah Arendt, writes:

> Where, indeed, was there better proof of the fantastic concept of a Jewish world government than in this one family, the Rothschilds, nationals of five different countries, prominent everywhere, in close cooperation with at least three different governments (French, Austrian, British), whose frequent conflicts never for a moment shook the solidarity of interests of their state bankers? No propaganda could have created a symbol more effective for political purposes than the reality itself.

Exactly because the involvements of these financiers extended beyond national frontiers, the Rothschilds and others found themselves forced into the role of active peacemakers. A casual review, for example, of the diary of the eminent British-Jewish investment banker, the genial centenarian Sir Moses Montefiore, reveals entries dealing not only with personal matters but also with portentous international affairs. There were references to rumors of war, to the health of the king of Portugal and of the emperor of Austria, to the Turkish policies of Czar Nicholas, to border disputes in India, to house calls on royalty and cabinet members. It was surely no accident that the bulk of Montefiore's entries dealt with peace, war, and international politics. Conflict between nations could mean economic disaster for Jewish investment bankers whose principal function was the extension of loans to governments. Regardless of which army defeated the other, the prodigious expense of a military campaign jeopardized the economy of victor as well as vanquished. Thus it was in the interest of these financiers to forestall the danger of war by whatever means, lest their international commitments be forfeited.

To the Rothschilds especially, the most inter-European of Jewish banking families, diplomatic crises were matters of the gravest concern. Issues of liberalism and conservatism, aggression or revolt, played little role in their thinking. The issues of rising or falling *rentes,* on the other hand, were of greater consequence to them. When, for example, France generated still another of its revolutions in 1830, the brothers Rothschild throughout Europe mustered all their vast influence, warning that they would withhold funds for military purposes, to contain the threat of military action by revolutionary or counterrevolutionary armies. "Our experience has taught us," wrote Rother, president of the Seehandlung Bank, to the king of Prussia that year, "that financial transactions in which the von Rothschild firm act not as intermediaries, but as opponents, are likely to collapse; and plans entered with men of affairs, such as we unfortunately find on our *Bourse* here, result in nothing." During the heyday of its influence, certainly, the massive weight of Jewish finance was a very real and deeply felt phenomenon. It expressed itself primarily in the withdrawal of funds and the consequent paralysis of aggressive foreign policies. Instances occurred in which the Rothschilds demonstrably altered the course of international politics: by canceling a Belgian loan in 1837 and thus ending the threat of a Belgian invasion of the Dutch Netherlands; by withdrawing funds from Louis Thiers, the bellicose French premier, during the Mehemet Ali crisis of 1840, thereby diminishing the possibility of war; by withholding funds from Austria when, twice in the 1850's, the Hapsburgs were on the verge of punitive action against Piedmont.

With the deaths of the five brothers who had comprised the second generation of Rothschilds, the close union among the branches of this powerful family was radically altered. This was due in part to the immersion of members of the third generation in the mainstream of their various national traditions. They were received in the highest social circles of France, England, Germany, Italy, and Austria. They were respected as philanthropists, as patrons of the arts, as fashion plates, as devotees of racing. The call of nationalism grew louder, at last, than the call of family. This metamorphosis was apparent in the regulation of Rothschild family property. In the days when old Meyer

Amschel was alive, the five sons shared equally in the profit and loss of every transaction. But by the 1860's, with each of the presiding firms in possession of its own private funds, it was only in rare and unusual instances that they acted together. By 1870 the House of Rothschild was legally and factually several national firms, and no longer one international bank. In the period immediately preceding World War I the English, Austrian, and French houses supported the foreign policies of their governments—although each of the firms did everything possible, within the limits of loyalty, to avoid the imminent catastrophe. When war broke out in 1914 the young male members of the various banks rushed to the colors of their respective countries. In 1917 Evelyn Rothschild, a scion of the British firm, fell in battle against the Central Powers. Demonstrably the National Affirmation had triumphed.

THE FRANKFURT TRADITION: ADDICTION TO AUTHORITY

In the discussion of the *Hofjuden* of an earlier era, it will be recalled that Jewish financiers were traditionally associated with governments, and quite divorced from contact with common people. These Jews extended services in return for protection and special privileges, rewards only the ruler could dispense. This tradition lingered on into the nineteenth century, as Jewish financiers, in the manner of the earlier Court Jews, continued to look to the sources of authority, whether liberal or autocratic, for the protection, honor, and recognition they expected as the reward for state service. Few of these bankers had qualms about transferring their support from one regime to the next. For governments alone—not people, policies, or principles—were the recipients of their loans. During the first half of the nineteenth century, the Habers, Oppenheimers, and Rothschilds actually preferred to deal with conservative regimes. They feared the damage that could be done to delicate financial negotiations by "unreasoning mobs," whether those mobs marched in the street or sat in legislative chambers to speak for the "commune." They feared governments based too directly on the will of fickle and easily inflamed populations. Occasionally, as in England, they found representative government palatable, but democracy they frankly distrusted.

Surely no man played a greater role in the destruction of the Bonapartist hegemony in Europe than did Nathan Meyer Rothschild. Yet it was not hatred of tyranny that motivated his actions. He did not hesitate, for example, to extend loans to the Restoration governments of the Bourbons throughout Europe. Nor was his brother Salomon unwilling to lend the Hapsburgs money with which to quell the Neopolitan uprisings in 1821. Rothschild and Bethmann loans were extended indiscriminately to the Pope, to General Louis Eugène Cavaignac in France, who crushed worker uprisings in 1848, to Metternich in Austria. Prince Metternich's right-hand man was Friedrich von Gentz, a talented but rapacious bureaucrat, who became an intimate friend of Salomon Rothschild in Vienna. Gentz exerted every effort to facilitate negotiations between the Jewish banking house and the government. Eventually Metternich was persuaded to deal with no other firm. It was Metternich's influence that raised Salomon Rothschild to the status of baron, that bound the solvency of the Austrian government to the Rothschilds so tightly that the chancellor, in a fit of melancholy, could confide to Salomon: "If I should go to the dogs, you surely would go with me." In later years Bismarck, too, came to appreciate the kind of service his government could command from Jewish finance; he emphatically insisted that only a Jewish banker, Baron Gerson von Bleichröder, be considered to supply Prussian state loans.

The rewards were more than financial. As in the eighteenth century, personal recognition was vital for these ambitious men, and often more compelling than quick profits. Titles and medals meant freedom of movement, freedom from anti-Jewish restrictions. It was, therefore, the motivation of self-interest, as well as the personal vanity of the self-made man, which animated Amschel Meyer Rothschild, son of the original founder of the firm, to plead obsequiously with the Austrian emperor for titles and recognition for services rendered. In 1816 he was rewarded with a patent of nobility, in an age when most of Europe's Jews were still restricted to squalid Jew-quarters. In 1822 Austria raised all the brothers and their descendants to the rank of baron, a tremendous coup of prestige for the house, and a cheap enough price for Metternich to pay for a loan. Soon the Rothschilds were acceptable at court, and in the "best" society.

The way was paved for similar recognition of other Jewish financiers: the Habers, Bleichröders, Bethmanns, Arnsteins, and others—all of whom soon proudly flaunted the coveted "von" before their names. In England Lionel de Rothschild, grandson of Meyer Amschel, was elevated to the peerage, and the honor of a baronetcy was extended later to Jews such as the Stern brothers, Ernest Cassel, and Edward Speyer. Eventually European court circles were liberally sprinkled with Jewish nobility, almost without exception bankers and financiers. The grimmest irony lay in the medals and orders with which they were rewarded for loans: the Order of Vladimir from Jew-hating Nicholas I; from Spain the Order of St. Isabella the Catholic, the queen who had expelled the Jews in 1492; the Order of St. George from Pope Gregory XVI. When Prussian Baron Becke sought to win a loan from James Rothschild in 1865 he conferred with Count Mulinen. "How would it be," asked Mulinen, "if we gave him the *grand cordon?* It was the Cross of Stanislaus that made the Russian loan. Has he the Iron Crown of the First Class? If not, can we let him hope for it . . . ?" But hope sprang eternal in the breasts of these bankers, whose idea of heaven frequently was the *Almanach de Gotha.*

THE FRANKFURT TRADITION: INTERCESSION FROM ABOVE

The indifference to liberal convictions of many of these bankers was a source of heartache to the millions of Jews who were deeply committed to the triumph of liberal principles, to the equality of opportunity which would surely accompany that triumph. Often they suspected that their most influential coreligionists had abandoned them. Actually, however, the disappointment of the Jewish liberals was only partially justified. It was true that the careers of these financiers were often linked to the citadels of conservatism. Yet, whatever their shortcomings, the bankers must have felt some inner misgivings about the gulf that separated them, ideologically as well as economically, from their fellow Jews. Whenever a serious crisis confronted their brethren, the Rothschilds and others did not hesitate to intercede with their governments; even for them, blood was thicker than coupons. Avoiding liberalism as the vehicle of Jewish emancipation, these wealthy intercessors preferred the *shtadtlan's* technique of a discreet word in an influential circle.

There were many instances of such philanthropic intervention. Early in 1818, for example, Amschel Meyer Rothschild hurried a dispatch to Prince Hardenberg of Prussia—aware of the statesman's friendship for the Jews —begging him to use his influence with the German Diet to alleviate Jewish disabilities. The gentle Hardenberg willingly promised to speak to the king of Prussia; and he did, in fact, succeed in modifying the monarch's obscurantist attitude toward the Jews. All the brothers Rothschild converged on the international Congress of Aix-la-Chapelle that same year. The dependable Gentz promised to urge Metternich to speak to the leaders of the Frankfurt Diet. A few weeks later Metternich issued a general expression of sympathy for the Jewish cause, pledging his colleagues in the diet to investigate Jewish disabilities. Nothing further happened; but Gentz, after all, had done his part. In 1837, again at Salomon Rothschild's request, Metternich arranged for a conference of foreign ministers to deal with the Jewish question. The result this time was an improvement in Jewish living conditions in the city of Vienna. We have already described (in Chapter V) the successful efforts of Lionel de Rothschild to secure concessions for his people in England.

It was moreover as a result of Baron James de Rothschild's influence on Napoleon III—the two elegant *viveurs* had great respect for each other— that the question of religious liberty in Romania and the Balkans was considered in the Convention of Paris in 1858. The *Alliance Israélite Universelle* stationed several representatives at the Congress of Berlin in 1878, when the Jewish question in Romania again was broached (see Chapter XII). But the most effective Jewish "lobbyist" was the banker, Baron Gerson von Bleichröder, who exerted his potent influence on Bismarck, and secured the Religious Liberty clause in the Convention of Berlin. Baron Alphonse de Rothschild declared that he would continue to keep a watchful eye over Jewish affairs in Romania. Nor was Alphonse's cousin in England indifferent to the cause of his people. When, in 1902, new disabilities were heaped upon the long-suffering Romanian Jews, Lord Nathaniel Mayer Rothschild successfully persuaded Foreign Secretary Henry Charles Lansdowne to make unofficial representations to the powers.

Perhaps the most dramatic example of the unique approach of the *shtadtlan,* the intercessor, lies in the career of Sir Moses Montefiore of England. Related by marriage to the Rothschilds, Sir Moses was in a position to amass a sizable fortune as a stockbroker and investment banker. His Jewish banking connections were a springboard for an unusually tenacious and single-minded devotion to the fate and fortune of his people. During the early period of his career, as president of the Board of Deputies of British Jews, he was conscientiously involved in the struggle for Jewish emancipation in England. His unremitting efforts on behalf of his brethren made a profound impression on young Queen Victoria, who experienced the curious sensation, whenever Montefiore was in her presence, of being face to face with a Biblical patriarch. He certainly looked the part: tall, dignified, bearded, his deep voice solemn with Hebraic allusions. In 1837 she knighted him.

During the course of Montefiore's long life, which spanned a century, he made a number of trips to the Holy Land, and contributed liberally for the construction of orphanages and schools. In 1846 he and wife Judith undertook the arduous journey to St. Petersburg to protest to Czar Nicholas the eviction of thousands of Jewish frontier families. Montefiore impressed the Russian monarch—so much so, in fact, that when Montefiore sought to defend the qualities of the Jews of Russia, Nicholas felt compelled to admit: "*s'ils vous ressemblent,*" "if they are like you." Wherever a Jewish community found itself in difficulty, Montefiore sought to intercede, occasionally traveling to the area to negotiate firsthand. His fame spread among the scattered Jewries of the world, many of whom hailed him as a modern Messiah. During his lifetime Montefiore became the principal spokesman of world Jewry. He is remembered particularly, however, as the man who resolved the most sensational *cause célèbre* of the mid-nineteenth century: the Damascus Blood Libel.

The facts were these: in 1840 the ruler of Egypt was Mehemet Ali, an Albanian soldier of fortune and, by right of conquest, overlord of Syria. The French Foreign Ministry nourished a peculiar regard for this adventurer; with sizable subsidies the Thiers administration had managed to transform him into a puppet of French Near Eastern policy. It was against this background, in February 1840, that a Catholic priest, Father Thomas de Camangiano, unaccountably disappeared from his lodgings in Damascus, capital city of the pashalik of Syria. The French consul in Damascus, a notorious deadbeat named Ratti-Menton, suggested that the case be turned over to the local Moslem sherif. This was an unusual procedure, for France traditionally exercised capitulatory supervision over local Catholics. Having abdicated his responsibility, however, Ratti-Menton was now free to suggest to the sherif that the local Jewish community ought to be charged with abducting Father Thomas. Perhaps, the Frenchman hinted discreetly, the Jews planned to use the body for ritual murder purposes. Of course there was no evidence whatever to support this allegation. But it seemed a convenient technique for sparing embarrassment for overlord Mehemet Ali, whose own people at this juncture could not be implicated.

A Jewish barber was therefore chosen at random to supply "evidence." The unfortunate wretch was tortured with true Oriental refinement, until he "admitted" that several of the town's leading Jews had done the monk to death and had used the blood for ritual purposes. Several prominent Jews were arrested. Clapped in a verminous dungeon, they were gently encouraged to confess: the prisoners were immersed in ice water; they were savagely beaten; the eyes of several victims were gouged out; the genitals of several others were crushed. Two Jews died, and one accepted conversion to Islam to escape further torment. Because one of the victims however, Isaac Picciotti, happened to be an Austrian subject, the Austrian consul general intervened. A full account of the Damascus Affair was instantly circulated throughout the chancelleries of Europe. The Government of France, concerned with maintaining unblemished Mehemet Ali's reputation as a modern and efficient governor, was seriously embarrassed. In the Jewish world, of course, the news of these tortures created consternation.

In August, Montefiore and Isaac Adolphe Crémieux—the latter a French-Jewish attorney, a noted liberal, and later president of the influential *Alliance Israélite Universelle*—departed for Alexandria, Mehemet Ali's capital. There the lordly Montefiore secured the combined support of all the consuls in the city, except the French, in "demanding" the exoneration and release of the Jewish prisoners. The British Foreign Office, determined to undermine the hegemony of Mehemet Ali (and France) in the Near East, backed Montefiore.and his group to the hilt. Ultimately, and with profound reluctance, French Premier Thiers decided that French Near Eastern policy was vulnerable as long as the hue and cry about the Damascus Affair continued. Against a backdrop of Jewish protest meetings throughout Europe and America, messages from British and Austrian statesmen, who were urgently prodded by the Rothschilds and the Arnsteins, Mehemet Ali finally agreed to"liberate" the prisoners. As far as the reading public of the time could discern, the climax of the affair came in human terms—when early in September, the prison gates swung open in Damascus and the surviving Jews, broken in body and mind, staggered out into sunlight. But the diplomats saw the deeper issue: the complex machinery of a modern foreign ministry had been thrown out of gear largely by the persistence of a handful of Jews.

It would be unrealistic, of course, to ignore the fact that the Damascus Affair was resolved by Anglo-French rivalry in the Levant. Nor can the liberal tradition exploited by Crémieux be ignored as an influential factor in the release of the prisoners. But of vast importance, too, was the profound respect in which Jewish wealth, represented by men like Montefiore, and the Rothschilds who stood behind him, was held by the diplomats of Europe. Thiers himself, in a particularly cunning speech before the Chamber of Deputies in the summer of 1840, made this clear: "And let them [the Jews] allow me to say," he declared, "that they are more powerful in the world than they believe; at the present hour they are appealing to all the foreign chancellories with an extraordinary zeal and an ardor which one cannot possibly imagine. It required courage for a minister to protect his representative [Ratti-Menton] under attack." For all his devious obfuscation, Thiers honestly reflected Christian awe of the influence of international Jewish finance. It should be added, too, that the banquets and parades with which the Jewish communities of Western Europe greeted Montefiore upon his return from Egypt, genuinely reflected Jewish awe of the mysterious power of the *shtadtlan*. That awe remained, and influenced Jewish community life, long after Jewish emancipation had been secured.

THE DECLINE OF THE FRANKFURT TRADITION

During the first half of the nineteenth century, the private fortunes of the Rothschilds and of other noted Jewish financiers undeniably provided the underpinning for many of the public enterprises of Europe's governments. But by the latter part of the century, the insatiable industrial and reclamation needs of Western nation-states required even more capital—more, indeed, than even these modern-day Midases could command. Innovations in banking called for new techniques. Incorporation, for example, was relied upon to tap the combined resources of thousands of small shareholders. The investment bank now became the joint-stock investment bank, its *petit-bourgeois* shareholders carefully protected against undue loss by limited liability laws. This joint-stock bank was largely a Berlin phenomenon—although originating in France—and came to be known as the German "Great Bank."

With the rapid growth of these German Great Banks, the Frankfurt tradition began to decline. In 1866, following the conclusion of the Austro-Prussian War, the city of Frankfurt itself was actually incorporated into the Prussian-controlled North German Federation. After this date the venerable community was left with little more status than a Prussian provincial town, although it still possessed the dubious privilege of electing one lone deputy to the Senate (and that man was Meyer Karl von Rothschild). The introduction of the new German currency resulted in additional losses for Frankfurt, and ended the city's function as an exchange center for provincial monies. Eventually Frankfurt was virtually ignored by the directors of the big joint-stock banks, who preferred to locate their key offices in other cities. The Frankfurt tradition terminated with a kind of poetic finality when Baron Wilhelm von Rothschild died in 1901, and the Frankfurt House of Rothschild was liquidated. The death of gentle old "Baron Willie" ended an association that had made Frankfurt a pioneering symbol of imaginative finance capitalism.

It is not to be concluded, however, that the Jews suddenly lost their importance in the world of finance. Until the twentieth century they were well represented among the bankers and brokers of Western and Central Europe. Frequently the principal promoters of the Berlin Great Banks were descendants of distinguished Jewish banking families: von Haber, Königswarter, Siener, von Wertheimstein—men who no longer single-handedly controlled the fortunes of these banks, to be sure, but who provided direction and guidance from long experience in finance. Many leading Jewish financiers now acted as directors, or as skilled and highly paid investment counselors. The leading executives of the Deutsche Bank, for example, the greatest bank in Germany, were the Wassermans of Hamburg, one of the most eminent Jewish banking families in the country. And this was not atypical, for most of the *Disconto* banks of Berlin, Dresden, and Darmstadt employed Jewish executives.

Yet Jews sitting as minority members on boards, or functioning as salaried executives, hardly resembled in wealth or prestige those Jewish financiers of the first half of the century who were at the heart of investment and diplomacy. For better or worse, the era had ended in which a few Jewish financiers could make or break the governments of Europe. In the new age, when the bond issues and industrial enterprises of Central Europe were controlled by the publicly accumulated fortunes of gigantic incorporated banks, the Frankfurt tradition, a tradition which Jews had largely fashioned, terminated forever.

CONCLUSION

The reader will have noted a paradox. We have seen in the preceding chapter that a characteristic behavior pattern of most Western European Jews during the nineteenth century was their determined effort to immerse themselves in the mainstream of national life, and to share a common national destiny with their Christian neighbors. The Jews had taken their National Affirmation to heart, and luxuriated in their new status as patriotic citizens. Yet the significance of Jewish high finance was its very anti-nationalism. The loyalty of these magnates was to the empire of their fortunes. While the leitmotiv of Jewish emancipation during the nineteenth century was the identification of Jews with liberalism, Jewish high finance scrupulously avoided political commitment. It associated, as a rule, with vested authority, irrespective of the ideological orientation of the regime in power.

We must not forget, of course, that we are speaking of only a handful of men when we discuss these financiers, men who surely were not typical of Jewry as a whole. They bore few resemblances to the impassioned masses of Jews who voted, marched, fought, and died for their security in the revolutionary cockpit of nineteenth-century Europe. Nevertheless, these financial titans deserve the space we have accorded them. For their accomplishments were the result of their Jewishness and the circumstances in which they found themselves as Jews—cosmopolitan, experienced in money matters, accustomed to viewing themselves, as their ancestors had viewed themselves, as dependents of the king's chamber. And their influence extended far beyond their numerical strength. Nations frequently governed their undertakings by the sufferance of these men, made peace, and obtained imperial concessions by virtue of these family fortunes. Truly they exerted a major influence on the modern history of Europe.

Although the contact of these investment wizards was never particularly intimate, except in a patronizing way, with the Jewish communities from which they had originally sprung, the impact of their careers was destined ultimately to foist their image upon all Jews. This image, in the century to come, would obscure the zealous identification with national fate and fortune which had characterized the majority of West European Jewry. A day would come in the twentieth century when the harassed and atomized masses of the nation-states, revolting against the orderly governmental traditions of their lands, would associate all Jews with the bureaucracies they despised. Then, too, would people hurl against Jewry the epithet "internationalist," at a time when the word assumed the most dangerous connotation in the vocabulary of modern politics.

Notes

Pages 121-2. Quotation from Israel Zangwill, *Children of the Ghetto*, pp. xvi and xvii of Proem.

Page 129. Quotation from Hannah Arendt, *The Origins of Totalitarianism*, p. 22.

Page 132. Quotation from Lawrence D. Steefel, "The Rothschilds and the Austrian Loan of 1865," *Journal of Modern History*, March, 1936.

VII

The Impact of Western Culture
on Jewish Life

COPING WITH JEWISHNESS

In 1772 a Leipzig publishing firm issued a collection of poems by a Polish Jew, Issachar Falkensohn Behr. The poems were written in the German language, and the entire collection was entitled, rather unimaginatively, *Poems of a Polish Jew*. After reading the collection Goethe remarked: "It is extremely praiseworthy for a Polish Jew to give up business in order to learn German, to polish verses and devote himself to the Muses. But if he can do no more than a Christian *étudiant en belles lettres,* then he does wrong, we think, to make such a fuss about being a Jew." Goethe's observation must have been shared by many of his Jewish contemporaries, for in the early part of the nineteenth century the Jewish intelligentsia of Germany, faced with the choice of "making a fuss" about their Jewishness or of aping their Christian neighbors, increasingly chose the latter alternative. Adaptation was the inevitable result of growing political freedom. And, in retrospect, it was natural and understandable that Jews should have abandoned their ghetto habits, should willingly have adjusted themselves to the tempo and cultural patterns of modern Western life. That adaptation not merely provided German Jewry with greater freedom of economic and social opportunity, it also produced the remarkable symbiosis of German and Jewish intellectual traditions which has been one of the glories of modern civilization. But these blessings notwithstanding, a basic characteristic of Jewish life during the years preceding complete emancipation was the very real difficulty experienced by "enlightened" West European Jewry in coping with the accident of their Jewish birth. Large numbers of talented young Jewish men and women began to desert their ancestral tradition and move, not only into the Christian world, but into Christianity itself.

There were several reasons for this disintegration of Jewish loyalties. For one thing, as Jews gravitated in greater numbers to the larger cities, they found their private lives less subject to scrutiny by their Orthodox Jewish neighbors.

It was comparatively easy to become lax in one's religious behavior, and more of a temptation, therefore, in an era of half-emancipation, to adopt Christian mores. Secondly, Judaism, as we recall, had become rigidly formalistic during the eighteenth century. The Judaic tradition, with its pilpulistic connotations, now began to lose its appeal when contrasted with the recently discovered attractions of Western culture; while significant numbers of Jews, too, identified Judaism with the squalid ghetto world, which they were on the verge of leaving. Moreover, the rise of the monolithic state, the growing fusion of nation and state, suggested that pluralism in cultures might be as outmoded as corporativism in government. Homogeneity of culture, on the other hand, was viewed as loyalty to the nation-state. This factor was important in Jewish thinking. The Jews of Germany had one foot in the ghetto and one foot in the free world; they had experienced emancipation, had summarily been deprived of emancipation after 1815, and yearned desperately for its return. They were willing to go to almost any length to prove themselves worthy of citizenship, even, in the case of some, if it meant sacrificing their religious identification.

To a degree, the situation in Germany was unique. In France, England, and the Netherlands emancipation came so rapidly, so uninterruptedly, that the self-conscious need for acceptance was never quite so apparent. Conversely, in the Hapsburg Empire, where emancipation did not make its appearance until the second half of the nineteenth century, Austrian Jewry continued to think of itself essentially as a corporate, or national, group. It was primarily in Germany, where the bulk of Western Jewry lived, that so much psychic confusion was to be found, the result of twilight emancipation, of brief and intensive contact with German intelligentsia and nobility. This was a period, therefore, in which the German-Jewish community was characterized by a wide variety of emotional disorders.

One of the results of this psychic insecurity was the emergence of a curious kind of Jewish self-hatred. It was a direct result of the Enlightenment, an age in which Moses Mendelssohn and his disciples were fawned over by Prussian intellectuals as the supreme proof that even Jews were capable of behaving like human beings. Increasingly, as a result, educated Jews found themselves faced with the ludicrous demand that they appear not only as exceptional Jews but also as exceptional specimens of humanity. Nor were they unwilling to play the role; for the more educated they were, the more "secular-minded," the more easily could they meet with their German neighbors on a social basis. Of course the best way for Jews to make initial contact with Christians was to take the initiative, to invite them to their homes. And, in their turn, the elite of the Prussian aristocratic and intellectual worlds responded to these invitations with alacrity, for the rise of Jewish salons filled a decided vacuum in their lives. Indeed, these affairs were a godsend to young noblemen who had been bored by the stiffness and conventionalism of their snobbish homes, with social gatherings that, until then, had been little more than noisy carousals. By the opening of the nineteenth century, as a result, Jewish salons in Berlin were well established as the center of German social life. The Jews, after all, were charming and witty hosts and hostesses; they were untrammeled by feudal traditions; they were plastic in their adaptability, alert to new literary and artistic developments. Writers, artists, intellectuals, and *viveurs* all found good food and even better conversation at these gatherings; while the clever and vivacious Jewish women who presided as hostesses delighted and fascinated their guests.

But what conflicting emotions churned within the breasts of these exotic salon Jewesses! Henrietta Herz, the wife of a prominent Berlin physician, was a woman of tact and intelligence, beauty and perception. She lacked only peace of mind; for her desire to win full acceptance in German society amounted virtually to an obsession. The problem would not have been so urgent for Henrietta Herz had she not come so tantalizingly close to achieving her goal. At her home the diplomats von Gentz and von Humboldt, the theologian Schleiermacher, the French political leader Mirabeau, were frequent guests; her soirees were little microcosms of the Enlightenment. And all her visitors flattered her, fawned over her—and expressed wonderment that a woman of her cultivation could remain loyal to Judaism. In 1817 Henrietta Herz finally yielded to a prevailing fashion of the day and accepted baptism into the Protestant faith.

Some of Henrietta Herz's contemporaries went even further. Rahel Levin, whose home was the meeting place for the most original minds in Germany, was a startlingly brilliant salon Jewess. Her ability to discern new talent was uncanny. It was Rahel Levin, for example, who first introduced Goethe and Ranke to the literary world. A veritable Rahel cult flourished throughout her life; she was called, rather extravagantly, the most gifted woman of the universe, a seeress with the influence of a Pythia, the first modern woman of German culture. But none of these encomiums brought her personal happiness. "How loathsomely degrading," she wrote to a friend, "how offensive, insane, and low are my surroundings, which I cannot avoid. One single defilement, a mere contact, sullies me and disturbs my nobility." That "defilement" was her Jewishness. "I imagine," she wrote, "that just as I was being thrust into this world a supernatural being plunged a dagger into my heart with these words: 'Now, have feeling, see the world as only a few can see it, be great and noble . . . But with one reservation: be a Jewess!'" In 1814, at the age of forty-three, she married a thirty-year-old Christian writer and diplomat, Karl August Varnhagen von Ense, and was baptized a Lutheran the same day.

A strange irony attached to the fate of Moses Mendelssohn's own children. His daughter, Dorothea, the wife of a Jewish industrialist, deserted her husband and their son and eloped with Friedrich Schlegel, a man eight years her junior, and was converted to Catholicism. Both her sons by her first marriage and a son by Friedrich Schlegel were baptized, and Dorothea lived to see them earn their livelihoods as painters of religious pictures in Rome. Abraham Mendelssohn, the son of Moses, also raised his children as Christians, explaining to them that his principal concern was for their social "adjustment." He himself at first hesitated to leave his ancestral faith. Later, however, his misgivings were dissipated by the persuasiveness of his brother-in-law Salomon, who had taken on the name of Bartholdy at the time of his own conversion. "You say," wrote Salomon, "you owe it to the memory of your father—do you really think you did something wicked when you gave your children the religion which you regard as better for them? It is rather a form of homage which you and all of us are rendering to the efforts of your father in behalf of true enlightenment."

The conflict of emotions that bedeviled these enlightened Jews was well stated by the gifted poet, Joel Jacob. Born in Königsberg in 1810, the son of a strictly Orthodox family, Jacob began his literary endeavors as a member of "Young Germany," and ended his career as a Catholic official in the Prussian propaganda service. In a small volume, *Lamentations of a Jew,* which he published in 1837, Jacob argued that Judaism's mission on earth had been fulfilled when it produced Christianity, and that the parent religion had lingered on ever after as a fossilized relic.

> Thou hast scattered us among all peoples [Jacob grieved] and hast extinguished our radiance. Thou hast made our body immortal in history and we wander corpse-like among these blossoming mortals . . . Lord, let us go hence! We are weak, we are tired, we yearn for the burial-vault . . . How I do love you, Germanic life, Germanic thought, Germanic history. You, my second fatherland—how I love your iron discipline, your moral seriousness, the world of your sages and the character of your peoples! As in my divine homeland do I feel myself amidst your old temples and a spirit of kinship wafts over me in these halls. Often have I unwittingly pressed my hot, tear-bedewed countenance to your cold marble, and a marvelous, home-like greeting floated down from your pillars . . .

The Germans, Jacob concluded, might be induced to assimilate the individual Jew, but they would not and could not assimilate the entire Jewish people.

Inability to cope with Jewishness was not always synonymous with an irretrievable break from the Jewish community. A second variety of Jewish disorder might well have been called ambivalence, the ambivalence of those who sought to move from the ghetto world into the glittering new world of Enlightenment and emancipation, but who found much to cherish and to despise in both worlds. Heinrich Heine was perhaps the most dramatic example of this kind of dualism. We have discussed Heine's role in the German revolutionary movement. But his career as a Jew was no less spectacular. During the impressionable years of his childhood, Heine's religious convictions, or lack of them, were probably affected by parental cynicism. His mother was an avid Deist of the Voltairian school; his father, too, fancied himself something of a rationalist but possessed a calculated respect for the proprieties. Thus, when Heine made ready to depart for school, his father warned him not to express atheistic theories around the neighborhood: "It would harm my business, were people to discover that my son does not believe in God. Particularly the Jews would stop buying velvets from me, and they are honest folk and pay promptly."

Heine came to Berlin as a student in 1821, during a period when the salons dominated German-Jewish life. From the very moment of his arrival the assimilated Prussian-Jewish circles did their utmost to make him one of their votaries, for his reputation as a writer and poet had preceded him. Even Hegel evinced a marked interest in him during this period, while the boisterous student drinking societies, too, welcomed him into their midst. It is remarkable, in the light of these "nonsectarian" influences, and in view, too, of his rather pagan extracurricular behavior, that Heine stubbornly preserved his Jewish loyalties, and even became a charter member of Leopold Zunz's "Society for Jewish Culture and Learning." Immediately following his graduation from law school, however, in 1825, and before entering the Prussian bar, Heine made a secret trip to Heilingenstadt, had lunch with the local divine, Father Gottlob Christian Grimm, and thereupon accepted baptism as "Christian Johann Heinrich Heine" (he had already exchanged "Harry" for its German equivalent). This sudden act of apostasy came as a surprise to Heine's friends, for his career up to the very moment of baptism pointed to a renunciation of the idea of conversion. Christianity had never represented anything more to him than a "stench of bedbugs." In letters to his colleagues in the "Society for Jewish Culture and Learning," he expressed the most withering contempt for Jews who converted.

There can be little doubt that Heine's decision was largely motivated by opportunism. He recognized, for example, that only members of the Christian faith were admitted to the Prussian bar; he must, therefore, have been referring to his baptism in the passage in *Travel-Pictures,* which described his climb to the peak of the Ilsenstein and his grasp of the iron cross that saved him from plunging into the abyss. Shortly after his baptism he wrote his friend Moses Moser: "If I could have made a living by stealing silver spoons without going to prison, I would never have been christened." Yet Heine did not practice law. His writings, the complex eroticism of his social behavior, all suggest another answer, as well. So, too, do the etchings that have been preserved of him. The delicate Semitic features, the eyes like almonds, the thin, gracefully curved nose, the long tapering fingers, convey the impression of an additional, perhaps a more subtle neurosis.

It is likely that Heine also viewed conversion as a "ticket of admission to European culture," as he put it frankly in a letter to a friend. As a typical child of the Enlightenment, he assumed that an open profession of Judaism limited the breadth of his humanity. "It would be wanting in taste on my part," he wrote, "and petty if, as they say about me, I had ever been ashamed of being a Jew; but it would be equally ridiculous if I professed to be one." Jewish life in those days was, for the most part, provincial, lower middle class; it must have constricted a man of Heine's intellectual and aesthetic sensibilities. Conversion probably offered him the opportunity for what Jean-Paul Sartre once called the "escape into the universal." Martin Greenberg put it well when he suggested that Heine was seeking, like so many Jews after him, to escape the Jewish condition not by negatively fleeing it, but by positively transcending it.

After his baptism Heine hurled himself into the liberal movement, into his writings, and into an unrestrained personal libertinism. He delighted, in this phase of his life, to identify himself as a "Hellene," as if in contrast with the sober Hebraism of his Jewish friends. And yet the call of his people continued to echo in his ears; and he would not turn away from that call as the salon Jews and Jewesses did. At the least, his bemused attitude toward his "conversion" took the form of open cynicism. Referring to the Sabbath dinners he continued to enjoy at Jewish homes, he wrote Moser: "I have become a typical Christian. I sponge on the rich Jews." But there was more than cynicism in his reaction; there was shame and self-contempt, as well. In December 1825, he offered a glimpse of his inner turmoil in a poem, "To an Apostate." It was written ostensibly in "honor" of the baptism of his friend, Eduard Gans. But it is not difficult to recognize the poem for what it really was—an example of self-flagellation:

> Out upon youth's holy flame!
> Oh, how quickly it burns low!
> Now, thy heated blood grows tame,
> Thou agreest to love thy foe!
>
> And thou meekly grovell'st low
> At the cross which thou didst spurn;
> Which not many weeks ago,
> Thou didst wish to crush and burn . . .

Equally masochistic were Heine's savage diatribes against the converted Jewesses of Berlin, "former daughters of Israel [who] wear crosses about their necks longer than their noses. . . ."

Nor did Heine spare Christian dogma itself, let alone the Christian partisans who had maneuvered him into baptism. He castigated Reform Jews on the grounds that they, too, were approaching dangerously near the despised Trinitarian creed. Orthodoxy, he insisted, was still the best antidote to the "poison" of Christianity. As the years passed, Heine began to yearn for his ancestral religion with an intensity that was almost physical: "I know the goal, and where it is—but I cannot reach it . . . We do not have the courage to wear the traditional beard, to fast, to protest, and suffer for the right to protest . . . I, too, lack the courage to let my beard grow and risk the taunts of children crying 'Hep! Hep!' or 'dirty Jew' after me."

The last six years of Heine's life were spent in a sickroom, where he wasted away in the living death of advanced syphilis, the agonizing consequence of a youthful indiscretion. But his mordant wit and keen aesthetic sensitivity remained alive to the very end. It was from this "mattress-grave" that Heine composed his *Hebrew Melodies,* poignant, enduring poems and reminiscences of his Jewish childhood, and of Jewish civilization as he now properly understood it. The poems ranged from "Princess Sabbath," reaching back to the visions and ideals of his ancestors, to "Judah ben Halevy," a deeply moving projection of the death of the medieval Spanish-Jewish poet. Indeed, the closer Heine himself came to death the more vapid his earlier "Hellenic" ideals seemed to him. As the consolations of the Psalms, the austere moral principles of the Torah loomed larger now in his consciousness, Heine penned his final evaluation of his heritage:

> Formerly I felt little affection for Moses, probably because the Hellenic spirit was dominant within me, and I could not pardon the Jewish lawgiver for his intolerance of images, and every sort of plastic representation. I failed to see that despite his hostile attitude toward art, Moses was himself a great artist, gifted with a true artist's spirit. Only in him, as in his Egyptian neighbors, the artistic instinct was exercised solely upon the colossal and indestructible. But unlike the Egyptians he did not shape his works of art out of brick or granite. His pyramids were built of men, his obelisks hewn out of human material. A feeble race of shepherds he transformed into a people bidding defiance to the centuries—a great, eternal, holy people, God's people, an exemplar to all other peoples, the prototype of mankind he created Israel . . . Now I understand that the Greeks were only beautiful youths, while the Jews have always been men, powerful, inflexible men. . . .

Then the light dimmed: "Can it be dusk so soon? Or is this deeper darkness? Is that you, Mother? How did you come? Where are the candles? . . . Over my bed a strange tree gleams—half filled with stars and birds whose white notes glimmer through its seven branches now that all is stilled. What? Friday night again and all my songs forgotten. Wait . . . I can still sing— *Sh'ma Yisroel Adonai Elohenu, Adonai Echod* . . . Mouche . . . Mathilde! . . ." To the last day of his life, Heine remained preoccupied with the problem of his true identification. He spoke for unnumbered thousands of nineteenth-century Jews who lacked his crystalline eloquence but who shared his tragic ambivalence.

Finally, there were those who coped with their Jewishness in an even more singular manner. It was the manner of unnatural aggressiveness, an almost bellicose assertion of one's Jewishness. The most vivid example of this kind of aggressiveness was to be found in the career of Benjamin Disraeli, the Earl of Beaconsfield. The facts of Disraeli's career as an English statesman are well-known: his dizzying ascent of the "greased pole" of English politics; his rise to the prime ministry on the Tory ticket; the imaginative social reforms he called "Tory democracy"; his purchase of the Suez Canal; his sponsorship of Queen Victoria as the Empress of India. Disraeli's career as a Jew is perhaps less well-known. He came from an entirely assimilated family. His father, who fancied himself an enlightened gentleman, had his son baptized to provide him with the opportunities of "ordinary mortals." Benjamin Disraeli's connections with Jewish society were minimal; he knew virtually nothing of the religion of his ancestors or of their customs. From the outset, therefore, Disraeli was in a position to tamper with the facts of Jewishness without the inhibition of actual knowledge.

Disraeli's notion of Jewry's world influence dated back to the time when he was a fledgling writer and had not yet begun his political career. In an early novel, *The Wondrous Tale of Alroy*, published in 1833, Disraeli first developed his theory of the Jews as history's most talented and creative race.

In a later novel, *Coningsby,* he elaborated upon this theme, depicting the Jews as the motive force behind the most fruitful accomplishments of modern civilization. In fact, the naïveté with which Disraeli ascribed to the Jews awesome, far-reaching, and certainly nonexistent powers, was in marked contrast with the shrewd economic and political good sense revealed in many of his novels of English life. As he had "divined" the "secret strength" of the Jews, so, too, did he detect the secret weakness of his Christian colleagues. For the truth was that the peerage of England, which year after year allowed a number of wealthy businessmen to buy titles, was haunted by serious doubts of its own value. Disraeli sensed instinctively how to exploit that aristocrat insecurity. Because he was intensely ambitious for social acclaim as well as for political power, he decided to beat the aristocracy at its own game of snobbery; he would summon up pride of race to confront pride of caste. Declaring in *Alroy* that "all is race," Disraeli brazenly insisted that Englishmen "came from a parvenu and hybrid race," while he himself had "sprung from the purest blood in Europe." He argued, moreover, that "the flower of the Jewish race is even now sitting on the right hand of the Lord God of Sabaoth." Nor did he hesitate to demand that "the Jews receive all that honour and favour from the northern and western races, which, in civilized and refined nations, should be the lot of those who charm the public taste and elevate the public feeling."

Incredible as it may seem, Disraeli managed in this fashion to turn the fact of his Jewish birth to his political advantage. He began to embellish "his olive complexion and his coal-black eyes" in such a way that he became, with "the mighty dome of his forehead—no Christian temple to be sure—unlike any living creature one has met." Disraeli's display of exoticism, strangeness, mysteriousness, appealed to the provincial and fogbound English public; and politicians were awed by the magician (Carlyle called him a conjuror) who invested boring business transactions with an Oriental flavor. His adventures in Asia particularly were attributed to his instinctive "Oriental" appreciation of the importance of the East in Britain's imperial future. To the very end of his life, Disraeli held fast to the credo of racial aristocracy. Whenever he engaged in conversation with his good friends the Rothschilds, he harped on the theme to the point of monotony—certainly to a point beyond their comprehension. But the imaginative "Dizzy" knew what he wanted: a place on the highest pinnacle of social acceptance. Eventually he got it, for he became Queen Victoria's closest friend. After all, with whom else would these two illustrious representatives of royal lines feel completely at ease?

The historian Hannah Arendt makes a penetrating observation on Western Jewish society in the nineteenth century. Nowhere did the fact of Jewish birth play a more decisive role, she points out, than in the private lives and careers of the assimilated Jews. The Jewish reformer who transformed a national religion into a religious denomination with the understanding that religion was a private affair; the Jewish revolutionary who pretended to be a world citizen in order to rid himself of Jewish nationality; the educated Jew, "a man in the street and a Jew at home"; or even, like Disraeli, the Jew who reversed the process and made Jewishness a privileged racial fraternity—each one of these succeeded in converting a national inheritance into a personal affair. The result was, as Arendt puts it, that their private lives, their decisions and sentiments, became the very center of their Jewishness. And the more the fact of Jewish birth lost its religious, national, and social-economic significance, the more obsessive Jewishness became. The behavior of a large number of enlightened Jews, certainly not all of them, differed significantly from the behavior of normal human beings: they continually justified not what they did, but what they were. They wavered between shame of birth and sudden aggressive pretensions to aristocracy. From the salon Jews who attempted to assimilate, to schizoid Jews like Heine, to consciously aggressive Jews like Disraeli, one phenomenon was most frequently apparent: the transformation of an un-self-conscious and public membership in a common tradition into a tortured and futile effort at redefinition. This was, perhaps, the principal characteristic of Western Jewish intellectuals as they struggled to cope with the age of emancipation: they had lost their peace of mind. While emancipation enabled them to make superb and enduring contributions to modern civilization as Germans or Frenchmen (see Chapter XIX)—only a few of them were capable any longer of releasing their full and unique potentialities as Jews.

PRELIMINARY EFFORTS AT REFORM

The impact of Western culture was responsible for changes not only in Jewish social behavior, but also in Jewish religious practice. One of the first manifestations of this change was the Occidentalization of Jewish religious services. There were many modern, acculturated Jews who were increasingly repelled by the synagogue's cacaphony: the nasal singsong, the selling of prayers, the gossiping of women in the gallery, the absence of decorum. In 1810 Israel Jacobsohn, a Jewish merchant of Seesen, Prussia, erected his own synagogue, and took the initiative in stripping away many of the "Orientalisms" in its services. Quiet and order were enforced, the sale of prayers was reduced, cantillation in prayer was eliminated. An organ was introduced into the Seesen temple as well as regular weekly sermons in the German language. These were modest reforms, hardly revolutionary in scope. But they frightened the Prussian Government no less than many Orthodox Jews. Once the Jews began reforming their religious practice who knew where they would stop? Perhaps they would move into politics with the same ideas. Jacobsohn was compelled to close down his temple in Seesen. Undaunted, however, he opened another synagogue in the city of Hamburg only a few years later, and continued with his innovations. He was determined to pattern his services on the Western style, and to make them aesthetic and dignified.

Those who followed Jacobsohn were less motivated by aesthetic considerations than by the prevailing rationalism of the Mendelssohnian Enlightenment. This was apparent in the career of David Friedländer, one of Mendelssohn's principal disciples. Friendländer was a wealthy man who had immersed himself thoroughly in German culture. Remarkably enough—for those days—he never lost his selfless idealism or his enthusiasm for Judaism. But he was determined, at the same time, to expose his coreligionists to modern secular influences. With this in mind, Friedländer founded the celebrated Jewish Free School in Berlin in 1781, and devoted much of his time to developing its curriculum. Courses included penmanship, mathematics, bookkeeping, drawing, geography, Hebrew, German, and French; and the teachers included both Christians and Jews. Friedländer made this school, and others that he helped found throughout Prussia, nurseries of German as well as Jewish culture. He was equally determined to cultivate this "modernization" within the framework of Judaism. Yet, like so many other products of the Enlightenment, Friedländer viewed Judaism as a "cult," in the fashion of the *philosophes* and Napoleon. He had as little understanding of history and its ramifications as his Orthodox contemporaries. He and his colleagues, Samuel Holdheim and the "Frankfurt Reformers," were determined to divest Judaism of all "Talmudical" anachronisms, of the vast and complex folklore that had developed since Biblical times. "If reason is not exercised," wrote Friedländer's friend, Gotthold Salomon, a pioneer preacher of the Hamburg Temple, "then customs and ceremonies come to be considered as religion itself." Such traditionally Jewish observances as the Saturday Sabbath, the rite of circumcision, the Hebrew prayers—all were to be discarded as anachronistic. Jewish life, which had heretofore been "unreasonably" contricted by "Talmudism," was now to be given an opportunity to respond "freely" to the needs of modern society.

Whether they consciously realized it or not, these early reformers were influenced by factors other than the desire to simplify and modernize. One of those factors was German Protestantism. When Samuel Holdheim, the radical rabbi of the Berlin Reform Society, argued that the modern life of the Jew demanded the end of rabbinical autonomy, the separation of religious affairs from civil and political issues, the recognition of marriage as a civil act, he was reflecting the Protestant view of the supremacy of State over Church. The use of German vernacular was not only a modernist innovation, it was a Protestant innovation, as well. The women's gallery in the synagogue was abolished by these early reformers not merely because it was outmoded, but because the Protestant family pew was the vogue in Germany. Many Reform rabbis dressed in the fashion of the Protestant pastorate, with black gowns and white wing collars. It was hardly an accident therefore that the Jewish Reform movement was to reach its fullest development in countries that were predominantly Low Church: Germany and then the United States.

But assuredly the most important influence in the early Reform movement was the lengthening shadow of the Paris Sanhedrin. German Jews seemed to be under a compulsion to "prove" their loyalty, their "alikeness," in order to wrest back from their grudging governments the emancipation they had once enjoyed. Thus the excision from the Reform liturgy of all Zion-oriented prayers was actually a declaration of loyalty to the particular German state. The reformers doubtless regarded it a master stroke, when it came to dedicating the Hamburg Temple, to choose as the date of the occasion the anniversary of the Prussian victory at Leipzig; they considered it equally fitting to call their house of worship a "temple," a term which had until then been reserved for the fallen sanctuary in Jerusalem. "Stuttgart," declared one Reform leader defiantly, "is our Jerusalem." Here, indeed, was convincing proof that the Jews were prepared unconditionally to accept the responsibilities of German citizenship.

While their motives may have been a mixture of idealism and expediency, these early reformers did establish clearly the need for some kind of liturgical readjustment in Judaism, if only for aesthetic reasons. Nevertheless, during this early pioneering period, between 1780 and 1820, Reform was a small and experimental movement; within the Western Jewish community there was as yet little serious agitation for religious change. It was only later, when Reform allied itself with the romantic movement, the great driving impulse of the nineteenth century, that basic modifications were effected in an ancient creed.

THE RETURN TO HISTORY

We have seen (in Chapter V) the intense devotion to history manifested by the thinkers and statesmen of nineteenth-century Europe. In contrast to the self-conscious rationalism of the eighteenth century, the nationalists of the nineteenth century, and the romantics who provided them with their *raison d'être,* emphasized emotion, individuality, personality, the color and pageantry of tradition. It was the contention of the romantics, for example, that the sentiments which attached men to larger groups and to the past were instinctive, and that the forces of history and tradition were the dominating factors in human behavior. Thus, to understand any belief or ideal, any custom or institution, one had merely to examine its gradual growth from primitive beginnings to its present form. The validity of any institution or idea was no longer to be measured by its reasonableness or utility, but rather by its origin and history. History, as Schiller put it, "is the final court of appeal."

Ironically, this principle had been enunciated in the "rationalist" eighteenth century by Pope, in his line "whatever is, is right," and by Gottfried Wilhelm von Leibnitz in his judgment on the "best of all possible worlds." These were men with whom Ranke and his school would have been loathe to be identified. But poor Candide went through all his sufferings in vain, for it was the nineteenth century that became the restless age of historical investigation. At first this investigation was the handmaiden of the conservatives, and as such was devoted to the justification of preconceived notions of what was desirable. But then increasingly, under Barthold Niebuhr and Ranke, historical research became an objective science. An army of trained historians emerged from the Hegelian school in Germany, ready and willing to apply the technique of historical criticism to every field of interest: literature, science, philosophy, law—and religion.

This emphasis upon the historical approach affected Jewish life as well.

By the end of the nineteenth century it was possible to acquire a fairly exact knowledge of Jewish life and thought merely by consulting an authoritative reference book. But at the beginning of the nineteenth century neither these books nor much of the information they contained were available. Most of the leaders of Jewish life frankly feared that the study of Jewish philosophy and history would undermine piety, and it was this fear which prevented all but the most daring from pursuing historical studies. The extreme Jewish rationalists, on the other hand, had little interest in this research, for their premises were logical, not historical. Whatever Jews knew of their post-Biblical history was to be found in the Talmud, the prayer book, or simply in folklore; while the actual facts of Jewish life in the medieval period were cloaked in myth and misinformation.

Under the influence of the new historical approach however, a small group of Jewish scholars now began systematically to raise Jewish post-Biblical history and literature from obscurity to the dignity of a science. Leading this research was the most commanding figure of Jewish learning in the nineteenth century, Yomtob Lipmann (Leopold) Zunz. His intellectual achievements were probably unmatched by any scholar or writer since the days of the Vilna *Gaon.* Zunz's career was all the more remarkable in view of the personal hardships that plagued his life. He was raised as an orphan in a Jewish foundling home in Wolfenbüttel. His early education was exclusively Talmudic—and pilpulistic at that. He did manage, however, to teach himself secular subjects by reading German books, wherever he could find them. Begging and borrowing, he managed to attend the University of Berlin, where he exposed himself to the full curriculum of scientific, philological, and literary studies. Even more than for studies the university was famous for its dedication to a *Weltbild,* an intellectual outlook that emphasized the continuing impact of history upon human affairs. Friedrich Karl von Savigny, for example, taught that law could not be understood except as an organic development embracing a people's history and folklore. In philology Friedrich August Wolf and in philosophy August Böckh similarly emphasized the organic approach to their fields. Historical criticism was emphasized in every department at Berlin, and although Zunz ultimately received his doctorate at the University of Halle, the historical approach of Berlin remained crucial in his thinking for the rest of his career.

In many ways Zunz was a rather forbidding man, with cold blue eyes, a hawklike profile, and a propensity for biting sarcasm that made it difficult even for his friends to work with him. But there was little enough in Zunz's personal circumstances to move him to geniality; nearly all his life he was engaged in a bitter, grueling struggle for economic security, indeed, for sheer survival. He first managed to earn his bread as a lay preacher for various Reform congregations. From 1825 to 1829 he was a director of a Sunday school. From time to time he returned to teaching and preaching at various congregations and Jewish seminaries. Although he lived to the ripe old age of ninety-two, he hardly experienced a year of freedom from the most degrading kind of poverty. In view of these obstacles and hardships his creativity was all the more amazing. In 1819 Zunz joined with Eduard Gans and Moses Moser to found the "Society for Jewish Culture and Learning." It was the acknowledged purpose of this *Verein* to master all the material incorporated in Jewish literature, to arrange it according to its historical development, to evaluate and relate it to world literature. The project was an immense one for young men, and it is perhaps not surprising that the members of the society simply ran out of energy within a year or two. In fact, many of them not only dropped out of the society, but were caught up in the salon world and became converts to Christianity. There was nothing for Zunz to do, therefore, but to carry on alone. The extraordinary fact was that, alone, he largely succeeded in realizing the ultimate goal of the society.

To Zunz Jewish post-Biblical literature was the mature product of a steady historical evolution and not a mere collection of stray writings for "moral" edification. His first work, *Studies in Rabbinical Literature,* written in 1818, was a brief review of all the post-Biblical Jewish learning of his time, and a formulation for its broader understanding. A splendidly conceived little volume, it was the first successful demonstration that scientific method and criticism could be applied to Jewish literature; indeed, it was the dividing line between the *lernen* of the ghetto and the true science of Judaism. A profusion of works flowed from Zunz's pen in the years that followed: essays on Spanish place names in Hebrew writings; a biography of Rashi, the medieval Talmudist; outlines of Jewish statistics. One of his most famous studies was his *History of the Jewish Sermon.* It was written in response to a Prussian law that forbade the innovation of the sermon in Jewish religious services. With masterly authoritativeness, Zunz provided historical evidence that preaching was as old as the synagogue itself, and that preaching in the vernacular was no less time-honored as an institution in Jewish life. In his most enduring work, *Contributions to History and Literature,* Zunz combed the vast reservoir of Jewish history to demonstrate that the Talmud, medieval poetry, ethics, homiletics, philosophy, folklore, liturgy—all belonged to the realm of true "literature"; these were literary, not merely theological, works, Zunz pointed out, and were an authentic expression of Jewish national life and thought. He demonstrated, too, the intimate connection between the political vicissitudes, the intellectual and moral cravings, and the literary productions of the Jews throughout the ages. With the publication of this work in 1845, no informed person could ever again assert that Jewish genius had exhausted itself with the Bible.

All of Zunz's works were rigorously scientific, precise, exact, in the best tradition of the new German historiography. Until he did his work, in fact, no one had really taken the study of Jewish literature or history seriously, except, perhaps, as background for the rise of Christianity. Zunz radically corrected this imbalance by revealing the wealth of the Jewish literary tradition, its animating philosophy, its orderly and progressive evolution. When he finished his active research in 1872, he had charted the main currents of Jewish literature and thought. He had not solved all the problems, by any means, nor did he have the historical tools which later became available. Marx had not yet turned Hegel upside down. Very little understanding of economics or social factors found their place in his work, or in the work of his disciples. But the giant steps taken by Zunz in recovering the mysteries of the Jewish past incalculably eased the task of all historians who followed. He deserves a secure place not only in Jewish scholarship, but in the general scholarly world of the nineteenth century.

Not the least of Zunz's contributions was the group of eminent disciples he managed to attract to the "Science of Judaism," people who gave further body to his preliminary chartings. The most conscientious of these disciples was Moritz Steinschneider, a Moravian Jew who received a splendid secular education at Vienna's Polytechnical Institute and the University of Berlin. Ordained as a rabbi in Prague in 1843, he followed the footsteps of his beloved master Zunz by forsaking the pulpit and devoting the rest of his life to Jewish scholarship. And, like Zunz, he earned his bread by teaching and lecturing, translating and tutoring. Before he was thirty, Steinschneider had completed his first volume, *Jewish Literature from the Eighth to the Eighteenth Century,* a work distinguished by the most scrupulous and detailed primary research in the "Berlin tradition." Within a year after its publication Steinschneider was called to Oxford to prepare the catalogue of Hebrew literature for the Bodleian Library.

Steinschneider gave to the Oxford assignment thirteen years of diligent, painstaking research; when he completed his task his reputation was established permanently. The catalogue, a huge compendium, filling 1,750 pages of double columns, became the single most important reference book for Jewish literature, the foundation, in fact, for all future Jewish scholarship in this area. Steinschneider provided similar catalogues for many of the famous libraries of Germany, and he did his work with the same unfailing objectivity, the same scrupulous concern for minute detail—and, it must be added, with the same heavy, pedantic German style. Tributes to his scholarly genius poured in: honorary doctorates from the University of Leipzig, Columbia University, and the Hebrew Union College. The Prussian Ministry of Education bestowed upon him the honorary title of professor at a time when no Jew could legally hold a professorship in Germany. The tribute was deserved. Along with Zunz, Steinschneider had succeeded in exhuming and reconstructing the rich and complex Jewish civilization of the Middle Ages.

Of the score of Jewish scholars who measurably enriched Jewish information during the nineteenth century, one other, the historian Heinrich Graetz, must be singled out for special comment. Indeed, Graetz is virtually the only representative of nineteenth-century Jewish science whose works are read in the twentieth century; for alone of the giant figures of German-Jewish scholarship he understood the benefits of a felicitous literary style. Like most of his colleagues, Graetz received a thorough Talmudic and secular education, including a doctorate from the University of Breslau. A few years later he became a professor of history at Breslau. It was there, between 1856 and 1873, that Graetz wrote his *magnum opus,* an eleven-volume *History of the Jews,* the most widely read and consulted work in modern Jewish life. Few other treatises, it must be added, have been so severely criticized. Graetz was quite scientific in assembling the facts for his history; but when he began interpreting them and interjecting value judgments, his personal biases, which were leveled at Orthodoxy, Reform, and Christianity, slipped through to arouse the anger of many of his readers. Steinschneider called him an ignoramus and a plagiarist; the Orthodox considered him an infidel; and many German Christians condemned him as a fanatic. Perhaps Graetz was not strictly objective at all times; but his perspective was generally sound. And the astonishing fact to the modern reader is the vast amount of correct information, covering the totality of Jewish history, he was able to accumulate, and the serene and Homeric style he used to describe it. If Graetz was not the Jewish Ranke, he was certainly the Jewish Macaulay. His rare synthesis of scholarship and style popularized not only the history of the Jews, but also the Science of Judaism to which he had made such an enduring contribution.

THE RISE OF "HISTORICAL JUDAISM"

The scientific, historical approach to religion effected a revolution both in Judaism and in Christianity during the nineteenth century. On the one hand, the return to history anchored men's loyalties to the past, to tradition, to ceremonialism. On the other hand, it produced a deadly weapon with which to attack traditionalism. Through historical criticism, for example, such distinguished Christian scholars as David Friedrich Strauss, Bruno Bauer, and Ludwig Feuerbach seemingly exposed the most sacred of religious symbols as mere atavistic relics of primitive and barbaric times. The biologist, Charles Darwin, struck at the very heart of religious fundamentalism with his daring theory of evolution. And the Science of Judaism, too, by demonstrating that Jewish religious practices were often the evolving customs of their times, dealt a serious blow to the Orthodox *status quo* of the nineteenth century.

It was this historical approach that was to be used now by the new generation of Jewish reformers. These men of the 1840's were not haphazard rationalists, as Friedländer's and Jacobsohn's generation had been. The new reformers were rabbis, many of them with doctorates; they recognized that pure rationalism would pare away Judaism, ceremony by ceremony, doctrine by doctrine, until little would be left except the innermost kernel of prophetic ethics. Hence they sought instead to substitute history for rationalism. History would decide what point of evolution Judaism had reached; it would decide what should be saved and what should be discarded. For did history not prove that there had always been adjustments and change in Judaism?

The outstanding personality of this new Reform movement was Abraham Geiger, a native of Frankfurt, trained at the universities of Heidelberg and Bonn, a rabbi, and a distinguished Orientalist. In 1836 Geiger founded a critical journal, the *Scientific Journal for Jewish Theology* (how magic the word "scientific" was in the nineteenth century!). Within a few years it had become famous for its scrupulously objective approach to Jewish history and theology. In 1838 the Jewish community of Breslau invited Geiger to become the associate rabbi. Believing that he was a staunch modernist, they expected Geiger to counterbalance the sternly Orthodox religious leader, S. A. Tiktin. Geiger accepted the invitation. When he arrived in Breslau, however, he discovered that his appointment had stirred up a hornet's nest. Tiktin and his adherents were enraged at Geiger's "intrusion," and fought savagely to keep him away from the pulpit. It took all of two years before Tiktin finally capitulated, and before Geiger was able to deliver his first sermon in Breslau. Later, when Tiktin resigned altogether, the way was open for Geiger to convert the Breslau pulpit into the outstanding forum of German-Jewish Reform.

If the Jews of Breslau had expected Geiger to play the role of the fiery iconoclast (he certainly looked the part, with his flashing black eyes and flamboyant mustache), they were destined to be disappointed. His genius lay in approaching religion not as a reformer, but as a student and a scholar. Geiger never failed to place emphasis upon the gradualism of Judaism's development. His approach was so mild, in fact, his reverence for tradition so manifest, that for a while even such respected conservatives as Solomon Rappaport and Zechariah Frankel followed his lead; while radical reformers like Samuel Holdheim of Berlin broke from him.

In order to clarify the Reform position on matters of theology and ritual, Geiger took the initiative in organizing a series of rabbinical synods. The first gathering of reformers met in Brunswick in 1844, while subsequent meetings took place through the 1850's and 1860's in Breslau and Frankfurt. It was through these colloquia that the basic paradox in the "evolutionary" approach emerged. Of course, history proved that Judaism evolved and must continue to evolve. But human beings would have to determine the pace of such evolution. Human beings would have to select and discard, and this left room for arbitrariness and error. The difficulty was most apparent at the Brunswick synod of 1844, where it was decided to eliminate all politico-national references from the liturgy. The prayers were judiciously divided between Hebrew and the vernacular. All anthropomorphic designations of the Deity were weeded out. But what about the Sabbath? Was it to be shifted to Sunday for the sake of the worshiper's convenience? That depended on whether the specific day was sanctified at Sinai or merely representative of man's need for weekly rededication. No agreement could be reached. Nor could agreement be reached on the matter of circumcision; Geiger and others viewed it as a "bloody practice." Not so many other reformers however. The fundamental anomaly of the proceedings was expressed by those who had at first sympathized with the "historical" approach, but who now left the gathering remarking, in effect: "True, we cannot return to the letter of the Bible and take this as our guide; but shall we be guided, on the other hand, by the spirit of the age? The spirit of the age is as changeable as time itself." In 1871, nearly six thousand members of the Jewish Reform Congregation in Berlin petitioned for supplementary Sunday services. This threw the synods into such a turmoil of confusion and indecision that the leaders of Reform Judaism refused to commit themselves further on doctrinal matters.

After its impressive beginnings, Reform Judaism in Germany reached a standstill by the latter part of the nineteenth century; later it actually began to decline. There were several reasons for this. For one thing, Prussian law required every confessing Jew to contribute to the maintenance of the principal congregation of his community. If he wished to belong to an independent (e.g., Reform) congregation, he was obliged to bear the additional burden of supporting two congregations. Few German Jews were willing to undertake this expense. Reform burned itself out, too, because it failed to offer the majority of German Jews the kind of definitive authority that pious people seek when they turn to religion. It was, in short, pliancy and uncertainty even more than radicalism that prevented Reform Judaism from exercising a greater appeal. The typical German Jew was confused by a movement which was continually in search of a theology, continually gestating, continually seeking a platform. Finally, Reform lost its momentum in Germany because the German *Weltanschauung* conditioned Jew and Christian alike to respect tradition and authority. Steeped in history though it was, Reform was increasingly identified with radicalism; and radicalism was alien to the sensibilities of the staid, middle-class, hierarchy-conscious German Jew. In liberal, experimental, empirical America, on the other hand, it found conditions perfectly suited for its most extensive growth.

Yet Reform Judaism fulfilled important functions for all of Western Jewry. For one thing, it created a service that was dignified, simple, and decorous. Moreover, by exposing many of the anachronisms and archaisms in Judaism, it liberated the educated Jews of the mid-nineteenth century from a literal belief in the Bible and Talmud, and obliged them henceforth to justify their religious tenets on historical premises. Under the impact of the "scientific" challenge of Reform, Orthodox Judaism was largely transformed into Conservative Judaism, a religion based on reason as well as tradition, on evolution as well as literalism. In truth, one of the most dramatic results of the romantic-historical approach was the rise of a new Conservative Judaism.

It was at the Frankfurt Synod of 1845 that Reform was split irreparably between radicals and conservatives. When the radicals sought to limit the use of the Hebrew language to a hard core of crucial prayers, the conservatives indignantly walked out of the conference. The man who led the secession was the true founder of Conservative Judaism in Europe, Zechariah Frankel, a rabbi whose monumental erudition was already a legend in the Jewish world. Born in Prague, educated at the University of Pesth, where he received his doctorate in classical philology, Frankel served as District Rabbi of Leitmeritz, and then as Chief Rabbi of Saxony. Frankel's success as a rabbi was all the more remarkable because his personality was that of the retiring "closet student," the dry, pedantic bookworm. It was, indeed, as a scholar that Frankel assumed his position of leadership among the rabbis of his time. His real superiority over almost every other Jewish scholar in Western Europe consisted in the fact that he united in himself solid Jewish *lernen,* which he pursued all his life, with the finest modern critical schooling. From his earliest youth he harmonized within himself the yeshivah bocher and the university scholar. None of his contemporaries, with the possible exception of Steinschneider, who scrupulously stayed out of theological controversies, surpassed him in the catholicity of his learning.

Until the synod at Frankfurt, Frankel had considered himself a member of the Reform movement. It was only when the proposal was made to eliminate Hebrew from the liturgy that he decided to leave the ranks of Reform. One may wonder that Frankel was able to sit calmly through the radical discussions concerning Sabbath and marriage laws, only to perceive a danger to the Jewish religion in the seemingly minor matter of the restrictive use of Hebrew. But this issue suddenly clarified in Frankel's mind his fundamental misgivings about Reform. For the extreme reformers Judaism was a creed, a theology, which had evolved from earliest times and was still in the process of evolution. Frankel viewed the matter differently. When he made his celebrated statement that "Judaism is the religion of the Jews," he was seeking to attest that Judaism was not exclusively a theology of ethical monotheism; Judaism was also the historical product of the Jewish nation, of the Jewish mind and soul. Hebrew, for example, was the language of the Jewish spirit, the language which gave *Judenschmerz* to Jewish religious services. Frankel, who had never really been an Orthodox Jew, certainly did not consider the Bible as the literal word of God. But he insisted that, for better or worse, the Bible had become the historic vehicle of Jewish religious feeling. Perhaps the sentence which gave the clearest clue to Frankel's historical approach was his reference to the Law as "a tradition of Moses from Sinai." It was apparent that he did not believe in the absoluteness of Sinaitic authority. He did believe, on the other hand, that these traditions had deeply influenced the minds and hearts of the Jewish people—and that they ought therefore to be respected.

Frankel's approach could be put another way. History was more than a convenient surgical instrument: it was living, breathing proof not of the anachronism, but of the endurance of Jewish tradition. The norm for change was simply this: whatever observance had become deeply embedded in community tradition must not be abrogated. By maintaining the general validity of traditional Jewish law and combining with it freedom of personal interpretation, Frankel and his successors hoped to preserve historical continuity. In practice this meant much greater adherence to ceremonialism, traditional ritual, daily prayer, the Hebrew language, and kosher diet. Change, when it came, was permissible not because history proved that a certain ritual or a certain ceremony was a relic of barbaric times; it was permissible because the rite or ceremony had gradually, inevitably, ceased to be meaningful to the Jewish people.

This was not very far from the view expressed by Samson Raphael Hirsch, Chief Rabbi of the Orthodox Jewish community of Frankfurt. A cross-eyed, round-shouldered little man, one of the most eloquent orators of his time, Hirsch recognized that pure literalism could no longer serve as a rationale for Orthodoxy. But as a disciple of Kant, he, too, had a critique of pure reason; he, too, recognized that the rational experience alone could not penetrate into the realm of the spirit. Hirsch emphasized instead the importance of symbolism in the Jewish tradition. Only a theology based on *Symbolik* could successfully navigate the murky depths of the spirit. This was not Orthodoxy in the literal sense, but rather a modernization, an intellectualization of Orthodoxy. Some called it Neo-Orthodoxy. And, indeed, that is what it was; for Hirsch viewed the statutes of Torah and Talmud primarily as symbolic lessons, offered to the Jews in order that they might become monitors and exemplars of God-fearing humanity.

In the end however the ritual and liturgy of Conservative Judaism, or "positive-historical Judaism," as Frankel called it, was accepted by most of the Jews of Central and Western Europe as the best possible compromise. Reform apparently was branded as too radical, Orthodoxy as too atavistic. Yet the truth was that the three branches of Judaism did not differ very much from each other by the end of the nineteenth century, certainly not nearly to the extent that they had differed in the first half of the century. All Jews—Orthodox, Conservative, Reform—now believed in the value of a good secular education. No Jew, like Mendelssohn or Zunz, was obliged to hide a novel dealing with Western European life under the bench in his *heder*. The religious leaders of the Jewish community were increasingly men of modern philosophical training. Very few of them, on the other hand, rejected tradition entirely; in fact, German Reform resembled American Conservatism more than American Reform. Yet, slight as the differences might have appeared among the various doctrinal viewpoints, they stimulated each group to create an exclusive network of religious institutions. Thus, each group maintained its own rabbinical seminary, its own teachers' training college. Until the advent of Hitler, moreover, the Reform *Lehranstalt,* the Orthodox *Rabbiner Seminar* (both in Berlin), and the Conservative *Judische-Theologisches Seminar* (in Breslau) were the citadels of Jewish scholarship in modern times.

In our discussion of Western Jewish religious life, little reference has been made to religious change among the Jewries of other lands. This omission has not been due solely to the obvious fact that the preponderance of Western Jews was concentrated in German-speaking countries. Rather there existed little religious ferment, of the kind we have described, among the Jews of France, England, Italy, or the Netherlands. Occasionally mild efforts at reform here and there created brief flurries of controversy. But for the most part the Mendelssohnian tradition and the psychic insecurities that gave rise to the German-Jewish *Kulturkampf* did not exist in the other lands of Western Europe. In Central Europe, in Austria-Hungary, two factors militated against major religious departures. The first was the policy of the Hapsburg government which, exercising a kind of consistorial control over Jewish religious life, identified religious reform with political intrigue; religious change was therefore sternly discouraged by the Ministry of Religion.

Moreover, the bulk of Hapsburg Jewry lived in Galicia until the twentieth century; and these were poverty-stricken Orthodox Jews who were identified much more closely with the cultural changes that swept through the Polish-Russian centers of Jewish life. These changes were of great consequence; but they are properly discussed elsewhere (see Chapter X).

CONCLUSION

Amy Levy, an Anglo-Jewish novelist who lived in the latter part of the nineteenth century, has left us some delightful sketches of the "transition Jews" of her time. There was the white-haired grandfather, his fortune made, who passed his leisure hours muttering mechanically at his Hebrew prayers. His grandchildren, too, conformed outwardly to the rites of their faith. But their ways were devious; some mumbled prayers in ignorance of their meaning, some with a kind of tender mockery, and some with grudging resignation. None, however, prayed with deep conviction of mind and heart. Observance of the Sabbath gradually was abandoned in the larger cities, and increasingly in the smaller towns, as well; at first, Jews surrendered the Sabbath secretly and shamefacedly, and then, bit by bit, publicly and openly. Israel Zangwill has portrayed, with a kind of wistful hilarity, the excitement of a community which discovered a Sabbath-breaker in its midst. The "renegade's" neighbors spared no effort to prevail over him. But when he refused to be won over, the townspeople had no choice but to yield and give up the Sabbath themselves. Actually, most Jews in the Western world were giving up much more than the simulacra of religious observance; they were also abandoning, in large measure, their traditional concern for religious values. The distinguished historian, Carleton J. H. Hayes, appropriately titled the second half of the nineteenth century the "Age of Materialism"; for everywhere, in Christian as in Jewish life, materialism was triumphing over religion.

Thus the doctrinal tempests of their scholars and rabbis notwithstanding, the majority of Jews was largely unaffected by changes in liturgy or shifting emphases in Jewish theology. By the end of the nineteenth century the same influences that had secularized European society had affected the Jews: the influences of urbanization, of Darwinism, of capitalism in its highest gear. Conservatism may have triumphed within the Jewish religion; but religion itself was steadily being undermined as a motivating influence in daily life.

The abandonment of Jewish loyalties was visible not merely in religious nonobservance; it was also apparent, as we have seen, in "ethnic disaffiliation." Throughout the course of the century the topsoil of Jewish intellectual life was steadily eroded by the departure of those for whom personal Jewishness had become an inconvenience and an embarrassment. In the pre-Emancipation period Jewishness had not been a matter of choice. It had been a matter of autonomous nationhood. And in spite of grave persecutions and physical insecurity, that nationhood had brought with it incalculable advantages: corporate status; international connections; a noble and austere religious philosophy as yet unchallenged by secularism or rationalism. But with the fall of the ghettos, the attractions—and indeed the blessings—of Western life very naturally exercised an irresistible appeal for thousands of literate and acculturated West European Jews. Many of them managed to preserve the best of both worlds; but there were many others who forsook their Jewishness altogether and submerged themselves biologically as well as culturally in the blood stream of European life.

Even for the great majority of Western Jews, however, who maintained their nominal Jewish connections, there was a growing tendency to forget the long, tragic, glorious history of autonomous nationhood. A rather significant number of German Jews, for example, preferred to think of themselves as Germans of the "Israelitish" or "Mosaic" persuasion. The long shadow of the Paris Sanhedrin reached across the century and blotted out the memory which, for hundreds of thousands of modern Jews, was associated only with suffering and bitter humiliation. Heine was writing for these people as well: "Over my head a strange tree gleams—half filled with stars and birds whose white notes glimmer through its seven branches now that all is stilled. What? Friday night again and all my songs forgotten?"

Notes

Page 141. Extensive translations of the "laments" of the salon Jews may be found in Sol Liptzin, *Germany's Stepchildren.*

Page 144. Translation of "To an Apostate" by G. Karpeles, *Jewish Literature and Other Essays,* p. 351.

Page 145. Translation of Heine's valedictory by Louis Untermeyer, *Heinrich Heine,* I, 384.

Page 146. For an original evaluation of Disraeli's attitude toward the Jewish "race," see Hannah Arendt, *The Origins of Totalitarianism,* p. 75 f.

VIII

The Rise of Jewish Life in the New World

THE STRUGGLE FOR RIGHTS IN COLONIAL AMERICA

It is probable that the most fateful date in the struggle for Jewish emancipation was neither 1791 nor 1848 nor 1870. Historians may yet decide that the crucial date was 1492. By a providential turn, the year 1492, in which two hundred thousand Jews were expelled from Spain by King Ferdinand and Queen Isabella, was also the year of Columbus's discovery of America. The New World was to draw the nucleus of the Jewish community which was destined, by the middle of the nineteenth century, to be the most fortunately placed on earth. In the minds of the Spanish-Jewish exiles, even the uncharted ocean, crawling with nameless sea monsters, even the aboriginal terrors of South American jungles, appeared preferable to clandestine existence in Spain. They endured appalling hardships to voyage to the Western Hemisphere, hopeful that at last they had escaped the Inquisition.

But at first they had not. A Jew was burned at the stake in Mexico in 1528, and a number of other burnings followed in the seventeenth century. In Spanish and Portuguese America, life in the shadow of the Church was far too uncertain to encourage significant Jewish immigration. The Jews did manage to find one oasis of toleration in the Dutch colony of Recife, Brazil; but even this oasis was short-lived, falling to the grim, pious Portuguese in 1654. Recife's Jewish settlers were compelled once again to board ship, this time embarking on a search for sanctuary in the Caribbean basin. Some of these wanderers reached Surinam (Dutch Guiana) and Dutch Curaçao, where they were treated quite generously, and where they formed the embryo of the Western Hemisphere's oldest existing Jewish communities. A few sought asylum in the French West Indies, in Guadeloupe and Martinique, where for a century and a quarter they fought a nerve-racking battle of wits with the Black Code, practicing their religion secretly until the Declaration of the Rights of Man in 1789 at last normalized the position of non-Catholics on the islands, as well as in France. And some of Recife's Jews found refuge in the British "Sugar Islands" of Jamaica and Barbados. Here they were extended grudging toleration; here, too, the enterprising among them managed to transform themselves into wealthy merchants and slave-owners. By 1740, when the British Parliament naturalized foreign Protestants and Jews in the Empire (although not in Britain proper), some two hundred Jews were comfortably established in the Sugar Islands—the outstanding Jewish community in the New World. As late as 1776, in fact, the British Government viewed its Jewish subjects in America primarily as West Indian colonials.

These were as yet all episodic migrations. The one which had enduring historic significance began in 1654 when twenty-four of Recife's fugitive Jews, cramped and ill in the fetid holds of the tiny vessel *St. Charles,* audaciously ventured north, beyond the blue waters of the Caribbean and into the slate-gray Atlantic. Early in September their anxious search was rewarded: Manhattan Island lay before their bowsprit, and on the tip of that island the squat little houses of the Dutch community of Nieuw Amsterdam. Nieuw Amsterdam was a trading community, the outpost of the Dutch West India Company in the New World. Accordingly, most of its inhabitants were interested in bullion rather more than in religion or in religious differences. Unfortunately for the Jewish newcomers, the governor of the outpost, Peter Stuyvesant, had prejudices of his own which he was not willing to abandon even for mercantilist considerations; Stuyvesant's community was Dutch Calvinist, and he was determined to keep it that way. Who knew what the consequences would be of allowing these gaunt newcomers to remain? "Giving them liberty," the governor observed in a letter to the Company headquarters in Amsterdam, ". . . we cannot refuse the Lutherans and Papists." It happened, however, that the Jewish stockholders in the West India Company were influential, too influential to risk offending; orders countermanding Stuyvesant were not long in arriving from Amsterdam. It would be best, suggested the home office, to admit the refugees "providing that they shall not become a charge upon the deaconry or the Company." Swallowing his chagrin, the governor allowed the Jews to remain—and a nucleus was established for the first Jewish community in North America.

Several years later a handful of Jews arrived in Massachusetts Bay Colony. Here they were extended a happier welcome. The theocratic fathers of this Puritan Canaan, who were themselves refugees from the Anglican High Church, admired Jewish lore, studied the Old Testament assiduously, even attempted to transpose their image of ancient Palestine to the shores of New England. The Jews were not extended full legal equality, to be sure, but they were permitted to build homes for themselves and to practice their religion. The same Puritan toleration characterized Connecticut, where a few families of Venetian Jews were accepted for settlement in New Haven. And in Rhode Island, founded by the sturdy nonconformist Roger Williams, freedom of conscience was an unshakable article of faith; even a brief retrogression following Williams's death could not undermine the essential security of the Newport Jewish community, the largest in the colonies. Simultaneously, in William Penn's domain on the Delaware, a tiny group of Philadelphia Jews acquired virtually all civic rights by the early eighteenth century, except the right to vote and hold office.

In the southern colonies, too, the Jews were permitted to exercise their religion, to ply their trades, and even, at the beginning of the eighteenth century in South Carolina, to vote in public elections. The charter of James Oglethorpe's Georgian colony promised liberty of conscience to all except "Papists"; as a result, the Jewish community of Savannah, composed of both Sephardim and Ashkenazim, expanded so rapidly that at one point Jews comprised a sixth of the city's population. Jews and Christians lived together in exemplary amity in Georgia. So cordial, in fact, were relations between the two groups that the Methodist pioneer John Wesley, who spent two unhappy years in Georgia, wrote in 1737: "I began learning Spanish, in order to converse with my Jewish parishioners, some of whom seem nearer the mind that was in Christ than many of those who call him Lord."

On the eve of the Revolution the American Jewish community was comparatively secure. In marked contrast to the wedding of Church and State which dominated European life, no one religious group preponderated in the colonies. Of course, each region, each section, each colony possessed a dominant religion. But the patchwork nature of the original colonial settlement operated in such a way that in fact, if not in law, Judaism, too, came to be viewed as simply one of a welter of sects struggling for survival on the Atlantic seaboard. On the other hand, civic equality, as distinguished from religious toleration, did not come as rapidly for the Jewish settlers. While restrictions on their livelihoods had virtually disappeared on the eve of the Revolution, the fence around political rights remained high; most Jews still were excluded from the franchise and from public office. These circumstances were easily endurable, however, for people whose grandparents could recall the horrors of the Inquisition.

It was only after the colonial struggle for independence that Jews in growing numbers began to chafe at their status as second-class citizens. On the one hand, the Northwest Ordinance of 1787 guaranteed political and religious liberty to all who settled in the virgin wilderness beyond the Allegheny Mountains. But the new Federal Constitution, on the other hand, left the right of suffrage to the separate states. Not all of these states were willing to qualify Jewish voters or office-seekers. Here, too, however, eighteenth-century rationalism began to chip away at archaic restrictions. In Virginia in 1786, Jefferson and Madison secured the passage of a law which, like the New York Charter of 1776, removed religious discrimination in all phases of public life (the law was passed, it is interesting to note, over the strenuous opposition of Patrick Henry). Georgia followed Virginia's lead in 1789, as did Pennsylvania and South Carolina in 1790. In other states religious tests were abolished more slowly, some of them lingering on into the nineteenth century. But, for the most part, the mood of Protestant, individualist America refused to countenance the union of Church and State "after so many ages during which the human mind has been held in vassalage by kings, priests, and nobles." "We hold these truths

to be self-evident," read the words of the Declaration of Independence—
"self-evident," not sanctified by the Bible, by Aristotle, nor even by courts
or legislatures, but evident rather to human reason. Rationalism dominated
the thinking of the Constitutional Fathers and the legislators of the early
United States as surely as it animated the decisive events of the early French
Revolution. Church establishment and religious intolerance were not "reasonable."

THE EARLY AMERICAN-JEWISH COMMUNITY

On the eve of the Revolution the Jews of North America, perhaps half
of whom already were Ashkenazim, numbered only two or three thousand
in a total colonial population of nearly three million. They were scattered
along the Atlantic seaboard, in the mercantile communities of New York,
Savannah, Charleston, Philadelphia, and Newport. As in Europe, the Jews
of colonial America were almost exclusively a trading people, active in
intercolonial, Indian, and foreign trade. Their experience, literacy, and
contacts overseas enabled them to play a disproportionately large role in
coastal shipping and ocean commerce. This period, as a result, gave rise
to many outstanding Jewish merchant-princes: Aaron Lopez, a marrano
of Lisbon, who settled in Newport and established the seaboard commerce
in spermaceti candles; Jacob Franks of New York, a shipping magnate who
became purveyor to the Crown during the French and Indian War; Moses
Lindo of Charleston, a pioneer in indigo exporting; Hayman Levy of New
York, the largest fur trader of the colonies, and the employer of John
Jacob Astor; Joseph Simon of Lancaster, one of the largest landholders in
Pennsylvania; the brothers Barnard and Michael Gratz of Philadelphia,
leading fur traders and speculators, and distinguished philanthropists. Many
of these eminent merchants, their twentieth-century descendants hasten to
inform us, lived the courtly and imposing life of the colonial squirearchy,
residing in elegant mansions, wearing silken knee-breeches, dancing minuets,
and, undoubtedly, riding occasionally to the hounds.

Most of these Jewish settlers—although by no means all of them—were
adherents of the colonial cause during the Revolution. As businessmen, they
could hardly take a kindly view of the British Acts of Trade. The emerging
concept of nationality, moreover, was no less attractive to them than it was
to their Christian neighbors. Approximately one hundred Jews enlisted in
Washington's army, half of them as officers. Haym Salomon, a Jewish
immigrant from Lissa, Poland, rendered valuable service to the cause of
the Revolution as a broker in Continental bills of exchange, although legend
has considerably embellished his importance. After the war the "silent
American Revolution," an inner social and political revolution, opened up
other avenues of public life. A number of Jews became active in Jefferson's
Democratic-Republican party; and one Jew, Jacob Henry, was elected a
member of the North Carolina legislature in 1808 and was re-elected the
following year.

But while the Jews established themselves economically and politically during the course of their first century and a half in America, they groped with much less certainty for a technique of sustaining their Jewish heritage. For those who were determined to remain faithful to their traditions, a vague, amorphous pattern of American-Jewish life was already apparent by the early 1800's. The Jewish community was synagogue-centered. Jews voluntarily grouped themselves in separate neighborhoods in order to be near their house of worship and their fellow *minyan*-members. On the eve of the Revolution there were organized Jewish congregations in a number of coastal cities—New York, Philadelphia, Charleston, Savannah, and other colonial ports. In Newport, Rhode Island, was to be found not only the wealthiest Jewish community on the continent but also the most beautiful synagogue and synagogue tradition. These synagogues were more than houses of worship; they were, also, as in Europe, Jewish communal institutions, the centers for an array of educational, philanthropic, and social activity. Indeed, the tiny synagogue schools, with their curriculum of Hebrew, Bible, and the three R's, provided Jewish children with the only elementary education they received in America. The variety of functions performed by the synagogue was not always apparent to the outsider. Thus, a Christian traveler who visited Newport's synagogue once commented, with sublime misunderstanding: "It will be extremely elegant when completed, but the outside is totally spoiled by a school which the Jews [would] have annexed to it for the education of their children." The synagogue was unquestionably responsible for holding the Jewish community together during the early years of American-Jewish history.

Ultimately, however, the self-conscious individualism characteristic of early American life had its effect on Jewish communal discipline. In 1825, for example, when the Sephardic officers of New York's *Shearith Israel* synagogue humiliated their Ashkenazic congregants by refusing them the right to introduce the Sabbath's Scriptural reading, the outraged German and Polish Jews withdrew to form their own congregation. Why, they asked, should tyranny be endured in the synagogue if it was not to be tolerated in the politics or in the society about them? Emancipated from the tight-knit official control of the European *kahal* or ghetto community, individual Jews could and did move freely into Christian society, enjoying a freedom which had never been theirs in the Old World. They were resolved, therefore, that they would resist any encroachments on their freedom in their Jewish religious and communal life.

On the other hand, there were innumerable instances in which this new freedom provided the opportunity for a complete abandonment of Jewish identification. The first Jew to set foot in Nieuw Amsterdam was Jacob Barsimson. Shortly after establishing himself there, Barsimson married a Christian woman; because his own religious observance was lax, his children were lost to the Jewish group. Barsimson's action portended an assimilation which contrasted profoundly with the old patterns in Europe. Virtually every Jew who settled in Connecticut prior to the Revolution intermarried with his neighbors and the children were reared as Christians. In 1777, a Hessian soldier, Johann Conrad Döhla, noted in his diary:

All . . . sects and Jews live in mutual trust and unity . . . The Jews, however, cannot be told, like those of our country, by their beard and customs, but are dressed like the other citizens, shave regularly, and also eat pork, although their religion forbids it. Jews and Christians, moreover, do not hesitate to intermarry. The Jewish women have their hair dressed and wear French finery like the women of other faiths.

Many Jews who attained prominence in American life—such men as August Belmont, the banker and a leader of the Democratic party, Judah P. Benjamin, the senator from Louisiana and later an active Confederate statesman, and David (Levy) Yulee, the Florida politician and senator—intermarried with native daughters. Untold numbers of immigrants in succeeding generations, made the same choice. Eventually, indeed, a majority of the descendants of colonial Jewry disappeared into their non-Jewish surroundings.

IMMIGRATION FROM CENTRAL EUROPE

Until the early part of the nineteenth century the racial composition of the United States was predominantly Anglo-Saxon. There was some admixture from Central Europe, most significantly the "Pennsylvania Dutch" of southern Germany; but, interspersed among the lanky Scotch-Irish and English farmers who peopled both sides of the Alleghenies, the German element was not significant. Then, in the nineteenth century, the population "explosion" discussed earlier (see Chapter VI) brought an unprecedented crisis to the Central European countryside. The old balance of society no longer could be maintained; overpopulation, land hunger, and unemployment were the topics that dominated all discussions. The post-Napoleonic years, thus, were marked by a rising tide of general emigration from Germany, primarily to America. The revolutionary unrest and the consequent reaction which followed 1848 may have accounted for some of the emigration; but economic insecurity, not the need for political asylum, was the primary centrifugal force.

In 1816 the ports of Holland were filled with Germans awaiting passage. Posters announcing the departure of vessels from Bremen, Holland, and Le Havre were to be seen on the walls of every German village and town. The following year it seemed as if southern Germany was about to be depopulated. Within a single fortnight four thousand persons left the little state of Baden; Württemberg lost sixteen thousand of its inhabitants by emigration before the year was over. In 1827-28 more than ten thousand Germans landed in New York and quite as many more in Philadelphia and Baltimore. In 1847 alone, fifty thousand Germans left for the United States. In the 1860's more than a million people arrived in America as part of this vast mid-century migration, raising the country's German population to six million by 1870.

Many settled along the Eastern seaboard. But the majority, intrigued by the opportunities in the undeveloped regions of the country, gravitated beyond the Alleghenies. America's population at mid-century churned with movement. When pioneer farmers departed for virgin lands further west, the immigrant farmers rushed into the vacuum to buy land that was already cleared. By greater patience and ingenuity, by a shrewd use of winter wheat or by a timely conversion to dairy farming, they succeeded in making their plots of earth productive. Many German immigrants who did not choose to become farmers made their homes in the burgeoning Midwestern cities of Cincinnati, Louisville, St. Louis, and Milwaukee.

The mass migrations from Central Europe included many thousands of German Jews. Actually, Ashkenazic Jews appeared on the American scene long before the German migration of the nineteenth century; from the early eighteenth century on, in fact, they outnumbered the original Sephardic community. But the first significant influx of Ashkenazim, or, for that matter, of Jews in general, did not begin until the great waves of nineteenth-century immigration we have just described. Political and civic discrimination undoubtedly played a part in moving these German Jews to America; e.g., the limitation upon the number of Jewish marriages in Bavaria, the flat, uncompromising expulsion of Jews by several German governments, the restrictions on Jewish businesses and professions in Württemberg, the "hep-hep" riots of Würzburg, Bamberg, Frankfurt, and the Hanseatic cities. During the first three decades of the nineteenth century, hostile voices were raised in Germany, urging the Jews to clear out. There were increasing numbers of German Jews who reluctantly agreed that migration to America seemed to be the only solution to Jewish insecurity. Jewish communities had long been accustomed to the loss of their young men who sought to remake their lives in other European countries; and, for centuries, Jewish girls had gone to Italy to serve as maids. Now, however, encouraged by glowing letters from across the Atlantic, the trend in favor of America acquired irresistible momentum.

The abortive revolutions of 1848, too, played their part in setting other Jews on the move. In some cases reactionary German monarchs tracked down Jewish revolutionaries. In other cases Jews were assailed by Slavic nationalists for their devotion to German culture. When, for example, the Czechs took up arms against Austrian rule, they unleashed a series of attacks on Jewish homes and businesses for they viewed their Jews as the advance guard for German culture. These outrages convinced many Bohemian Jews that emigration to America was the only solution. Some echoed the lament of Leopold Kompert, eminent Czech-Jewish novelist: "On to America," he cried, "no relief has been brought to us. The sun of liberty is up for the Fatherland; but for us it is like the screaming mews during a storm. . . . There is no other desire among us than to get away from this 'freedom.' Our goal must, therefore, be emigration, the founding of a new fatherland, the immediate achievement of freedom. . . . Let us go to America!" Among those who departed from Prague in 1849 was Adolf Brandeis, father of the eminent jurist Louis Dembitz Brandeis. Despairing of the possibility of living happily in the Empire, he was the forerunner of a group, including his future wife, who later that year sailed via Hamburg for the United States. "In a few months you will be here yourself," Brandeis wrote to his fiancée in Prague, "and you will be able to see, judge and decide. To your own surprise you will see how your hatred of your fellow-man, all your disgust at civilization, all your revulsion from the intellectual life, will drop away from you at once. You will appreciate that these feelings are solely the products of the rotten European conditions."

But, as in the case of German immigration in its larger contours, economic pressure exerted the major influence in stimulating the flight of German Jews to the United States. It was virtually impossible for Jews to subsist as petty retailers if the peasants with whom they dealt were abandoning the countryside for larger cities or for America. Moreover, the Jewish population was growing phenomenally—at a rate higher, in fact, than the incredible increase of the non-Jews. The number of Jews in Europe tripled during the nineteenth century, and the need for wider economic opportunities made emigration literally a matter of life or death. At the least, the Enlightenment had instilled in the more resourceful Jews the conviction that self-improvement was necessary and right.

By the 1840's migration took shape as an organized process. In the Hapsburg monarchy, for example, emigration societies were organized in Vienna, Budapest, Prague, and Lemberg to provide financial assistance for destitute emigrants. Jews and Germans leaving the south of Germany together usually went by local stage to Strasbourg. There, bag and baggage, they were loaded into wagons that carried them on to Paris. In Paris, they were transferred to river steamers that bore them up the Seine to Le Havre. Meanwhile, from northern and central Germany the Polish-speaking Jews of Posen traveled up the Elbe and Weser rivers to the harbors of Hamburg and Bremen. The emigrants who huddled on the docks of these harbors, especially those from Posen and Austrian Galicia, carried with them precious baggage: a scroll of the Torah, a *Megillah,* a shofar, as well as other ritual objects used for services. They would turn often to the sections in their prayer books written specifically for those sailing the high seas. The prayers were needed: during the first half of the century the emigrant ship was a fragile vessel, usually an old cotton or timber ship coming back to America in ballast. The steerage, in which most of these "passengers" were dumped, was hardly more than six feet from floor to ceiling; a ladder leading down from a hole in the deck was its only means of entrance. Around the side of this enclosure ran two layers of berths, cumbersome shelves wide enough for five persons, and filling most of the floor space.

We find an account of a typical voyage in the diary of Bernhard Rosenbaum, a Bohemian Jew. He journeyed from Hamburg to New York in 1847 aboard the two-masted brig *Colibri.* It was a painfully slow trip, encompassing weeks of boredom and illness. The passengers were crowded into the reeking steerage together with foul-smelling hogs, cattle, and hens. "The food is so bad," Rosenbaum wrote, "that, in comparison, the pigs in Bohemia are fed with delicacies." He added later, "in four weeks I have eaten meat only once; for it is so bad that most of the passengers say that it must be horse meat, and, unfortunately, it is easy to believe." Not infrequently the scramble for precious drinking water resulted in fist fights, scratching, gouging—even killing. Fish, the only fresh and tasty food, could not be served because it gave rise to thirst. The supplies of bread and butter, rice and potatoes, were consumed rapidly. It is not difficult to understand why Rosenbaum regarded the day that the New York pilot boarded the boat as the happiest of his life: "forgotten are all sufferings and inconveniences; I have seen America; my desire is fulfilled." It should be added that by the 1860's and 1870's travel to America was both more rapid and more comfortable.

By mid-century New York had largely superseded Boston and Philadelphia as the principal gateway for European immigrants, and was already well on its way to becoming America's largest and wealthiest city. Once the awed and open-mouthed immigrant arrived in this bustling metropolis, he was often reluctant to move inland. Business opportunities looked good, often deceptively so. Most important, ties of *landsmannschaft* tended to keep many of the immigrants in the New York area. Although the majority of Jews moved on, so many remained that the Jewish population of New York grew from a handful in 1795 to 40,000 by 1859. Eventually, the number of Jewish immigrants arriving from Central Europe in the period between 1830 and 1860 may have been as high as 200,000. This inflow, together with natural increase, raised the total Jewish population of America to 300,000 in 1870. German-Jewish emigration had provided solid bedrock for what was ultimately to become the largest community in the history of Jewish life.

THE ECONOMIC DEVELOPMENT OF THE GERMAN-JEWISH COMMUNITY

IN AMERICA

Most of the Jews who arrived in the United States during this German wave of immigration were dirt-poor. Indeed, in the 1850's nearly 20 per cent of those who reached New York found themselves dependent upon the Jewish charities of the city. They were confused and appalled by the size and impersonality of American economic life. The alternatives for immigrants were all too limited. Only a handful possessed some modest capital and could begin their new lives with the exhilaration of hope. Industry called for laborers but there was little attraction when the possibility of advancement was so remote. Agriculture was an alien livelihood and held little appeal. Inevitably then, at the outset, the immigrants poured into petty trade. They were quite familiar with its twists and turns in the old country. It asked only for a strong constitution and a thick skin and required very little capital. Thus it was that hand-to-mouth trade and peddling became the chief economic outlet for the German-Jewish immigrant group.

During the mid-century period most of these peddlers depended upon their ports of debarkation—Philadelphia, New York, Baltimore—as the supply centers and headquarters from which they fanned out into small towns and rural districts. They hoped to find their best customers among the Germans who had moved inland, and with whom they would have little difficulty in communication. Sometimes working for others, sometimes on their own account, they moved out into the West, ranged the countryside, joined the covered wagons headed for the Western trail, followed the gold rushes to the Pacific. In his *Reminiscences,* Rabbi Isaac M. Wise described the stages of the German Jew's economic progress:

> Our people in this country may be divided into the following classes: 1. the basket-peddler—he is as yet altogether dumb and homeless; 2. the trunk-carrier, who stammers some little English, and hopes for better times; 3. the pack-carrier, who carries one hundred to one hundred and fifty pounds upon his back, and indulges the thought that he will become a businessman some day. In addition to these, there is the aristocracy, which may be divided into three classes: 1. the wagon-baron, who peddles through the country with a one- or two-horse team; 2. the jewelry-count, who carries a stock of watches and jewelry in a small trunk, and is considered a rich man even now; 3. the store-prince, who has a shop, and sells goods in it . . . At first one is the slave of the basket or the pack; then the lackey of the horse, in order to become finally the servant of the shop.

These Jewish peddlers—or drummers, for those who were graduated to the more profitable status of traveling salesmen—were usually the only Jews that inland communities knew; often their caricature, speaking broken English or a few Yiddish words, joined Irish Pat and German Fritz on the vaudeville stage as a stock type.

Some Jews accumulated enough of a reserve to transform the pack into a settled retail establishment, a general store, or a secondhand store. In a surprisingly short time several thousand of these immigrants achieved *petit-bourgeois* status, and not a few of them rose to upper-mercantile ranks. Wise's semisatirical description notwithstanding, the Jewish peddler's rise to economic security was a formidable, indeed, a rather heroic accomplishment. It was in peddling, for example, that some of the most eminent Jewish magnates began their careers: Meyer Guggenheim, the mining czar, Joseph Fels, the soap manufacturer, Henry Frohman, the father of the famous theatrical family, Adam Gimbel, the department-store magnate of Philadelphia, Marcus Fechheimer, the pioneer Cincinnati clothing manufacturer.

The progress of the German-Jewish immigrant is perhaps most dramatically symbolized in the career of the Straus family. In 1852, Lazarus Straus came to the United States from Bavaria, settled in Georgia, and became a peddler. Two years later he was joined in the little town of Talbotton, Georgia, by his wife and four children. Within a decade, he had accumulated enough capital to open a general store. In 1863, the family packed up again, moved to Columbus, Georgia, and branched out with an even larger establishment. After the Civil War ended, the restless father was tantalized by yet new visions of opportunity, and decided to move to New York. There Lazarus and his sons launched a wholesale crockery business. Several years later they acquired control of the retail store originally pioneered by a Captain Macy; by shrewd financing, they soon managed to transform the enterprise into the leading retail establishment in the United States. It was, in fact, the younger Strauses who made a new art of merchandise retailing. One brother, Oscar, backed by the family fortune, became a power in the Democratic Party, and was appointed Minister to Turkey by President Cleveland. Isidor Straus held a number of civic, political, and philanthropic posts in his city and state, served a term in Congress, and for nearly twenty years was President of the Educational Alliance in New York. In 1912 Isidor and his wife, Ida, were on the *Titanic* when it struck an iceberg; Ida refused the rescue which was offered her, preferring to die with her husband. Still another brother, Nathan, was recognized as one of America's foremost philanthropists, especially for his research subsidies in public health, and for his major contributions to the development of Palestine.

Success was not always the end of the story, however. Many hapless Jewish peddlers fell by the wayside. Our friend Rosenbaum of Bohemia, upon arriving in America, settled in Allentown, Pennsylvania; and the last pages of his diary bespeak complete disillusionment:

> O, how sanguine were my hopes when I turned my back on the unfree city of Hamburg on the 19th of May, 1847, in order to go to free America. Oh, how very much have I sacrificed: how I have renounced everything that was dear to me, separated from my mother . . . torn myself from my brother and sister; renounced the home of Cohn; all that in order to suffer in America and to go peddling. O, had I been able to see into the future, how different things would be with me now, how content I would have been in Lamstedt, how economical, secluded . . . But it is past, what has happened cannot be undone. Here I am buried alive. Here I must go peddling and cry "Do you want to buy?", sweat, and carry my basket.

This plaint must have been often repeated by immigrant sons, lying friend-less and alone in Midwestern country inns, listening to the call of strange birds in the woods, the raucous laughter of raw-boned frontiersmen rising from the public rooms below. Far away they were, irretrievably cut off from their families and from the scenes of their childhood.

Yet tens of thousands of German-Jewish immigrants gambled on the future of the lonely towns of the American hinterland. Sizable Jewish communities had already been established in metropolitan New York and Philadelphia; and there were growing Jewish communities in Baltimore, Boston, and New Orleans. But by mid-century new Jewish centers sprang up, far from the Atlantic seaboard: in St. Louis, Cincinnati, Louisville, Cleveland, Milwaukee, Detroit, Pittsburgh, Chicago, San Francisco. There were important advantages to be gained from such dispersion. Unlike the Irish who clung together clannishly on the Atlantic seaboard, and unlike the Russian Jews of half a century later, who came as families, or even as whole villages, the German-Jewish immigrants came primarily as individuals, and were able eventually to move somewhat more easily into the main-stream of American life. In this way they avoided the unemployment and pauperism, the slum housing and disease that plagued the less mobile, or the less ambitious, who remained in the Eastern cities.

GERMANISM AND AMERICANIZATION

During the voyage to America ties were formed between Jews and Germans that were rare in the old country, and these ties persisted with surprising tenacity in the New World. The shared memories of the past, the common motivation for emigration, the ability to converse with one another in a mother tongue—all this sustained at least a mild comradeship. German Jews streamed into German reading circles, dramatic clubs, choral groups, and gymnastic societies. Many of the later German arrivals were professional men with a persistent sense of liberalism; their friendship with Jews was often a matter of principle. But even those who brought their ancient prejudices with them to America sensed that the Jews could be depended upon to strengthen the German cultural position in the new country. The Jews, for their part, relinquished their Germanism and their German contacts as slowly and reluctantly as possible. Jewish religious instruction was imparted in the German language. When German-Jewish immigration was at its height, even Jewish newspapers printed in English were obliged to publish some of their contents in the old vernacular. Jewish loyalty to German culture was highly developed and was stubbornly maintained.

And yet, the German-Jewish newcomer, no less than the non-Jewish expatriate, ultimately came to terms with American civilization. Most of the younger immigrants were determined to become full-fledged Americans. In order to make Americanization fashionable and attractive, the specifically Jewish fraternal orders—B'nai B'rith, B'rith Abraham, and others—borrowed national symbols and ceremonies for their programs. In the 1850's, another favorite vehicle for nativizing was the Jewish young men's literary society and association. Rejecting the secret ritual of the fraternal orders, these groups concentrated on cultural and social programs, on debates, poetry readings, plays, and song fests, as well as elaborate dress balls and parties. Their membership was almost exclusively German-Jewish; but the programs were significantly void of German, or Jewish, content. For the clear, though unacknowledged, purpose of these associations was the Americanization of the younger immigrants.

Economic and political factors also played a role in this acculturation. One we have mentioned: the dispersal of German-Jewish immigrants throughout the country, and their business dealings with native Americans as well as German-Americans. Another was the land policy of the American Government. In 1818 the Irish societies of New York and Philadelphia petitioned Congress for a land grant in the West upon which they might settle their charity cases. Congress refused, agreeing with the report of a special committee that it would be undesirable to concentrate alien peoples geographically. If a grant were made to the Irish, the Germans would be next, then the Swedes, and then who knew to how many other immigrant groups. Probably no decision in the history of American immigration policy was ever more significant. It avoided a patchwork nation of foreign settlements, and it aborted many tentative schemes for buying up tracts in Texas or Michigan to form colonies within colonies.

Surely of profound importance, too, was the American Civil War, which broke out before the main wave of German-Jewish immigrants had become completely settled. The war accelerated the pace of Americanization for those Jews who participated in the fighting; but none could remain aloof from the struggle. All groups, immigrant and native, became partisans, sharing the privations and, to a lesser degree, the passions and prejudices of their neighbors. All groups felt that they had earned their stake in their country. They belonged to it, for they had suffered for it, and this feeling of belonging affected significantly the inner life of American Jewry during the post-war generation. Reform Judaism, for example, consciously adapting American and Jewish traditions, entered its greatest period of expansion after the war. By the 1880's the German-Jewish immigrants of the early and mid-nineteenth century had virtually completed the process of acculturation.

COMMUNITY ORGANIZATION IN THE "GERMAN" PERIOD OF IMMIGRATION

Following the pattern which dominated the early years of Jewish settlement in the New World, American Jews continued at first to make their houses of worship the focal points of their communities. Until about 1820, it was not uncommon for parochial schools, charitable and philanthropic societies, and fraternal organizations to remain as integral components of the synagogue-center, giving it vague resemblance to the old synagogue of the European ghetto. But even before the beginning of the German migration of the 1820's and 1830's, this all-embracing synagogue-complex began to decline. It was, first of all, rather too authoritarian to survive in democratic America. The incubus of the European caste system, where the wealthy alone could afford pews, where the rich alone were eligible for synagogue honors, provoked the less affluent immigrants into founding their own congregations. And there were secessions from these new synagogues as well, notably in New York City. It has earlier been cited how, in 1825, disaffected Ashkenazim seceded from *Shearith Israel,* the original Sephardic congregation of the city, and founded Congregation *B'nai Jeshurun.* No sooner, however, was *B'nai Jeshurun* established than, in 1828, a number of its Polish-Jewish members withdrew to form the *Anshe Chesed* synagogue. This process repeated itself many times. By mid-century New York alone possessed some fifty or sixty Jewish congregations. The proliferation of these synagogues was due less to secession, however, than to the natural growth of the Jewish population in America. Indeed, most of the congregations emerged out of simple gregariousness, out of the desire of kindred folk to worship together. The immigrants, flooding into the country in ever-increasing numbers, exulted when they discovered, for the first time, that they were free to worship wherever and with whomever they pleased.

It was not only the fragmentation of religious units, however, but also the multiplicity of Jewish communal activities which doomed the over-all synagogue domination. The problem of raising and distributing funds for the crush of frightened, penniless Jewish immigrants who arrived after 1820 simply became too large for the synagogue to handle—especially if, as was increasingly the case, the congregations themselves were breaking up into new groups. Besides, a man who could not afford to be a pew-member of a congregation could belong to a *hevra,* a burial society, for a mere three dollars a year. In 1860 there were some thirty-five permanently organized burial, mutual aid, and charitable societies in New York, twenty-three in Philadelphia, and several in each of the small Jewish communities of the Midwest. Even New York's Hebrew Benevolent Society, a general communal charity rather than a mutual benefit association, felt compelled, in the 1850's, to relinquish its narrow synagogue affiliation. Eventually, in fact, this Society became the outstanding Jewish philanthropic organization in the city. It is significant that the Jews were usually willing to establish their own institutions at considerable expense rather than rely upon public welfare agencies. Their sense of insecurity, a heritage of many centuries, made them take with the utmost seriousness the stipulation by which they had first been permitted in Nieuw Amsterdam—that they "not become a charge upon the deaconry or the Company." Conversely, the very existence of specifically Jewish philanthropies served to accentuate and perpetuate a sense of Jewish cohesiveness and group identity.

For many thousands of lonely and isolated German Jews, dispersed throughout the United States, some sort of organization was needed to supply the comradeship and sense of "belonging" which, as aliens, they did not possess. The local synagogue certainly could not meet the need— especially the synagogue of a small Jewish community. In the first half of the nineteenth century, one of the noteworthy features of the American social scene was its large number of Masonic lodges, *Turnvereinen,* and other fraternal orders. These groups usually started out functionally, by providing the burial and insurance benefits that were important for native and immigrant alike. Frequently, members were prevented by pride from accepting charity; but they could meet their problems and still retain their self-respect through help from the society's treasury. As the burial society was the forerunner of the mutual aid society, so the mutual aid society was the forerunner of the lodge and the fraternal order. And the nation-wide fraternal order, the capstone of the whole hierarchy, offered something far more mysterious and wonderful than mere financial aid; it offered prestige, strength, comradeship, ceremony, ritual, and honorific title.

The confluence of these factors was most apparent in the operation of America's first Jewish fraternal group, the Independent Order of B'nai B'rith. Founded in New York in 1843, B'nai B'rith combined mutual aid functions with purely fraternal features. It did not hesitate to borrow its secret ritual from the Masons. In fact, the earliest founders of B'nai B'rith—Henry Jones, William Renau, Isaac Rosenberg—were all Masons of high degree. The Order prospered. B'nai B'rith lodges sprang up in Cincinnati, Baltimore, and Philadelphia. By 1860 B'nai B'rith was organizing District Grand Lodges to supervise and centralize the activities of its more than fifty local units. The Order's annual conventions, drawing their delegates from all over the country, began to attract nation-wide attention in the American press. B'nai B'rith's officials luxuriated, as did their Christian counterparts in the Masons, in a glamorous world of make-believe. Usually they borrowed their exalted titles from Jewish lore. Thus, the Grand Master became the Grand *Sar;* the Grand Secretary was the Grand *Mazkir;* the highest ruling body burgeoned out as the Grand *Zekenim.* The proceedings of the typical early B'nai B'rith meeting were characterized by secret passwords drawn from German and Hebrew sources, inner and outer guards, regalia, rosettes, initiations, and other elaborate solemnities. Affiliation with a B'nai B'rith lodge was a coveted social distinction among the German Jews of the mid-nineteenth century.

With this fraternal order, and with others less widely established, the German Jews broadened, if they did not at first deepen, the basis of Jewish life in the United States. By making efforts to unite on a national scale, they battered down the self-contained, independent "Jewries" of separate synagogues which the immigrants had initially transplanted in America. Of course, fraternal orders such as B'nai B'rith could not represent American Jewry "officially," for they were primarily social organizations. But, with a membership of fifty thousand Jews by 1860 as contrasted with a combined synagogue membership of only fifteen thousand, they could speak with a measure of authority. After all, the fraternal orders were democratic; they accepted anyone who could pay his dues and acquire a sponsor. They were not ridden with theological disputes. It is significant that the words of the B'nai B'rith Charter promised to "banish from its deliberations all doctrinal and dogmatic discussions," for these were the bane of the synagogue, "and by the practice of moral and benevolent precepts bring about union and harmony" among the Jews. The term "Jew" now assumed a broader meaning for the lodge member, a meaning which transcended synagogue membership and came also to mean fraternal and social camaraderie.

Even education, the last of the synagogue's extrareligious responsibilities, was now detached and transferred. For by mid-century Jewish children were at liberty to abandon the parochial school for the free, secular, and eventually compulsory public school of New York and other American cities. Soon worship alone remained the function of the venerable old institution, whose shadow had dominated Jewish life in Europe for nearly two thousand years.

RELIGIOUS AND CULTURAL DEVELOPMENTS WITHIN THE AMERICAN-JEWISH COMMUNITY

We have discussed (in Chapter I) the awesome penalty which the European Jewish community imposed upon those of its members who defected from the Jewish group: excommunication beyond the pale of Jewish society. A Jew so ostracized found himself in a bleak "no man's land" between equally hostile Jewish and Christian worlds. In the United States, however, there were no effective penalties. Here a Jew who dared to be lax in his religious observances found himself in a goodly company, Christian as well as Jewish. Christians flouted the desiccated "blue laws" openly. Piety apparently was not the prevailing custom any longer. Why, therefore, should it dominate the lives of Jews when social and legal compulsions no longer acted upon them? When economic and social contacts among Christians were open and often quite cordial? As German-Jewish peddlers fanned out into the American prairies and plains, it became increasingly difficult even to assemble a *minyan* for worship. Intermarriage was not uncommon, although neither was it as common as among the earlier Sephardic community, and many hundreds of individuals and families simply lost contact with the Jewish community and fell away. This "leakage" from the Jewish group did not affect all Jews by mid-nineteenth century, nor even most of them. But a far larger minority was lost in the process of Americanization than was the case even in Germany proper.

Perhaps the dilemma of the newly arrived immigrants could also be attributed to another factor: the absence of dynamic leadership. No single lay leader of the pre-Civil War era achieved national prominence. There was no American counterpart to Europe's Moses Montefiore. As late as 1840, spiritual leadership rested not with rabbis, but rather with cantors or teachers who discharged official functions because they were the only ones available, often with a minimal Jewish background. Isaac Leeser was one of the earliest of these lay preachers to offer the American-Jewish community anything approaching authentic leadership. Born in Westphalia in 1806, Leeser arrived in Richmond, Virginia, at the age of eighteen to enter his uncle's business. While training as a bookkeeper, he volunteered to conduct services at the local congregation. His offer was gladly accepted for he was the only Jew in the community who could remember the fundamentals of his early religious instruction. In his spare time Leeser dashed off for the Richmond *Whig* several articles in defense of Judaism. To his amazement the articles attracted nation-wide attention. The following year, 1829, Philadelphia's distinguished *Mikveh Israel* congregation asked him to become its cantor-preacher. Leeser, barely twenty-three years old, accepted.

For thirty-nine years this scholarly, bespectacled string bean of a man served Philadelphia Jewry with love and devotion. He was an astonishingly creative person. It was Leeser who tried to organize a Jewish Publication Society; a similar, later organization became the principal vehicle for promotion of popular Jewish literature in America. The monthly journal which Leeser edited, *The Occident,* was basic pabulum for thousands of literate Jewish families on the Eastern seaboard. His English translation of the Bible remained standard for American Jewry until the twentieth century. It was Leeser, too, who introduced the regular sermon in English. He did this quietly, unobtrusively, at a time when the issue of the sermon was tearing German Jewry apart. Many of his ideas, such as the establishment of a Jewish-sponsored institution of higher learning, were so new and revolutionary that they failed during his lifetime. It was rather difficult to associate this kind of prescience and imagination with a man whose personal mannerisms were so difficult and eccentric, whose sermons and writings were so maddeningly long-winded and pedantic. Yet, but for Leeser's efforts, traditional Judaism might not have survived in recognizable form in the period before the Russian-Jewish immigration.

Meantime the rise of Reform Judaism generated a basic controversy out of which a number of new dominating personalities emerged. It was a controversy not unaffected by the individualism and noncomformity which characterized American life in general, and American religious life in particular. In the period before the Civil War, a developing folk-movement of Protestants was in open rebellion against the static ecclesiasticism of the country's established churches. Denominations and theological schools were rent by strife and ill feeling. Mormonism was in its period of gestation. Emerson, Alcott and the Transcendentalists, the Millerites and Unitarians preached their gospels during the "restless 30's and 40's." It was against this background of religious unrest and schismatic violence that Reform Judaism made its way in the New World.

The first inkling of "revolt" appeared in 1824, in the synagogue of Charleston, South Carolina. A handful of congregants sought to transplant some of the reforms of Germany's Hamburg Temple: insistence upon greater decorum, modification of ritual, abridgment of the Sabbath service, prayers in the vernacular. The effect of this minority effort was to stimulate into existence a few quasi-Reform congregations. The movement gained depth with the arrival of large numbers of German Jews, whose religious and lay leaders had been trained in Germany and had brought with them carefully prepared doctrinal and philosophic conceptions. Such men were Rabbi David Einhorn of Baltimore's *Har Sinai* Congregation, Rabbi Samuel Adler and Rabbi Gustave Gottheil of New York's illustrious *Emanu-El* synagogue. And yet, although a good deal of the dogma of Reform was imported from Germany, the motivation and climate of the movement were essentially native. Unfettered either in expression or in organization in America, Reform was at liberty to go to more radical extremes. There were some Reform congregations, for example, that abolished not only the incidental anachronisms of Jewish ritual, but also some of the most fundamental and characteristic Jewish laws and practices—and this at a time when Reform Judaism in Germany, for reasons mentioned earlier, tended to become more conservative.

Reform Judaism in America reached its maturity under the guidance of one of its most eloquent and gifted leaders, Isaac Mayer Wise. Born in Bohemia, where he received his rabbinical training, Wise came to the United States to accept a pulpit in Albany in 1846. Already in these early years of his service in upstate New York, he demonstrated the qualities which were to make a major impact on the American-Jewish scene: tireless energy, pugnacity, and organizational genius. In 1854 he accepted the call to a prominent pulpit in Cincinnati, where he remained for forty-six years until his death in 1900. Within half a decade of his arrival in Cincinnati, Wise became the most active and renowned rabbi in the United States. He was the author of numerous articles on theology and history, wrote a dozen novels (fair to mediocre) and two plays (bad). He edited two truly splendid newspapers, *The Israelite* and *Die Deborah,* one in English, the other in German. These journals were read avidly by Jews scattered throughout the continent, and were authoritative sounding boards of Jewish life. Wise was active, too, in the civic life of Cincinnati; he spoke frequently at public forums on behalf of the Democratic Party and the anti-abolitionist cause. A liberal in so many ways, he nevertheless maintained an equivocal attitude on the question of slavery; his admirers insisted, however, that this was merely his technique of maintaining contact with Southern Jewry. Wise's hurried, bandy-legged gait and mutton-chop whiskers eventually became as familiar to the Christians as to the Jews of Cincinnati. His principal claim to fame, however, lay in his herculean efforts to formulate a rationale for Reform Judaism and to buttress it with appropriate and enduring institutions.

Soon after Wise's arrival in the Midwest he published a new prayer book, *Minhag Amerika*—"the American Rite." A coldly modern work, it divested the liturgy of most of the Hebraisms, anachronisms, along with most of the warmth of the old-fashioned *Siddur.* Its influence was far-reaching; indeed, the Einhorn prayer book, which later became the forerunner of the standard American Reform prayer book, was largely based on Wise's *Minhag.* After completion of the prayer book, Wise directed his efforts to the successful creation of a formal union of Reform congregations. In 1873 one of his enduring monuments came into being, the Union of American Hebrew Congregations, comprising both lay and rabbinical representatives. Two years later, the indefatigable Wise organized America's first rabbinical seminary, the Hebrew Union College, strenuously Reform in curriculum and orientation.

The principles of the American Reform movement were not formulated systematically, however, until 1885. It was then that a conference of Reform rabbis, meeting in Pittsburgh, officially endorsed a manifesto, a statement of the Reform position. The statement was written primarily by Kaufman Kohler, but it was Wise's skill and tact in negotiation which brought about its acceptance. The Pittsburgh "Platform" was not intended to be a creed, but rather a set of guiding principles. As in Germany, it insisted that Judaism was an evolutionary faith. The preservation of historical identity was urged, but not the continuity of tradition. The Talmud was to be considered not as legislation but as nothing more or less than "religious literature." The synagogue liturgy was "de-Orientalized." With the publication of these "suggestions," the Reform movement made a clean break with the nominally Orthodox tenets of the older American-Jewish community. Wise was determined, moreover, that Reform would never lack for authorized spokesmen and interpreters; in 1889 he culminated a lifetime of organizational accomplishment by establishing the Central Conference of American Rabbis, the official "legislature" of Reform Judaism in America.

It was Wise's fond hope that the institutions he created—the Union, the College, the Conference—might include all elements of American Judaism. But he was doomed to disappointment, for the Orthodox and Conservatives recoiled from them in horror. The fruits of Wise's incredible energy and administrative skill were sufficiently abundant, however; by the end of the 1880's Reform Judaism had been accepted by the majority of America's German Jews. When the devout, skullcapped Russian immigrants arrived in the United States at the turn of the century, bringing their deep-rooted religious traditionalism with them, the established German Jews disdained to dispute any longer over points of theology. Reform, by then, had become the citadel of their established nativism.

EFFORTS TO UNITE

Persistent efforts were made during the course of the nineteenth century to create a united American-Jewish community. An instrument was sought to transcend the unofficial fraternal or religious groupings of the country, and to facilitate unity of action on philanthropic matters and on matters which affected American Jewry as a whole. Leeser led such an attempt in 1841 and Wise made the effort in 1848. But the plans of both floundered because the devotees of Orthodoxy and Reform were continually at each other's throats. It was, moreover, the mutual and personal hostility of Wise and Leeser, both of them prima donnas of classic stature, which undermined the most promising attempt at union: the Board of Delegates of American Israelites. This was an organization founded in 1859 by Rabbi Samuel Isaacs of New York in shocked reaction to the Mortara case, the kidnaping of a Jewish child in Italy for the purpose of forced baptism. The response to Isaacs' appeal was initially encouraging; the conference call was answered by many congregations, including thirteen from outside New York. A constitution was drawn up, officers were elected, and the first authentic nation-wide colloquium of American Jewry came into existence. But the effort collapsed only a few years afterward. Wise, an advocate of religious Reform, was continually at swords' points with Leeser; moreover, the "aristocratic" Sephardic congregations of New York and Philadelphia refused to be swallowed in a democratic body dominated by German and Polish Jews. The basic cleavages were then deepened by the Civil War, in which Jews largely shared the sectional passions and prejudices of their neighbors.

Essentially, however, it was heterogeneity of background which divided the Jews. Unlike such national immigrant groups as the Irish, the Germans, the English, or the Swedes, the Jews had come to America from widely separated European areas. They spoke different languages, and represented a variety of cultural backgrounds which embraced hundreds of rooted and distinctive customs and traditions. Groups of immigrants formed their own synagogues with these differences in mind. Even in as small a community as Zanesville, Ohio, the Jews were unable to organize a congregation, because they could not agree upon any one of the four rites among them. In New York, in 1860, French, Polish, Portuguese, English, Russian, Dutch, German, and Bohemian Jews all insisted upon maintaining synagogues of their own. If Jews were so divided by linguistic and cultural barriers that even local differences could not be transcended, it was little wonder that they should have found it impossible to unite on a national scale. Of course, American freedom offered a welcome escape from the iron discipline European Jewry had endured for centuries under authoritarian governments and government-sponsored *kahals*. And, too, anxiety about prejudice was undoubtedly a factor which frightened many Jews away from the projects for national union. Significant numbers of the newcomers were determined to blend quietly with their surroundings, to avoid giving offense or the impression that there was a Jewish bloc or, perhaps, a Jewish "vote." Who knew but that American Protestants would misunderstand the purposes of such union? It could easily be confused as a counterpart of the Catholic hierarchy which the Know-Nothing crusade had stigmatized as un-American.

And yet, despite the failure of all attempts to create a formal, nation-wide, fully representative Jewish organization, there already existed a kind of emotional American-Jewish unity as early as mid-century. Bertram Korn has shrewdly pointed out that this feeling of mutual comradeship revealed itself in many actions and reactions that were shared by the overwhelming majority of American Jews. They were, for example, bitterly opposed to all attempts to convert them; they were still the "stiff-necked people," even in the pioneer towns of Texas or Nebraska. Occasionally they would intermarry, but formal conversion to Christianity was not common. They fought unremittingly for the constitutional rights of their people; for equal treatment before the law; for the excision of exclusive references to Christianity in public proclamations and documents; for repeal of religious tests for office in the few states that still maintained such tests. They responded eagerly to Moses Montefiore's appeals on behalf of the oppressed Jews in Morocco or Persia; they shared the anguish of their European brethren over the Damascus Blood Libel and the Mortara case. This sense of community overcame snobbery and the hauteur of caste. It provided the sustaining basis for aid and comfort when, a few decades later, millions of bedraggled, exotic-looking Eastern European Jews shuffled off the gangplanks and into the waiting rooms of Castle Garden and Ellis Island.

CONCLUSION

German-Jewish life in America was characterized by much more than a sense of mutual community. It was characterized by freedom. The Jews of America were free, profoundly free, freer than Jews anywhere else on the face of the earth. They were free from the ecclesiastical-feudal tradition of Jew-hatred which prevailed in the Old World, and which sputtered anew from time to time out of the recesses of the constitutional West. They were free, too, from blind reaction on the Russian model, from the medieval Judeophobia of the Orthodox Church, and the kind of clumsy autocracy represented by Czarist cameralism. The United States, after all, had been forged from its very colonial beginnings in the mold of eighteenth-century rationalism; and with the exception of the Old South, the American people were little preoccupied with feudal traditionalism, which had never taken root in the first place.

There had been ugly episodes, especially during the Civil War, when partisanship was sometimes stigmatized in anti-Jewish terms. But while such manifestations were far from uncommon in nineteenth-century America, rarely did Christians react to their Jewish neighbors in terms of cold vindictive malice. As yet, no frame of reference existed for enduring religious hatred in a country which had been created of many persecuted sects and peoples, and which had scrupulously and painstakingly constitutionalized their security. It was perhaps the very vulnerability of America's peoples which made them invulnerable. It is not unlikely, too, that the Civil War, into the vortex of which was projected nearly every variety of fratricidal impulse, delayed for several decades the advent of organized anti-Semitism; for a while the country had purged itself of its hostilities. Most important of all, however, was the abundance of other preoccupations: too much frontier land to conquer; too many resources to plumb; too much money to make. Throughout the nineteenth century opportunities—for economic enrichment, political advancement, intellectual and religious self-expression—dazzled the view of native and immigrant alike. They looked not at each other, but at vistas of personal fulfillment those opportunities opened.

Notes

Page 165. Döhla's diary extract may be found in Rudolf Glanz, *Jews in Relation to the Cultural Milieu of the Germans in America*, p. 20.

Pages 166-7. Quotations from Kompert and Brandeis from Mark Wischnitzer, *To Dwell in Safety*, pp. 18-19, 22.

Pages 167, 170. Rosenbaum's diary extracts appear in Guido Kisch, "A Voyage to America Ninety Years Ago," *Publications of the American Jewish Historical Society*, XXXV, 1939.

IX

False Dawn in the East

In 1855 Nicholas the barracks master died, and the prestige of his regime died with him. As a direct result of inefficiency and corruption in high places, Russia had suffered disastrous military defeats in the Crimean War. The Russian people were shaken to their depths, not merely by the thousands of wasted lives, but by their sudden awareness that the autocracy's very *raison d'être*—military efficiency—had been proved worthless. A revulsion against the sterile apparatus of repression began to sweep through Russia; people desired a change, and began at last to express that desire openly.

It was in the midst of this growing unrest that the new czar, Alexander II, ascended the throne. Immediately following his coronation, Alexander issued a pronunciamento to his people. It was his intention, he declared, to provide "education, equal justice, tolerance, and humaneness" for every citizen in Russia. The statement, which today reads as an innocuous political platitude, generated indescribable excitement among the Russian people of Alexander's time. The very words—"equal justice, tolerance"—had not been part of the czarist vernacular for decades; their use now seemed to betoken monumental improvements in the public welfare. Wherever the thirty-seven-year-old czar went, he was cheered enthusiastically. His tall, erect figure and calm, china-blue eyes inspired confidence in all who saw him. "There are periods in history," wrote Michael Katkov in 1857, " . . . when to the depths of the innermost soul one clearly hears the answers which bring peace and blessed-ness to the heart . . . when people with a quickening of the heart merge in the common cause and feeling. Happy are the generations which are destined to live in such a period. Thank God!—we are privileged to live in such an epoch." Hardly had the young czar moved into the royal palace at St. Peters-burg than he was acclaimed as "Czar-Liberator" by ecstatic crowds milling in the public square below.

In Alexander II were to be found many of the qualities that had char-acterized his uncle Alexander I. He, too, was a vaguely good-hearted man.

He, too, had been influenced by the humanitarian ideals of his tutor—in this case, the poet Vasili Zhukovski—and was not unwilling to take measures for the alleviation of suffering. But, again like Alexander I, the new czar was at cross-purposes with himself. Fundamentally he had little real sympathy for the cause of liberalism. Throughout his reign he maintained a police regime of exceptional severity, and was responsible for sending thousands of people into Siberian exile without the formality of a trial. Some historians have divided Alexander's reign into an early, liberal period, and a later, reactionary period. But such a division is artificial. Whatever liberal measures he enacted during the early years of his reign were made grudgingly, as half-hearted concessions to a dangerously disaffected people; and even these reforms were at best half-measures of exasperating incompleteness.

No one, however, could predict that the czar would ultimately reverse himself; and the edicts with which he opened his reign seemed to augur well for the future. The censorship of the press was relaxed. Virtually all restrictions on foreign travel were removed. The inquisitorial "Third Section" of the Ministry of Interior was deprived of its power and authority. Universities were opened to students drawn from all economic groups. In 1861 Alexander turned his attention to Russia's forty-seven million serfs, whose status was perhaps the principal anachronism of the times. He granted these peasants their legal freedom, at the same time compensating the landowners with funds raised by a huge bond issue. It was at best a complicated and unsatisfactory solution; for until they repaid this loan, the peasants were not permitted to own their plots of land except as co-operative members of a mir, a collective farm. Nevertheless, the fact that the peasantry had at last won its legal freedom represented a landmark in Russian history. And there were other reforms, too. Representative government was cautiously introduced through a system of advisory local assemblies known as zemstvos. The judicial system was reconstructed on Western lines; jury trials were permitted for the first time in Russian history. Military service was reduced from the living death of twenty-five years to a maximum of six years. These measures may have been inadequate, but they gave the impression that Russia was at last advancing into a new era of enlightenment and toleration.

ALEXANDER II AND THE JEWS: FIRST PHASE

No people held higher hopes for the future than the three million Jews in the Pale of Settlement. They sensed in the young czar a modern-day Cyrus, and they waited breathlessly for the chains of Babylon to be struck off. The times were auspicious for Jewish emancipation. Liberal sentiment in Russia was already far ahead of official reform. By the middle of the nineteenth century European culture was no longer remote; the typical educated Russian counted the Western humanist tradition as part of his heritage. One result of this intellectual maturity was a significant decline in the old medieval-religious suspicion of the Jew. This was particularly apparent in the Russian press. In 1858, for example, an article in the *Russky Invalid* ("Russian

Veteran"), a publication of the Ministry of War, evidenced the welcome spirit of friendship:

> Let us be worthy of our age; let us give up the childish habit of pre-senting the Jews in our literary works as ludicrous and ignominious creatures. On the contrary, remembering the causes which brought them to such a state, let us not forget the innate ability of the Jews for the arts and sciences; and by offering them a place among us, let us utilize their energy, readiness of wit, and skill as a new means for satisfying the ever-growing needs of our people.

The influential *Russky Vestnik* ("Russian Messenger") also pleaded the cause of tolerance: "The time for making attacks on the Jews has passed forever. Rather let us defend ourselves against their justified attacks, and through our actions nullify the truth of Shylock's famous words: 'The villainy you teach me, I will execute.' " The provincial government attorney, I. N. Kozakovski, begged the czar and his advisers to remove the

> disabilities imposed on the Jews; organize commercial and trade schools for them; and that same people which at present is regarded as the scourge of the population of the Western provinces, will be transformed into arteries, carrying life-giving sap into all parts of the empire.

These public appeals for brotherhood and understanding were hailed with enthusiasm by Jewish writers. The Jewish novelist Lev Levanda ventured to equate Russia's philo-Semites—Kozakovski, Lanskoy, Stroganov—with Macaulay and Disraeli.

Had the Jews really understood the "Czar-Liberator's" attitude toward them, they would have been less than optimistic about the likelihood of com-plete emancipation. The truth was that Alexander shared Nicholas's distrust of the "stiff-necked" people, and the notion of granting them full civil equality frankly horrified him. When, therefore, Lanskoy, the Minister of the Interior, urged that the Pale of Settlement be abolished as a first step toward "amalgamating" the Jews with the Russian people, the czar flatly demurred. Nor was he influenced by the opinions of high local and central administrative officials who urged the removal of residence restrictions and other oppressive disabilities. Alexander had no confidence whatever in the honorable qualities of the Jews; like his father, he expected them to "earn" their civil rights through "moral improvement."

Alexander's dislike of the Jews notwithstanding, the tenor of the times demanded some improvement in Jewish status, if only as a more modern and effective translation of the old ideal of "amalgamation." One of the first problems to claim the czar's attention, therefore, a relic of his father's un-successful Jewish policy, was the six-year period of military "cantonment," the creeping horror of Russian-Jewish life. In 1856 he issued a ukase abolish-ing it. The joy this edict aroused within the Jewish community may well be imagined. A former Jewish cantonist recalled that "the news was to us as the sound of the great shofar which will awaken the dead on the Day of

Resurrection." Throughout the Pale, synagogues were filled to overflowing with Jews who came to observe special thanksgiving services. The Jewish children who had been coerced into Christianity during their term of military service were not allowed to return to their families. Still, coming as it did with the suspension of Russia's twenty-five-year draft, the abandonment of the cantonment system lifted the single most unbearable incubus of Jewish life.

Meantime Alexander ordered a reappraisal of the harsh "amalgamation" laws of his imperial predecessors, a reappraisal not for their cruelty, but for their inefficiency. He realized that new techniques must be devised for a more practicable "fusion" of the Jewish and Russian peoples. Whereas Nicholas had penalized "useless" categories of Jews by heaping disabilities upon them, Alexander reversed the process by rewarding the more "useful" elements among the Jewish population, people of superior financial or educational potentialities. The more valuable a class of Jews became to the state, the more, in turn, would its rights be enlarged. This policy bore a striking resemblance to Frederick the Great's system of "general privileges"; as always, Russia panted a steady century behind the times. In 1865 a government decree permitted "large-scale" Jewish merchants, Jewish university graduates, and skilled Jewish artisans to move into the Russian interior. It was the czar's devout wish, as it had been Frederick's a century earlier, that Jewish capital might be attracted to Russian industrial ventures, that Jewish artisans and mechanics might provide valuable services to Russia's backward rural population. Educated Jews were welcome, too, because they were more likely to "have renounced the errors of fanaticism."

The irony of Alexander's policy was that it opened the Russian interior precisely to those privileged Jews who suffered least from the Pale's congestion. On the other hand, Jewish peddlers and shopkeepers, for whom congestion and competition had become virtually insupportable, were specifically denied permission to leave the Pale. Hence, many of the more desperate moved into the interior anyway, disguising themselves as artisans or professional men. Their position was precarious in the extreme. They lived by sufferance of police bribery, and were never quite certain when an ominous knock on the door would signal their arrest and expulsion.

Alexander II's "emancipation" continued. His national reforms were not tarnished by the old formula *Kromye Zhydov*—"except the Jews." All Jews possessing the necessary agricultural or commercial qualifications were granted "active" and "passive" suffrage within the scheme of zemstvo self-government. In the southern provinces, in fact, Jews not only participated in these rural assemblies but occasionally were appointed to rural office. Nor did the liberally conceived Judicial Regulations of 1864 contain any significant discriminations against Jews; within a few years a number of Jewish lawyers attained prominence as members of the Russian bar. The old czarist missionary zeal began at last to decline. The bribery, the torture, the economic pressure once employed by the government to encourage Jewish apostasy now were gradually abandoned; after all, under Nicholas, these techniques had not succeeded. Alexander recognized, too, that political and cultural "amalgamation" did not necessarily require religious homogeneity. Thus, in 1873, the ill-considered Crown school system, which for years had persisted in theory only, was done away with once and for all. It hardly mattered; Jews by the thousands began to matriculate in Russian schools. The Russian bureaucracy noted with astonishment and pleasure that the new system of "quasi-emancipation" was infinitely more effective than the old techniques of force and repression.

Both within the Pale and beyond, new Jewish communities were established, composed primarily of wholesale merchants, industrialists, financiers, academicians, artisans, and discharged veterans—Jews whose vocations brought them into closer contact with Russian life and rendered them more susceptible to "amalgamation." They were quick to adopt the Russian language and Russian habits of dress and behavior; they sent their children to Russian schools and brought them up in the Russian manner. As the new "aristocrats" of Russian-Jewish life, they encouraged their fellow Jews to follow their example, to "Russify" themselves, and in this fashion to win commensurate privileges from the government. When Moses Montefiore returned to St. Petersburg in 1872 he was astonished to discover there a Jewish community which had advanced by centuries beyond the Jewish towns and villages of the Pale.

> I conversed [he noted in his Diary] with Jewish merchants, literary men, editors of Russian periodicals, artisans and persons who had formerly served in the imperial army, all of whom alluded to their present position in the most satisfactory terms. All blessed the Emperor, and words seemed wanting in which adequately to praise his benevolent character. The Jews now dress like ordinary gentlemen in England, France, or Germany. Their schools are well attended, and they are foremost in every honourable enterprise destined to promote the prosperity of their community and the country at large.

As in Western Europe, the Russian program of "quasi-emancipation" fostered an intense feeling of national pride among the Jews. In the memoirs of his childhood, a Jewish writer recalls the enthusiasm with which his parents and teachers hailed the emancipation of the serfs in 1861. "Their faces glowed with joy," he wrote, "just as though they themselves had been liberated." Panegyrics extolling the "Czar-Liberator" and the new era he had inaugurated filled the pages of Hebrew periodicals. One of these magazines greeted the end of Russian serfdom with the verse from Solomon's Song of Songs: "The time of the [birds'] singing is come, and the voice of the turtledove is heard in our land." Jews who had once been compelled to live in seclusion in the Pale of Settlement were unrestrained in their warm affection for the language and culture of "Mother Russia." "Our motherland," declared *Razvet,* the Russian-Jewish newspaper, "is Russia. And just as her air is ours, so, too, must her language be ours." Zeiberling, the Jewish social worker, strongly advised his fellow Jews to engage Russian nurses for their children, in order that the Russian "spirit" and language might be absorbed from infancy. *Razvet* advocated, too, that the Russian language be adopted in Jewish government schools in place of German, which until then had been the *lingua franca* of secular instruction. German, the paper argued, could not possibly take the place of "the beautiful and rich Russian language, which is the inheritance of everyone who calls Russia his motherland."

Accustomed originally to a purely separatistic environment, Russian Jews had never been particularly concerned about the attitudes of their Christian neighbors. Now, however, as many of them emerged from their isolation, they became quite sensitive to non-Jewish opinion, and increasingly conscious of their own dignity. Friendly gestures on the part of Russian officials evoked enthusiastic comment in the Jewish press. In the 1860's government representatives often appeared at celebrations in Jewish schools, at farewell dinners, even at occasional *bar mitzvot* (confirmations). Jews in turn were occasionally admitted into Russian social circles and Russian clubs. These manifestations of interest and regard were joyously welcomed, particularly by the "enlightened" Jews of the time. In some ways the growing *haut monde* contact between Russian and Jew was not unlike Berlin's "salon era" of nearly a century earlier. The ecstatic outburst, for example, with which a Jew of Kovno announced his election to the nobility club, might have been lifted directly from the memoirs of the Mendelssohnian Enlightenment: "What happened! ... What miracles! ... They elected me not in spite of my being a Jew but because of it, so that I might serve as an instrument for the expression of their highest ideas." In their eagerness to bridge the gulf separating them from their Christian neighbors, many Russian Jews interpreted a friendly gesture on the part of non-Jews as evidence of a complete change of heart. "Soon, soon," declared Lev Levanda, "perhaps the door of our little hut, too, will open and we will rush forth to the great celebration of our good mother." As it turned out, "Mother Russia" was still determined to distinguish between her children and her stepchildren.

REACTION UNDER ALEXANDER II

In 1863 "Congress" Poland revolted against Russian rule. The uprising was long and bloody, and it failed. Its most disastrous effect was to release Czar Alexander's long dormant instinct for reaction; he hardly needed convincing now that the Polish revolt was the direct result of his earlier concessions to "Westernization." What Russia needed, apparently, was a firm hand and a clear-cut policy of strict conservatism. The period following the Polish uprising stood out, therefore, in grim contrast to the first eight years of Alexander's reign. All reforms were abruptly halted. The murderous "Third Section" of the Ministry of the Interior was revived and ordered to hunt down liberals and the associates of liberals in all corners of the Empire. The secret police were particularly harsh with Russia's national minorities, for they were under a cloud of suspicion as a result of Polish "disloyalty." At the same time, Alexander and his advisors gave increasing attention to Slavophilism, a nativist philosophy of Orthodoxy and Great Russian nationalism which rejected the ideals of the West and all the trappings of liberalism.

The Jews, the least popular of the Empire's ethnic minorities, took the full brunt of the furious reaction. Once again czarist bureaucracy began to debate the sinister old question: Were the Jews useful or harmful to the State? To what extent, the government wondered, had the Jews "amalgamated" with the Russian people? The answer was that though the urge for Russification was strong among the new Jewish intelligentsia and industrial aristocracy, the broad masses had responded very little to the "reforms" of Alexander's early years. The few gratuities offered them thus far had been insufficient to fill them with a burning desire to "fuse" with the Russian people. The government was little interested in explanations, however; it had found the excuse it needed to reverse its policies in the Pale.

There were others who welcomed the reimposition of Jewish disabilities. For the emergence of a significant Jewish middle class in the interior had aroused the jealousy of the Russian *petit-bourgeoisie*. Actually these Russian small businessmen and white-collar workers suffered very little from Jewish competition; but their frustration when they did not share in the Russian industrial boom was directed, characteristically, against the Jews. In fact, the industrial and mercantile development of the Russian hinterland owed a great deal to the Jews (see page 188 ff.). It was to profit further from their enterprise that Alexander had originally encouraged Jewish settlement beyond the Pale. Now, however, the very success of this scheme provided the rationale for ending it. The Russian middle class, it was decided, had to be protected from "cutthroat Jewish competition."

In reviving its anti-Jewish policy, the czarist regime employed a contemptible technique. It was the technique of the paid government informer. The most notorious of these men was an embittered Jewish apostate named Jacob Brafman. As a youth, Brafman had been impressed into the Russian army by Jewish *khappers*. He never quite recovered from this traumatic experience, and was determined, as a result, to wreak his vengeance on the Jewish community. Appointed an instructor of Hebrew at a Greek Orthodox seminary, Brafman devoted his every spare moment to the mission of luring Jews into baptism. Failing in this effort, he became a full-time lobbyist for anti-Jewish legislation. During the early 1860's he spent months at a time roaming the corridors of government buildings in Vilna and St. Petersburg, buttonholing bureaucrats, and warning them of a "secret" Jewish government which, ostensibly, was inciting the Jews against the State. The "secret" Jewish government to which Brafman referred was none other than the *kahal*; it had never really gone out of existence, he argued. His solution was quite simple: the government must eradicate the last vestiges of Jewish communal autonomy by closing all religious and charitable *hevras*. Eventually Brafman's persistence was rewarded. By order of the Czar himself, the Government Printing Office published the apostate's "revelations" in a rather murky pamphlet entitled *The Book of the Kahal*. It was a hopelessly confused collection of misquotations from Talmudic literature, all of them seemingly hostile to Christianity. Although the pamphlet was easily exposed by competent rabbinical authorities, *The Book of the Kahal* was circulated to Russian officials throughout the country and used as "evidence" of Jewish disloyalty.

Once again, storm clouds gathered over the Pale. In 1871 the Council of

State set up another of its innumerable Jewish "Commissions" to investigate Brafman's accusations against the Jews. The Commission came to few definite conclusions during its haphazard sittings, except to recommend that all vestiges of Jewish separatism must be abolished: the Jewish schools, the mutual relief societies (the *hevras*), anything that tended to foster "communal cohesion among the Jews." While the Commission produced little in the way of anti-Jewish legislation, its hostile spirit put the Jews on notice that the barometer of toleration was falling. Already municipal zemstvos were restricting their Jewish members to one third of their total representation, even in communities that were almost entirely Jewish. Physical requirements for Jewish conscripts were arbitrarily lowered. Here and there ritual murder charges cropped up. On the fringes of the Pale there were increasing numbers of "spontaneous" outbreaks against Jews. During the 1870's it was apparent that the "enlightenment" of Alexander II's early years had hardly been more than a false dawn.

LIFE IN THE PALE: THE ECONOMICS OF LIVING

All their sufferings and tribulations notwithstanding, the Jews of Eastern Europe did manage to reproduce themselves at an extraordinary rate. Even czarist persecution could not counteract the decline in infant mortality. At the opening of the nineteenth century the Jewish population of Russia totaled perhaps a million; fifty years later the number reached three and a quarter million; by the end of the century it grew to nearly five and a half million. These people were concentrated in an area—the Pale of Settlement—of 362,000 square miles, encompassing 20 per cent of European Russia, 4 per cent of the entire Russian Empire. According to the census of 1887, fully a million and a quarter Jews were to be found in former "Congress" Poland; southern Lithuania and White Russia each contained approximately three quarters of a million Jews. Nearly half of this immense Jewish population was to be found in towns and cities; the rest were spread through the villages and the hamlets of the rural areas. By mid-century perhaps 40 per cent of the Jews were engaged in commerce; the others were fairly equally divided between artisanry and personal service. Even this sizable figure of 40 per cent was a much lower proportion of Jewish businessmen—ranging from peddlers to exporters—than in the West. But if not all Jews were merchants, nearly all the merchants of the Pale were Jews. It was this fact which enabled, even if it did not cause, the Russian government to refer contemptuously to Jewish "parasitism," to Jewish overconcentration in trade and commerce.

It was true that the Jews were exceptionally influential in the upper levels of commerce. For one thing, until the second half of the nineteenth century they dominated the liquor traffic of Russia, even as they had Poland's a century earlier. As the principal middlemen in the commerce between city and country, they had learned to avoid the risk of perishable crops and uncertain markets by converting grains and cereal products into mash for distilling purposes. During the first half of the century, therefore, wherever one traveled in Russia, the tavern or inn or liquor store was likely to be

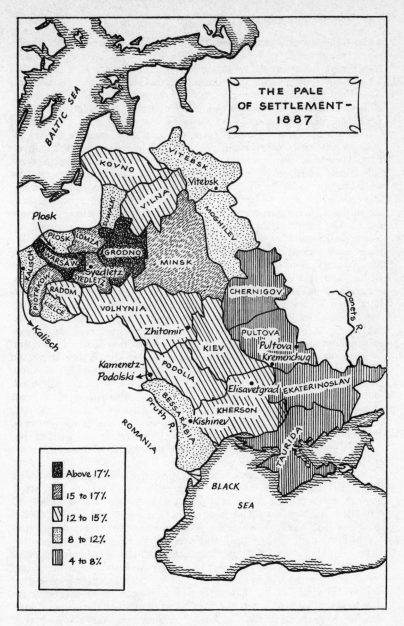

THE PALE OF SETTLEMENT IN WESTERN RUSSIA
(based on statistics of the Russian census of 1887)

under Jewish proprietorship. Above the rank and file of tavern-keepers there was a large minority of Jewish tax-farmers, who enjoyed a monopoly of the collection of liquor excises throughout the Pale, and even within Russia. In 1861, however, the Russian government itself took over the sale and distribution of liquor. While occasional Jewish innkeepers still remained, thousands of Jewish wholesalers, tax agents, distillers, and company agents soon were forced into other occupations.

The capital of these liquor dealers, as well as of other Jewish businessmen, was applied to new enterprises during the 1860's. The Jews who were admitted into the Russian interior during the early years of Alexander's reign were able to take advantage of the industrial awakening which characterized the second half of the nineteenth century. Jewish funds were diverted increasingly into railroad building. In fact, it was the initiative of Jewish contractors that accounted for the construction of fully three fourths of the Russian railroad system. The Poliakovs, the Kronenbergs, the Nathansons, the bankers Efrosi & Co., the Rafaloviches, the Günzbergs, were Russia's most prominent railroad tycoons. They had the most available liquid capital and the best international connections for securing additional funds from their fellow Jews in Berlin, Paris, and Warsaw.

Largely for the same reasons—easy access to capital and advantageous international relationships—Jews were able to lay the basis for modern Russian banking Beginning in 1859 in St. Petersburg, Baron Horace Günzberg established the foundations for one of the largest investment banking systems in Russia; the second largest bank in the capital was that of Meyer & Co. In Warsaw the leading bankers of the second half of the century were the Wawelbergs, the Kronenbergs, and the Frankels. In Odessa the Efrosi Bank played a crucial role in the grain export trade. In the 1870's the Poliakovs founded the Moscow Agrarian Bank, the Moscow International Bank, the Don Agrarian Bank, and the Azov-Don Bank. Another area of Jewish investment, too, was the sugar industry. Here Jews pioneered in the purchase of the beet crops from the estates of Russian aristocrats; they extracted the sugar in their own refineries. Of the three hundred Russian refineries in existence in 1914, one hundred were owned by Jews.

Nevertheless, for most Jews of the Pale, the term "business" hardly meant this kind of industrial or financial pioneering. The Poliakovs and the Günzbergs were as much the exception as were the Court Jews of eighteenth-century Germany. Business meant small shopkeeping and petty trade. "Retail commerce" was the term which the government applied to nearly half the Jewish inhabitants of the Pale. Yet the term "retail commerce" hardly described the kind of marginal existence eked out by hundreds of thousands of miserably impoverished people. It barely described the grocer whose "store" was a rickety stall by the side of a dirt road, the clothing salesman who hawked the virtues of the cloth he carried on his back as he shuffled from door to door. Nor can the term "artisan" properly describe the wagoner who slept in the same stable with his lone, emaciated horse, the carpenter who ate not by virtue of the wages he earned but by sufferance of the weed-strewn truck garden he cultivated behind his shack, the glazier who patched up windows not with glass but with wood planking and rags.

Life in the Pale of Settlement—as, indeed, in all Russia—was grudging and bitter; competition was keen and continual. The typical breadwinner, driven frantic in his efforts to provide for his family, undertook any kind of exhausting and degrading work; he bore, if necessary, the insults and browbeatings of the peasant or local magnate as long as his work led at least to a minimal degree of independence. Yet there were certain well-defined limits beyond which no self-respecting Jew would go. If a Jew kept a shop by which he earned his livelihood, no other Jew presumed to open a shop in immediate competition. If a petty trader haggled with a peasant over the price of a bag of grain, no one else, however anxious he may have been for the profit, intervened. Encroachment was considered a profoundly anti-social act and could even lead to ostracism in the community.

Maurice Samuel, the most discerning Jewish folklorist of our own day, describes the *shtetl* of Kasrielevky, a typical Jewish hamlet in the province of Poltava, whose citizens were immortalized in the writings of the nine-teenth-century Yiddish author Sholom Aleichem:

> Kasrielevky is also Kozodoievka and Bohopolie and Bohslav and any one of a hundred Jewish or half-Jewish centres in old White Russia. The town itself is a jumble of wooden houses clustering higgledy-piggledy about a market-place at the foot of a hill. All around is the spaciousness of mighty Russia, but Kasrielevky is as crowded as a slum, is in fact a slum. . . . The streets of Kasrielevky—let us be courteous and call them that—are as tortuous as a Talmudic argument. They are bent into ques-tion marks and folded into parentheses. They run into culs-de-sac like a theory arrested by a fact; they ooze off into lanes, alleys, back yards, like a thesis dribbling into an anti-climax. Sewerage and paving are as un-known in Kasrielevky as the steam train. . . . Most of the market-place was occupied by pedlars, hangers-on, parodies of commission men, women with a basket of eggs or a bundle of old clothes. And the richest Jew in Kasrielevky could be bought out on the lower margin of four figures. Rich or poor, pedlars or artisans, their livelihood was drawn from the market-place, and from semi-annual fairs. It depends, naturally, on what you call a living. . . . Yerechmiel Moses, the Hebrew teacher, blind in one eye and short-sighted in the other, used to wear spectacles without lenses. Asked why, he would answer triumphantly: "Well, it's better than nothing, isn't it?"

It was certainly better than the life of the Russian peasant. It was better, too, than Russian-Jewish life after the 1880's. For until the reign of Alexan-der III, existence in the Pale remained tolerable—barely tolerable. The notion of political or social protest was never seriously entertained.

A HOLY LIFE

As always, the chief sustaining influence for the Jew was his religion, and piety dominated and suffused every aspect of his life in the Pale. To go on without the facilities of a synagogue, a cemetery, a burial society, a ritual pool for women, without provisions for kosher slaughter—all this was simply unimaginable to the inhabitants of the typical *shtetl*. In the early nineteenth century the *ḳahal* had painstakingly supervised and regulated Jewish religious observance; in later years voluntary committees insured that there were *mezuzot* (hallowed parchment) on every Jewish doorpost, that Jewish worshipers wore their phylacteries properly on their arms, that women scrupulously attended the ritual bath once a month. There were even boards of morals to direct and regulate private lives. When the *ḳahals* were officially abolished in 1844, most of their supervisory functions passed to the special synagogue-boards that maintained intact the full spectrum of Jewish religious observances.

In the typical *shtetl* the rabbi was both the religious and secular leader, while the synagogue remained the religious, cultural, educational, and social center. There was always at least one synagogue, even if it had to be built by borrowing from neighboring communities. The synagogue, or *shul*, was rarely imposing. A slate-gray house, almost invariably dilapidated and leaking, it was quite ugly by any aesthetic standard. Nevertheless, a seat in the *shul* was highly prized. It was either purchased for life or rented annually; for without such a seat a man was not eligible for the exalted honor of introducing the weekly Scriptural reading. In the larger communities there were two varieties of synagogues: one, the *bet ha-ḳneset*, was exclusively a house of prayer, and was closed during the other hours of the day; the other, the *bet ha-midrash*, was open throughout the day for study and for social and communal as well as for religious uses. In the larger communities there were many private synagogues, belonging to the well-to-do; still others were maintained by various occupational groups, *hevras* of butchers or tailors, or even chimney sweeps. In Vilna, by the end of the century, there were no less than one hundred and ten such establishments, and these were exclusive of numerous Hasidic prayer rooms.

The variety of synagogues was exceeded only by the bedlam of devotional practices within. The writer Isaac Baer Levinsohn described the disorder which prevailed in the Volhynian *shul* of the mid-nineteenth century:

> Each chapel or house of prayer or synagogue abides by its own rules; there is no uniformity of service, only general disorder. This one demolishes what another has built; this one jumps while the other shouts; this one moans his loss while the other one complacently smokes; this man eats while that man drinks. One has just begun his prayer as another has finished it, one converses while the next one chants. Here one deliberates on the events of the day and there another indulges in ridicule; this one jokes and that one pulls by the ear. Quarrels and

fisticuffs often ensue about private as well as public matters. This one follows the Ashkenazic ritual, the other the Sephardic, and a third one the Italian. One aspires to the honor of being the sixth to come up to the Torah, another seeks the honor of taking the Torah out of the Ark and often they quarrel on that account, and strive and fight. Absence of decorum was the rule, the gossiping in the women's gallery above calmly ignoring the strenuous entreaties of the beadle to quiet down.

Yet, for all the absence of decorum, and all the interruptions and discursions in the service, the Jews in the synagogue prayed—prayed deeply, devoutly, emotionally, emptying their hearts to God in thankfulness for having been permitted to endure in the midst of a sea of enemies.

In the years before the development of an effective Yiddish press, the synagogue served as the information center of the community. Here, too, matters of equity or personal grievance could be brought to public attention. In fact, it was not uncommon for an aggrieved party to interrupt the reading of the Torah until his tormentor was shamed into giving satisfaction. The *shul* was also the center for the collection and distribution of charity. Many *hevras* and relief organizations derived their regular income from *pushkas,* charity boxes, prominently displayed at entrance or exit. Jewish travelers who were lodged in the annex were cared for with an especial refinement of hospitality because they were under the roof of a holy place. The *shul* also served the community as a semirecreational retreat, a place where people could indulge in friendly, intimate chats and gossip. In the twilight of a winter's day, particularly after long hours of work, groups of Jews would cluster around the warm stove, reminisce about family matters, speculate about the world around them, and deliberately put out of their minds the sordid routine of the struggle for bread. The synagogue, too, was the social club in which the wealthy and ostentatious displayed their rich garments and jewels, the gold-embroidered collars of their prayer shawls, and the silk skullcaps. Family festivities were held in the *shul,* confirmations and weddings and circumcisions. As the celebrants drank wine, ate cake, danced a spirited *freilach* (a Jewish folk dance), it hardly mattered to them that the building in which they were meeting was old and decaying, dirty and ill-smelling.

Far from exacerbating the hardships of life, the Pale's tenacious religious tradition was the principal source of consolation, even of recreation. In the Jewish and Oriental world, all life flowed within the estuaries of the religious experience; and joy was part of life. On the eve of the Sabbath, the Jew threw off his weekday worries; he washed and donned his clean Sabbath clothes; every nook of his house was spotless and shining. His wife, who during the week had been drudging in her kitchen and haggling in the market place, lit the Sabbath candles and self-consciously assumed, once again, the revered role of a queen in the household of Israel. Gone was monotony and dreariness, bitterness and humiliation. The holy Sabbath, the day of rest, the sublime, peaceful day, brought into the Jewish home an added warmth, a precious serenity. Whenever possible the householder shared his Sabbath joy with a dinner guest, for no matter how good the fish and how well-cooked the noodles, they lost much of their savor without a guest at one's elbow. A. S. Sachs recalls how even the shabbiest little Jewish holiday procession generated excitement and delight among its participants and spectators:

> All the houses that lined the route of the procession were duly illu-
> minated by candles placed in the front windows, the youth of the town
> also carrying lighted candles or tapers in their hands as they marched
> bravely along. But all these bright lights were thrown completely in the
> shade by the bright glow of the faces of the Jewish children in their
> experience of a great and holy ecstasy. The band marched at the head,
> playing its tune, the *Hazzan* (cantor) and the choir following directly
> behind them, chanting their songs, while the public at large indulged
> in song and dance. The young and innocent Jewish maidens lined the
> streets, casting admiring glances upon the proud and fresh and happy
> faces of the grown boys, while the happy mothers of the little boys wept
> out of sheer joy. Even wrinkled grannies pushed back their Turkish
> shawls, clapping their hands, the while the grand-dads chimed in by
> the clapping of hands and the snapping of fingers.

It was not all gall and wormwood for the Jews of the Pale.

A PROCESS OF LEARNING

Because cultural activities were steeped in the religious spirit, there was little secular education in the Pale of Settlement until late in the nineteenth century. There was virtually no illiteracy among Russian Jewry, to be sure; learning was a universal pursuit. It was simply that this learning was exclusively religious. At the tender age of four the male child embarked upon his school career at the *heder,* the little private primary school which was usually conducted by a *melamed* of the father's choice. By mid-century there were perhaps six thousand such private schools in the Pale, with about fifteen thousand *melamdim.* The hierarchy of the educational system began with the *heder,* continued with the *Talmud Torah* (secondary school), and was crowned by the *yeshivah* (Talmudical Academy), which was the equivalent of a seminary, and which was usually attended by a select minority of talented students.

The caliber of instruction in the Jewish educational system was probably even more primitive than in the Christian schools. It was not simply that the curriculum of the typical *heder*—consisting of *Alef Bet* (alphabet), *Ivri* (Hebrew), *Humash* (Torah), *Gemara* (the core of the Talmud)—was hopelessly inadequate. There were other factors, too: the rote memorization which substituted, in those days, for understanding; the lamentable physical condition of most of the schools; the damp, foul air, the filthy, spittle-strewn floors, the racking cold in the winter, the endless swarms of flies in the summer. But the most unfortunate anachronism of all was the instructor. The poor *melamed* could never rise above his preoccupation with sheer survival. Tuition fees were modest, and even then hardly ever paid on time. However disciplined his needs, the *melamed* rarely managed to make ends meet. The more he worried, the more irritable he became; and the more restive the *melamed,* the more rebellious the students. When, therefore, the unfortunate children allowed their attention to wander, or occasionally whispered to each other, they were reviled, or slapped, or whipped by their teacher. Shmarya Levin recalls:

> I would not be wrong in saying that one-third of the *heder* hours were taken up by the stupid, ugly squabbles between Rebbi (the *melamed*) and the pupils; the remaining two-thirds poisoned by the first. Who knows how many genuine talents have been brutally done to death by the lash of the *Rebbi,* how many victims remained buried forever under the ruins of that institution known as the *heder?* . . . I cannot stress too often, the dominating, the exclusive role which the *heder* played in the life of the young Jewish boy. He saw his parents only for half an hour in the morning—before first prayers—and then for an hour in the evening, before he went to sleep. . . . Thus the *melamed* became the lord and master of the Jewish child, and the *heder,* the narrow one-roomed school, lightless, unclean, laid its stamp on the Jewish child and brought ruin and misery on its tenderest years. In my time the Jewish *heder* was already an institution rotten in every corner. . . . Only the very few, the chosen ones of fortune, escaped from those years of oppression more or less unharmed, with minds and bodies unruined.

No definite age limit or formal educational accomplishment marked the end of a pupil's school career. If the financial circumstances of his parents permitted, or if he were primarily devoted to scholarship, the student might attend a *yeshivah,* an academy which was built around the personality of a particularly learned rabbi. It happened that the ambition of every noted rabbi was to raise for himself a following of advanced students, and the organization of a *yeshivah* was usually a means to this end. Only three *yeshivot* achieved wide renown, however, all of them in Lithuania, the citadel of Jewish intellectualism. One was located in Volozhin, one in Mir, and one in Vilna. Virtually all of the students who attended the *yeshivot* were quite poor, and could hardly be maintained except by contributions from the general community. Since many came from outlying areas, it was the practice of the *yeshivot* to send collectors throughout Europe and America to raise money. Even with the help of this philanthropy, the typical *yeshivah bocher* lived on the shadow of a mite. He received perhaps seventy-five kopecks a week on which to maintain himself and he waited pathetically for the Sabbath, when he might be invited out for a meal by one of the families. The weekday meal, however, rarely consisted of more than grits cooked in water. It was from this kind of diet that students somehow generated the endurance to study from five in the morning until eleven at night. Most of them slept in the school.

Because knowledge of the Talmud was considered to be a supreme attainment—except in the most ardently revivalist of Hasidic communities—not only the *yeshivah bocher* but virtually every male Jew studied its writings at one time or another in his life. In fact, it was not uncommon for the most practical-minded businessman to spend a few hours weekly at the synagogue after evening services to join in study. If there was such a thing as a typical melody in the Pale of Settlement, it was the soft crooning of voices intoning the Talmudic text, as heads and bodies rocked back and forth over the precious script. Where else but in the Pale were scholars the princes of the community, prized far above the richest of men? It is worth noting, too, that Russian-Jewish culture, while strongly religious in its emphasis, was not entirely unworldly. For the Talmud discussed a wide variety of "practical" matters—civil damages, physical science, sexual relations. The transition from religious to secular education offered no real hurdles for the young people of the *Haskalah* (see Chapter X); this kind of Talmudic training had sharpened their intellects. Nor was it an accident that the first Jewish revolutionary circle in Russia was established at the rabbinical seminary of Vilna. The Talmudic emphasis on humanitarianism prepared the *yeshivah bocher* for the burning idealism of the revolutionary movement.

LIFE IS WITH PEOPLE

We have seen that the Russian government left virtually no stone unturned in its efforts to destroy Jewish separatism: under Nicholas I the bureaucracy resorted to conscription, persecution, Crown schools, and abolition of the *kahal*; in the early years of Alexander II it resorted to blandishments and rewards. But whichever guise the czarist attack assumed, Russian Jewry stubbornly and successfully preserved its communal integrity. In defending themselves against despotism from without, however, Jews frequently created despotisms of their own. Even during the "quasi-emancipation" period of the 1860's the lives of most Jews in the Pale were dominated by an inflexible traditionalism. A short jacket or a trimmed beard were viewed as symptoms of dangerous free-thinking. The old scheme of Jewish family life, with all its patriarchal survivals, remained in force. In spite of the Statute of 1835, which fixed the minimum age of bridegrooms at eighteen and of brides at sixteen, the practice of child marriages nevertheless continued and parents imperturbably arranged alliances between adolescents of thirteen and fifteen. It was not uncommon, as a result, for boys of school age to become husbands and fathers, continuing their education at the *Talmud Torah* or *yeshivah* after their marriage. Not the least of the Pale's tragedies was the fact that children rarely knew what it was to be young and, scarcely out of their teens, they frequently bore the harassed, care-worn appearance of middle-aged men. Moreover, the overemphasis on Talmudic study quite often produced men who were entirely unfit for the battle of life, and it became necessary, in such cases, for dynamic and resourceful wives to take charge of business affairs and become the breadwinners. It achieved little to revolt against the relentless conservatism of Jewish life, especially after the promises of Alexander II had been proved bankrupt. Until late in the nineteenth century, those who ventured to protest against the usages and customs of the Pale were crushed back into conformity by the massive weight of tradition.

Lest the undue reverence for ancient usage be judged too harshly, it is well to recall that it was also responsible for some of the truly noble and exemplary characteristics of Jewish life. Crimes of violence were virtually unknown. More common, perhaps, were such offenses as tax evasion, smuggling, and similar extralegal derelictions that resulted, inevitably, from imposed official disabilities. Infidelity and drunkenness were extremely rare. Talmudic law, which exercised so profound a moral influence, guided the Jew in his social responsibilities. It was this influence, indeed, which accounted for the extraordinary proliferation of charitable agencies in the Pale—the soup kitchens, poorhouses, dispensaries, Passover loan societies, and philanthropic institutions of every variety. Even before the barbarous May Laws of the 1880's, fully a fifth of the Pale's population were the recipients of charity. Those who dispensed this philanthropy were themselves, with but few exceptions, on the borderline of poverty, even of mendicancy. But as long as one had, one gave. In those days there was no compromise on matters of morality and social conscience.

One final word should be added about life in the Pale: it was austerely parochial, insulated even from physical contact with the Russian people. Occasionally, information about the Czar and his family would filter into the Pale through the medium of Hebrew newspapers, the *Hameliz* or the *Hazefirah*. But the political events and activities of official Russia were as foreign and remote to the dwellers of the typical *shtetl* as the secrets of the Persian Court. Although this insularity was modified, as we have seen, during the early years of Alexander II's reign, contact between Russians and Jews remained extremely superficial, and was confined almost exclusively to intermittent business dealings. The Russian population lived on a far lower cultural level than the Jewish population. Russian life was a life of the earth, a life Jews did not understand, which, indeed, they did not care to understand. "What are they shrinking from?" asked Maurice Samuel of the Jewish inhabitants of Kasrielevky. "Perhaps the loneliness and formlessness of space, perhaps the world of the uncircumcised, perhaps the brutalizing influence of untamed nature. They fear the bucolic. They fear, instinctively, the Man with the Hoe, not because they live any better than he, but because his jaw hangs down." Even during the "quasi emancipation" of the 1860's, only a small minority of Jews took the trouble to learn more than a smattering of words in the Russian language. Not that separation between the two peoples necessarily meant hostility:

As far as I remember [wrote Shmarya Levin] the relations between the Jews and the Gentiles in our town were friendly enough. . . . True, we lived in two distinct worlds, but it never occurred to us that *their* world was the secure one, while the foundations of *ours* were shaky. On the contrary, we accounted our world the nobler, the finer, and the higher. Of course we learned even as children that we Jews were a people in exile, such being the divine decree, but that had nothing to do with the details of our daily life. . . . In the interim we did not stand on a lower level than the Gentiles.

This parity of "levels" would change radically within a few years.

CONCLUSION

Both Nicholas I and Alexander II were much preoccupied with the problem of "amalgamating" the Jews with the Russian people. Nicholas, however, confused apostasy with amalgamation, and, as a result, failed to make Russians of his Jews. Alexander's emphasis on secularism and toleration was rather more enlightened—and certainly more successful. But during the latter part of his reign he lapsed again into reaction and Slavophilism and abandoned his comparatively sane and practical approach to the Jewish problem which came remarkably close, had he but known it, to the successful integration of the Jewish community into Russian life. Once he slammed all doors to emancipation save apostasy, the possibilities of "amalgamation" vanished.

Apostasy never exercised any gravitational pull upon the Jews. As far as they were concerned Slavic culture was still too primitive to be worth the "passport" of conversion. After the "betrayal" by Alexander II they were more self-consciously independent than ever, tenaciously holding to religious and social forms which became symbols of loyalty as much as expressions of piety. Yet even the disillusionment which followed Alexander's relapse into reaction could not too long postpone the basic changes which were stirring in the Pale. By the 1870's, as we shall see, a new humanism, a revived interest in secular affairs, opened the way to a complete reorientation of Jewish life.

Notes

Pages 183, 185, 186. Translation of newspaper articles from Louis Greenberg, *The Jews in Russia,* I, chapter VI.

Page 191. Quotation from Maurice Samuel, *The World of Sholom Aleichem,* p. 26.

Page 194. Quotation from A. S. Sachs, *Worlds That Passed,* pp. 36-37.

Page 195. Quotation from Shmarya Levin, *Childhood in Exile,* pp. 47, 62-63.

Pages 197-8. Quotation from Levin, *op. cit.,* pp. 36-37.

X

Jewish Humanism in Eastern Europe

CONTACT WITH THE WEST

One of the most fascinating phenomena of European history has been the immensely influential, the larger-than-life, role played by tiny handfuls of individuals—the artists of the Italian Renaissance, the writers of Elizabethan England, the *philosophes* of eighteenth-century France—in shaping and altering the course of human affairs. In the nineteenth century, too, just such an influential minority made its appearance in the dreary Jewish world of the Pale of Settlement. It was composed of thinkers and writers called *maskilim,* humanists. And like the artists of Florence, the poets and scientists of the rationalist era, these *maskilim* made a profound and enduring impact on the life and times of their people and its civilization.

Their appearance was by no means premature, and the regeneration they achieved could not have been more timely. Unquestionably moral, ethical, and humane, Russian-Jewish life was nevertheless narrow and provincial, its religious expression frequently lapsing into narrow pietism, its concern with commerce very often degenerating into unproductive petty trade and cheap-jack peddlery. It was in the midst of this intellectual parochialism and vocational marginalism that a few writers turned to the study of *humanus,* of secular man in the modern world. The emphasis they placed on the importance of "practical" knowledge, of "well-balanced" economic activity, ultimately touched off an intellectual revolution, historically referred to as *Haskalah,* best translated as "Enlightenment." But "Enlightenment," strictly speaking, does not capture the entire flavor of the revolution. The humanistic preoccupation with the pleasures of full-orbed secular activity was more evocative of the Italian Renaissance than of the classically formalistic eighteenth century. And like the Renaissance, the age of *Haskalah* was memorable for what it foreshadowed rather than for what it created.

The awakening of secular intellectual interests among the Jews of Russia was an integral part of a larger Russian response to Western ideas. As late as the French Revolution those ideas were meaningful, east of the Elbe, only to a handful of well-traveled courtiers; for the first major penetration of

Western thinking came only after the Congress of Vienna, with the substantial increase of trade between East and West. Merchants and other men of affairs who visited Germany and France returned with glowing accounts of Western science, Western energy, Western liberalism. During the early decades of the nineteenth century, therefore, Russian writers concentrated increasingly on the task of incorporating into the Russian political and social system the most relevant theories and techniques of Western life.

The leading "Westernizers"—Pushkin, Herzen, Belinski, and later Pisarev and Chernyshevski—had no wish to abandon the authentic and enduring values of Slavic civilization. Pushkin, for example, mocked the Russian noblemen who toyed with the decorative graces and fashionable externals of French and German society. Herzen and Belinski poured scorn on the fops whose understanding never reached beneath the façade. These writers hoped to effect a deeper kind of ideological fusion between East and West.

> The destiny of Russia [wrote Belinski] is to take into herself those elements of European and world civilization as is sufficiently shown by her historic development, geographical position and the variety of races composing her. Of course the reception of those elements cannot be mechanical or eclectic, but must be organic and concrete.

Turgenev went further, urging the kind of drastic, even violent reforms that had characterized the reign of Peter the Great. None of the "Westernizers," with the possible exception of the "Positivists" who witnessed both the half-hearted liberalism and the stern reaction of Alexander II, lived to share in the root-and-branch reconstruction of Russian society. But they did, at least, succeed in generating among their people a wider awareness of the West. It was an awareness which for several decades became the principal obsession of Russian intellectual life, and which, for a time, seemed likely to effect practical amelioration.

The reaction of Russian writers to the tempo and secular efficiency of Western life was duplicated, in many respects, among the *maskilim* in the Pale of Settlement. Even before the nineteenth century, brief flashes of secular humanism made their appearance in the Eastern Jewish world: in the days of the Polish monarchy before the Chmielnicki horrors of the seventeenth century; during the lifetime of the Vilna *Gaon* in the eighteenth century. But these were at best fitful manifestations, notable by their very exception. It was only with the great increase in world trade, early in the nineteenth century, that the intellectual horizons of Eastern European Jewry widened. Galicia was the crossroads of commerce between "enlightened" Germany and backward Russia, and the Galician cities of Lemberg, Brody, and Tarnopol, together with the southern seaport of Odessa, were the principal entrepôts of that commerce. It was no accident, therefore, that the Jewish communities of Galicia and Odessa, communities of business people who participated in the upswing of European trade, were most directly influenced by European ideas, and became the principal advocates and disseminators of *Haskalah*.

The middle-class outlook of *Haskalah* was evident throughout the history of the movement, as evident, indeed, as the bourgeois outlook in the European Enlightenment of a century earlier, and, to a lesser extent, of the Russian awakening of the early nineteenth century. Virtually all of the pioneering humanists came from wealthy merchant families. Thus, Solomon Rapoport was the son of a well-to-do tax assessor of Lemberg; and Rapoport was himself employed for many years as manager of an association of meat-tax-farmers. Joseph Perl was the son a meat-tax-farmer of Tarnopol. Nahman Krochmal was also a tax-farmer for distilleries in the district of Zolkiew. Many others among the leading Jewish *maskilim* were physicians, government employees, and professional people. There were poor *maskilim*, too, but they usually obtained patronage from wealthy Jewish merchants, and had a tendency, as a result, to mirror the middle-class viewpoint of their benefactors.

The very watchword of *Haskalah*—secular Jewish education—emerged from the circumstances and demands of life related to a merchant class. The small tradesman was not penalized in his commercial activities if he commanded only a smattering of Polish or Ukrainian. But the big businessman with connections in Leipzig, Berlin, and Vienna, or even with local authorities, could not function without mastery of German or Russian and familiarity with geography, literature, and other secular subjects. This middle-class orientation explained, too, the social philosophy of the *maskilim*. They urged that the Jews "productivize" themselves, move into useful, dignified livelihoods. Actually, the "productivization" of the Jewish masses was directly in the interest of the rising Jewish capitalist class; for the impoverished nonproductive peddlers and hawkers, who dominated the population of the Pale, were a handicap to the expansion of the internal market. Finally, the *maskilim* honestly believed that secular education would endow all Jews with greater dignity, greater "poise," vis-à-vis their non-Jewish neighbors.

Like the French bourgeoisie of a century earlier, and like the "enlightened" Jews of Mendelssohnian Germany, the Jewish merchants of Galicia and Odessa were determined not merely to break out of their intellectual ghettos, but also to equalize themselves socially with their "betters," in this case, the Russian and Austrian middle classes. They were determined to prove to their Christian neighbors that Jews, too, were capable of "civilized" behavior, that they were not necessarily obscurantists, disguising their ignorance of the world's affairs under a cloak of *pilpul*. Samson Bloch, a *maskil* of the early nineteenth century, gave the clue to this bourgeois humanism when he spoke of "the shame of ignorance and the disgrace of idleness and poverty." Like their predecessors in France and Germany, however, the *maskilim* of Eastern Europe advanced their program not in the name of the class whose interests they represented, but in the name of their entire people. They were convinced that their program of enlightened secularism would solve most of the cultural, economic, and political problems of Jewish life.

Yet the beginnings of *Haskalah* in Galicia, in Odessa, in St. Petersburg, and later in Lithuania, did not take the form of Russification. Here, indeed, was the crucial difference between Jewish secular humanism in Eastern and Western Europe. In the first part of the nineteenth century Russian culture itself was still in too embryonic a stage to be worth emulating. Rather, most of the early *maskilim* were admirers of Germany. German culture, which had so deeply influenced the "salon Jews" of the post-Mendelssohnian era, exercised the same fascination for Galician Jewry, who were in closest contact with the German world. Frequently, indeed, the *maskilim* were stigmatized as *Berlinchiks* or *Deitscher* by the pious inhabitants of the Pale. But it was an unwarranted censure, for admiration of German culture, to the *maskil,* was limited simply to German dress, German decorum, German emphasis upon science and academic research, German technology. Like the Russian "Westernizers," the humanist Jews of Eastern Europe never for a moment contemplated Germanizing themselves spiritually, emotionally, or religiously. In contrast with many of the Emancipation-obsessed Jews of Germany, the more traditional Russian Jew, if he was a humanist, sought to create the modern Jew, and not simply the modern Jewish-German or Jewish-Russian. In fact, *maskilim* of the caliber of Joseph Perl, Meyer Letteris, Solomon Rapoport, or Nahman Krochmal were devoutly religious Jews, infused with a genuine devotion to Jewish tradition and its perpetuation. These early humanists had no intention whatever of ridiculing Judaism—only the superstitions and obscurantist folkways of the Pale.

THE SCIENCE OF JUDAISM

It was this reverence for Judaism which largely accounted for the choice of the Hebrew language as the medium of the Eastern *Haskalah*—largely, though not entirely, for reliance upon Hebrew was yet another way by which the middle-class *maskilim* distinguished themselves from the Yiddish-speaking masses. Hebrew was the language of the Bible and of Jewish history. Its use signified that the humanists intended to remain within the mainstream of Jewish life, and not to parochialize themselves, as so many German Jews had done when they chose the German vernacular. In short, they remained continually preoccupied with the Jew, qua Jew. Thus, one of the earliest uses to which the revived Hebrew language was put in Poland and Russia, and one of the first expressions, therefore, of the *Haskalah,* was an Eastern version of the Science of Judaism. Beginning close to the core of Jewish tradition, scholars such as Solomon Rapoport and Nahman Krochmal sought to analyze Jewish history and literature objectively, to peel away the layers of myth and religious obscurantism that shrouded the Jewish past.

In many ways, Solomon Rapoport was the typical *maskil.* He was, as was noted, a *Galizianer,* born in Lemberg in 1790 of well-to-do parents. In the best middle-class tradition of the *Haskalah,* he earned his living as manager of a tax-farming corporation, and married into yet additional wealth. Like most *maskilim,* he remained an Orthodox Jew, even receiving ordination as a rabbi in Tarnapol. But the importance of secular information was basic in his background, and he was determined to apply the secular approach to the understanding of his own people. The first fruit of Rapoport's research appeared in 1829; it was a masterfully "scientific" biography of Rashi, the most authoritative of the medieval Talmudic commentators. This study was followed by five other historical monographs of first rank. They were not lengthy works. Certainly in quantity of production Rapoport could not compare to Leopold Zunz. But each monograph, whether a biography of the Saadia *Gaon* or Nathan of Rome, or some other historic Jewish personality, excelled in quality of research and critical acumen. These tracts endure, in fact, even today. Rapoport's intellectual reputation was so widespread that scholars throughout Europe corresponded with him to seek his advice on various knotty problems of Jewish historiography. The volumes of this collected correspondence are not the least valuable of Rapoport's contributions to the Science of Judaism. Working respectfully within the framework of Jewish tradition, he was the first major Jewish intellect since the Vilna *Gaon* to give impetus to the objective-secular approach to Jewish history, and to obtain acceptance for it in Eastern Europe.

The pioneering effort to create a Science of Judaism was immeasurably enhanced by the contributions of another Galician *maskil,* Nahman Krochmal. He was a contemporary of Rapoport's, born in Brody in 1785, and, like Rapoport, the son of a wealthy merchant. During numerous business trips to Berlin the father had become an admirer of the Mendelssohnian Enlightenment and he provided his son with a splendid education, secular as well as Jewish. Nahman earned his living as a liquor-tax-farmer, but he managed to spend virtually every leisure hour in scholarly research. He was determined to follow Rapoport's lead in applying the "scientific" technique to the re-evaluation of Jewish history and philosophy. Krochmal was a brilliant conversationalist and teacher; indeed, his reputation extended far beyond the Pale and into Western Europe—where he was known as the "Mendelssohn of Galicia." It was a well-meant sobriquet, but hardly an accurate one; for in depth and originality of thought, Krochmal far transcended Mendelssohn. Unlike Mendelssohn, however, Krochmal was not a prolific writer. So much of his time was devoted to the disciples who flocked to his home at Zolkiew to study with him that it was only in the last decade of his life that he began to publish some of his articles, the result of years of research and reflection. Most of his career, in fact, was spent in the preparation of one definitive work, a volume which was destined to become his *magnum opus*: the *Guide to the Perplexed of Our Time.*

The *Guide* was published eleven years after his death, and its impact on the world of Jewish scholarship was truly prodigious. In the manner of the German Idealists, Krochmal sought to identify the characteristics which made up the historic Jewish "spirit." Ultimately, he discovered that "spirit" in the Jewish people itself. By subsuming religion in the larger concept of nation, Krochmal laid the groundwork for the secular-nationalist philosophy of Jewish history which was ultimately to become so important in Zionism. In the first half of the nineteenth century, however, Krochmal's shift in emphasis was important both for its challenge and for its method. The challenge came in the vigorous avowal that the "spirit" of the Jewish nation in the modern world was being constricted by Hasidism and pilpulistic

Talmudism. The method of detachment in research gave respectability to the scientific approach to Jewish history. It was an approach soon to be preempted by the polemicists of *Haskalah*.

PROSE AND POETRY: THE EARLY YEARS

The humanistic yardstick was applied not merely to scholarship, but also to life itself. After the initial period of the Science of Judaism, *Haskalah* creativity unfolded in four principal phases. The first was the polemical-rationalist phase, which concentrated on battering down the intellectual confines of the Pale, with its dogmatism and its emphasis on the minutiae of pietistic observance. The second stage sent the *maskilim* back to a rather overglorified past; it was responsible for the romanticism and stylistic exaggerations of men like Abraham Mapu and Abraham Bar Lebensohn. The third stage, that of "Positivism," brought the humanists into the broad currents of European culture. Many lost their moorings and were swept away into complete assimilation. Others gave strength to their Jewish background by enriching it with the experience of the European world. The final stage, represented by Perez Smolenskin (and discussed at greater length in Chapter XIV), encompassed the union of *Haskalah* with Jewish nationalism, the pride of ancestry and the aspiration for corporate rebirth.

In the first phase, during the 1820's and 1830's, the "enlightened" Jews of Galicia made a fetish of broadening the horizons of Jewish life, appealing to their fellow Jews to expose themselves to European literature, to natural science, to vocational training. Outside the *heder* and the market-stall the world in all its glories awaited the Jew if only he were willing to train himself to appreciate it. All that was required, apparently, was modern education. ". . . Because God loved man," wrote Isaac Satonov, "he sent Wisdom to walk upon the earth, that her delightful employ be with man, who would choose her in order to survive unto great salvation." The humanists concentrated their attacks upon the ignorant Hasidic Jews of the countryside, the *pilpul*-tyrannized Jews of the towns. Once these "benighted" people exposed themselves to modern secular ideas, the *maskilim* argued, they would become "whole" human beings. Endowed with a "modern" education, they would abandon their unwholesome vocations of peddling and liquor dealing and move into large-scale commerce, manual labor, perhaps even onto the soil. They would "productivize" themselves.

On the issue of "vocational readjustment," it is now clear that the *maskilim* evidenced a very real blindness to the circumstances of Russian-Jewish life. There were, to be sure, all too many Jews who were peddlers, liquor dealers, secondhand-clothing merchants, and petty proprietors of various sorts—far more, proportionately and numerically, than among the neighboring Russian and Polish peoples. But if the Jews had more than their share of peddlers and *luftmenschen* (*melamdim*, Talmudic students, Jewish communal workers), they also had more than their share of artisans. For the typical Jewish *shtetl*-inhabitant was much more likely to be a shoemaker, a carpenter, a blacksmith, or a porter than a haberdasher or a synagogue sexton. Indeed, the Jews performed virtually all the skilled labor, and very often the unskilled labor, for their non-Jewish neighbors. Jews built and repaired Russian homes, mended Russian wagons, sewed Russian clothes, carried Russian lumber. They were not farmers, of course, but that depended far less on Jewish vocational training than on Russian land law. All these facts notwithstanding, the *maskilim* persisted in criticizing their brethren in the *shtetl* not merely for their cultural parochialism (and here the *maskilim* were on solid ground), but for their alleged aversion to "wholesome" manual labor. No criticism could have been less well-founded.

The emphasis of Galician *Haskalah* literature in the 1820's and 1830's lay in prose, in tracts that satirized the lamentable backwardness of life in the Pale. The Galician *maskilim,* Joseph Perl and Isaac Erter, concentrated on essays and quasi-novels that caricatured the Jewish world around them in the most lurid and heavy-handed fashion, grossly exaggerating the obscurantism, the sordidness, the pettiness of Jewish existence. In the manner of the *philosophes* of eighteenth-century France, they frequently resorted to the device of "dreams" or "visions" or "letters" from "travelers" in the Pale to expose the shortcomings of the world they sought to reform. In Erter's *Gilgul Nefesh* ("Transmigration of a Soul"), for example, the author hit upon the vehicle of reincarnation in order to parody the Pale's "typical" personalities. Thus a pompous Talmudic scholar reappeared as a helpless, wriggling mackerel; a cantor, endowed with every musical talent except a decent voice, assumed the shape of a hound, baying endlessly at the moon—off-key, of course; while other caricatures, running the gamut of ghetto types, were portrayed even more graphically and, if possible, less subtly. There was nothing gentle about these early polemicists.

It was during the 1820's, too, that humanism began to strike root simultaneously in the northern Pale, in Volhynia and Lithuania. In the densely Hasidic province of Volhynia one man, Isaac Baer Levinsohn, did virtually all the basic pioneering work of *Haskalah*. Like his colleagues in the early decades of the movement, Levinsohn, scion of a wealthy mercantile family, had all of the advantages of a thorough secular education. He was, in fact, one of the few Jews of his time with knowledge of the Russian language. Later he became so ardent a champion of "modernization" that Czar Nicholas I awarded him a subsidy of a thousand rubles in gratitude for his effort to end Jewish "fanaticism." His influence on the intellectuals of Volhynian Jewry won him the title, "prince of Hebrew letters." He was not, to be sure, a particularly profound writer; his talent lay primarily in pathfinding. He advocated "enlightenment" more lucidly and convincingly than any of his contemporaries, and buttressed his appeal by ingenious references to Jewish historical precedent. He went on to propose the usual program of "practical" improvements for Jewish life: secular education and a more "wholesome" vocational diversification in manual labor and agriculture. In everything he wrote, Levinsohn was so manifestly respectful of Jewish tradition that even his severest critics were obliged to admit that his suggestions were neither heretical nor revolutionary. In Lithuania, meanwhile, a small circle of humanists borrowed Levinsohn's approach of "proof" from history.

The leading spirits here—Mordecai Aaron Günzburg and Abraham Bar Levensohn—defended the cause of enlightenment with a combination of scholarly exposition and poetic satire. Abraham Bar Levensohn's *Emet ve-Emunah* ("Truth and Belief") was perhaps the finest epic poem of this early period of *Haskalah*. It was an allegorical portrayal of the battle between knowledge and ignorance; in the best Goethian manner, the leading protagonists were "Wisdom," "Truth," "Reason"—and their counterparts, "Ignorance," and "Superstition."

During the 1840's and early 1850's, the emphasis shifted from the polemical-rationalist phase of *Haskalah* to a romantic appreciation of the beauties and lush grandeurs of the world outside the Pale. The time was propitious for this emphasis; the era of Nicholas I was the zenith period of Russian Romanticism. The Russian language, which Pushkin had almost single-handedly purged of its ancient Slavonic encumbrances, was used with rare expressiveness by Lermontov and Gogol. The richness and color of historical pageantry which characterized the writings of these Russian giants, and which filtered through to the Jewish intellectual world only after their deaths, exerted a significant influence on the Jewish humanists.

As far as the Jewish reading public was concerned, romantic literature provided a welcome escape from the harsh realities of life under Nicholas I. In 1848, therefore, when a Vilna *maskil,* Kalman Schulman, translated into Hebrew Eugene Sue's exotic and rather garish *Mysteries of Paris,* the Jews of the Pale astonished both author and translator by purchasing tens of thousands of copies; for the book—shallow stylistic period piece though it was—answered their yearning for beauty, for an outgoing life of action and emotion. Other Jewish humanists responded increasingly to this nostalgia. Nature, beauty, love, action—all were now re-examined by the translators, novelists, and poets of the *Haskalah*. Must Jewish life forever be identified with the squalid *shtetl,* these writers asked? "Mikaele," the talented son of Abraham Bar Levensohn, provided his own answer:

> Once in a leafy tree, there was my home.
> Torn from a swaying branch, friendless I roam.
> Plucked from the joyous green that gave me birth,
> What is my life to me, and of what worth?
> Thus do they haunt me, with none to save,
> Prey of the whirlwind, the storm and the wave.

Unquestionably there were glorious episodes in the past, life "in a leafy tree," the robust, agricultural life of ancient Judah, the secure and dignified life of the Spanish Golden Age. These periods were now exhumed, reconstructed, and often overidealized in the poems and novels of "Mikaele," Schulman, and, above all, in the colorful historical romances of Abraham Mapu.

Reared amidst poverty and squalor in Slobodka, Lithuania, Mapu was educated in the most rigid pilpulistic tradition. He probably would have become a professional Talmudic scholar if his first tutorial assignment, in his early twenties, had not brought him to the home of a Jewish farmer. Close communion with nature made a lasting impact on Mapu's impressionable mind; so, too, apparently, did the writings of the European romanticists, whose works he digested after he had taught himself French and Russian. "I was raised to live in the atmosphere of the dead," he recalled, "and here I am cast among people who lead a real life, in which I am unable to take part." But while Mapu was barred both by physique and economic circumstances from sharing in the idealized life of the soil, or in the "emancipated" secular activities of Western Europe, he was determined to re-create on paper the "heroic" existence he attributed to the Jews of Biblical times.

In 1853 he published a historical romance, *Ahibat Zion* ("The Love of Zion"), a florid melodrama dealing with the wars and loves of King Ahab of ancient Israel. *Ahibat Zion* was a contrived, implausible work, its characters flat and one-dimensional. Yet its effect upon the younger generation of Lithuanian Jews, who were usually obliged to read the novel surreptitiously, often hiding it inside the pages of their Talmud texts, was truly remarkable. It opened to untold thousands of ghetto Jews the world of action, love, romance, even violence. Later, when writers like Abraham Bar Gottlober of Odessa gathered up the thread of this romanticism and wove it into novels, essays, histories, poems, and reviews, the reservoir of *Haskalah*-oriented readers in the Pale increased significantly. After all, these exuberant and imaginative period pieces provided entertaining reading, far more palatable, certainly, than the carping, single-minded polemicism of the rationalists. Indeed, the emphasis upon historical pageantry was ultimately responsible not merely for the growing secularization of life in certain areas of the Pale, but also for the revival of Jewish nationalism. The romantic mood of *Haskalah,* its sentimental tribute to ancient Zion, was revived in the 1880's, and directly influenced the emergence of cultural Zionism.

THE AGE OF REFORMS

The third phase of *Haskalah* was mainly brought on by the climate of reform in the early years of Alexander II's regime. All of Russia stirred as if in a gigantic thaw. With favorable opportunities suddenly opened to undertake major social and economic improvements, Russian writers dropped their preoccupation with ornate, bombastic extravaganzas in the romantic genre. *"Chto delat?"*—"What is to be done?"—asked Chernyshevski. This question penetrated to the very roots of the Russian social system. The time for theorizing had passed; the time for action had arrived. The essayists Chernyshevski and Pisarev, who called themselves "Positivists" after their hero, August Comte, belabored their people to think in terms of immediate practical reforms. Confronted with a situation offering infinite possibilities of self-improvement, the Jewish humanists, too, began to veer off on a new trend. Who knew how much longer this golden opportunity would continue, these men asked? Jews dared not waste precious time reconstructing the glories of ancient Israel, or digging away at some point of medieval history. Steps must be taken immediately, they insisted, for practical social and economic improvements. This emphasis upon tangible reformist action accounted for the decline of novels, poetry, and satire during the 1850's and

1860's, and for the emergence, in their place, of Hebrew-language journals, scientific essays, and manuals devoted to educational and vocational reform.

The most brilliant and influential spokesmen for this "Positivist" phase of *Haskalah* were Judah Leib Gordon and Moses Lilienblum. Gordon, who was born in Vilna in 1830 and given a typically Talmudic education, broke violently from the pietistic tradition while still in his teens. For twenty years he earned his livelihood as a teacher in one of the Crown schools established by the government. Later, as secretary for the Society for the Promotion of Culture among the Jews of Russia, he was victimized in a case of mistaken identity, and was briefly imprisoned as a political conspirator, with effects disastrous to his health. The early phase of Gordon's career as a *maskil* was largely devoted to romantic-Biblical epics, to fables centered about the lives of King David and King Solomon, to lyric poetry on pastoral themes, in the style of the 1840's and early 1850's. His powerful historical ballad, *Zidkiyahu be-Bet ha-Pekudot* ("Zedekiah in Prison"), was perhaps his finest work in this vein, and indicated that a tough streak of realism was already showing. An imaginative reconstruction of life in Biblical days, the poem managed, at the same time, to ridicule the obscurantism of rabbis and priests in the early days of Hebrew history.

The completion of the *Zidkiyahu* ballad was the turning point in Gordon's literary career. Thereafter, his poetry and essays became exclusively "Positivist," cold, clinical analyses of the shortcomings of contemporary Jewish life. The dialogue he provided for his protagonists was strictly reformist. A husband in one of his works declared:

> Slaves we were in the land of Egypt, and what are we now? Do we not sink lower from year to year? Are we not bound with ropes of absurdities, and with cords of quibbles, with all sorts of prejudices? . . . The stranger no longer oppresses us, our despots are the progeny of our own bodies. Our hands are no longer manacled, but our souls are in chains.

What, then, was the answer? Be modern, Gordon urged his readers; dress and talk like Russians; read Russian literature; take an interest in Russian life. Did this mean forsaking one's Jewish loyalties? Not at all, Gordon insisted. But, he added, with a scornful glance at the caftaned Hasidim, the skullcapped pietists around him, "be a Jew at home, and a man in the street." It was, in some ways, a revolutionary concept. It suggested, in the Western fashion, that what was needed was not the modern Jew, but rather the modern Russian of Jewish faith.

Gordon's contemporary, and fellow townsman, Moses Leib Lilienblum, took an even more extreme position. As a child, Lilienblum had been apprenticed to a backward and tyrannical *melamed*; later his parents married him off at the age of thirteen. Although Lilienblum's instinct was to revolt against the social and educational system which had ruined his youth, he was compelled for years to earn his livelihood within that system as a teacher of Talmud. The ambivalence of this kind of existence destroyed his health, and very nearly forced him into starvation. For his articles in the journal

Ha-Meliz went so far as to urge major reforms in Talmudic law, something unheard of until then, even within the *Haskalah* tradition. Lilienblum spoke as a believing Jew, but—insisting that even the Talmud was permeated with the spirit of reform—he urged the rabbis to interpret the law in a way which would ease the rigorous legalism of life in the Pale. "I plead with you, leaders of the people," he wrote in one impassioned essay, "accept the voice of one who loves his people and his faith."

The answer of the pietistic elders of the community was to drive Lilienblum out of town, and to boycott his father-in-law's business. Broken in spirit, ill and penniless, Lilienblum moved on to Odessa, where he barely supported his family as a bookkeeper. Here, at least, in the Black Sea port, the center of southern *Haskalah,* Lilienblum could express himself as he pleased. He wrote prolifically during this period, insisting, with all the eloquence and sincerity at his command, on a more "positive" attitude toward the problems of Jewish life—especially toward the problem of religious reform.

> At a time [he wrote] when all thinking elements in Russia are aroused by the new ideas of Chernyshevsky and Pisarev, which offer a solution to the great problem of universal happiness, our honored men of letters make a big noise about some comment on a Biblical text, and pore over ancient tomes whose ideas are as dried up as withered leaves.

These were strong words. Indeed, they marked the most extreme position taken by *Haskalah* in the nineteenth century.

It was significant, too, that during the period of Gordon and Lilienblum, the leaders of *Haskalah* were no longer a tiny minority. Undoubtedly, the majority of Jews still remained pietistic, and allowed themselves to be governed by the old social and educational traditions. The idea of religious reform may have been too extreme even for the majority of *maskilim*. But tens of thousands of Russian Jews had become familiar at last with secular ideas and values; after all, these were the palmy days of Alexander II's quasi emancipation, when sizable numbers of Jews were beginning to enter into Russian economic and social life. The devotees of *Haskalah* began to take very seriously Gordon's injunction to "be a Jew at home, and a man in the street." When the Russian intelligentsia demonstrated their willingness to treat the Jews with sympathy, the *maskilim* responded with almost embarrassing alacrity. Some of them, in fact, moved very close to the kind of groveling apologetics that characterized the German-Jewish humanists of half a century earlier, overemphasizing their patriotism, minimizing their ethnic distinctiveness as Jews. Sarin, the *maskil* of Lev Levanda's novel *Fervent Days,* could declare: "My heart tells me that in time the Russians will come to love us. We will make them love us. How? By our own love."

The approach of the German-Jewish *Meassefim* was daily becoming more attractive to these Russian-Jewish humanists, who decided now that they were Russian by nationality and Jewish by religious observance only. Even the medium of the Hebrew language was declared expendable. Thus Ioakhim Tarnopol and Osip Rabinowich obtained permission, in 1856, to issue a Russian-language Jewish weekly called *Razvet* ("Dawn"), for the purpose of preaching "patriotism, emancipation and modernism." The foremost contributor to this journal was the novelist Lev Levanda, a Vilna-born *maskil,* instructor in the Crown school of Vilna, and a feverish advocate of Russianization. Levanda, Rabinowich, and Tarnopol made the pages of *Razvet* fairly crackle with their denunciation of the formerly well-respected *Haskalah* vehicle of Hebrew; for, by their lights, the use of Hebrew constituted "treason" to the ideal of Russification.

In the early 1860's, the wealthy Jewish bankers and railroad kings of St. Petersburg and Odessa took the initiative in creating a "Society for the Promotion of Culture Among Jews." Its self-announced purpose was to educate Jewry into "readiness for citizenship." Its three basic techniques were to promote the Russian language among the Jews, to underwrite the cost of secular education for needy Jewish children, and to subsidize the publication of books on "useful" knowledge. The Society also sponsored a Russian-language literary journal devoted to the scientific study of Judaism and one of its recurrent themes was the crucial need for linguistic and cultural reform. Probably the Society's most enduring accomplishment was the translation of the Old Testament into Russian in 1871, fully three quarters of a century after Mendelssohn had performed the equivalent service for German Jewry. Here was practical action. Here, apparently, was "Positivism" in operation.

The literary quality and scientific standards of the Russian-Jewish press during the reign of Alexander II were really quite high, reflecting impressive cultural progress in a short span of time. The progress of acculturation was evident, too, in the increase of Jewish students who attended Russian universities and *gymnasia*; between 1856 and 1871 their number quadrupled. The sanguine conviction that Jews and Russians were brothers produced some remarkable observations from the *maskilim*. The Jewish philologist I. Warshavski asserted, for example, that the spirit of the Russian language, according to his linguistic research, was uniquely similar to that of the Hebrew language; while I. G. Orshanski viewed the Jew as the most effective medium for the Russification of the various racial groups within the Russian Empire.

The expansion of Jewish cultural boundaries was apparent, as well, in former "Congress" Poland. This was a territory which had only recently been incorporated into Russia proper, after the uprising of 1863, and in which, as a result, the full scheme of czarist anti-Jewish disabilities had never been thoroughly operative. Four hundred thousand Jews lived here. They were subject to discrimination, to be sure; but the discrimination was never as severe as in Russia proper. Moreover, western Poland was in close touch with the West, economically and intellectually. The Jews, as the people with the most extensive mercantile experience, were able to profit from that proximity. A comfortable Jewish bourgeoisie developed, Jews with sufficient leisure to familiarize themselves with the Polish language and Polish cultural traditions. Accordingly, the Jewish middle class provided the base for a significant Polish-Jewish intelligentsia, which made its appearance during the 1860's. Jews found employment in the banks, commission houses, export concerns, and in the liberal professions. Jews, too, were often the patrons of the most important Polish journals and newspapers. The Natanson family, for example, owned the largest Polish publishing house. For that matter, the book trade, the theatrical and concert booking offices were almost entirely in Jewish hands. Until the Polish Revolution of 1863, the Jews of "Congress" Poland were perhaps the outstanding contributors to Polish cultural life; their sons were writers, doctors, scientists, philologists, musicians, actors, painters, sculptors. Indeed, the rate of Jewish acculturation in "Congress" Poland was much faster than in the Pale of Settlement.

Both in the Pale and in "Congress" Poland the passion to adopt non-Jewish mores was responsible for conversion to Christianity of a significant minority of Jews. The factors of insecurity, of culture nostalgia that had operated in post-Mendelssohnian Germany, now began to operate in Eastern Europe during the 1860's. Of course, conversion was not nearly as common among Russian and Polish Jews as it had been in Germany; but its very existence was striking evidence of how far *Haskalah* had come since those early days of Joseph Perl and Isaac Baer Levinsohn when it had been considered blasphemous to read an occasional book on a secular subject.

SMOLENSKIN: THE PENDULUM SWINGS BACK

The lucid, intelligible realism which has been the crowning glory of modern literature awaited its pioneers in Russia until the late nineteenth century. Then the giants made their appearance: Turgenev, Tolstoy, Dostoevski, men who pierced to the very center of human issues. Their novels were credible at all times; the contours of their plots were recognizable; their protagonists brimmed with the authentic sap of life. The course these writers charted in developing the modern novel was followed, too, by the one Jewish novelist who dominated *Haskalah* prose in the second half of the nineteenth century, a writer whose mastery of the realistic technique, imperfect though it was, brooked no comparison among his fellow *maskilim*. He was Perez Smolenskin, and his career represented the watershed of the *Haskalah*. Smolenskin's youth in White Russia was the typical traumatic experience of the Pale: pilpulistic education; a brother dragged off to oblivion by *khappers*; the wretched, poverty-stricken existence of Hebrew teaching; the escape—in Smolenskin's case by freight car to Odessa, and then later, in 1868, to Vienna. Our only photograph of him shows us a man bearing a striking resemblance to Edgar Allan Poe: flashing dark eyes, rich black hair, elegant mustache and goatee, dressed, significantly, in formal Western style, with wing collar and cravat.

It was in Vienna that Smolenskin realized his long-cherished dream of founding a Hebrew-language literary monthly, *Ha-Shahar* ("The Dawn"); he served as the journal's editor for twelve years and made it the finest, most influential forum of *Haskalah* writing. His editorial contribution, by itself, would have established his reputation permanently. But he was, in addition, the journal's principal contributor. In the columns of *Ha-Shahar* appeared the installments of his six novels, books that laid the basic foundations of literary realism in the Hebrew language. Like so many of their predecessors, Smolenskin's volumes ground the secularist ax of *Haskalah*. Their plot structures were often contrived, and not infrequently the leading protagonists were drawn without any marked psychological insight. Yet the descriptive material was photographically honest. It was honest not merely in scope—Smolenskin had traveled extensively in the Pale—but honest, too, in its objectivity. Although his heroes advocated secular humanism, he refused to idealize them; indeed, he described many of them for what they were—thinly veiled assimilationists. Conversely, he possessed a genuine appreciation for those qualities of ghetto life that were decent and noble. Two of his most exalted characters, Simon, in the novel *Simhat Ha-Nef* ("The Joy of the Flatterer"), and Isaiah, in the novel *Gemul Yesharim* ("The Reward of Righteousness"), were former *yeshivah* students; Smolenskin did not hesitate to ascribe their spirituality to their Talmudic training. With his highly refined capacity for realistic description, Smolenskin was able effectively to discredit the desiccated romantic tradition, founded by Mapu, which for thirty years had dominated *Haskalah* fiction.

It was, in fact, Smolenskin's deeply embedded reverence for the Jewish people which ultimately thrust him into the onrushing path of *Haskalah*. Like the Russian Slavophiles, disenchanted with the "false blandishments" of the West, Smolenskin was one of the first to sense, in the late 1860's and 1870's, the dangerous implications of *Haskalah* extremism: that it was leading not merely to Russification, but to the abandonment of Jewish loyalties altogether. He expressed his concern trenchantly and unequivocally, as he transformed *Ha-Shahar* into a weapon of war not merely against the obscurantism of the Pale, but also against modern assimilation. In article after article, Smolenskin exhorted his fellow *maskilim* to stand firm for Judaism and the Jewish tradition.

> The wilfully blind [he wrote] bid us to be like all other nations, and I repeat after them: let us be like all the other nations pursuing and attaining knowledge, leaving off from wickedness and folly, and dwelling as loyal citizens in the lands whither we have been scattered. Yes, let us be like all the other nations, unashamed of the rock whence we have been hewn, like the rest in holding dear our language and the glory of our people.

Such was Smolenskin's reputation, his eloquence, the mastery of his idiom, that virtually single-handed he gave pause to the "Russificators" and "emancipators." It is pointless to speculate whether he alone could have blocked the progress of *Haskalah*; hardly had he issued his warnings than Alexander II himself closed the door to Jewish emancipation and made it plain that the "fusion" of the Russian and Jewish peoples was an empty dream. Smolenskin's campaign against assimilation picked up momentum after Alexander's "betrayal." He blazed away now, in articles that were frankly polemic, on behalf of the Hebrew language and the vast skein of historical associations embodied in that language.

In 1872 Smolenskin published his most significant essay, *Am Olam*

("Eternal People"), a trenchant and memorable defense of Jewish national-ism. The post-Mendelssohnian ideal of Judaism as a religious confession was bankrupt, he insisted. So, too, was Gordon's concept of the duality of the Jew—"in the home" and "in the street." The time had come to gird for the moral, even the political, resurrection of the Jewish people as a national entity. Smolenskin devoted several moving essays to this rather revolutionary notion in the last decade of his life. He died in 1885 before he could develop the concept fully, but even before his death others had begun to support his cause. In 1880, Judah Leib Gordon, the arch-exponent of Russification, in one of the last poems of his life, *L'Mi Ani Omel?* ("For Whom Do I Labor?") wrote "For whom have I labored all my best years, denying myself contentment and peace? . . . My fellow *maskilim,* possessed of true knowledge, once loosely attached to the idiom of their people, now but scorn the faithful old mother. . . ." Isaac Erter, one of the earliest humanists, now in the twilight of his life, also divined the crude self-seeking of "emancipated" Jews who "cast off the folly of their own people in order to indulge in the folly of the Gentiles." Thus, within the space of Smolenskin's own lifetime, *Haskalah* had swung full-circle: from humanism to assimilation back to national regeneration. The Hebrew writers who followed Smolenskin eventually transformed the prophetic language into the vehicle of the Zionist movement.

THE RISE OF YIDDISH LITERATURE

During the nineteenth century, while the *maskilim* self-consciously em-ployed Hebrew as the instrument of their program, and as the symbol of their separation from the masses, Yiddish, the vernacular of the Pale, con-tinued nonetheless to grow freely and richly, even though untended and elbowed away from "the places of honor." It was a hybrid language, a transliteration into Hebrew characters of the German phonetics that the Jews had adopted during their medieval residence in the German world. Since then, this Yiddish patois had been liberally sprinkled with both Slavic and Hebrew words, a kind of linguistic trail of Jewish movement eastward and inward. It was a virile and stubborn vernacular; but it was hardly a literary medium, certainly not a medium which presumed to compete with Hebrew, the language of the Prophets. Whatever writing appeared in Yiddish until the eighteenth century was in the nature of *Spielmann* romances, religious fables, and folk songs. In these earlier stages, Yiddish limited itself to its role as a recreational or a woman's language.

During the course of the eighteenth and nineteenth centuries, however, two factors energized Yiddish into increasing use as a literary medium. The first was the rise of Hasidism, a movement which validated the aspirations and mores of the common people, and with it their language. The poet-sages of the Hasidic period expressed their deeply moving allegories in the Yiddish language, infusing it with a warmth and passion it had not known before. Secondly, the *Haskalah* itself was indirectly responsible for the rise of Yiddish literature, for it sponsored the idea that a secular career as a writer was worthy of a mature Jewish intelligence. Occasionally such eminent *maskilim* as Isaac Baer Levinsohn and Judah Leib Gordon, much as they urged Jews to drop their "jargon," relaxed, yielded to the spirit of abandon, and wrote poetry in Yiddish. But Yiddish writing on a truly "literary" level emerged only in the 1870's, when the full force of Hebrew *Haskalah* literature was on the wane.

It was near the end of the nineteenth century that writers influenced by *Haskalah* realism, as well as by an appreciation of the value of a mass audience, began to shape the basic lineaments of Yiddish prose literature. The first Yiddish writings were merely translations of European secular literature; there were, as well, a few polemical tracts and articles on *Haskalah* themes, turned out by such minor talents as Israel Oxenfeld and Solomon Ettinger. Ettinger, however, was one of the first to refine Yiddish, to purge it of some of its medieval anachronisms; while his contemporary, Yeshue Mordhe Lifshitz, compiled a German-Yiddish dictionary, which was not published, and a Russian-Yiddish dictionary which was published; he intended them for the specific use of a new Yiddish literature. But Yiddish as the medium of modern prose was given little serious consideration until it was linked with the pulsating life-force of the *shtetl*. As such it was repudiated by those whose major preoccupation was secularism or "modernization" and who identified Yiddish with the life of the *shtetl*. But people who remained in the Yiddish-speaking milieu, and who understood its vitality and warmth, turned instinctively to the earthy vernacular of the Pale.

The transition from *Haskalah* to Yiddishist realism was initiated by Sholom Abramovich, the "grandfather" of modern Yiddish literature, who is best remembered today by his pen name of Mendele Mocher Sforim—Mendele the bookseller. Mendele was a Minsk-born Jew who considered himself a *maskil,* but who was compelled to support himself during most of his life by directing a *Talmud Torah* in Odessa. His early writings, all in Hebrew, were masterpieces of realism, in the best Smolenskin tradition. When he finally reverted to the Yiddish language, he did so exclusively to establish communication. "I closely observe the mode of life of our people and want to relate it afterwards in the sacred tongue. But the majority of the people do not understand this language and speak Yiddish. Of what good then are the writer's efforts and his soul's desire if he cannot serve the people?" For the first twenty years of his Yiddish literary career Mendele was the fighting satirist, concentrating his attacks on the squalor, ignorance, and uncouthness of ghetto life. Chaim Tschernowitz recalled of this little patriarchal man: " 'There is in me two Mendeles,' he used to say—the wise, pious Jew of the *Beth Ha-Midrash,* and the modern skeptic. He loved Jews and Judaism, but he also criticized trenchantly the pettiness he found in Jewish life in the Diaspora. . . ."

What the Talmud called "the chastisements of love" were best expressed in his satires on Jewish community life, *Die Klyotsche* ("The Nag"), *Dos Kleine Menschele* ("The Parasite"), and again in his recollections, in fictional form, of his experience with wandering beggars during the early years of his life, *Die Takse* ("The Tax"), *Fishke der Kruhmer* ("Fishke the Lame"). Perhaps his finest novel was *Benyemin Hashleshi* ("Benjamin the Third"), a picaresque work, in which Don Quixote was his model, about a timid and vacillating Yiddish adventurer who wandered aimlessly through the Pale, encountering everywhere superstition, uncleanliness, backwardness. There was much of the carping polemicist in the early Mendele. Indeed, his first Yiddish writings, with their self-conscious sense of "mission," bore little relation to the masterful realism of his earlier Hebrew prose. His plots, too, were weak in structure, often involving little more than a string of anecdotes.

The more Mendele wrote, however, the greater refinement his work achieved. He polished and repolished. His tempo remained slow, as slow and club-footed as the tempo of the ghetto itself. But his style, his use of the Yiddish idiom, vastly improved in resourcefulness and precision. Under his guidance Yiddish eventually became a language of arch mimicry. In a revised edition of *Dos Kleine Menchele,* for example, Mendele conjured up the city of "Glupsk":

> Glupsk was the city that pleased me most. Glupsk is a large Jewish city with many fools who love to be led by the nose. They come running to greet you, thrusting their noses forward, shoving each other, each one striving to offer his nose first, because they believe that to be so led is an obligation—a Jewish custom which should not be violated. Glupsk is a city with many societies, heads of synagogues, officials and magnates. And the good Lord who feeds all, from the horned buffalo to the larva of the louse, also provides for these creatures as well. In short, Glupsk pleased me immensely, as if it had been designed for me. Glupsk was for me what the stagnant, slimy swamp is for the frog, a place where it can croak and enjoy its domain.

In later years Mendele's writing acquired further depth. He did not cease to satirize the life of the Pale; but increasingly the satire was tinctured with tenderness, with wistful irony, with a sharper delineation of character. Because Mendele loved his people, his works breathed with compassion, with an understanding which the Hebrew language, no matter how fastidiously applied, could not duplicate. Mendele did not merely attune the Yiddish language to literary needs; he attuned the language to his people. It was only a beginning; but it laid the groundwork for the Chekhovian portraiture of Sholom Aleichem, and the psychological incisiveness of Peretz.

Few writers have so completely captured the imagination of their people as did Sholom Aleichem, the culture-hero of the Pale of Settlement. Like Mendele, he came from Minsk. His real name was Sholom Rabinowitz. But, again like Mendele, he chose to write under an easily recognizable nom de plume: Sholom Aleichem. Because Sholom Aleichem had the good fortune to marry the daughter of a wealthy landowner, he was able, for many years, to travel and write extensively. For a time he lived in Switzerland and he accepted extensive lecture tours through Europe and the

United States. When World War I exploded he fled to Denmark, and from there to America where he settled late in 1914. His literary productivity was enormous. From his first Yiddish story in 1883 until the autobiography on which he was engaged at the time of his death in 1916, a steady stream of forty volumes of stories, novels, and plays poured from his pen. Moreover, he founded the distinguished Yiddish literary journal, *Die Yiddishe Bibliothek,* and the well-known Yiddish writers of the time whom he assembled helped to produce a Yiddish literary Renaissance.

While Sholom Aleichem embarked upon his literary career by frankly imitating Mendele's moralistic approach, he soon abandoned the moribund cause of *Haskalah,* as had Mendele himself. He concentrated instead on the task of developing an authentic literature of recreation and delight for the readers of the Pale. Indeed, it was as a gentle, relaxed—even discursive—humorist that Sholom Aleichem became the most beloved Jewish writer of modern times. He chose the short story as his principal medium, and the plain folk of the typical *shtetl* as his subject matter. And what people they were! Not merely Tevye the dairyman, the poverty-stricken, wryly optimistic Jewish philosopher, the character who appeared again and again in Sholom Aleichem's stories. Not merely Menahem Mendel, the dauntless optimist and harebrained promoter; nor Hapke, the pock-marked maid. But also Rabtchik, the Jewish dog, Methuselah, the Jewish horse, and untold numbers of Jewish goats, cats, and chickens. His characters were walking clinical exhibits, suffering from every well-known affliction of the Pale: scurvy, cataracts, tuberculosis, and asthma. Although Sholom Aleichem's characters were types, they were never caricatures; neither were they, on the other hand, probing psychological studies.

Sholom Aleichem's true genius lay in his ability to master completely the emotional rhythm of Jewish life, in his willingness to dispense with "philosophy" for the sake of teaching his fellow Jews to laugh at themselves and at their suffering. And since he aimed primarily at the risibilities, he chose not to describe as much as to discurse, not to speak, as much as to *shmoose,* to chatter casually.

> Take my word for it, Mr. Sholom Aleichem [says Tevye the dairyman], the story is worth hearing. I'll sit down for a little while here near you on the grass. Let the horse do a little nibbling meanwhile. After all, even a horse is one of God's living creatures. Well, it was late spring, around *Shevuos* time. But I don't want to mislead you; it may have been a week or two before *Shevuos,* or—let's see—maybe a couple of weeks after *Shevuos.* Don't forget, this didn't happen yesterday. Wait! To be exact, it was nine or ten years ago to the day. And maybe a trifle more. In those days I was not the man I am today. That is, I *was* the same Tevye, and yet not exactly the same. The same old woman, as they say, but in a different bonnet. How so? I was as poor as a man could be, completely penniless. If you want to know the truth I'm not a rich man now either. . . .

How Sholom Aleichem's readers laughed—and cried! His reproduction of *shtetl* life was an exquisite balance of tact and humor, realism and pathos. He was content at all times to write of and for the plain people he knew. He did not moralize as did Mendele; he did not probe as did Peretz. But he exalted the commonplace by his sympathy, humor, his unerring ear for the authentic. Truly he was the folk-writer of his people, instinctively trusted, instinctively believed, more widely appreciated and understood than any of his contemporaries.

With Isaac Loeb Peretz, classical Yiddish literature reached the zenith of its belletristic development. Peretz, the ideologue of Yiddishism, was very much the student of European thought and literature. He was born in Poland, and his early manhood was scarred by misfortune: an unhappy marriage and divorce, disbarment from the practice of the law because of a brief flirtation with the revolutionary movement. Ultimately Peretz was compelled to earn his bread as a bookkeeper at the Warsaw Jewish Community House. Nearly every leisure moment of his life was spent in writing. Like his predecessors and contemporaries, Peretz passed through a "patrician" period, using the Russian, Polish, and Hebrew languages. Not until he was forty did he arrive at Yiddish, as a "last stop" in literary expression.

Peretz's writing was far from Mendele's picaresque moralizing, however, and far, too, from Sholom Aleichem's leisurely reflection of the nuances and foibles of *shtetl* life. It was instead stylistically "sophisticated," suffused with the electric nervousness of Jewish Warsaw. Unlike Mendele and Sholom Aleichem, therefore, Peretz was the hero of the intellectuals. It was he, more than anyone else, who elevated Yiddish literature to the level of European realism, who endowed it with insight, with crisp, gripping dialogue, with clinically accurate descriptions that rank his work even today with some of the finest products of Hauptmann and Péguy. Peretz was a *maskil* in the best sense of the word, attacking the fanaticism of ghetto life, its dirt and needless squalor, and yet retaining at all times an unshakable loyalty to his fellow Jews.

It was not merely his sophistication which prevented Peretz from embracing secularism as the one true *Weltanschauung* for his people. He was also a traditional and sensitive Jew. It was, in fact, his profound personal religiosity which led him into an exploration of the unadorned private faith of the ghetto-dwellers, into the field of their folklore, their wondrous and supernatural folk tales. Peretz gloriously embellished these tales. In the area of folklore, therefore, we find some of his most enduring writing: in *Bontsche Shweig,* for example, an account of a poor, helpless, uncomplaining clod of a man who even in the Kingdom of Heaven asks for only the most modest reward; *Even Higher,* the tale of a kindly Hasidic *rebbe* who proves his worth even to the most uncompromising opponents of Hasidism. There were many other tales in this genre.

It was this love and respect for the piety of simple people which led Peretz into a re-examination of Hasidism, a re-examination, as it turned out, that anticipated the writings of Martin Buber, the neo-Hasidism of the years immediately following Peretz's death (see Chapter XIX). In this sense, perhaps, Peretz was influenced by the Europe-wide re-evaluation of mysticism, which was pioneered, during his lifetime, by such men as Baudelaire, Mallarmé, Verlaine, and Maeterlinck in Western Europe, by the Polish dramatist Stanislaus Wyspianski, and the Russian novelist D. S. Merezhovski. Peretz's splendid tale *Zwischen Zwei Berg* ("Between Two Mountains") was an affirmation of the importance of faith in a materialistic world:

> That which I saw differed in no way from what I had seen on previous occasions; but the manner of my seeing it was different. It was as if scales had fallen from my eyes. . . . On the meadows, among the flames and grasses, little groups of Hasidim walked to and fro. Their satin gabardines—and even those of plain cotton—glittered like mirrors: all of them, even those that were ragged. And the flames that danced among the grasses touched the holiday attire of the Hasidim and played with it; it was as if every Hasid was surrounded with exultant, joyous fire. And the Hasidim turned their longing eyes to the veranda, and the light in their eyes was drawn from the eyes of their Rabbi. And as the light grew, their songs became louder, gayer, and even more sacred. Every group sang its own melody, and the melodies mingled in the air and came to us in a single harmony. And not only they sang; the heavens sang too, the upper spheres sang, and the earth under their feet sang; the soul of the world sang—everything sang. Lord of the world! The sweetness of it melted my heart!

But even in his most romantic and mystical moments, Peretz always retained a sense of realism, a crispness of style, and a psychological insight into the labyrinths of character.

There were other gifted Yiddish writers who followed this classical trio of Mendele, Sholom Aleichem, and Peretz into the twentieth century: Sholem Asch and I. J. Singer, the authors of monumental neo-Tolstoyan novels on Jewish life in Eastern Europe; Joseph Opatoshu, Zalman Schneur, David Pinski, men who worked out new styles that were frequently naturalistic, erotic, often coarse as well as vivid. Even as Yiddish was rising to the stature of a major European literary medium, however, it was increasingly identified as a propaganda medium—at least in the Pale of Settlement—by the emergence of the Bundist movement (see Chapter XIV). Precisely because Socialism idealized Yiddish as the language of the proletarian masses, the ranks of the Yiddish writers were swollen by hundreds of Bundist professionals, who stamped their partisan imprimatur on the new Yiddish literary tradition. By the eve of the first World War, as a result, the majority of Yiddish writers in the Pale (not all of them, to be sure) had become official or unofficial publicists for the Bundist cause.

With the first World War, the future of Yiddish literature as a medium of belletristic expression hung in the balance. Within the space of three years Mendele, Sholom Aleichem, and Peretz all died; the enormous crowds that attended their funerals attested to the vast and enduring impact of their writings. Even as this trio was passing from the scene, the Bolshevist

Revolution eradicated the old Russian Empire. Yiddish literature split into three principal sectors: Soviet, American, and Polish. In Russia, Yiddish rapidly became the State-serving vehicle of sovietization, and thus lost its creative *élan* in the land of its birth. In the United States, Yiddish was increasingly transformed into a journalistic medium for Americanization. Poland alone remained, for the brief years before the Nazi holocaust, the world center of creative Yiddish writing. The very feverish intensity with which the Polish-Jewish community produced its novels and plays signified little more, ultimately, than the final flaring of the candle before it guttered out.

CONCLUSION

One of the reasons for the decline of *Haskalah* in Eastern Europe was the fact that it devoted its principal efforts to self-justification; it presented Russian Jewry with virtually no original ideas—save the idea that secular literature had a right to exist in the first place. It is little wonder that the first breath of political reaction in Russia was enough to rout the kind of naive reformism which believed that all salvation lay in reading Western books and getting back to nature. Yet we must not underestimate the function *Haskalah* performed for the Jews of the Pale. It purified their writings and made significant progress in cleansing the recesses and cul-de-sacs of ghetto obscurantism. By creating a literate Jew, a Jew with an ear for practical as well as spiritual inspiration, the *Haskalah* justified even the most contumacious of its advocates. Socialism and Zionism would never have been possible without the secularistic groundwork laid by the *maskilim*.

During the early years of the twentieth century Hebrew writers spent much less of their time in justifying Enlightenment, and a great deal more in examining the meaning and values of Zionism. This meant that their major attention and talents were devoted to movements that were not predominantly literary or cultural, but activist, that is to say, political and economic. Of course, there were poets and novelists who were drawn to Zionism, ever more of them as the movement gained in strength and maturity. Yet most of the literature produced by this new crusade in its early years was statistical, pragmatic, programmatic. In the long view, this proved to be a blessing, even for the cultural Zionists. For it was from the terra firma of Jewish settlement in Palestine that yet a new Hebrew literature sprang into existence—a literature authentic, imaginative, creative beyond the most far-visioned hopes and dreams of the Hebrew writers of nineteenth-century Russia.

Notes

Page 206. Translation of "Mikaele's" poem by Meyer Waxman, *A History of Jewish Literature*, III, 234.

Page 214. For an excellent analysis of the development of Yiddish literature, see the introduction in Irving Howe and Eliezer Greenberg (edd.), *A Treasury of Yiddish Stories*.

Page 215. See Chaim Tschernowitz's portrait of Mendele in "Grandfather Mendele as I Remember Him," *Commentary*, November, 1948.

Page 218. The luminous translation from Peretz is included in Maurice Samuel, *Prince of the Ghetto*, p. 238.

Page 219. For a valuable analysis of the decline of *Haskalah* see Simon Halkin, *Modern Hebrew Literature*, pp. 67-73.

XI

The Emergence of Anti-Semitism

GERMANY: CONSERVATISM TRIUMPHANT

In 1870, the *annus mirabilis* of modern European history, a powerful German Empire suddenly emerged from a chaos of independent, factious sovereignties, and cast its shadow over all Central Europe. The new empire was an authentic political miracle; and it was brought into existence by a gruff, walrus-mustached miracle-maker named Otto von Bismarck, the "Iron Chancellor" of Prussia. Bismarck's achievement was all the more remarkable in that he was not obliged to invoke the liberal-romantic tradition of 1848. Instead, he forged the new Germany out of the "blood and iron" of the Franco-Prussian War; he appealed to the national pride and the voluntary allegiance of Germany's principalities by producing the bogey of a common French enemy. The ruse worked; the states of Germany rallied to the Prussian cause—and then remained with Prussia when the war was over. While some trappings of democracy were adopted to make the new empire more palatable—two houses of Parliament, for example, and universal suffrage—German "constitutionalism" was largely a sham. Parliament could not initiate legislation, nor could it demand ministerial recall. Only the Kaiser was permitted to appoint the officials of government; and Bismarck saw to it that old Wilhelm I chose such officials from the arch-conservative Prussian Junker class.

All in all, Bismarck had a right to be satisfied with himself. He not only created an empire, but he created it in his own conservative image. During his career as chancellor of the new Germany, he was able to rely on a powerful coalition of supporters from among the Junker aristocracy of his native Prussia and from among members of the conservative Catholic Center party. Even the middle-class industrialists, with their painfully nurtured notions of liberalism and constitutionalism, were cajoled into co-operation. Bismarck closed their eyes to the authoritarianism of his regime by offering them a huge, unrestricted market for business, the glittering new slogan of "nationalism," and the bait of some civil rights, especially the right to make money. By the 1880's the National Liberal party, the citadel of the industrial middle class, was no longer a serious danger to the monolithic conservative State-machine. Germany was on its way to becoming a mailed fist.

There are few arguments as powerful as those that are rooted in success. Unquestionably, it was Bismarck's achievement in building the new Germany which accounted for the significant growth of German statist literature in the latter part of the nineteenth century. For that matter, the whole period was marked by a Europe-wide intellectual reaction against the "mobocracy." Russia had its Pobedonostev and Dostoevski, Italy its Carducci, France its Taine, England its Carlyle and Rhodes. But the implications of this revived conservatism were most fully apparent in Germany. For in Germany conservatism worked: it created the State; it created prosperity; it created power. For sixty years before the emergence of the empire, Kant, Fichte, Herder, and Hegel had argued that the needs of the Christian-German State took precedence over the needs of the individual. Droysen and Ranke delved deep into German history to support this contention. Now, in one massive *coup de main*, Bismarck validated all the theorizing that had gone before. If conservative nationalism had been a respectable philosophy in pre-Bismarckian days, it seemed positively irrefutable after 1870.

Among the supporters of statism was the philosopher Friedrich Nietzsche, one of the most provocative writers of his time, and certainly among Germany's most brilliant stylists. Profoundly impressed by the growth of the German State-machine, Nietzsche was unsparing in his contempt for the "outworn" values of the old order—"philistine slave-morality," democracy, and middle-class self-satisfaction. After all, none of these "ornaments" of Western civilization had contributed to Germany's ascendancy. Nietzsche's most celebrated works, *The Will to Power* and *Thus Spake Zarathustra*, provided the intelligentsia of Central Europe with morbidly attractive slogans: "might makes right," "blond beast," "superman." Distorted and misappropriated by Nietzsche's more impressionable readers, these were slogans that eventually became the ideological tools of aggressive nationalism.

Nietzsche was joined in his contempt for "nineteenth-century morality" by Heinrich von Treitschke, perhaps the most eloquent and formidable of pre-Nazi German ideologues. Treitschke envisaged the State as the true embodiment of mind and spirit, as an all-embracing self-determined entity, unbound by rules of behavior or morality, by any limitation save its own carnivorous power to grow. The State was, in sum, the "divine will" as it "exists on earth." The writings of Nietzsche and Treitschke were extraordinarily influential. Indeed, they became Scripture for tens of thousands of young German intellectuals who thus buttressed the political triumph of conservative nationalism. Only a few additional weapons were needed to render the Leviathan-State impregnable. One of these weapons was anti-Semitism.

WHY THE JEWS?

For those who have followed our narrative thus far, a description of the Jew-hatred which obstructed Emancipation hardly requires repetition. We recall that in the minds of some Europeans (of Voltaire, for example) the Jews were relics of a barbarous and obscurantist past, and as such were unworthy of the rights of free men. Yet even this kind of intellectualized contempt, however bitingly expressed by Europe's cleverest minds, was swallowed up in the lingering backwash of peasant fear and distrust. As late as the nineteenth century Europe was still predominantly agricultural; and because the peasantry had not yet entirely shed its religious traditions and superstitions, the medieval conception of the Jew as Christ-killer, as blood-sucker, as well-poisoner, had not completely vanished. In the folklore of the countryside, the Jew continued to represent the incarnation of the devil. The "diabolization" of the Jew may have been declining in a world growing progressively secular; but it still endured with enough strength, even in Central and Western Europe, to stigmatize the Jews as a people apart, a people under a historic cloud of suspicion, barely to be tolerated. Occasionally these old suspicions flamed into active hatred. In 1882, for example, in the Hungarian village of Tisza-Eszlar, the disappearance of a local girl revived the medieval canard of Jewish ritual murder. For a year and a half a group of Jewish villagers were imprisoned, and ruthlessly cross-examined and tortured, in an attempt to extract from them a confession of their "heinous" religious practice. Ultimately they were released for lack of evidence. But the fact of their release could not obscure the alarming credulity of Europeans so late in the nineteenth century. In the decades that followed, other ritual murder charges made their appearance. "Religious" suspicion was a comparatively dormant phenomenon in the twentieth century, but it did endure.

There were other factors that compounded this "religious" distrust. The fact that the Jews were circumcised suggested weird characteristics to the unconscious of the typical European: that the Jews were castrated, enfeebled, and impotent men, perhaps even females in disguise. Freud theorized that Christians resented Jews because of the son-father tension in the superego. Maurice Samuel went further in suggesting that Jew-hatred sublimates the yearning of Christians for the freedoms of the pagan world. They resent Christian morality as the strait jacket that inhibits the release of their pagan instincts. Yet they are unable to attack Christianity without destroying the foundations of their society. Hence they vent their spleen on the Jews, the people who produced Christ and Christianity. In this fashion anti-Semitism gives the Christian the opportunity to rebel against and at the same time to respect authority. Conversely, modern man, covetous of his "civilized" reputation, fears the animal, the destructive instincts that emerge occasionally in his unconscious. He projects those instincts, the existence of which both frightens and confuses him, onto a people he fears and cannot understand, viz., the Jews.

In modern times the rise of nationalism gave an even more tangible contour to the unique and anomalous status occupied by Jews in Christian thinking. Who were the Jews? Where did these mysterious and potent wizards come from? They bore, as Leo Pinsker suggested in his penetrating little volume, *Auto-Emancipation* (see Chapter XIII), all the attributes of nationality but they had no country of their own. They skulked like faceless gypsies through Europe's cities. They pledged loyalty to the lands of their domicile, and yet they were a people with international ties, and they expressed their ethnic cohesion in a hundred different religious and philanthropic ways. In addition, their international bankers had been identified indiscriminately with all the major dynasties of Europe. Of course, these dynasties had freed themselves from the Frankfurt tradition by the latter part of the nineteenth century; but loss of Jewish banking power merely aggravated nationalist suspicions. The international Jewish bankers now maintained their position of world prestige without sufficient power to justify it. As de Tocqueville suggested of eighteenth-century France, and as Hannah Arendt has observed of these international bankers, society, like nature, abhors a vacuum. Wealth without visible function was much more intolerable because nobody understood why it should be tolerated.

These, then, were at least some of the factors that accounted for the anti-Jewish resentments and suspicions that lay dormant in the psyche of European Christendom. By themselves they were not likely to sputter into flames. They had to be ignited for pragmatic ends by experts in mob psychology. In the latter part of the nineteenth century such experts appeared as the agents of conservative nationalism.

CHRISTIAN SOCIALISM: THE REVOLT OF THE LOWER MIDDLE CLASS

Even before Jew-hatred was systematically exploited as a political weapon, a number of German nationalist-conservative ideologues had prepared the intellectual groundwork for modern anti-Semitism. It was Treitschke, for example, who encouraged German conservative nationalists to identify the Jews with the twin dangers of liberalism and internationalism, an identification which had merely been toyed with by conservatives during the 1848 period. What stake could the Jews possibly have in the future of the German State, Treitschke asked? Were they not everywhere revolutionists or atheists? In a series of articles in the *Preussische Jahrbuch* in the autumn of 1879, Treitschke called attention to the growing power of "Jewish solidarity," to the emergence of a separate German-Jewish caste. Accordingly, he warned his countrymen that Germany must be transformed into a Lutheran *Kultur-Staat,* and cleansed of all "cosmopolitanism" influences. Treitschke argued, too, that an international "network of Jews was using liberalism to fasten a strangle hold on German life; after all, what were big business and dynamic capitalism if not Jewish creations? It was a theory which exercised an irresistible appeal to the lower middle class, the people who most feared modern capitalism.

The 1870's were, in truth, critical years for the lower middle class. They were years of depression in which the shopkeeper and schoolteacher were driven perilously close to loss of white-collar status. It was during this period of national malaise that Adolf Stöcker, one of the cleverest demagogues of modern times, came to prominence. The son of a jail warden who barely managed to provide him with schooling, Stöcker eventually rose to the position of Protestant chaplain at the Imperial Court. Sharing the passions and prejudices of his royal and Junker parishioners, Stöcker loathed the industrial middle class and feared its growing power. It was, in fact, precisely because he himself experienced a kind of valetlike antipathy for the intrusion of parvenus into German society that he was able to appreciate the bitterness of the small businessmen of his time. He understood the pride which prevented them from moving into Marxian Socialism cheek by jowl with the working proletariat.

Stöcker was determined, therefore, to provide the lower *Mittelstand* with a species of nonproletarian socialism that would bring it back into alliance with the Protestant conservatives. To that end, he founded a Christian Social Workers Party in 1878, and undergirded it with a broad program for social reform: trade corporations, government-controlled insurance schemes, prohibition of Sunday work, and a number of other "welfare" ideas that yet fell short of classic Marxism. Later, as he stumped through lower-middle-class neighborhoods, Stöcker gradually perfected a technique which was destined to make his program even more appealing to harassed white-collar workers. "I have emphasized," he said, "that the social revolution has to be overcome by healthy social reform, built on a Christian foundation. . . . I do not want culture that is not Germanic and Christian. That is why I am fighting against Jewish supremacy."

Anti-Semitism exercised a peculiar fascination for the lower middle class. When they resented the success of big business, assaults on Jewish big businessmen enabled them to express their resentment without espousing socialism. Desperately in need of self-assurance, white-collar workers were obliged to grope at threadbare and pitiful rationalizations to explain their lack of success and standing. The groups from which Stöcker recruited his followers were, in fact, entirely lacking in social cohesion and unity of purpose. Cohesion and purpose, therefore, were the qualities Stöcker taught them instantly and instinctively to attribute to the Jews. Curiously enough, it was the democratization of government in the nineteenth century which gave fillip to this kind of political anti-Semitism. The "mob," despised and feared by aristocrats, now had become the arbiter of issues. It was the "mob," therefore, to which Stöcker appealed as he harangued his audiences with blunt, primitive references to the "conspiracy" of an unpopular and suspected people.

Stöcker was the man who first made anti-Semitism a national issue in Germany. His power of oratory was extraordinary—indeed, he was elected to the Reichstag intermittently throughout the 1880's. More than any other personality, it was he who lured the lower middle class permanently away from Marxism and into the camp of the squirearchy. It was Stöcker, too, who rekindled social anti-Semitism: during the 1870's and 1880's restrictive placards began to appear in the leading hotels, restaurants, and resorts of Germany; and anti-Semitic epithets were mouthed without hesitation by civil servants, shopkeepers, schoolteachers, and even professors. Stöcker was too cautious a man, perhaps even too sincere a Christian—according to his own lights—to espouse the doctine of racism. By twentieth-century standards his anti-Semitic strictures were rather mild and bore little relation to the wild nihilism of his successors; he demanded little more than "reasonable" restrictions on Jewish immigration and on Jewish participation in economic life. But Stöcker's "moderation" notwithstanding, he did succeed in saturating the lower middle class with Jew-hatred and, thereby, laid the groundwork for the racists who followed.

There were politicians in the Hapsburg Monarchy equally willing to exploit white-collar anti-Semitism. They were concentrated, for the most part, in two rival groups: the Pan-German Party (see p. 237, below) and the Christian Socialist Party. Of the two, in the 1880's and 1890's it was the Christian Socialists, backed by the full power of the Austrian Catholic clergy, who achieved the greater degree of prestige, especially in the capital of Vienna. They were led by Dr. Karl Lueger, a man quite similar in ideology and purpose to Adolf Stöcker. In some ways, in fact, Lueger surpassed Stöcker in calculated demagoguery and political acumen. He was elected as mayor of Vienna several times during the 1890's, although it was not until 1897 that Emperor Franz Josef, who feared the "antisocial" consequences of Lueger's anti-Semitism, finally confirmed him in office. Lueger was a curious combination: vision and courage walked hand in hand with cynicism and unscrupulousness. He was Europe's first pioneer, together with Joseph Chamberlain of England, in the field of municipal socialism. He municipalized Vienna's gas, water, and street systems, and drafted a series of insurance programs for the lower middle class which spared them the "humiliation" of having to join labor unions. But he maintained his alliance with conservative clerical forces; and at all times he employed anti-Semitism as the principal bait for his party. Like Stöcker, Lueger avoided appeals to racism; nor did he ever actively persecute Jews after he assumed office as mayor. But throughout his career he maintained a steady drumbeat of anti-Semitic abuse and vilification, shrewdly identifying the Jews with the despised upper middle class. Lueger's enduring significance, perhaps, was to be found in his impact on a shabby Austrian ne'er-do-well named Adolf Hitler. For it was from Lueger that Hitler learned the expediency of bypassing the established, more cautious classes, and of appealing rather to economic groups that felt themselves threatened with loss of status—groups that were willing, therefore, to fight vigorously.

In the late 1870's and early 1880's, as Christian Socialism developed into a movement of not inconsiderable consequence throughout the German-speaking world, increasing numbers of German conservatives awakened to the uses that could be made of anti-Semitism. In Germany itself, several Conservative party journals tried to discredit the National Liberal party by identifying it with such prominent Jewish leaders as Eduard Lasker and Ludwig Bamberger. They made snide references to "fellow citizens of

Semitic race." Bismarck himself, however, the titular leader of the Conservative party, was at first quite unwilling to ride the hobbyhorse of political anti-Semitism. After all, he had pioneered Jewish emancipation in Germany; he had once made the memorable statement that the breeding of a "German stallion" and a "Jewish mare" would provide the country with its most valuable offspring. In addition, Bismarck was personally associated with several Jewish bankers, particularly the Bleichröders, and he respected them highly. Yet, as the exigencies of domestic politics drove him into greater dependence upon Stöcker and other questionable politicians, even Bismarck eventually felt compelled to reconsider his position vis-à-vis the Jews. In the spring of 1881, persuaded that anti-Semitism was an indispensable weapon in wooing lower-middle-class support, the Chancellor permittted himself to observe: "I should like to see the State which for the most part consists of Christians—penetrated to some extent by the principles of the religion it professes." In November of that year Bismarck informed his Minister of Agriculture that "while he was opposed to anti-Semitic agitation he had done nothing against it because of its courageous stand against the Progressives." With these words Bismarck provided German anti-Semitism with a necessary ingredient: respectability.

It was, therefore, with Bismarck's tacit approval that the leadership of the German Conservative party turned increasingly in the 1880's to Stöcker's Christian Socialists—a *mariage de convenance* which anticipated the twentieth-century alliance between the German nationalists and the Nazis. In 1892 Stöcker engineered his most effective coup: he persuaded the Conservative leaders that they must endorse the cult of Jew-hatred if they wished to channel a mass movement of disgruntled white-collar workers into their party. Accordingly, at the Tivoli Convention of 1892, the Conservatives adopted a mildly anti-Semitic plank, deprecating "Jewish influence" in national life. This success came too late for Stöcker, however; within a month of the Tivoli Convention he was fired by the new Kaiser, Wilhelm II, for "irresponsible extremism"—the extremism of socialism, not anti-Semitism. With Stöcker's disgrace the Christian Socialist movement sank into oblivion. But not organized anti-Semitism. Jew-hatred was respectable now; it had been endorsed by the aristocratic Conservative party, and was destined, as a result, to endure as a basic political weapon of the German right.

FRANCE: THE REVOLUTION CONTINUES

France, too, witnessed the revival of a dangerous conservative nationalism. It is a basic axiom of French history that the great Revolution of 1789 never really ended. Throughout the course of the nineteenth century, royalists and clericals fought bitterly, and with occasional success, to stem the liberal tide. They managed to dispose of the first two French Republics, and were convinced that the third, which had been rather precariously established out of the shambles of the Franco-Prussian War, was equally vulnerable. Nor were the conservatives unsuccessful in developing an appealing intellectual rationale. The Positivist August Comte censured republicanism for its inefficiency. What France needed, Comte insisted, was a political-intellectual dictatorship of philosopher-kings, men capable of formulating national policies on the basis of science and technology rather than on the basis of popular whim. Hippolyte Adolphe Taine appealed to French nationalism and pride, both grievously wounded by the Prussian victory in 1870, by extolling the virtues of militant Statism, and by assuring Frenchmen that they bore the same relation to the national State that the single cell bore to the mature organism. Monarchy, Aristocracy, and Catholicism, declared Taine, were the historic influences that had shaped the French nation; it was a nation, he warned, which was now being seriously debilitated by dangerous notions of democracy. Maurice Barrès endorsed this approach, arguing that the moral unity of France must be the Frenchman's first concern, and that only a historic dynasty could create that unity; if France wished to be strong, she must first purge herself of liberals and internationalists, of aliens and Jews. To prepare for this purge, Charles Maurras emphasized the importance of "direct action." His hoodlum band of followers, the *Action Française,* specialized in felonious assaults on liberals, Protestants, and Jews; indeed, it was the *Action Française* which represented Western Europe's first sinister transformation of modern anti-Semitic ideology into organized physical violence.

Both in France and Germany, therefore, powerful nationalist movements developed, attached themselves to political conservatism, and crowded out the more inept (because they were more scrupulous) varieties of liberal nationalism. And in both countries, conversely, there were conservatives aplenty willing to embrace nationalism as the logical weapon with which to disarm their adversaries. In France, for example, the aristocracy and royalists drew much of their support from a militantly vindictive Catholic Church. The clerics lived in mortal dread of "Republican secularism," especially the belligerent secularism of Léon Gambetta and his radical colleagues. To be sure, Pope Leo XIII had urged French Catholics to accept the Republic, and to defend the cause of the Church within the framework of Republican politics; but his words fell on deaf ears. During the 1880's the Jesuits, infiltrating back into France, established close connection with the royalist cause. They issued shrewd appeals to French "nationalism," urging patriotic Frenchmen to repudiate a Republic which was the "captive" of Protestants, Freemasons, internationalists, and Jews.

In 1900 the Jews who "held France captive" numbered at most eighty thousand, perhaps thirteen hundredths of one per cent of the country's population, and most of them in the lower-middle income bracket. Yet, because there were also a few millionaires among them, some disquieting, if transitory, suggestions of anti-Semitism appeared among French Socialists. The more blatant anti-Semitism was soon pre-empted, however, by the conservatives. Their most eloquent and effective spokesman was a venomous little journalist named Edouard Drumont, who earned his livelihood variously as a clerk, traveling salesman, police agent, government spy, and finally as a reporter. He was a man consumed, too, with *petit-bourgeois* bitterness;

although he was hard-working and ambitious, his personal and sexual life, as well as the erratic course of his career, was a continual frustration to him. Deeply sentimental, then progressively superstitious, Drumont carried a mandrake root and consorted with seers and spiritualists. It was out of the ferment of such bitterness and obscurantism that he produced, in 1886, his notorious anti-Semitic harangue, *La France Juive.*

It was an easily readable book, written in the raciest of prose, filled with the most sensational and farfetched "revelations." The story was an old one: the Jews were the principal source of France's misfortunes; they could be distinguished by their hooked noses, eager fingers, and unpleasant odors; every Protestant was a half-Jew; the Jews were the principal innovators of liberalism. In fact, it was through the medium of the liberal upper bourgeoisie that the Jews and Freemasons conspired to control the country. Page after page of *La France Juive* was filled with "documentation" and variations of this theme. The success of the book was phenomenal. Before the end of the year, over one hundred thousand copies had been sold, and installments of its chapters had appeared in the leading royalist newspapers of France. For a while Drumont sought to exploit his success by working out a kind of fuzzy-minded program of Christian Socialism; unlike Stöcker and Lueger, however, he ultimately dropped the idea and concentrated, with disastrous effectiveness, on naked anti-Semitism. It was Drumont, more than any other man, who gave the anti-Republican forces in France their most lethal weapon. Royalists and clericals had long sought to popularize the notion that liberalism was a "secret conspiracy"—of Protestants, Rosicrucians, Freemasons—even Anabaptists! Now the success of Drumont's work convinced them that Jew-hatred was the most perfect catalyst. The royalist press launched a steadily mounting campaign against the Jewish bourgeoisie.

Yet reaction did not enjoy the prestige of success in France as it did in Germany and in the Hapsburg Monarchy. The administration remained in the hands of the Republicans; as a result, anti-Semitism was not invested with the respectability of government approval. Thus, by the mid-1890's, Jew-hatred began to lose some of its effectiveness as a political force in France; it was simply impossible to exploit. For a while, to be sure, it appeared as if the failure of the government-backed Panama Canal project might provide the royalists with the necessary opening. This widely publicized undertaking, it was revealed, had been riddled by corruption and bribery; a number of liberal deputies and Jewish financiers, the most conspicuous of whom was Baron Jacques de Reinach, had participated in some of the shady dealings. Before the royalists could effectively dramatize their advantage, however, the facts revealed that significant numbers of their own group were equally implicated, and the rightist press hastily buried the incident.

Then, suddenly, a made-to-order "scandal" exploded just in time to give renewed power to anti-Semitism as a weapon of the right. It was out of the furor of the Dreyfus Case that the fate of clerical reaction, of anti-Semitism, indeed of the Republic itself, was ultimately to be decided.

THE DREYFUS AFFAIR

In September of 1894 a French counterespionage agent discovered a suspicious piece of paper in the wastebasket of the German military attaché; he promptly delivered it to his superiors. On the *bordereau,* as the paper was later called, appeared a promise, written in French, to deliver a valuable French artillery manual into German hands. Colonel Sandherr, Chief of French Military Intelligence, was unable to identify the handwriting authoritatively; neither could the handwriting experts whom he consulted. Eventually, however, he was persuaded by his aide, Colonel Henry, that the most likely culprit was an artillery officer, a Captain Alfred Dreyfus. It hardly mattered that the handwriting bore little resemblance to Dreyfus's script; the man was vulnerable on other counts. He was rich; he was snobbish; and he was a Jew. His very presence in the midst of the Jesuit-trained aristocrats at military headquarters was a festering source of irritation. In a matter of days, therefore, Dreyfus was summarily arrested, jailed, held incommunicado, and then dragged before a cold-eyed military court-martial and formally accused of treason. Colonel Henry, who had first devised the idea of arresting Dreyfus, informed the panel of officers that he had "other" information implicating Dreyfus, information "of such secrecy" that it could not be revealed without jeopardizing France's military position. At first, the court-martial hesitated to pass judgment against Dreyfus on the basis of the meager "evidence" before it. But the vindictive clamor of Drumont and the royalist press soon forced the issue; headlines and editorials devoted to the "international Jewish conspiracy" convinced the presiding officers that it would be politically expedient to convict Dreyfus. Accordingly, the unfortunate man was banished from the Army and sentenced to life imprisonment in exile. Dreyfus was transported in chains to a pestilent prison island off the coast of French Guiana. The case was apparently closed.

Then Sandherr retired as Chief of Intelligence and was succeeded by Lieutenant Colonel Picquart. In March of 1896 the counterespionage agent who had uncovered the original *bordereau* discovered—in the same office of the German military attaché—a new piece of paper, a small special delivery letterette which promised new deliveries of French military secrets. More important, the handwriting was identical with that found on the original *bordereau.* Inasmuch as Dreyfus was locked away on Devil's Island, it was clear that he could not logically have been the author of the original treason. Checking carefully, Picquart managed to trace the writing to another officer, Walsin Esterhazy, a notorious profligate and roué. When Picquart revealed his findings to Henry, whom he had inherited as his assistant, he was astonished at his subordinate's reaction. How, asked Henry, could the Army admit that it had made a mistake without tarnishing its honor? Henry must have left a few thoughts unspoken, as well: would the Army not compromise itself as the glittering instrument of the royalist cause? Was it not for the sake of embarrassing the Republic, of investing the Republic with the incubus of "Jewish treason," that he, Henry, had invented the story of other "secret" information about Dreyfus? The case had to be kept closed at all costs. In a sweat, Henry rushed out of Picquart's office, found scissors, paste, and invisible ink, and began to forge additional "evidence" against Dreyfus. Simultaneously, he notified his superiors that Picquart was about to make embarrassing investigations into the original conviction. Thus, before Picquart could take further action on his own, he found himself summarily ordered off to Tunisia.

Virtually on the eve of his departure, Picquart transmitted the crucial new information to his attorney who, in turn, brought it to the attention of Scheurer-Kestner, the liberal vice-president of the French Senate. Scheurer-Kestner recognized at once that the Army's determination to protect its "honor" undermined equality before the law, the very foundation of republican government. Almost immediately, therefore, he and his colleagues in the liberal wing of the Senate began to campaign for a retrial. At approximately the same time, Mathieu Dreyfus, the brother of the imprisoned officer, managed to secure a facsimile of the original *bordereau*. He submitted it for examination to a number of bank officials, and within a matter of weeks they identified the handwriting as Esterhazy's. When the information was released to the press, the military had no choice but to bring Esterhazy before a court-martial. The evidence against him was serious. It was not merely a matter of handwriting, but of motive as well. Esterhazy was a chronic gambler and playboy; his adventures at the gaming table and in the boudoir left him continually short of cash. Moreover, his diaries revealed his secret detestation for his adopted land. None of this mattered to the uniformed aristocrats who heard the evidence: the original account of "Jewish treason" could not be undone. Nor could the Army sully its "honor" by convicting one of its own. Esterhazy was acquitted.

By 1898 the Dreyfus Affair had become a public scandal, the most explosive issue in national politics. The press was filled with the bitterest of diatribes on both sides of the issue. Families and friendships were broken, duels were fought over the *Affaire*. The organized royalist anti-Semitic campaign gained momentum daily; it was largely directed, later evidence revealed, by the administrative staff of the Vatican Secretariat of State. More was at stake, clearly, than the guilt or innocence of a Jewish officer. Liberal politicians such as Georges Clemenceau and Aristide Briand, liberal writers such as Anatole France, Charles Péguy, and Emile Zola openly branded the anti-Dreyfusard assault for what it was: an attempt by the royalists to liberate the Army from the civilian processes of government—with consequences that might well mean the demise of republican government.

In the summer of 1898 events approached a climax. A disgruntled relative of Esterhazy's, one of many whom the officer had swindled, charged that the so-called "secret" evidence against Dreyfus was a fraud. General Cavaignac, the new Army Chief of Staff, was by no means a defender of republican government or a friend of the Jews; but he was an honest man, and he did feel obliged to investigate the charge. He recalled Henry and demanded the "secret" Dreyfus dossier. It was only a matter of minutes before Henry's "evidence" was exposed for the clumsy forgery that it was. Henry himself was unceremoniously thrown into jail. That night he drank two bottles of rum, wrote a terrified and incoherent letter to his wife, and cut his throat. The news of his suicide struck France like a bombshell. The royalists, although horrified, were far from willing to admit defeat. A "Henry Memorial Fund" was established, and hundreds of Catholic clergy joined the officers and aristocrats who subscribed to it, including one prelate who "wished that he could wield a sword as well as a holy water sprinkler," and another who wished to "circumcise the Jews up to the necks." Nevertheless, it was now perfectly apparent that a retrial for Dreyfus could no longer be postponed.

Ever since the winter of 1894 Dreyfus had been left to rot, half insane, in a vermin-infested cell in Devil's Island. Each day his view was restricted to the little beach fronting his hut; each night he was chained to his cot. The worst of the tragedy was, however, that for four years he believed himself a forgotten man. The fact that his conviction had created a furor in France was never revealed to him until June of 1899, when he was suddenly ordered to dress and board a cruiser for his return to France. He was carried back across the ocean, reunited with his family in the military headquarters of Rennes, and told to prepare himself for a retrial. Still dazed by the sudden turn of events, Dreyfus walked into the courtroom, bent, gaunt, bald, except for a fringe of white hair. He was thirty-nine years old. As the trial proceeded, the anti-Semitic diatribes of the army officers and the royalist-Catholic press reached new levels of irresponsibility, including the warning that the Jews faced "mass extermination." Yet, the evidence for Dreyfus was irrefutable: the *bordereau,* Henry's forgeries, newly revealed facts of Esterhazy's complicity. Nevertheless, it took the court-martial of army officers only an hour to reach a verdict: they pronounced Dreyfus guilty. They were willing, however, to reduce his sentence to ten years because of "extenuating circumstances."

The liberal reaction to this verdict, both in France and the rest of Western Europe, was emphatic and violent. Fortunately, the new President of the French Republic, Emile Loubet, was himself a liberal; he hastened to silence the uproar by promptly pardoning Dreyfus. After all, there was the forthcoming Paris Exposition to think about. Dreyfus's good name, on the other hand, could hardly be cleared except by complete judicial exoneration, and this did not come until seven years later. But it hardly mattered. If the Catholics and royalists had hoped to return to power through the military, their hopes now were doomed; the Army had seriously compromised itself as the shining repository of French glory. The royalists and clericals, too, by their unequivocal support of the anti-Dreyfusard campaign, had decisively destroyed their effectiveness as a major political force. Within a few years a Radical Parliament was able to separate Church and State, to reaffirm the abiding liberal principles of French republicanism, and, as if to symbolize the unshakable security of French Jewry, to honor Dreyfus himself with membership in the Legion of Honor.

The victory of the liberal forces was unhappily overemphasized. For many years after the vindication of the Jewish army officer and the discomfiture of the reactionaries, it seemed conventionally sound to refer to the

Dreyfus Case as a turning point for all of Europe, a harbinger of a new day. No political illusion was ever more widely cherished—or more cruelly shattered. For the sinister gestation of German racism eventually proved the Dreyfus Affair to be little more than a fretful rehearsal for the incalculable horrors of the twentieth century.

THE RISE OF RACISM

We have discussed the confluence of nationalism and conservatism which dominated political events in Germany and France: in the former successfully, in the latter much less so. Near the end of the nineteenth century, a number of German conservative nationalists began tentatively to experiment with a new doctrine, racism. The doctrine appealed to the rightists for two principal reasons. First, it supplied Germany's iron State-machine with a biological rationale: "proving" German racial superiority over neighboring peoples, the disciples of Nietzsche and Treitschke lent further credence to the irrestistibility of the German "will to power." Secondly, because the rightists had found anti-Semitism a valuable weapon in maintaining the political *status quo,* they were able to strengthen its usefulness by adding racial contempt to the backlog of Jew-hatred.

German racism grew out of the "Aryan" myth, a myth which found its "scientific" beginnings in the eighteenth century. It was the Frenchman Buffon who created the modern concept of genus and species; while Camper, a Dutchman, tentatively suggested that there were basic differences in physiognomy between groups of human beings. The Semitic languages were identified and classified at the end of the eighteenth century, and in 1833 the German Franz Bopp traced the Romance, Germanic, and Slavic tongues back to a common Aryan source. Here science ended and pseudoscience began, for European scholars erroneously assumed that a common language meant a common race. A. F. Pott and Theodore Pösch reconstructed a mythical Aryan people, blond and blue-eyed, who apparently migrated to Europe from Central Asia. Then, in 1855, Count Joseph Arthur de Gobineau, a French diplomat, published a widely influential two-volume book entitled *Essai sur l'inégalité des races humaines.* In this treatise Gobineau argued that "the history of mankind proves that the destinies of people are governed by racial law." He deduced that all civilization flowed back to the Aryan race, ostensibly the purest and most creative of the historic races of the world. Gobineau concluded that the descendants of the Aryan race were now to be found only in Central Europe. Gobineau's curious idealization of a mythical people had not yet reached its final apogee, however. During the second half of the century the legend of Aryan superiority was taken over by a number of German historians and anthropologists, nearly all of whom were conservative and nationalist in their political orientation. It was hardly surprising that these scholars—Friedrich Ratzel, Karl Lamprecht, Leopold von Ranke, Ernst Curtius, and others—should have identified the Germans as the living representatives of the Aryan race, or that the vernacular of pseudoscience should have been employed to accentuate the alleged differences between the modern German-Aryan and his non-German, and non-Aryan, neighbors.

The racists found a basis of comparison within Germany, too, by fastening upon the least popular of Europe's ethnic groups. It was a comparison between the boundless superhumanity of the German people and the "debilitating subhumanity" of the Jewish people.

> How can the race difference between a German and a Slav, of a German and a Dane [wrote Otto Wigand in 1858] be compared to the race antagonism between the children of Jacob, who are of Asiatic descent, and the descendants of Teut and Hermann, who have inhabited Europe from time immemorial; between the proud and tall blond Aryan and the short, black-haired, dark-eyed Jew! Races which differ in such degree oppose each other instinctively, and against such opposition reason and good sense are powerless.

The eminent composer Richard Wagner warned that the German people faced "racial degeneration." "We should seek to take earnest account of this [degeneration]," he wrote, "if we wish to explain the decay of the German folk which is now exposed without defense to the penetration of the Jews." In 1879, Wilhelm Marr, a sensation-mongering journalist and the son of a Jewish actor, published a pamphlet which he called *Der Sieg des Judentums über das Germanentum*—"The Victory of Judaism over Germanism." In this tract, which brimmed over with the most vulgar kind of scurrility, and which first launched the term "anti-Semitism," Marr warned that the Jews were not only perpetually at war with the Germans, but that they were winning that war. According to Marr, the Jews were born materialists; they developed industry and commerce in order to achieve world domination, and cultivated liberalism as the façade for their activities. Marr himself may have been scum; but his followers and successors, many of whom joined his Anti-Semitic League, were not. Ernest Dühring, Otto Ammon, and Ludwig Wilser were university professors, and they supplied quasi-anthropological and quasi-historical "evidence" that the German blood mixture was in danger of contamination by sexual contact with Jews.

Nietzsche was, technically speaking, no racist; he actually warned his followers to have no part in the "mendacious race-swindle." But if Nietzsche was not actually a racist, his writings lent themselves to use by those who were. He observed, for instance, that "in the Latin *malus* ... the vulgar man can be distinguished as black-haired, as the pre-Aryan inhabitants of the Italian soil, whose complexion formed the clearest feature of distinction from the dominant blonds, namely, the Aryan conquering race." He reveled, as we have seen, in the concept of the "blond Teuton beast," and urged castration for decadents. In 1899 Nietzsche lost his mind; his friend Overbeck found him in his humble, furnished room in Turin, plowing the piano keyboard with his elbow, singing and shrieking in demented self-glorification. It was during those last years, when Nietzsche was unable to defend his writings against misinterpretation, that sizable numbers of Germans began to twist his ideas into full-blown theories of superior races and species. Most of the soundest scholars resented and condemned racism as a hoax and a disaster to society and State. But there were not lacking respectable historians, men like J. G. Droysen, Constantine Frantz, and Heinrich von Sybel, who subscribed to notions of German superiority and, conversely, of Jewish inferiority.

Curiously enough, the most influential exponent of racism in nineteenth-century Germany was a foreigner, the Englishman Houston Stewart Chamberlain. Chamberlain was born in Southsea in 1855, the son of a British admiral and a German mother. Traveling to Germany in his early manhood, he became a disciple of Wagner's Aryanism, and eventually settled in Germany to write the *magnum opus* of German racism, *Die Grundlagen des Neunzehnten Jahrhunderts*—"The Foundations of the Nineteenth Century." Later he fell in love with Richard Wagner's daughter, and she became his second wife. Chamberlain's masterpiece was a beautifully written polemic, perhaps the most eloquent statement of the racist pseudoscience. In *Die Grundlagen* Chamberlain traced the history of the Aryan race with impressive, if specious, documentation. He sought to "prove" that the most cherished creations of nearly every civilization were the result of German-Aryan influence. Even Jesus was transformed into an Aryan. The Jews, Chamberlain insisted, were a race of cheap-jacks, who produced nothing of value in their entire history, not even the Bible; he warned that it was their mission on earth to contaminate the German racial stream, and to "produce a herd of pseudo-hebraic mestizos, a people beyond all doubt degenerate physically, mentally, and morally." It was necessary that the Germans fight back, therefore, not merely to survive, but to conquer; for they were destined to be a people of masters, to govern the "chaotic jungle of peoples . . ." These ominous words won for Chamberlain the warmest approbation of his friend and admirer Kaiser Wilhelm II. They were words that ultimately became the central refrain of twentieth-century German history.

There was another factor, imperialism, responsible for the rise of modern racism. It was a factor which was borrowed but not discovered by the Germans. Imperialism gave dignity and importance to racism at the end of the nineteenth century, and body and substance to the psychotic theories of the German racists. In the minds of Boer, British, and Belgian colonial officials —although perhaps not in the minds of the peoples themselves—the black natives of Africa or the disease-ridden *fellahin* of Egypt were subtly but surely downgraded from human beings into a species of quasi-humans. Through the simple device of administrative bureaucracy a handful of colonial bureaucrats transformed themselves into a master race. Imperialism, in fact, with its notion of the "white man's burden," provided the rationale in the scramble for African territory. When German political groups borrowed imperialism's "administrative racism," adapted it to Aryan theory, linked it to the driving power of the German people—as imperialist racism had never been linked to the British or Belgian peoples—and made available to it a bureaucratic machine of diabolical efficiency, the stage was set for the Nazi horrors of the twentieth century.

THE RISE OF RACIST SPLINTER GROUPS

The idea of German racial superiority, in its more general terms, was embraced by a significant number of conservative nationalists. But anti-Semitism of the racist variety was treated more cautiously. The rightists believed that anti-Semitism was a legitimate issue as long as it left the Jews the safety valve of conversion or occupational reform. But the relentlessness of racial anti-Semitism, the fact that a Jew, by definition, was reduced to the inescapable status of a vampire bat, was a considerably more dangerous doctrine. As a rule, it was repudiated by the tradition-bound Junkers, the "respectable" anti-Semites of the German Conservative Party. To them, racist anti-Semitism, or simply anti-Semitism in its literal meaning, seemed to possess uncontrollable and nihilistic potentialities. The racist Jew-baiters were, rather, the wild-eyed political reactionaries and expansionists, the people least willing to accept the civilized restrictions of law and order either in the domestic or in the international community. They were to be found in the splinter groups that festered in the nooks and crannies of German political life.

The idea of a political grouping based only on radical and racial anti-Semitism was first propagandized by Moritz Busch, Bismarck's press attaché in the Foreign Office, and later by Wilhelm Marr and Ernst Henrici, in the 1870's. Marr founded a League of Anti-Semites, Henrici an anti-Semitic Social Reich party. Both failed to gain significant numbers of adherents. In 1887, however, Otto Boeckel was elected to the Reichstag, the first anti-Semitic deputy who remained independent of official Conservative sponsorship. A few other racists were elected to the Reichstag in the late 1890's. These men made it clear that they could no longer be counted reliable allies of the Christian Conservative State. Arrogant and uncontrollable, they hardly troubled to disguise their fundamental hostility to the orderly transaction of public affairs.

Such a man, for example, was Hermann Ahlwardt, the most celebrated anti-Semitic rabble rouser in Germany in the period after Stöcker's decline. Ahlwardt originally held a position as principal of an elementary school, but in 1890 was fired for filching money from the school treasury. Shortly thereafter he launched himself on a political career by writing a series of bitterly anti-Semitic essays. The German public had by then become accustomed to anti-Semitic writings; but Ahlwardt's were the ultimate in vituperation, irresponsibility, and sheer madness. He was, in fact, imprisoned repeatedly for criminal libel and slander. But social responsibility meant far less to Ahlwardt and his ilk than it had to Stöcker; for those people aimed their diatribes not only against the Jews, but against the Junkers and the middle class, the government and civil rights, against the very machinery of civilization with which the Jews were identified. It happened that Ahlwardt won little power in his own time; but he and his followers were symptomatic of an ominous transition in German political thinking at the turn of the century. Thus far, Ahlwardt's brand of racist anti-Semitism failed to achieve the respectability of the older Judaeophobia; but the growth of respectable political movements willing to pay homage to the "idea" of race indicated that its time was coming.

One of those movements was Pan-Germanism. While never a large movement, it reflected the sentiments of Kaiser Wilhelm II and of an influential group of German industrialists and army officers. Pan-Germanism was a peculiarly German reaction to the age of imperialism. During the years in which Britain and France were swallowing up Africa and large tracts of Asia, a land power such as Germany was obliged to think in terms of expansion on the continent of Europe itself. The origins of this expansionism could be traced to a kind of tribal nationalism. There were German communities in every corner of Europe, in Austria, in Russia, in Poland, in the Baltic and Black Sea regions, in the backwaters of other nations. Because Germans lived in large numbers in the belts of mixed populations where no territorial identification was possible, tribal loyalty, the idealization of race and culture, took the place of territorial allegiance. This Europe-wide loyalty of Germans to each other provided a perfect rationale for German expansionism. "It cannot be a matter of indifference to Germany," declared the secretary of the Pan-German League in 1903, "whether the Saxons and Swabians are Magyarized or Germans in Switzerland or Flemings in Belgium are Gallicized."

The Pan-Germans, with fanatic ardor, set out on their "mission" of educating the German people in common patriotic beliefs, of cultivating German "national values" all over the world, of "encouraging the preservation of German culture in Europe and overseas," and of establishing "closer ties among all peoples of Germanic stock." In 1897 Ernst Hasse, Chairman of the League, voiced the mood of the Pan-Germans when he declared, solemnly, that "our future lies in our blood." Houston Stewart Chamberlain, a member and shining light of the Pan-German League, echoed Hasse's sentiments. The racist bias in Pan-German propaganda became increasingly apparent over the years. Indeed, the League ultimately made its orientation quite clear when it officially barred Jews from membership. Quite aside from matters of "blood and race," the Jews were singled out as European internationalists at a time when Pan-German ideology had little patience with "good Europeans." It was easy to attack the European balance of power by striking first at the Jews as the symbols of internationalism.

Pan-Germanism was exploited in the Hapsburg Empire as well. In Austria, the leader of the movement was Georg von Schoenerer, the son of a wealthy railway pioneer, and heir to a newly created patent of nobility. Schoenerer was a monomaniac on the issue of union with Germany, and was determined, if necessary, to rip the patchwork Hapsburg Empire to bits in order to achieve that union. He was one of the most effective rabble rousers of modern times. In fact, he pioneered many standard Nazi propaganda techniques: Pan-German songs, post cards, beer mugs, matches, signboards. With the aid of these techniques he built up a network of followers throughout Austria. And he continually badgered Bismarck for some sign of encouragement in his effort to transform Austria into an appendage of the German Reich. But the old chancellor remained stonily indifferent to Schoenerer's blandishments.

Schoenerer was the first demagogue who understood the importance of utilizing anti-Semitism to undermine the structure of the Hapsburg regime. He invoked the well-worn specter of the Jewish banker, and associated that specter with the Austrian government; indeed, he identified the Jews as the secret and sinister force behind every imperial institution in the Hapsburg Empire. No Jew was exempt from the damning identification; for, after all, Jewishness was no longer a matter of religious loyalty, but rather racial inheritance. Schoenerer urged the government to enact a truly "effective" series of anti-Jewish laws. But the violent measures he demanded would hardly have been possible within the legal and economic structure of the State. This was particularly true in Austria, where the non-German nationalities were obliged, for their own sake, to oppose such innovations vigorously. It was Schoenerer's hope that Austria's German population would ultimately be provoked into a mass uprising against the "obstructionist" Austrian government—for the sake of "ridding the country of the Jews." Once this was accomplished, Schoenerer was convinced, union with Germany would follow automatically.

At the very moment that Schoenerer's propaganda campaign appeared to be gaining its greatest momentum, it was ruined by a spectacular blunder. In 1888 a liberal newspaper prematurely published a notice of the death of the German Emperor, Wilhelm I. Acting on the erroneous information, Schoenerer suddenly raided the newspaper's office in order to proclaim his loyalty to the Hohenzollern dynasty. Presumably he believed that the Crown Prince of Germany, the future Emperor Friedrich, would respond by annexing Austria. All Schoenerer accomplished, however, was to get himself arrested and imprisoned for disorderly conduct. The Austrian government, its patience exhausted by Schoenerer's near-treason, seized upon this latest indiscretion as the opportunity to disfranchise him, to disbar him from serving as a deputy in Parliament, and to deprive him of his patent of nobility. Schoenerer's power was broken. In 1904 he dissolved his Pan-German Union and declared the struggle for union hopeless. Actually, however, he gave up too soon—as he himself later recognized. It must have given him melancholy satisfaction to witness the dissolution of the Hapsburg Empire at the close of the first World War. His satisfaction was surely compounded in the postwar era as the cancer of racism, which had been kept alive through the medium of Pan-Germanism, spread into every part of the German-speaking world.

CONCLUSION

On the eve of the first World War anti-Semitism as an organized movement temporarily declined. Aggressive German nationalism was directed outward, in the *Drang nach Osten* toward the Balkans and Near East. When the drive stopped, however, with the defeat of Germany, anti-Semitism revived once again as a factor in the embittered domestic politics of Central Europe. It revived not merely intact, but infinitely more vicious than before, for it was preserved by old-fashioned conservatives who used it to exploit lower-middle-class discontent. It was intensified by the racist nationalism of postwar Pan-Germanism. Most important, it was shrewdly transformed and reoriented by the racist splinter groups, groups that fixed their sights on nothing less than the destruction of the orderly processes of law and government. It was this last transformation, particularly, which was destined to be the crowning horror of the twentieth century. For fifteen centuries the chasm had widened between the Jew and his neighbors. It was a chasm which the mild nostrums of nineteenth-century liberalism were unable to bridge in time.

One aspect of this discussion of modern anti-Semitism may have struck the reader: it has dealt with Christians, and not with Jews.

Notes

Page 234. A good, brief analysis of the rise of racism will be found in Marvin Lowenthal, *The Jews of Germany.*

XII

Beginning of the End for Russian Jewry

THE PERVERSION OF SLAVOPHILISM

The Russian variety of resurgent nationalism was Slavophilism. Formulated in the 1840's by Ivan Kireevsky and Alexis Khomiakov, Slavophilism was given its most felicitous literary expression by Ivan Aksakov in the years following the humiliating defeat of the Crimean War. It was summarized in Aksakov's famous phrase *"Para Domoi!"*—"It is time to go home!" It was time, Aksakov insisted, to stop aping the "decadent" West, with its materialism, its socialism, its autocratic Roman Catholicism. Russia must be herself, and assert herself in the community of nations through her own authentic institutions: her mir, her peasant commune; her pacifism and "spirituality"; her "true and glorious" Orthodox Church. In 1871 Nicolai Yakovlevich Danilevsky elaborated upon this doctrine in his celebrated volume, *Russia and Europe.* Danilevsky called attention to those unique characteristics of life east of the Vistula, especially the passivity and "moral consciousness" of the Slavic peasantry, that the West and Russian admirers of of the West failed to understand or appreciate. Any attempt to introduce the social organization or the political methods of Western Europe into Russia, Danilevsky insisted, would surely destroy the integral foundations of Slavic civilization.

Initially, perhaps, there was nothing particularly antidemocratic about this philosophy. After all, Slavophilism did venerate the *narod,* the common folk. A Slavophile poet, Tyutchev, could idealize

> These poor villages,
> this sterile nature,
> homeland of patience,
> land of the Russian people!
> The proud glance of the foreigner can neither see nor observe
> that which pierces through and shines hidden in its humble nakedness.

But in the last years of Alexander II's reign, as the Czar grew progressively disenchanted with his earlier "liberal" ideals, he and his advisors became devotees of the new Slavophile doctrine and systematically stripped it of its democratic trappings. It was the Orthodoxy of Slavic civilization, the "uniqueness" of Russian autocracy, the "instinctive" love and obedience extended to their czar by Russia's common folk that were increasingly contrasted with the decadent "parliamentarism" of the West. By the time Alexander III assumed the throne in 1881, Slavophilism was transformed altogether from a uniquely Russian form of nationalism into a deliberate rationale for reaction. Personally, the Czar hardly needed to be persuaded that Russia's long-range interests, and his own, were best served by a policy of uncompromising autocracy, and of equally uncompromising nationalism. A stocky, powerfully built soldier, a devoted husband and father, he was a man endowed with a grimly insular view of the world. "We can have no other policy," he announced in April 1891, "except one that is purely Russian and national."

Whatever imagination Alexander III lacked for implementing his philosophy was supplied for him by Constantin Pobedonostsev, the arch-ideologue of reactionary nationalism. A distinguished jurist and coauthor of the reform of the law courts, Pobedonostsev served, from 1880 to 1905, as the Chief Procurator of the Holy Synod, the lay director of the Orthodox Church. In earlier years, he had also served as Alexander's tutor, and his influence on his pupil, even after Alexander became czar, was little less than hypnotic. Eventually, Pobedonostsev became the most powerful man in Russia. He was the bureaucrat par excellence, "a kind of wooden ruling machine in human shape," wrote a Russian journalist of the time, "to whom the living units of mankind are nothing, while the maintenance of bureaucratic 'order' is everything." Unlike the "pure" Slavophiles, Pobedonostsev had little faith in the common people; indeed, he once described Russia beyond the imperial palaces as "an icy desert and an abode of the Bad Man." An uncompromising Russian nationalist himself, he looked to the autocracy and the clergy as the exclusive source of Russia's leadership; as far as he was concerned, parliamentarism and constitutionalism were "the great lie of our age." Pobedonostsev poured hundreds of thousands of rubles into the school system maintained by the Church; for Orthodoxy, in his eyes, was the ideal instrument to insure that the Russian people remained "a colossal herd, obedient to the arbitrary will of one man."

Pobedonostsev wasted little time before implementing his philosophy of government. In the first year of Alexander III's reign he drafted the notorious "Police Constitution," giving arbitrary powers of arrest to the governors of the various provinces. The judicial and educational systems were radically revamped in favor of the aristocracy. Censorship was imposed on every medium of public opinion. Both liberal and terrorist leaders were hunted down and shot. Non-Russian minorities were subjected to a far-reaching campaign of "Russification." Germans, Poles, Estonians, Latvians, Finns, Armenians—all saw their school systems drastically restructured and their religious institutions restaffed with Russian puppets. The use of their native languages was forbidden in school and courtroom, in state bank, railway office, or in any state enterprise. Even for such "fellow Slavs" as the Poles, the unremitting policy of Russification made it perfectly apparent that Slavophilism was to be synonymous with pure Russian nationalism, and that this meant naked reaction. A decade after Alexander's coronation, the extent of this reaction was described by the Moscow correspondent of the London *Times*:

> One must go to Moscow to comprehend the strength of this feeling [Slavophilism] and the tremendous fascination it has for the Russian mind. A dozen years ago it seemed to be the exclusive property of a small though influential group of reactionary thinkers—the Aksakovs, Katkov, Ignatiev, and others less well known to European fame. Today it literally possesses the nation. . . . The signs of this reaction force themselves upon the attention at every corner in inner Russia. Gentlemen and officers who fifteen years ago affected rationalism in religion, and left the demonstrative part of Church ceremonial to the monks and the *moujiks,* now ostentatiously halt before every shrine and church edifice to bow and cross themselves. . . . Another indication, perhaps even more significant, is found in the immense proportional increase of books printed in the Russian language.

It was not to be expected that Alexander III's bureaucracy would deal less gently with the Jews than with other minority peoples. Moreover, Jew-hatred might well be as useful a weapon to the Russian government as it was to the reactionaries of Germany, Austria, and France. Riding the wave of Slavophile nationalism, the czarist administration borrowed the rightist techniques of Central Europe and stigmatized "liberalism" as the instrument of the Jews. It was no longer, therefore, a question of "amalgamating" the Jews, or even of Russianizing them. Political expediency dictated a change of approach: the time had come for the Jews to be cordoned off even further from Russian life and identified as the head and front of all Russian ills. With simple-minded directness, Czar Alexander himself pointed out "that it was the Jews who crucified our Lord, and spilled his precious blood." Pobedonostsev, Count Dmitri Tolstoi, Minister of the Interior, Wenzel von Plehve, Chief of the Secret Police, were Jew-haters of long standing; they sensed—at the same time that they caused—the disproportionately large role played by Jews in the subterranean revolutionary movement (see Chapter XIV). Accordingly, they subsidized the influential conservative and nationalist press in its persistent and insidious campaign of Jew-baiting.

In Russia, unlike in Central Europe, there existed no significant lower middle class to provide fuel for the anti-Semitic assault. Consequently, the latent prejudices of the Russian people had to be much more strenuously, and artificially, fanned into life. On the other hand, the czarist government, unlike those of Germany, Austria, or France, was in a position to move beyond mere journalistic warfare. Exactly because the Russian State was structured on Byzantine lines, the bureaucracy was in a position to condone anti-Jewish attacks without compromising its authority or prestige. Thus, the government was able instantly to exploit the fact that Alexander II had been killed by a revolutionist's bomb, and that a Jewess, one Hessia Helfman, had been involved in the assassination plot. Shortly after Alexander II's funeral the press began to hint darkly at a "secret Jewish conspiracy" against the Motherland. Czarist officials mysteriously appeared and disappeared in cities of the Pale; rumors were circulated, and later authenticated, of police collusion in the preparation of anti-Jewish riots. Then, in the spring and summer of 1881, the worst of Jewish fears were realized, as a succession of pogroms "spontaneously" exploded throughout southern Russia and the Ukraine. In Kiev, in Balta, even in Warsaw, hundreds of Jewish homes and shops were gutted and looted, and nearly one hundred Jews killed and maimed. Everywhere, too, the police remained significantly inactive, intervening only when it appeared that damage might spread to non-Jewish establishments. "The entire behavior of the police," wrote the Austrian consul in Kiev after the April pogrom of 1881, "leads one rightfully to the conclusion that the disturbances are abetted by the authorities."

A shudder of fear passed through the Jewish community of the Pale. It was apparent that renegade Russian nationalism, the Government's determination to identify the revolutionary danger with the Jews, placed the very existence of Russian Jewry in question. Grandparents with memories of the *khappers* and mass expulsions of Nicholas I's day were convinced now that something even worse was brewing. They were not mistaken. On August 22, 1881, Alexander issued an ominous ukase. It dwelt on the "abnormal relations" between the Jews and the Russian people, and ordered an investigation into "injurious" Jewish economic activities. Manifestly, the Czar anticipated a recommendation to destroy the economic basis of Jewish life altogether. So, too, did Count Ignatiev, who had just succeeded Tolstoi as Minister of the Interior, and who was placed in charge of the "Jewish problem." When Ignatiev failed, therefore, to obtain a particularly harsh anti-Jewish report from the provincial bureaucrats whom he had entrusted with the investigation, he appointed his own "Central Committee for the Revision of the Jewish Question." October 1881 was a dividing line in Russian-Jewish history. For with the appointment that month of Ignatiev's Committee a paralyzing grillwork of legal disabilities was dropped on the Jews which was not lifted until March 1917. After a century of governmental indecision and equivocation, of assaults, retreats, cross-purposes, and half-measures, Russian Jewry was at last about to be placed under sentence of slow death.

THE MAY LAWS

The dominating influence in the Central Committee was Minister of the Interior Ignatiev himself. Nikolai Pavlovich Ignatiev was a Slavophile reactionary of the most militant variety, a man grimly determined to extirpate "sedition" wherever he found it. Personally, he detested Jews and made no secret of the fact. "What can we do," he explained to the American chargé d'affaires in St. Petersburg, "if on the one hand there are five million Russian Jews and on the other hand there are eighty-five million Russian subjects who insist that we expel from the Empire these five million Jews?" Yet, in spite of his convictions, Ignatiev remained open to bribery until the end of his life, a habit he had acquired during his days as ambassador to Constantinople (he was known in St. Petersburg as "Liar-Pasha"). Several times, in fact, Ignatiev hinted to Baron Horace de Günzburg that a million rubles deposited to his account might significantly change his attitude toward the Jews. Little of this cynical latitudinarianism was evident, however, in the report issued by the Central Committee.

The preamble of the "Ignatiev Report," which was submitted in the spring of 1882, stated bluntly that Alexander II's policy of toleration had failed, that the rise of the "popular protest in Russia itself" proved that new measures would have to be taken against Russian Jewry. The Committee's recommendations were shortly thereafter enacted by the Czar in the form of "Temporary Rules," without the customary ratification of the Council of State. Because the "Temporary Rules" were passed on May 3, 1882, they have been remembered ever after as the "May Laws." The May Laws, alas, were far from temporary; they remained in effect, with progressive stringency in their enforcement, until the Russian Revolution.

According to the May Laws, no Jew henceforth was permitted to settle "anew" in any rural area in Russia, not even within the Pale of Settlement. At one stroke, all exits from the crowded cities to the villages were sealed off. But the legislation was aimed no less at Jews already living on the countryside—perhaps two fifths of the Pale's Jewry. For the Russian inhabitants of the villages were given the right to expel "vicious" inhabitants by a special "verdict," and the provincial governors saw to it that the intoxicated, half-illiterate *muzhiks* frequently signed such verdicts against Jews. Those who left their villages for a few days and who sought to return were classified as "new visitors" and prohibited from entering. Jews who rented their homes were denied new leases and forced out of town. Jews moving from village to village looking for work were classified as "new settlers" and expelled. A Jew was not permitted to take in his widowed mother from another village, inherit a father's business in another village, or go to a hospital in another village, without facing expulsion. Provincial authorities arbitrarily reclassified thousands of small towns as villages, which, as rural settlements, were thereby closed off for Jews. Many Jews managed to stay on in rural areas by recourse to bribery; but the great majority was forced out. Jews by the hundreds of thousands began to pour from the countryside into the congestion of the cities. Ultimately the rural Jewish community was all but obliterated.

The May Laws established a strict *numerus clausus* for the Russian school system. Jewish quotas for the gymnasia and universities were slashed so radically that many thousands of young Jewish men and women were obliged to travel abroad for their education. Most of them flocked to Central and Western European universities—and returned later with carefully nurtured revolutionary and Zionist ideas. Every effort was made to dislodge the Jews from the liberal professions and "respectable" trades that enabled them to live outside the Pale. Jewish doctors and lawyers were deprived of their positions under central or local authorities. The proportion of Jews permitted membership in the Russian bar was reduced from 22 to 9 per cent. Any Jew living in the Russian interior who sought to enlarge his sphere of economic activity was promptly sent back to the Pale. Similarly, large numbers of Jewish artisans were expelled from the interior because their trades were summarily removed from the classification of artisanry. If a Jew used a machine in any phase of his craft, his status as an artisan was cancelled. A watchmaker who sold watch chains he had not made himself, or a pastry cook who served coffee with his pastry, was stamped as a merchant and his right of domicile declared forfeit. Families whose credentials were found to have the most trivial discrepancies were rooted out and forced back into the Pale. Often they were given only twenty-four hours notice to move, with virtually no opportunity to sell their homes or businesses. There was one incredible episode of a young Jewess who had come to St. Petersburg to enter the college courses for women; in order to obtain the right of residence she was obliged to "take the yellow ticket," i.e., to register as a prostitute. When the police discovered that the young woman was engaged in studying, instead of plying her "official" trade, she was banished from the capital.

The May Laws reached their climax of brutality with the eviction of the Jewish community of Moscow. In 1891 Alexander III's brother, the Grand Duke Sergei, in comparison with whom even the Czar was a liberal, was appointed as the city's Governor-General. In honor of his arrival, an Imperial ukase was issued on the first day of Passover, ordering the expulsion of Moscow's twenty thousand Jews. While the authorities offered rewards to citizens who would track down "rightless" Jews, the police spread a solid cordon around the city, conducted their searches during the dead of night, and marched their captives—men, women, and children—in manacles to the railway stations. The famous Moscow Synagogue was boarded up and its use forbidden. In this manner a cultivated and comparatively prosperous Jewish community was uprooted. The mass expulsion of a city's Jewry was repeated, with only minor variations, in St. Petersburg and Kharkov.

The Pale of the *shtetl*—the little Jewish townlet—was fast approaching its end. In its place now appeared the Pale of the city and town, an area resembling the string of congested urban ghettos in which Western Jewry had lived in the seventeenth and eighteenth centuries. The working population, fairly equally divided now between artisans and petty traders, barely managed to keep alive. As he watched the influx of rural Jews into his jurisdiction, Ussarov, the Governor of Bessarabia, commented:

The observer is struck by the number of Jewish signs in Bessarabian towns. The houses along second-rate and even back streets are occupied in unbroken succession by stores, big and small, shops of watch-makers, shoe-makers, locksmiths, tinsmiths, tailors, carpenters, and so on. All these workers are huddled together in nooks and lanes amidst shocking poverty. They toil hard for a living so scanty that a rusty herring and a slice of onion is considered the tip-top of luxury and prosperity. There are scores of watch-makers in small towns where the townsfolk, as a rule, have no watches. It is hard to understand where all these artisans, frequently making up seventy-five percent of the total population of a city or town, get their orders and patrons. Competition cuts down their earnings to the limit of bare subsistence on so minute a scale as to call in question the theory of wages.

The Jews of Russia were driven steadily toward pauperism. By the end of the nineteenth century, 40 per cent of Russian Jewry were completely dependent on charity; while in the province of Minsk fully half the Jewish population lived on the dole provided by their more fortunate brethren. There had never been oppression like this before, even in the worst days of Nicholas I. Even the most resourceful and imaginative members of the Jewish community seemed to be temporarily without a solution. But Pobedonostsev apparently had prepared his own solution when he frankly stated to a group of Jews who petitioned him in 1898: "One third will die out, one third will leave the country, and one third will be completely dissolved in the surrounding population."

> Neither storm, wind, nor starshine by night
> And the days neither cloudy nor bright—
> O my people, how sad is thy state,
> How gray and how cheerless thy fate.

The poet Simon Frug was speaking for a people rapidly sinking into shock.

NICHOLAS II: THE REVOLUTION LURKS BENEATH

In 1894 Alexander III died in agony from nephritis. His successor, Nicholas II, was as weak and pliable as his father had been stern and inflexible. In truth, it was difficult for the inner bureaucracy at St. Petersburg to take seriously a man who at the age of twenty-six was still playing hide-and-seek with his friends, and filling his diary with ecstatic accounts of picnics and hunting parties. Nicholas II was particularly susceptible to personal influences at Court, and these were mainly reactionary. There was the evil genius, Pobedonostsev, whom Nicholas inherited. There was the notorious roué and blackmailer, Prince V. P. Mescherski, editor of the Slavophilist newspaper, *Grazhdanin*. Above all there was Nicholas's wife, the former Princess Alix of Hesse-Darmstadt, a woman ridden with fundamentalist superstitions and obsessions. With the confluence of these minds and wills pressing in upon him, it was not surprising when Nicholas declared that he would maintain his father's autocracy intact in every respect.

But this was more easily said than done. The famine and cholera epidemic of the early 1890's produced rumblings of discontent throughout the empire, and they could not be entirely muffled by the police regime. Social

Revolutionary propaganda in the countryside, Marxist propaganda among the urban proletariat, grew rapidly. A rising wave of terrorism, sponsored by the Populist People's Will party, accounted for the assassination of some three thousand members of the Russian bureaucracy. The revolutionary conspiracy was a source of mortal terror to the regime; Russian officials literally took their lives in their hands whenever they ventured out of their offices. The terminology of Slavophile nationalism, as a result, had to be worked overtime in an attempt to abort the revolution; and, consequently, Alexander III's fourteen-year war against the Jews had to be continued. Nicholas II needed little encouragement in this direction. He loathed the Jews. He used the word *"zhyd"* as synonymous with "enemy"; *"zhidy"* was his term of opprobrium for all his pet hates, especially the English and Japanese. He was quite willing to continue the May Laws with all the harshness that his father had developed. He and his advisors were determined methodically and systematically to debase the Jews in Russian eyes as the source of Russian poverty and weakness.

In 1902 the czar turned over the Ministry of the Interior to Wenzel von Plehve, a squat, bull-necked Baltic German. According to his contemporaries, von Plehve entertained few personal anti-Jewish opinions; in fact, he frequently expressed the belief that the government's anti-Semitic policy was a mistake. But if the czar so desired, von Plehve would make a good job of Jew-baiting. It was von Plehve who decided to transcend the legal limitations of the May Laws, to resort to systematic murder and pillage—an approach which had been abandoned after the first year of Alexander III's regime. It took a man of von Plehve's stripe, the cool bureaucrat without personal scruples, to engineer this transition to violence. The Russian lower middle class, unlike its German counterpart, was hardly large enough to play a significant role in anti-Semitic demonstrations. And unlike the literate and embittered white-collar worker of Central Europe, the typical Russian peasant, ignorant and lethargic, was not, as a rule, a cruel or violent man. The most ingenious and cunning technique was needed to involve the Russian people in "spontaneous" uprisings against Jewish "exploitation."

The first test of this technique was made in Kishinev, the capital of the province of Bessarabia, where the Jews had lived for years in traditional friendship with their Russian neighbors. The only newspaper in the province, the *Bessarabetz,* was a sensation-mongering anti-Semitic journal. Von Plehve not only refused to license any other paper, but actively subsidized its editor, Krushevan, from a special slush fund. Krushevan was soon presented with a splendid opportunity to endear himself to his patrons. Early in 1903 some peasants living in the outskirts of Kishinev discovered the mutilated body of a Russian boy. Although the boy's uncle openly confessed to the crime, the *Bessarabetz* hurled the charge of ritual murder against the Jews. On Easter eve a group of government emissaries arrived in Kishinev to engage in secret conversations with Krushevan and provincial officials. Shortly thereafter, handbills, printed by Krushevan on the *Bessarabetz* press, were scattered about the city urging the inhabitants to inflict a "bloody punishment" upon the Jews. In the saloons and teahouses there was open discussion of the approaching pogrom.

On Sunday, April 6, 1903, a mob of Russian teen-age ruffians, undoubtedly acting upon a given signal, rushed through the city streets to attack and loot Jewish stores and homes. The police made no attempt whatever to interfere. In the evening, looting gave way to killing. For nearly twenty-four hours, while the local police studiously avoided leaving their barracks, Jews were hunted down and murdered. At last, at 5:00 P.M. of the afternoon of April 7, a telegram was received from von Plehve himself, and an hour later large detachments of troops, fully armed, appeared on the central streets to disperse the mobs. By then, of course, the rioters had largely accomplished their task. Fifteen hundred stores and homes had been gutted. Forty-five Jews had been killed, eighty-six wounded or crippled. Russian eye-witnesses described people torn in two, babies' brains splattered, bellies split open, tongues cut out, women with breasts cut off, men castrated, blinded, hanged, hacked to death. The news of the massacre spread not only through Russia—where many members of the Russian intelligentsia issued statements of shocked outrage—but also through Europe and America. Mass meetings of protest, under both Jewish and Christian auspices, took place in the major capitals. So great, in fact, was the world uproar, that the Russian government felt obliged to take a few tentative steps to appease public opinion. Von Plehve replaced the Governor of Bessarabia, and brought a few of the male-factors to trial. But the government attorneys who handled the prosecution in good faith were hampered at every turn, and the sentences imposed upon a few convicted rioters were quite nominal.

Von Plehve was not yet finished. In August of 1903 a government-insti-gated pogrom broke out at Gomel, in the White Russian Government of Moghilev, where twenty thousand Jews formed half the city's population. In spite of a rather well-organized Jewish defense effort—the Jewish poet Bialik had savagely, and unjustly, excoriated his brethren for their passivity at Kishinev—some 250 Jewish homes were destroyed and twelve Jews killed. For the remainder of the year pogroms erupted in rapid succession through-out White Russia and the Ukraine. In January 1904, von Plehve called together a committee of governors and other high officials from the Ministry of the Interior, and warned them not to get squeamish. The government, he stated, was unalterably opposed even to the slightest mitigation of Jewish disabilities: their task was not to modify Jewish legislation, but to systema-tize it. A few days later, however, the Russo-Japanese War broke out, and anti-Jewish measures were temporarily suspended. Because Jewish com-munal leaders asked their people to support the war effort, von Plehve allowed the families of Jewish soldiers to be left in their places of residence, "pending the termination of the war." The passions kindled by wartime nationalism could easily have been exploited for anti-Semitic agitation; but the government concluded that pogroms might disrupt the economy, and the Jews were given a breathing spell. Yet until the very end of the war the reactionary press, led by the *Novoye Vremya,* continued to circulate rumors that the Jews were secretly providing aid for the Japanese, "their kinsmen by race."

It is of interest, from the vantage point of the second half of the twentieth century, to review the world reaction to merely one pogrom, that of Kishinev. The German Kaiser protested personally to the Czar, as did the Austrian Emperor. Resolutions adopted by mass meetings in Britain were forwarded by the Foreign Secretary to the Russian Foreign Ministry. In the United States, President Theodore Roosevelt sent a personal note of deep concern to Nicholas II. Referring to the mass protest meetings in New York, Philadelphia, and Chicago, and to the Joint Resolution of protest passed by Congress, Roosevelt stated: "I have never in my experience in this country known of a more immediate or deeper expression of sympathy for the victims . . . [of oppression] or of horror over the appalling calamity that has occurred." Forty years before the Nazi death camps, the murder of forty-five Jews could elicit this kind of shocked reaction from the Christian world.

THE REVOLUTIONARY EPOCH

The departure of the Russian army for Manchuria gave the revolutionary forces in Russia an unprecedented opportunity for effective protest against czarist despotism. For the first time large numbers of factory workers enrolled themselves in the Social Democratic cause; these were people capable of striking, of rioting, if necessary even of paralyzing the entire economy of the country. Nor were the terrorists inactive: in July 1904 von Plehve was slain by a bomb thrown under his carriage as he drove to make a report to the Czar at Peterhof. Genuinely frightened, Nicholas at last began to make a few concessions: the censorship was relaxed; State workmen's insurance was established; the jurisdiction of the zemstvos was enlarged. But it was not enough. The number of strikes and assassinations multiplied rapidly. On "Bloody Sunday," January 22, 1905, czarist guards fired into a parade of working people, killing and wounding some fifteen hundred men and women. The Social Revolutionaries retaliated the following month by blowing Grand Duke Sergei to bits. When the Russian army was decisively defeated in the Far East, and Nicholas was compelled to sue for peace with the Japanese, revolutionary discontent reached a climax. In October 1905, a massive nation-wide strike, sponsored by the Marxist Social Democrats, paralyzed the entire economy of Russia. On October 30 a thoroughly demoralized monarch capitulated to the strikers. Nicholas issued a manifesto which promised his people a constitution, basic civil rights, and a Duma—a parliament—chosen by a wide franchise and with full authority to veto undesirable legislation. Throughout the empire thousands, hundreds of thousands of people paraded, demonstrated in jubilation. Apparently the day of liberation had arrived; the incubus of oppression at last was to be lifted.

But the manifesto of October 30 was no sooner issued than it was subverted. The government recognized that its opponents were divided. The

Constitutional Democrats ("Cadets") wanted a limited monarchy. The laboring populations of St. Petersburg and Moscow, represented by the Social Democratic party, were thinking in terms of a proletarian regime. The "Octobrists" were willing to stand pat on the Czar's October manifesto. None of the groups fully appreciated the importance of establishing a solid front with the others; the government, in turn, took advantage of this confusion to whittle down the earlier concessions. By the spring of 1906, moreover, the army had returned from Manchuria, and the presence of tens of thousands of armed soldiers in St. Petersburg had a remarkably calming effect on Nicholas's composure. Swarms of police spies began making wholesale arrests. On April 27, 1906, only three days before the opening of the first Duma, an Imperial decree restored to the czar much of the power he had surrendered in October. By significantly raising property requirements for the franchise, and by dividing the Duma into "curias"—estates—the Duma's authority was seriously limited. P. A. Stolypin, the active head of the czarist regime, was prepared now to go even further. Moving troops into the capital, he suddenly ordered the Duma dissolved, only two months after its opening, and arrested many of the liberal legislators. "First order," Stolypin warned grimly, "then reform." Subsequent Dumas, meeting during the next few years, found themselves left with hardly more than advisory powers. By the eve of the first World War, czarist autocracy in all its insupportable cruelty was fully reinstalled in Russia.

During the early months of the revolutionary spiral, late in 1904, the Jews of Russia began contributing actively and openly to the clamor for reform. In March of 1905 a national conference of Russian Jews gathered in Vilna; there a program of "demands" (not requests) was formulated for presentation to the government. It was no time for timidity, for the life of an entire people was at stake. Nearly every political party in the Jewish community was represented at Vilna, from socialists to middle-class liberals. Whatever the political orientation of the various Jewish spokesmen, they were determined to remain united on the issue of Jewish emancipation; to that end they banded together in a League for the Attainment of Complete Equality for Russian Jewry. The delegates demanded more than equal rights as Russians, however. They demanded national rights as Jews, rights embracing communal autonomy, and official recognition of Yiddish as the Jewish national language (see Chapter XIV). At first, it was uncertain whether or not the government would permit Jews to sit in the first Duma. Even as reasonable a statesman as Count Sergei Witte counseled the Jews to stay out of Russian politics: "It is not your business to teach us," he warned. "Leave that to Russians by birth and civil status and mind your own affairs." After a long discussion, however, the Council of Ministers decided in favor of Jewish representation. The Ministers were convinced that the property qualifications required for voting would pit the Jewish proletariat against the Jewish bourgeoisie. This shrewd evaluation was borne out as the Bund, the Jewish Socialist Organization, boycotted the elections for the first Duma.

Internecine rivalry notwithstanding, the remaining Jewish political groups, banded together in the League, were able to conduct a remarkably vigorous election campaign, and succeeded in electing twelve Jewish deputies to the first Duma. The spokesman for this Jewish "bloc" was a St. Petersburg lawyer, Maxim M. Vinaver, the most eminent of the bourgeois Jewish leaders. Vinaver was a tall, dignified man of rare cultivation and charm; during the course of his career he had become a respected member of the Constitutional Democratic party. He played a leading role in the Jewish community and was one of the founders of the League for the Attainment of Complete Equality for Russian Jewry. He was astute enough to recognize that political and doctrinal differences would prevent the Jewish deputies in the first Duma from voting as a bloc on all issues. But he managed, at least, to persuade his Jewish colleagues to work and vote together on all matters of vital Jewish interest. Now that the Jews had at last found a public forum in which to express their grievances, they were determined not to let disunity destroy a historic opportunity.

Vinaver's immense prestige, his truly brilliant tact in negotiation, won the support of the Cadets, the most influential party in the Duma, for an omnibus measure of civic equality for all minority groups. "We Jews," Vinaver cried, in fluent Russian, "representatives of one of the most tormented nationalities in the land, have never uttered a word about ourselves, because we did not consider it fitting to speak in this place about civic equality." All his people asked, he insisted, was a law to normalize the status of every inhabitant of the empire. When Vinaver sat down, trembling with emotion, the Cadets gave him a rousing ovation. On May 15, 1906, a declaration, proposing the enactment of a basic law on civil equality, was signed by 151 Cadets and introduced in the Duma. The measure was sent to committee and appeared certain of approval for final passage. In nearly every city and town in the Pale, Jews gathered in their synagogues to conduct passionate prayer meetings for the success of the legislation. They had committed themselves to the revolution; they had gambled everything on its triumph. Few of them had any illusions about their fate if the revolution, and Jewish emancipation, failed. Before the conclusive vote could be taken, however, the first Duma was suddenly dissolved by czarist troops.

Today, with the hindsight of many decades, it seems clear that Vinaver and his associates did not work fast enough, and erred on the side of restraint. But even if the measure had passed the Duma in time, it would almost certainly have been vetoed by the Czar. One significant moral gesture was made, however, two days before the Duma was dissolved. The deputies solemnly placed the responsibility for the anti-Jewish pogroms on the government. In a genuine parliamentary regime such an expression of censure would surely have caused the fall of the Ministry.

The Duma had produced no practical gains for the Jews. None of the evils under which they were living was removed. None of their larger political aspirations was realized. Yet even after the dissolution of the first Duma Jewish hopes remained high. Later Dumas, it was believed, would surely bring more tangible results. Had the Jews but known it, the crest of the revolution was passed. Stolypin, the Minister of the Interior, hounded down and everywhere arrested liberal leaders. By May of 1907, some six hundred constitutionalists had been sentenced to hang by czarist tribunals, the infamous "Stolypin neckties." The second and third Dumas were considerably chastened bodies, while the fourth Duma was hardly more than a rubber stamp. The number of Jewish deputies in these Dumas steadily declined, even as did the number of Christian liberals. Only four Jews sat in the second Duma, only two in each of the last two. Whenever they ventured to raise the question of Jewish emancipation they were reviled and hooted down by the rightists who increasingly dominated the proceedings. With the decline of revolutionary momentum the League for the Attainment of Jewish Equality split apart: first the Zionists broke away, then the Jewish People's Group, then the *Volkspartei*—the autonomists—and finally the assimilationist Jewish Democratic Group. A leaden despair overwhelmed all the politicians from Vinaver on down. It had become apparent, at last, that the solution to Jewish persecution lay either in emigration or—and they shuddered to think of it—in a bloody revolution of truly massive proportions.

STOLYPIN'S NECKTIE

In the long list of Russian anti-Semites, from Uvarov to Pobedonostsev, from Ignatiev to von Plehve, Peter Stolypin ranks as perhaps the most cunning and the most lethal of all. As governor of the provinces of Saratov and Grodno, Stolypin succeeded brilliantly both in effecting land reforms and in smashing peasant uprisings. His administrative skill, his personal courage, and his militant Russian nationalism led to his appointment, in 1906, as Minister of the Interior. From this vantage point he was prime minister in all but title. Personally, Stolypin was a genial and charming person, handsome, superficially friendly, a devoted husband and father. He was by no means a blind reactionary; he understood the importance of primary education and of thoroughgoing land reform, and he encouraged these projects at every opportunity.

Yet, at the same time, Stolypin was unshakable in his determination to crush the revolution; and as far as he was concerned, oppression was at least as valuable a counterrevolutionary technique as amelioration. Thus, he openly subsidized gangs of hooligans to terrorize opponents of the government; and he organized a secret police force which honeycombed the empire with informers and counterinformers. It was Stolypin's uncompromising chauvinism, moreover, which drove him to extraordinary excesses of Russification. He purged the zemstvo boards of all "aliens," and expelled from the various branches of government all civil servants who were not of Great Russian birth. While he had little personal feeling one way or the other about the Jews, and was undecided at first about treating them differently from Russia's other "alien" peoples, eventually he was persuaded by Nicholas II and the Council of State that the revolution could best be "drowned in Jewish blood." Once he accepted this approach, Stolypin cracked down on the Jews with as much enthusiasm as if he had originated the policy.

Stolypin inherited a weapon custom-made for Jew-baiting, the notorious Union of the Russian People. This was an organization established in St.

Petersburg in October 1904, under the leadership of a number of prominent boyars and high government officials. Nearly all the Union's following came from Russia's incipient and irascible lower middle class, and from minor government officials, people who believed themselves closed out of the benefits of the burgeoning Russian capitalism. Most important, the Union enjoyed the blessing of the czar, who wore the Union's badge proudly on his breast. The Union of the Russian People was the first really modern instrument of Russian anti-Semitism: for it aimed not merely at the Jews as an "unassimilable" people; it aimed, as well, at the emergent liberal middle class of Russia—which was stigmatized, in the best Central European fashion, as the "Jewish middle class." The Union had compiled a list of people to be assassinated, and nearly all the prospective victims were prominent industrialists of constitutional leanings. The activist arm of the Union, the so-called "Black Hundreds," exterminated hundreds of these bourgeois liberals, including several Jewish members of the Duma. By 1906 the protective attitude of the government enabled the Union to build up a network of three thousand local cells.

Even before Stolypin's accession in 1906, therefore, Jew-hatred was skillfully exploited by a quasi-monarchical organization of terrorists. To the slogan of the revolutionary and liberal movement, "Down with the Autocracy," the Union of the Russian People responded with "Kill the *zhidy*." During the revolutionary period of 1905, Nicholas himself launched the Black Hundreds on their "mission" with the ominous statement: "I shall set the underworld in motion." Bands of thugs began to terrorize outlying Jewish districts in Kiev, Odessa, Bialystok, and Minsk. At the same time the Union's agents distributed handbills in town squares, warning the Russian people that the Jews were their true oppressors, that the Jews were in league with the German factory-owners, the Japanese, the Poles, and the English. After Stolypin's accession to power, the Union became virtually a second government. Assured of the Czar's approbation, the Black Hundreds hardly let a month go by without an assault on some crowded Jewish community. Carrying in front of them portraits of the Czar, national flags, and Church banners, these mounted hoodlums galloped through the Pale, burning, pillaging, raping, and killing.

But Stolypin did not stop with pogroms. Together with physical attacks in the streets came intensified legal assaults on the Jews. The May Laws were applied with such brutish cruelty that even von Plehve's administration seemed favorable by comparison. The wholesale expulsion of Jews from cities outside the Pale, and from villages within the Pale, assumed the character of an epidemic. Jews were ousted from the Russian school system altogether, while Jewish cultural and religious institutions were denied police protection and were frequently compelled to close down. Government newspapers branded the Jews as "werewolves," "a criminal race," "bloodsuckers," and "traitors." Witte noted in his memoirs: "The Jewish question was never before handled in such a cruel way, and never before were the Jews subjected to such vexations as at the present time. One who is not a Jew-hater cannot achieve a reputation as a real conservative." Later, when the ruination of Jewish economic life became so apparent as to make the charge of Jewish "exploitation" increasingly ineffectual, the desiccated old canard of ritual murder was revived by the nationalist reactionaries.

On March 20, 1911, the dead body of a boy, Andrei Yustshinski, was found in the outskirts of the city of Kiev. All available evidence indicated that the child had been murdered by a whore named Vera Cheberiak, apparently because he had threatened to expose a den of thieves of which she was the chieftain. Almost immediately, the Kiev cell of the Union of the Russian People organized a mass demonstration against Jewish "ritual murder." The case was quickly taken in hand by Stolypin, who sensed a priceless opportunity to divert revolutionary unrest; he ordered the Kiev district attorney to make as much capital as possible out of the Union's charge. What next occurred bore all the characteristics of a medieval nightmare. Two medical professors were bribed, as they later admitted, to testify that the child had apparently been drained of his blood while still alive. Then the Jewish manager of a brick factory, Mendel Beilis, was arbitrarily arrested and formally accused of the crime of "ritual murder." Every conceivable device of cross-examination and torture was employed to "persuade" the unfortunate prisoner to confess. When Beilis nevertheless continued to protest his innocence, "cell-mates" were produced by the prosecution to testify that Beilis had admitted his guilt to them. The district attorney brazenly placed Vera Cheberiak on the stand—a woman with a long record of convictions—and elicited from her the "information" that she, too, had learned of Jewish plans for ritual murder long before the child's death.

By the middle of 1912 the transparent ludicrousness of the prosecution's case had become an insult to all but the most demented mind. Even the accusation against Dreyfus in France had initially been based upon more plausible evidence. Later in 1912 a liberal journalist named Brazul-Brushkovsky began to make his own investigations. He discovered that Vera Cheberiak had co-operated with the government in planting the dead boy's clothing in Beilis's home. He learned, too, that she had killed her own son rather than run the risk of his disclosing the true facts of the original murder. After Brazul-Brushkovsky published the information, the leading attorneys of the Kiev and St. Petersburg bars publicly announced their belief in Beilis's innocence; several of them even volunteered their services to him. Later, when the district attorney went so far as to trot out "Talmudical proof" of "ritual murder," mass strikes and protest meetings on behalf of the Jewish prisoner spread as far as St. Petersburg, where mobs demonstrated in the public squares.

Russia was far from a modern country; few were the villagers who did not fear the evil eye and evil omens, who did not consult sorcerers and faith healers for their illnesses and domestic difficulties. Yet even a jury composed of typically superstitious *muzhiks* could not bring itself to convict Beilis. More than two years after his arrest, he was finally acquitted. Remarkably, the government behaved as if it had scored a moral victory in "alerting" the Russian people to the Jewish "menace." Nicholas II himself distributed honors, titles, orders and promotions, gifts and money to those who had participated in the prosecution. In 1817 Alexander I had issued a publication condemning the blood-libel as a "superstitious belief . . . unworthy of discussion." Now, nearly a century later, a Russian government could make the blood-libel a pillar of its policy. Unquestionably, czarist reaction had reached its ultimate depravity.

ROMANIA: "LATIN ISLAND"

As the Slavophile assault gained momentum in Russia, the neighboring Romanian-Jewish community, a community of sizable proportions, also fell victim to a savage brand of renegade nationalism. It was a xenophobia which emerged from the peculiar, the rather desperate circumstances of Romania's struggle for sovereignty in the nineteenth century. Like the Greeks and Serbs, the Romanians had experienced centuries of humiliating vassalage under the barbaric and corrupt Ottoman Empire. But unlike the Greeks and Serbs, the Romanians won their independence piecemeal, after several Russo-Turkish wars and the Crimean War. The long and tortuous process of liberation involved quasi-autonomous status, an "international protectorate," and division into the two Danubian principalities of Wallachia and Moldavia. In 1859, however, a Moldavian colonel, Alexandru Ioan Cuza, finally managed to unite the Danubian principalities into one Romanian kingdom under his "dynasty." For all practical purposes, Romania had at last become independent.

But the struggle for national sovereignty had been a long and costly one—indeed, final *de jure* recognition was not won until 1878—and Romanian nationalism remained a sensitive and easily exacerbated emotion. The Romanians were convinced that they had reason for their exalted national pride. They were, their historians insisted, a Latin people, descendents of the Roman settlers of ancient Dacia. The quality of Latinism was not merely a matter of race, of the dark complexions and black hair that as late as the nineteenth century distinguished the Romanians from other Balkan peoples. The historians claimed that this Latinism was also a matter of culture. In truth the Romanians were mainly ignorant peasants, illiterate, profoundly superstitious, hardly more elevated in abilities or sensibilities than their Balkan neighbors. Nevertheless, the Romanian intelligentsia chose to encourage the notion that, in some fashion or another, their nation was cultivated, Western-oriented, nothing less, in fact, than an island of Latin culture in a Slavic ocean. Alien influences, therefore, had to be extirpated. Of course, each Balkan people fought savagely to preserve its individuality amidst the *mélange* of races elbowing for position and territory within the Balkan jungle. But national homogeneity was particularly important for the Latin Romanians, for they wished to preserve their status as a "Western" race. Turks, Serbs, Magyars, Slavs of all varieties were ruthlessly hounded out of Romanian territory. And there were Jews, too, to be considered.

The length of Jewish settlement on Romanian soil has long been a matter of debate. Romanian historians, most of them biased against the Jews, contended that the mass of Romanian Jewry "invaded" the country in the period from the late eighteenth century to 1860. Actually, Jews were living in Romania before the conquest of Dacia by Trajan; they were reinforced by small numbers of Jewish traders in the Middle Ages, when the Danubian principalities were the nexus of the commercial highway connecting Poland with Turkey. But the bulk of Jewish settlers did indeed come in during the second quarter of the nineteenth century, primarily Russian Jews in flight from the conscription horrors of Nicholas I's regime. By the end of the nineteenth century the Jewish population of Romania had grown to nearly a quarter of a million in a Romanian population of five and a half million.

Jewish disabilities, like Jewish settlement, predated Romanian autonomy. In the first half of the nineteenth century, both Turkish and Russian over-lords arbitrarily expelled Jewish families from selected cities and towns, and denied to all Jews even the limited communal privileges vouchsafed the Romanians. All the while, the oppressed Romanians regarded their Jewish neighbors as less than pariahs. Then, for a brief period, it appeared as if the Jews might win a guarantee of civil rights during the Congress of Paris in 1858, which followed the Crimean War. It was at this gathering that Baron James de Rothschild exerted his potent influence on Napoleon III, the unofficial protector of the Romanians. The banker asked his emperor, who was also his debtor, to raise the question of political equality for Romania's religious and ethnic minorities. Napoleon III agreed most will-ingly to do whatever he could; but on this issue, as on nearly every other matter that he touched, the French ruler was as ineffectual as he was amiable. The article in the Treaty of Paris which resulted from his efforts was less than satisfactory: its guarantee of political rights was extended merely to the Christian peoples who were not members of the Romanian Orthodox Church. The Romanians maintained their bitter animus against the Jews, and continued to deprive them of the rights and opportunities of Romanian citizenship.

When Cuza united the Danubian principalities into the single state of Romania, it again appeared as if the fate of the Jews might take a turn for the better. On New Year's Day, 1864, Cuza excited the hopes of a visiting Jewish delegation by remarking, with some feeling, "I wanted to give you all, but I could not. You will be gradually emancipated. Wherever I have been, I have liked you, and I have never discriminated between religions." Cuza did his best to keep his word; he ordered a legislative commission to prepare the groundwork for Jewish emancipation. Cuza's liberalism on the Jewish question was rather typical of his vaguely progressive attitude on a number of important political and economic issues. But it was an attitude which did not suit the tastes of Romania's powerful boyar nobility. In 1866 Cuza was overthrown, and Carol of Hohenzollern-Sigmaringen was brought in as the new Romanian monarch. The "democratic" constitution which the new king was expected to enforce was largely a sham, for control of the government remained firmly in the hands of Romania's propertied families. Among the most powerful of these families were the talented and rapacious Bratianus, whose ancestral holdings in northwestern Romania were the largest in the entire Balkans. From 1866 down to the first World War, Ioan Bratianu and his brothers and sons were the leading political figures in Romania. Although Bratianu's party was known as the Liberal Party, it was far from liberal; in alliance with the country's conservative boyars, it was more than willing to invoke strident Balkan nationalism and anti-Semitism as a diversion for social unrest.

Upon forming a government in 1866, Bratianu served notice upon the Jews that they could expect little sympathy from him. As the moment approached for the Romanian Parliament to ratify the new constitution, Bratianu persuaded the deputies to postpone their approval of Article VI, which would have extended political freedom to all religious groups. One of the truly unique aspects of Romanian anti-Semitism was its bland hypocrisy. When Adolphe Crémieux, President of the *Alliance Israélite Universelle,* rushed to Bucharest to plead with the Romanian government for a more tolerant attitude toward the Jews, Bratianu received him with the utmost cordiality, even promising to support Article VI. After all, Romania had need of its friends in France, the only real friends it had in Europe. Later, the distinguished French Jew received a standing ovation when he appeared in the Romanian Chamber of Deputies. No sooner had Crémieux left the country, however, than gangs of ruffians, hired by the government, reappeared in the streets, attacking Jews, and inveighing against Article VI as the "treason clause." In an impassioned speech to the Chamber, Bratianu himself stigmatized the Jews as a "social wound," and implored his countrymen to save the country from "that leprosy." Article VI never passed.

From then on the Jews of Romania were victims of a systematic "cold pogrom." Whenever revolutionary unrest threatened the economic oligarchy which backed the Bratianu regime, the government invoked anti-Semitism as a routine matter of public policy. In 1867, for example, Jews were forbidden to live in the Romanian countryside or to operate inns and taverns; instantly thousands of Jewish families were bankrupted. Even after the Jews poured into the cities, they found little in the way of security. Several thousands of them were arbitrarily driven out of Jassy, on the pretext that they were making the city "a dangerous focus of infection." The fact that these people were penniless, that hundreds of children and old people among them collapsed on the roads from exhaustion and exposure, made little impression on the government. Occasionally the consuls of foreign countries, particularly those of England and the United States, felt morally obligated to protest against this kind of State sadism. Bratianu's response to these protests was typically cunning. To underscore the serious problem of unassimilability which plagued his country, he ordered his agents to circulate abroad photographs of Romania's poorest, most wretched Jews, creatures who must have appeared bizarre indeed in all the splendor of their torn caftans, long beards, and earlocks.

At the Congress of Berlin in 1878, which followed the Russo-Turkish War, the question of the final *de jure* validation of Romanian independence was put on the agenda. So, too, once again, was the question of Jewish emancipation in Romania. This time the pressure brought to bear by Jewish bankers, the most influential of whom was Baron Gerson Bleichroeder of Berlin, was particularly unrelenting. The representatives of the Western Powers responded to such pressure by insisting that Romania must guarantee Jewish political emancipation before her sovereignty could be recognized. The Western statesmen followed up this ultimatum by drafting the guarantee themselves and incorporating it in the Treaty of Berlin as Article XLIV. It was couched in clear and unequivocal language, much clearer, in fact, than the abortive Article VI of the Romanian Constitution. But again the Western nations underestimated Romanian deviousness. While accepting the provision "in principle," the Romanian Parliament insisted that it would extend citizenship to "aliens" on an individual basis only. In practice, this counterproposition would have required that the citizenship of each Jew be voted by the Romanian Chamber of Deputies and then be approved by the king. At first the Western Powers indignantly rejected the Romanian plan as a "moral betrayal." The Romanian government was patient; it knew its bargaining power. Germany, for example, was especially eager to secure railroad concessions in Romania; so, too, was France. In February 1880, exactly as Romania's nationalist politicians had predicted, Britain, France, and Germany "expressed confidence" that the Bucharest regime would conform to the spirit of the Treaty of Berlin; a month later they announced Romania's complete *de jure* sovereignty. Romanian Jewry, as a result, lost its last best hope of international guarantee. Down to 1919 the Jews continued to exist as "aliens," burdened with all the disabilities—and more— suggested by that status. As it turned out, the disabilities continued long beyond the World War.

Most of Romania's 250,000 Jews lived in the largest cities, particularly in Bucharest and Jassy, where they had gradually returned after their initial expulsion. Essentially a commercial people, they survived marginally as petty storekeepers, peddlers, and artisans. In urban areas Jews were barred from export trade, from the professions, from all state employment. In the countryside Jewish physicians were permitted to practice only in those localities that were scorned by Romanian physicians; the moment that a Romanian physician appeared on the scene the Jew was obliged to clear out. The number of Jewish patients admitted to hospitals was strictly limited. In 1891, the Bratianu Government evicted all Jewish children from the Romanian school system; when the Jewish community attempted, with the financial aid of the *Alliance,* to establish a school system of its own, the government obstructed this effort by the simple device of requiring instruction to be given on the Jewish Sabbath. All the while these hardships and grievances were exacerbated by the government's systematic encouragement of pogroms. Each election season, Bratianu incited the chauvinism of his countrymen by announcing a program of "repression of the Germans and of the Jews who are everywhere their advance guard." Bands of thugs, fed and housed by Bratianu's supporters, roamed Jewish neighborhoods, attacking Jews, looting Jewish stores and homes.

At the turn of the century the sheer physical survival of Romanian Jewry was becoming a matter of doubt; tens of thousands of Jews were completely dependent upon the charity of the *Alliance* for their daily bread. As a result, a major tide of Jewish emigration began, blending with the exodus from Russia, and directing itself primarily toward America. So large, in fact, had the proportion of Romanian Jews pouring into the United States become, that in 1902 the American Secretary of State, John Hay, felt obliged to submit a note of protest to the Romanian government. In exceptionally strong language, Hay notified the Bucharest regime that the United States could not remain indifferent to a policy of maltreatment which each year drove thousands of destitute aliens to America's shores. The "interest of civilization," Hay warned, required an end to the persecution. The note had some effect; the Romanian government paused on the eve of new and even more severe anti-Jewish legislation. But after a few years, the thread of Jew-baiting was picked up again, both by the government and by Romania's opposition parties. Far from diminishing in intensity, Balkan nationalism reached even higher temperatures, sputtering into two small wars and ultimately into the first World War. Anti-Semitism was much too valuable a campaign slogan to be relinquished by ambitious politicians.

Ultimately, the Jews of Romania became the most wretched minority in all of Europe. Romanian anti-Semitism was even more pathological than Russian. For it was the small, poisonous, mean-minded anti-Semitism of a "have-not" nation aping and compounding the vices of its larger and more powerful neighbors. Like the lower middle class of Central and Western Europe, a third-rate power like Romania was convinced that it could best preserve its status, in this case within the hierarchy of nations, by demonstrating its "superiority" over the "aliens" in its midst.

CONCLUSION

In Western Europe the classical middle-class liberalism which had insured Jewish security during the nineteenth century was now beginning to run dry. The threat of socialism was driving increasing numbers of industrialists into alliance with the old aristocracy. In Germany, particularly, this new alliance shrewdly wooed the lower middle class with the slogans of nationalism and anti-Semitism, and circulated the sinister doctrines of race, Jewish banking power, and Jewish internationalism. But open violence against the Jews, even active legislative discrimination, was usually abjured. In Eastern Europe, on the other hand, exactly because there was less likelihood of identifying anti-Semitism with any large economic stratum, the Romanov regime was compelled to use a much heavier hand in alerting the Russian people to the Jewish "menace." The approach was one of blunt, primitive appeals to chauvinism and to Russian peasant superstition. In the long run, the labyrinthine complexities of the German psyche would result in the most calamitous Jew-hatred of human history. For the immediate future, however, the brutal and simple-minded anti-Semitism of czarist Russia, and the vindictive Balkan xenophobia of Romania, appeared to present by far the graver threat to the continued existence of the largest Jewish community in the world.

In 1882, shortly after the enactment of the May Laws, a Jewish intellectual poured out his heart in the pages of the Russo-Jewish journal, *Razsvet*: "When I think of what was done to us," he wrote, "how we were taught to love Russia and the Russian word, how we were lured into introducing the Russian language and everything Russian into our homes; that our children know no other language but Russian, and how we are now rejected and hounded . . . my heart is filled with corroding despair from which there is no escape." But, of course, there had to be some form of escape. The search for a way out of the constricting vise of East European oppression was responsible for a major revolution in Jewish life. It was the revolution of activism. While retaining their trust in God, the Jews of Russia and Romania prepared at last to abandon prayer as their principal means of salvation. The time had come to assume a more dynamic role in the long and bitter travail of survival.

XIII

The Rise of Zionism

THE IDEA OF NATIONALISM

Surely one of the central motifs of European history in the nineteenth century was the rise of nationalism, and the progressive self-liberation of Italian, German, and Balkan peoples which was its result. The revival of this passion for self-determination could be traced, in large measure, to the influence of modern romanticism. It was romanticism, as we have seen, which appeared to extol emotion in preference to reason, and which encouraged writers, clerics, and statesmen alike to re-evaluate the cumulative wisdom of earlier centuries. Within the space of a few decades after the Congress of Vienna this veneration of history, however opportunistically it may at first have been manipulated by conservative politicians, awakened in the races of Europe a renewed appreciation of their spiritual and cultural heritages. Respected scholars—the Czech Dubrovsky, the Greek Karais, the Italian Leopardi, the German Kleist—busily engaged themselves in the study of the languages, folkways, music, and history of their native lands. At first, indeed, modern nationalism was almost literally the creation of the intellectuals at the top—the historians and lexicographers, the philologists and musicologists—and was embraced only gradually by the general population. From historical researches and linguistic studies flowed the art and literature, from ancient mumbled folk tunes were created the symphonies and operas that reminded the members of Europe's principal linguistic groups that they possessed a collective genius, and, because of this, a collective destiny.

The rise of nationalism was a Europe-wide phenomenon, and it affected the Jews no less profoundly than other European peoples. For if one truth emerges from modern history it is that Jewish nationalism was not merely a reaction to anti-Semitism—any more, indeed, than German nationalism was merely a reaction to Napoleonic invasion. The history of modern Jewish nationalism begins with the basic fact of a cohesive ethnic group, living as a separate nation in Eastern, but not in Western, Europe, a "nation within a nation" the czars called it, apparently unassimilable, clinging tenaciously to ancient folkways, costume, diet, language, as well as to a common religion. Of course a people can share certain ideals and memories without the commitment to a common destiny. It was still necessary for such writers as Mazzini and Manzoni in Italy, Herder and Ranke in Germany, to jar sleeping aspirations into creative movement. Within the Pale of Settlement equally resourceful minds were required to encourage the Jewish population to productive acts of self-emancipation.

Such minds did, in fact, exist within the Jewish community. The conscious cultivation of Jewish nationalism may be traced back to the historical and philosophical investigations of Nahman Krochmal, Solomon Rapoport, and Samuel David Luzzatto, scholars who were convinced that they were exposing to view the rich and colorful folklore of a historic nation. Luzzatto, a native of Padua, Italy, and the most erudite Hebrew philologist of the early nineteenth century, bitingly criticized the "emancipation" complex which apparently obsessed the Western students of the Science of Judaism. His research was conducted, as was Krochmal's and Rapoport's, with the express aim of reacquainting Jews with their national heritage. It was with some feeling that Luzzatto wrote to Lazarus Geiger in Germany: "And may this year see an end to the servility and spiritual degradation of those who say: 'We are Germans, we are just like you, your culture is our culture, your morality is our morality!' It is not so! It is not so!"

When the early *maskilim,* the romanticists Micah Joseph Lebensohn and Abraham Mapu, depicted the lush pastoral glories of ancient Palestine, their purpose was not merely to encourage their people to return to the soil, but also to remind them that a proud sovereign nation of kings and warriors had once lived in Palestine. Nearly all the *maskilim,* for that matter, even those whose goal was to modernize and occidentalize life in the Pale, were as tenacious in their use of the Hebrew language as were such conscious nationalists as Krochmal, Rapoport, and Luzzatto. In his autobiography, Chaim Weizmann recalled the extent of Hebrew usage among literate circles in the Pale of Settlement: ". . . I, for instance, never corresponded with my father in any other language [except Hebrew], though to mother I wrote in Yiddish. I sent my father one Yiddish letter; he returned it without an answer." Whether used by nationalists or *maskilim,* the Hebrew language increasingly became the vogue among Jewish intellectuals, and it could not fail to evoke a chain of historic associations.

Jewish nationalism emerged, too, during the Russian-Jewish "honeymoon" of Alexander II's regime, by way of reaction to the dangers of assimilation. We recall (from Chapter X) the dismay expressed by Judah Leib Gordon and Perez Smolenskin as they suddenly recognized that *Haskalah* "modernism" was becoming a façade for the abandonment of Jewish loyalties. It was to stem the tide of this assimilation that Yehiel Michel Pines and Zeev Wolf Jawitz returned to a re-evaluation of the ghetto world, and discovered in that world a depth and a tenderness they had not formerly recognized or appreciated. But it was Perez Smolenskin, particularly, who reasserted, in such works as *Am Olam* ("Eternal People"), the identity and individuality of the Jewish people. In Judaism, he insisted, religion and nationalism went hand in hand. "And like [the other nations]," he declared, "let us treasure and honor the language of our people! Just as other subjugated nations are not ashamed to hope for their national redemption, neither is it a disgrace for us to hope for an end to our exile." Frankly doubting the permanency of emancipation, Smolenskin argued that the hope of return to the Promised Land was essential for the preservation of the Jewish people. Although Smolenskin did not at first preach or envisage a program of practical reconstruction in Palestine, he was the "bridge" between Jewish cultural nationalism and modern Zionism.

In addition to the regenerative impulse latent in *Haskalah,* the example of other European nationalist movements also served to stimulate the rise of Zionist activism. The passion and virility of Germany's *Jung Deutschland,* for example, made a powerful impact on Micah Joseph Lebensohn when he lived in Berlin; Hungarian and Slovakian nationalism had a similar effect on Smolenskin during his stay in Vienna. Eliezer Perlman, a writer who later assumed the pen name of Ben Yehudah, was notably impressed by the intensified Pan-Slavism which swept through Russia and the Balkan States during the Russo-Turkish War of 1877-78. One night, according to Ben Yehudah's memoirs, as he was contemplating the depth of Russian feeling for the Pan-Slavist cause, he thought of his own people: "Why should we be any less worthy than any other people?" he asked himself. "What about our nation, our language, our land?" The idea continued to prey on his mind, until at last he made the decision to devote his efforts to the actual resettlement of Palestine. Writing in the pages of the Hebrew-language journal *Ha-Shahar,* Ben Yehudah insisted that the Jews possessed all the attributes of nationhood: a common history, a common memory, a common language. All that was needed was a "national center to serve as the heart feeding the blood arteries of the nation." He urged Jewish writers to enlist in this cause and to organize a society for the promotion of colonization in the Holy Land.

Perhaps the most interesting example of Jewish reaction to European nationalism was to be found in the career of a German Jew named Moses Hess. It was a rather bohemian career. Although Hess came from an Orthodox family, he exhibited little Jewish loyalty in his early years. While a student at the University of Bonn he married a Christian girl, threw himself heart and soul in the socialist movement, and studiously avoided any contact with Jews or Jewish traditions. After the failure of the 1848 uprisings in Germany, he was obliged to flee for his life and to spend most of his remaining years wandering aimlessly from country to country. In the 1850's Hess at last abandoned his cosmopolitanism. He had been dabbling in ethnology, and had come to the conclusion that mankind was divided into groups of nations, each distinct in physical type and mental characteristics, each characteristic primal and inherent. Hess was particularly impressed by the writings of the Italian patriot Mazzini. If the Italians were entitled to their *Risorgimento*—the product of the unique characteristics Mazzini attributed to them—why were the Jews not entitled, as well, to their own national awakening and homeland? If the liberation of Rome was an act of historic justice, why not the liberation of Jerusalem? In 1862 Hess developed these ideas in a small volume entitled *Rome and Jerusalem*. It was the work of a prophetic idealist rather than a practical statesman. Even as Mazzini projected his vision of Italy as a unifying influence among the nations, so Hess envisaged a rejuvenated Jewish nation in Palestine as the moral messiah of the world. "March forward, Jews of all lands!" wrote Hess, in the ornate and florid style of his time:

> The ancient fatherland of yours is calling you, and we will be proud to open its gates for you. March forward, ye sons of martyrs! The harvest of experience which you have accumulated in your long exile will help to bring again to Israel the splendor of the Davidic days and rewrite that part of history of which the monoliths of Semiramis are the only witness.

It is only against this background of gestating national sentiment that the revived pogroms of the 1880's can be said to have intensified the urgency of Jewish nationalism. Weizmann put it well: "In the depths of the masses an impulse arose, vague, groping, unformulated, for Jewish self-liberation. It was genuinely of the folk; it was saturated with Jewish tradition; and it was connected with the most ancient memories of the land where Jewish life had first expressed itself in freedom. It was, in short, the birth of modern Zionism." Many young Jews, formerly indifferent to Jewish values, now were spurred by the pogroms to take an interest in the fate and fortune of their people. Jewish self-defense units were established in the leading cities of the Pale. Even the former Russophile Lev Levanda was moved to address a Jewish public prayer meeting, to exhort his brethren to return to their traditions, to begin thinking in terms of national rejuvenation.

The first clear-cut appeal to Jewish nationalism as an answer to the new anti-Semitic terror, rather than as a fulfillment of a "mission," was sounded in 1882. It was contained in a pamphlet written by Dr. Leon Pinsker, a former *maskil* from Odessa, and was entitled *Auto-Emanzipation* ("Self-Emancipation"). Pinsker, a physician, approached the problem of anti-Semitism "scientifically." Concluding that Jew-hatred was a phenomenon lying deep in human psychology, he made this observation:

> Nations live side by side in a state of relative peace, which is based chiefly on the fundamental equality between them. . . . But it is different with the people of Israel. This people is not counted among the nations, because since it was exiled from its land it has lacked the essential attributes of nationality, by which one nation is distinguished from another. . . . True, we have not ceased even in the lands of our exile to be spiritually a distinct nation; but this spiritual nationality, so far from giving us the status of a nation in the eyes of the other nations, is the very cause of their hatred for us as a people. Men are always terrified by a disembodied spirit, a soul wandering about with no physical covering; and terror breeds hatred.

Pinsker, in short, provided a scientific rationale for the growing numbers of Russian Jews who sensed that Jewish nationhood must now be transformed into urgent physical formulation.

As we review the rise of nineteenth-century nationalism, we note that the German, Italian, and Balkan nationalist movements could count upon a priceless asset, an asset perhaps even more important than a sense of history, a common folk music, a common language, or a common memory. That asset was the ancestral land itself: the land with familiar hills, contours, valleys, familiar graves, place names, relics, and markers. When European peoples spoke of "freedom" they spoke of a land to be cleared of alien soldiers, of subjugated provinces to be reunited. One wonders, at first, how revived Jewish nationalism could be taken seriously without the asset of a land. But for the Jews of Eastern Europe there was a land. It was as real for hundreds of thousands of them as if they had actually been living on its soil. When they spoke of it, prayed for it, yearned to be reunited with it, time and space disappeared, and it assumed a tangibility as concrete as anything in their practical experience. The land was Palestine.

THE IDEA OF PALESTINE

It was a burnt-out and eroded little wedge of soil, and after the last Jewish uprising against the Romans in the second century A.D. its history had little to do with the Jews. Invaded, looted, and despoiled by succeeding waves of Romans, Persians, Byzantines, Crusaders, and Arabs, it fell at last into the hands of the Ottoman Turks in 1517. Brave and savage warriors, the most ruthless conquerors in Near Eastern history, the Ottomans were destined to hold Palestine until 1917. During the four centuries of their rule the Ottoman sultans did nothing to improve the province and much to ravage it; the land which had once flowed "with milk and honey" lay blighted and depopulated. Rains eroded its hillsides; its valleys became malarial gullies. Its forests disappeared and the remaining vegetation was exposed to the goats, which the Bedouin nomads drove unhindered through the land.

Yet always there remained a handful of Jews, dark-skinned, poverty-stricken people, hardly distinguishable from the Arabs who inhabited the country after the seventh century. Their numbers were slightly augmented by refugees from the Spanish Inquisition, and by pious Hasidim who, during the nineteenth century, settled in the four "holy" cities of Jerusalem, Tiberias, Safad, and Hebron. They were abjectly poor, living like Arab slum-squatters, dependent on *Chalukah* (charity from abroad), for which each of the groups among them sent out periodic solicitors. A deadly inertia lay on these relics; if the restoration of Zion had depended upon them alone, Jewish nationalism would indeed have been a forlorn cause.

Zion, however, was not just the chimera of the living dead. It was enshrined in the hearts of Jews in every part of the world. It was never divorced from Jewish thinking and religious experience through all the centuries of dispersion. On the ninth day of the month of Ab, for example, which commemorated the destruction of the Temple by the Romans, Jews of a hundred generations later fasted and mourned as though they had been witnesses and victims of that ancient catastrophe. Maurice Samuel recalls:

> I have sat on the floor in stockinged feet among fellow-mourners, listened to the sobbing recital of the Lamentations of Jeremiah and, by the light of the commemorative candles, seen the tears run down the cheeks of grown men. This was no mechanical ritual. It came from the heart of a frustrated people. It was real, poignant and terrifying, a Fourth of July in reverse.

The obsessive presentness of Palestine in their lives was a fact. At Jewish weddings the groom crushed a glass underfoot to commemorate the lost Temple of Jerusalem. Three times a day, and oftener on special occasions, pious Jews prayed for the Restoration. The prayers for timely rains and abundant harvests were inevitably phrased in terms evocative of the Holy Land; morning and evening they called upon God to send them the *yoreh* and the *malkosh,* the "former" and the "latter" rains, in due season. They might have been living in the Arctic where there were no rains, or in the tropics where rain was a disaster; they were, in fact, usually city dwellers to whom rain had little personal meaning. It did not matter; the chronology of a Jew's life was still measured by the calendar of ancient Palestine. Jews living in the slate-gray wastes of northern Lithuania continued to erect the *Sukkah,* the tabernacle of desert foliage, during the season when once the Palestine harvest was due. In the midst of the insupportable sufferings of the medieval period, tens of thousands of piteously credulous Jews were deluded into following false Messiahs—Solomon Molcho, David Reubeni, Sabbatai Zevi—in expectation of imminent return to the Holy Land.

For most Jews, however, the notion of a physical return to Palestine was as farfetched as the arrival of an authentic Messiah. It was the rise of Hebrew literature, of Jewish nationalism, and of czarist persecution which combined to convert the thought of a Return from a pious hope to a dramatic salvation. *Haskalah* literature, for example, from the beginning of its history to the end of the nineteenth century, referred explicitly and repeatedly to Palestine: the land Palestine, not merely the national destiny of the Jewish people. This was most apparent, as we have seen, in the lyric and romantic literature of Micah Joseph Lebensohn, Kalman Schulman, and Abraham Mapu. Even before the pogroms, *Haskalah* authors were developing solutions for the Jewish problem that were not merely nationalist but also Zionist—Palestine-oriented—in everything but name. Perez Smolenskin did not formally embrace Zionism before the 1880's; but as early as 1868 he declared that it was not at all inappropriate for the modern Jew to aspire to political independence in a Jewish state in Palestine. After the pogroms, Smolenskin urged that Palestine be considered not only as a refuge for the persecuted Jews of Russia, but also as a territorial and spiritual center for the Jewish people—the kind of center America could never be. "Even if that land were inferior to all other countries," he wrote, "even if much work and effort be required to rebuild its waste lands, we should still choose Palestine, for that land is the symbol of our nationhood."

Smolenskin was joined in his Zionist appeals by Yehiel Michel Pines, Moshe Leib Lilienblum, and, most important of all, by Eliezer Ben Yehudah, to whom the cultivation of the Hebrew language and literature was not enough. "If I did not believe in the possibility of Israeli's redemption," Ben Yehudah declared in 1881, "I would discard the Hebrew language as a worthless thing." He issued an appeal for mass emigration to Palestine, for the physical cultivation of its soil, the use of its hallowed shrines as a stimulus for revived Jewish cultural and religious creativity. Thus, by the year 1881, sixteen years before the first Zionist Congress, Ben Yehudah, Smolenskin, Pines, and Lilienblum had already formulated the basic contours of the Zionist idea.

THE RISE OF ZIONISM

It was not as simple, however, to transform an inspiring idea into a viable movement. What responsible Jew would give even momentary consideration to settlement in a land parched and arid, snagged and straitened by the Turkish master? The Jews of Russia may have found sentimental outlets in dreams of Zion, but their immediate haven of refuge was bountiful America. To be sure, such eminent Western Jewish leaders as Moses Montefiore and Charles Netter, the latter representing the *Alliance,* visited Palestine, and established a few schools there for the children of the *Chalukah* mendicants; but this philanthropy was animated by no Jewish national purpose. More specific Zionist contact with the land of Palestine was needed to prime the pump of emigration there. It was to this end of reviving interest in the Holy Land, during the 1880's, that small numbers of nationalist zealots organized Zionist groups in the cities of the Pale.

The *Hoveve Zion*—Lovers of Zion—collected money, conducted courses in the Hebrew language and Jewish history, organized glee clubs. In the classic pattern of all embryonic national groups they pioneered gymnastic and self-defense organizations which they called Maccabee clubs. Of course these meetings had to be conducted secretly, often disguising themselves as wedding parties, for Zionism was an illegal movement in Russia. When the *Hoveve Zion* conducted their national convention, in 1884, they were obliged to meet in the city of Kattowitz in Upper Silesia, then a part of Germany, where they elected Dr. Leon Pinsker as president of the organization. In large part, it was this need for secrecy which centered leadership in the Russian-Jewish students who were registered at German and Austrian universities. They were mobile, unhampered by police investigation, and in intimate contact with the financial and cultural resources of the West. Even as the bourgeois university student was the classical carrier of modern nationalism, so, too, it was the Russian-Jewish student, moving from one German university to another, who carried with him the torch of national revival.

Jewish emigration from Russia after 1881 was unquestionably motivated by the czarist pogroms. But it was principally as a result of *Hibat Zion* propaganda that some seven thousand Jews departed in 1882 for Palestine. These young zealots were blissfully unpreoccupied with practical considerations. They did not know how long the suspicious Turkish administration would permit them to stay; nor did they know how they would support themselves once they arrived. After they reached Palestine, therefore, many of them drifted aimlessly into the cities of Jerusalem, Jaffa, Haifa, and Hebron. A few opened shops; others were artisans. Most of them lived on what they had brought with them, and a few even found it necessary to fall back on *Chalukah*. But while these early settlers who came to Palestine in the first *Aliyah*, the first wave, did not fulfill the Zionist ideal of creating a virile new agricultural society, they did nevertheless bring into the country human material which served as the indispensable nucleus for further settlement.

They fared better, at least, than the tiny group of three dozen Russian Jews who called themselves BILU (from the Hebrew initials of "House of Jacob, Let Us Go"). The BILUim, all of them young men in their teens and early twenties, combined Marxist zeal with Jewish nationalist fervor. They were determined to settle in Palestine as farmers or laborers and to avoid at all costs, on the ancestral soil of Zion, the stereotype of peddlery and petty trade that they identified, perhaps unfairly, with Jewish life in the Pale. Few of these youths had the foggiest notion of Palestinian conditions, climate, soil, or resources. Some of them hoped to receive financial aid from a sympathetic British-Christian writer, Lawrence Oliphant, whose sentimental good will was confused with realistic support. This assurance of security vanished when Oliphant failed to raise money from among his friends in the West. It was a serious blow, but the BILUim were endowed with the blindest of faith and they refused to be deterred. In 1882, with hardly more than the clothes on their backs and a total common treasury of a few hundred rubles, they departed for Palestine.

On their way to Constantinople the BILUim issued a naive and touching document which expressed the hope that "the interests of our glorious nation will rouse our national spirit in rich and powerful men, and that everyone, rich and poor, will give his best labors to the holy cause. Greetings, dear brothers and sisters,"—and then, combining this passionate nationalism with a very un-Marxian religiosity, they added: "Hear, O Israel, the Lord our God, the Lord is One, and our land, Zion, is our only hope." Once arrived in Palestine, the real hardship began. Instead of building co-operative colonies of their own, as they had planned, they were obliged to hire themselves out as farm hands on a plantation established by the *Alliance*. Exhausting physical labor under the blistering desert sun, years of crop failures and illness, destroyed their illusions. Some of the BILUim died of malaria; some returned to Russia; and some severed their contact with their fellows and strayed off into limbo.

There were, however, several hundred *Hoveve* Zionists of the first *Aliyah*, uncommitted to the socialist ideals of the BILU, who founded a thin line of agricultural settlements—Rosh Pinah, Zichron Ya'akov, and Petah Tikvah—

and who managed to survive as farmers. They had few scruples about hiring Arab labor to do the heavy work for them. Nor were they unwilling to accept subsidies from Baron Edmond de Rothschild of Paris. This dilettante philanthropist was no Zionist, but he welcomed any experiment which could produce Jewish agriculturists, and he made the struggling colonies his pet project. His intentions were honorable but in effect he succeeded only in undermining the initiative of the new settlements. For example, the enormous wine cellars he constructed for them produced little in the way of marketable vintage; yet he was never unwilling to buy the wine at prices well above the market.

Nevertheless, these first Jewish farmers, by their very willingness to remain on the soil, to endure the desert heat, the dangers of malaria and Arab bandits, played an influential role in securing the first modern Jewish settlement in Palestine on nationalist premises. What discouraged them was not the compromises they were obliged to make with the original austere ideals of Zionism. These could be endured. But to what end if they continued to live in the Holy Land without the protection of juridical status; if they were as much at the mercy of venal Turkish officials in Palestine as they had been of czarist bureaucrats in the Pale? Had they come to Palestine, the *Hoveve* Zionists wondered, merely to resume the statuslessness which had cursed their life in Russia? The more they brooded about it, the more they were convinced that mere settlement could not create the homeland; by itself settlement was far too tortuous and precarious. A bolder and more drastic solution was needed. In 1896 such a solution was formulated by an assimilated Western Jew.

THEODOR HERZL

On a May day in 1895, Baron Maurice de Hirsch, the eminent Jewish philanthropist, was sitting in the drawing room of his Paris mansion when his valet ushered in a visitor, a rather impressive man, tall, broad-shouldered, with piercing black eyes, a strong, well-shaped brow, and a long, rich "Assyrian" beard. After introducing himself as Theodor Herzl, a Jew from Vienna, the caller plunged into a discussion of the Jewish problem. He denigrated de Hirsch's scheme for transporting Russian Jewry to the Argentine. "You breed beggars," he stated bluntly to de Hirsch. "This philanthropy debases the character of our people." De Hirsch smiled, and asked Herzl what his alternative was. "My alternative," Herzl said, "is to call a congress of Jewish notables to discuss migration to a sovereign Jewish State." De Hirsch stared at his guest incredulously for a moment, and within a matter of minutes succeeded in closing the interview. What manner of man, he wondered later, could utter thoughts so shockingly at variance with the National Affirmation—the Sanhedrin's dominating tradition in Western Jewish life?

History was to prove that Herzl was eminently sane and sensible. He was the son of assimilated Hungarian-Jewish parents. In his early twenties he acquired an excellent legal education at the University of Vienna. Shortly after receiving his doctorate of jurisprudence, however, he decided to abandon the law for a career in writing. His confidence in his literary ability, as well as in the family fortune which assured him security, was justified; within a few years he achieved a reputation as one of the most brilliant feuilletonists in Central Europe. In 1887 he was appointed feuilleton editor of the *Wiener Allgemeine Zeitung*; and within ten years the liberal daily, the *Neue Freie Presse*, the most distinguished paper in the Hapsburg Empire, offered him the enviable position of Paris correspondent.

His professional accomplishments notwithstanding, Herzl was not a happy man. His best friend committed suicide in 1891. His wife, Julie Naschauer, a lovely Bohemian Jewess, lived in a childlike world of personal whims and caprices, and frequent separations between the two ultimately led to permanent estrangement. Perhaps the most decisive factor in Herzl's deepening melancholy was the bitter anti-Semitism he encountered everywhere in Europe. A man of almost morbid sensitivity, he had suffered keenly, while a student in Vienna, from the frigid correctness of his non-Jewish classmates. As a journalist he was obliged to attend political rallies and public conventions at which anti-Jewish epithets and slogans were far from uncommon. It is likely that Herzl was seriously preoccupied with anti-Jewish discrimination long before he encountered the insane Jew-baiting of the anti-Dreyfusards in civilized Paris, or the malevolent political anti-Semitism of Mayor Lueger in Vienna. He first expressed himself on the Jewish problem, in 1894, in a rather superior play, *The New Ghetto*; the drama dealt with the tragedy of modern Jew-hatred in conventionally liberal terms. Shortly thereafter—exactly when we do not know—the idea of a Jewish homeland began to take shape. By early May of 1895, the rough contours of his concept had become sufficiently definite to be boldly presented in the interview with Baron de Hirsch which opened his Jewish political career.

Undaunted by the failure of his mission to de Hirsch, Herzl cast about for new allies. His diary for the year 1895 tells of a vision of "immeasurable greatness" which obsessed him every waking moment. "It has the appearance of a stupendous dream," he wrote, "but for days and weeks it has absorbed me to the point of unconsciousness. It accompanies me wherever I go, it hovers over my ordinary conversation, looks over my shoulder during my ridiculously petty journalistic work, haunts and intoxicates me." In November 1895, he presented his plan for a Jewish State to the celebrated Jewish publicist, Dr. Max Nordau. Apparently the concept moved Nordau deeply; according to Nordau's daughter, he clutched Herzl in his arms. "If you are insane," he cried, "we are insane together. Count on me!" Measurably encouraged by Nordau's support, Herzl hurled himself into the literary formulation of his "solution." The small volume was completed in 1896, and bore the dramatic and unequivocal title, *Der Judenstaat*—"The Jewish State." "The idea which I have developed in this pamphlet is a very old one," Herzl began; "it is the restoration of the Jewish State. The world resounds with outcries against the Jews, and these outcries have awakened the slumbering idea." This last sentence was the clue to Herzl's theme: the Jewish State was to be created as an answer to anti-Semitism. The deeply rooted facts of Jewish nationalism, of Jewish cultural traditions, of historic

Jewish affinity for Zion, had apparently not occurred to him. The book was devoted to the practical physical functions to be performed by a homeland in which Jews would never again be subjected to anti-Semitism.

It was, however, this very insularity which gave the book its strength. For Herzl entered into the most detailed discussion of the needs of the State: the need for a congress of Jewish representatives, for money, for engineers and technicians. Nowhere did he make it clear that Palestine must be the site of this State. At one point he even touched upon Argentina as its possible location. But Herzl's naïveté was overshadowed by his audacity. The Jews of Western Europe may have mocked him. The German and German-Jewish press may have cracked jokes about the "Jewish Jules Verne" and taken him to task for his betrayal of the tradition of the National Affirmation. But for the Jews of Eastern Europe, even for those who were angered by Herzl's transparent ignorance of the depth and roots of Jewish nationalism, the publication of *Der Judenstaat* was an historic event. Chaim Weizmann recalled:

> I was in my second year in Berlin when, in 1896, Theodore Herzl published his tract, now a classic of Zionism, *Der Judenstaat*. . . . It was an utterance which came like a bolt from the blue. . . . Fundamentally, *The Jewish State* contained not a single new idea for us; that which so startled the Jewish bourgeoisie, and called down the resentment and derision of Western Rabbis, had long been the substance of our Zionist tradition . . . Not the ideas, but the personality which stood behind them appealed to us. Here was daring, clarity, and energy. The very fact that the Westerner came to us unencumbered by our own preconceptions had its appeal. . . . We were right in our instinctive appreciation that what had emerged from the *Judenstaat* was less a concept than a historic personality.

It was precisely this instantaneous and enthusiastic Russian-Jewish response which changed the course of Herzl's plans. As an "aristocrat," with an instinctive distrust of the masses, Herzl had initially gravitated for help to the wealthy and distinguished among his people. But when, in 1896, Edmond de Rothschild and several of his banking colleagues turned down his request for funds and moral support, Herzl began to pay closer attention to the crowds of cheering Galician and Russian Jews who met him at railway stations in his travels through the eastern provinces of the Hapsburg Empire. On July 21, 1896, he communicated his decision to Jacob de Haas, the honorary secretary of the Zionist movement in London: "There is only one reply to this situation: let us organize the masses immediately." It was the fateful moment in the rise of modern Zionism.

DIPLOMATIC AND PARLIAMENTARY MANEUVERS

Herzl determined to summon a World Zionist Congress, to provide the movement for a Jewish State with a mass base. It was a daring, certainly a presumptuous move for one man to make. Ninety years earlier Napoleon

Bonaparte had summoned an international colloquium of Jews; but Napoleon was the conqueror of Europe, and even then he had restricted his "invitation" to the Jews of France and Italy. Yet Herzl was not without qualifications for the task he had undertaken. He possessed a superbly commanding presence and personality, a sound legal background, and years of journalistic experience covering the workings of Western parliaments. Of course, his decision to summon a Congress met with strenuous opposition. The leaders of Western Jewry, particularly, were horrified by the announced project. Was Herzl mad, they asked, to summon this kind of international gathering in the presence of the whole world, to publish openly the "treasonable" view that the Jews were not simply a religious community, but rather a separate nation? If Herzl was given pause by the violence of this Western Jewish reaction, he received significant reassurance of support from the thousands of followers who sent delegates to the first Zionist Congress. When the Congress opened, on August 29, 1897, in the Swiss city of Basel, some 204 delegates had arrived from all corners of the world, including 80 from Russia and a handful from America. The delegates were young and old, bourgeois and socialist, Orthodox and nonobservant—all of them surcharged with a sense of historic mission.

As Nordau opened the first session in the dignified Basel Concert Hall, as the delegates, secretaries, and spectators took their seats, Herzl found it difficult to control his emotions. Here, he recognized, was a dramatic reassertion of the dignity of the Jewish people in the midst of their European degradation, an answer of at least a significant portion of world Jewry to Bonaparte's Sanhedrin of nearly a century earlier. Herzl, unanimously elected President of the Congress, presented a clear and intelligible program. Emancipation had proved to be an illusion, he declared; Jews were everywhere the objects of renewed hatred and contempt. The one, the only intelligible solution to the Jewish problem was the re-establishment of a Jewish homeland in Palestine, a homeland which would be *"offentlich, rechtlich"*—openly recognized and legally secured. Because he did not wish to offend the Turks, with whom he hoped soon to open negotiations, Herzl did not deem it expedient to speak openly in terms of Statehood. But the delegates sensed the political realism which tempered his remarks and voted overwhelmingly in favor of the platform he presented. A World Zionist Organization was established, with Herzl as its president; a Jewish flag and a national anthem, *Hatikvah,* were adopted; an Actions Committee was set up in Vienna. By the elevated level of their discussions and the sobriety of their decisions, the delegates to the first Zionist Congress made it patently clear to Christians and Jews alike that they were in deadly earnest. It is difficult today to take issue with the words Herzl penned in his diary: "In Basel, I created the Jewish State."

After establishing the basic machinery of the Zionist movement, Herzl determined now to concentrate on diplomatic negotiations. His goal was nothing less than a charter for his people from the Turkish government, a charter which, in one fell swoop, would legalize Jewish settlement in Palestine on a corporate basis. Ever the aristocrat, the student of international intrigue, Herzl was convinced that a chain of influential contacts was all that was necessary to win the co-operation of the Sultan. He began by tracking down the Sultan's friend and ally, Kaiser Wilhelm II of Germany. After protracted negotiations with the Kaiser's uncle, Count Philipp zu Eulenburg, and the German ambassador in Vienna, Herzl managed to obtain his interview with Wilhelm II in Constantinople in October 1898. One must smile today at the solemn faith Herzl placed in these interviews. He fancied he understood royalty and knew how to deal with it. Unquestionably Herzl's aristocratic bearing, carefully cultivated, made an impression on the Kaiser. During the course of the hour-long interview the flamboyant German emperor seemed favorably disposed to the Zionist idea. "There are among your people," the Kaiser observed, "certain elements whom it would be a good thing to move to Palestine." Chancellor von Bülow, standing beside the two men, smiled an anti-Semitic smile of agreement. The interview ended with the Kaiser's promise that he would take up the matter of a "Chartered Company" with the Sultan when the two monarchs next met. In October, Herzl followed the Imperial German cortege to Palestine (where he himself was shadowed by Turkish detectives). He was again greeted by the Kaiser, who still appeared to be sympathetic to the idea of a Jewish homeland in Palestine. And then months went by, and nothing happened. It gradually dawned on Herzl that his request had been politely ignored.

Between 1899 and 1901 Herzl made a concerted effort to reach the ear of the Sultan directly. It was a complicated and expensive project, for baksheesh was the only sure route to the Yildiz Palace, and Herzl had already used up the larger part of his private fortune in organizing the Zionist movement. But eventually he made some headway through the clotted throng of avaricious Turkish officials. By the expeditious use of an influential Jewish apostate, one Armin Vámbéry, Herzl at last obtained his interview with the Sultan in May 1901. The sight of the ugly, hook-nosed little degenerate, the murderer of hundreds of thousands of Armenians, physically revolted Herzl; but he masked his feelings and launched into a two-hour conversation. The Turks were up to their ears in debt, Herzl pointed out. Indeed, the bondholders of Europe had placed a "lien" on Turkey in the form of an Ottoman public debt. In return for a charter of Jewish settlement in Palestine, Herzl shrewdly suggested, perhaps the wealthy Jewish bankers of Europe might be willing to pay off the debt. It was pure bluff: Herzl had no such contacts, but he was convinced that the promise of a charter would produce them. The Sultan was interested. He plied Herzl with cigarettes, the Grand Cordon of the Order of the Medjidje, and the vague promise of a charter; but he also wanted to see the color of Herzl's money. Herzl promised to have an answer for the Sultan soon. He rushed back to Paris, tried desperately to get some kind of a commitment from Rothschild—and failed. In February 1902, he returned to Constantinople and attempted to maneuver the Sultan into making a firm bid. But this time the Sultan was more explicit: the Turkish government would approve Jewish settlement throughout the Ottoman Empire, but not as a corporate group in Palestine. Herzl's heart sank; he recognized that the Sultan had made a fool of him, and was using the threat of a Jewish loan to obtain better interest terms from French creditors. Herzl's morale badly shaken, he gave serious consideration now to resigning from the presidency of the movement.

Had Herzl but known it, the Zionist movement was beginning to make encouraging progress; it was progress which dwarfed in significance the failure of his diplomatic negotiations. In the year which followed the first Zionist Congress, as a direct result of the "Basel Platform," the number of Zionist societies throughout the world increased from 117 to 913. Each subsequent Congress lent new strength and enthusiasm to the movement. In 1901 the Jewish Colonial Trust was established; and while the Trust had sold only a million dollars worth of shares by 1904, out of this modest beginning arose the Anglo-Palestine Company, which in years to come was to play a leading role in the development of Palestine. The Jewish National Fund was founded at the behest of an eminent German Zionist, Professor Hermann Shapira. Because its purpose was to purchase land in Palestine as the inalienable property of the Jewish people, the Fund ultimately made possible the impressive social experiment of co-operative farm settlement. Each Zionist Congress attracted as its delegates some of the finest minds of the Jewish world, and of the Eastern European Jewish world at that. It was, in fact, the infusion of large numbers of Russian Jews which insured the strength and permanency of the Zionist movement. For these were the zealots, men for whom Zion was not merely a solution to political problems, but rather a fact of the deepest cultural and religious significance, and for whom, therefore, the short-term success or failure of diplomatic negotiations brought neither elation nor dismay.

THE GREAT CRISIS

Still unwilling to abandon the "diplomatic" approach altogether, Herzl proceeded to cultivate contacts in England. There was always an outside possibility that London might prove to be a better avenue to Jerusalem than Berlin or even Constantinople had been. It was in London that Herzl won the friendship and admiration of Lord Nathan Rothschild, who in turn secured an interview for him with Joseph Chamberlain, Britain's Secretary of State for Colonial Affairs. Bluff, genial Joe Chamberlain was not without sympathy for the Jews of Russia; but his principal motivation in receiving Herzl was to find a solution to the congestion of London's East End. Like most non-Jews, he was favorably impressed by Herzl's bearing and eloquence, and he offered to help. Herzl suggested that El Arish in the Sinai Peninsula might be a feasible area of settlement. El Arish was adjacent to Palestine, and possessed historic Jewish associations. When Chamberlain countered with the suggestion of some other spot in Egypt, Herzl remarked: "Egypt? No, Mr. Secretary, we will not go there. We have have already been there." Chamberlain grinned appreciatively, and agreed to explore the possibilities of El Arish with Foreign Secretary Lansdowne, with the British agent in Egypt, and with Zionist officials in England. Herzl returned to Vienna to await developments. The El Arish plan, unfortunately, was soon entangled in a Gordian knot of Egyptian and Turkish intrigue and came to nothing. But Chamberlain promised to explore other alternatives and to notify Herzl if a solution presented itself.

One wonders if, at this point, Herzl were willing to dismiss Palestine altogether as the site of a Jewish State. Certainly the torment of Romanian and Russian Jewry affected him deeply; he was convinced, in fact, that an immediate asylum for these wretches had become a matter of life or death. More important, Herzl was obsessed with the need to present his followers with a tangible diplomatic coup in the near future, lest—in his opinion— the Zionist movement collapse for lack of hope and inspiration. For that matter, Herzl did not know how many more years of leadership he personally could offer. He had already suffered several heart attacks, the direct result of annoyance and overwork.

One gains insight into Herzl's thinking by reading a short novel he dashed off as a form of therapy during the black days of 1902. It was called *Altneuland* ("Old-New Land"). *Altneuland* dealt with Herzl's vision of a Palestine recreated by Zionist enthusiasts. The mediocre plot and the uninspired character sketches were so thinly contrived that they need hardly preoccupy the reader today. Obviously, he was no novelist. But he was truly prescient in his detailed discussion of the new society. His descriptions of modern trolley cars, of electric turbines, of theaters, commercial enterprises, clinics, research institutions, were unexceptional. Through his protagonist, Friedrich Lowenberg, Herzl repeatedly assured the reader that Altneuland represented the synthesis of the best technology and the ideas of the West. His notions of Altneuland's cultural future, an amalgam and refinement of Jewish linguistic and intellectual accomplishments in Europe, were curiously pedestrian and superficial. Hebrew, to be sure, occupied a place in the new society; but so did French, German, Italian, Spanish, and Yiddish. The sturdy peasants of Altneuland spoke Russian or German, and gave Russian or German names to their model villages and their children. Herzl neither foresaw nor apparently hoped for a Hebrew press, Hebrew assemblies, Hebrew schools, nor did he foresee a life thoroughly rooted in the Hebraic idiom. Altneuland, in sum, was viewed as a political and technological answer to Jewish oppression—little more.

It was in this respect that Herzl was destined to come a cropper in his dealings with the vast hinterland of world Jewry, the Jewish community of Eastern Europe. For the Zionists of Russia and Romania were even then under the spell of one of the most influential personalities in modern Jewish history. He was Asher Ginzberg (1858-1927), a man who refracted and distilled in brilliant literary form the innermost religious and cultural traditions of the Pale. Ginzberg was a Ukrainian Jew who managed, at heavy personal sacrifice, to obtain a modern education at several Western European universities. Like many of his generation, he was caught up in the restless surge of Jewish nationalism, and joined the *Hibat Zion*. Yet, while not devout, but as a proud and tradition-minded Jew, Ginzberg was disturbed by Zionism's emphasis upon the physical rebuilding of Palestine. In 1881, he published an article in a Hebrew journal over the pen name by which he was henceforth known: *Ahad Ha'am*—"One of the People." The article was entitled *Lo Zeh Ha-Derech* ("This Is Not the Way") and it attracted wide attention among the Russian-Jewish students of Germany. Virtually overnight Ahad Ha'am became the spiritual conscience of Jewish nationalism.

There was too much concern in Zionism, Ahad Ha'am insisted in *Lo Zeh Ha-Derech* and in subsequent writings, for the physical safety of the Jew. Instead, Jewish nationalism ought properly to be concerned with reviving the cultural loyalties and spiritual productivity of the Jewish people. ". . . The whole point of the material settlement [in Palestine] consists, to my mind, in this . . ." he wrote, "that it can be the foundation of that national spiritual center which is destined to be created in our ancestral country in response to a real and insistent national demand . . . Not twenty agricultural colonies, not even a hundred . . . can automatically effect our spiritual salvation." The mission of Zionism, in Ahad Ha'am's thesis, was to solve the problem not merely of the Jew, but of Judaism as well. Convinced that Palestine offered little solution to Jewish political disabilities, that most Jews would continue to live in the Diaspora for many generations to come, Ahad Ha'am urged the Zionists to concentrate their energies on evolving in Israel's historic land a community which would be a "true miniature of the Jewish People." He likened Palestine to a hub and the outer Jewish community to the spokes of the wheel of Judaism. This spiritual revival, of course, depended almost exclusively upon the prophetic and spiritual significance of Palestine, the only land which possessed uniquely Jewish historical associations.

The theory was attractive. And yet Ahad Ha'am was no mere theorist, dreamily ignoring the routine necessities of Jewish life. In his own career, for example, he was an eminently practical person. The great tea firm of K. W. Wissotzky sent him to London to manage its English branch, and he did this extremely well. It was the clarity of his mind, and the beauty of his Hebrew idiom, which made his arguments irresistible. Weizmann recalled the personal magnetism of this spare little man, with his sunken cheeks, carefully trimmed goatee, and pince-nez—and his remarkable influence over his Zionist colleagues:

> He had the profoundest effect on the Russian-Jewish students in Europe. . . . The appearance of one of Ahad Ha'am's articles was always an event of prime importance. He was read and discussed endlessly. . . . He was, I might say, what Gandhi had been to many Indians, what Mazzini was to Young Italy a century ago.

Ahad Ha'am's suspicion of Herzl's political Zionism was perhaps overstated. It was little short of ludicrous for him to say, for example: "At the first festive gathering in Basel, I sat like a mourner at a wedding." But he reflected the misgivings of ever larger numbers of Russian Zionists, men like Weizmann, Yehiel Tchlenov, Menahem Ussischkin, Shmarya Levin, who called themselves the "practicals." Strongly influenced by Ahad Ha'am, they placed little faith in Herzl's diplomatic Zionism—the Zionism of the "politicals"; they preferred to concentrate on the day-to-day construction of a Jewish community in Palestine, and on an equally steady program of Zionist education throughout the Jewish world. Because they represented the masses of devout, impoverished Russian Jewry, the "practicals" had little patience with what they considered to be the aristocratic "pretensions" of Herzl and his German-Jewish colleagues, people who flaunted their contacts with "influential" European statesmen. Weizmann recalled Herzl's attempt to put Sir Francis Montefiore, a nonentity, into the office of vice-president of the World Zionist Organization. "But Dr. Herzl," protested Weizmann, "the man's a fool." To which Herzl replied, with immense solemnity, *"Er öffnet mir königliche pforten"*—"He opens the portals of royalty to me." When Weizmann could not help smiling, Herzl turned white. "He was full of Western dignity," the Russian Jew added, "which did not sit well with our Russian-Jewish realism." It was this dichotomy between the Western-Jewish "aristocratic" approach, seeking a quick political solution to the Jewish problem, and the approach of the Russian-Jewish traditionalists, who sought in Palestine a touchstone for Jewish cultural rejuvenation, which was intensified now by the abortive Uganda project.

In the summer of 1903 Herzl was suddenly called back to London for another interview with Joseph Chamberlain. The Colonial Secretary had just returned from a trip to Africa. "On my travels," he said, "I saw a country for you: Uganda. On the coast it is hot, but in the interior the climate is excellent for Europeans. You can plant cotton and sugar. I thought to myself: that's just the country for Dr. Herzl. But *he* must have Palestine and will move only in its vicinity." The news of the Kishinev pogrom had just reached Western Europe, and Herzl was no longer certain that he ought to wait for Palestine. He asked Chamberlain for time to consider the proposal. Later in the summer he visited the Pale personally and witnessed at firsthand the desperate conditions of Russian-Jewish life. The sight of the squalor and beggary in the Pale's ghettos horrified him; it was much worse than he had ever imagined. Thus, when the British Foreign Office offered Uganda to him officially, in August 1903, Herzl reluctantly decided to accept it as a temporary asylum, and to present the project for ratification to the sixth Zionist Congress, scheduled to meet in Basel.

Herzl expected opposition from the Russian-Jewish delegates. So, too, did Max Nordau, who presented the plan at the opening session of the Congress. Nordau pointed out, with grave eloquence, that Uganda was not meant to serve as a permanent solution, but rather as a *nachtasyl,* a mere haven for the night. Neither, however, anticipated the heat of Russian-Jewish reaction. A deadly silence followed Nordau's address; he recalled later that hate and fury from the floor of the auditorium seemed to well up toward him in waves. Herzl's personal prestige was such that the Uganda plan was accepted on the first balloting; but the margin of approval was extremely narrow—and when the delegates from Eastern Europe indignantly walked out of the auditorium en bloc it was apparent that the vote itself was of much less consequence than the imminent disruption of the Zionist movement. Herzl watched the departure of the Russian Jews with his mouth agape, and then commented to a friend, with sublime misunderstanding of the kind of Zionism that animated the *Ostjuden*: "These people have a rope around their necks, and still they refuse!"

During the next few days the Zionist movement was threatened by an irrevocable schism. The Russian-Jewish delegates, the "practicals," met in a rump session and hooted down Herzl's efforts to pacify them. The Congress remained in a state of high tension; family bonds and lifelong friendships were shattered. When the proceedings ended, the Russian Zionists departed for Kharkov. There they convened their own conference and committed themselves permanently and exclusively to the idea of Palestine—even issuing a brutal denunciation of Herzl. But it hardly mattered; the Uganda question was soon to become academic. Public opinion in England was running strong against turning "rich" Uganda over to the Jews; and in response to this public clamor, as well as to the evident division on the matter within Zionist ranks, the English government made a graceful withdrawal. The passions and the resentments of the debates died down, and the Zionist movement was not shattered. It was the ideological chasm momentarily revealed by the Uganda issue, however, which made it clear to Herzl for the first time how profound was the yearning for Palestine in the racial memories of his kinsmen east of the Elbe. It was then, too, that Herzl grasped an inescapable portent: it was only a matter of time before the potent reservoir of *Ostjuden* would take over the movement altogether.

The strain of this last battle proved too much for Herzl's weakened heart. In May of 1904 he began spitting blood and was rushed off to Franzensbad for a rest cure. On July 3, at the age of forty-four, he died at Edlach. His body was sent back to Vienna, draped in a Zionist flag, and carried through the streets of the city. An immense procession of ten thousand Jews followed his funeral cortege to the graveside, arousing the wonder and awe of Christian bystanders. Throughout Europe, even as far away as Vilna and Odessa, streets and highways in the Jewish sections of town were packed with mourners. Old acrimonies were forgotten when the giant passed away; only his dedication and devotion to his people were remembered. Perhaps the best epitaph for the man was penned by Herzl himself in a diary entry of January 24, 1902:

> Zionism was the Sabbath of my life. I believe that my influence as a leader is based on the fact that while as man and writer I had so many faults, and committed so many blunders and mistakes, as a leader in Zionism I have remained pure of heart and quite selfless.

History has not dimmed the judgment.

The Zionist movement was severely shaken, but not destroyed, by Herzl's death. The accomplishments which had been telescoped into the seven years since the first Congress could not easily be erased: there was the World Zionist Organization, the Congress itself, the Jewish Colonial Trust, and the Jewish National Fund. There were intangible assets, too: vigor, international sympathy, momentum. The new president, David Wolffsohn, was, to be sure, no Herzl; but he was a congenial and diplomatic man. Born in

Lithuania and settled in business in Cologne, Germany, he served as the ideal intermediary between Westerners and Easterners, "politicals" and "practicals." It was largely due to Wolffsohn's talents for compromise that the Zionist movement was opened on a federative basis to groups that had formerly avoided Zionism as too relentlessly doctrinaire. Orthodox Jews now entered Zionism through the Mizrachi party to stand guard against the impairment of traditional Judaism in the affairs of the Movement. Socialist Jews entered through the Labor Zionist (Poale Zion) party to strive for a co-operative commonwealth in Palestine without "exploiters or exploited."

The highest tribute to Wolffsohn's healing leadership was the "official" fusion of "practical" and "political" Zionism at the 1907 Congress. A resolution of the gathering pledged the Movement not merely to the quest for a charter, but to the physical settlement of Palestine, to the moral strengthening of Jewish consciousness, and to the revival of the Hebrew language. In that year, too, the Palestine Department of the Zionist Organization was created, and Dr. Arthur Ruppin was placed in charge of colonization. For the next decade the decisive developments in the Zionist movement were to take place in Zion itself.

PALESTINE BEFORE THE FIRST WORLD WAR

By 1907 there were perhaps 70,000 Jews in Palestine; most of them were city dwellers, and of these at least 60 per cent were *Chalukah* mendicants. While there were some 5,000 Jewish agriculturists living on twenty-two farm colonies, the majority of these colonies were still controlled by the paternalistic Palestine Jewish Colonization Association—PICA—of Baron Edmond de Rothschild. A number of excellent citrus crops were undoubtedly produced by these colonies; but most of the settlers were hardly farmers in the classical sense. Indeed, they had grown into a miniature planter aristocracy, supervising large gangs of Arab laborers who did the actual drudging spadework on the soil.

A change in orientation was foreshadowed in 1904, when a new wave of Jewish immigrants, the second *Aliyah,* departed for Palestine. Most of the 15,000 to 20,000 pioneers of this second *Aliyah* were resolved, first and foremost, to be men of the soil. They despised the urbanization of Jewish life in the Pale, and were determined to transform themselves into a race of hardhanded farmers or die in the attempt. The most articulate spokesman for this return-to-the-soil movement was Aaron David Gordon, the "Tolstoi of Palestine." For twenty-seven years Gordon had served as administrator on one of the estates of Baron Günzberg. Then, at the age of fifty, he followed the pattern of Tolstoi's flight to Yasnaya Polyana and he joined the second *Aliyah.* Heroically he worked out, on his own aging body, the painful transformation which he demanded of a whole people. Gordon did not believe in waiting for the improvement of the social order to bring about an improvement of the individual. He insisted that labor, the dedication of one's body to creation, was the proper function of man. "Too long," he observed, "have the hands been the hands of Esau, and the voice the voice

of Jacob. It is time for Jacob to use his hands, too." A people compelled
by persecution to live by its wits had forgotten the exaltation of manual
labor as it was known to the men of the Bible.

While Gordon himself was not a socialist, most of the would-be farmers
of the *Aliyah* were. They were influenced to some extent by the Socialist,
or Labor, Zionism of Nachman Syrkin (1867-1924) and Ber Borochov
(1881-1917)—although neither of these men ever settled in Palestine. Syrkin
was an evolutionary socialist, the founder of the Poale Zion party; Borochov
was a Marxist, the founder of the radical Hapoel Hatzair party. The
ideological points of difference between them, and the partisan rivalry of
their adherents in Palestine, were less important, however, than their points
of agreement. In fact, the two groups ultimately merged in the Mapai party
in 1930. Both Syrkin and Borochov held that Zionism and socialism, far
from being incompatible, were actually complementary. Zionism was needed
to liberate the stateless Jewish people; the Jewish State could be created only
on socialist principles. The settlers of the second *Aliyah* believed, moreover,
that a return to the soil was a tangible fulfillment of socialist ideology.
From Marx to Lenin, socialist thinkers had cited the absence of a Jewish
peasant class as evidence that the Jews were not a nation, but rather a
peculiar racial or functional entity. Many of these young Jews were determined to disprove the charge.

Syrkin and Borochov stirred the minds and shaped the spirit of the
second *Aliyah;* they channeled into the Zionist movement, and into Palestine
proper, thousands of formerly intransigent Bundists (see Chapter XIV). Yet
the labor ideology of the second *Aliyah* was less the creation of these two
men than of the collective experience of the early settlers themselves. Indeed,
those who came in the 1904-14 period were destined to be the most influential
pioneers in the history of the Zionist movement. Included in the second
Aliyah, for example, were the brothers Lavee of Plonsk, Berl Katznelson
of Bobruisk, Isaac Ben Zvi of Poltava, David Remez of Mogilev, Aaron
David Gordon, Joseph Baratz—the founding fathers of what was to be a
new age in Palestine. One of the recruits was a tough-minded young man,
David Green, from Plonsk, Poland, who changed his name, shortly after
arriving in Palestine in 1906, to David Ben-Gurion. Ben-Gurion's career in
Palestine was quite typical of the second *Aliyah*. Like the others, he was
imbued with the agriculturist ideals of A. D. Gordon and with the socialist
aspirations of Labor Zionism. He wrote later of his first night in Palestine:

> It was sealed in my heart with the joy of victory. I did not sleep. I was
> among the rich smell of corn, I heard the braying of donkeys and the
> rustle of leaves in the orchards. Above were massed clusters of stars
> clear against the deep blue firmament. My heart overflowed with happi-
> ness, as if I had entered the realm of legend. My dream had become a
> reality!

But it had not. As Ben-Gurion and his colleagues encountered the planter
aristocracies at Petah Tikvah, Rishon l'Zion, Zichron Ya'akov, and Rehovoth,
as they were compelled to work as Judean farm hands for a few piasters a
day, often collapsing from the blistering heat of the sun, or from malaria or

hunger, they recognized that the ideals of socialist agriculture would have to be won painfully. They organized into unions, under Poale Zion or Hapoel Hatzair auspices, edited their own newspapers, made desperate attempts to begin their own collective settlements. Ben-Gurion himself took the lead in these efforts. When his father begged him to return, he wrote back furiously: "These mummified Diaspora Jews wouldn't emerge from their bog even if they heard the streets here were paved with gold. But the new Jew is proud and full of fight. He won't turn back. I only feel sorry for those petty-minded people who have fled the battleground and then try to foist the blame on bad conditions here." Ben-Gurion, Ben-Zvi, and those who came with them did not retreat.

It would have been profoundly difficult, however, if not impossible, for these courageous zealots of the second *Aliyah* to realize their goal, had it not been for the sympathetic support of Ruppin and the Palestine Department. With money from the Jewish National Fund, Ruppin purchased for them the Kinereth tract lying on the eastern side of the Jordan River. It was on this tract that the collective settlements of Daganiah A and Daganiah B were founded, and the nucleus laid for others to be established later. When the first World War began there were forty-three Jewish farm colonies, of which only fourteen stood to the credit of the Zionist Organization. But a wave of hope swept over the land. Jews took heart at last in the knowledge that they could work in the fields in a productive way, without "exploiting" others. While the discipline and dedication of Ben-Gurion and his friends brought no immediate fulfillment, their efforts were destined to shape the economy—indeed, the entire social philosophy—of Jewish Palestine.

Another towering accomplishment of the embryonic settlement in Palestine was the transformation of the Hebrew language into a living vernacular. It was a transformation which took place only after a bitter *Kulturkampf*. The struggle resulted partly from the fact that Hebrew was, for most of the settlers, an alien tongue. Accordingly, the German and French Jews, who administered the best-equipped schools in Palestine, argued that it was necessary for youngsters to be taught a practical langauge. German or French—even Yiddish—were practical languages; Hebrew was not, for it could not be used in business or professional life. Why, therefore, must children be compelled to study a language which was valuable only for reading the Bible or the Talmud? There was another factor, too. As the Ottoman Empire continued its steady decline, the various European powers began using their hospices and monasteries, their schools and hospitals in Palestine as the cultural advance guard for their imperialist designs. Perhaps the French-Jewish administrators of the *Alliance's* network of schools, or the German-Jewish administrators of the *Hilfsverein's* school system, were not conscious imperialists; but as patriotic citizens of their lands they felt it their duty to encourage the use of their native tongue on Palestinian soil.

The Zionist educational system established by the colonists had little in the way of physical or financial resources to match the powerful institutions of the *Alliance* and *Hilfsverein*. But the settlers, particularly those of the second *Aliyah,* were grimly determined to create a Hebraic culture for Palestine, and they resolutely placed their children in Hebrew-language schools. Moreover, they made every effort to use Hebrew as their daily idiom in the home and field. It was an excruciating discipline for Yiddish-speaking immigrants, but they submitted to it willingly. They received effective assistance from the Zionist intellectuals. The philologist and philosopher Ben Yehudah spent the last three decades of his life tracking down the root of every Hebrew word, and creating a monumental Hebrew dictionary which became the basis for the modern Hebrew language. Ahad Ha'am, Reuben Brainin, and Chaim Nachman Bialik gave the language extraordinary literary and practical suppleness. Above all, it was the settlers themselves, by their iron self-control and devotion to the most deeply felt ideals of cultural Zionism, who transformed Hebrew into a living tongue. By the first World War Hebrew had taken precedence over all other languages as the vernacular of Palestine.

How far, then, had the Jewish awakening to the Return developed? So far, indeed, that by 1917, on the eve of the Balfour Declaration, the Jews were sufficiently advanced by preparation and effort to make the offer of a Jewish Homeland reasonable. The awakening was made possible not merely by the organization of the World Zionist Organization, and by the instruments of that Organization, the Jewish National Fund and the Anglo-Palestine Bank; it was made possible, too, by the presence of 90,000 Jews in Palestine, nearly 10 per cent of them on the soil—many of them speaking Hebrew, their hands on their own plows and their own guns. Had the policy of extending Jewish holdings in Palestine not been followed, there is little doubt that the Zionist Movement throughout the world, waiting breathlessly for some miracle of statecraft, would have died of inanition. It was between 1907 and 1914, therefore, that the foundations of the Jewish Homeland were laid. "Above all," reflected Weizmann, "we got the feel of things so that we did not approach our task after the Balfour Declaration like complete beginners."

CONCLUSION

We have seen that much more than post-pogrom despair was responsible for the rise of Zionism in Eastern Europe. The basic sediment of Jewish national feeling pre-existed; it was cultivated, too, by the scholars of Judaism and the Hebrew writers of the *Haskalah,* many of them inspired by the romantic movements of Europe. But in the West the rise of Zionism was a much slower process, for here the National Affirmation had long since triumphed over Jewish separatism. When Western Jews thought of nationalism they meant the greater glory of France, Germany, Austria, Hungary, or England, and there was no identification with a Jewish nation. It was for this reason that Zionist sentiment, when it did emerge in Western Europe, developed not as the logical capstone of Jewish religion and folklore, but as a tentative solution to Jewish political insecurity. The Zionism of Western Jewry, a much weaker and less fashionable Zionism than its counterpart in the Pale, was born of expediency, not of deep-rooted traditionalism.

The basic dichotomy of approach between Eastern and Western European Jewry was eventually resolved in favor of the *Ostjuden*. On the eve of the first World War, the German-Jewish "politicals" were at last compelled to relinquish control of the World Zionist Organization to the much more numerous and infinitely more passionate folk-Zionists of the Pale. From 1914 on, the movement was destined to be nurtured and directed by the great Jewish populations of Eastern Europe, and then later by their blood brothers in America.

Notes

Page 262. These remarks of Chaim Weizmann, and all others quoted from him, are found in his autobiography, *Trial and Error*.

Page 266. Quotation from Maurice Samuel, *Harvest in the Desert*, p. 14.

Page 281. Quotations from Barnet Litvinoff, *Ben-Gurion of Israel*, pp. 52, 56.

XIV

The Growth of Jewish Socialism

As the Jews of Eastern Europe groped desperately for an answer to the poverty and persecution of life in the Pale, some of them looked beyond Zionism to another activist solution, the solution of socialism. It was a plan of action formulated originally by a group of Western European Jews —although hardly as an answer to the Jewish problem. Ironically, in nearly every instance these early Jewish socialist pioneers were unrepresentative not only of Jewish ideals and aspirations, but also of the Jews who later became socialists, and who rejected the sanguinary techniques of class revolution. Karl Marx, for example, the original prophet of the classless society, far from being a practicing Jew, had actually been baptized in his youth by apostate parents. A native of Trier, Germany, with the advantage of an unexceptional education in the social sciences at the Universities of Berlin and Jena, Marx began his career in the field of journalism as a conventional liberal. Only after a period of study in Paris, where he met his ally and supporter, Friedrich Engels, and where he enjoyed a wider opportunity to absorb the new economic theories of his time, did Marx formulate his philosophy of class warfare. First in the *Communist Manifesto* of 1848 and then later in his ponderous *Das Kapital* of 1867–95, Marx warned Europe's bourgeoisie that its days were numbered; that the vast unpropertied mass of the world's workingmen were preparing for the inevitable revolution; that all powers in the State, all means of production, were to be turned over to the proletariat. One would hardly have expected so cataclysmic a theory from this gentle, full-bearded little man, who, though suffering from boils of Jobian proportions, was known for personal kindliness and sweetness of disposition.

But Marx was in deadly earnest. He sought to put his ideas into operation by founding an international organization of workingmen. But apparently he was a better theorist than a politician, and his creation, the First International, foundered for lack of support. It was hardly possible to fuse laboring men internationally until they had first been united into national political parties of their own. Eventually, when this logic became irresistible, the technique of establishing Socialist parties on a national basis was begun. In Germany it was initiated under the direction of another Jew, Ferdinand Lassalle.

It was Lassalle's eloquence and his mastery of political compromise that shaped a viable political organization out of a morass of ideological confusion and personal jealousies. A brilliant and wealthy lawyer, a roué and a dandy, Lassalle was in every respect the temperamental opposite of the stolid, "respectable" Marx. At the very moment of political success, in 1864, Lassalle ended his promising career in a harebrained duel over the daughter of a Bavarian diplomat. But during the course of his brief career, Lassalle proved the efficacy of political action well enough to stimulate the creation of a network of Socialist parties in other lands: in France, Italy, Scandinavia, Holland, and Belgium. In 1889 all these parties combined in the Second International. Because Western Europe was industrializing rapidly, the Marxist leadership was able to recruit followers from an expanding reservoir of workingmen. By the opening of the twentieth century, socialism had won recognition as a movement of far-reaching economic and political influence.

By now most of the Jews of Germany and the Hapsburg Empire were solid middle-class businessmen, and staunchly liberal in their political and economic orientation. It happened, nevertheless, that a large proportion of the leaders of German socialism was Jewish. One of the reasons for such involvement was a sense of betrayal, for German liberalism, to which Jews had heretofore committed themselves almost as a matter of instinct, had recently sold out to Bismarck, and was acting now in placid co-operation with his authoritarianism and nationalism. Another factor was the opportunity which socialism offered to promote international co-operation. The fraternalism of the Second International was self-conscious and often bombastic, but it emphasized inter-European brotherhood. This appealed to cosmopolitan-minded Jewish intellectuals, threatened as they were by the brutal chauvinism which increasingly characterized the politics of their native lands.

Internal changes in the structure of socialism meantime further strengthened its appeal. At the turn of the century, "Revisionism" gradually superseded the older variety of doctrinaire Marxism in the socialist movements of Central and Western Europe. Men like Jean Jaurès in France and Eduard Bernstein in Germany labored to modify classical Marxism's relentless emphasis on political revolution, and offered in its stead a gradualist approach to economic and political reforms. They urged their fellow socialists to co-operate with all forces in modern society that were willing to fight for political democracy, for pacifism, and for industrial and economic reform. Ultimately, Revisionism was accepted as the official platform of the German, French, and Austrian Socialist parties. With their traditional addiction to social justice, their fear of renegade nationalism and militarism, many Jews found this new Revisionist approach quite irresistible, especially in Imperial Germany, where a large minority of Jews abandoned the National Liberal party and entered the socialist camp.

Finally, the socialist principle sternly eschewed anti-Semitism and this was often decisive for an increasingly harassed Jewish community. Marx himself, to be sure, was no admirer of the Jews, the people who had produced him. For one thing, he viewed both Judaism and Christianity as a kind of "opiate" which dulled the economic sensibilities of suffering proletarians. For another, he despised the Jews as the worst marginal representatives of the "parasitical" middle class. "What is the worldly basis of Judaism," Marx sneered, "if not practical need, egoism? What is the worldly cult of the Jew? Huckstering. What is his worldly god? Money." Nor was Lassalle more charitable than Marx in his evaluation of his own people, whom he viewed as economic bloodsuckers and artists of exploitation. When, however, the conservative nationalists transformed Jew-baiting into a major political weapon, the principal socialist spokesmen of Western Europe repudiated anti-Semitism unequivocally. From the rise of the Social Democratic parties in the 1860's to the second World War, the socialist leadership expressed unswerving opposition, in both word and deed, to any kind of discrimination against Jews.

For all these reasons, therefore—socialism's internationalism, its pacifism, its Revisionism, its repudiation of anti-Semitism—Jews moved in growing numbers into the Social Democratic parties of Western Europe. Of the sixty Jews who served at one time or another in the German Reichstag from 1871 to 1930, thirty-five were Socialists, while the rest were National Liberals, Progressives, and Communists. In 1912 twelve of the one hundred Social Democratic Reichstag members were of Jewish descent, including the distinguished Revisionists Eduard Bernstein and Otto Landsberg. At the same time, the leading journalists in the German Social Democratic party were Georg Gradnauer and Josef Bloch; the leading theorists (aside from Bernstein) were Adolf Braun and Simon Katzenstein; the leading specialist in municipal adminstration was Hugo Heimann, in electoral law Leo Arons, in youth organization Ludwig Frank—all Jews.

Jewish socialists were particularly influential during the chaotic days of Germany's collapse at the end of the first World War. It was a period when the vacuum created by the fall of the discredited Imperial regime was filled by leftists. In the provisional government established after the flight of Wilhelm II, two of the six cabinet members were Jews, Otto Landsberg and Hugo Haase. The Social Democrat Dr. Hugo Preuss was largely responsible for the formulation of the Weimar Constitution, and served as Minister of the Interior in the new Weimar Republic. The courageous pacifist Kurt Eisner led the socialist uprising in Bavaria during the last days of the Empire, and served as Prime Minister of Bavaria from November 1918 to February 1919. As Bavarian representative to the first postwar International Socialist Conference at Bern, Eisner made a confession of the war guilt of the German nation, and for this "antipatriotic" gesture he was later assassinated by a Nazi gunman. Georg Gradnauer served as Socialist

Prime Minister of Saxony from 1919 to 1921. Paul Hirsch was Socialist Prime Minister of Prussia from 1918 to 1920. Kurt Rosenfeld, leader of the Independent Socialists after the death of Hugo Haase, was Prussian Minister of Justice in 1918.

The majority of Jews, certainly, continued to identify themselves as middle-class liberals; conversely, most of the German and Austrian Socialists were non-Jews. It was, however, the disproportionate participation of Jews in the Social Democratic parties, their frequent intellectual superiority over their proletarian colleagues, the years of dedicated pioneering spadework they contributed to the socialist cause, that accounted for their remarkable influence, their authority, and their conspicuousness in postwar Germany—and later in France and Austria.

THE BEGINNINGS OF RUSSIAN-JEWISH SOCIALISM

The impact of the German-Jewish socialists notwithstanding, Marxism was destined to play a much greater role in the lives of Russian Jewry. This was not apparent at first, because Russia moved very slowly toward industrialization, and, as a result, traditional Marxism had no impressive following until quite late in the Empire of the Czars. Yet even before the emergence of a proletarian class, there were collectivist movements which served as forerunners. In the 1860's and 1870's the *narodniki,* agrarian populists, issued urgent—and ineffectual—appeals to the lethargic and unimaginative Russian peasantry. In the 1880's and 1890's there was the People's Will party, the majority of its members half-crazed mystics who specialized in murderous assaults on czarist officials; most of these terrorists were gradually tracked down and executed or exiled to Siberia. By the turn of the century, however, the expansion of Russian railroads, iron and steel mills, and textile factories created a labor force of 1,600,000 men. Witnessing the growth of this urban proletariat, agrarian socialists like George Plekhanov were able for the first time to contemplate salvation along Marxist lines. In 1898 Plekhanov joined with other former *narodniki*—Paul Axelrod, Lev Deutsch, and Vera Zasulitch—to found the Russian Social Democratic party. The party's platform was blunt and uncompromising: first, all efforts must be directed toward the establishment of a middle-class constitutional regime in Russia. Once this was accomplished, and once the laboring population had grown in numbers and discipline, the middle-class regime was to be overthrown in favor of a "classless" society. But until that time came, laboring men were to be organized into trade unions and indoctrinated by means of strikes and mass protest meetings.

Few Jews were represented in the early Russian revolutionary movement of the 1860's and 1870's. In the Pale there had always been a tradition of abstinence from political affairs, and of obedience to established authority. The leaders of *Haskalah,* on the other hand, were far too absorbed in their struggle against cultural and religious obscurantism to give serious attention to the day-to-day problems of the Jewish working masses. Yet, paradoxically, it was *Haskalah* which was largely responsible for the rise of Jewish socialist activity, for the *maskilim* had secularized the outlook of tens of thousands of their fellow Jews. At first, such socialist activity took the form of a preliminary involvement in the agrarian populist—*narodnik*—movement. A group of young Jewish intellectuals, willing to go virtually to any lengths to demonstrate their kinship with the Russian people, left their urban surroundings and self-consciously toiled in the fields at the side of the peasants. Unfortunately for these would-be Jewish *narodniki,* agrarian populism was narrowly nativist, even erupting, from time to time, in anti-Jewish demonstrations. When the Russian *narodnik* leaders welcomed this Jew-hatred as "proof" of revolutionary awakening, the Jewish partisans dispiritedly left the movement.

Because of the structure of Jewish economic life, it was hardly surprising that Marxian socialism, the socialism of the cities, proved to be the principal magnet for politically minded Jews. By the 1890's, in fact, the Jews of the Pale were more urbanized, more impoverished and proletarianized than any other ethnic group within the Russian Empire. Marxism was now the panacea for the nightmare of czarist oppression; its program for reconstructing society from top to bottom appeared far more thoroughgoing than staid liberalism, and far more applicable than agrarian populism to the needs of the harassed Jewish working classes. Two of Plekhanov's principal associates were Jews: Paul (Pavel) Axelrod and Lev Deutsch. Axelrod, one of the two or three outstanding pioneers in the early history of Marxian socialism, not only helped create the Russian Social Democratic party, but, with Karl Kautsky and Eduard Bernstein of Germany, was one of the founders of the Second International. For almost sixty years this gaunt, intense man, with his beetling brows and piercing eyes, was the guide and tutor of two generations of Russian and European socialists. Zederbaum, Lenin, Trotsky, Kautsky, Bernstein, and scores of other prominent figures of modern Marxism all came under the spell of his brilliant intellect.

A great many of the Jewish Social Democrats of the nineteenth century were *émigrés.* The Russian secret police were vigilant and their hunt for radicals was as nerve-racking as their hunt for Zionists. Moreover, Jewish students, fated by the May Laws to seek their educational opportunities in Central and Western Europe, were particularly susceptible to the "intellectualism" of Marxist theorizing. They were tantalized by the exciting Bohemian life of the European socialists, a life of sexual freedom and of romantic conspiratorial intrigue. Many of the Jewish Marxists of this "university" period served as intermediaries between Russian and Western Socialism. Gera Dobrodzanu became famous as literary critic, publicist, and pioneer of Marxist socialism in Romania. Another Russian-Jewish *émigré,* Anna Kuleshov, organized the Italian Socialist party and for thirty-five years edited *Kritica Sociale,* the organ of the party.

Social Democratic cells sprouted rapidly in the Pale, too, during the 1880's and 1890's. Almost every substantial Jewish community produced at least one Marxist "study group." Yet the language of propaganda was Russian, and there was nothing "Jewish" in its tone. The agitators were usually men who had come from assimilated Jewish families—typical mutants of *Haskalah* secularism—and who had not the slightest intention of dealing with specifically Jewish problems. The characteristic attitude of these early Russian-Jewish Marxists was summarized by a May Day orator of 1892:

> We Jews repudiate all our national holidays and fantasies which are useless for human society. We link ourselves up with armies of Socialism and adopt their holidays. Our holidays, which we have inherited from our ancestors, will vanish together with the old social system. . . . Although the majority of us are convinced that Socialism must inevitably come, it will not come by supernatural miracles. The Torah of Socialism will not descend from the heaven of Sinai in thunder and lightning, and the Messiah will not come riding on a white horse.

As far as these pioneer Jewish Marxists were concerned, the Jewish problem would simply cease to exist once the class revolution destroyed the apparatus of czarist and bourgeois oppression, and reconstructed Russian society from top to bottom.

THE FORMATION OF THE BUND

There existed in the Pale, merely waiting to be tapped, a number of vital ingredients for the devolopment of a mass Jewish socialist movement. These ingredients included: the resentment of the Jewish poor for the Jewish rich, which stemmed from the tyranny of the *kahal* tradition, and which was expressed as far back as the Hasidic protest of the eighteenth century; *Haskalah* secularism, without which any form of political activism would have been impossible; the *hevras,* in a sense the forerunners of Jewish trade unions (as the guilds of Western Europe were the forerunners of European trade unions); and, not least of all, the prophetic yearning for social justice— the very bedrock of the Jewish faith, which endured long after traditional pietism declined. Yet the factor most responsible for the rise of Marxism in the Pale was the structure of the Jewish economy, which was profoundly altered by the Russian industrial boom of the late nineteenth century. Textile shops and factories sprang up in the Lodz and Bialystok regions; tanneries were constructed in Smorgon and Shavli in Lithuania; tobacco factories appeared throughout the Ukraine. This new industrial development created a sizable Jewish laboring class which, for the first time, abandoned petty artisanry to work in the factories for fixed wages. By the turn of the century, perhaps 40 per cent of the Jewish population of the Pale were proletarianized. Working conditions in the typical small Jewish textile shop were hard— bitterly hard. Tending the looms seventeen and eighteen hours a day, men and women worked under exceptionally dangerous and squalid conditions; and the wages were the lowest in Russia. After the May Laws, indeed, the competition for jobs in the congested Pale rendered the Jews far more vulnerable to exploitation than their Russian neighbors. In his volume, *The Jewish Worker* (Yiddish, 1905), Jacob Lestschinsky described the destitution, poverty and privation, need and hunger in the fullest meaning of the word, sweating-system, shrunken chests, lifeless eyes, pale faces, sick and tubercular lungs—this is the picture of the Jewish street, these are the conditions under which the Jewish worker had to fight for social reforms, for the future ideal of socialism.

The cradle of the Jewish socialist movement was Vilna. There, in the early 1890's, a group of rabbinical students, thoroughly disenchanted with the apparent irrelevance of their studies to the burning social issues of the day, decided to preach the new Marxist dogma to the poverty-stricken artisans and wage earners of the Pale. At the beginning, their organizational effort was pathetically ineffectual. For one thing, Marxist propaganda was completely assimilationist in character and Russian in form and content. The Jewish workers, on the other hand, insisted on remaining Jewish in their personal and cultural lives. Moreover, Revisionism had not been accepted by the Russian Social Democratic party, and the majority of Jewish workingmen rejected the idea of a bloody class revolution; violence of that sort was completely alien to their tradition. In truth, they were far less interested in Marxist dialectic than in obtaining higher wages and shorter hours; they wanted less abstract theorizing and more collective bargaining. Hence, when groups of Jewish workers precipitated successful strikes entirely on their own in 1895 and 1896, they caught the Marxist propagandists as much by surprise as they did the employers. The theorists of Vilna decided, therefore, to capitalize on this latent discontent by switching from dialectical propaganda to strike agitation. But this meant, too, that they were obliged to switch from Russian to Yiddish as the language of socialist propaganda. It was with the adoption of the Yiddish language that the socialist movement of the Pale assumed more of a folk quality and became more distinctively Jewish in character. By the end of 1896 the Vilna "intellectuals" decided—reluctantly, to be sure—that, if socialism were to become an effective mass movement in the Pale, an independent Yiddish-speaking labor group would have to be formed.

Thus, in the winter of 1897—the same year in which Herzl summoned the first Zionist Congress—a group of fifteen Jewish socialists assembled in the back room of a Vilna blacksmith's house to establish the Jewish socialist organization—the Bund. Of the fifteen men present, the only one who was not a worker was Arkady Kremer, the Bund's presiding officer and first president. Kremer was hardly a romantic figure, neither a spellbinding orator like Ferdinand Lassalle nor a conspiratorial intellectual like Paul Axelrod. He was a stolid, practical man, an engineer by training, who had been lured into the Russian revolutionary movement while still a student at the Riga *Polytechnikum*. As a dabbler in *Haskalah,* Kremer had little appreciation for what he considered the outworn values of Jewish culture. Yet it was this very "scientific objectivity" which convinced him of the unshakable ethnocentrism of the Jewish people, and of the need for a separate Jewish socialist organization. Kremer himself set the rationale of the Bund during the back-room meeting in Vilna:

A general union of all Jewish Socialist organizations will have as its goal not only the struggle for general Russian political demands; it will have the special task of defending the specific interests of the Jewish workers, carry on the struggle for the civic rights of the Jewish workers and above all carry on the struggle against discriminatory anti-Jewish laws.

It is difficult to know how much this deference to the "Jewish problem" was mere lip service on Kremer's part. After the founding of the Bund, he paid little attention to the problem of Jewish political or cultural aspirations, and concentrated almost exclusively—often at great personal peril—on organizing strikes in the Jewish industrial areas of the Pale. If Kremer was merely being opportunistic, however, his strategy was apparently successful. At the turn of the century the Bund's ranks had been augmented by tens of thousands of young Jewish men and women, youths for whom the Bundist promise of a land liberated from czarist and capitalist oppression was irresistible. Moreover, membership in the Bund seemed to bring tangible bread-and-butter results; the early Bundist strikes won significant improvements in working conditions from grudging employers. And all the while the Bund leadership exultantly defied the secret police, for their cells were skillfully hidden behind the façade of "mutual aid societies."

In its early years, nevertheless, Jewish socialism in its Bundist form was intellectually sterile, slavishly imitating the formulas and programs of the Russian Social Democratic party. If the initial momentum of the movement were to be preserved some new way of establishing rapport with the Jewish community would have to be found. For every Jewish laboring man who joined the Bund, there were two who were repelled by Kremer's ambivalence. The leaders of the Bund were not obtuse: as they, in their turn, sensed the recurrent suspicion of their fellow Jews, they recognized the importance of making even further compromises with Jewish folk tradition. This is why they now willingly, even eagerly, paid attention to the theories of several thoughtful and discerning non-Bundists. One was Dr. Chaim Zhitlowski, who argued that "cosmopolitanism," whether Marxist or czarist, was merely a cloak for the Russification of minority peoples within the Empire. The other was the eminent Jewish historian, Dr. Simon Dubnow, who provided an exceptionally appealing rationale with which to win prospective recruits away from Zionism. It was Dubnow's contention that the Jews were indeed a separate nation, but that national autonomy could be achieved elsewhere than in Palestine, perhaps even within the Russian Empire. Those who endorsed Dubnow's position argued that there was nothing heretically anti-Marxist in his national-autonomist approach; after all, the Brno Congress of the Austrian Social Democratic party had but recently endorsed the principle of territorial and extraterritorial cultural autonomy for non-Austrian peoples. Why not the same concessions for Russian Jewry? At the fourth convention of the Bund in 1901, leading delegates did, in fact, express this demand. "This convention," their resolution declared, "maintains that . . . not only must one class not be permitted to oppress another, not only must the government not oppress citizens, but no nation must oppress another, and no language must take precedence over another." The assembly did not go so far as to endorse national autonomy for the Jews, for fear of provoking the charge of "chauvinism"; it did ask for an end to any further infringement of "legitimate Jewish national rights."

The assimilationist veterans of the Bund were rather bewildered by this torrent of nationalist emotion but they were not prepared to resist it. The challenge came rather from the infuriated Jewish members of the Russian Social Democratic party. In typically vitriolic language, the "hard-core" Marxists—Axelrod, Trotsky, Martov, Riasanov, and Deutsch—admonished the Bundists to fuse with the Russian proletariat, to end their dangerous "deviationism" at once. Otherwise, they threatened, "dire" consequences would follow. These grim warnings had little effect on the Bundists. They knew what they wanted. Besides, they had now found a new and eloquent spokesman for their cause, a blond, blue-eyed, mild-mannered young man named Vladimir Medem. In this nationalist phase of the Bundist movement, from 1901 on, it was Medem who took over the mantle of leadership from Arkady Kremer. Medem's full-hearted devotion to the cause of the Jewish working population climaxed an extraordinary spiritual odyssey. He was born in Libau, in 1879, of a completely assimilated Jewish family; while he was still a child his parents had him baptized. Later, as a law student at the University of Kiev, he divided his spare time studying Marx's *Das Kapital* and the Bible—which he had expected to "expose." Caught up in the socialist movement, Medem found himself, simultaneously, almost against his will, groping his way back to his own people. He became an ardent Bundist and the Bund's most eloquent exponent of Jewish "autonomism."

It was Medem who led the Bundist delegation to the second Congress of Russian Social Democrats in London. There, a youngster of twenty-four, standing alone before a suspicious, even hostile audience, he boldly demanded autonomy for the Bund on a federative basis within the Russian Social Democratic party. When the Congress indignantly rejected his demand, Medem calmly declared the Bund's independence and left the convention hall. This courageous show of independence, far from weakening the Jewish socialist organization, actually strengthened its hold among the masses of Jewish laboring people. For once the die of secession had been cast, the way was opened for an intensification of nationalist, as well as socialist activity. In 1905 Medem and his colleagues endorsed the ideal of cultural autonomy for Russian Jewry; they demanded, as well, that the State recognize Yiddish as a legal language of the realm and provide funds for the establishment of a Yiddish school system. The very audacity of these demands evoked the widespread admiration of the Jewish working population, an admiration which enabled the Bund to play a crucial role in the life of East European Jewry.

THE ZENITH OF THE BUND

In the decade before the first World War the Bund was never without competition for the political allegiance of the Jews of Russia. For example, the "assimilationist" Marxism of the Russian Social Democratic party always exercised some appeal, particularly for the intelligentsia. Some Jews, too, were wooed by the czarist government into a kind of "economist" socialism; it was a socialism which concentrated upon economic gains without embracing a political creed, and, consequently, eliminated the risk of police interference. But "economism" rarely made serious inroads among the Jewish working masses, for it was always suspect as "police socialism." Much more formidable as critics of the Bund were the religious traditionalists; the majority of Russian Jews were still devoutly Orthodox, and they viewed with misgivings the Bund's strenuous emphasis on secular and economic matters. It did not help that the Bundist leadership was less than politic in its contemptuous identification of Orthodox Judaism with "bourgeois Reaction." Conversely, there were many employers, who did not hesitate to appeal to the Orthodox traditions of their workers for opportunistic reasons. In his novel *The Brothers Ashkenazi*, I. J. Singer described the cautious opening of a bargaining session between Max Ashkenazi, the employer, and Nissan, the representative of the workers. Ashkenazi spoke first:

> "Do you know, I still remember the last lesson we did together; I can repeat it by heart . . ." And he began to chant the Talmudic text, word for word, glancing at the other two delegates. "Do you remember it, Nissan?" he asked. "I don't spend any time on Talmud these days," answered Nissan coldly. . . . Max Ashkenazi glanced from [the other delegates] to Nissan. Decidedly he was not getting far with this sudden burst of scholarship. He reverted to his other self, Max Ashkenazi the factory director. . . .

The truth was, however, that most factory owners were not religious traditionalists, and most religious traditionalists were not reactionary. Neither, for that matter, were the bulk of the Jewish workers atheists. In fact, by 1905, the spokesmen for the Bund found it necessary to tone down their antireligious statements; they had learned by then that the typical Bundist, while perhaps not an ardently traditional Jew, was nevertheless unwilling to abandon a traditional respect for the prophetic values of his ancestral creed. Had the leadership not made such ameliorative gestures, it is unlikely that the Bund could have exerted its considerable influence during the Octobrist uprising.

Yet the Bund's major rival was neither the government nor the employers. It was the Zionist movement. Zionism succeeded in capturing the loyalty of greater numbers of Jews than any other political movement in the Pale. The majority of Bundists despised Zionism as "bourgeois Utopianism." It implied dependence upon the good will of the reactionary Turkish sultan and other bourgeois governments; it required aid from Jewish capitalists and philanthropists. Further, Zionism ignored the very real political and economic problems of the Jews within Russia proper. This failure of identification the Bundists could neither understand nor forgive. In 1918, a full year after the Balfour Declaration, Vladimir Medem, his sense of *"Galuth*-patriotism" outraged by Zionist propaganda, burst into a Zionist meeting and shouted:

> Journey preparations, travel-fever! Pack your belongings! Turn your back on our life, on our struggle, on our joys and sorrows. You have decided to desert the *Galuth* [life outside of Palestine]! Well, leave it in peace. Don't interfere in our affairs, don't show your generosity by throwing alms . . . [to us] . . . from the window of your rail carriage— and, please, don't talk about defending our rights here.

The struggle between Zionism and Bundism was waged with particular savagery for the minds and souls of Russian-Jewish students at Western universities, the young people who were destined to become the intellectual elite of the Jewish community. There were occasional ideological compromises between the two movements, as in the Poale Zionist party (see Chapter XIII); but for the most part the Zionists and Bundists remained poles apart. Zionism drew its strength from the middle and lower middle classes of the Pale; Bundism commanded the allegiance of the Jewish proletariat.

It was exactly because of its commitment to economic and political improvement within the Pale that the Bund became the most dependable instrument of pragmatic Jewish protest on Russian soil. It was a protest that carried considerable peril. Police brutality drove the Bundist leadership from one hiding place to another; unscrupulous Jewish factory owners and police informers often undermined their socialist opponents and showed no compunction when they were led off to imprisonment in Siberia. All such dangers notwithstanding, the Bund exercised an unprecedented influence on the Jewish working population between 1900 and 1914. The daring exploits of Bundist strike organizers, their cool disdain for their own personal safety, became legend throughout the Pale. Few Jewish employers could withstand the pressure of a disciplined Bundist strike: wages were forced upward; working hours were reduced; and with each victory the Bund's reputation and membership increased. In the smaller Jewish cities and towns the word of the Bund became law. Its orders were obeyed without question by the devoted masses of Jewish workingmen. Again, in *The Brothers Ashkenazi,* I. J. Singer effectively captures the spirit of this period:

> A tremendous change had come over Balut since Nissan had last walked its streets. He realized it now in the synagogue, and realized it even more strongly later, when he went out and took up his work with the committee. Crowds gathered everywhere fearlessly, ignoring the police and their armed attendants. The workmen's circles were well organized, and worked day and night. Their membership had grown beyond all expectation and included every class of worker: weavers, shoe-makers, leather-workers, stocking-knitters, cobblers, irreligious Jews in modern clothes, religious Jews in long gabardines, women in wigs

and women who had refused to shear off their hair after marriage, but wore a red kerchief around their heads. Meetings were in progress everywhere, councils sat, strikes were called, literature was distributed openly, speakers addressed crowds in the streets . . . The workers' circles were all-powerful at this time in Balut. There was no appeal from their decision, and there was no way of bribing them; they listened to no arguments, and could not be cited before the courts, for any attempt to call in the authorities would have meant exposing oneself to the concerted vengeance of the entire workers' movement.

During the revolutionary era of 1904-5, the Bund organized massive strikes in the industrial cities of Lodz and Bialystok; its leaflets were distributed by the hundreds of thousands; while its protest meetings and street demonstrations attracted tens of thousands of people. Its reputation as an anti-czarist force was so high in those days, in fact, even among the Jewish middle class, that rabbis frequently closed their eyes to socialist "secularism" and offered the use of their synagogues for Bundist strike rallies. For every striker arrested—and during the summers of 1903 and 1904 over 4,500 of them were taken into custody— two took their place. On May Day of 1905 the Bund participated in a paralyzing walkout of nation-wide proportions, making the most disciplined contribution of any ethnic proletarian group to the ominous public unrest. All through the year a mounting succession of strikes in factories, on railways, in sweatshops and textile mills, whipped up Bundist enthusiasm into a kind of dedicated frenzy.

As it turned out, 1905 was the zenith of the Bund's activity and power. Afterward Stolypin's savage counterrevolutionary efficiency made political and economic protest exceptionally dangerous. Throughout the Empire liberals, conservatives, and reactionaries alike co-operated in squeezing the Jewish socialists out of the cities and villages. Moreover, the leaders of the Bund had made a fatal mistake in boycotting the Duma elections; their boycott enabled the bourgeois Jewish leaders to speak in behalf of the entire Jewish population, to claim exclusive representative authority. In addition, these middle-class spokesmen made extensive use of their "connections" with the leaders of the local Jewish communities to "lock out" and even arrest Bundist strikers and agitators. Bundist strength declined steadily, although there was a brief resurgence during the economic boom of 1910-14. The Bund was then able to take advantage of better times to organize a number of effective strikes in the industrial centers of the Pale. Then came the outbreak of the first World War, which put a stop—a permanent stop, as it turned out—to its activities.

Nevertheless, the impact of the Bund on the Jews of Russia lingered long after the actual demise of the organization. For one thing, the crucial decade of the Bund's influence in the Pale brought with it an attendant Yiddishist cultural renaissance. Socialism was conceived by the Bundists not merely as a new system of social economy, but as a new civilization, as an entirely new way of life. As a consequence, Yiddish, the proletarian language, was galvanized into renewed usage in all fields of expression: poetry, fiction, and philosophy. Inevitably, however, much of this Yiddish writing was tinctured with the Bundist viewpoint, and it fell into the category of evanescent socialist propaganda.

Of more lasting significance among the Bund's achievements was its role in bringing the Jews out of their spiritual isolation. The Jewish socialists found themselves united not only with non-Jewish comrades in Russia, but also with a world-wide political and economic movement. For the textile worker sweating in the noisome factory, for the porter staggering under a back-frame of lumber, for the intellectual, frustrated and lonely at his accountant's copy desk, the Bund meant friends and comrades stirring in sympathy in the farthest reaches of Europe. "Belonging" ceased to be strictly synonymous with membership in a Jewish slum-community. In this sense, therefore, Bundism represented a radical but logical extension of *Haskalah's* secular horizons.

Finally, the spirit of socialist revolt provided the impoverished Jewish population of the Pale with a new sense of dignity. The fact that Jews, who had always quaked at the sight of police or Cossacks, now dared openly to defy the authorities and to offer armed resistance, was ample testimony to the Bund's effectiveness.

Thus, Jewish socialism, like Zionism, was a clear-cut manifestation of Jewish national consciousness. Secularism, dignity, national revival—these, together with the promise of economic security, were the factors that stamped the tradition of radicalism irrefragibly upon the souls of untold thousands of Russian-Jewish young people. It was a tradition not easily abandoned.

THE WAR BREAKS

On June 28, 1914, the assassination of Austrian Archduke Franz Ferdinand at Sarajevo brought the festering Austrian-Russian rivalry in the Balkans to a climax. With the Austrian invasion of Serbia, a complicated series of alliances and alignments pitted Russia, and her allies England and France, in war against the Central Powers. In the four and a half years of bloodshed that followed, each of the belligerent Powers suffered cruel and bitter losses of manpower and material. Yet, with the possible exception of the Armenian massacres of 1915, no tragedy of the World War compared to the long horror of the campaigns on the Eastern Front, as vast armies, sweeping back and forth over wide regions, brought ruinous destruction in their train. For the Jews of Galicia and the Pale of Settlement the World War was a virtually unimaginable catastrophe. The battlefields converged on Jewish territory, and the march and countermarch of armies hopelessly disrupted organized Jewish life.

In the early months of the fighting, Russian forces under Generals Ruzsky and Brusilov poured into Austrian Galicia and Bukovina, ripping Lemberg and huge segments of territory from the enfeebled control of the Hapsburgs. In mortal terror of czarist domination, hundreds of thousands of Galician Jews, Hapsburg citizens, were compelled to flee for their lives to Vienna and western Austria. There they survived, quite miserably, on a dole provided by Austrian-Jewish philanthropy. It was impossible for these refugees to return to their homes, for eastern Galicia and Bukovina remained in Russian hands until 1917; the rest of Galicia was devastated so thoroughly that, even when liberated, it was unable to support its original inhabitants.

The tragedy was compounded when the tide of battle shifted and flowed the other way. Late in 1914 and early in 1915, General Ludendorff's German divisions battered their way from East Prussia into Russian Poland. There, for the moment, it appeared as if the fate of the million and a half Jews who fell under German domination might take a turn for the better. Ludendorff summarily repealed the czar's anti-Jewish legislation. Determined to win the loyalty of the Jewish population, he went so far as to dedicate synagogues and issue proclamations of friendship—"An Meine Libe Yiden in Poilen"—in choicest Yiddish. But though the occupation authorities had no desire to increase the suffering of the Jewish population beyond the measure inevitable in war, the occupied areas in Lithuania, northwest Poland, and the Ukraine were too devastated to offer their Jewish inhabitants any economic security whatever. By 1917 the plight of the Jews in the German zone had become so desperate that people were driven to subsistence on cooked weeds and grass dug up from the fields.

It was the Jewish population remaining under Russian control, however, which endured the cruelest hardships of all. When the war broke out the bureaucracy in St. Petersburg decided, after some hesitation, to maintain the entire apparatus of Jewish disabilities. Apparently the government was convinced that Jewish loyalty could not be depended upon in any case; it would be futile, therefore, to make hypocritical gestures of friendship at this late date. As a consequence of this decision, military and civil authorities vied with each other in dealing with the Jews precisely as they would deal with the population of an enemy territory. Yiddish was declared an alien language, and its public use was banned. The day after their discharge, Jewish veterans were deported back to the Pale. Jewish mothers were not permitted to visit their wounded sons in hospitals outside the Pale. There were sporadic expulsions of Jewish inhabitants in localities which the authorities desired to clear for military operations. At the very moment when 300,000 Jews were serving in the czarist armies, Russian Jewry was branded publicly as a race of spies, cowards, and deserters. Fantastic stories were circulated of Jews extending aid and comfort to the Germans, tying gold under the wings of westward-flying geese, sending secret nocturnal messages to German couriers.

The hammer blow fell with its most lethal effect during the Russian retreat in the winter of 1914-15. Grand Duke Sergei, the Russian Commander in Chief, announced that the Jewish population of the Pale could not be trusted to remain in territory invaded by the Germans. In March of 1915, therefore, the army began systematically to expel the Jews from the Polish provinces, and from the governments of Kovno in Lithuania and of Kurland. It was only the rapid invasion of this territory by the Germans that prevented the complete expulsion of every one of the two million or more Jewish inhabitants. As it was, perhaps 600,000 Jews were forcibly driven from their homes into the Russian interior.

The agony which resulted from this forced expulsion was unprecedented, even for czarist Russia. Hundreds of thousands of people were hurled onto the roads of the Pale and driven like beasts to unknown destinations. Dzubinsky, a non-Jewish deputy in the Duma, later recollected:

> As a representative of our Fifth Siberian Division I was myself on the scene and can testify with what incredible cruelty the expulsion of the Jews from the province of Radom took place. The whole population was driven out within a few hours during the night. At eleven o'clock the people were informed that they had to leave, with a threat that any one found at daybreak would be hanged. And so in the darkness of the night began the exodus of the Jews to the nearest town, Ilzha, thirty versts away. Old men, invalids, and paralytics had to be carried on people's arms because there were no vehicles. The police and gendarmes treated the Jewish refugees precisely like criminals. At one station, for instance, the Jewish Commission of Gomel was not even allowed to approach the trains to render aid to the refugees or to give them food and water. In one case a train which was conveying the victims was completely sealed and when finally opened most of the inmates were found half dead, sixteen down with scarlet fever and one with typhus.

Because most of the able-bodied Jewish men were at the front, those affected by the expulsions were people least able to endure physical hardship: old men and women, children, the sick, even wounded and crippled Jewish soldiers. Women in labor were denied special consideration, and many births occurred along the route; mothers were separated from their children; entire families were broken up and dispersed to different areas of the interior. Where transportation was provided, the exiles were packed into freight cars and forwarded to their destination on a waybill. Elsewhere, thousands of Jews were compelled for weeks at a time to remain in congested villages, or to sleep in wagons, boxcars, or in open fields.

One hundred thousand Jews died of starvation and exposure during the great expulsion of 1915. The uprooting destroyed the economic security of an additional 600,000, for virtually all Jewish homes and businesses were burned and gutted. After 1916 some 200,000 refugees attempted to return to their homes in northwestern Poland and Lithuania. They discovered, however, that there was no employment to be had; the provinces were ravaged wastelands. And yet even the calamity of this unprecedented expulsion paled, as we shall see, beside the postwar horrors in the Ukraine and Poland. Time was rapidly running out for the historic Jewish hinterland of the East.

THE RISE OF BOLSHEVISM

The outbreak of the war found the Russian Social Democratic party seriously rent by factional disputes; by *Oborontsy* who wished to support the war effort; by Mensheviks who advocated a two-stage approach to economic and political revolution; by a hard core of Bolsheviks who aimed at the establishment of a totalitarian Communist regime. None of the Social Democrats, however, not even the Bolsheviks, expected that the opportunity for revolution would appear as quickly as it did. The czarist military machine, horribly battered by the German invasion of 1915-16, ground slowly to a halt. Corruption and mismanagement from the Court at St. Petersburg, under the influence of the wild-eyed Siberian charlatan, Rasputin, down to regimental supply offices, hopelessly obstructed the effective prosecution of the war. Whenever the Czar's intimates ventured, however tactfully, to suggest reforms, Nicholas rejected them out of hand. It was precisely this pigheaded obstinacy which sealed the government's doom. In 1917 the long-suffering Russian people at last reached their limit of endurance. Soldiers, insufficiently clothed, were found frozen in their trenches. Workers, yellow with hunger and fatigue, began to collapse by their workbenches. In March bread riots and troop mutinies forced the resignation of the czarist ministry. Shortly thereafter, even before the astounded Russian people could grasp the significance of what was happening, rioting soldiers compelled Nicholas II, Czar of all the Russians, to abdicate his throne and the incubus of Romanov oppression was lifted forever.

Within a few weeks after the Czar's abdication, Alexander Kerensky, Minister of Justice in the new provisional government, assumed the direction of Russian affairs. Kerensky was a well-meaning liberal; but his efforts to keep Russia in the war failed to rally public support. Even as he spoke of effecting ultimate reforms, peasants clamored for land and workers for bread. Mutiny spread through the army. In November of 1917, Lenin, the bullet-headed, slant-eyed Bolshevik leader who had recently returned from exile in Switzerland, decided that the time had come to strike down the ineffectual Kerensky regime. It was far from Lenin's intention, however, merely to replace the bourgeois liberal government with a democratic socialist administration. Lenin had in mind something far more drastic, nothing less, in fact, than the establishment of a Bolshevik dictatorship, its supporters recruited from "soviets," or workers' councils. His fellow Bolsheviks protested that the moment was not opportune, that there had not been sufficient opportunity to organize, to cope with the sudden onrush of developments in Russia. Lenin sneered at them, browbeat them, galvanized them into action. On the morning of November 7, Kerensky awoke to encounter the hard faces and gleaming bayonets of the St. Petersburg garrison's mutineering soldiers. He needed no further persuasion to resign. The Bolsheviks took over.

The Jews of Russia viewed the onrush of events from March to November with mixed emotions. The original March uprising, which brought in a democratic, if bourgeois, regime, seemed to augur well for them. Virtually all elements among the Jewish population, not excluding the Bundists, threw their support to Kerensky, even to Kerensky's policy of continuing the war. For Kerensky had promised national autonomy to non-Russian peoples; in the case of the Jews he had even begun to implement that policy in the Ukraine. Whether he would actually have given the Jews the full degree of national and cultural autonomy they sought must always remain a mystery; he was out of office before he could put his program into effect. There is no doubt, however, that during the nine months' breathing space granted Russia before the Bolshevik uprising in November, most Jews—the Bundists among them—were opposed to Bolshevism and to the Bolshevik scheme for a totalitarian government. Every one of the eight Jewish members of the first St. Petersburg Soviet, the group which overthrew the Kerensky regime, voted against the Bolshevik plan of action. Trotsky later recalled that during the famous mass demonstration of June 18, 1917, when the working population of St. Petersburg swarmed out into the streets carrying banners with Bolshevik mottoes, only three small groups appeared bearing slogans in favor of Kerensky's provisional government. One of those groups was composed of Jewish Bundists.

It was, in fact, during this "inter-Revolutionary" period, between March and November of 1917, that the essential points of difference between Bundist socialism and Soviet Communism became most apparent. Bundism's central concern was for Jewish national autonomy, and for a democratic Russian government committed to gradualist public ownership of the means of production. The kind of ruthless proletarian dictatorship established by Lenin and his supporters violated the deepest instinct of nearly every Russian Jew, socialist or nonsocialist. The typical Bundist had never expected, for example, to see his Jewish neighbors dragged into the street and shot for the "crime" of being employers or of owning property. The complications of Marxist doctrine which had plagued or confused Jewish workingmen from 1897 to 1917 were quite effectively resolved with the Bolshevik Revolution. Hundreds of thousands of Jewish proletarians, whose frustrations were, after all, more the result of czarist domicile restrictions than of capitalist exploitation, suddenly recognized that their socialist Utopia and Lenin's godless and cynical execution-machine were by no means synonymous.

There were, however, individual Jews who played a role in the Bolshevik uprising which was quite out of proportion to the number of Jews in the Russian population or even in the Bolshevik party. Jacob Sverdlov was the first President of the Central Executive Committee; Grigori Zinoviev became President of the Third International—and was eventually shot after the Tukhachevski purge trials of 1936; Maxim Litvinov became Soviet Commissar for Foreign Affairs; Karl Radek was Soviet Press Commissar; D. Riazanov was Chairman of the Marx-Engels Institute and the leading Marxist historian; Jakob Yoffe, Lev Kamenev, Lazar Kaganovich all became leading figures in the Soviet regime, the latter two commissars and members of the Politburo.

Perhaps the most influential Jewish Bolshevik of all, standing next to Lenin himself, was the fiery and audacious Leon Trotsky. His neatly trimmed little goatee, his pince-nez and jackboots were caricatured so frequently in the European press that, for non-Russians, they virtually became trade-marks of the Revolution. Trotsky was the son of a Ukrainian-Jewish farmer. He was still in his teens when he came in contact with Marxist ideology, enrolled in the Russian Social Democratic party, and decided to dedicate his life to the establishment of a proletarian dictatorship in Russia. Before Trotsky was twenty years of age his powerful intellect and almost superhuman energy gained him access to the party's inner councils. After the Bolshevik Revolution, he was appointed Commissar of Foreign Affairs, and then Commissar of Defense. It was Trotsky, a Jew, who organized the Red Army, and as Commander in Chief brilliantly planned, and personally led, the military campaign against the counterrevolutionary forces. He remained high in Soviet ranks until Lenin's death in 1924. After that date, however, the Revolution began to devour its own; in a protracted and grueling struggle with Joseph Stalin, Trotsky, in 1929, was finally outmaneuvered and exiled.

In no other period in modern times, not even in the Metternichian era during the heyday of the Rothschilds, did Europe produce so influential a minority of powerful Jews. And yet, almost without exception, these prominent Jewish Bolsheviks severed their connections with the Jewish people, were fanatically Russian in their cultural orientation, and almost uncontrollably vindictive in their attitude toward Jewish nationalism.

This vindictiveness was not uninfluenced by the patent anti-Bolshevism of the Russian-Jewish masses. To be sure, the Russian civil wars, the pogrom-ridden nationalist uprising in the Ukraine, produced a marked shift to the left in the loyalty of younger elements of Russian Jewry. The Bolsheviks, after all, did their best to protect the Jews from the anti-Semitic savagery of the Ukrainian and White armies; and in certain Ukrainian provinces, where pogroms were particularly severe, a number of Red detachments consisted almost exclusively of Jewish soldiers. Yet the bulk of Russian Jewry stubbornly refused to support the Bolshevik cause. From bitter experience they found little real difference between revolutionary and counterrevolutionary terror; it was merely a choice between one form of tyranny and another. In his story, *Gedalli,* Isaac Babel described the plight of the Jew caught between the Red and White armies:

"Revolution? 'Yes' we say to it, but shall we say 'no' to Sabbath?" " 'Yes', I cry out to the revolution, 'yes,' I cry out to it, but it hides from Gedalli and answers only with bullets. . . . 'You don't know what you like, Gedalli. I am going to shoot at you and then you will know, and I cannot help but shoot, for I am the revolution. . . .' 'But the Pole shot at me, my kind Pani, because he is the counter-revolution. You shoot at me because you are the revolution. . . . Who will tell Gedalli where is the revolution and where the counter-revolution?' "

In March 1919, after heated and passionate debate, the all-Russian Conference of the Bund decided to accept the "platform of a soviet government"; but they condemned the terrorist practices of the Communist party and called for the democratization of the Soviets, and for freedom of speech and press. The Bund's halfhearted acceptance of the Bolshevik program convinced the Soviet leaders that it could no longer be permitted to exist as an autonomous party. In 1921, accordingly, the Bund's registered membership was officially attached to the *Yevsektsia,* the Yiddish-language section of the All-Union

Communist party. For all practical purposes, Russian-Jewish socialism had come to an end.

THE LAST PHASE OF JEWISH PAUPERIZATION

As far as the Jews were concerned, even the 1915 exodus and the drastic economic dislocations that resulted from the Bolshevik Revolution were eclipsed by the horrors of the Russian civil wars of 1918-21. In November 1918, the German armies evacuated their holdings in western Russia; immediately thereafter, the Bolshevik regime in Moscow prepared to reannex the Ukraine to Russia. This annexation was stoutly resisted by the Ukrainian people, however. Ardent nationalists and brave soldiers, they enlisted by the thousands in the guerrilla bands of their hetman, Simon Petlura, and prepared to battle the Soviet armies to the death. Ukrainian hatred of the Russians was compounded when it came to the Jews. Quite aside from the backlog of Jew-hatred which was an integral part of their folklore, the Ukrainians were convinced that a definite connection existed between the Jews and the Bolshevik regime. Many of the minor Communist officials in the Ukrainian cities and towns happened to be Jews. These Jewish Communists represented only a small proportion of the Ukraine's Jewish population; and they were, after all, the only literate group whose services could be exploited for Soviet administrative purposes. But the typical Ukrainian nationalist was uninterested in explanations; he knew only what he saw. As a peasant who had suffered intensely from Communist grain requisitions, he was more than willing to wreak his vengeance upon the Jewish "antichrist" whom he identified with an alien and godless regime.

Pogroms, which Petlura publicly condemned and privately encouraged, broke out on a large scale early in 1919, and swept rapidly through every province in the Ukraine. Roaming like wild horses through the cities of Ovruch, Berdichev, Zhitomir, and Proscurov, Petlurist rioters shot up Jewish neighborhoods, moved from house to house in their hunt for "hooked-nosed commissars." In the town of Novo Mirgorod, the guerrillas systematically cut down every Jewish man, woman, and child they could find; then they flung their victims into wagons and dumped the bodies in huge limed mass graves. In Uman, while Jews were being slaughtered, Christian neighbors in the same houses found it necessary to protect themselves by hanging crosses on the walls. Years later, in 1926, Petlura was assassinated in Paris. The trial of his assassin, Samuel Schwartzbard (who was acquitted by a French jury), produced evidence that the Ukrainian guerrilla bands had committed no less than 493 pogroms during the year 1919, and had killed upward of 70,000 Jews.

At the end of the summer of 1919, General Denikin's White armies moved into the Ukraine and triumphed briefly over both Petlurist and Bolshevik forces. There was destined to be no respite, however, in Jewish suffering. Denikin and his men, in typical czarist fashion, identified Jewry with the Revolution (had not the Bolsheviks outlawed anti-Semitism?). The wholesale murders, looting, and rapine erupted once again, and life for the Jewish population of the Ukraine became a hell on earth. A hostile observer, the anti-Semitic publicist V. V. Shulgin, described the agony of Jewish existence during the Denikin period:

> A dreadful medieval spirit moves in the streets of Kiev at night. In the general stillness and emptiness of the streets a heart-rending cry suddenly breaks out. It is the cry of the Jews, a cry of fear. In the darkness of the street appears a group of "men with bayonets." At this sight large five- and six-story houses begin to shriek from top to bottom. Whole streets, seized with mortal anguish, scream with inhuman voices.

If there were any distinguishing characteristics between Petlura's pogroms and those of Denikin, they were to be found only in the military character and mass violation of women which characterized the latter. At least 50,000 Jews died at the hands of Denikin's soldiery. In all, perhaps a quarter of a million Jews—men, women, and children—were slain or allowed to starve to death in the period between 1915 and 1921. And yet the era of the first World War was only the second phase, as the era of the May Laws had been the first, of the unfolding destruction of the largest Jewish community in the world. While the third phase, the period of Adolf Hitler, was, to be sure, the grimmest of all, the mounting horror of phase II was not an inconsequential prelude.

In 1920 the Red forces rallied and drove the counterrevolutionary armies permanently from the soil of Russia. Yet the Jewish survivors in the Ukraine, gazing about at the gutted skeletons of their homes and shops, must have recognized that there was little possibility any longer of reconstructing a decent, orderly life for their families. Even before Lenin's bureaucrats had an opportunity systematically to destroy the Jewish middle class, the pauperization of the Jewish community of Russia was completed. The process was begun in the last days of the Polish monarchy in the eighteenth century. It was further accelerated by the establishment of the Pale of Settlement. The enactment of Alexander III's May Laws undermined Jewish security even more thoroughly. And now the war, the horrors of the 1915 retreat, the Ukrainian pogroms of 1919-21, beggared the Jews of Eastern Europe so completely that a calculated Soviet purge was hardly necessary. By 1920, ironically, when resurgent anti-Semitic propaganda in the West accused the Jews of monopolizing the world's wealth, most of the Jews of Europe were impoverished beyond hope of recovery.

CONCLUSION

There was never a moment in the twentieth century when European Jewry abandoned its traditional alliance with political liberalism. Both in Western and Eastern Europe Jews by the thousands, by the tens of thousands, were actively represented in nonsocialist liberal movements. Yet even in Western Europe the alert, sensitive, urbanized Jewish intelligentsia participated in the socialist movement to a degree, and with an effect, out of proportion both to their numbers and to their own involvement as proletarians. For socialism, as we have seen, was regarded by many Jews as a more effective instrument for peace, for industrial democracy, and for international brotherhood than classical middle-class liberalism. And in Eastern Europe, the overwhelming fact of an impoverished Jewish working-class population, permanently impoverished, as it turned out, by a frightful series of wars, placed the stamp of radicalism upon myriads of Jews who did not necessarily owe their allegiance to the murderous Bolsheviks.

It was the prominent appearance of Jewish names upon the rosters of Socialists and—to a much smaller extent—Communist parties, which provided the reactionaries of the twentieth century with a most effective political weapon. In the nineteenth century, conservative aristocrats, seeking to preserve the political *status quo,* had found it convenient to brand liberalism as Jewish. In the twentieth century, a nervous race of agrarian and industrial monopolists sought, with equal desperation, to find a political technique for preserving the economic *status quo.* They found it by stigmatizing Marxism (together with the old chestnut of international banking) as a Jewish phenomenon. As we shall see, this political technique was applied with notable success in Poland, in Romania, in Hungary—and in Germany.

Notes

Page 289. May Day quotation from A. L. Patkin, *The Origins of the Russian-Jewish Labour Movement,* pp. 126-127.

XV

The Great Migration and Settlement in America

EMIGRATION FROM THE PALE BEGINS

Referring to the immense migrations of the late nineteenth century which transcended in numbers and diversity all the earlier movements of East to West, a gifted American poet, Paul Engle, wrote:

> Who knows
> What strange multi-fathered child will come
> Out of the nervous travail of these bloods
> To fashion in a new world continent
> A newer breed of men?

The progenitors of the "newer breed of men" now came primarily from Eastern and Southern Europe, driven by poverty, the curse of overpopulation, and restricted native opportunities. The principal immigration reservoirs of the past, the countries of Northern and Western Europe, had become fairly well stabilized; wages were improved, birth rates had leveled off, religious and political persecution had almost completely disappeared. But in the distressed agricultural belt—Italy, Serbia, Croatia, Romania, Poland, and the Russian Pale—populations grew out of hand, social and political reforms remained negligible, and the vital and the ambitious felt increasingly constricted. Fortunately, the Italian and the Pole, the Magyar and the Slovak, no longer found it necessary to remain tied to the ancestral plot of earth. They had been liberated from the thrall of serfdom; if the West now beckoned irresistibly no feudal authority attempted to stop their departure. Little wonder, therefore, that the peasant populations of Southern and Eastern Europe were restive, that rumors of the fortunes to be made in the New World increasingly excited their imagination. Immigration agents, *padroni,* and other middlemen hired by American employers took advantage of the unrest, and they swarmed through the European hinterland with glowing accounts of opportunities in the United States. Steamship agents, aware that

305

the immigrants were lucrative cargo—they loaded and unloaded themselves and their miserable baggage—added their blandishments to the emigration propaganda, emphasizing the safety and convenience of modern ocean travel. Between 1876 and 1926 some fifteen million Italians moved westward, over half of them to America. A million and a half Poles crossed the ocean, together with half a million Magyars, half a million Slovaks, half a million Croats and Slovenes. And then there were the Jews, too, whose poverty and restricted opportunity were compounded by the nightmare of czarist oppression. Each time the Romanov autocracy tightened the vise on Russian Jewry, the tempo of exodus was accelerated and, after the May Laws and the pogroms of 1881, the flight burst through all restraints. During the entire period between 1800 and 1881 the total emigration from Eastern to Western Europe and the United States was approximately 250,000, a yearly average of about 3,000. From 1881 to 1899, the number of Jewish emigrants rose to 450,000 for a yearly average of nearly 23,000.

It was the United States, more than any other land, which drew the emigrant. In her autobiography, *From Polotzk to Boston,* Mary Antin recalled that

> America was in everybody's mouth. Businessmen talked of it over their accounts; the market women made up their quarrels that they might discuss it from stall to stall; people who had relatives in the famous land went around reading letters for the enlightenment of less fortunate folks, the one-letter-carrier informed the public how many letters arrived from America, and who were the recipients; children played at emigrating . . . all talked of it, but scarcely anybody knew one true fact about this magic land.

The first catch basin for this new emigration was Brody, the frontier station between Russia and Austrian Galicia. Thousands of refugees, the first victims of the May Laws, began encamping there in 1881-82. In later years, other routes of exit largely by-passed Brody. Perhaps the most widely trafficked of these routes was the one which crossed Northern Russia and Old Poland by Dünaburg and Vilna, and entered East Prussia at Eydtkuhnen. The central section of the Pale, on the other hand, the district along the line from Moscow to Brest-Litovsk, sent its Jews through Warsaw to cross the frontier on the Vistula at Thorn. In the southern Pale, the vast population reservoir beyond Kiev and Odessa was drained by the railway which crossed the Austrian frontier at Podvolochesk, and also—to a lesser degree—by the line which entered Romania at Ungheni. With the exception of those traveling by the last-mentioned route, the fugitives all made their way to Hamburg and Bremen.

By the time they reached the frontier, the refugees had been packed into third-class railway cars for some twenty to sixty hours, and were usually exhausted and half-stupefied. Climbing out of the trains at the border stations, they encountered strange new sights: tall buildings, storage depots, warning flares, booted soldiers and policemen, and, everywhere, hundreds of confused passengers milling about aimlessly. The usual routine was for the emigrants to line up and to show their passports and their police stamps of permission to leave the Empire. Without the exit permit, passage across the border to Austria or Germany was prohibited; and Russian bureaucrats, determined to maintain a reservoir of able-bodied men for conscription purposes, denied such permits more frequently than not. Moreover, if there was the slightest discrepancy in the passport, or if the examining Russian gendarme chose to suspect a discrepancy, the Jew was roughly thrust to one side, perhaps to be detained at the local prison, perhaps to be sent back to the Pale. It was the endless red tape, the insistence that all papers had to fulfill every last technical requirement, which frightened the travelers most of all. Jews therefore frequently chose to by-pass the capricious tyranny of passports and bureaucrats by crossing the border surreptitiously at night. Often they disguised themselves as *muzhiks*, or bribed guards to permit them passage. Occasionally they hired guides who led them on foot or in boats across forest swamps and rivers. The danger of murder, robbery, and rape was never absent; yet tens of thousands of emigrants were willing to take the chance rather than risk the whims of the dilatory Russian bureaucracy.

The promulgation of the May Laws, and the massive exodus of Russian Jews which was its result, took the leaders of Western Jewry completely by surprise. Throughout 1881, hundreds of immigrants, shabby and penniless, kept arriving in Brody daily. Their arrival placed their Austrian and German coreligionists in a quandary. What was to be done with these *Ostjuden*? How were they to be fed and housed? The comfortable middle-class Jewish community of Central and Western Europe looked instinctively to the *Alliance Israélite Universelle*, the world's largest and most respected Jewish philanthropic agency, to bring order out of chaos, to cope with the huge influx of newcomers. The directors of the *Alliance* were willing to try. They sent a representative, Charles Netter, to supervise the temporary housing and feeding of the fugitives, and also to arrange for their transport from Brody to Hamburg. Ahad Ha'am described the hope which Netter brought to the distraught *émigrés* in Brody:

> The city was full of refugees from Russia. Charles Netter and his aides stayed there, directing group after group to America. One of the groups was in the train in which I traveled to Vienna, and I could see Netter, that worthy man, standing in the station and distributing money to the refugees. His face expressed the kindness and compassion he felt for them. The refugees were gay and in high spirits. One could read in their eyes how hopefully they looked into the future. As the train started to move, they called out: "Long live Netter! Long live the *Alliance*!"

But the refugees cheered the Western philanthropists prematurely. The directors of the *Alliance,* in common with many other French and German Jews, soon wondered if they had not been too impulsive in undertaking the responsibility. Would their help not encourage Russian Jews to move westward in uncontrollable numbers? Even Netter, "that worthy man," felt obliged to write his headquarters in Paris, urging that "the emigrants . . . be checked; otherwise we shall receive here all the beggars of the Russian

Empire." The Paris office agreed and blandly instructed Netter to "persuade" the refugees to return to Russia. One can well understand the reaction to such completely impersonal and unrealistic snap judgments where life and death issues were at stake. The fugitives angrily refused to budge; many of them even threatened suicide. Taken aback by the vehemence of their reaction, the *Alliance* finally emerged with a compromise proposal: those Jews who were already in Brody would be sent on to America, but no newcomers would be given passage money. The *Ostjuden* ignored the warning; they continued to cross the border into Austria, hundreds each day. When they found the *Alliance* unwilling to subsidize their passage to the United States, their determination to go on was in no wise modified. Those who could, managed somehow to beg or borrow funds from other sources. The others flatly refused to budge. By 1882, 23,000 Jews huddled in the Brody border station. Netter and his colleagues hardly knew what to make of the situation; it was costing 30,000 francs a week to feed and clothe them. Eventually, the distraught *Alliance* officials decided to call in the help of German and Austrian philanthropy; soon thereafter, as the tide of emigration temporarily ebbed after 1882, Netter and his colleagues wound up their work and withdrew from the border area. They were morally convinced now that it was the willingness of Western philanthropic agencies to provide funds—not poverty and persecution in Russia—which was principally responsible for the swelling tide of emigration. They were determined, therefore, to close the dam gates before the tide swamped all orderly procedures.

The reaction of the *Alliance* was an extreme, but not an unusual example of the irritation of Western Jewish leaders over the undisciplined and intransigent behavior of the Russian Jews. Why were they so insistent upon solving their problems with such impatience and with this inconvenience to their well-wishers! Were not the philanthropic agencies doing all they could? They organized protest meetings against czarist oppression, often under distinguished Christian as well as Jewish auspices. There were impressive prestige names on all the relief committees: the Mansion House Fund in London, the German Central Committee Aiding Russian Jewish Refugees, the *Israelitische Allianz* of Austria, the Brussels Emigration Committee, and numerous others. If the initial protestations of sympathy were not always followed up with devoted care, it was only because the problems multiplied vexingly. The phrase *verfallen wie in Brod*—"lost as in Brody"—became current among the East European refugees, and it needed no commentary.

The possibility of transshipping the derelicts of Brody through Western Europe met with stiff resistance from local community leaders. Sir Julian Goldsmid of the London Mansion House Fund cabled his representatives in Paris, urging them not to commit the Anglo-Jewish community to accept any of the newcomers. The leaders in Germany and Austria went so far as to issue solemn "warnings" to the refugee Jews to stop coming to Brody. The admonition of Dr. Rülf, rabbi in Memel, was more specific; Russian Jews who came to Hamburg would "be exposed to starvation, Heaven forfend, as has already happened." Rülf added that aid would be extended only to those who were compelled to leave their homes because of actual pogroms, while "all others would not receive a penny." There were ugly incidents when Hungarian and Belgian Jews met refugees at railway stations in Budapest and Antwerp and offered them money to return to Russia.

The German-Jewish community in the United States, some 300,000 strong by 1881, reacted similarly. Max Lilienthal, now a practicing rabbi in America, who had seen at firsthand the conditions of Russian-Jewish life several decades earlier, could suggest in 1881 that the stream of emigration from Russia ought to be diverted to Palestine. He was not a Zionist, and his advice was not motivated by his loyalty to a Jewish homeland. His main concern was to prevent the creation of a "problem" in America. A decade later Jacob Schiff actually sailed from New York to Europe to plead with Jewish leaders there to direct the emigration away from the United States. In the same spirit, the leaders of B'nai B'rith informed their European representative, Nissim Behar, that the continued influx of Russian and Romanian Jewry would jeopardize the Jewish position in America. They pointed out that the control of municipal elections in New York by the immigrant Jews of the East Side would provoke a "commotion." The problems of Russian Jewry, they insisted, would have to be solved in Russia.

The truth was that the Jews of Western Europe and America were caught in a critical dilemma. As decent, well-meaning human beings, they sympathized deeply with the plight of the refugees. On the other hand, they had labored for many decades to achieve and maintain their status as Westernized nationals and were convinced that they would jeopardize that status, and would lend credence to the emergent anti-Semitic propaganda, by identifying themselves with the bearded, Yiddish-speaking, frequently exotic-looking "alien people" from Eastern Europe. Nor were all the leaders of Western Jewish communities necessarily motivated by selfishness or insecurity. Many of them simply were unprepared psychologically to organize relief on the major scale demanded by the new emigration. The very concept of hundreds of thousands of people moving away from their native land was beyond their comprehension. Never certain whether the movement was a temporary or a permanent phenomenon, the immigration committees were unable to perform their tasks efficiently or scientifically: they had formulated no master plan. Two decades passed before the Jews of Western Europe came to terms with the fact that the flood of emigration was not likely to run dry.

THE DIKES BREAK

Eastern Jewish emigration was divided roughly into two stages. The first began in 1881, reached its peak the following year, and then leveled off and declined until 1891. During this period some 135,000 Russian Jews entered the United States, while another 15,000 went to other countries. Emigration on a scale truly immense began after 1891. In the quarter-century until the first World War approximately 1,314,000 flooded in, and more were still to come! On the average, of every 1,000 Jews in the Russian Empire, 156 emigrated between 1898 to 1914. A flight of such proportions could not have been the result of isolated attacks; it was the result, rather, of the systematic program of anti-Jewish restrictions which rapidly cut Jews off from their few remaining rights. It involved the whole complex of Slavo-phile horrors: the May Laws, the expulsion from Moscow, the Kishinev massacre, Stolypin's "neckties," the revival of the Blood Libel. Simultaneously, there was a vast upswing in Romanian-Jewish emigration, as Jewish disabili-ties in the Danubian basin became increasingly insupportable. In just the five years between 1899 and 1904 perhaps 60,000 Romanian Jews fled, an average of 323 emigrants for every 1,000 Jews in the country. Although the exodus was halted temporarily by the World War, the flow of Jewish emigrants broke through again in 1921. The movement seemed unending; in the early postwar era, the number of Jews moving westward averaged a quarter of a million a year! From 1881 to 1930, in sum, there emigrated from Eastern Europe to the United States, South America, the British Empire, and Western Europe approximately four million Jews! It was the most far-reach-ing and significant transplantation in Jewish history.

By the turn of the century, the philanthropic organizations of Western Jewry finally resigned themselves to the fact that the exodus was a con-tinuing phenomenon, and that the responsibility for organizing and directing it could no longer be avoided. Once this decision was taken, a chaotic flood tide was transformed into a somewhat more orderly and systematic migration. In 1904 the presidents and directors of Europe's leading Jewish relief organizations—save the *Alliance,* which had lost face and was dis-credited—met together at an international conference in Frankfurt. There a Central Office of Migration Affairs was established to co-ordinate all immigra-tion activities. By 1905 twenty-four immigrant aid committees were success-fully organized in the key cities of Eastern and Central Europe. Austria's *Israelitische Allianz* supervised migration through Austria-Hungary. The Berlin Central Committee, with its two offices in Hamburg and Bremen and its network of branches in the leading border towns and rail centers, regulated the movement of refugees through Germany. Hundreds of thou-sands of Russian-Jewish emigrants were met at border stations by Austrian- or German-Jewish philanthropic representatives, and were provided with clothing, medical care, and kosher food. Western Jewish interpreters boarded the trains with the emigrants and remained with them during the long rail journey to the German ports.

The trek across Central Europe was only slightly less terrifying for the refugees than the original flight from Russia or Romania. The memory of furtive border crossings and suspicious frontier officials was still fresh in their minds, and they found it difficult, as a result, to adjust to the fact that they were among friends. At first, for example, emigrants hesitated to eat the food set before them for fear that it was not kosher, or to exchange their currency or tickets, for every stranger was a possible swindler. When their train entered the tunnel of Berlin's Charlottenburg Station, many of the refugees imagined, with sinking hearts, that they had been brought to a Russian prison, that the train had carried them to Siberia instead of Germany. But the presence of friendly fellow Jews from Western Europe was re-assurance enough for most of them. Indeed, from Russian or Romanian border to port of debarkation they remained continually under the benevolent protection of Western Jewish philanthropy. During the ocean crossing the refugees rejoiced that the Hamburg branch of the Berlin Central Committee had provided for their religious needs. There were stores of kosher meat and bread on the ship, a Jewish kitchen, a *mashgiach* (ritual inspector), and a doctor. Thus, the earlier failure of Western Jewish philanthropy was redressed, and the ancient Jewish tradition of solicitude and concern staunchly and permanently reasserted.

TO "GOLDEN AMERICA"

The exodus from Eastern Europe led to many lands, to Western Europe, to the British Commonwealth, to Latin America. But welcome as these sanctuaries were, they attracted only a small fraction of the Russian and Romanian Jews. To most of them there was only one goal, the United States, and between 1881 and 1920 nearly three million fought through every obstacle to reach its shores. They came primarily by families, indeed, often by whole communities, and they came determined to stay.

This migration would not have assumed such proportions had it not been for vast improvements in ocean transportation. Some million and three quarters Jews arrived from Bremen and Hamburg on German liners, and perhaps three quarters of a million from Liverpool on the mighty Cunarders. These vessels had room for many hundreds of passengers in their cavernous steerages. There was usually a spring bed for each person, a towel, a bar of soap, and a life preserver. The berths were arranged two, four, and six in a cabin. As a rule, married couples were allowed a room to themselves, even in steerage. British emigrants were ordinarily lumped together, as were Scandinavians, Jews, and Russians—in order that each person in the cabin would understand the others' language. In most cases, kosher food and facilities were available as a special provision of the company or of Jewish philanthropic agencies.

Of course, steerage trips were no pleasure cruise and the heartache of uprooting could not be easily or quickly dissipated. Yet despite physical discomfort or the gnawing desolation of homesickness, the voyager's spirits must have been buoyed immeasurably by his first glimpse of the American skyline. "The magnificent verdure of Staten Island," Abraham Cahan recalled, "the tender blue of sea and sky, the dignified bustle of passing craft—above all, those floating, squatting, multitudinously-windowed palaces which I consequently learned to call ferries. It was all so utterly unlike anything I had ever seen or dreamed of before. It unfolded itself like a divine revelation."

There was an exhausting ordeal ahead, to break the spell. For many decades the immigration station for New York harbor was Castle Garden, under the supervision of the State of New York. Then, in 1890, a celebrated Supreme Court decision gave the Federal government jurisdiction over immigration. Shortly thereafter, the United States Treasury Department transformed the tiny harbor defense of Ellis Island into its principal inspection depot for newcomers. To millions of aliens the name Ellis Island became a painful memory of endless red tape, days, even weeks, of waiting, questioning, examining. The doctors were ever on the hunt for granuloma, trachoma, and other communicable diseases common to Eastern Europe. Those who were afflicted could be sent back and the tragic scenes which ensued were like those after a sentence of death. The officials were tireless: Have you ever been arrested? For a crime involving moral turpitude? Have you got a job in America? (This was a dangerous question; if the immigrant said "yes" he could be deported, for it was a violation of American law to contract for foreign labor.) Are you an anarchist? Are you willing to live in subordination to the laws of the United States? Are you a polygamist? Have you any friends in New York? Give me the address. How much money have you got? Show me, please. "They are not a bit better than Cossacks," Cahan's hero, David Levinsky, remarked to his friend. "But they neither looked nor spoke like Cossacks," he reflected, "so their gruff voices were part of the uncanny scheme of things that surrounded me."

The immigrant sorely needed aid and counsel as he moved through the labyrinth of the immigration routine. To meet the challenge, in 1902, a group of recently arrived Russian Jews, most of them members of the Independent Order of B'rith Abraham, established the Hebrew Immigrant Aid Society. At Ellis Island and at immigration stations in other American ports, HIAS representatives served as interpreters and voluntary attorneys, protecting the newcomers from misinterpretation of the law, and from the abuse of discretionary powers vested in the Board of Special Inquiry. Jewish immigrants were taken in charge by HIAS until they were safely placed with their relatives and friends; where friends or relatives could not be located, HIAS inserted advertisements in the Jewish dailies in an effort to find them. In addition, HIAS conducted an employment agency and a temporary Shelter House in New York.

In 1893, under the leadership of the German-Jewish group, the National Council of Jewish Women was created to protect immigrant Jewish girls from the predatory white slavers who awaited them on the docks. In later years yet other agencies were established to provide additional services. For the most part, however, these services were confined to the immediate disembarkation needs of the immigrants. Usually the United Hebrew Charities of New York assumed responsibility for the newcomers who required long-range relief and rehabilitation after passing through Ellis Island. The calls for such help were frequent; as late as 1907 at least two fifths of the Jews from Eastern Europe arrived destitute, having spent their last penny for tickets or other items of transportation. In the years to come the problem became much less acute, for by then the majority of Jewish immigrants were on the way to join relatives and were assisted by them.

Even as Jewish philanthropy both in Europe and America spread a protective canopy over the refugee population, a powerful anti-immigration sentiment emerged in the United States. As early as the 1880's Congress began to impose qualifications on the American tradition of asylum, by levying head taxes on immigrants and forbidding contract labor. In 1891, a statute ordered the return to Europe of immigrants suffering from "loathsome and contagious" diseases; it was a law of some concern to Jewish immigrants, many of whom were afflicted with trachoma. In 1907 yet another Act of Congress raised the head tax to four dollars per immigrant, and forbade entry to imbeciles, idiots, criminals, polygamists, anarchists, prostitutes, persons with contagious diseases, contract laborers—and "persons likely to become a public charge." This last clause seemed for a while to pose a serious obstacle to Jewish immigration. But eventually American-Jewish philanthropic representatives convinced the authorities that Jewish newcomers, penniless though many of them were, were not typical indigents—and that they required only a minimal transition period before they were able to earn their own livelihoods. Qualifying legislation became increasingly restrictive. In 1917, for example, a literacy test was passed over President Wilson's veto. Few Jews were ·literate in any save the Yiddish language, and it took prolonged negotiations before the immigration authorities were persuaded to accept Yiddish as an "authentic" tongue.

It was during the first World War period that opposition to immigration reached truly ominous proportions. The primary source of such opposition was the trade union movement, whose leaders expressed concern at the threat presented by "cheap, immigrant labor." Another source of anti-immigration sentiment was America's educated "elite," who argued that "bossism" was battening on the insecurity and political ineptitude of the immigrant populations. America's farmers, too, were troubled by the transformation of metropolitan areas into "hives" of alien, and Catholic and Jewish, "corruption." At the same time, German racism, making its appearance in the United States in the quasi-scientific guise of the "eugenics" doctrine, suggested to white Protestant Americans that they were in danger of being "mongrelized" by the "rabble" of Italian slums and Russian ghettos. After the Bolshevik Revolution of November 1917, a more potent argument was added: the imminent danger of infiltration by East European "radicals"; it was the very real fear of this infiltration which finally convinced the Daughters of the American Revolution, the American Legion, and other traditional patriot groups, that America's doors ought to be closed. In 1921 Senator Thomas ("Tomtom") Heflin voiced their convictions when he drew a distinction between the earlier type of immigrants "who built America" and "some of the miserable horde that is coming now."

In March 1921, responding to the pressure of the "exclusionists," President Warren Harding called an extra session of Congress to rewrite America's immigration laws. Within eleven days Congress passed the legislation Harding requested. By its terms, the annual immigration of aliens of any nationality was limited to 3 per cent "of the number of foreign-born persons of such nationality who were resident in the United States according to the census of 1910." Here was a group test obviously aimed at immigration from Southern and Eastern Europe. Although the measure expired in 1924, it was swiftly superseded by a permanent immigration law. Under the terms of this new Act—popularly known as the Johnson Act, after its sponsoring Senator, Magnus Johnson of Minnesota—the annual immigrant quotas were further reduced to 2 per cent; and the base year was changed from 1910 to

1890, a period before any significant numbers of Italians, Slavs, or Russian Jews had arrived in the United States. After 1927 the total annual quota from all sources was to be reduced to 150,000. Thus, with the Johnson Act, the door was slammed permanently on all but the most nominal immigration from the southeastern hinterland of Europe.

The tragedy of this restrictive legislation was not merely that it denied Jews and other suffering peoples access to "the Promised Land," but also that it set a precedent for other nations. In 1923, a Canadian Order-in-Council inaugurated a closed-door policy against all immigration from Eastern Europe except "bona-fide" agriculturists. England, Australia, Argentina, and Brazil all quickly followed America's lead. As far as the Jews of Eastern Europe were concerned, this string of laws ultimately became a hangman's noose. Polish Jewry was sealed off from the West; the migrations came to an end suddenly and catastrophically less than a decade before the rise of Adolf Hitler.

THE MEANING OF THE GREAT MIGRATION

A half-century of migration had significantly redistributed the Jews of the world. Between 1880 and 1933, the movement westward of four million Jews drained off the entire natural increase of the main reservoir of Eastern European Jewry, leaving the Jewish population of the Pale, and later of postwar Poland, virtually stationary. French, Belgian, and German Jewry, whose numbers had not significantly increased between 1870 and 1880, whose birth rates had begun to drop, and whose Jewish loyalties had become attenuated, now were suddenly reinvigorated by tranfusions of Eastern European coreligionists: 60,000 in France, 50,000 in Belgium, 100,000 in Germany, many of these after the first World War. But the great migration made its deepest impact on the American-Jewish community, whose numbers, by 1933, soared to four and a half million in a world Jewish population of fifteen and a half million. The percentage formed by East European Jewry

TABLE I

VOLUME OF JEWISH MIGRATION OVERSEAS AND

CHANGES IN THE DISTRIBUTION OF THE JEWS OF THE WORLD*

Years	United States and Canada	Argentina and Brazil	Other American Countries	Palestine	Others	Total
1840-1900	890,000	28,000	2,000	35,000	30,000	985,000
1901-1925	1,823,000	149,000	19,000	76,000	52,000	2,119,000
1926-1939	173,000	107,000	58,000	233,000	83,000	654,000
Total	2,886,000	284,000	79,000	344,000	165,000	3,758,000

* From Mark Wischnitzer, *To Dwell in Safety*, Jewish Publication Society.

sank from 75 per cent to 46 per cent. The proportion inhabiting Western and Central Europe remained virtually unchanged as against 1880—about 13.5 per cent. But the United States and other overseas countries, which in 1880 had only 3.8 per cent of world Jewry, now had approximately 30 per cent.

The shift in the center of Jewish life from east to west was both a demographic and a sociological revolution of the profoundest importance. While the Jews had ceased to be a predominantly Oriental people by the end of the

TABLE II

DISTRIBUTION OF JEWISH POPULATION

1880		1933	
World Jewish Population	10,000,000	*World Jewish Population*	15,500,000
Eastern Europe	75 %	*Eastern Europe*	46 %
Western and Central Europe	13.5%	*Western and Central Europe*	13.5%
North and South America	3.5%	*North and South America*	30 %
Near East	8 %	*Near East*	5.7%
		Other Areas of the World	4.8%

nineteenth century, the fact that most of them continued to live in the Pale of Settlement prevented them from taking on the personality of the West. They no longer belonged to the one, but they could not become the other. By Western standards they remained backward, poverty-stricken, unhygienic, frequently quite ignorant of the world's most cherished secular values. Here, of course, they hardly differed from their Polish and Russian neighbors. Suddenly millions of these impoverished, devoutly religious Jews were hurled into the West, primarily into the United States, the most materialistic, the most modern, the wealthiest of all Western lands. Would they follow the example of earlier immigrant groups, forsake their Old Worldly ways, abandon their deeply rooted religious and cultural traditions, and remold their lives on Western lines?

The true significance of the Jewish migration to the United States was the willingness of the newcomers to adapt themselves to the speed, the tempo, the efficiency of American life; but also their unwillingness to follow the path marked out by most of the Sephardic and many of the German Jews who preceded them: namely, their unwillingness to abandon their ethnic and cultural inheritance. It was this fusion of New World efficiency and wealth with Old World ethnocentrism which enabled the American-Jewish community to move into the center of the stage of Jewish history for the seventy years that followed the May Laws, and to dominate that history until the rise of the State of Israel in 1948.

THE IMMIGRANTS SETTLE

When the newcomers disembarked at New York harbor, they were faced with the problem of finding homes and jobs. Few of them had any fixed notion of where they would settle. Some of the immigrants moved inland, in the manner of their German-Jewish predecessors. A tiny minority among them, perhaps four thousand, were animated by the agriculturist ideals of the *Haskalah*; with as much naïveté as audacity, they sought to create agricultural colonies in such unlikely places as Sicily Island, Louisiana, Cremieux, South Dakota, or New Odessa, Oregon. Although encouraged and subsidized by the Baron de Hirsch Fund, these would-be farmers found the bucolic life too lonely and too much divorced from their traditions; most of them drifted off into the cities.

Perhaps 60,000 immigrants were moved into the smaller communities of the American interior by an Industrial Removal Office, an organization which wealthy, nativized Jews of German descent had established in the hope of relieving the squalid congestion of the metropolitan ghettos. There were, in addition, approximately half a million East European Jews who were attracted to the larger inland cities—Cincinnati, Cleveland, Detroit, St. Louis, Minneapolis, Chicago—entirely on their own. It was a spontaneous process by which, for example, an immigrant heard rumors of a better opportunity inland, a peddler in his travels saw and liked another town, a worker with savings heard from a friend in the Midwest, a shoemaker barely eking out a living read in a newspaper of openings elsewhere. By 1930 perhaps 35 per cent of the Russian-Jewish immigrants had turned their backs on the more crowded Atlantic coastal area.

Withal, 65 per cent of the newcomers remained in the great cities of the East—as, in fact, did most of the immigrants who came from Southern and Eastern Europe. The choice was natural both because of inclination and because of major changes in the American economic structure which favored and accelerated urbanization. Americans—native Americans—by the millions were leaving the countryside for the burgeoning industrial complexes of the Atlantic seaboard. Although the city had always played an important role in American life, and had been growing steadily during the nineteenth century, it was not until the 1880's that it assumed its titanic historic role. For the turn of the century was a period of immense technological advance in American industry. Factories, in their thousands, now produced rails, bridges, agricultural implements, machines, and household appliances of countless shapes and functions to serve the new era. At the same time opportunities on the countryside diminished steadily. By 1890 America's large homesteaded agricultural areas had been virtually pre-empted; while advances in scientific farming undermined the security of several million "superfluous" farm families. These developments—the advancement of industry, the diminution of farm opportunity—influenced immigrants no less than natives, and were as decisive as ethnic solidarity in creating the heavy concentration of newcomers in the metropolitan areas of the East.

There were additional factors that accounted for the urbanization of the Jews. As a people whose experiences with agriculture had been quite minimal, even in the Old Country, it was hardly surprising that they continued to think in terms of petty trade. Again, because most of the Jewish immigrants, at least on arrival, were still observant religionists, it was natural for them to seek close contact with their fellow Jews; in larger organized Jewish communities they could better sustain their religious practices. It happened, moreover, that the ocean liners unloaded some three quarters of all Jewish immigrants at the port of New York, the largest city in America even before 1881. Hundreds of thousands of these immigrants simply remained in the metropolitan area; here they could quickly and conveniently dispose of their labor; from New York they could easily maintain contact with opportunities in Philadelphia or Boston. On the eve of the second World War New York City accounted for 46 per cent of all American Jews— 2,300,000 out of 5,000,000. This was 30 per cent of the city's entire population, and represented six times the number of Jews in Warsaw, five times the number in Moscow—the largest Jewish communities in Europe.

Originally, in each of the major cities, there was an area of primary settlement: the Lower East Side in New York; the North End in Boston; downtown in Philadelphia; the West Side in Chicago. These were all slum districts, even then, with the lowest rentals available for immigrant families. Thus, New York's East Side was transformed virtually into a Jewish city; as early as 1890 its Tenth Ward encompassed some 330,000 Jews, all living within an area of one square mile. It need hardly be added that the German or Hungarian Jews who had inhabited this area now fled uptown in terror. By 1917, no less than 700,000 Jews were jammed into the East Side; while in the slum area of Brooklyn, the Brownsville section, an additional 200,000 were congested so tightly that, up to the age of twelve, a Brownsville child scarcely encountered non-Jews, except for teachers and policemen, and hardly ever considered himself a member of a minority group. "I don't think my contemporaries and I believed that the figures who loomed largest in our imagination—say, George Washington, Nathan Hale, Tom Mix, Babe Ruth, and Jack Dempsey—were actually Jewish," recalls one writer who was raised in the Brownsville section, "but we never clearly thought of them as anything else."

After arriving in New York most of the immigrants made their homes in five-story tenements. Nearly all the tenement flats were of the same size and shape: a room with windows opening upon a court, and at the rear a small black bin or pen for the bed. The room was perhaps twelve feet square and the bin was six. The flat may have been squalid, but it was also cheap. usually renting for about six dollars a month. Even at this rental it was not uncommon for immigrant families to live ten and twelve in a flat, their unwashed children spilling out into the dark hallways, the filthy cellars, the garbage-strewn alleyways and streets. The typical tenement building literally trembled beneath the weight of humanity, and was notorious as a firetrap.

As in the Pale, the market place remained the center of activity in Jewish neighborhoods. In New York's East Side, for example, the public shopping area was Hester Street, known by the less than affectionate title of *chazer-mark*—"Pig Market." In this area of hardly more than three square blocks, bearded Jews and beshawled Jewesses hawked the virtues of the merchandise they carried in their pushcarts—pencils, tin cups, eggs, horseradish, articles of clothing, and nearly every other portable item conceivable. The cacophony was earsplitting. Through his protagonist, David Levinsky, Abraham Cahan recalled his experience as a typical pushcart peddler:

> I rented a push-cart and tried to sell remnants of dress-goods, linen, and oil-cloth. This turned out somewhat better than basket peddling; but I was one of the common herd in this branch of the business as well. Often I would load my push-cart with cheap hosiery, collars, brushes, hand-mirrors, note-books, shoe-laces, and the like, sometimes with several of these articles at once, but more often with one at a time. In the latter case I would announce to the passers-by the glad news that I had struck a miraculous bargain at a wholesale bankruptcy sale, for instance, and exhort them not to miss their golden opportunity. I also learned to crumple up new underwear, or even to wet it somewhat, and then shout that I could sell it "so cheap" because it was slightly damaged. . . . I hated the constant chase and scramble for bargains and I hated to yell and scream in order to create a demand for my wares by the sheer force of my lungs. Many an illiterate dolt easily outshouted me and thus dampened what little interest I had mustered.

Tens of thousands of Jewish children were raised in these clamorous catch basins. At school most of them were remarkably good students, and they adjusted rapidly to their new language and environment. But the struggle for economic security was severe; many Jewish youngsters were obliged to leave school before they reached their teens, to work in the streets as newsboys, shoeshine boys, or porters. Very often, especially when they ventured into non-Jewish neighborhoods, they were beaten, robbed, or —as in the case of Irving Berlin—nearly drowned. Often, too, they were lured into bands of young ruffians who specialized in petty pilfering and, in rarer instances, were not averse to robbery by assault. At the age of thirteen, Eddie Cantor was famous as a "strong-arm" member of a gang of strikebreakers, led by "pock-faced Sam, chief terror of the local strikers." To combat such delinquency settlement houses were established in New York and Chicago. These institutions were not without influence on Jewish immigrant children, and unquestionably helped to save large numbers of them from criminal careers. Social workers such as New York's Lillian Wald and Chicago's Jane Addams were responsible, in no small degree, for the many judges, teachers, musicians, playwrights, and public figures who sprang from the fetid soil of America's ghettos.

AMERICA'S JEWISH PROLETARIAT

The immigrants who poured into the United States between 1880 and 1924 were grist for the mills of America's manufacturers. For immigrant labor was cheap labor, cowed and docile. The newcomer was willing to take any kind of work as quickly as he could get it, to endure long hours and low wages in the mines, steel mills, and factories. Jewish immigrants, too, gravitated to the bewildering complex of manual trades: in the building industry, as independent painters or carpenters; as cigar and cigarette makers; as jewelry workers. It should be noted that few of them were attracted to heavy industry. For one thing, they were subject to frequent manhandling there by German, Irish, or Slavic workers. Most Jews, too, were not physically or temperamentally inured to the brutish labor of the mill or foundry. They were, on the other hand, well acquainted with the needle trades—as peddlers, tailors, cap-, shawl-, and dressmakers; they brought with them years of experience as garment workers in the Pale of Settlement.

It happened, moreover, that the garment industry in New York was largely in the hands of German Jews, people whose parents and grandparents both in Europe and America had moved up the hierarchy from rag-pickers to peddlers to retailers to manufacturers. During the Civil War, most of those who were tailors or textile manufacturers had profited from the huge orders for uniforms placed by the Union army; and, within a generation, had managed to transform their shops into large factories. In their willingness to hire Russian Jews, the factory owners combined philanthropy with a natural desire to take advantage of cheap immigrant labor. When, for example, the Eighth Street Jewish Charities sent out a circular to Jewish manufacturers, in 1892, urging them to hire Jewish immigrants, it was emphasized that the newcomers "are people who obey the law, are God-fearing, patient, industrious, and satisfied with little . . ."

Perhaps more than any other single factor, it was the invention of the sewing machine which made it possible for the garment manufacturers to hire Eastern European Jews in large numbers. The sewing machine introduced the mass production of ready-made suits and dresses and stimulated the establishment of hundreds of clothing factories. The new technique called for men rather than women to operate the heavy new cutting-knives. The production of ladies' cloaks and skirts also became a man's job; women were now used primarily for trimming and finishing. Thus, over the turn of the century, 150,000 to 200,000 Jewish immigrants, together with their wives and children—perhaps a million people in all—depended on the needle trades for their daily bread. After 1890, in fact, the manufacture of clothing in the United States became very literally a "Jewish" industry, operated, directed, managed, and increasingly owned by Eastern European Jews.

The garment industry did not fall into the pattern of American monopoly, the giants absorbing the little men and producing "efficiency." As a result the industry encouraged endless fragmentation, with all of its concomitant problems. Because mechanization never rendered small enterprises impractical in the needle trades, any worker who raised enough money to buy a few sewing machines could set himself up as a "contractor." These shoestring entrepreneurs received unfinished material from the large factory owners, and then hired immigrants, at marginal wages, to do the finishing for them. It was perhaps a circuitous technique of production, but the manufacturers encouraged its use, for the dog-eat-dog competition among the contractors ultimately lowered the cost of production. So thin, in fact, was the line between contractor and worker that the two often operated the sewing machines side by side. Indeed, most of the "outside" shops were located in tenement houses, in the one- or two-room flats of the contractors, where fifteen or twenty men and women—operators, pressers, and finishers—usually were crowded together in joint labor. Although they often began working at dawn and stopped only at ten or eleven at night, some workers were so poorly paid that they were obliged to carry straw mattresses with them and sleep in the halls outside at night. The shop-flats were invariably airless and unlighted. The walls, moist and rotting from lack of sunshine and dry air, bred germs—and fires. These were the tragic "sweatshops" that formed so integral a part of the immigrant's early years in America. Jacob Riis wrote during this period:

> Take a Second Avenue Elevated and ride up half a mile to the sweat-shop district. Every open window of the big tenements, that stand like a continuous brick wall on both sides of the way, give you a glimpse of one of those shops as the train speeds by. Men and women, bending over their machines or ironing boards at the windows, half-naked. . . . The road is like a big gangway through an endless workroom where vast multitudes are forever laboring. Morning, noon, and night, it makes no difference; the scene is always the same.

In the beginning it rarely occurred to the immigrants that they were being exploited. After all, the contractors were almost as poor as they were, and most of them seemed like decent, religious men. Did they not protect the Sabbath and ritual rights of the workers? It was quite common, moreover, for contractors to seek out their *landsleute,* neighbors from the Old Country, and, in the guise of benefactors, to take these "greenhorns" into their shops. The *landsleute* connection was crucial in determining the personnel of the various trades. The skilled machine operator would take in as a learner a newly arrived *landsmann.* The latter would do the same favor for another neighbor who arrived months later. It gradually developed that one particular *shtetl* in the Pale "produced" mostly cloak operators, another, knee-pants operators, and still a third, dress pressers. From single towns this occupational relationship spread to chains of neighboring communities. This loyalty-to-a-countryman relationship proved to be a most serious obstacle to union organization, for in the early days it was impossible to make any "greenhorn" believe that a *landsmann* would take advantage of his helplessness as a stranger. Only gradually, as the socialist organizers made it plain that sweatshop conditions were unconscionable—even by the standards of an immigrant community—did the Jewish worker venture an occasional complaint.

It is not surprising that the first authentic Yiddish literature to emerge from the American scene was a literature of protest against the rigors of the needle trades. The four most gifted Yiddish poets of the time, Morris Winchevsky, Morris Rosenfeld, David Edelstadt, and Yossef Bovshover, all were united by the single purpose of fighting the wretchedness of the sweatshop. Their poems, particularly those of Rosenfeld, bemoaned the harshness of life in the garment district, and described the pale overworked wives and emaciated children in the most graphic and piteous terms. They heaped scorn, too, on the "bloodsuckers" and "fleecers," and projected a militantly socialist picture of a classless society where hunger would be banished and the brotherhood of man would triumph. Rosenfeld, the "Dante of the sweatshop," earned his livelihood operating a heavy pressing machine; his wife supplemented their income peddling *sheitels*—wigs for Orthodox Jewish women—from door to door. Although Rosenfeld was acclaimed by William Dean Howells as one of America's notable poets, he died penniless. His moving poem, "In the Shop," authentically conjures up the image of those early days in the garment industry.

> The sweatshop at midday—I will draw you a picture:
> A battlefield bloody; the conflict at rest;
> Around and about me the corpses are lying;
> The blood cries aloud from the earth's gory breast.
> A moment . . . and hark! The loud signal is sounded,
> And dead rise again and renewed is the fight. . . .
> They struggle, these corpses; for strangers, for strangers!
> They struggle, they fall, and they sink into night.

The loneliness of the German-Jewish settler in 1850 was the physical isolation of the peddler in a tiny prairie town. The loneliness of the Russian-Jewish immigrant in 1900 was the psychic rootlessness of the garment cutter in a congested urban slum.

CONCLUSION

In spite of the hardships that surrounded them, the Jewish immigrant's standard of living was never lower than it had been in the Pale. Undoubtedly, the pressure of the sweatshop, the squalor of the tenement, were quite oppressive; so, too, was the feeling of insecurity and tension in a strange land. Still, life was generally better and freer than in the Pale of Settlement. Unemployment was rare; food was plentiful, if expensive. Physical security was assured, for there was no danger of discriminatory legislation or political persecution. One always had the hope of saving enough money to buy a flat or to send a son through college. What made the sweatshop system particularly difficult to accept, therefore, was the fact that it was permitted to flourish in a land which symbolized opportunity; that the Jews, as foreigners, could be exploited so shamelessly without arousing the traditional American spirit of fair play. Jewish immigrants were not ungrateful when they cried out against injustices which they had borne more patiently abroad. It was an expression of their faith to expect more from a republic whose promise of freedom had drawn them from the ends of the earth. Their assaults were "the chastisements of love."

Notes

Page 317. Quotation from William Poster, " 'Twas a Dark Night in Brownsville," in Eliot Cohen (ed.), *Commentary on the American Scene.*

Page 321. Morris Rosenfeld poem translated by Melech Epstein, *Jewish Labor in the United States,* I, 282.

XVI

Russian Jewry's "Liberal" Tradition in America

The sudden influx of East European Jews, millions of intense, energetic, resourceful people, significantly enlivened the pattern of American civilization. They added their traditions of business acumen, unparalleled powers of self-expression, and a brooding intellectualism; above all, they made an enduring contribution by their devotion to the ideals of industrial democracy. It was the same passion, indeed, which created Bundism in Russia and which identified Jews with the liberal and socialist movements of Central and Western Europe. The Jews of Eastern Europe brought with them, in short, an austere social conscience which they expressed more articulately than any other ethnic group in twentieth-century America.

A million Jewish immigrant families had departed for the United States with shining visions of political freedom and economic advancement. Few of the newcomers had anticipated that their first introduction to "Golden America" would come through the verminous tenement and the squalid and oppressive sweatshop. The shock was a bitter one. Yet it was precisely because the Eastern European Jews had so tenaciously guarded their illusions of American opportunity that they were prepared, once convinced that they were being exploited, to fight back with all the means at their command. At first, however, those means were limited. The political process was comparatively unfamiliar to them. For generations, in fact, they had regarded the State as an impersonal and rather cruel monolith, its officials to be avoided or, if necessary, bribed into indifference. In Europe, the significant Jewish participation in political—and revolutionary—activity was only just beginning. In America, movement into the realm of politics was no less tentative.

As immigrants now in a strange land, the Jews preferred, at first, to avoid the unknown, to depend upon the friendship and patronage of Tammany Hall rather than to seek redress by political techniques. Tammany's ward bosses, making the most of this passivity, handled the East Side with particular shrewdness. They discreetly established relations with Jewish saloon-keepers, "fixed" infractions of city ordinances, provided destitute families with food and clothing, placed young people in minor city jobs, sent district captains to Bar Mitzvahs, weddings, and funerals, with gifts and flowers —and brazenly bought Jewish votes outright. There were occasional Jews in New York and elsewhere who held public office, and a few Tammany clubs were primarily Jewish in membership. But during the early years of their settlement, most of the Jews in New York's East Side were too inept politically to challenge the power of Tammany Hall or the Irish politicians. Ironically, the most powerful Jewish political figures of the period, "Czar" Harry Bernstein in Cleveland, Abe Ruef in San Francisco, arose in cities without large Jewish populations; and there were Jewish governors in Idaho, Oregon, and Utah long before any were elected in populous New York and Illinois.

Around the turn of the century, however, increasing numbers of immigrants began to familiarize themselves with the workings of the American political system. Their willingness to learn was born of necessity, for exploitation in the sweatshops became progressively more difficult to endure. The second wave of mass immigration included a large number of tough, dedicated Bundists who never tired of presenting the collectivist ideal. They could do this without violating the American democratic tradition; for collectivism, as interpreted by Eugene Debs's Socialist party, was strictly Revisionist, unequivocally rejecting the notion of class warfare. While advocating public ownership of the means of production, Debs made it perfectly plain that he intended this to be accomplished by strictly peaceful, democratic means. It was a viewpoint which accorded completely with the Bundist position.

Actually Socialism had never been without strength in the East Side; but until now the Anarchists and Socialist Laborites, both activist, semirevolutionary parties, had dominated the Jewish political scene. In the early 1900's, socialist study groups of the Bundist—and Debsian—variety began to meet on the roofs of the tenements, or in the little East Side cafés, and to conduct endless discussions on the economic and political problems of the Jewish working population. Socialism seemed to bolster the immigrants' faith in themselves, to offer to the worker in the sweatshop the prospect of dignity and respect. By 1910 the American Socialist party had solid anchorage in the East Side of New York, especially in the predominantly Jewish Twelfth Congressional District.

Professing themselves shocked at the "ingratitude" of the inhabitants of the East Side, the Tammany politicos fought back with every device at their disposal—bribery, strong-arm methods, rigged ballot boxes. But by November 1914, the fervor and discipline of the Socialist campaign achieved results. Meyer London, a Russian-Jewish immigrant and a lifelong Socialist, was elected to the United States House of Representatives from the Twelfth Congressional District. London was a trained lawyer, a man of uncommon oratorical ability, with a truly saintly concern for his fellow Jews in the garment district. His election, it should be noted, created consternation among America's more affluent German Jews, who viewed this East Side radicalism as a serious threat to American Jewry's good name. But the masses of the East Side saw nothing "unrespectable" about breaking the Tammany strangle hold and cleansing their neighborhoods of officially protected prostitution and gambling. They elected London to Congress for three consecutive terms, and permanently destroyed Tammany's power in the garment district. And yet Jewish Socialist activity in the political sphere was bound to be ineffectual. London was a lonely man in Congress; none of his colleagues was interested in his theory of reconstructing the national economy. Actually, in an essentially capitalist country like the United States the only kind of economic reform that had a chance lay in the direction of antimonopoly legislation; and this legislation would have little effect on the sweatshop.

Fortunately the Jews of the garment district had never placed too much reliance on political action. They had early recognized that sweatshop conditions could best be remedied through the direct negotiation of trade unions. At first, the process of organizing Jewish workingmen was made particularly difficult by the chaotic state of the American labor movement. There were internal conflicts between the skilled and the unskilled workers which prevented a common front. In 1886, the bombing of Chicago's Haymarket Square, presumably by an anarchist, created a revulsion of public feeling against all forms of organized labor activity. Jews who sought to organize the early unions found that their normal difficulties as immigrants were aggravated by a rather generalized public suspicion of collective bargaining. Undoubtedly they possessed certain advantages over other exploited immigrant groups, for they were grouped together cohesively in the garment industry. Even so, the first Jewish garment unions of the 1880's were shortlived, called into existence for the duration of a strike, and then dying out. Moreover, the socialists who led these early strikes were usually bookish theorists, with little understanding of specific Jewish problems. They were not even realistic enough to communicate with the workers in Yiddish, the only language which could reach them.

Eventually even the most doctrinaire Marxist intellectuals accepted the facts of life. They resorted increasingly to Yiddish in their recruitment drives and in the exposition of union objectives. In 1888 they went so far as to establish the United Hebrew Trades, and announced that the purpose of the organization was to create "Jewish" unions for the "Jewish" garment industry. Morris Hillquit, the group's first secretary, conducted all his official correspondence in Yiddish. In the first year of its existence the United Hebrew Trades established three unions in the needle industry. By 1890 the number had risen to twenty-two, with a membership of nearly 6,000. In order to build membership, Hillquit and his colleagues continued to appeal both to socialist and to Jewish loyalties. It was not uncommon for delegates at United Hebrew Trades rallies to wave banners emblazoned with Talmudic and Biblical quotations. Close ties with the American Socialist Labor party were maintained, and thousands of Jewish workers were recruited by the United Hebrew Trades to participate in May Day parades. In the beginning, the goals of the organization were eminently practical. Its leadership agitated for the eight-hour day and for paid vacations, for the abolition of the pestilent sweatshop and child labor. These practical aspirations proved no less important than Marxian dialectic in attracting Jewish needleworkers into the labor movement.

Now the leadership of the United Hebrew Trades decided to test its strength by organizing several strikes in the ladies' garment industry. Although conducted with enthusiasm, virtually all of these walkouts failed. For one thing, they were ineptly organized. For another, the garment industry was highly seasonal; workers were often laid off for long periods of time and were unable to accumulate enough savings to contribute to union strike funds. Many of the immigrants, too, it must be added, viewed labor in the sweatshop as a kind of temporary employment—until the time came when they could go into business for themselves. As a result the turnover of the Jewish labor force was quite high. Of course, strike organization on such a basis was extremely difficult. Finally, the United Hebrew Trades encountered an ideological crisis in the 1890's which ultimately proved its undoing. Large numbers of Jewish workers fell under the spell of Daniel De Leon, the president of the American Socialist Labor party. De Leon was a brilliant and erratic Venezuelan, the descendant, some said, of Sephardic Jews. As a young man he had studied economics at Columbia University, had traveled widely, and had become a passionate and dogmatic socialist. By the time he was thirty he had committed himself to propagandizing the socialist cause on a full-time basis. De Leon's power of oratory was nothing less than hypnotic, and workers by the thousands, immigrants and natives alike, flocked to his cause. At first he had little difficulty in winning the loyalty of the U.H.T. leadership. For a year and a half they followed him blindly into strike after strike. In response to his direction, their picketing was clamorous, occasionally even violent. It soon became apparent, however, that De Leon was little interested in the practical improvement of working conditions, and far more obsessed with the notion of communizing American society. His strikes quite effectively demoralized the needle industry, but they won few tangible benefits for the workers. One walkout followed another; and no appreciable "bread-and-butter" gains resulted. Nor was it possible to persuade De Leon to modify his approach, for his insufferable egotism and explosive temper made him virtually unapproachable. The United Hebrew Trades, which had entered the 1890's with thirty-three member unions, ended the century with barely three. By then most of the Jewish workers had learned their lesson: the doctrinaire socialism of the De Leonists had burned itself out.

THE TRIUMPH OF JEWISH TRADE UNIONISM

No trade union movement could possibly have succeeded in the United States if it carried the incubus of the Marxian dogma. The immigrant had to face the practical reality that he lived and functioned in a powerful and expanding capitalist economy. By the early twentieth century most Jews who were attracted to socialism by temperament or economic orientation had made the adjustment as part of their "Americanization." Ironically, one of the agencies most responsible for mellowing the Jewish working-man and familiarizing him with the context of American life was the Yiddish press. The newcomer needed a reliable guide to adapt himself more easily to American mores, and the Yiddish press served as that guide, even as the German-language press had served as a guide for the earlier Jewish immigrants. As the immigrant population grew, Yiddish newspapers sprang up in profusion, so many, in fact, that by 1895 twelve Yiddish dailies were being published in New York alone. Most of them represented definite economic and political points of view; they included, for example, the anarchist *Warheit,* the socialist *Die Naye Zeit,* and the De Leonist *Arbeiter Zeitung.*

By far the most influential of these journals was *Der Forverts*—the *Jewish Daily Forward.* Its editor was Abraham Cahan, the outstanding personality of Yiddish journalism in the United States. A Russian-Jewish immigrant, Cahan first earned his living in New York as a cigar maker; later he sup-plemented his income by tutoring his fellow Jews in the English language. As a dedicated socialist, he contributed prolifically to the *Arbeiter Zeitung,* the organ of the Socialist Labor party, and even served for a while as the paper's editor. By 1896, however, Cahan found it impossible any longer to endure De Leon's dogmatism and militancy, and he resigned. Together with a group of other "moderates," he founded the *Forward* in 1897 and threw its support to Eugene Debs's Socialist party. Eventually the *Forward* became the representative voice of American Jewish socialism, a socialism far milder and more pragmatic than the De Leonist variety.

For a brief period Cahan left the *Forward* to serve as a reporter for the New York *Commercial Advertiser.* It was there, working closely with Lincoln Steffens and Hutchins Hapgood, that he perfected his crisp jour-nalistic technique. When he returned to the editorship of the *Forward* in 1902, he had acquired the necessary experience and skill, and, above all, the moderation, to transform it into a national organ of Jewish life. Within a few years, the *Forward*'s circulation reached the impressive total of 200,000. Cahan remained a devoted socialist; his editorials, vitriolic in their denun-ciation of the sweatshop, continued to reflect his economic viewpoint. But it was not necessary to be a socialist to enjoy the *Forward.* The paper's "journalese" was simple and direct; its columns were filled with tales of human interest, particularly the column called *Bint'l Brief* ("Bundle of Letters") which answered requests for advice on domestic and personal matters. Jewish holidays and religious observances were treated with defer-ence for the feelings of Orthodox Jews—an attitude unprecedented in the radical community. The *Forward* forbearance was summarized in an early editorial admonition: "Free thinkers, don't be fanatics."

Moreover, Cahan understood the role of his paper as an instrument of Americanization. His features and weekly supplements, the construction of his news items, gradually familiarized the immigrant readers with the workings of American life. In the "light" category were so-called human interest happenings retold and interpreted from the Socialist-Jewish point of view. The more serious articles would deal with a debate in Congress, the seasonal trend in a garment industry, international affairs, or American history, government, and customs. The distinguished American philosopher, Morris R. Cohen, spoke for hundreds of thousands of Jewish immigrants when he observed:

> I owe a good deal of my education to the Yiddish press. It taught me to look at world news from a cosmopolitan instead of a local or provincial point of view, and it taught me to interpret politics realistically, instead of being misled by empty phrases.

But there were other factors, too, that helped to modify the ardent radicalism of many of the Jewish newcomers. One of those factors was European Revisionist socialism, the impact of which in the United States was mainly responsible for the decline of such extremist groups as the "Molly Maguires," the I.W.W.'s, and the De Leonists of the Socialist Labor movement. In the American-Jewish community the Revisionist point of view was advocated not merely by Cahan, but also, as we have seen, by thousands of former Jewish Bundists who poured in after 1900. Yet another factor was the career of a gnomelike little man, Samuel Gompers, who was to dominate the American labor movement. His appearance—short legs, stocky torso, huge head, sharp pointed nose, and tiny near-sighted eyes—belied his stature as the authentic giant of trade unionism. The son of Sephardic Jews, Gompers was born and raised in London. He came to the United States in 1863, settled in New York, and became a cigar maker in an East Side tenement. It was a hard and bitter trade, one of the lowest paid in the country, and among the first, therefore, to generate a labor revolt. Gompers belonged to the militant group of organizers that managed ultimately to establish a cigar makers' union. The struggle nearly killed him; but it also provided him with the basic, and hard-won, philosophy of trade unionism which animated his subsequent career.

It was a philosophy of pragmatism; while emphasizing the importance of fighting for fewer hours, higher wages, better working conditions, it also eschewed utopian notions of creating a socialist society. Gompers profited, too, from the lessons of internecine warfare which had wrecked earlier union efforts. He was convinced that trade union membership ought to be restricted, at least initially, to skilled laborers, those workingmen who could employ their bargaining power to greatest effect. It was out of these convictions that he founded, in 1881, the forerunner of the American Federation of Labor, a federation of unions of skilled craftsmen. The period of foundation-laying was long and tortuous. Gompers was hard-put to fend off the doctrinaires of the Socialist Labor party, to maintain worker discipline during long and seemingly profitless strikes against powerful and stubborn employers. But eventually, with infinite patience and endurance, these obstacles were overcome, and Gompers succeeded in steering the AFL to a membership of five million men and women by 1914. By then, too, the unions of the AFL managed to win sizable "bread-and-butter" gains in the form of shorter working hours, higher wages, and better working conditions.

Even the most radical of Jewish garment workers could not fail to be impressed by the tangible results achieved through the "Gompers method." Growing numbers of Jewish workers, through their unions in the various branches of the needle trades, returned now to a United Hebrew Trades thoroughly purged of De Leonist influence. They pledged their loyalty to the AFL and linked themselves integrally to the main body of American organized labor. Once the decision was reached to concentrate on limited pragmatic objectives, the Jewish needleworkers became a dynamic force in the trade union movement, and won far-reaching concessions for themselves. Between 1909 and 1914 a series of carefully organized, tightly disciplined strikes paralyzed successive areas of the garment industry. In American-Jewish labor history these five years are remembered as the "great revolt." Massive strikes of shirtwaist makers, cloak makers, and skirt makers took the factory owners and contractors completely by surprise; they had never for a moment imagined that mild, apparently docile tailors and seamstresses, burdened with all the limitations and insecurities of an immigrant people, could command such enthusiasm, discipline, tenacity, and defense in depth.

It is worth noting that the strikes involved far more for the Jewish garment workers than merely laying down tools. Employers could call in powerful allies to fight back—strikers who picketed faced police brutality and arrest on the spurious grounds of "disturbing the peace." For Jewish seamstresses strikes frequently meant incarceration in the city jail together with hardened women of the streets—a particularly horrifying experience because, according to New York law, all arrests were duly noted on marriage licenses. Since jail sentences for women in those days were usually associated with prostitution, many a woman striker risked paying for her convictions with a permanently ruined reputation.

Yet the self-sacrifice of the garment workers eventually achieved its goal. The contractors and factory owners were compelled to capitulate and agree to shorter hours, higher wages, and better working conditions. These gains in the needle industry were eventually consolidated in a settlement known as the "Protocol of Peace"; it was an agreement largely worked out by the brilliant attorney and labor advocate Louis Brandeis, then at the beginning of his spectacular career. By its terms, the Protocol further adjusted hours and wages; it also abolished the curse of subcontracting, and obliged the factory owners to recognize and deal with the union leaders. A Joint Board of Sanitary Control was established for the purpose of supervising sanitary conditions in the factories. The Protocol also provided for a Board of Arbitration, composed of representatives of workers, owners, and a disinterested third party, to adjudicate on all workers' grievances. In this way employers and employees alike hoped, in the future, to avoid the possibility of crippling strikes.

By 1913 most of the employees in the women's garment industry were effectively enrolled in the International Ladies' Garment Workers' Union, one of the most powerful associations in the country. The ILGWU was governed by a succession of dedicated presidents, all of whom were Russian-Jewish immigrants, all former workers themselves; in innumerable bargaining sessions, arbitrations, and occasional strikes, they pressed home to eventual realization the demands of the Jewish needleworkers. There was John Dyche, a conservative "evolutionist," the first to liberate the garment unions from the Socialist Laborites; and Dyche's successor, Benjamin Schlesinger, a somber, melancholy, rather Lincolnesque man, racked by the illnesses of a lifetime in the sweatshops, who bargained tirelessly and ingeniously—and with almost invariable success—on behalf of his constituents. Morris Sigman, a former De Leonist, led the ILGWU during the factious era of the Communist "civil wars" of 1925-26 (p. 331, below), and succeeded ultimately in wresting the union back into the hands of the moderates. There was David Dubinsky, a stocky, amiable organizational genius whose apprenticeship had been spent as a Bundist official in czarist Russia, and as a prisoner in a lice-ridden Siberian prison. Dubinsky was one of the ablest exponents of conservative "business" unionism. Whenever possible he rejected strikes and concentrated on detailed and protracted negotiations. It was he, for example, who pioneered in time-study plans which enabled employers to provide wage increases without loss of profits. During his administration, the ILGWU emphasis was on workers' insurance programs, adult education courses, nurseries, clinics, and summer resorts. "Business" unionism notwithstanding, it was also under Dubinsky's leadership that the ILGWU forthrightly sponsored a wide variety of liberal programs in public and political affairs. Indeed, the ILGWU has almost invariably joined the progressive and left-wing unions in the AFL conventions—in opposition to the stand-pat attitude of the Federation oligarchy.

The progress of the women's garment workers was largely duplicated in the men's clothing industry. This was due, almost invariably, to the tireless energy and pugnacity of Sidney Hillman, a former Kovno Rabbinical student. Hillman came to the United States while still in his teens, beginning his career in the garment industry as a cutter in the Chicago clothing factory of Hart, Schaffner and Marx. In 1914, at the age of twenty-eight, he founded and was elected first president of the Amalgamated Clothing Workers of America, an all-encompassing union of men's clothing workers —only about half of whom, incidentally, were Jews. Patiently engineering a succession of strikes, Hillman eventually won a formidable series of concessions from the employers. By 1919 he had matched the gains of the women's garment workers point for point: a forty-four-hour week, better working conditions, arbitration and sanitary boards. After 1919, as owners became more conciliatory and strikes less frequent, the "Amalgamated," like the ILGWU, managed to concentrate on "business unionism." Pension and insurance funds were established for the pressers, spongers, cutters, and fitters who made up the union's membership. While the pure and simple unionism of the decades after the World War may have lacked the flaming idealism and intellectual sparkle of the earlier period, it was incalculably more productive in terms of solid workers' benefits.

Quite aside from the determination, courage, and practical moderation of the workers, there were other factors that accounted for the success of the Jewish labor movement. For one thing, the Jewish working force was concentrated in light manufacturing, a production-area much easier than heavy industry to organize for trade-union purposes. It helped, too, that both owners and employees were Jews; for while little love was lost between the "German" manufacturer and the "Russian" needleworker, at least they could talk to each other. Eminent Jewish communal leaders such as Louis Marshall, Rabbi Sabato Morais, and Rabbi David Philipson were prepared to intercede, whenever necessary, for the sake of the "good name" of the Jewish community.

THE COMMUNIST CRISIS AND THE TRIUMPH OF THE NEW DEAL

At the very apex of its hopes the Jewish labor movement was suddenly overwhelmed by a crisis which at first had little to do with events in the United States, but much indeed to do with events in Russia. It was the Bolshevik Revolution, which hopelessly divided the American Socialist party, and drove its majority membership, including many of its Jews, away from Marxian socialism. Within the labor movement, and especially within the Jewish labor movement, events in Soviet Russia created an even deeper schism. The great majority of Jewish immigrants possessed bitter recollections of czarist persecution; many of them, as a result, felt an instinctive gratitude to the Soviet regime for its suppression of counterrevolutionary anti-Semitism. This gratitude rendered many thousands of Jewish workingmen particularly susceptible to the blandishments of Communist labor organizers.

The Communist battle for control of the unions was fought with every stratagem of demagogy and personal vilification. Indeed, for a while, in 1925, the Reds succeeded in capturing the most important New York locals of the International Ladies' Garment Workers' Union. Within a year, however, the Communists undermined their own cause, when they engineered a disastrous strike and then refused to negotiate with the employers. It became transparently clear that their purpose was not to win gains for the workers, but rather to demoralize the garment industry. The strike virtually crippled the ILGWU, and it took years to rebuild its membership and financial reserves. But it revealed the moral bankruptcy of the Communist party and the garment workers learned a lesson they would not soon forget. The Communists never again succeeded in penetrating their organization. There were a few "Jewish" unions—the cigar makers, the furriers—in which Communists managed to entrench themselves until the late 1940's. But they embraced only a small minority of Jewish working people.

No sooner, however, had the crisis of the 1920's ended than the Communists found another opening: the great Depression of 1929. The stock market collapsed, banks failed, savings were wiped out, factories closed, unemployment rose—eventually to fifteen million. The apparently invincible American industrial machine ground to a halt. For a while, indeed, it seemed as if the entire social system would be swept away. Throughout the early years of the Depression, the Communists were frequently first on the scene among the unemployed. They organized unemployment councils and led noisy marches on Washington, on state legislatures and city halls. They played their game with their usual shrewd opportunism, denouncing the bread lines and the mortgage foreclosures, but attacking Federal and state aid, with equal simulated passion. Helping the hungry in this way was "paternalism," and "bourgeois fake."

Along with other Americans, the Jews suffered bitterly during the Depression. Their ordeal was exacerbated by anti-Semitic discrimination, for Jews were often the first to be fired by retrenching industries. In such a time of confusion and anxiety, Communism made deep inroads. Curiously enough, it was not the Jewish workingman who succumbed to its influence. As far as the typical Jewish needleworker was concerned, unionism had already proved to be the most effective solution to economic insecurity. Rather Communism won its largest Jewish following among lower-middle-class shopkeepers and intellectuals. The former were chagrined at their imminent loss of status, yet could hardly turn to fascism as a release. The latter were convinced that Marxist dialectic provided an intellectual answer both to the renegade business cycle and to anti-Semitism. It was the children of the immigrants who were among the most susceptible. They were in their teens and twenties when the Depression struck. It was shattering to learn that the accepted virtues of hard work, intelligence, and ambition were a mockery and a delusion. Morris Freedman recalls the impact of Communism upon his classmates at New York's City College:

> Anyone who has not lived through it . . . cannot fully appreciate the intellectual terror . . . that the Communists exercised on the campus. Always small in number, they were the most dedicated and fearless of missionaries. In the basement alcoves at City College . . . the party adherents held regular sway with booklets on tables, placards announcing rallies, speeches going on to nobody in particular. In this atmosphere, it took unusual courage and unusual apathy to remain outside the church, especially since joining up was supposed to be a practical demonstration of idealism and humanism.

Eventually the advance of Communism was checked; and more than any other factor it was the New Deal which checked it. Franklin Roosevelt emerged from the debris of depression and fear and attempted vigorously to restore faith in the American dream. He established NRA codes to provide for the participation of employers and organized labor in each industry, and to determine maximum hours and minimum wages. The Wagner Act of 1935 protected the right of workers to bargain collectively through their own chosen representatives; for the first time in American history organ-

ized labor could expect fair play from the government and greater acceptance by society as a whole. Thus amply protected, membership in the
ILGWU and Amalgamated grew spectacularly during the Depression
years. Moreover, Jewish workers and small businessmen alike were deeply
impressed by the President's unequivocal rejection of anti-Semitism, and
by his known reliance upon many Jewish friends and associates in Washington.

During the mid-1930's, as a result, most of the Jewish needleworkers,
together with the majority of Jewish shopkeepers and Jewish intellectuals,
transferred their political allegiance to Franklin Roosevelt. They would not
register as Democrats, to be sure, for the memories of Tammany Hall were
still too fresh in their minds. They preferred instead to organize their own
American Labor party in the East Side and the Bronx. But it was through
this party that Jewish workingmen managed to vote both for Roosevelt
and for the more leftist Congressional candidates who were closer to their
socialist traditions—although those traditions were fading fast. Later, when
the Communists succeeded in infiltrating and dominating the American
Labor party, the Jewish workers and lower middle class of New York took
the initiative, in 1944, in creating a Liberal party free from Communist
influence. Like its predecessor, the Liberal party extended full support to
Roosevelt, as well as to subsequent Democratic presidential candidates. It
has since become a decisive factor in New York City and State elections.

By mid-century the Jewish laboring group, a small minority now, even
within the American-Jewish population, had won a major degree of security
for itself. The typical Jewish worker was protected by law and by union,
by minimum wages, pensions, and a wide variety of insurance and retirement benefits. He enjoyed, as well, the services of union nurseries for his
children, of adult education classes, clinics, and summer resorts for his
family. Ensconced in his modern apartment in the Bronx or in a two-
family house in Flatbush, the garment worker had forgotten, or chosen to
forget, the old socialist tradition of the early twentieth century. "Karl
Marx or no Karl Marx," writes Wallace Markfield, "they can never prove
to him that a summer at Grossinger's is not better than a summer at Coney
Island." While still actively associated with many "progressive" causes, the
Jewish laboring man had long since made his peace with American industry.
In fact, his son and grandson had probably become entrepreneurs them-
selves.

Yet the passion for social justice which the Jewish immigrants communicated to the American labor scene had not been dissipated. Rather
it was applied increasingly to other areas of national life. One of those
areas was encompassed by the political process. In the early 1900's Jewish
liberalism did not, as a rule, take the form of loyalty to the Democratic
party. Most of the German Jews voted Republican, for the Republican party
was still associated, in those days, with Lincoln and abolition; the Democrats, on the other hand, were identified with the South and insurrection.
While large numbers of Russian-Jewish immigrants voted Socialist, there
were many others who were impressed by the apparent liberalism of the

Republican cause, especially when it was interpreted for them by older and "wiser" heads in the German-Jewish community. Besides, nearly all the newcomers felt a deep sense of gratitude to the administrations that had granted them refuge; and in the majority of instances these were Republican. Finally, in the mind of the typical immigrant, the Democratic party was associated with the Irish and Tammany Hall. One voted either Socialist or Republican, but never for Tammany Hall.

It was not until 1924 that Jews in large numbers began to transfer their political loyalties to the Democratic party. Two factors were responsible for the change. The first was the steady decline of socialist influence among the rapidly prospering Jewish immigrant group. The second was the resurgent liberalism of the Democratic party itself, as evidenced in the forthright and progressive platform adopted by Al Smith of New York in his successful gubernatorial campaign of 1924. Four years later Smith was nominated for president. With the help of his active collaborator and speech-writer, the brilliant Jewish attorney, Joseph Proskauer, Smith conducted an even more aggressively liberal campaign than he had for Governor. The election of 1928, as a result, was the first in which more Jews voted Democratic than Republican. Yet it was not until 1932, with the election of Franklin Roosevelt as President, and Herbert Lehman as Governor of New York—the latter New York's first Jewish governor—that a tentative Jewish-Democratic alliance was transformed into a basic fact of political life. The vigor and courage with which Roosevelt and Lehman attacked the crisis of the Depression appealed to the Jews—not merely as a "marginal" economic group but also as a group traditionally devoted to reformist ideals.

Franklin Roosevelt not merely reflected a characteristic Jewish viewpoint on economic and social issues; he was actively influenced by that viewpoint. When he moved into the White House in 1933, he inaugurated the most sweeping series of legislative changes since the Civil War period. Bank insurance, social security, industrial and labor codes, agricultural allotments were enacted into law in swift succession during the early years of the New Deal, evidencing an entirely new concept of the Federal government as a partner in the national welfare. It was a concept which borrowed from the mavericks of the past: from the Progressive tradition of Theodore Roosevelt and the La Follettes of Wisconsin, from the Wilsonian concept of the New Freedom. But in no small measure it drew, as well, from the strenuous preoccupation with social justice which was formulated by outstanding Jewish liberals. It has been argued, with considerable merit, that the intellectual foundations of the New Deal were vitally influenced by the legal briefs and judicial dissents of Louis Dembitz Brandeis.

Brandeis's parents were political refugees from Bohemia who settled and prospered in Louisville, Kentucky. They were able to provide their son with a superior education at private German academies both in Louisville and in Dresden, Saxony. Later, young Brandeis received his undergraduate training at the University of Louisville, and his legal training at the Harvard Law School—where he attained the highest grade average, until then, in Harvard's history. He practiced law in Boston, very successfully, on behalf of conventionally capitalist clients; indeed, he became a millionaire several times over. His interest in reform developed rather slowly. The turning point of his life was not reached until 1890, when he married into the liberal-minded Goldmark family. Simultaneously, he reacted to the shock of the Homestead steel strike and to the ruthless violence perpetrated on the striking steelworkers. It was the age of the "robber barons"; and the more Brandeis contemplated predatory capitalism, the more he determined to transform the law into an instrument of social reform. His clients now included labor unions (many of them Jewish), small manufacturers, farmers' co-operatives, and minor stockholders. Brandeis filed actions on their behalf against some of the towering monoliths of American capitalism: the utility companies, the railroads, the insurance corporations. While never questioning the right of these institutions to exist, he did question their right to become carnivorous. Capitalism, he warned, was in danger of becoming "runaway" capitalism.

Two unique characteristics distinguished Brandeis's briefs: one was a truly fantastic thoroughness of preparation, an exhaustive accumulation of data and statistics from the inner workings of business economy; the other was the frank invocation of social ethics as a criterion for legal decision. Brandeis was among the first to insist that law did not operate in a vacuum; that it must be constructed rather "in harmony with conditions prevailing from time to time." On such issues, for example, as shorter hours or improved working conditions for women, which he advocated before state and Federal courts, Brandeis submitted a few pages of law and several hundred pages of the "world's experience," documentation on the moral, physiological, and social effects of overwork. It was an extraordinary construction of the law; but gradually it left its impact on American legal thought. In 1916 President Wilson decided that it was not too audacious to appoint Brandeis to the Supreme Court; and while the representatives of big business both in and out of the Senate raised a hue and cry, they failed to block ratification.

For over twenty years, Brandeis sat on the high court, a slim spare man with mild blue eyes and thick graying hair. His legal opinions were invariably expressed in dry, factual prose, stripped, as Solomon Bloom has put it, of "all allusion, verbiage, or penumbra." While his opinions usually expressed the minority viewpoint, they ultimately formed the ideological premise for much of the New Deal legislation of the 1930's. Closer regulation of banking, the stock exchange, and holding companies, the careful and scrupulous protection of the investor, the separation of investment from deposit banking, the recognition of labor's bargaining rights, the establishment of social insurance—these were warmly advocated and defended by Brandeis, and they were all eventually translated into law by Franklin Roosevelt, who affectionately referred to Brandeis as "Isaiah."

For many years one of Brandeis's closest intellectual disciples and allies was Felix Frankfurter. Like Brandeis, Frankfurter was the son of Central European Jews—he himself arrived from Austria at the age of twelve—and a graduate of the Harvard Law School. Unlike Brandeis, however, Frankfurter acquired his legal experience, not as a private lawyer, but, from 1906 to 1912, as a government attorney and later, until 1939, as a professor at the Harvard Law School. While Frankfurter was a passionate liberal—he was one of the most ardent defenders of Sacco and Vanzetti—and a legal scholar of unchallenged erudition, he was also a hard-minded realist who worked diligently during the 1930's to help shape the legislation of the New Deal. Both as Professor of Administrative Law at Harvard and as a widely respected consultant in Washington, Frankfurter exerted a major influence in the establishment of many of Roosevelt's administrative agencies. It was Frankfurter's student, for example, James Landis, a former Brandeis law clerk, who drafted the Securities Act and later became Chairman of the Securities and Exchange Commission. Indeed, not the least of Frankfurter's contributions during the Roosevelt administrations was the large number of students and disciples he placed in government service. In 1939 Roosevelt appointed him to the Supreme Court, where he served for the next two decades. For all his involvement in academic and government responsibilities, Frankfurter remained active in Jewish affairs, particularly in the Zionist activities that had claimed his interest and support as far back as the first World War.

The dedicated liberalism of the American-Jewish community was apparent, too, in the college-trained sons of Jewish immigrants who poured into Washington during the New Deal. Many entered the government civil service because they could not find positions in industry or at universities, where jobs were scarce, and where Jews were rarely welcome. But many became government workers because they were raised on the pabulum of social reform, and they shared the Brandeis and Frankfurter viewpoint. The minds of these young men were keen, their devotion to the New Deal unquestioned. Franklin Roosevelt wanted them for his "team"; he depended on them and he liked them. "No Jew ever let me down," the President once confided to an intimate. Their names were as well known as collaborators of the New Deal as those of Tommy Corcoran, Harold Ickes, or General Hugh "Iron Pants" Johnson.

There was Mordecai Ezekiel, the senior agricultural economist of the Department of Agriculture, and later economic adviser to the Secretary of Agriculture. Ezekiel was the intellectual father of the controversial Agricultural Adjustment Act. Isador Lubin, a brilliant economist from the Brookings Institute, became Commissioner of Labor Statistics and Chairman of the Labor Advisory Board of the Public Works administration. Later, as special statistician to the President, Lubin became a member of the White House staff. Both Ezekiel and Lubin were among the leading economic technicians of the New Deal.

With the exception of Louis Howe and Harry Hopkins, the two men closest to Roosevelt were Judge Samuel Rosenman and Henry Morgenthau, Jr. In 1928 Rosenman met Roosevelt on a boat crossing the Hudson River. The two men took to each other immediately and became fast friends. After Roosevelt's election to the governorship of New York, Rosenman became his chief legal counselor, and later was appointed a judge of the New York State Supreme Court. When Roosevelt went to the White House, Rosenman became the unofficial leader of the President's "Brain Trust" and the President's principal speech-writer. Morgenthau, the son of a former American ambassador to Turkey, served as Roosevelt's Secretary of the Treasury, and was one of the few Jews in the executive branch of the government who did not come from a Russian-Jewish background. A somber, humorless man of unshakable integrity, he was largely responsible for assembling the experts who restored public confidence in government securities and in the banking system, who stabilized the dollar through the Gold Reserve Act of 1934, and who reconstructed the tax laws on the basis of ability to pay. By the time Morgenthau and his aides completed their wide-sweeping economic changes, it was a common saying that the financial capital had finally moved from Wall Street to Washington.

David K. Niles, like Rosenman the son of Russian-Jewish immigrants, spent his entire career as a steward of liberal causes, having served variously as Chairman of the Sacco-Vanzetti Defense Committee, Director of the National Committee of Independent Voters for Al Smith, and Director of the National Progressive League for Roosevelt in 1932. After Roosevelt's election, he became general assistant in charge of labor liaison under Harry Hopkins for the Works Progress Administration in 1935. Later he served variously as labor advisor for the War Production Board, and then as Special Assistant for Minority Affairs under both Roosevelt and Harry Truman. Niles was an inconspicuous, tight-lipped man, with a treasured passion for anonymity. During the presidency of Harry Truman he served as the principal White House liaison between the administration and the Jewish community. From the point of view of American Jewry, he was perhaps the most influential Jew in the White House staff (see Chapter XXII).

All these men—Ezekiel, Lubin, Morgenthau, Rosenman, Niles—as well as Ben Cohen, Jerome Frank, Robert Nathan, Anna Rosenberg, and hundreds of other Jews at lower echelons of public service, were ardent exponents of the New Deal philosophy. They were profoundly convinced that the Democratic party was the most effective political vehicle of American progress. Certainly not all American Jews, even those active in government, were liberal in their political convictions. The eminent financier Bernard Baruch, for example, while a registered South Carolina Democrat, was never particularly progressive in his political and social views; yet his services as an industrial mobilization expert were highly valued by Wilson and Roosevelt. There were other Jews, men such as Admiral Lewis Strauss and Judge Cyrus Sulzberger, who were quite active and influential in Republican political circles. Since the days of the New Deal, however, the preponderance of American Jews continued to identify themselves closely with the Democratic party.

It was an identification that persisted long after the Jews had graduated from their "proletarian" status. While their middle-class Christian neighbors demonstrated an unmistakable tendency to vote according to economic self-interest, the Jews were obliged to take other factors into account when they cast their ballots. The factor of political and economic liberalism, for example, represented more than the afterglow of East Side radicalism; more, certainly, than the influence of Jewish "social ethics." As a minority group, the Jews remained sensitive to the strength of racial tensions in America. Those tensions could best be minimized in a healthy economy. Conversely, economic disaffection, the restiveness of labor or small business-men, provided the reactionary and the rabble rouser with an opportunity to exploit group friction. Few Jews had to be reminded that anti-Semitism both in Europe and America was the classical weapon of economic oligarchy. They recognized that the Republicans were no less concerned than the Democrats about the well-being of the national economy and the danger of racial hatreds. They believed, nevertheless, that the Democratic party tradi-tionally evidenced more awareness of the role of government in protecting the national welfare. Because Jews recognized, too, that a narrow nationalism usually brought anti-Semitism in its wake, they preferred to support the more internationalist of the two parties. Thus, from the point of view both of social "conscience" and internationalism, the Democrats seemed to be the safer choice.

By the 1950's, however, one of the most significant developments in American-Jewish life was the growing prosperity of the Jewish middle class, the movement of tens of thousands of Jewish families into the fashionable suburbs of America's cities. As these wealthy businessmen graduated into the higher tax brackets, their economic interest crowded out traditional senti-ment and they were found to be defending a more "Republican" view of political issues. In the presidential election of 1956, as a result, a great many—by no means a majority—of American Jews crossed party lines to vote for the Eisenhower-Nixon ticket. They were convinced that "Eisen-hower Republicanism" would protect their interests as businessmen and they hoped that the party could emancipate itself from its former tradition of laissez-faire economics and isolationism. It seemed likely that this defection would continue, for both parties increasingly borrowed each other's prin-ciples and programs in an effort to capture the independent voter. Yet, as late as 1956, most Jews continued to cast their ballots for Democratic candidates. Whatever the defection of Jewish businessmen to the Re-publican party, by far the larger majority of Jewish voters, "brain trusters," and campaign workers was still to be found in the Democratic camp. The contours of American-Jewish history suggested that the Jewish liberal tradi-tion was less likely to be abandoned than wooed into new and shifting alliances.

ANTI-SEMITISM IN AMERICA

As late as 1880 it did not appear as if the American-Jewish community needed to give more than nominal attention to the problem of anti-Semitism. It was true that a distorted image of Jews existed in many American minds, the image of the German-Jewish peddler with the thick accent, hooked nose, and derby hat. But such a stereotype seemed hardly more offensive than the stage symbol of the drunken Irishman, the chicken-pilfering Negro, or the parsimonious Yankee. The caricature became somewhat less casual a decade later, in the era of the Greenback and Free Silver movements, and the agrarian Populist revolt. During the 1890's the hated money-changer, the manipulator of hard currencies, was often associated with such prominent Jewish financiers as the Levis, the Montefiores, the Rothschilds— or, in America, the Belmonts and the Lehmans. The hard-pressed Protestant farmer did not find it difficult to believe that the Jews were members of a "great international conspiracy" to prevent cheap money from reaching the market, and to keep American farm families in chronic debt. When men like Governor Tom Watson of Georgia and William Jennings Bryan of Nebraska drew attention to the "mysterious, invisible money powers" of the world, they wittingly or unwittingly lent credence to the emergent Jewish stereotype of a "Shylock" or "octopus" of the world's finances. *Caesar's Column,* a Utopian novel written in 1890 by the Populist Ignatius Donnelly, painted a vivid picture of the future domination of Europe by "the Israelites, the great money-getters of the world who rose from dealers in old clothes and peddlers of hats to merchants, to bankers, to princes." The novel's ominous reference to "international Judaism" was lent verification, in some minds, by the Zionist Congress in Basel in 1897.

Yet the attitude toward the Jews of most Americans was, at the worst, merely vague suspicion; men like Donnelly still spoke primarily for the lunatic fringe of American life. The first serious change came with the spectacular growth of America's cities after the turn of the century. The rise of the American "Mammon" was a terrifying phenomenon for Southern and Midwestern farmers, people who found their credit and markets, their very livelihoods, governed by far-off metropolises. Bryan expressed their fear in his description of "Babylon the great, the mother of the harlots and of the abominations of the earth . . . drunken with the blood of the saints, and with the blood of the martyrs of Jesus." The cities were filled with more than harlots and dance halls, however, more than bankers and creditors. After 1900 they were filled with foreigners, with immigrants speaking strange tongues, worshiping the Pope in cathedrals, or denying the Trinity in synagogues. In time, it was primarily the Jew whom rural Americans identified with the city. Returning to the United States in 1907, as civilized and cultivated a person as Henry James could profess shock at the "Hebrew conquest of New York," which, he insisted, was transforming that city into a "new Jerusalem." To rural Americans, every Jewish storekeeper was the advance guard of the new commercial civilization, and bore the standard of the dread forces that threatened their security.

This suspicion was buttressed by a recrudescent race doctrine which made its appearance in the United States early in the twentieth century: the theory that men were divided into biological breeds, each incapable of "wholesome" fusion with the other. In the South the doctrine had long been applied to Negroes, and on the Pacific Coast to Orientals; and now, for the first time, it was applied to the "alien" Slavic-Jewish-Italian "islands" in the East. Prescott Hall and William Z. Ripley professed grave concern that the "Anglo-Saxon breed" was about to be inundated by the "hordes" of the big cities. Their fears were given even more "respectable" literary formulation when the writings of Count de Gobineau and Houston Stewart Chamberlain began to reach the United States. By 1914 increasing numbers of Americans were conditioned to the view that the Jews were as a race apart, members of the "Semitic" as distinguished from the "Aryan" race. Even such distinguished intellectuals as John R. Commons, Edward A. Ross, and Henry Pratt Fairchild misapplied sociological and anthropological terminology to urge that society be structured along sound "eugenic" lines; in this manner, they explained, Anglo-Saxons would avoid admixture with "inferior" breeds. The weird pseudoscience of eugenics was widely popularized by Alfred P. Schultz's *Race or Mongrel?* (1908), and Madison Grant's *The Passing of the Great Race* (1916)—two of the most colorful and effective apologias for Anglo-Saxon superiority. By 1920 an influential minority of Americans had swallowed whole the notion that the "great American race" was in danger of permanent contamination by Negroes, Latins, Slavs, and Jews.

These racist fantasies were intensified by the isolationism and xenophobia that followed the first World War. The high tariffs, the virulent nationalism, the rejuvenated religious Fundamentalism of the 1920's, the revival of Ku Klux Klan terrorization in Catholic and Jewish neighborhoods of the South and Midwest—all were merely the outward manifestations of a deeply rooted fear of contamination by alien ideas. Certainly the most sinister of those imported ideas was "Bolshevism"—or "anarchism" or "syndicalism": they were all of a piece in the mind of the typical provincial American. "Once lead this people into war," Woodrow Wilson had predicted, "and they'll forget there ever was such a thing as tolerance." Wilson's Attorney General, A. Mitchell Palmer, now proceeded to justify this prediction by conducting a series of lawless raids on private houses and labor headquarters, rounding up thousands of aliens, holding them incommunicado, and subjecting them to drumhead interrogations. Even the courts bowed before the wind, construing the wartime Espionage and Sedition Acts with inflexible harshness. It was the age of the Sacco-Vanzetti case, of an unreasoning fear of radicalism, of antipathy to foreigners, and especially of antipathy to Jews, who, after all, came from the land of the Bolshevik Revolution, and who were hardly conservative in their own political and economic orientation.

Into all of these combustible elements there was now dropped an evil little pamphlet which had originally been circulated throughout Eastern Europe and Germany as a calculated means of promoting Jew-hatred. *The Protocols of the Elders of Zion* first appeared in 1905, as an addendum to a hopelessly confused religious tract written by Serge Nilus, a czarist civil servant. According to Nilus, the wise men of Zion had entered into a "secret" plot to enslave the Christian world. The leaders of the Jewish world government, who were variously identified as the chiefs of the twelve tribes of Israel and the leaders of world Zionism, planned to employ the institutions of liberalism and socialism to ensnare and befuddle the simple-minded "goyim." In the event of discovery, the Jewish Elders apparently had made plans for blowing up all the capitals of Europe. The implication was plain: that resistance to liberalism and socialism was vital if the world was to be rescued from a malevolent Jewish conspiracy.

In 1921 the London *Times* exposed the *Protocols* as a crude forgery of a lampoon on Napoleon III, written as far back as 1864. Notwithstanding the exposure, it was in the interest of reactionaries everywhere to promote the circulation of the Nilus pamphlet. In the United States, Boris Brasol, a czarist *émigré,* persuaded a group of American business leaders, among them the motor magnate Henry Ford, to publicize the *Protocols.* Ford was a capable enough automobile manufacturer; but his understanding of world affairs was astonishingly limited, and even more profoundly illiberal and bigoted. For several years his private newspaper, *The Dearborn Independent,* quoted liberally from the *Protocols,* and issued repeated warnings against the "Jewish menace." Not until 1927, when a Jewish attorney, Aaron Sapiro, brought a libel suit against *The Dearborn Independent,* did Ford repudiate his anti-Semitism and issue a public apology.

The confluence of all these factors—American provincialism, rural suspicion of the cities, the eugenics theory, the fear of alien radicalism, even, perhaps, *The Protocols of the Elders of Zion*—had its cumulative impact. It was felt not simply in the steady growth of the Ku Klux Klan, nor even in the anti-immigration legislation of 1921 and 1924 which closed America's doors to the fugitives of southeastern Europe; it was felt, too, in the adoption of nation-wide Jewish "quotas" by colleges and professional societies. In 1922 President Abbott Lawrence Lowell of Harvard gave these quotas "respectability" when he sought openly to introduce them at his own institution. Similarly, medical and law schools began limiting the admission of Jews to a small fractional percentage of the total enrollment. Eventually employment agencies and large corporations adopted the same practice. Soon the exclusionist policy was extended into the field of housing. Through voluntary covenants of real-estate owners, large areas of many cities were abruptly closed to persons of "Hebrew descent."

During the Depression period, anti-Semitism proved to be a ready-made defense for some of the bigoted vested interests that feared "that man" Franklin Roosevelt's sweeping social reforms. A number of demagogic politicians, most of them the hired spokesmen for large industrial concerns, stigmatized the New Deal as the "Jew Deal," and identified trade unionism with "Jewish Bolshevism." Scores of organizations—the Silver Shirts, the Khaki Shirts, the Militant Christian Patriots, the Green Mountain Boys, and others —many of them creations of cranks and rabble rousers, but some of them financed by well-known corporations, drenched the United States with an avalanche of appeals to racial and religious hate. Fingers were pointed at the unusual numbers of Jews in Washington, and especially the Jews close to Roosevelt. Even such respected figures as Theodore Dreiser, Representative Louis T. McFadden of Pennsylvania, the eloquent Catholic priest Father Charles Coughlin of Detroit, the national hero Charles Lindbergh attacked the Jews variously as radicals, international bankers, Reds, materialists, or warmongers.

During the late 1930's American anti-Semitism was given further direction and financial support by Nazi Germany. Hitler's most dependable agents in this campaign were German-Americans, many of them recent immigrants to the United States, veterans of the Kaiser's army, and now ardent partisans of the Third Reich. The Nazi propaganda bureau supplied them with organizational leadership, funds, and endless quantities of uniforms, insignia, and propaganda literature. In 1934 many of America's German culture *vereinen* were reorganized and centralized in the German-American Bund. Under the successive leadership of Heinz Spanknoebel, Fritz Gissible, Fritz Kuhn, and Wilhelm Kunze, the Bund set about popularizing the doctrine of Hitler's New Order. Of course, anti-Semitism was the most convenient propaganda device of all. The Nazis contributed large sums of money to nativist "hate" groups. They shrilled their anti-Semitic slogans at mass meetings in Madison Square Garden and at the Philadelphia Municipal Stadium. Anti-Semitic literature was distributed to the American team as it departed for the Berlin Olympic Games in 1936. German-born professors frequently served as Nazi agents on university campuses.

Despite the many sewers from which the filth flowed, it is doubtful if the systematic "hate" campaign made a significant impact except on those who were already inclined to anti-Semitism. For the most part, the coverage given by the American press to Nazi barbarism in Europe effectively counteracted the efforts of paid German propagandists in America. It was, in fact, the appropriation of the anti-Semitic movement by the Nazis which ultimately doomed organized Jew-hatred in the United States. When America went to war against Hitler, anti-Semitism at last became clearly identified in the public mind with an alien and subversive ideology. After 1945, organized American anti-Semitism made little significant headway. For one thing, the economic boom of the postwar era left few racial tensions for hate groups to exploit. Most Americans, too, were deeply moved by the courageous struggle of the Jews, as "underdogs," to win Statehood for themselves in Israel. They were impressed by Israeli military valor, and by the new Israeli Republic's devotion to the democratic way of life. Moreover, the rise of a Jewish sovereign State endowed the Jews with standing in the eyes of the Christian world; they were no longer "gypsies," begging crumbs of hospitality from others. The B'nai B'rith Anti-Defamation League was able to report, in 1950, that anti-Semitism in America had fallen to an "all-time" low. Yet it is doubtful if Jew-hatred, even at its peak, was ever a major threat to the essential security of the Jewish community in the United States. The problem was rather one of Jewish social acceptance—the opportunity of Jews to gain entrance to colleges, legal and professional societies, restricted areas of employment, exclusive neighborhoods. These were unfortunate survivals which were not to be easily eliminated even with the lifting of depression or the termination of war. But they were mainly in the category of irritants. They were not really an overwhelming menace to the security of the American-Jewish community.

JEWISH LIFE AT MID-CENTURY

By mid-twentieth century the basic contours of American-Jewish economic life were becoming clear. The Jews remained an urban people: not merely urban, indeed, but metropolitan. Sixty-five per cent of America's 5,200,000 Jews were still to be found in New York, Chicago, Los Angeles, Philadelphia, Boston, and Miami Beach. This was a higher percentage of urbanization, certainly of metropolitanization, than could be found among any other ethnic group in the United States. Most of the remaining 35 per cent were located in cities of intermediate size. The "small-town" Jews, perhaps 150,000 in 1950, were disappearing rapidly, moving into—or being absorbed by—larger urban areas.

But while the demographic patterns were not changing, the economic patterns were. If the preoccupation with political and economic liberalism was one basic concern of Jewish life in the New World, the unremitting struggle for economic security was another. It was the driving passion of every Jewish immigrant family to rise above proletarian levels, to afford a more fashionable neighborhood, to belong to a socially more "acceptable" synagogue, to marry children into a better economic and social stratum. By mid-century the transformations in the social structure were impressive and significant.

With the end of mass Jewish immigration and the rise of the second generation of Russian Jews in America, the percentage of Jews involved in physical labor, in the needle trades, for example, began to decline markedly. As early as 1930, for that matter, the "Jewish" unions of the garment district had ceased to be predominantly Jewish; by 1957 they were largely Italian and Puerto Rican. In the biggest cities, particularly in New York and Chicago, there were still large numbers of Jewish garment workers to be found, together with Jewish glaziers, painters, and plumbers, and cigar makers. But by the 1950's these vocations encompassed a far greater percentage of non-Jews. Ever-increasing numbers of Jews were becoming white-collar workers, independent proprietors, and professional men; no less than 60 per cent of the Jewish population in large cities were business or professional people, and the proportion rose steadily in the smaller cities. In the middle-sized and smaller cities of America, Jews not only were heavily concentrated in small businesses, but small businesses frequently were concentrated in Jewish hands. In a typical "middle-sized" city such as New Haven, Connecticut, over 50 per cent of the town's small business was owned by Jews; yet only 15 per cent of the town's population was Jewish.

It was now possible to make a few generalizations about trades and industries in which Jews played an important role. Scrap iron and steel was a billion-dollar business by the end of the second World War, providing the steel foundries with half their metal requirements; 90 per cent of the industry was owned by Jews. After all, they had generations of experience behind them in the junk and scrap businesses of Europe, livelihoods that traditionally had been outside guild jurisdiction. As a scrap collector in

America, moreover, the immigrant was able to keep his own hours and holidays, and could transact business with a minimum of proficiency in the English language. In 1950 the largest scrap companies in the United States—Luria Brothers of Philadelphia, Hyman Michaels of Chicago, Luntz Iron and Steel of Canton, Ohio—were all Jewish owned. The traditional Jewish association with the clothing industry remained, too, but increasingly on an entrepreneurial basis. In the production of men's and women's apparel—in its final stages of cutting and sewing, not of textile spinning—in the production of underwear and lingerie, Jewish control was virtually absolute. The fur industry was 95 per cent Jewish; the shoe-and-boot industry, 40 per cent.

As in Europe, Jews were heavily concentrated in tobacco buying; they owned three of the four leading cigar-manufacturing concerns, including Fred Hirschhorn's General Cigar Company which manufactured every seventh cigar smoked in the United States. In cigarettes, on the other hand, Jewish interests were confined to P. Lorillard and Company. As for the liquor industry, long an area of Jewish concentration in Europe, nearly half the main distilling concerns of North America were Jewish, including Schenley and Seagram. In retailing, at least 90 per cent of the apparel-store chains were Jewish; and in New York City most of the department stores were Jewish owned—including Macy's, Gimbels, Abraham and Straus, Bloomingdale's, and Hearn's. Farther West, the proportion of Jewish-owned department stores was much smaller. Such chains as May, Allied, Interstate, and Saks Fifth Avenue (a subsidiary of Gimbels) were Jewish; but the five-and-ten-cent-store chains such as Woolworth and Kresge were not. In the food-and-grocery field where the greatest number of chain stores operated, only 15 per cent were Jewish—although there is evidence that this proportion is increasing as Jews move into the supermarket area. In the mail-order field, the mammoth firm of Sears Roebuck and Company was the creation of Julius Rosenwald; but by mid-century the family possessed only a minority of the company's stock. And yet, while Jews owned only a small proportion of America's retail establishments, American Jewry produced a higher proportion of retail proprietors—perhaps 35 per cent—than any other ethnic group in America.

The Jews made one of their most enduring contributions to the economic and cultural life of the United States in the field of general entertainment. It was a contribution which included scores of distinguished Jewish playwrights and composers, among them Elmer Rice, George S. Kaufman, Moss Hart, Lillian Hellman, Sidney Kingsley, Edna Ferber, Clifford Odets, Sam and Bella Spewack, Arthur Miller, George Gershwin, Irving Berlin, Rodgers and Hammerstein, and Lorenz Hart. It encompassed, as well, many celebrated Jewish actors and actresses, and a powerful group of producers and entrepreneurs who literally transformed Broadway and Hollywood into major institutions of American life. The business organization of the legitimate theater in America was the exclusive accomplishment of a handful of Jewish producers: Abraham Erlanger, Marc Klaw, Charles and Daniel Frohman, David Belasco, and Sam, Lee, and J. J. Shubert—men who, in the aggregate, owned most of the theaters on Broadway and produced the vast majority of its plays. No complete statistics have been compiled on the number of Jews who own or manage the various night clubs and cabarets in America's larger cities; but there is little doubt that this number totals well over 50 per cent.

The motion picture industry was pioneered almost entirely by Jews. In 1903, Adolf Zukor began producing films in New York for use in the penny arcades that he owned jointly with Marcus Loew. A few years later, Jesse L. Lasky, who had formerly been a vaudeville manager, entered the motion picture business in partnership with his brother-in-law, Samuel Goldfish— or, as he became known later, Samuel Goldwyn. Lasky and Goldwyn opened the first film studios in Hollywood and produced America's earliest full-length motion picture. In 1914 the Lasky-Zukor enterprises merged as Paramount-Famous Players-Lasky, and then as Paramount Pictures. Later other firms were founded under Jewish auspices: Universal (Carl Laemmle), Twentieth Century-Fox (Sol Brill and William Fox), Metro-Goldwyn-Mayer (Marcus Loew, Louis B. Mayer, Samuel Goldwyn), Warner Brothers, Columbia Pictures (Jack and Harry Cohn), United Artists (Al Lichtman).

Motion pictures were by no means America's largest "Jewish" industry. Textiles, scrap iron, shoes, retail clothing—all represented a much more substantial capital investment. All played a much more basic role in the functioning of the American economy. But no industry, Jewish or non-Jewish, exerted so profound an influence on American cultural life; for the movies shaped—even more than they reflected—the mores of the American people. Three generations of Americans patterned their social and sexual lives after the heroes and heroines of the silver screen. In the movie emporium, farmers, factory workers, and shop girls found recreation and escape from the drudgeries of the workday. The wonders of ancient history and foreign civilizations were reproduced on the screen for the isolated citizens of the smallest country towns. The Jewish pioneers of the film industry had "inherited" no genius for entertainment. They were businessmen who happened to be operating a handful of vaudeville houses and nickelodeon parlors because such buildings rented cheaply. The talent of these men lay in the speed with which they were able suddenly to sense and answer the public's long-neglected need for "escapism." It was a talent conditioned by the identical circumstances that had made Jews the mercantile pioneers of modern Europe: adaptability, the result of freedom from the inhibitions of archaic business traditions; and the passion of the ghetto dweller—in this case the immigrant—for economic security and independence. With the recent incorporation of most of Hollywood's major film companies the controlling interest passed from Jewish hands. Even then, however, fully 40 per cent of the film industry's personnel, its writers, musical directors, producers, and technicians, continued to be Jewish. Jewish influence in the radio and television industry was no less notable. The Columbia Broadcasting System, the National Broadcasting Company, and the American Broadcasting Company were all controlled by Jews—William Paley, David Sarnoff, and Leonard Goldenson.

Another significant development in American-Jewish life after the 1920's was the marked increase in the number of Jewish professional people, often as high as 15 per cent of the Jewish population in some middle-sized and smaller cities. This was a striking proportion in view of the difficulty encountered by Jews in entering medical, dental, or law schools. Yet more than the traditional Jewish respect for intellectual discipline was responsible for attracting the young people into professional training. The professions required little initial capital, and they offered self-employment and comparative freedom from anti-Semitic discrimination. The vision of a son becoming a doctor or a lawyer kept many a Jewish parent unwearyingly at the needle or the cutting machine, and the hardships of the daily routine were more patiently borne. So many Jews now achieved distinction in professional life that each new honor or appointment no longer created a sensation. Three Jews—Louis Brandeis, Benjamin Cardozo, and Felix Frankfurter—were appointed to the Supreme Court, and countless other Jews served on lower Federal courts, on state supreme and divisional courts, on municipal courts, as chairmen and as members of innumerable administrative and arbitration commissions. Medicine produced large numbers of brilliant researchers: Jacobi, Sulzberger, Waksman, Salk—to mention only the smallest proportion of the truly great. There were, in addition, many hundreds of Jewish medical professors, as well as tens of thousands of outstanding practitioners. Among the country's most eminent philosophers were Felix Adler, Morris R. Cohen, and Irwin Edman; among the social scientists were I. A. Hourwitch, E. R. A. Seligman, Franz Boas, Charles Gross, and David Riesman. The world of journalism produced Joseph Pulitzer, Adolph S. Ochs, Walter Lippmann, and Raymond Clapper. In the musical field there were hundreds upon hundreds of Jewish instrumentalists who staffed the country's orchestras, who achieved fame as artists on the concert stage or as distinguished conductors.

By 1957, perhaps the most characteristic feature of the economic pyramid was the narrowness of its base: the paucity of Jewish unskilled workers or farmers. Conversely, some 20 per cent of America's 9,000 millionaires were Jews. These latter were rarely multimillionaires, however, for they were little involved in the key capital industries—coal, steel, banking, oil, automobiles, shipping, transportation—that produced America's staggering fortunes. Most American Jews were to be found neither among the very rich nor among the very poor, but rather in the "middle" middle class. It was a respectable status; as "typical" American businessmen they had come a long way. Hardly more than half a century had passed since their parents and grandparents had arrived at Ellis Island with just the clothes on their back and little more. No immigrant people had ever responded to opportunity with more willingness or resourcefulness; no ethnic group had ever proved itself less "likely to become a public charge."

CONCLUSION

It was a Jewish community on the move. The immigrant grandparents had made the big jump over the water and settled in the slum neighborhoods of New York, Chicago, and other populous cities. As opportunities improved, the newcomers, Jews and Christians alike, moved on again, traveling from the East Side to the West Side of Manhattan or to the Bronx, from Brownsville to Flatbush—or perhaps to Long Island. Like their non-Jewish neighbors, they rented two-family houses or triple-decker flats. And soon the second generation, the children of the immigrants, or, increasingly, the third generation, the grandchildren of the immigrants, reached out for suburban areas where there were lawns, grass, trees, and, above all, space. Each city had its well-defined Jewish neighborhoods; the original settlement points, only sparsely inhabited now by the very poor, or the very Orthodox (usually both); the Jewish Bohemia, more shabby than picturesque; the Jewish middle-class area; and the new Jewish suburbs.

The Jews who lived in the newer neighborhoods remained, for the most part, politically liberal—even if they voted occasionally for a Republican candidate. But their private lives were quite conservative, even staid, anchored in middle-class morality. They were middle class, too, in their pleasures and relaxations, their B'nai B'rith or Temple Sisterhood membership, their love of a friendly game of pinochle or gin rummy, their fondness for trips to the seashore in the summer, their appreciation of comfort and the good life. David Riesman has suggested that Jews were among the pioneers of "comfortable" living because their adaptation to metropolitan status was never "internalized": that is, few Jews learned to substitute a devotion to vocation for a devotion to family. Thus, they were prepared, somewhat in advance of other groups, for the general shift of urban America toward leisure-minded rather than work-minded attitudes. It might also be added that, with newly won security, they were determined to enjoy the fruits of their labor. In their emphasis upon the "good things," the good "material things," American Jewry had largely abandoned both the fervor of the old radical tradition and the fervor of the old religious tradition. They were increasingly willing to settle for the practical advantages of the *status quo*.

Notes

Page 328. Quotation from Morris R. Cohen, *Reflections of a Wondering Jew*, pp. 32-33.

Page 332. Quotation from Morris Freedman, "The Jewish College Student: New Model," in Eliot Cohen (ed.), *Commentary on the American Scene.*

Page 338. The best available account of the development of American anti-Semitism is to be found in Oscar Handlin, *Adventure in Freedom.*

Page 347. David Reisman expresses his theory in his introduction to Eliot Cohen, *op. cit.*

XVII

The Jews of Eastern Europe

Between the Wars

RUSSIA: THE TRAUMA OF "COLLECTIVIZATION"

It is virtually impossible to study the history of the Jews from the May Laws to the rise of Adolf Hitler without detecting a kind of Greek prelusiveness in the unfolding course of events. In Eastern Europe, particularly, it was as if each new horror was merely a rehearsal for tragedy to come. Physical pogroms may have ended with the triumph of the Red armies in 1921; but in the successor-states, systematic "cold" pogroms, in the form of economic discrimination, laid the groundwork for the dehumanization of the Nazi period. Even in Russia, as we shall see, economic and political standardization were merely the overture to spiritual and cultural slavery.

After the Bolsheviks assumed power in 1917, they set about implementing Lenin's motto—"Bread, Peace, and Land"—as quickly and as thoroughly as possible. Peace, albeit an ignominious one, was secured by the Treaty of Brest-Litovsk. Vast areas of land, too, were confiscated and communalized into collective settlements. Factories were sequestered by tough little soviets of workers, soldiers, and Communist bureaucrats. It was perhaps the reckless speed of this collectivization which accounted for the dreadful economic paralysis of 1920. Throughout Russia factories closed down for lack of raw materials; market stalls were boarded up for lack of food. Finally, in 1922, Lenin was compelled to compromise with harsh reality by returning, in the New Economic Policy, to a kind of quasi capitalism. Goods and staples began once again to circulate, although not before hundreds of thousands of Russians had starved to death in the famines of 1921-22. For nearly five years the members of the Bolshevik inner council were obliged to "co-exist" with capitalism in the NEP. It was not, in fact, until 1927 that they were sufficiently emboldened to launch a new drive toward a truly Communist economy; it was then that the Soviet planners devised a crash program for industrializing Russia within half a decade. Industrialization, they expected, would create the mass proletariat required by the Communist

348

regime for its base of power. The birth trauma of the Five Year Plan, from 1928 to 1933, was, in fact, responsible for a notable enlargement of Russian industrial capacity. But it postponed, too, most of the pleasures and amenities, the leisures and little freedoms that made life meaningful.

The Jews were hardly less affected by these developments than other citizens of the Soviet regime. After the World War, some 2,500,000 Jews remained in postwar Russia. The other 3,500,000, who had formerly been citizens of the Czarist Empire, now were parceled out among half a dozen successor states. The majority of Russian Jews continued to live in the Ukraine and White Russia, the territory which had once been part of the Pale of Settlement. At the same time the official abolition of the Pale, which was one of the Soviet regime's first acts, permitted many thousands of Jews, perhaps 750,000 by 1939, to move into the cities of the Russian interior. Movement inland relieved some of the economic pressure on Russian Jewry, but hardly enough to compensate for the inevitable tragedy of Communist displacement. Perhaps 400,000 Jews found employment in the Soviet bureaucracy, and another 750,000 in factories and in other varieties of industrial labor. But this absorption still left nearly 1,000,000 bewildered petty tradesmen and artisans who now found themselves even more "economically superfluous" than they had been in czarist times. The transition to proletarian life was eased somewhat by Lenin's New Economic Policy; but even during the NEP period of qualified capitalism, fully a third of a million Jews remained economically unclassifiable. Many of them eked out a meager existence as part-time stocking-weavers, as peddlers, or as mendicants living on the dole of the Joint Distribution Committee. As late as 1926 70 per cent of their children suffered from tuberculosis, while unnumbered thousands of others perished altogether.

The Soviet bureaucracy recognized that the plight of this minority people was not the result of Jewish laziness or ineptitude; it was the consequence, rather, of years of economic disability under the czars. A group of state officials, led by President Kalinin, decided, therefore, to make special provisions for Jewish resettlement. They requisitioned large fertile tracts of land in the Ukraine, in the Crimea, and urged Jews to settle there on a collective basis. Kalinin gave his personal assurance that all Jewish farmers would receive the fullest possible government co-operation; and unlike the czarist officials of the nineteenth century, he meant what he said. When Kalinin broached his idea to representatives of the Joint Distribution Committee, the German *Hilfsverein,* the ICA, and other Western Jewish philanthropic agencies, they immediately threw their support behind the agricultural resettlement plan, offering all reasonable help in funds and equipment.

The Jewish response to these offers was not unenthusiastic. Under the leadership of an aggressive, bullnecked Jewish agriculturist, one Lurie-Larin, Jewish collective farm settlements were established both in the Ukraine and Crimea. By 1935, indeed, there were no less than fifty such settlements in the Crimea alone; and perhaps twice that many in the Ukraine. With the help both of the government and of the Agro-Joint, the agricultural branch of the Joint Distribution Committee, these Jewish settlers became solid, reliable farmers. Their dairy farms, particularly, were among the best in Russia—frequently winning state prizes for quality of production. And yet, while the back-to-the-soil movement proved successful for those Jews who actually became farmers, the urban traditions of centuries were not so easily abandoned. As late as 1939 no more than 175,000 had settled on the soil in Russia—at best a small proportion of the Russian-Jewish population.

The Five Year Plan was responsible for a much more significant revolution in Jewish life. The immense project of industrializing backward Russia within a few decades absorbed the energies of hundreds of thousands of Jews. The Jewish tailor went down into the mines; the shoemaker found his way to the unexplored timber regions; the petty tradesman tasted the rigors of frontier life in the oil fields. In the metal factories of Dnepropetrovsk alone, 10,000 young Jews labored to prepare the fabricated sections of the giant new hydroelectric dam. The industrial cities of Magnitogorsk and Kuznetskstroi were built under the supervision of Jewish engineers and technicians; while several thousand Jewish workers could be found in the plants and on the girders. By 1930, only two years after the launching of the Five Year Plan, more Jews were employed in the metal industries than in the traditionally Jewish needle and leather trades. By the end of the Five Year Plan, in 1932, 750,000 Jews were absorbed in the mighty industrial effort, treading the causeways of dams, hammering rivets in steel beams, working jackhammers in coal mines. Jews by the thousands had been manual laborers long before the Soviets came to power; but that labor had been artisanry as much as factory work. Now, for the first time, most Jewish workers had become proletarians working with machines in the factories and mines, and working, too, for state wages.

From the point of view of the Jews themselves, the most gratifying Soviet achievement, initially, was the government assault on organized anti-Semitism. During the 1920's the Reds associated this curse of the czarist days with the counterrevolution, and made anti-Semitic violence a capital offense, punishable by death or long imprisonment. Nor did Soviet officials confine their strictures against Jew-hatred to legal penalties. An assiduous Soviet program of education was launched to root out all symptoms of anti-Semitism from the army, from the factories, and from the countryside. From time to time there were poster campaigns during elections, which called upon loyal Communists to "fight ignorance, alcoholism, and anti-Semitism." Examples were made of those who were arrested for anti-Semitic activity. Widest publicity, even to the extent of national radio hookups, was given their trials. As the years passed, however, and as Joseph Stalin consolidated his power in Russia, disturbing symptoms of government-sponsored anti-Semitism made their appearance once again. The purge trials of the 1930's, for example, which ended in the imprisonment or execution of such prominent Jewish Communists as Radek, Zinoviev, and Kamenev, produced a significant revival of thinly disguised Jew-hatred—as if to insure public support for the Party's destruction of its pioneer Old Guard. In certain key industries and government bureaus discrimination against Jews became quite common. But at no time before World War II was this anti-Semitic revival of sufficient proportions or endurance to jeopardize Jewish security. It was only after the Nazi invasion, ironically, that official anti-Semitism became sufficiently overt to cause serious concern among Russian Jewry.

THE DISSOLUTION OF JEWISH COMMUNITY LIFE

By creating a Union of Soviet Socialist Republics in 1922, Lenin and his followers evidenced their willingness to placate the nationalist sensibilities of the Ukrainians, the Uzbeks, the Georgians, and others of Russia's minority peoples. Nevertheless, the concept of national self-determination was anathema to the ideologues of Communism, and was discouraged whenever possible. When, therefore, Jewish Bundist leaders requested that communal autonomy be extended to the Jews, they were rejected out of hand. For the sake of convenience, the Soviet government did establish a special Jewish section of the Bolshevik party, the *Yevsektsia*—but merely as a kind of ideological instrument with which to enlist the Jewish masses in the cause of the Revolution. A Commissariat for Jewish National Affairs was also established under the direction of Semin M. Dimanshtein, to govern the Jewish community until the Jews were completely integrated into Russian life.

Dimanshtein, an old Bolshevik, found his task to be much more difficult than he had originally anticipated. Most of the Jewish Bolsheviks whom he recruited to serve on his staff could not even speak Yiddish, much less edit the Yiddish newspapers that were needed as propaganda organs. Their ignorance of Jewish life led them into egregious errors: e.g., serving pork products in a Jewish home for the aged, thereby starving the inmates to death; provoking suicides in Jewish hospitals by failing to provide religious facilities for the devout. Soon Dimanshtein abandoned the technique of gradualism altogether. He summarily abolished all Jewish political parties and independent organizations, and nationalized Jewish orphan and old folks' homes, hospitals, and libraries. Once this was accomplished, by the mid-twenties, both the Jewish Commissariat and the *Yevsektsia* were dissolved, and the separate Jewish community, which had withstood the most determined assaults of the Romanovs for a century and a quarter, virtually ceased to exist.

Whatever their dislike of minority nationalism, the Communists were not unwilling for the various minority peoples to use their own languages as vernaculars and as vehicles of literary expression. Because of its antinationalist dogmas, Communism could hardly idealize Russian at the expense of other tongues, especially when they were employed as instruments of Communist ideology. The Jews, too, were permitted to use their native language, which was judged to be Yiddish. Hebrew was identified with Zionism and bourgeois imperialism; while "proletarian" Yiddish was rooted in the folk aspirations of the working masses. Large numbers of Jewish schools were established in the Ukraine and White Russia during the 1920's; and while the curriculum of these institutions was strictly secular, the language was Yiddish. In areas with large Jewish populations—again, primarily in the Ukraine and White Russia—Yiddish was used as the official language of the courts, and the newspapers, journals, and scholarly magazines were usually published in Yiddish. In the Jewish agricultural colonies, secular Yiddish culture was actively encouraged by the government. For a while there was a brief renaissance of Yiddish literary creativity which manifested itself most notably in the field of drama. A product of the twentieth century, the Jewish theater had scarcely grown beyond the experimental stage when the Soviets suddenly furnished it with unprecedented quantities of technical resources. After all, it was free from any counterrevolutionary political blemish, and met with full acceptance as a vehicle of pro-Soviet culture.

Yet the material which emerged from the multitude of Yiddish theaters, newspapers, journals, and libraries was pathetically stereotyped, drained of any real originality or Jewish feeling. The theme was usually related to tractors and wheat fields and the glories of the Five Year Plan. Young Alexander Bezymenski, a well-known Russian-Jewish poet of the 1920's, could write, typically:

> You know? I'm happy that I live
> My Days recruited in the ranks of struggle
> and love, anger, pain and laughter.
> Like my brothers of the Komsomol I love,
> All things are dear to me,
> Deeds and men, Days and Years
> The timid walk the livelier pace
> Of my fields and factories.

Eventually the single-minded concentration on the goal of collectivization, and the equivalent lapse of interest in Jewish cultural and spiritual values, doomed even Yiddish as the language of the Jewish people. By 1939 it was spoken by less than a quarter of Russian Jewry.

In view of Communism's hostile attitude toward Jewish nationalism, it seemed at first rather surprising that the Soviet government should have attempted to create a Jewish Autonomous Region in Eastern Russia. But here again, as in its encouragement of the Yiddish language, the Communist leadership had its own ulterior motives. In 1926 Soviet officials had become quite concerned over the infiltration of Chinese into the province of Birobijan, just north of Manchuria across the Amur River. It was a matter of some urgency for the Soviet regime to create a buffer state there in the event of a Far Eastern war. While Birobijan was rich in timber and mineral resources, its climate was exceptionally harsh, and few Russians could be induced to brave its severity. Perhaps, however, under the guise of "national autonomy," large numbers of Russian Jews could be persuaded to settle there.

The plan may have had intrinsic validity but its implementation was hardly less clumsy than earlier czarist projects for Jewish relocation. No arrangements were made for sheltering the settlers or for assigning land to them on other than a communal basis. Most of the Jews who arrived between 1927 and 1939 were unable to endure the rigorous climate. Some went back, while others hung about the market areas of Tikhon'kaya (Birobijan City) and Vladivostok, and drifted once again into petty trade. By 1939 the total Jewish population of Birobijan was only 20,000, less than 1 per cent of the Jewish population of Russia. Some of the Jews persisted and became successful as farmers; in fact, by the eve of the second World War, there were some 70 collective farm settlements in the district. Presumably they were proud of the "official" status of autonomy which was granted them. Soviet press releases intended for Jewish consumption abroad described Jewish life in Birobijan in the most glowing terms. Nevertheless, in the light of the very meager results, Jews and Soviet officials alike recognized that the project had failed.

One of the most melancholy facts of Jewish life under the Soviets was the persistent Communist assault on Jewish religious loyalties. In Soviet Russia all religious groups were treated with equal contempt and derision; but the Jews were the most unfortunate victims because religion was the last citadel of their ethnic separatism. While religious observance was never officially prohibited for Russian or Jew, both the church and the synagogue were deprived of their time-hallowed jurisdiction over education and philanthropy. The Jewish parochial school system was abolished. When synagogues fell into disrepair, they could not be repaired. Cemeteries were converted into parks or used as the sites of public buildings. As new proletarian calendars came into use, the Sabbath and other Jewish festivals were abolished. Bibles were smoked up as cigarette paper. The League of Militant Atheists vowed to "dethrone the heavenly czars as we have dethroned the earthly ones," and circulated its propaganda through newspaper and schoolroom. In 1932 a central antireligious museum in Moscow opened a special Jewish department, satirizing the "stupidities" of Judaism. As a rule, it was the vindictive Jewish Communists who went to the most cunning extremes—preparing public banquets on Yom Kippur, conducting mock trials of "bourgeois" Jewish patriarchs during the Passover Seder—to demonstrate their contempt for the "superstition" of Jewish practices.

As an entire generation of young people grew up in this rabidly atheistic environment, Jewish religious loyalties faded rapidly. Some of the harshest antireligious legislation was repealed in 1934 and 1936; but by then the Reds could afford to be confident, believing—correctly for the most part—that the new generation had been completely "emancipated" from religion. With their ethnic individuality under assault, their cultural and religious loyalties ridiculed and largely destroyed, the Jews were in many ways more to be pitied than in the days of the czar. They were no longer persecuted as Jews—not, at least, before World War II; but as the generations went by, the historic beliefs and traditions that had made life meaningful to them were gradually dissipated. There were some notable exceptions to this trend as late as 1957; clandestine Jewish religious education was never eradicated, and many young Russian-born Jews retained their Orthodoxy. For the most part, however, whatever feeling for tradition still persisted was more in the nature of folk nostalgia. What had once been the most fecund Jewish community in modern times now dropped out of the mainstream of creative Jewish civilization.

THE STRUGGLE FOR MINORITY RIGHTS IN EASTERN EUROPE

The Paris Peace Conference detached almost 100,000,000 people from the great prewar empires. But in redrawing the maps of Europe the peace-makers found it impossible to dispose of the compact minority groups—some twenty to twenty-four million people in Central and Eastern Europe. Terrified at the thought of living among alien majorities, most of these minority peoples were determined to win legal guarantees for themselves and also, if possible, the coveted rights of national autonomy. For the Jews such rights were critical; without them they were doomed to permanent minority status wherever they lived, and they had no recourse to the protection of a neighboring "brother" state in the event of persecution.

The Jews of Eastern Europe were in no position to fight for the precious boon of self-determination. They were weak, divided, and such earlier programs as projected by the Bundists had been smothered to death by the World War and the Bolshevik Revolution. The initiative in battling for Jewish "national" rights came, instead, from the East European Jews of America, close to their kinsmen abroad and remembering well the cultural aspirations of the communities they left behind on European soil. The American-Jewish delegation at the Paris Peace Conference laid siege to the Allied plenipotentiaries. Such distinguished Jewish spokesmen as Louis Marshall, Stephen Wise, and Julian Mack were in continual contact with President Wilson and Colonel House, and their testimony on behalf of their fellow Jews was eloquent and persuasive. Jews living in backward successor-states, they insisted, had a right to receive legal guarantees of physical safety; they had a historic right; too, to their own school systems, to the legal recognition of their own national language, and to their own state-subsidized community institutions. The American Peace Delegation was inclined to sympathize with this view. Professor A. C. Coolidge assured Wilson that guarantees for Jewish national rights were entirely consonant with the American doctrine of self-determination. Once Wilson was convinced, it was not difficult to win the support of other Allied delegations. By December 1919, a Special Minorities Committee of the Council of Four had formulated the basic provisions of such guarantees.

It was one thing, however, to write the guarantees, but quite another to persuade the successor-states to accept them. The Romanian, Polish, and Yugoslavian delegations put up a bitter and stubborn battle, protesting that they would compromise their sovereignty by creating autonomous enclaves of minority peoples within their midst. The proponents of guarantees pointed out, in response, that special school systems and language rights in no sense implied minority disloyalty. Moreover, the long history of festering nationalism in the successor-states, the certainty that its consequences were no longer predictable, was additional evidence that the minority peoples required assurances of physical and cultural protection. Eventually, biting nails, the Poles, Romanians, Hungarians, Estonians, Lithuanians, and Turks agreed to sign the guarantees; for the Allies made their agreement a firm condition precedent to the recognition of successor-state sovereignty.

The minority peoples were at last guaranteed full legal and civil equality. They were guaranteed, as well, the use of their own languages in the courts; adequate facilities for primary education; the establishment of religious and welfare institutions, schools, and other educational facilities under their own control, as well as an equitable proportion of state and communal expenditures as a subsidy for these institutions. The Jews were deeply gratified by these assurances, for specific and unmistakable references to them had been written into the Romanian and Polish treaties. It was apparent that the diplomats at Paris had been thoroughly apprised of the intensity of Polish and Romanian anti-Semitism. In the Romanian treaty, for example, a clause provided that Romania "undertakes to recognize as Romanian nationals, ipso facto and without the requirement of any formality, Jews inhabiting any Romanian territory, who do not possess another nationality." The Polish treaty was no less explicit in guaranteeing the scrupulous protection of Jewish equality before the law. Both treaties, moreover, recognized Yiddish as an "official" language, and authorized the use of public funds for the support of Jewish school systems and public welfare institutions.

The Jews of Eastern Europe had long lived as a separate nation within a nation; but now their status as a separate nationality was recognized officially, as a matter of international law. This was perhaps the first unequivocal admission by Jews and Christians alike that the National Affirmation—the Napoleonic Sanhedrin's declaration of citizenship—had no relevance in the areas where most Jews lived. Given such an admission, it became a matter of some urgency to make provision for effective international protection. The Jews of America and Western Europe, together with the Allied statesmen at Paris, were convinced that they had succeeded in doing this. But they were tragically mistaken. There was the matter of enforcement of the Minority Treaties. No provision had been made for that.

POLAND: SUCCESSOR-STATE NATIONALISM

One of the authentic miracles of modern European history was the rebirth of the Polish state a century and a half after its destruction by the rapacious empires of the East. The Allies took cognizance of the sufferings, the courage, the endurance of the Polish people by insuring that Poland reborn should be provided with every possible advantage as she embarked upon her newly won sovereignty. Awarded vast expanses of Ukrainian, German, and White Russian territories, independent Poland emerged from the Paris Peace Conference as the fifth largest state in Europe. But if Poland acquired new territory, she also inherited the people who lived there: no less than 11,000,000 non-Polish people, including 6,000,000 Ukrainians and White Russians, 1,000,000 Germans—and more than 3,000,000 Jews.

At first, the minority guarantees seemed to the non-Polish groups to offer evidence of Polish good will. But 19,000,000 "racial" Poles regarded their huge inheritance of "foreigners"—many of whom had lived in the land for centuries—with anything but good will. Poland's frontiers, endowed with few natural defenses, were threatened by enemies on all sides, especially by Russia and Germany. From the crusading Soviets the cry was heard: "The emancipated workers know no historical frontiers"; from sullen, humiliated Germany came the echo: "Blood knows no state boundaries." Few Polish statesmen went to sleep at night without the thought that the partitions of the eighteenth century might some day be repeated, and that the huge minority populations might be the secret instruments of such partitions. It was fear, therefore, even more than hatred, which led Poland into a policy of repression, of applying to her minority peoples the same galling discriminations from which she, herself, had suffered for centuries.

It was not long before 3,000,000 Jews of Poland learned that the change of political jurisdictions meant little more than a transfer from one variety of tyranny to another. Their first encounter with postwar Polish nationalism took place under the most tragic of circumstances. In 1920 the Polish warrior hero, Pilsudski, taking advantage of Soviet Russia's civil wars, launched an ambitious invasion of the Ukraine, and penetrated as far as the Ukrainian capital of Kiev. The Soviets counterattacked briefly, but their offensive was quickly smashed, and the Polish armies, with French assistance, forced the Russians to peace terms. By the Treaty of Riga of March 1921, the Poles carved out for themselves perhaps a third of the vast Ukrainian hinterland. It was during the course of this invasion that the Polish armies moved through areas thickly populated by Ukrainian Jews. The Poles bore little affection for these unfortunate people. The typical Polish peasant-soldier, ardently—even fanatically—Catholic, had been weaned on anti-Jewish folk legends. His hatred was fanned when he identified the Jew with the Bolshevik regime. Moreover, the Poles realized that these poor caftaned wretches, with their long beards and earlocks, their strange alien jargon and religion, were prospective citizens of the new Poland; if fewer of these Jews survived the inevitable hardships of war, there would be fewer to plague the new Polish regime.

In their advance and retreat, the Polish armies laid waste Jewish communities that had already been thoroughly demoralized by the peasant bands of Petlura and by the czarist regulars of Denikin. As a rule, the Poles stormed Jewish neighborhoods exactly as if they were military objectives—shelling houses, setting fire to shops, lining up Jewish captives and systematically machine-gunning them to death. Perhaps thirty thousand Jews were killed by Pilsudski's armies; and tens of thousands were wounded and violated. The mass murders ended only after the Allies threatened to intervene. As it developed, the Ukrainian expedition was an augury of the hostility with which all Jews, even those in integral Poland, were to be dealt. Sporadic rioting continued for two more years after the organized killing had stopped. During the Polish elections in the summer of 1922, Jews in Warsaw and Lodz hardly dared to appear on the streets. Anti-Semitic societies circulated incendiary literature, persistently identifying the Jews with godless Bolshevism. Occasional pogroms erupted in crowded Jewish neighborhoods.

Most of Poland's minority peoples possessed reserve strength and were able to resist occasional harassment, for they had powerful "brother" states near by to intercede for them. But the Jews had no one, and the Poles were quite aware of their helplessness. As a result, the Polish government cynically began to reduce its subsidies to the Jewish school and welfare system. Shortly thereafter, in 1923, the government devised the "cold pogrom," the policy of systematically eliminating Jews from the economic life of the country. In justification, government officials explained that the Jews were "superfluous," their economic position in the country was an "intrusion," and their elimination in favor of "purely Polish" elements was desirable and necessary.

This militant Polish anti-Semitism was animated by more than successor-state nationalism, however. During the entire period between the two World Wars the Polish economy tottered precariously on the brink of bankruptcy. Tariff barriers deprived the crucial Polish textile industry of its customary markets in Germany, Russia, Austria, and the Baltic States. With the crisis in industry and the collapse of urban purchasing power, the agricultural price system was adversely affected, and thousands of Polish peasants were driven to ruin. As the sons of these impoverished farmers moved into the cities, they seemed to encounter Jews everywhere they went. In Warsaw alone, two fifths of the population was Jewish, and the proportion was only slightly less in most of Poland's other chief communities. Commerce, moreover, was very largely in Jewish hands. While it was true that less than half the Jewish population of Poland was engaged in trade, fully a third of the mercantile class was Jewish. In 1931, for example, 3.7 per cent of Poland's total population was employed in commerce; but about 34 per cent of these merchants were Jews, most of them engaged in petty trade. Nationalist agitators made the most of these facts in stimulating Polish hostility. "If the aboriginal nation reaches economic maturity," one Polish senator declared, "the immigrant nation must step aside." The majority of Poles were convinced that a "native" middle class could develop only through the displacement of the Jews.

Was this true, one wonders? Was Poland in fact so poor that one of its peoples could survive only at the expense of another? Actually, in fertile land and in economic resources—in coal, lumber, oil, and zinc—Poland was one of the richest countries in Europe. But these resources had never been intelligently exploited, nor the land equitably distributed. The monopolist landowners, the *Pans,* and the Catholic Church were quite unwilling to have the *status quo* tampered with. It was the inflexibility of these vested interests, together with the loss of foreign markets, which was the root of Polish poverty. Nevertheless, under continual nationalist pressure, the Polish government decided that the displacement of the Jews was now a fundamental goal in its economic policy.

Initially, the assault did not take the form of specifically anti-Jewish legislation. It was not until the mid-1930's, in fact, that the Polish government ventured to repudiate its obligations under the Minority Treaty. During the 1920's the government resorted instead to *étatism,* a kind of state capitalism which nationalized the tobacco, liquor, salt, and match industries, together with all branches of public transportation. It was no accident, of course, that these were industries in which the Jews had long been prominently represented—which, in fact, they had virtually created. Now that the government took them over, however, all Jewish employees were summarily dismissed. In addition, Jews were completely frozen out of all civil service positions, and from all government contracts.

As tens of thousands of Jews found themselves without livelihoods, the collapse of their purchasing power affected nearly every stratum of Jewish life. The Jewish artisans of Warsaw pointed to some melancholy statistics, gathered in the mid-1920's. Of 2,800 Jewish shoemaking establishments, 2,060 were closed. Of 3,000 tailoring shops, 2,560 were closed. Of 180 embroidery shops, 108 were closed. Of 100 brush factories, 50 were closed. Of course, this attack on the Jews did not solve Poland's economic problems. Neither did loans from the United States. A wild inflation drove the Polish regime once again to the verge of bankruptcy. It was at this juncture, in 1926, that old *Dziadek* ("Grandpa") Pilsudski, who had withdrawn from active participation in the state he helped create, suddenly marched on Warsaw with a legion of followers, overthrew the government, and transformed Poland into a dictatorship. One of Pilsudski's first acts was to end the government's policy of anti-Semitism; for much as he loathed Jews personally—as he had proved in the 1920 invasion—he recognized that the officially condoned policy of Jew-hatred had proved a blind for corruption. Yet Pilsudski's ban on "official" anti-Semitism came too late to help the Jews. Less than three years later the world Depression struck Poland.

All Poles suffered bitterly from the disaster; but the Jews, already weakened by *étatism,* were driven to an economic marginalism from which they never recovered. In 1931 a million Polish Jews belonged to unemployed families. Lodz, once the outstanding textile center of Eastern Europe, was transformed into an industrial morgue. Jewish neighborhoods—the Nalewki district in Warsaw, the Poddenbem in Lemberg, Leather Street in Vilna—soon became the most wretched slum sections of Eastern Europe. In Warsaw, the *Beth Lechem,* a Jewish charitable association, was obliged to maintain relays of bread and tea wagons to keep famished Jews from fainting in the streets. Jewish parents actually put advertisements in Polish newspapers offering to sell their children in return for food. In damp and cold dwellings five or six persons lived together in a wretched little room. Children slept there, sometimes without undressing for weeks, huddled together, several in one bed. The reports of TOZ, the Jewish health agency in Poland, provided grim evidence of the Jewish economic collapse. In Grodno it was noted that 57 per cent of the boys and 39 per cent of the girls were underweight; 48 per cent of the boys suffered from undernourishment and 21 per cent were anemic. In Vilna 80 per cent of the children in the school were tubercular or anemic. Children who had the strength to come to school usually required feeding. Inasmuch as the means of assistance were quite limited, a meal of bread and milk was served at eleven o'clock in the morning to take the place of both breakfast and lunch.

Jewish communities abroad, particularly in America, did what they could to help. The American Joint Distribution Committee, that superb philanthropy which had proved its indispensability in the Eastern war zone during the first World War, supported schools, loan societies, medical and sanitary facilities, and allied social-welfare institutions. The Joint's revolving loan funds alone kept no less than 150,000 families alive each year during the 1930's. It was the Joint, moreover, which maintained TOZ, and its wide network of dispensaries and X-ray centers. American-Jewish philanthropy might have sustained the better part of the Polish-Jewish population through the agony of the Depression—if Poland's poverty and successor-state nationalism had not been exacerbated by new political factors.

THE RISE OF POLISH FASCISM

As the great Depression paralyzed one segment of the national economy after another, ominous rumblings of discontent could be heard from Poland's peasantry and urban working population. The growth of this unrest convinced Poland's economic aristocrats that their own vital interests would have to be safeguarded from possible legislative interference. It is one of the tragedies of modern history that the Polish Republic failed to deal swiftly and sternly with its legacy of economic oligarchism. While the vast majority of farmers and agricultural laborers lived in a state of semiserfdom, a relatively small group of Polish nobles and clerics continued, as we have seen, to maintain a tight grip on most of the arable soil of the country. In addition, the powerful Catholic hierarchy, the largest of Poland's landowners, was in control of the country's educational system, and did not hesitate to use the schools as well as the church pulpits to defend the inviolability of the *status quo*.

In the urban areas, too, Poland's heavy industry was largely concentrated in the hands of a few dozen enormously wealthy businessmen. Banded together informally in the "Leviathan," a kind of Polish National Association of Manufacturers, the industrialists managed to raise the prices of their products to a level utterly out of relationship to the laws of supply and demand. None of these groups—the aristocracy, the Church, the Leviathan—was willing to accept a change in the economic fabric of the country. As in Western Europe, moreover, they were able to count on the support of the embittered lower middle class, that pathetic and threadbare collection of shopkeepers and white-collar workers who cast about desparately for some "conspiratorial" explanation for their imminent proletarianization.

All these vulnerable interest groups were willing to exploit anti-Semitism to its fullest degree, for the sake of diverting peasant and labor unrest from the true sources of Poland's economic difficulties. A collection of fascist paramilitary organizations, the most notorious of which were the *Endeks* and the *Naras,* mushroomed throughout the country, openly encouraged by Catholic propaganda, and subsidized secretly by the gentry and the Leviathan. Roaming the streets in uniforms, the rightist strong-arm gangs indiscriminately attacked Jews (were they not all Bolsheviks?), socialists, and liberals. By 1933 the problem of Jewish survival in Poland was seriously complicated, as a high-powered, carefully nurtured program of fascist anti-Semitism was added to the economic disaster of the Depression. With the example of Hitler now before them, the *Endeks* and *Naras* grew steadily more brazen: advocating the total elimination of Jews from gainful employment; provoking riots, disturbances, synagogue and cemetery desecrations. In a pastoral letter of 1936, Cardinal Hlond, the Primate of Poland, publicly urged a boycott of Jewish businesses; while in the spring of that same year, in the city of Przytyk, Jewish students who sought to resist the assaults of anti-Semitic thugs were thrown in prison by the government magistrates. By the end of 1936, indeed, dictator Smigly-Rydz, who had succeeded Pilsudski on the latter's death, now deemed it politically expedient to compromise with fascist anti-Semitism whenever possible.

Hardly a session of the *Sejm*—the Polish Parliament—now passed without reference to the "surplus" Jewish population. Government leaders explored every possible avenue of facilitating Jewish emigration to Palestine, even making representations to the Mandatory Power, Britain, not to lower the Jewish quota. A series of laws was passed placing merchants and artisans at the mercy of license examiners; and thus, through an ingenious manipulation of rules and regulations, tens of thousands of Jews were driven out of business altogether. *Endek* and *Nara* picket lines and boycotts, all set up with official police protection, reduced other thousands of Jewish businessmen to peddlery. Nor were the universities free from Jew-baiting. By the mid-1930's the violent clamor of nationalist student groups compelled nearly every university in Poland to adopt an "unofficial" *numerus clausus* against Jewish students—while less than twenty Jews remained on the teaching faculties of the country's higher educational institutions.

The *Endeks* and the *Naras* prepared now to press their advantage to the limit. They demanded ghetto benches for those few thousand Jewish students who remained in the universities, and sought to implement this demand by clubbing Jewish classmates, wrecking lecture halls, insulting and hooting down liberal professors. At last, in 1937, after two years of this kind of skirmishing, the government authorized the universities to allocate the left side of classrooms for Jews where special benches would be available. Although they were exhausted and demoralized by years of discrimination and humiliation, the Jews of Poland, especially the younger generation, were determined not to suffer this ultimate affront without protest. On October 20 the entire Jewish working class laid down its tools and went on strike; they were joined, too, by liberal and labor groups throughout the country. Jewish students stood throughout their classes rather than sit on the ghetto benches, and occasionally a university official resigned rather than compel the Jews to comply with the regulations. Ultimately, however, after weeks of public clamor, the government managed to enforce the decrees.

By 1938 it was apparent that Poland's fascist elements had succeeded in transforming Smigly-Rydz into their puppet, and he spoke of Jews as if he were editing the fascist press. "[The Jews] have separate national aims," he declared. "They weaken Polish national forces. They interfere with national evolution." It was under cover of this anti-Semitic smoke screen that the government carefully made its preparations to crack down on— perhaps even eliminate altogether—Poland's articulate liberal, labor, and socialist organizations. Sensing the imminence of the danger, the country's democratic forces conducted a desperate campaign in advance of the election of 1938; and, almost miraculously, they prevented the Smigly-Rydz coalition from winning a majority in the *Sejm*. It actually appeared for a moment as if Poland might still escape being swallowed by outright fascism.

The Jews of Poland, beggared, demoralized, living every moment in expectation of expulsion or final starvation, waited to learn if this last-minute reprieve meant the birth of a new era or if it was a last cruel delusion. One sees them yet, frozen in anticipation of changes the consequences of which they dared not predict: bearded Orthodox Jews; caftaned Hasidic Jews; tough Jewish Bundists with their cloth caps thrust aggressively forward; cultivated Jewish doctors and lawyers, clean shaven, their clothing worn Western style; Jewish writers and artists, singers, and musicians. And their women and children. Three million human beings, the heirs of one of the most vibrant, fecund, and humane communities in Jewish history. While they waited, Adolf Hitler was making preparations for the Nazi invasion of Poland.

ROMANIA AND HER JEWS

The first World War converted Romania from a tiny, provincial country, smaller geographically than England, its population scarcely 7,000,000 people, into the largest of the Balkan States, with a population of 18,000,000. Romania's territorial gains, carved out of the ruins of the Romanov and Hapsburg Empires, were proportionately larger than those of any other country; while the mineral resources—in oil, timber, and wheat land—of these new acquisitions were no less impressive. But, like Poland, Romania also inherited national minorities—over 4,500,000 of them: 1,400,000 Hungarians, 1,100,000 Ukrainians, 800,000 Germans, 800,000 Jews, 300,000 Bulgarians, and perhaps 300,000 Ruthenians, Poles, and Serbs.

The Romanians feared these minorities not only for their irredentism, but also for their economic and intellectual vitality. The Jews and Germans, particularly, occupied strategic positions in the commercial and cultural life of Romania. The typical Romanian was a shepherd or a peasant, wearing hand-woven clothes and living in a primitive thatched hut. The typical Romanian Jew, a city or village dweller, was not, as a rule, much better off; for he had been driven to economic marginalism by the savage Judaeophobia of successive prewar Romanian governments. Nevertheless, the success of an influential minority of Jewish businessmen on the one hand, and the prominence of Jewish names on Communist rosters on the other—combined with the wild xenophobia which Romanians displayed toward all non-Romanian peoples—foredoomed the one minority people in Europe which could not appeal to a protecting "brother" state.

Before the first World War there were approximately 250,000 Jews in Little Romania. The new provinces added another 550,000. Although these people were specifically protected by the Romanian Minority Treaty, the Bucharest government waited little more than a few months before demonstrating its contempt for the agreement. It promptly denationalized some 200,000 of the Jewish newcomers when they lacked proof of ten years of previous continuous residence. The protests of the League of Nations and the European Powers were unavailing; Romania, in its best time-honored fashion, brazened out its violations. The 200,000 stateless Jews found themselves without consular protection, without rights under Romanian law, without opportunity for government employment. Living in limbo, they were subject to the whim of the authorities even for the right to remain on Romanian soil.

Denationalization was only the beginning of a systematic anti-Jewish program. Throughout the 1920's the government issued a steady stream of decrees designed to protect the "pure" Romanian population. The Jewish school system and welfare organizations, their autonomy and financial support explicitly guaranteed by the Minority Treaty, were systematically disallowed. The heaviest taxes were imposed on non-Romanian peoples, and the rate was highest for the Jews. As in Poland, a government policy of *étatism* froze the Jews out of their traditional livelihoods in the tobacco, salt, match, and transportation industries. In Romania's four overcrowded universities Jews were insulted and often beaten by student nationalists, and eventually almost entirely eliminated through the device of the government-inspired *numerus clausus*. In the countryside bands of nationalist hooligans attacked Jewish travelers, broke the windows of Jewish village inns. With few exceptions, police protection was rare. Other minority groups, too, were subjected to occasional physical abuse, but less frequently and less boldly; there was always the danger of reprisal from "brother" states. In 1928 these nativist assaults halted briefly after the electoral triumph of Dr. Julius Maniu and the National Peasant party. Maniu, a liberal and a man of highest personal integrity, inaugurated a program of domestic and agrarian reforms; at the same time he sternly suppressed all antiminority and anti-Semitic agitation. But the ravages of the world Depression, the racial hatreds that sprang out of economic discontent, eventually doomed Maniu's Government. The Liberal party, actually one of Romania's most reactionary political organizations, took office again, and the Jews braced themselves for storms to come.

The widespread unemployment, the sullen restiveness of the men who stood for hours in bread lines, created grave concern among Romania's propertied aristocrats: the handful of boyar landlords and the powerful Romanian Orthodox clergy who owned most of the arable soil of the country; the Bratianu family and their network of alliances who controlled many of the banks and most of the heavy industry in Romania; the distaught *petit-bourgeoisie* of the land. Each of these groups lived in constant apprehension of a peasant or worker uprising. In search of a plausible diversion, they were not unwilling to appeal to the worst instincts of Balkan xenophobia, or to exploit the backlog of Romanian Jew-hatred. Many of these rightists were convinced that their economic interests could best be safeguarded by transforming the country into a fascist dictatorship. To be sure, the magnates and their allies faced an obstacle in King Carol; but they battered away at that obstacle by continually and contemptuously drawing public attention to the scandal of Carol's love affair with the Jewess, Magda Lupescu.

Effective spokesmen were not lacking for the new campaign against the Jews. There was the seasoned old patriarch of Romanian anti-Semitism, Alexander Cuza, who had advocated the expulsion of all Jews from Europe long before Hitler was born, and who now lent his support to the organized parties of fascism. There was the doggerel poet, Octavian Goga, for whom anti-Semitism was essentially a convenient weapon of personal advancement, and whose political creed was little more than a rank and semiliterate chauvinism. There was the half-Romanian, Cornelius Codreanu (his father was a Pole), a typical swaggering gangster, whose militantly fascist paramilitary group, the Iron Guard, thrived on assassinations and terrorism, and whose partisans possessed less of an economic and political program than an unadulterated lust for totalitarian power. Finally there was the Grand Patriarch of the Romanian Orthodox Church, Miron Christea, whose views were evidenced in his comment of 1937: "One feels like crying with pity for the good Romanian nation, whose very marrow has been sucked from its bones by the Jews. To defend ourselves is a national and patriotic duty, not anti-Semitism." These were the men who assumed the direction of the anti-Semitic campaign of the 1930's; and behind them, egging them on with funds, were the boyars, the clerical leaders, and the industrial magnates. There was one other interest group, too, which did its best to fan the flames of racial hatred: it was the Nazi party of Germany, which used its propaganda resources to wean Romania away from the Little Entente, and to secure Romania as an ally in its strategy to destroy the Treaty of Versailles.

By the end of 1935, as Cuza, Goga, and Codreanu joined their forces into a United Front, only King Carol, apparently, and the rather shaky Liberal Government stood in the way of a pro-Nazi coup. For the next two years the Jews were exposed to new and increasingly violent waves of anti-Semitism. In November 1936, the United Front staged the greatest anti-Semitic demonstration in Romanian history; no less than 280,000 marchers participated in the parade in Bucharest. The Liberal Government, which hated the Nazis, but had always been more than willing to court the anti-Semites, did not protest; on the contrary, it placed 2,000 railroad cars, free of charge, at the disposal of the "pilgrims." The Romanian Orthodox Church added its blessing, too, as the Patriarch Christea urged a final eradication of the Jewish plague from Romanian life. Archdeacon Jon Mota called for drastic treatment on the lines of the "great master, Hitler." The more enlightened forces wavered and broke ranks. Several leaders of the National Peasant party, long the bulwark of democracy in Romania, now began to flirt with anti-Semitism. The bar associations of the leading communities eliminated their Jewish members. The Romanian Culture League proclaimed a boycott against the Jews.

Through all these developments the government scarcely stirred, except to promise that racial standards would be established in employment, and that at least 75 per cent of all working positions would be reserved for those of "pure Romanian origin." The enactment of this legislation did not, however, alleviate the lot of the landless peasant or of the struggling wage earner; their poverty worsened daily. They were probably vaguely aware that they were being exploited; but, drugged by anti-Semitic propaganda, they fastened on the Jew as the exploiter. If one wonders how an entire nation could go berserk, completely oblivious to the economic and political inequities that were the authentic sources of national poverty, it should be remembered that the political literacy of the Romanian people had been dulled by centuries of Turkish rule, with its torpor and graft, its corruption and baksheesh. Blindly and befuddled, the Romanians staggered their way to the slaughterhouse.

The indecisive election of 1937 was destined to have tragically decisive results. Issues sharply centered on foreign policy. The National Peasant party stood firm for the Little Entente. The United Front of Goga, Cuza, and Codreanu was pledged to the Axis. The result of the election was an apparent deadlock; neither group succeeded in winning a clear majority. It was at this moment that King Carol made an astonishing move. Unaccountably, he called upon Octavian Goga to form a government. Perhaps Carol thought it better to compromise with a mild fascism than run the risk of being swept into an Iron Guard bedlam. Whatever the King's motives, his decision achieved no political stability. Goga's Government lasted only seven weeks before it collapsed under the weight of its own ineptitude, but it managed to pass a series of sweeping laws against the Jews. All Jewish newspapers were closed. All Jews were dismissed from government service. Jews were barred from obtaining foreign currency for travel abroad. Twelve thousand Jewish families were pauperized overnight through the annulment of their liquor licenses, and many times that number by the prohibition of Jewish commercial activity in any village where they were in competition with Christians. Romanian Jewry, like the Jews of Poland, faced beggary.

Then, as in Poland, there was a moment of respite. Goga died of apoplexy in May 1938. Shortly thereafter, Codreanu and his immediate followers, implicated in a plot to overthrow the Monarchy, were gunned down by King Carol's bodyguard. Premier Christea, who succeeded Goga, died of pneumonia. Cuza alone remained of the Old Guard Jew-baiters; but he was now past eighty-two and quite senile. For a brief interval it seemed that reaction had burned itself out. The Jews of Romania, perhaps the most thoroughly demoralized Jewish population in Europe, hoped that they might now count upon a reasonably secure existence. But their optimism, like Polish Jewry's, was premature. A year later World War II began, and Romania became a Nazi ally.

HUNGARY AND REVISIONIST NATIONALISM

If Poland and Romania emerged from the first World War as the fortunate recipients of new territories, Hungary, which had been allied with the Central Powers, was the unhappy victim of drastic diplomatic surgery. By the Treaty of Trianon the Magyar state was deprived of two thirds of its territory and half its population. 1918-19 were years of unalleviated horror for the Hungarian people. The inflation and food shortages of the immediate postwar period were intensified by a relentless, and gratuitous, Allied blockade. The blockade, in turn, undermined Hungary's economy so thoroughly that no democratic politician could take responsibility for the future of the country. On the other hand, the Communists, ever on the alert for opportunities to exploit human misery, were quite prepared to move into the political vacuum. Before the citizens of Hungary quite realized what was happening, a Red dictatorship set itself up in Budapest.

By a tragic turn of destiny the leader of the Red regime was a Jew, Béla Kun, born Berele Kohn, the son of a Galician peddler. He had been an officer in the Hungarian army and his conversion to Marxism took place in 1915 after he had fallen prisoner to the Russians. His sudden accession to power gave him an opportunity to implement much more than his Marxist ideology; apparently there was a deeply rooted personal sadism which had also to be appeased. For three dreadful months Kun worked out plans for a thoroughgoing economic and social revolution which included the nationalization of all land and industry, and the execution of thousands of "class enemies," many of them Jews. Eventually Kun's regime was overthrown by counterrevolutionary forces under the command of Admiral Nicholas Horthy—but not before Kun had been diabolized as the "antichrist" in nearly every Hungarian home.

The fact of Kun's Jewish birth was an incalculable disaster for the Jews of Hungary; it made it much easier for the Admiral's feudal supporters to stigmatize the Jews as the spawn of Bolshevism, and to incite excesses against them. In truth, the typical embittered Hungarian nationalist, for whom Magyarization had always been a basic axiom of policy, needed little excuse to vent his spleen on any of Hungary's ethnic minorities—Germans, Slovaks, Serbs, or Jews. But the 600,000 Jews who lived on Hungarian soil were especially vulnerable: they alone were without protection, save for the worthless scrap of paper known as the Minority Treaty. As in Poland and Romania, too, the Jews were ideal scapegoats for Horthy's supporters, the aristocrats who owned most of the arable soil of the country, and who lived in mortal dread of peasant unrest. It mattered little that the Hungarian-Jewish community was one of the oldest and most distinguished in Europe, with a long tradition of bourgeois respectability and leadership in the literary and musical life of the land. The White Terror fell with indiscriminate fury. For two years the Jews of Budapest were subjected to assaults by nationalist rowdies, pilloried as Red agents and horsewhipped, scores dragged to the river and drowned or shot. The massacres spread through the country. Perhaps 5,000 Jews were slain during 1919 and 1920, and many times that number were maimed or economically ruined.

Even after the shootings stopped, in the autumn of 1921, most of the miseries that plagued Jews in the rest of Eastern Europe were repeated in Hungary—the same chauvinistic propaganda, the riots, and the boycotts. There was one variation, however: Hungary was the first nation which dared to flout the Minority Treaty openly by establishing a *numerus clausus* in the universities, legally limiting the Jewish registration. The bill, which went through Parliament in September 1922, restricted Jews to 6 per cent of the university enrollment; shortly thereafter, the League of Nations admitted Hungary to membership. Successive appeals to the League ultimately brought about the modification of anti-Jewish restrictions; but the modification was quite nominal, and operated only in theory. Yet as Hungary began to move out of its economic doldrums, the more overt and violent forms of revisionist nationalism began to decline. In 1925 Count Stephen Bethlen, the new Prime Minister, announced that anti-Semitic excesses would no longer be tolerated. For a moment the Jews breathed easier.

The respite was only temporary. The world Depression struck in 1930, and the Magyar magnates sought once again to invoke nationalist agitation as a diversion from economic unrest. The feudal lords found leverage in the diplomatic reorientation in Europe which resulted from the rise of Adolf Hitler. They willingly financed a high-powered campaign to lure Hungary into the fascist orbit, and to follow the irredentist path marked out by Germany and Italy. There was no better driving wedge for their purposes than a furious anti-Semitism, more efficiently mounted by collaboration with experts in Berlin. The prime mover in this new campaign was General Gyula von Gömbös, one of the brains behind the White Terror of the 1920's. Gömbös, who was reared in the German section of Hungary, publicly boasted of his long friendship with Adolf Hitler. From 1931 to 1936 he was Prime Minister of Hungary; and during his premiership the Jews lived again through the panic of the postwar period. Little actual legislation was passed; but anti-Semitic propaganda, assaults, and boycotts were stepped up to such a point that Gömbös's successors, Darani and Imredy, encountered few obstacles when they piloted the most extreme anti-Jewish laws.

In 1938 quotas were established for Jews in the economic life of Hungary. Jews were not permitted to occupy more than 20 per cent of any business or profession; nor were the total wages and salaries paid to Jews permitted to exceed 20 per cent of the total expenditures in any one economic area. Later in the year Prime Minister Béla Imredy announced a plan by which Jews would be purged from the theater and press altogether, and limited to 6 per cent in the professions and 12 per cent in commerce and industry. All Jews naturalized since 1914, moreover, would be summarily denaturalized— a measure which affected more than half the Jewish population of Hungary. Ironically, the discovery that Imredy had a Jewish great-grandmother forced his resignation from office. But the denaturalization law passed anyway in May of 1939. Two thirds of Hungarian Jewry, a cultured, middle-class community, faced complete economic collapse. By then, however, time had run out for them altogether. Within a few months the second World War began, and Hungary had the honor of becoming Nazi Germany's first East European satellite.

The melancholy history of Jewish life in Poland, Romania, and Hungary, was duplicated with only minor modifications for the 150,000 Lithuanian Jews and the 90,000 Latvian Jews. The Minority Treaties again failed to protect either the Jewish school and welfare systems or Jewish economic and political opportunity. The rise of fascism in the 1930's resulted in the usual economic purges. Of course, Lithuania and Latvia, as in the other States of Eastern Europe, all minorities were the victims of xenophobia; while the Lithuanian and Latvian peoples themselves suffered dreadfully during the great Depression. But again, as in Hungary, Poland, and Romania, the Jews were marked out for special treatment. For they alone of all minority peoples had no influential intercessor in Europe to speak and, if necessary, retaliate on their behalf.

CONCLUSION

All the glowing hopes of the early postwar years quickly turned to ashes. The merciless political anti-Semitism of the czarist regime in Russia was gone; the status of Russian Jewry was equalized vis-à-vis the other inhabitants of the Soviet Union. But there were other ways in which the Soviet regime proved as oppressive to the Jews as to the other citizens of Russia, and even more oppressive after 1939. The Communists strangled organized Jewish community life, Jewish religious institutions, and the opportunity for economic advancement or individual self-expression. Nor was there much for Jews to prefer in lands liberated from Romanov or Hapsburg domination. For in nearly every country of Eastern Europe Jews found themselves the victims of two oppressive inheritances. One inheritance was the vindictive nationalism of minority peoples suddenly become sovereign majorities, people who now turned upon their own minorities, and especially upon the Jews, the full force of a long-repressed ethnocentrism. The other inheritance was a corrupt economic system; so corrupt, indeed, that its defenders—the magnates, the industrial cartelists, the *petit-bourgeoisie,* the land-glutted Church hierarchies—turned instinctively to anti-Semitic propaganda as the technique with which to engineer the establishment of protective fascist regimes.

In view of the poverty, the illiteracy, even the brutishness of these East European peoples, one might have expected that the initiative for the final extermination of Jewish life would come from East of the Elbe. Ironically enough, precisely the opposite was the case. Anti-Semitism reached its ultimate, its most lethal intensity in cultured Germany. Here Jew-hatred was

The Course of Modern Jewish History

transformed into far more than an instrument of political reaction; it became a fearsomely effective technique with which to attack and undermine the structure of Western civilization itself.

Notes

Page 352. The translation of the Bezymenski poem quoted in A. L. Sachar, *Sufferance Is the Badge*, pp. 168-69.

XVIII

The Palestine Mandate

As one notes the ebb and flow of Jewish fortunes through the centuries, it appears almost as if a principle of compensation is at work. When darkness blots out civilized values in one part of the world, the lights go on in another; when death strikes here, life emerges there. The destruction of independence in Palestine was paralleled by a revival of Jewish life in Babylon: the eclipse in Babylon was matched by the glories in Spain; the fall in Western Europe was offset by the revival in Poland—and so it went. At no time, however, did the principle of compensation seem to function more providentially than in the twentieth century. During the years in which the European Jewish community—the largest in Jewish history—was placed under sentence of death, a creative new era was in seed, surely in the nick of time, on the ancestral soil of Palestine. The idiom in Jewish tradition that summarizes the recurrent miracle is happily phrased: God sends the *refuah,* the remedy, before he inflicts the *makah,* the plague.

When the first World War began, the *Yishuv,* the Jewish settlement in Palestine, was placed in a precarious, even desperate, position. Blockaded by the Allied fleet, denied access to Western markets, the country faced economic paralysis. Those Jews who lived in pious mendicancy in Jerusalem and Safad found that even the flow of *Chalukah* charity from Eastern Europe was cut off. Meanwhile Djemal Pasha, the surly and suspicious Turkish governor of Palestine, indiscriminately arrested the leaders of both Arab and Jewish nationalist groups. The Zionist activists were faced with the choice either of leaving Palestine or of languishing in verminous Turkish prisons. Most of them—Ben-Gurion, Ben-Zvi, Shertok—took advantage of their exile to continue their planning from other vantage points. At the same time, the World Zionist Organization itself, whose branches were located in countries that were at war with each other, was faced with the problem of conflicting loyalties. Eventually the Zionist leadership attempted to resolve the dilemma by opening up "neutral" offices in Copenhagen. It was no solution. The transfer to Denmark, far from the vital centers of Jewish life, virtually emasculated the organization's effectiveness.

It happened, however, that a member of the Zionist Executive, the eloquent tribune, Shmaryah Levin, was en route from America to Europe when the war began. His ship turned back immediately and Levin remained in New York to establish a Provisional Executive Committee for General Zionist Affairs. It was this vigilant liaison which ultimately saved the Zionist movement—and the Jewish community in Palestine. For by 1914 there were about two and a half million Jews in the United States, most of them of Eastern European origin, and eager to lend their support to the Zionist cause. Moreover, the president of the Provisional Executive Committee, Louis Brandeis, was a man of national prominence in American life. He had acquired a warm appreciation for the aspirations of East European Jews during his experience as an attorney for the Jewish labor unions in the needle trades. As a result, he was predisposed toward Zionism even before Jacob de Haas, editor of the Boston *Jewish Advocate,* acquainted him with the full political and cultural potentialities of the Zionist movement. Equally prominent was the American ambassador to Constantinople, Henry Morgenthau, Sr., a non-Zionist. The matchless reputation these men enjoyed in American political circles convinced the Turks that Jews were disproportionately powerful in American life; that it would be wise to cultivate their good will if the United States were not to intervene on the side of the Allies. When, therefore, Ambassador Morgenthau made representations on behalf of the Jews of Palestine, the Turkish government was constrained to listen. Djemal Pasha still continued to arrest or exile Zionist leaders wherever he could find them; but even he felt it politic to allow the occasional distribution of American food and clothing among the Jewish population. It was largely the influence of American Jewry, both reputed and real, that enabled fifty-five thousand Palestinian Jews to survive the war.

Meantime the political fate of the *Yishuv* was on the diplomatic chessboard. Turkey had been counted as a historic British ally. But at the very beginning of the war the Sultan defaulted to the Central Powers, removing the "buffer" from Britain's Suez life line to India. British statesmen were obliged to cast about for new friends and confederates in the Near East. In this dark moment an unexpected ally appeared. The Sherif Husein, the patriarch of the powerful Hashemi family, sent his son, Abdullah, on a mission to the British Agency in Egypt. Would His Majesty's Government be interested, asked Abdullah, in supporting an Arab revolt against the Sultan? The British officials in Cairo were taken completely by surprise. They had never contemplated the Arabs as possible allies, and still less as a potential buffer against Turko-German expansion; Husein's overtures opened out entirely new areas of exploration. Of course, "His Majesty's Government" was very much interested. Negotiations between High Commissioner Henry McMahon and the Hashemi family continued throughout 1914 and 1915. Eventually a bargain was struck. In October 1915, McMahon sent to Husein a note which the Arabs henceforth recognized as their "Declaration of Independence." By the provisions of the note, McMahon declared Britain's willingness to recognize the independence of the Arabs, both in the Levant and in the Hejaz.

But McMahon stipulated, too, that certain areas were to be exempted from Arab control. The exemptions were destined later to complicate seriously the problems of Near Eastern peace. The Arab portions of the Turkish Empire were divided into administrative units known as vilayets and sanjaks. Palestine, for example, was divided into the sanjaks of Acre and Nablus, both of which belonged to the vilayet of Beirut, and the independent sanjak of Jerusalem. The areas exempted from Arab control by the Mc-Mahon note included "Syria west of Damascus, Homs, Hama, and Aleppo." If, as the British later insisted, "Damascus" meant the vilayet, and not the city, of Damascus, then virtually all of Palestine was excluded from Arab control. The Arabs, however, insisted that "Damascus" meant the city of Damascus—which left Palestine in their hands. In 1915, however, none of these problems of interpretation occurred to Abdullah or Husein, and they agreed to British terms. In June of 1916 the tribes of the Hejaz revolted against the Turks and placed themselves under the command of a British officer, the brilliant Oxford classicist, T. E. Lawrence. It was not much of an uprising, as military efforts went. At the most ten thousand Bedouin guerrillas were involved, nearly all from the Hejaz, and their fighting was confined to occasional raiding and looting forays against Turkish railroads. These raids, nevertheless, were effective enough to disrupt the Turkish communication system during a crucial phase of the war, and to establish the basis of Arab claims at the Paris Peace Conference.

Yet British plans for the Near East were not altogether encompassed in their promises to the Arabs. It seemed obvious to Colonial and Foreign Office officials that an area so crucial to British interests should not be turned over unequivocally to a backward and unstable people. There were 25,000,000 Arabs in the vast reaches of the Near East, but the British were not impressed; all they saw were hordes of diseased and poverty-stricken illiterates. The Colonial officials, men of the stature of Sir Henry McMahon, Ronald Storrs, and Gilbert Clayton, were not incapable Colonel Blimps. But the notion of building permanent British security on the flimsy foundations of Arab nomadism seemed to them highly unrealistic. With modern hindsight by which to judge, it appears that they were seriously underestimating the potential strength of Arab nationalism. Since the early nineteenth century it had been gestating slowly among Arab merchants in the coastal cities of the Levant and among Arab officers in the Ottoman army. It had also been inculcated, in large measure, by American and French missionaries in Beirut, who encouraged their Moslem students to evaluate Arab history from a national point of view and not to limit themselves exclusively to the religious experience. Hence, when the Sherif's son, Abdullah, offered to fight at the side of the British, he was perhaps mainly motivated by dynastic ambition, the hope to emerge as the overlord of an Arab empire. But he was also responding to the maturing passion for Arab national independence. All of this the British missed, even as the later Zionist leaders, in their oversimplification of complex issues, also missed it.

In any case, in the spring of 1916, acting on such misgivings, the British, French, and Russians entered into an agreement for their own postwar disposition of the Levant. By the terms of the Sykes-Picot-Sazonov agreement, Britain reserved for herself the area which later became Trans-Jordan, while all of Iraq except Mosul and its district, Syria, and Cilicia, were allocated to France. Russia, in turn, earmarked Constantinople and the Armenian vilayets of Turkey. Later the Arabs denounced the Sykes-Picot agreement as a rather cynical piece of double-dealing, not merely because it contradicted the McMahon pledge to Husein, but also because it partitioned the Arab rectangle in such a way as to place artificial obstacles in the way of Arab unity. Even the Sykes-Picot arrangement, however, was not the final word on the Near East. By its provisions, one part of Palestine was to be internationalized, and the other part was assigned to France. Within a year Britain, harassed by the exigencies of the war, was eager again to reconsider the provisions of the allocation agreement.

THE BALFOUR DECLARATION

One of the incentives for such reconsideration was provided by a Jewish scientist named Chaim Weizmann. Weizmann was born in Russia, nurtured on the warm Jewish folk traditions of his native *shtetl* of Motel, near Pinsk, and educated in the finest universities of Switzerland and Germany. Equipped with a doctorate in chemistry from the University of Freiburg, he obtained a readership in chemistry, in 1904, at the University of Manchester. Because he had been an ardent Jewish nationalist all his life, Weizmann enrolled in the English Zionist movement almost immediately after settling in Manchester. His reputation as one of the most brilliant chemists in England, and the fervor that he brought from his native background, earned him, within less than a decade, the leadership of Anglo-Zionism. By 1914 he was able to count on the devotion and loyalty of many of England's leading Jews: its chief rabbis, Herz and Gaster; its financiers, Lionel and James Rothschild; its intellectuals, Herbert Bentwich and Harry Sacher.

When the war began Weizmann was called to London to devise a process for synthesizing acetone, an ingredient vital in the production of the explosive, cordite. Eventually he succeeded in working out an effective technique of fermentation, and won from the War Office both gratitude and a large cash award. But the successful fermentation of acetone was the least of his accomplishments; for he also made valuable contacts and converts to Zionism among England's top public figures. Weizmann was certainly not the first to bring the Zionist idea to England, nor even to call it to the attention of government officials. We recall the favorable impression made by Herzl in his interviews with Baron Lionel Rothschild and Joseph Chamberlain, the Colonial Secretary. But Weizmann was the first to persuade significant numbers of English public figures to give practical consideration to the concept of a Jewish homeland in Palestine. Charles P. Scott, editor of the Manchester *Guardian,* and Henry Wickham Steed, editor of the London *Times*, became Weizmann's devoted friends. He won the ear and sympathy of Winston Churchill, then first Lord of the Admiralty, of David Lloyd George, then Minister of Munitions, and of Arthur James Balfour, who was soon to become Foreign Secretary. All these men were well disposed to Weizmann, not merely for his scientific war contributions, but also for his contemptuous refusal to deal with the "neutral" Zionist Bureau in Copenhagen, his insistence that the future of Zionism was linked with the triumph of the Western democracies. Then, too, Weizmann was a man of great personal magnetism. He made a striking appearance with his massive bald head, finely etched with veins, deep piercing eyes, dignified mustache and goatee. When he warmed to his subject, his dignity and eloquence left an enduring impact on his listeners. Years later the British Governor of Jerusalem gave this description of him:

> An almost feminine charm combined with a feline deadliness of attack; utter disillusion over both Gentile and Jew, together with burning enthusiasm and prophetic vision of what negotiation may still win from the one for the other . . . a brilliant talker with an unrivalled gift for lucid exposition. . . . As a speaker almost frighteningly convincing, even in English . . . in Hebrew, and even more in Russian, overwhelming; with all that dynamic persuasiveness which Slavs usually devote to love and Jews to business, nourished, trained, and concentrated upon the accomplishment of Zion.

By the end of 1916 Weizmann had won allies from among the top echelons of English life, particularly in government and journalism; his colleague, Nahum Sokolow, made equally staunch friends among the leading Anglican clergy, including the Archbishop of Canterbury. Meanwhile Bentwich and Sacher had written an effective little volume dealing with the aims of Zionism which won an unusually wide distribution in the general market. The only strenuous opposition to the Zionist idea seemed now to come from a small, well-placed group of wealthy English Jews, who were concerned lest Zionist propaganda expose Anglo-Jewry to the charge of "dual loyalty."

By January 1917, Weizmann decided that the time had come to press the British government for a statement of pro-Zionist sympathy. There was no thought in his mind, or in the minds of his colleagues, of asking Britain to assume a protectorate over the Jewish National Home—not, at least, as early as 1917. Neither, on the other hand, did Weizmann or his friends have any inkling that Britain was precluded by the Sykes-Picot agreement from disposing of Palestine for the benefit of the Jews or anyone else. The Secretary of the War Cabinet, Sir Mark Sykes, one of the signatories to the agreement, was a loyal friend of Weizmann's; even he, however, could not divulge to the Zionists the nature of the secret pact, or the fact that the British government was forestalled from making an official statement on behalf of the Jewish National Home. Not until April of 1917 did Weizmann learn of the Sykes-Picot agreement from Charles P. Scott, who had uncovered the information in Paris. Of course he was shocked and dismayed: apparently the decision on Palestine had been up to France all the time.

As it happened, key Foreign Office officials had their own reasons for dissatisfaction with the Sykes-Picot agreement. For one thing, the British were bearing the major burden of military operations in the Near East, and felt that they were entitled to more for their efforts than the agreement provided. They were entitled, for example, to control of the eastern flank of the Suez Canal: namely, the Sinai Peninsula and Palestine. Yet the Foreign Office had no "moral" justification for a British protectorate over Palestine. It occurred to Lloyd George that a Jewish National Home might well provide that justification.

Then, too, the war was going badly. Russia had virtually been knocked out of the struggle; the French army clung to its trenches; the Italians had been disastrously defeated at Caporetto; enemy U-boats were playing havoc with Allied shipping; and American manpower was not yet engaged in telling numbers. In this desperate predicament, Lloyd George was willing to grasp at any straw. It was possible, he believed, that a British-sponsored homeland for the Jews in Palestine would favorably excite some powerful Jewish elements in America and Russia; perhaps if enough of them were influenced they would intercede with their governments on behalf of the Allied war effort.

Thus it was, in April of 1917, that the British themselves offered the Zionists a solution to the impasse created by the Sykes-Picot agreement. Lord Robert Cecil, Under-Secretary for Foreign Affairs, discreetly hinted to Weizmann that the British government would be willing to issue a statement endorsing a Jewish National Home in Palestine. In return, Cecil expected that Weizmann and his colleagues would appeal for a British protectorate in the area. Cecil hoped, too, that the Zionists would persuade their fellow Jews everywhere to mobilize world opinion on behalf of the Allied cause. Weizmann instantly grasped the implications of the offer, and agreed without hesitation to both stipulations.

Weizmann ardently hoped for an Allied victory primarily because he was a devoted friend of his adopted land. His love for the British people and his admiration for British values were basic motifs in his career. He could therefore make his appeals on behalf of the Allied war effort with no misgivings. Yet in his heart he must have known how futile his appeals would be. As a man of the highest intelligence, he surely realized that no conceivable *force majeure* was capable of shaking the loyalty of German and Austrian Jewry to the cause of the Central Powers; and he had enough understanding of American Jewry to recognize that they placed American national interest above all other considerations. As for the Jews of Russia, it was likely that their attitude to the war would be influenced by their loyalty to the new Kerensky regime—and little else. All this Weizmann must have known. But if Lloyd George and his associates credited him with more power than he had, it was not for him to disillusion them.

By July Weizmann and his colleagues completed a memorandum which they submitted to the Lloyd George Cabinet. It proposed the establishment *of* Palestine *as* a national home for the Jewish People; it called for full Jewish autonomy in the Holy Land, and for freedom of Jewish immigration there. On September 19, Lloyd George and his colleagues discussed the text draft. It is conceivable that they might have endorsed it then and there, had it not been for the vehement, tearful protest of the one Jew in the Cabinet, Edwin Montagu, Secretary of State for India, a bitter anti-Zionist. Balfour and Lloyd George sent for Weizmann, who had been asked to wait in another room. Trivialities can carry heavy consequences; the messengers failed to locate him. Lacking the data necessary to rebut Montagu, and knowing, too, that he spoke for some of the most "aristocratic" Jewish families in England, the two statesmen felt compelled to withdraw the draft from the agenda. The opposition of one man had destroyed a historic opportunity for a maximum British statement on behalf of the Jewish National Home.

Eventually a compromise formula was worked out by Sykes and Balfour; it was a formula with which Weizmann and his colleagues dared not tamper for fear of jeopardizing the project altogether. Before the British were willing to approve even a compromise draft, however, they insisted upon endorsement from the American government. The text of the proposed declaration was communicated to the White House by Colonel House, President Wilson's personal emissary in London. Wilson approved it without hesitation. The British government then moved ahead quickly, stating its position on November 2, 1917, in the form of a letter from Foreign Secretary Balfour to Lord Rothschild, President of the British Zionist Federation.

> Dear Lord Rothschild [the letter read], I have much pleasure in conveying to you, on behalf of His Majesty's Government, the following declaration of sympathy with Jewish Zionist aspirations which has been submitted to, and approved by, the Cabinet. His Majesty's Government view with favour the establishment in Palestine of a national home for the Jewish people, and will use their best endeavours to facilitate the achievement of this object, it being clearly understood that nothing shall be done which may prejudice the civil and religious rights of existing non-Jewish communities in Palestine, or the rights and political status enjoyed by Jews in any other country. I should be grateful to you if you would bring this declaration to the knowledge of the Zionist Federation.

"In" Palestine "of" a national home—a phrase which left the national home without defined boundaries, vulnerable to the successive attenuations of Jewish territory in Palestine for which later British governments would be responsible. Montagu had done his work better than he knew. At the time the Declaration was issued, however, the Lloyd George Cabinet had no intention of aborting the possibility of an ultimate Jewish commonwealth in Palestine. The Prime Minister himself later confirmed this unequivocally in his autobiography, as did Balfour, Cecil, and Churchill in subsequent public statements.

When the news of the Balfour Declaration was released, Jewish communities from Odessa to Shanghai went wild with happiness, dancing in the streets, cheering British and American consular officers, and deluging Whitehall and Washington with telegrams of gratitude. Only a month later, and by a prophetic coincidence, on the Jewish festival of Chanukah, General Allenby's British legions liberated Palestine and its Jewish population from the Turks. It appeared as if an era of incalculable promise and glory was unfolding for the Jewish people. There were many among the Orthodox who wondered if the Messianic deliverance had not begun.

THE STRUCTURE OF THE MANDATE

Then the war ended, and the delegates of the victorious Allied Powers assembled in Paris to rechart the world's boundaries. Britain had little difficulty in persuading the French to part with Palestine; in return Lloyd George promised Clemenceau diplomatic support on the issue of the Rhineland. But the Arabs, remembering McMahon's promise to the Sherif Husein, were less easily appeased. The Emir Faisal, Husein's brilliant and ambitious son, arrived in Paris to stake his claim for Arab independence. He was studiously ignored by Clemenceau and Lloyd George, and insulted by meaningless promises of autonomy under projected Anglo-French mandates. Bewildered and enraged, the Emir returned to Damascus; there he unilaterally "accepted" the kingship of the entire Arab rectangle. It was an audacious move: his "army's" equipment consisted of little more than ancient rifles and fowling pieces. Within less than a month, as a result, the French occupation forces broke the back of the uprising. Later, when Faisal's allies in Iraq sought to engineer a similar revolt against the Anglo-Indian regime there, they were crushed with even less difficulty. Overwhelmed by heavier firepower and superior technology, the Hashemi dynasty lost its bid for control of the Arab world. Faisal then grudgingly accepted the puppet throne of Iraq, which the British offered him in compensation. But he viewed this acceptance merely as a temporary, tactical retreat, until the time arrived for a new uprising. The Arab nationalists were adamant. They would not accept even temporarily the "intrusion" into the Arab Near East of a people whose rights they categorically denied.

At first, to be sure, the Emir Faisal had expressed no hostility toward the Balfour Declaration. In fact, he hoped to make allies of the Zionists. He had met with Weizmann early in 1919, and seemed satisfied with the Jewish statesman's assurances of friendship. In March of 1919, during his stay in Paris, Faisal even wrote a cordial letter to Felix Frankfurter, a member of the American Zionist delegation, promising that "we will do our best . . . to wish the Jews a most hearty welcome home. . . ." At San Remo, too, the Arab leaders remained silent while the peace conference awarded the Palestine Mandate to Britain and authorized the British to implement the Balfour Declaration. For their part, the British sought to insure Arab friendship for the Jewish National Home by detaching Trans-

Jordan from Palestine and awarding it to Faisal's brother, the Emir Abdullah. But eventually these mutual professions and concessions proved unavailing. The Arab nationalists were convinced that McMahon's letter of October 24, 1915, precluded the possibility of "alien" domination in Palestine. When it became apparent that the Zionists could not be won over as allies in the struggle against British and French domination, the Arabs, Faisal among them, began protesting ever more vigorously against Jewish immigration to Palestine. Moreover the enthronement of Faisal in Iraq, and the installation of his brother Abdullah across the Jordan, encouraged the Palestine Arab leaders to demand the immediate annulment of the Balfour Declaration.

In May of 1921 the Palestine Arabs resorted to violence. Riots, burnings, killings spread from Tel Aviv to the colonies—Petah Tiqva, Kfar Saba, Hadera, and Rehovot. While the casualties were not large—less than a hundred on both sides—they were evidence, nevertheless, that Arab nationalism would not confine itself merely to Syria or Iraq. The violence had the effect, moreover, of forcing the British further to "redefine" the area encompassed by the Balfour Declaration. It was the beginning of a process of attenuation that during the next twenty-seven years would steadily erode the letter and spirit of the Declaration. Weizmann, representing the World Zionist Organization, was eventually compelled to accept a White Paper (the "Churchill" White Paper, after the Colonial Secretary who sponsored it) which reaffirmed the Balfour Declaration, but which stated that the Zionists must not contemplate transforming Palestine as a whole into a Jewish National Home. At the same time the Arab community in Palestine was assured that it would not be inundated by Jewish settlement. Only after Weizmann yielded did Britain submit the mandate to the League of Nations Council. It was on the basis of these modifications that the League ratified the mandate in September 1923. Britain could now redefine its responsibilities in the hope of appeasing the Arabs.

The British Mandatory Government for Palestine was fairly unexceptional as far as it went. The legal system was set up along Anglo-Saxon lines—without including the jury system, however—and was staffed by British magistrates. The law itself was based on both Anglo-Saxon and Ottoman precedents. Efficient postal, railway, and telephone systems were installed throughout Palestine, together with hospitals and dispensaries. The mandatory's Education and Agriculture Departments devoted themselves primarily to Arab needs, assuming perhaps that in these fields the Jews were more than able to provide for themselves. By appointing an advisory council under his own chairmanship, the High Commissioner for Palestine sought to bring the representatives of the population into consultation on matters of public policy; to that end he reserved ten places for high British officials, four for prominent Moslem Arabs, three for Christian Arabs, and three for Jews. Actually, it was the government's hope eventually to give the council full legislative authority in all matters of internal affairs. But it was a foredoomed hope, for the Arabs steadfastly boycotted its sittings; and whenever, as in 1929, the project of creating a truly effective legislature was broached, it was swiftly abandoned in the face of Arab opposition. This left the mandatory little alternative but to deal with two separate entities, each with its own political structure.

In the case of the Jews, the structure was rather complicated. It involved an internal government for the Yishuv and a shared government for the Jewish National Home which linked the Palestine-Jewish community with the Jews of the world. The Yishuv encompassed only those Jews permanently resident in Palestine. The Jewish National Home involved a much broader formula, a special relationship between world Jewry and the revived national life emerging in Palestine. As far as the "community" was concerned, the Jews of Palestine elected members to their own national assembly, and exercised jurisdiction over purely domestic matters—health, education, religion. Equally significant, however, was the apparatus established for the administration of the Jewish National Home. The terms of the mandate laid down that "an appropriate Jewish Agency shall be recognized as a public body for the purpose of advising and cooperating with the Administration of Palestine in such economic, social, and other matters as may affect the establishment of the Jewish National Home." Provisionally the World Zionist Organization itself was accepted as such an agency. Thus, the W.Z.O. carried on all negotiations with the mandatory power on matters concerning the National Home. This included colonization and settlement, training and selecting immigrants, and until 1929 governing the policy of the Jewish National Fund and the *Keren Hayesod*.

But Weizmann, President of the World Zionist Organization—an honor extended to him after he secured the Balfour Declaration—was far from satisfied with this arrangement. Too many friendly and influential non-Zionists were prevented thereby from lending their talents, prestige, and resources to the creation of the Jewish National Home. Weizmann therefore sought to expand the basis of the Agency beyond the Zionist Organization; he hoped, in particular, to include some of the wealthy and powerful Jewish leaders of the United States and Western Europe. By 1929 this expansion was nominally accomplished; the Jewish Agency was broadened to include spokesmen from the non-Zionist world. Among the new members were Louis Marshall, Felix Warburg, and Léon Blum—men whose names lent added dignity to the Jewish effort in Palestine, and who were willing to stand side by side with the Zionists in the practical work of building up the homeland. For all normal purposes, however, the Executive of the Jewish Agency remained in the hands of the Zionists; during the diplomatic crises of the 1930's, when the harassed Zionists had little time to spare for public-relations niceties, the Jewish Agency reverted once again to a thinly disguised façade for the World Zionist Organization.

Under this arrangement, it was clear, the Agency was the mainspring of Jewish quasi government. The Agency's political department, for example, operated as the National Home's foreign office, negotiating with the British officials in Palestine, with the London Cabinet, and with the League of Nations on all matters affecting mandatory policy toward the building of Jewish Palestine. The Zionist organizations of other countries had representation on the Agency, but in reality, and increasingly so as the years passed, the fulcrum of the quasi government centered in the Yishuv and its leadership. By the mid-1930's the Jews of the Yishuv outnumbered all others on the Agency Executive; in this fashion they received invaluable experience in self-rule. Moreover the various departments of the Agency were staffed from within the Yishuv, so that a core of civil servants was continually being trained. The Jews even maintained their own militia, the Haganah, a powerful defense force which they established after the first Arab attacks of 1921, and which, though never really legalized by the British, numbered nearly twenty thousand men by 1936. A strong and continuing base for this quasi government was insured through excellent Jewish schools, which constituted one of the most effective instruments of nationalism. "From this educational 'melting-pot,'" observed the Royal Commission of 1936-37, "emerges a national self-consciousness of unusual intensity." Jewish teachers in the Yishuv believed that the encouragement of this national self-consciousness was their basic mission in the Holy Land.

An overwhelming majority of the Jews of Palestine respected the authority of the quasi government. Competition for control of its administration was keen, for with control went the right to determine policy, to manage large and growing national wealth, and to negotiate with the Mandatory and British Governments for changes in legislation for Palestine. This control was usually dependent upon the election results of the World Zionist Organization and of the Yishuv itself. The Zionists did not, as a rule, vote for candidates, but rather for party "lists" or tickets, and the key political planks were pledges to develop the National Home in specific ways. For example, one party envisaged a national home based on the theocratic ideal; another on capitalist and still another on socialist premises. Some parties developed combinations, elaborations, or refinements of their programs that rivaled the most factious characteristics of Balkan or Latin politics. By 1936, however, Mapai, the Labor Zionist party, which had been created out of the merger of Poale Zion and several smaller leftist groups, had become dominant in the World Zionist Organization, as well as in Palestine proper. It was destined, more than all others, to shape the unique framework of the Jewish National Home.

BUILDING THE JEWISH NATIONAL HOME

At the end of the first World War there were a mere fifty-five thousand Jews in Palestine, a demoralized, impoverished little community, still over-balanced by *Chalukah* mendicants. After the Balfour Declaration and the establishment of the mandate, successive Aliyot, waves of immigrants, settled in the country. Until the mid-1930's most of these Aliyot came from Poland, and each seemed to have a special character. The first Aliyah, from 1882 on, represented the emerging will to return; the second, from 1906 to 1914, was responsible for gradually turning from the mysticism of sentiment to more practical problems of colonization; the third, from 1919 to 1924, devoted itself to the preparation of the land for subsequent migrations.

The immigrants of the second and third Aliyot were true *Chalutzim,* pioneers, and most of them were imbued with the Labor Zionist viewpoint. Supported to the limit by the Jewish National Fund, they drained the swamps, plowed the fields, established the collective colonies—and sought to realize in their own lifetimes the ideal of physical rejuvenation preached by A. D. Gordon.

Not all immigrants were idealists, of course. The thirty-four thousand Polish Jews—the fourth Aliyah—who arrived in 1925 were refugees, pure and simple, from Polish anti-Semitism. Peddling, setting up the petty shops and *gazoz* (confectionery) stands by which they had earned their livelihoods in postwar Poland, they very nearly transformed the Zionist institutions into relief organizations. Eventually however even this fourth Aliyah was absorbed into the economy of the Yishuv; it played a historic role if only because it so materially augmented the Jewish population of Palestine. The rise of Hitler added still other refugees but now the mainstream was coming out of Central Europe. To a total Jewish population of 84,000 in 1922, 345,000 were added in the course of the following twenty-three years. The Jewish Agency's immigration department maintained offices in the larger cities of Europe to organize and direct this new inflow. As a rule, the department was careful to give priority to young Zionists, and, whenever possible, youngsters were trained in agricultural and manual work, and educated in the use of Hebrew at special camps operated by various branches of the Zionist Organization. As a direct result of this immigration policy, by 1936 85 per cent of the Jews of Palestine were under forty-five years old, and the average age was twenty-seven.

It was superb raw material, and the leadership of the Zionist movement was resolved not to waste it. The Jewish Agency exerted every effort to insure that the disproportionate economic concentration of the European epochs would not be duplicated in Palestine. It was not always a simple matter to move the newcomers into agriculture. Palestine was only 160 miles long and 70 miles wide. Of the four principal geographical divisions of the country—the hills of Galilee in the north, the west central plains, the flat and dusty Beersheba area in the south, the arid Negeb Desert in the southeast—only the first two were suitable for normal cultivation. Even these were swampy, malarial, dependent upon irrigation from wells, and under continued assault by Arab marauders. It was a tribute to the effectiveness of Zionist indoctrination as well as to the courage and tenacity of the pioneers that such large numbers were willing to remain on the soil in spite of a wide variety of physical and psychological obstacles.

Whenever possible, the Jewish National Fund purchased agricultural land as the "inalienable property" of the Jewish people, and then leased it at a nominal rent to Jewish farmers. By 1939 approximately 30 per cent of Jewish farmland was on loan in this way. A second fund, the *Keren Hayesod,* purchased tools, housing, and equipment for the settlers. The combined efforts of these two agencies proved to be exceptionally valuable in creating the nucleus of a Jewish agricultural class. In 1919 there had been less than fifty Jewish agricultural settlements in Palestine, sustaining a population of 12,000. Ten years later the number of settlements had risen to one hundred and twenty, with a population of 40,000. With the help of agricultural experts imported by the Jewish Agency, most of the farmers were able to apply the most modern scientific techniques of irrigation and crossbreeding. Their success was most notable in the development of citriculture; by 1937 the Yishuv was exporting eleven million cases of citrus fruit annually. There was little, perhaps, that was really spectacular in Jewish agricultural achievement in these years. The historic achievement was not in economic statistics or in unique institutions; it was in the psychological victory of untrained Zionists who remained on the soil, who were determined to stake out a claim on the land, to prove that it had absorptive capacity, and that Jews could reorient their economic energies if given the opportunity.

One of the most significant characteristics of Jewish agriculture was its emphasis upon the Labor Zionist ideal of collectivism. Perhaps the pioneer farmers did not really have much choice. The soil of Palestine was submarginal; the one crop that it could produce naturally was oranges, and citriculture was early pre-empted by capitalist farmers. If Jews wished to produce normal staple crops—vegetables, wheat, cereals—they could hardly survive as private owners on the Western model. Barren, waterless soil, unrelenting sun, malaria would have broken the will of the most pugnacious individualist. Collective farming was the only effective technique to redeem the earth of Palestine. Fortunately the Jewish National Fund and the *Keren Hayesod* opened up the land and supplied the equipment which gave the settlers the opportunity to test the techniques of collective farming.

The co-operative effort took several forms. One was the *kvutzah*, the completely Socialist colony, where families tilled the soil and poured their profits back into the land, taking nothing for themselves beyond their basic needs. Another form was the *moshav*, which combined co-operative and individualistic functions. Here each family worked on its own strip of land, owned its own home, and retained its own income. All farm machinery and farm equipment was owned in common, however, and the policies of the colony were democratically decided by an elected committee. In between the two was the *kibbutz*, a "*kvutzah* in the making." The *kibbutzniks* lived together on land assigned by the Jewish National Fund, shared a common kitchen and nursery, a common social and cultural life; but they supplemented their work in their own fields by accepting employment on the outside, pooling all their earnings in a common treasury.

In the collective settlements one man's work usually counted as much as any other's. Thus, equality in the distribution of goods and services remained the norm, and all the farmers and their families shared the same food. In some collectives, even private gifts of radios and books were absorbed into a communal pool and were rotated among the members. The colonists were no less egalitarian in their political viewpoint. In many ways *kibbutz* politics were akin to the primal democracy of the New England town meeting. Once or twice a week *kibbutz* members gathered in a "general meeting," the colony's supreme governing body. It was this assembly which voted the annual budgets, elected the members of committees, considered appeals from committee decisions. The general meeting largely absorbed the member's "leisure" hours. The evenings not devoted to government affairs were usually spent on watchtowers, guarding against Arab marauders. Since private leisure was rare and precious, many *kibbutz* members preferred an individual family life, and insisted that children and parents should live together. Others believed that an intimate family life would interfere with the communal spirit of the settlement. Yet none, not even the most Socialist-oriented among them, were "robotized" by their experience. In their private lives most of them seemed actually to become more deeply entrenched in their individualism than the typical capitalist. Perhaps it was a form of compensation. In time the typical *kibbutznik* could usually be identified not merely by his toughness, but also by an almost arrogant self-confidence. He was no ghetto type.

Not all Palestinian Jews were farmers, of course. As late as 1939 less than 25 per cent of the inhabitants of the Yishuv lived on the soil. In 1914 the population of Tel Aviv was 2,000; by 1939 it was 150,000; while the Jewish populations of Haifa and Jerusalem grew from less than 10,000 each in 1919 to 60,000 and 90,000 respectively in 1939. Neither, on the other hand, did most Jews return to their old vocations of petty trade or peddling. By 1942 less than 15 per cent of the Yishuv's breadwinners were engaged in any form of commerce whatever, even in its productive and lucrative branches. Most of them were employed in labor and in light and heavy industry as masons, glaziers, street-cleaners, electricians, plumbers, steel-workers; it was their labor which made possible the Yishuv's rapid urban and industrial development. The growth of Palestine was also promoted, in large measure, by the Palestine Economic Corporation, a private enterprise run on sound business principles, although not primarily for profit, which invested in such basic industries as the Palestine Electric Corporation and Palestine Potash, Ltd.

The Palestine Electric Corporation was largely the creation of Pinchas Rutenberg, a hard-driving, rather eccentric Russian-Jewish engineer. Rutenberg planned and supervised the construction of several large hydroelectric dams on the Jordan river; by 1936 these plants generated approximately 70,000,000 kilowatt-hours of electricity. Together with the Reading generators in Tel Aviv, constructed a few years later, the Rutenberg works brought a significant improvement in living standards for most of the Jews of Palestine; for the first time many of the pioneering families knew what it was to enjoy efficient illumination and refrigeration. Electrification made possible, too, the rapid expansion of other industries: the Nesher Cement Works, the Shemen Oil Works, the Rothschild Flour Mills, Palestine Potash, Ltd. By the late 1930's, indeed, the Yishuv was changing from a pioneer outpost into something approaching a frontier of modernity in the Near East.

The dominating influence on the economy of the Yishuv, permeating every aspect of personal and social living, was the all-embracing Histadrut, the Federation of Jewish Labor. It was founded by Berl Katznelson, one of the foremost pillars of the second Aliyah, a disciple of Syrkin and

Borochov. From the early 1920's to the end of the second World War Katznelson was the intellectual leader and spiritual counselor of the Yishuv's labor movement. Ben-Gurion, for example, the Executive Secretary of the Histadrut, was his disciple and protégé; it was under Katznelson's influence that the future prime minister built the organization into a vast workers' collective-bargaining agent. It was Ben-Gurion and Katznelson, too, who transformed the Histadrut into one of the principal investing agencies in the Yishuv. By 1929 the sprawling federation sponsored at least five hundred co-operatives, operating in every economic sphere: in agriculture, construction, manufacturing, marketing, purchasing, insurance, and banking. The objective of the co-operative movement was not only to promote the immediate interests of its members, but also to expand the absorptive potential of the Yishuv. Even public health was considered an appropriate area of responsibility for Histadrut. Co-operating with the Hadassah Medical Organization, it maintained a wide network of hospitals, dispensaries, clinics, and infant-feeding stations throughout the country. Together, the two organizations employed hundreds of physicians, dentists, and nurses. The result of this emphasis on medical care was a dramatic drop in Palestine's mortality rate, together with an equally notable drop in the incidence of malaria and trachoma.

Progress in education was equally noteworthy. The small group of schools which the Zionist Organization took over in 1914 after the bitter language struggle with the *Hilfsverein* had grown by 1929 to a total of 220 with some 20,000 students—and had doubled again within another decade. A Hebrew university was established in Jerusalem in 1925 as an act of faith in the Yishuv's future, and within ten years had established first-rate undergraduate and graduate divisions, staffed by some of the outstanding scholars and scientists of Europe.

The cultural level of the Yishuv was remarkably high; in literacy its people perhaps ranked highest in the world. It was not surprising that a brilliant, vital group of literary giants, who were early attracted to Palestine, should find there the deepest respect and encouragement, and the perfect opportunity for the fulfillment of their promise. There was Chaim Nachman Bialik, poet laureate of the Hebrew language, whose superb command of haggadic traditions and rabbinic lore was a prime factor in the Hebrew renaissance. There was Joseph Chaim Brenner, novelist and short-story writer, who treated the problems of the self-questioning Jewish intelligentsia with rare sensitivity. Tragically enough, just as he was reaching the fullest power of his artistry, he was killed in the Arab riots of 1921. There were others: S. J. Agnon, the Yishuv's most sympathetic interpreter of East European traditional Jewish life; the lyric poet, Saul Tchernichovsky, who worshiped physical beauty with an ardor that was more Hellenic than Hebrew; Zalmon Schneur, Yitzhak Lamdan, Uri Zvi Greenberg—all poetic craftsmen of the first rank, who wrote prolifically despite, at least at first, the comparatively narrow base of their Hebrew-reading public. The tradition of plaint and sorrow, of self-pity and protest against the cruelity of fate, of weeping and wailing over victims and martyrs—all of this was submerged in a new tradition of pride and hope and thanksgiving, for the freedom that emerged from hardship, for the honey and the oil that came from the flint and the rock. The motif in early Palestinian poetry which recurred most often and evoked most passion was the "religion of labor," the exaltation experienced in rebuilding the sacred homeland with the sweat of one's brow and the brawn of one's back. The poetess Rachel Bluwstein expressed the mood of the second and third Aliyot:

> A jug of water in the hand, and on
> My shoulder—basket, spade and rake.
> To distant fields, to toil, my path I make.
>
> Upon my right the green hills fling
> Protecting arms; before me—the wide fields!
> And in my heart my twenty Aprils sing . . .
>
> Be this my lot, until I be undone;
> Dust of the road, my land, and thy
> Grain waving golden in the sun.

In the Jewish-inhabited areas Palestine was actually becoming an attractive and civilized country in which to live. It was certainly exciting and stimulating. This was the land that Herzl had envisaged in his novel, *Altneuland*—except that the language, traditions, and aspirations of the real *Altneuland*—*1939* were authentically Hebraic. By then there were 550,000 Jews in Palestine, exactly ten times the number that had lived there twenty years earlier. They had created their own quasi government, their own agricultural and industrial economy, their own distinctive Hebraic culture. The achievements were not to be measured in statistics nor to be compared by Western standards. They were to be measured in the context of the problems of an uprooted people who were determined to create a well-balanced, "normal" society. They came to their historic task with ready hands and hearts, and, above all, with a determination to cut through old forms and conventional patterns, to experiment boldly with new social forms. The determination was all the more exceptional by contrast with the squalor and lethargy of the neighboring Arab community.

THE RISE OF PALESTINE ARAB NATIONALISM

The seven hundred thousand Arabs of Palestine were concentrated principally in the hill districts of the central and northern part of the country, and to a lesser extent in the coastal plain. Most of them were *fellahin,* peasants, who tilled the soil as tenants of the small circle of Moslem families that owned virtually all the Arab land of Palestine, and dominated the Arab social system. The peasantry's standard of living was among the lowest on earth. Without the faintest notion of the purposes of sanitation, burning camel dung for fuel, tethering animals in the tents where they slept, nearly 90 per cent of the *fellahin* were critically infected with syphilis and bilharziasis. The Jews stimulated considerable economic activity, but the money spent by them among the Arabs rarely reached the *fellahin*; it usually ended up in the hands of the feudal landlords of the hill areas or the Christian Arab real-estate dealers in the coastal cities. The political structure of the Arab community also differed radically from its Jewish counterpart. The Arabs were governed by clans; and these clans, usually pyramidal in organization, led up to the unchallengeable authority of two or three powerful landowning families. The ruling oligarchy had a vested interest in maintaining the *status quo,* and, far from encouraging, it staunchly resisted any attempts to inaugurate shared government on Anglo-Saxon lines. As a result, the Arab communities gained virtually no experience in self-rule.

The leading families were all bitterly anti-Zionist. In some instances this anti-Zionism was rooted in fear of Jewish free labor and collective farming, and of the dangerous ideas these innovations would implant in the minds of the tenants. For the most part, however, the most articulate Arab opposition to Jewish immigration was the result of genuine folk pride. Increasing numbers of Arabs were awakening to their "destiny" as a people, and they resented the intrusion into the Levant of an alien nation from the West. While most of the *fellahin* remained quite ignorant of political developments—they were 90 per cent illiterate—the Arab upper middle class, the professional people, the businessmen, as well as the landowners, viewed the Zionist experiment with growing concern. They frankly feared that these European Jews, with apparently limitless financial and technological resources, would some day engulf all of Palestine, and transform the country into a Jewish state, a dagger poised at the Arab heart. In Arab newspapers, in political discussions in cafés, and in occasional street rallies, this resentment of Jewish infiltration was expressed with bitterness and passion. Nor, for that matter, was it difficult to arouse anti-Jewish feeling among the devout and superstitious peasantry, for the Jews were identified with an alien religious tradition.

The leadership of the anti-Zionist movement was largely centered in the influential Husseini clan, which owned most of southern Palestine, and traditionally had provided the mayors for the cities of Jerusalem and Haifa. In 1922, the mandatory granted the Arabs permission to establish their own Supreme Moslem Council, ostensibly to co-ordinate the religious activities and institutions of the Palestine Arab community. Inasmuch as Islam was— and is—a socio-political creed, the Council took over virtually unchallenged political power. The Council was controlled by the Husseinis; its lifetime president, or mufti, was Haj Amin-al-Husseini.

With his gentle moon face, blue eyes, and red hair and beard, the Mufti appeared to be the mildest of men. In conversation his manner was quiet and ingratiating; in correspondence he was the model of delicacy and tact. But his mildness was deceptive, for he was destined to become the most belligerent nationalist and anti-Zionist in the entire Arab world. An astute and ambitious politician, Haj Amin al-Husseini took full advantage of his position as mufti, and of his unlimited rights of appointment and dismissal, to create a personal, country-wide political machine. He did not hesitate for a moment to bribe the officials of dependent religious establishments with money taken in as the Council's annual revenues; for through these officials he was able to reach the illiterate *fellahin* and appeal to their religious fanaticism. For a while the mandatory hoped to use the Mufti as a puppet through whom it could maintain contact with Moslems in other Arab countries. But within a few years it became apparent that his nationalism was directed as much against the British as against the Jews. The colonial officials in Palestine then sought to whittle down the Mufti's powers and prerogatives, and to build up the more conciliatory Nashashibi family into an effective counterpoise. But by then it was too late.

In the summer of 1929 the Mufti prepared to intensify his attacks against the Yishuv. In July his agents circulated rumors that the Jews were planning an assault on Moslem shrines. On August 15, Arab nationalists used a traditional Jewish religious demonstration in front of the Wailing Wall of Jerusalem as the pretext for a nation-wide pogrom. In the week that followed, Arab bands swooped down on Jewish homes and settlements, gunned down Jewish farmers and their families, and inflicted nearly five hundred casualties. The raids seriously shook the complacency of the mandatory; British officials in Palestine had not been aware until then that the Arab nationalist movement extended beyond the boundaries of Syria and Iraq. Lord Passfield, Britain's Colonial Secretary, immediately dispatched two investigating commissions to the scene of the riots. The first commission was led by Sir Walter Shaw, a former colonial jurist, the second by Sir John Hope Simpson, an expert on economic matters. Both investigating groups spent nearly three months in Palestine, studying the country's legal and economic problems, and listening to witnesses for Jews, Arabs, and the mandatory administration.

To the amazement of the Zionists, the report of the Shaw Commission completely absolved the Mufti and the Arab Executive of any complicity in the riots. Intimating that the country was not capable of absorbing further Jewish immigrants, the report urged a restatement of policy which would "safeguard the rights of the non-Jewish communities in Palestine." The conclusions of the Simpson Commission were even more extreme, condemning virtually every phase of the Zionist effort in Palestine. Jewish industry was unsound, the report declared; the policy of the Jewish National Fund, which required that its farm settlements should employ only Jewish labor, was reprehensible; the social objectives of the Histadrut were undesirable. The commission recommended that Jewish immigration, as well as Jewish land acquisition, should be drastically restricted.

If the reports shocked the Zionists, the consequences of the reports were even more stunning. The Colonial Secretary of the British Labour Government was the eminent Fabian Socialist, Sidney Webb, later Lord Passfield. Zionism had long been anathema to him; his wife and collaborator, Beatrice, had once remarked to Weizmann: "I can't understand why the Jews make such a fuss over a few dozen of their people killed in Palestine. As many are killed every week in London in traffic accidents, and no one pays any attention." It was of little consequence to Passfield that the Jews were building in the midst of the feudal Arab world precisely the kind of Socialist economy that British Labourites admired most. The Histadrut, which Simpson condemned so vigorously, represented the type of public-welfare planning that the Colonial Secretary had advocated in a lifetime of writing. He stigmatized Zionism as an "imperialist" and "colonial" movement; he was ready to scuttle the Yishuv on the very imperialistic desire to safeguard Britain's colonial position in the Near East by placating the Arabs and their feudal overlords. In 1930 he secured permission from Prime Minister Ramsay MacDonald to issue a White Paper which virtually "interpreted" the Balfour Declaration to death. The Passfield White Paper prohibited any further Jewish purchase of agricultural land in Palestine, and served notice that Jewish labor immigration into Palestine would henceforth be severely curtailed.

Outraged by this "betrayal," Weizmann resigned as president of the World Zionist Organization. Protests poured in on Whitehall from Jews and non-Jews throughout the Empire. It was, indeed, impossible for a labor government, dependent upon the good will of liberals and humanitarians, to ignore the cumulative impact of the protests. Within a year MacDonald himself was compelled to write Weizmann, assuring him that there would be no change in the government's attitude toward the Balfour Declaration, and that the normal growth of the Jewish National Home would not be inhibited by political considerations. In effect, MacDonald's letter was a repudiation of the Passfield White Paper. For the moment, at least, the Zionists breathed easier. And yet, in the light of the continued Arab political pressure and of the ambiguous phraseology of the Balfour Declaration itself, the Jews had a sobering insight into the Yishuv's vulnerability. Even before Hitler assumed power in Germany, they sensed the urgency of consolidating their strength and their numbers in Palestine. From 1930 to 1936, under the aegis of the friendly High Commissioner, Sir Arthur Wauchope, the efforts of the Palestine Jewish community to drain and reclaim the soil, to industrialize and electrify their cities, were even more feverish. During those six years, too, the population of the Yishuv rose by another 200,000.

THE ARABS STEP UP THE ATTACK

Meantime an endemic Arab guerrilla campaign in the areas surrounding Palestine won far-reaching concessions from the Mandatory Powers. In 1930 the British decided to grant Iraq its full independence, and to support Iraq's admission into the League of Nations. In Egypt, too, Britain gave ground and permitted a fuller measure of *de facto* independence, exchanging ambassadors and, as in the case of Iraq, supporting Egypt's admission into the League. In Syria and Lebanon the French Mandatory relaxed its autocratic grip; after a series of bloody revolts and equally bloody suppressions, France granted these countries their independence in 1936 and supported their entrance into the League. In each case British and French military interests and air and naval bases were protected; but what loomed largest in the Arab mind was the lesson that nationalist pressure could and did bring results.

The retreat of the Mandatory Powers was motivated by more than a tolerant appreciation of Arab nationalism. It was judged that if the Arabs were not swiftly placated they would move into the camp of powerful rivals. In the 1930's the growing strength of the Axis Powers, Italy and Germany, presented a serious threat to the Anglo-French position in the Mediterranean. Mussolini cultivated Arab nationalism at every opportunity, viewing it as a weapon with which to dislodge the English and French from the Mediterranean. The powerful radio station at Bari beamed Arabic broadcasts into the Levant at all hours of the day and night, striking equally at British and French imperialism, and at Zionism as the alleged instrument of that imperialism. The Nazis simultaneously maintained a propaganda apparatus in Palestine proper, staffing it with German shipping agents, commercial travelers, students, businessmen, and permanent residents, along with professional propagandists. The official German News Agency supplied the Arab press of Palestine, Trans-Jordan, Syria, and Lebanon with news handouts; the Agency's director, Dr. Franz Reichert, became a close personal friend of the Mufti. Even the Templars, members of a German religious sect in Palestine, maintained contacts with the Arabs, and effectively allied them to long-range Nazi objectives. Arab editors borrowed freely from Nazi anti-Semitic clichés. One Arab journal declared:

> Hitlerism is violently but nevertheless truly symptomatic of a world which is sick to death of the pedestrian materialistic civilization of the industrial countries, which gave the subversive activities of Judaism the chance to develop a stranglehold on international economics.

When Mohammed's birthday was celebrated in May 1937, German and Italian flags, pictures of Hitler and Mussolini were prominently displayed by Arab paraders in Palestine, while Arab newspapers hailed this display as a "significant gesture of sympathy and respect . . . with the Nazis and Fascists in their agony and trials at the hands of Jewish intrigues and international financial pressure . . ." The Palestine Arab revolt was not altogether engineered and financed by the Axis; but the weapons supplied by the Germans and Italians, together with their funds and military direction, was a significant contributing factor.

The Axis intrusion into the Mediterranean magnified the position of Palestine in Britain's strategic planning. For after the grant of independence to Iraq and Egypt, Britain was obliged to place greater reliance on its military installations in Palestine and Trans-Jordan from where British forces could operate radially. The port of Haifa was a key naval base, as well as a vital terminus for the oil pipe line from Iraq. Haifa could supplement, or in case of need, replace Alexandria as a naval base in the southeastern Mediterranean; while the Negeb might be used as an alternative to the Canal Zone in the defense of Suez. None of these considerations escaped the Arab leaders. Precisely because they understood the precariousness of Britain's position in the Near East, the vital importance of Palestine in British military and naval thinking, they suspected that Whitehall might be willing to throttle the Jewish National Home as the price for Arab co-operation in Palestine. They were determined, at any rate, to find out.

In 1936 the Palestine Arab nationalists established an executive agency under the presidency of the Mufti, which they called the Arab Higher Committee. It was perhaps the first truly effective instrument of the Arab nationalist movement in Palestine. With Axis backing, the Committee launched a nation-wide propaganda campaign designed to provoke anti-Jewish assaults. The campaign was successful. Beginning in April 1936, bands of armed Arabs raided Jewish settlements, cutting telephone wires and trees, shooting down villagers. From the start, the neighboring Arab countries supported the guerrillas by sending large numbers of "volunteers" into Palestine. One of the guerrilla leaders was the Lebanese-born Fawzi Kaukji, who resigned his commission in the Iraqi army to assume supreme command of the rebel units. While the Jews resisted direct attacks on their settlements, they were under instructions from the Jewish Agency to avoid, at all costs, reprisals on Arab communities. This was the beginning of the Jewish policy of *Havlagah,* "restraint." By a refusal to engage in counter-terrorism, the Yishuv hoped to place the onus of the attacks unmistakably on the Arabs. They expected, as well, to deny the British any possible excuse for a further attenuation of the Balfour Declaration—by bracketing Jews and Arabs "impartially" in the "disturbances."

During the early months of the Arab attacks, the mandatory studiously avoided making more than a nominal effort to protect the Jewish settlers. In a choice between Arab and Jewish good will, the colonial officials in Palestine had long since decided in favor of the Arabs. In later months, however, as Arab guerrilla bands began to launch direct attacks on British garrisons as well as on Jewish settlements, the High Commissioner was compelled to call for sterner discipline. Unfortunately the acute international crisis in Europe in 1936 prevented the War Office from sending necessary reinforcements to Palestine, and the mandatory watched helplessly as arms and money from German and Italian agents passed into Arab hands. Nor could the few thousand British troops in Palestine, with their orthodox battle training and their unfamiliarity with the terrain, cope effectively with the lightly armed, fast-moving Arab raiders. The defense of the Yishuv during those critical years devolved principally upon the Jews themselves.

Very reluctantly, the British permitted the Jews to train their own militia, the Haganah, and for a while even supplied limited light arms with which to protect outlying Jewish farm settlements. Many of the Jewish soldiers, or "supernumerary Jewish police," as the British called them, were trained in counterterrorist tactics by a British army officer, Captain Orde Wingate. Wingate was an extraordinary figure. A daring and imaginative soldier, he was also a devout student of the Bible. Indeed, it was through religious conviction that Wingate became a passionate Zionist, and volunteered for the job of training a Jewish defense force. Weizmann's recollection was eloquent:

... I can testify that he was idolized by the men who fought under him, and that they were filled with admiration for his qualities of endurance, courage, and originality. There are hundreds who recall how, having to cope with the Arab guerillas who descended on the Haifa-Mosul pipe line from time to time, destroyed a section of it, and retreated as fast as they had come, Wingate created a special motorcycle squad to patrol the whole length of the line, and by matching speed against speed, eliminated the threat. The Jews under his command were especially feared by the Arabs. Wingate used to tell me that when, at the head of a Jewish squad, he ambushed a group of raiders, he would hear a shout: "Run! These are not British soldiers! They are Jews!"

They were Jews quite unlike those of whom Bialik had written after Kishinev:

> Do not pity them! The whip has burned them,
> But they are used to sorrow and intimate with shame. . . .

It was a different generation now; and the training they received from Wingate was to stand them in good stead in the years to come.

By 1937 the heaviest fighting subsided; it was, after all, costing the Arabs enormous losses in wasted citrus crops. But sporadic shooting continued until 1939. By then the estimated fatalities for the three years of violence included 2,287 Arabs, 450 Jews, and 140 Britons. Actually, however, the attacks had accomplished their purpose long before 1939, for they compelled Whitehall to re-evaluate completely the Palestine Mandate. In November 1936, the British Government sent a Royal Commission to Palestine with instructions to make a detailed and widespread investigation of the tensions there. Lord William Robert Peel, who headed the group, was a former Secretary of State for India, with a reputation for the highest objectivity and integrity; most of the other members were equally distinguished. The Commission spent two months listening to the testimony of Jewish, Arab, and Mandatory representatives. Throughout the hearings Peel presided with patience and fairness, in spite of the agonizing stomach cancer which was even then eating away at his life.

The Commission's report, issued in July of 1937, was an exceptionally detailed document, packed with statistics and factual data. It found no basis for the Arab claim of exploitation. Stating, instead, that the Arabs had benefited measurably from the growth of the Yishuv, the report deprecated the Mandatary's "policy of conciliation." But it concluded by declaring the Palestine Mandate unworkable—in view of irreconcilable Arab and Jewish interests—and recommended in its stead the partition of Palestine into separate Arab and Jewish States. It was a drastic and revolutionary proposal, but the government was prepared to endorse it. Hopefully the recommendation for partition was submitted to the Jews and Arabs for their consideration.

It was a sorely beset Zionist Congress which met in Zurich in August 1937. The issue of partition convulsed the delegates no less profoundly than had the issue of Uganda thirty-four years earlier. There were many, particularly among the Orthodox and the Revisionists, who believed that the Yishuv had already beeen disastrously truncated by the Trans-Jordan "surgery" of 1921. Acceptance of the proposal was a betrayal of history and would close out all hope for the development of a productive and defensible Yishuv. There were others, however, Labor and the General Zionists among them, who felt that the offer might appropriately be explored. Weizmann was the spokesman for this second group. He argued that partition did, after all, involve an outright acknowledgment of the possibility of Jewish statehood, a possibility which no responsible Zionist had ever before presumed to utter publicly. The compromise was costly, but the gains would be breath-taking. Eventually Weizmann's prestige carried the issue; after bitter debate the Congress gave him a vote of confidence, and authorized him to enter into negotiations with the British government "with a view to ascertaining the precise terms of His Majesty's Government for the proposed establishment of a Jewish State."

Had the delegates but known it, all their debate and controversy was academic. In the summer of 1937 a sudden flare-up of Arab terrorism killed and wounded several hundred more Jews. This factor, together with the unalterable opposition to the partition plan of the colonial career officials in Palestine, convinced the British government that no solution for Palestine was feasible which did not have the prior consent of the Arabs. In April 1938, a British "Partition" commission headed by Sir John Woodhead arrived in Palestine. After a month of investigation, Woodhead and his colleagues concluded that the Peel plan for partition could never produce "viable" Arab and Jewish states. With the Woodhead report as its pre-text, the British government decided to attempt an entirely new approach to Arab-Jewish *rapprochement*.

In December 1938, spokesmen for both Arabs and Jews were called to London to participate in a series of round-table conferences on the future of Palestine. The London Conference began in February 1939, at St. James's Palace, and was presided over alternately by Prime Minister Neville Chamberlain, Foreign Secretary Lord Halifax, and Colonial Secretary Malcolm MacDonald. The term "round table" was a misnomer, for the Arabs adamantly refused to sit in the same room with Weizmann and his colleagues; they announced, moreover, that they would agree to no solution which envisaged the continuation of Jewish immigration into Palestine. Given this intransigent attitude on the part of the Arabs, it soon became clear that no voluntary agreement could be reached between the two groups. For several weeks the separate conversations meandered along hopelessly and meaninglessly. Then, in March of 1939, the British government sum-marily terminated the Conference, and announced that it was preparing to impose a solution of its own. Britain was already in the Munich climate; its solution for Palestine reflected its authentic spirit.

Even before the public announcement, Weizmann was prepared for the new plan; a clerk in the Colonial Office had inadvertently sent the Jewish delegation a copy of the British draft statement. As Weizmann read the document he could scarcely believe his eyes; it was outright capitulation to the Arab extremists, for it envisaged the complete termination of Jewish immigration to Palestine after a period of five years. Weizmann confronted Malcolm MacDonald with the copy and accused him to his face of betrayal. "MacDonald was very crestfallen," Weizmann recalled, "and stammered some ineffective excuses, falling back always on the argument that the document did not represent the final view of His Majesty's Government." But that was exactly what the document did represent. When the British government revealed its policy officially in May, the White Paper fully confirmed Weizmann's worst anticipation. It set a maximum total of 75,000 Jewish immigrants into Palestine over the next five years, and then decreed that further Jewish immigration would be stopped altogether.

The evisceration of the Balfour Declaration, which began with the "redefinition" of 1921 and continued with the Passfield White Paper and later with the Woodhead report, was now complete. Sucked into a desperate international crisis, the Chamberlain Government concluded that the Jewish National Home was not less expendable than the Sudetenland had been a year earlier. The decision made no pretense at ethics or sentiment. *Realpolitik* has no morality; and it was obvious that the Jews could not go over to the Axis camp, whatever the British decided. But the Arabs could, and they must be held in line at all costs. The tragedy was that England's appeasement of the Arabs was unavailing. When World War II broke, the Arabs defected to the Axis, anyway, even as the Zionist leaders had predicted.

CONCLUSION

Black as circumstances appeared in 1939, there was a significant reservoir of achievement from which to draw strength and inspiration. For one thing, when the first World War ended, few Zionists, even the most optimistic among them, could have envisaged the extraordinary progress of the next two decades. The Yishuv's growth in population, productivity, health standards, and nationalist spirit was an astonishment even to the maximalists of the Zionist movement. But the historic impact of the new land went far beyond the Yishuv. The romance of pioneering gave verve, meaning, and inner dignity to Jewish life everywhere. Perhaps its most enduring influence was exerted on the education of the young. In Eastern Europe—Poland, Lithuania, and Romania—the Zionists established educational systems of their own under the name of *Tarbut,* "Culture." In these school networks Hebrew was the language of instruction, and the vigorous Zionist ideal permeated the curriculum. It was significant that *Tarbut* schools attracted far more students than the institutions established by rival Socialist or Orthodox groups. Among young, and not so young for that matter, in nearly every Jewish community in the world, save for Nazi- or Soviet-occupied territory, a quickening of the Jewish spirit was apparent: it reflected itself in a renaissance of Jewish folk music, Jewish drama and opera, Jewish art and belles-lettres, Jewish religious expression—even in Jewish athletic and gymnastic activity. By the eve of the second World War it appeared as if the dreams of Ahad Ha'am were to find major fulfillment.

Freedom, physical and spiritual awakening, dignity, self-assurance—they were all embraced in the resurgent nationalist experience. It was an experience that quickened the hearts of caftaned Jews in Eastern Europe, lifted the spirits of frightened and assimilated Jews in Central Europe, elicited the sympathetic interest of those American Jews whose roots lay in the Zionist terra firma of Poland and Russia. The schoolboy in Warsaw, the seamstress in New York's garment district, the disillusioned Jewish intellectual of Berlin, all were stirred by the concept of a bronzed new race of Jews who spoke their own Hebrew language, worked their own plows, loaded their own rifles, sang their own songs, and never hushed their voices or looked back in fear over their shoulders. Arab nationalism was a fact and a reality which the twentieth century could not ignore. But the vague mystic sense of peoplehood that had reappeared in the Pale of Settlement in the nineteenth century had also become a reality on the soil of Palestine within the space of two generations. It was full-blooded Jewish nationalism, no less deeply anchored or sincerely felt than its Arab counterpart. And like Arab nationalism, it, too, would have to be reckoned with some day.

Notes

Page 373. Description of Weizmann quoted in Ronald Storrs, *Orientations*, p. 439.

Page 384. Translation of Rachel Bluwstein poem by Simon Halkin, *Modern Hebrew Literature*, p. 127.

XIX

The Impact of the Jews on Western Culture

THE PHENOMENON OF JEWISH INTELLECTUALISM

In 1926 an Austrian Protestant, Hugo Bettauer, published a provocative little novel which he called *Stadt Ohne Juden*—"City Without Jews." For the most part the book was a thinly veiled satire on the anti-Semitic politics of the author's native Vienna. Bettauer's villain, the Chancellor, decided to expel all Jews who lived in the capital city; he justified the expulsion on the basis of Jewish "domination." "With their uncannily keen intelligence," the Chancellor explained, "their worldliness and freedom of tradition, their catlike versatility and their lightning comprehension—with all their faculties, accentuated by centuries of oppression, they overpowered us, became our masters, and gained the upper hand in all our economic, spiritual and cultural life." Unfortunately for the Chancellor's plans, the elimination of the Jews resulted in calamitous changes in the economic and cultural life of the city. Without Jewish patronage, the opera closed, as did the theaters, the art salons, the publishing houses, and libraries; without Jewish doctors and lawyers, the hospitals and law courts became hopelessly congested with patients and litigants. The paralysis ultimately became so severe that the Chancellor was left with no choice but grudgingly to reverse himself and to recall the city's Jews. The novel concluded with a description of the Christian population joyously welcoming back its Jewish neighbors.

Bettauer's satire provided a revealing insight into the Central European world of his time. By the turn of the century, and especially by the end of the first World War, Jewish participation in European cultural life had assumed major dimensions. There was virtually no field of intellectual activity in which Jews did not play a crucial, at times even a dominating, role. In the field of music, for example, Jews were among the most numerous and esteemed of Europe's instrumentalists, both as members of orchestras and as concert performers. In the field of science Jewish influence was no less significant. As faculty members of universities and as researchers in industry,

Jews in numbers far out of proportion to their percentage in the general population were among Europe's leading chemists, biologists, physicists, and mathematicians. The proportion of Jews in the field of medicine was truly astonishing (see pp. 399-400). As historians, philosophers, sociologists, Jews were among the most distinguished scholars of Central Europe; they were, as well, outstanding editors, art, music, and literary critics. There were Jewish writers, doctors, musicians, scholars, professors—not to mention untold tens of thousands of Jewish patrons of the arts, letters, music, and humanities—in numbers far beyond the fondest hopes and dreams of Moses Mendelssohn and the *Meassefim* of a century earlier.

This extraordinary efflorescence of Jewish intellectual activity was not a mere coincidence. In modern times the commonwealth of intellect had never been the closed preserve of the aristocracy and the Church. Most of the old Junkers and Austrian nobles still maintained their precarious control of the civil service and the army; but, with the exception of occasional nonconformists, they were much too preoccupied with the problem of political and economical survival to crave identification with the arts and sciences. Writing, musical composition, library and laboratory research were largely left to the middle class; and of all the bourgeoisie, the Jews were the people most willing to move into the "emancipated" professions. One very obvious reason was the desire of Jews to free themselves from economic discrimination by becoming self-employed. The safest professions, from the point of view of Jews without sufficient capital to set themselves up in business, were medicine and law. Thus, in 1924, of the 28,987 doctors in Prussia, 4,505 were Jews—15.5 per cent. Of the 8,559 lawyers in Prussia, 2,239—26 per cent—were Jews. In Berlin during the 1920's, there were actually more Jews than non-Jews who practiced law.

The proliferation of Jews in all fields of intellectual endeavor, the purely humanistic as well as the practical, found further explanation in the Jewish intellectual tradition. Historically, the Jews valued intellect perhaps more than any other people since the ancient Athenians. As a "this-worldly" religion, Judaism had produced a sacred literature which was largely legalistic, and which required, for its comprehension and observance, the most diligent kind of mental concentration. Throughout Jewish history, therefore—with the exception of the Hasidic movement in Eastern Europe—piety and scholarship were virtually synonymous terms; it had become almost axiomatic that study was a form of worship. Even after religious observance declined in emancipated Western Europe, as the principal motivating factor in Jewish life, the concern for scholarship remained—translated, however, into secular terms. During the twentieth century the prize catch for the daughter of a wealthy Jewish family was a professional man, a doctor, lawyer, scholar, or, though less frequently now, a rabbi. This deference to intellect may have been partly responsible for the fact that, among Jewish families, the drive for wealth was frequently exhausted within two or three generations. The Lord Rothschild who became an ornithologist, the Warburg who became an art historian, the Cassirer who became a philosopher, the Sassoon who became a poet, were typical of thousands of sons of Jewish businessmen who were determined to free themselves from cold money-making, to flee from the clamorous market place into the respected and sheltered retreat of the intellect.

Finally, many talented Jews discovered that while mere wealth did not always bring with it social equality, fame almost invariably did. It was still possible to exclude a Jewish parvenu millionaire from a fashionable upper-bourgeois salon; but it was unthinkable to close the door on a world-renowned artist or scientist. The European *haut monde* idolized genius; and the "radiant power of fame," as Stefan Zweig put it, was a very real force by which social outcasts were able at last to establish a home. Throughout Europe, talented Jews sensed this opportunity, and were not slow to take advantage of it. By the eve of the second World War, Jews had contributed eleven out of thirty-eight German Nobel prize winners, three out of six Austrian Nobel prize winners, or twenty-nine times their "proportionate share" compared to the non-Jewish population. "They came," wrote Jakob Wassermann, "imbued with a fierce resolution to hold their own; they came as conquerors. . . ." And as conquerors they battered down the social barriers of Europe.

SOME CHARACTERISTICS OF JEWISH INTELLECTUALISM: INNOVATION

It is not improbable that the same motivations that drove Jews into intellectual activity—their economic marginalism, their desire to acquire dignity among Jews through identification with the intellectual tradition, and among Christians by attaining distinction within that tradition—largely explained Jewish intellectual primacy. Motivation, after all, accounted for the extraordinarily large numbers of Jews who became intellectuals; and the larger the base of Jewish intellectual participation, the larger, according to the law of averages, the apex of truly brilliant minds. Motivation may have accounted, too, for Jewish diligence in research, for the willingness of Jewish scientists and scholars to persist in the wearing trial and error of experimentation, or in the dogged discipline of refashioning, rephrasing, repolishing in literary endeavors.

Within the framework of Jewish intellectualism, there appeared to be certain characteristics that distinguished Jewish creativity. One of these was a palpable willingness to innovate, to fashion new ideas, to break with old ways of thinking. Assuredly this did not mean that all Jewish intellectuals were pioneers of original thoughts, ideas, or techniques. Far from it: most Jewish composers, writers, scientists moved with the times, keeping up with new ideas and theories, but rarely demonstrating a personal willingness to pioneer themselves. Nevertheless, the Jewish intellectual community did manage to produce an exceptionally large minority of "revolutionaries," much larger, numerically as well as proportionately, than its counterpart in the Christian world.

One of the clearest examples was offered by the field of music. At the close of the nineteenth century, the mighty figure of Richard Wagner dominated the musical scene, and, inevitably, most of the composers who were over-whelmed by his towering genius, produced work which was, consciously or unconsciously, derivative. It fell to two Austrian-Jewish intellectuals to trans-form elements from Wagner's music drama into altogether new channels, expanding yet further the bounds of musical expression.

Gustav Mahler, the almost legendary conductor of the Vienna Opera, brought Wagner's music drama into the symphony. For Mahler the sym-phony was not merely an abstract classical form but an extremely dramatic form as well, a vehicle for a vast panorama of expression. There was room in the symphony for all varieties of emotion, the nostalgically recollected innocence of childhood, ghostly gaiety, martial feelings, power, frenzy, despair, exaltation, and sometimes sheer sentimentality. Mahler's innovations in form and orchestration allowed the classical symphony to incorporate a range of emotion and ideation never dreamed of before. Arnold Schönberg perceived the possibilities of Wagnerian harmony whose lushness had already blurred the listener's awareness of key. Schönberg's twelve-tone formula audaciously, yet systematically, eliminated tonality altogether, and he thereby wrought a revolution in musical syntax.

In brief, both Mahler and Schönberg added new dimensions to music. Mahler's contribution was greater in form and orchestration, and it had enduring effect upon composers of the caliber of Schönberg himself, Alban Berg, Dimitri Shostakovich, Benjamin Britten, Aaron Copland, and Leonard Bernstein. Schönberg's twelve-tone system found its way not only into orchestral and chamber music but into the opera and modern musical comedy. Indeed, he influenced the musical language of composers who were poles apart from him, and the time came when even a bitterly critical Stravinsky paid him the compliment of adopting his technique.

In the field of drama it was the Jewish producer, Otto Brahm, who intro-duced Ibsen realism to Germany in the latter part of the nineteenth century. Brahm underwrote and occasionally directed a whole series of realistic dramas, often at great financial risk; almost single-handedly he thereby steered realism to its eventual conquest of the German stage. Not the least of his accomplishments was his discovery and sponsorship of the young actor-director, Max Reinhardt, whose name is still synonymous with the most colorful period in the history of the German stage. During the 1920's and early 1930's, Reinhardt merged the orthodox, one-sided naturalism of the prewar era with a sensual and versatile style, which mastered the services of all allied arts, the dance, music, pantomime, painting, and architecture. It was Reinhardt, too, who set the example for a new type of playhouse with his introduction of the *Kammerspiel,* the play presented in a tiny, intimate theater fitted with club chairs only, and its counterpart, the all-dimensional theater-circus of the masses. Reinhardt's influence was felt not only in Germany and Austria where he himself produced and directed, but in countless theaters of the Continent where his students were employed. One devoted disciple, Leopold Jessner, directed the *Berlin Staatstheater;* another, Victor Barnowsky, staged productions in three of Berlin's most famous theaters. In the period between 1914 and 1933, Jewish producers and directors were so numerous and influential that it is hardly an exaggeration to describe the modern German and Austrian stage as their creation.

Jewish intellectualism was even more revolutionary in the field of science. It was a field, we recall, in which the Newtonian concept of a mechanical universe governed all basic research until the discoveries of a Swiss patent-inspector named Albert Einstein. In a dazzling succession of daring formulations—the essential facts of the theory of the equivalence of matter and energy, the expansion of the theory into the more generalized theory of relativity, its proof by astronomical observation—Einstein established the most fundamental scientific premises of the century. It is worth noting, however, that other Jewish scientists played a disproportionately large role in laying the foundation for Einstein's theory of relativity. It was Hermann Minkowski who first devised the concept of a four-dimensional time continuum. Tullio Levi-Civita developed the absolute calculus, the mathematical instrument with which Einstein reached his conclusions. Confidence in the simple mechanical universe was first shaken in 1887 when Albert Abraham Michelson disproved the existence of ether as the medium for the transmission of light rays. The theory of relativity was first interpreted in the United States by Leon Silberstein and in Germany by Max Born. Later so many Jews left applied physics for nuclear research that the Nazis contemptuously dubbed this new wing of science *Judenphysik*.

The genius for innovation which drove Mahler, Schönberg, Reinhardt, Minkowski, Einstein, and hundreds of other Jews in all fields could not be explained on a racial or religious basis, as Sombart had once sought to explain Jewish pre-eminence in capitalist enterprise. Certainly a Darwinian interpretation for Jewish intellectual leadership—that is, the notion that persecution somehow enables the fittest to survive—has been decisively disproved by the frequent degeneration of productive Jewish intellectualism under adverse circumstances—viz., in the ghetto. Perhaps the simplest and most plausible explanation was offered by Sigmund Freud in his letter of thanks to the B'nai B'rith Lodge of Vienna, which in 1926 celebrated his seventieth birthday. ". . . Only to my Jewish nature," wrote Freud, "did I owe the two qualities which had become indispensable to me on my hard road. Because I was a Jew I found myself free from many prejudices which limited others in the use of their intellect, and, being a Jew, I was prepared to enter opposition and to renounce agreement with the 'compact majority.' " Here, surely, was a penetrating insight into a root cause of Jewish innovation. The very minority status which had divorced the Jews from feudal land law and ecclesiastical loyalties, which had made them mobile, resourceful, imaginative businessmen, was the status which liberated them from the intellectual dogmas and prejudices of the "compact majority." Such status, together with the secular education available in emancipated Western Europe, enabled a crucial minority of Jewish scientists, philosophers, writers, and critics to view the world about them, to probe the universe, the mind, the body, the folk mores of their neighbors, with a freedom from tradition and inhibition not ordinarily vouchsafed their Christian colleagues.

RESPECT AND COMPASSION FOR LIFE

In exploring the distinguishing characteristics of Jewish intellectualism in the twentieth century, there is an interesting clue in the concentration of Jews in the profession of medicine. Medicine was, assuredly, a profitable field in many ways: it offered an opportunity for self-employment, and for a reasonable degree of financial success. Even so, these purely practical considerations probably would not by themselves account for the fact that Jews in medicine represented thirty times the proportion of Jews in the population of Central and Western Europe. In the 1920's, moreover, the Jews represented 25 per cent of the German doctors who had abandoned the lucrative opportunities of practice for full-time higher research. The names of the most eminent of these Jewish medical scientists read like a roll call of modern medical history. Ferdinand Cohn was the founder of bacteriology. Moriz Schiff laid the basic groundwork for the science of endocrinology. The founders of the field of otology, the study of the diseases of the ear, were the Austrian Jews, Politzer and Bárány. Paul Ehrlich, the first pioneer of chemicotherapy, and the discoverer of salvarsan for the treatment of syphilis, was the greatest biochemist of modern times. August von Wassermann originated the famous Wassermann test for syphilis. Waldemar Haffkine devised the method of inoculation against cholera. Bernard Zondek codeveloped the Zondek-Ascheim test for pregnancy. The micrococci of pneumonia were isolated by Albert Frankel. Vitamins were discovered by a Polish Jew, Casimir Funk. Countless diagnostic and surgical techniques were pioneered by Jewish medical men.

Surely one of the factors responsible for this remarkable Jewish concentration in medicine was the enormous prestige with which the Jewish tradition endowed the medical profession, a prestige which no other calling shared, neither law, nor teaching, nor even the rabbinate. It is impossible even for the most tough-minded realist to account for this idealization of the healing art without reference to the central meaning of the Jewish religious tradition: the sanctification of life. The uniqueness of Judaism was its rejection of the indifference to life which characterized the pagan world; and its corollary rejection of emphasis on life in a world-to-come—an emphasis which, with a few notable exceptions (the most important of which were Anglican evangelicalism and Protestant missionary medicine in the nineteenth century), seemed to characterize Christian doctrine until very recent times. Reverence for life on earth was basic; it was concretized in countless Jewish regulations, injunctions, and blessings covering the most prosaic as well as the most sacred deeds of man's daily life; it was symbolized in the cryptic phrase with which Jews toast each other, *L'Chaim*—"To Life." The concept has been abused and pulpiteered, but its vulgarization has not drained it of its validity: the passion for life counted as a more effective instrument than economic and political factors in enabling the Jews to survive as a people down to modern times.

It is not to be suggested that Jewish doctors were responding directly to an ancient religious sanction; indeed, most of them, as most Christian doctors, were probably irreligious. But the veneration of life had lingered long enough in the Jewish tradition to invest with particular prestige and honor the man who could save life: in sum, the Jew who had earned the medical degree. Medicine was a dignified calling in the Christian world; among Jews the profession was nothing less than exalted. And it was primarily among Jews, after all, that the majority of Jewish doctors would be living.

One branch of medicine, psychiatry, was, at least in its beginnings, virtually a Jewish monopoly. It was a field which did not so much as exist before Freud: for the study of mental disorders, until then, was confined either to the realm of philosophy and religion (disorders of the "soul") or to the realm of pure physiological science. Freud's own epochal discoveries are now integrated into the cultural, as well as the purely medical, vernaculars of the twentieth century: his exploration of the hidden iceberg of the unconscious; his compartmentalization of the unconscious into the id, ego, and superego; his use of the technique of analysis to probe the dreams, obsessions, and traumas of childhood and infancy; his ability to relieve psychiatric disturbances by teaching his patients to recognize and work through the origins of their neuroses. Nearly all Freud's associates and disciples in the Vienna Psycho-Analytic Society were Jews: Max Kahane, Rudolph Reitler, Alfred Adler, Hugo Heller, Max Graf, Isidore Sadger, Maximilian Steiner, Hans Sachs, Hilbert Silberer, and many other followers abroad. It was for the sake of releasing psychiatry from a purely Jewish identification that Freud was willing, for so many years, to tolerate the heresies of Jung, a non-Jew. "Most of you are Jews," Freud explained to his colleagues, "and therefore you are incompetent to win friends for the new thinking." Ernest Jones, one of the few non-Jews in Freud's coterie, found that a knowledge of Judaeo-German colloquialisms was indispensable in capturing the full flavor of the interchange between Freud and his colleagues. Jones recalled:

> When the Nazis entered Vienna we tried to save whatever was possible and [the Society] decreed that only an "Aryan" should be allowed to conduct the Psychoanalytical Clinic. Unfortunately the only member of the Vienna Society answering this description had just fled over the mountains to Italy. On hearing this, I cried out: "Oi weh, unser einziger Shabbat-Goy ist fort," a remark that dispelled for a moment the gloom of the gathering.

While the freedom from traditionalism we have discussed earlier enabled Jews to pioneer in this field, it is possible that two other factors also accounted for the unusually large Jewish concentration in psychiatry. One was the unconscious desire of Jews, as social pariahs, to unmask the respectability of the European society which closed them out. There was no more effective way of doing this than by dredging up from the human psyche the sordid and infantile sexual aberrations that were frequently the authentic sources of human behavior, or misbehavior. Even Jews who were not psychiatrists must have taken pleasure in the feat of social equalization performed by

Freud's "new thinking." The B'nai B'rith Lodge of Vienna, for example, delighted in listening to Freud air his theories at a time when Viennese medical and ecclesiastical authorities yearned to see him behind bars.

Yet if many Jews entered the field of psychiatry to "unmask," they were also motivated by the desire to ameliorate and cure, responding, in no small degree, to their exceptional sensitivity to the psychic pain of their patients. The point need not be labored (nor must it be stretched) that a suffering people, a minority people plagued by every variety of personal and social insecurity and frustration, was capable of greater empathy with the suffering and pain, the insecurities and frustrations of others. Few Jewish psychiatrists escaped these Jewish-rooted insecurities. Even Freud, for all his tough-mindedness and aggressiveness, was inhibited for decades from visiting the city of Rome because, according to his biographer, Ernest Jones, he experienced an unconscious fear of the center of the Christian world which had brought little but grief and persecution to the Jewish people. Plagued by uncertainty, by social ostracism, by cultural ambivalences, by a search for status and appreciation, the Jew developed a unique capacity for understanding the sources of emotional suffering in others. Nor is the point invalidated by the "cold-blooded" scientific objectivity which Freud and his disciples brought to their craft, and without which even the best motivation in the world would have been rendered futile. There is a necessary distinction between the sensitivity which attracts people into a profession, and the calm craftsmanship with which they learn to perform their professional duties. This sensitivity, together with a Jewish veneration of life—and the lifesaver—appears to have been one of the most noteworthy, as well as one of the most productive, characteristics of Jewish intellectualism in modern times.

ALIENATION

The mastery of European belles-lettres, which characterized the career of Moses Mendelssohn, the pioneer of intellectual emancipation, reached its most dramatic culmination in the early years of the twentieth century. Between 1900 and 1930 Jewish writers, novelists, essayists, literary and drama critics were widely recognized as the most penetrating and influential interpreters of European culture. In this sense, perhaps, they were fulfilling an interpretive role which extended back to the days of Jewish settlement in Moslem Spain. It was the classic role of Jewish "outsiders," who found themselves in a position to evaluate the life and mores of their countries, free from the preconceived notions and prejudices of their non-Jewish neighbors. It was a role, too, which modern Europeans expected of their Jews; it precluded the necessity of inventing "Persian" or "Chinese" visitors, as in the days of the eighteenth-century rationalists.

Not all Jewish intellectuals, certainly not the large number of Jewish writers who made enduring contributions to the vernacular literature of their lands, were conscious of being outsiders, or consciously fulfilled the role of outsiders. There were no more typically English playwrights than Arthur

Wing Pinero and Henry Arthur Jones; no truer *boulevardiers* than Adolphe
Philippe d'Ennery or Henry Bernstein in France; no Germans more militantly
Prussian than Ernst Lissauer or Walther Rathenau. Yet even in the case of
some of these, particularly the Germans, the intensity of their passion for
complete cultural identification—the right to be evaluated with the cherished
adjective, "typical"—may in itself have been evidence of their fundamental
insecurity as outsiders, evidence, as in the days of the "salon Jews," of the
need to prove their Europeanization. One thinks of Stefan Zweig, the gentle
Viennese, and his fixation for collecting mementos of Mozart, Beethoven,
Blake, Claudel, Rolland, his concern lest Jews occupy too prominent a position in public life—"thus arousing envy"; of Lissauer, on the other hand,
whose desire to belong took the narrower and more parochial form of German
chauvinism, and whose "Hymn of Hate" was the single most popular
patriotic song in German during the first World War. One thinks particularly of the children of Jewish millionaires, who crowded into the arts
and belles-lettres, patronized museums and art galleries, aspired to appear
in the rotogravures as fashion plates, but studiously avoided contact with
or mention of Jewish cultural associations. A French Christian, Jacques
de Lacretelle, captured this insecurity in his memorable portrait of the
Jewish schoolboy, *Silbermann*:

> "Oh, I'm not going to deny my origin," [Silbermann] said decidedly,
> with the little quiver of the nostrils which with him indicated a feeling
> of pride. "On the contrary, to be a Jew and a Frenchman seems to me
> the most favorable condition possible for accomplishing great things."
> He raised a finger prophetically. "Only I want to form the genius of my
> race according to the character of this country; I want to unite my
> resources with yours. If I write, I want to make it impossible to be
> reproached with the least sign of a foreign characteristic. I do not want
> to hear, of anything I produce, the judgment: 'It is thoroughly Jewish.'"

Such alienation was only occasionally glimpsed when the Europeanization was just a touch too deliberate or when the patriotism was just a percentage point or two beyond one hundred. It was rather more apparent in
works which frankly rendered judgment, from a distance, on the European
society of the times. One senses this in Marcel Proust's reconstruction of
fin de siècle French society. For all this half-Jew's Parisian sophistication,
there is a tone of lamentation and complaint resounding through his *Remembrance of Things Past* which is really very un-French and far more akin
to Prophetic Jewish literature. In his autobiography, Jakob Wassermann, one
of the most perceptive of German-Jewish novelists, candidly expressed this
sense of alienation, of approaching life as an outsider. "I am a German and a
Jew," he wrote. "I am completely permeated with elements from both
spheres, the Oriental and the Occidental." Although he penetrated with rare
insight into the life and soul of the German people, Wassermann confessed
that his work was the expression of a Jewish mind and a Jewish heart.
His life struggle was typical of Max Brod, Ernst Toller, Franz Kafka, Arnold
Zweig, and a number of other Jewish writers of Western Europe, who

recognized the estrangement between themselves and the people among whom they moved and to whose culture they made such enduring contributions. It was perhaps this very estrangement which frequently permitted them to detect the approaching crisis of European civilization more rapidly and with clearer vision than their non-Jewish colleagues.

The mood of estrangement was particularly evident in the writings of Franz Kafka. In the twelve years between 1912 and 1924 this slim, introspective Prague Jew produced some of the most fearsome commentaries on the condition of man ever to appear in modern Europe. His stories are quite stark, almost surrealistic in their detachment from time and place. Immemorial dreams, primeval shapes emerge from mistlike surroundings; arrests, executions, transformations into vermin are described in the most casual, even pedestrian, terms. Together with a variety of complex and subterranean meanings, the theme of alienation reveals itself in almost everything Kafka wrote. If man, according to Kafka, is alienated from his fellow human beings—the idea is the central motif of his novel, *The Trial*—he also appeared to be alienated from God. The entire narrative of *The Castle* revolves around the effort of a surveyor to obtain an interview with the Lord of the Manor. It is a fruitless effort which consumes all the surveyor's time and energy. When at last he attempts to telephone the Lord, the superintendent of the castle observes sardonically:

> You haven't once up till now come into real contact with our authorities. All those contacts of yours have been illusory, but owing to your ignorance of the circumstances you take them to be real. And as for the telephone: as you see . . . there's no telephone. . . . There's no fixed connection with the Castle, no central exchange which transmits our calls further. . . . For who would take the responsibility of interrupting in the middle of the night the extremely important work up there that goes on furiously the whole time, with a message about his own little private troubles?

Kafka's preoccupation with the problem of estrangement may have derived partly from the barrier which separated him from his father (see p. 407): partly, too, from his inability to savor fully the physical and material pleasures of life, for he suffered from a laryngeal tuberculosis which eventually killed him in 1924. But much of it probably stemmed directly from his insecurity as a Jew—a Jew of Prague at that, a minority within the German minority. The word "Jew" does not appear in *The Castle,* but the Jew's isolation is there. The surveyor—K, as in *The Trial*—is lost in a strange village. Exhausted, he asks an old peasant, "May I come in for a while?" The peasant mumbles something indistinctly. Later K asks an unfriendly schoolmaster whether he may visit him sometime. The schoolmaster responds: "I live at Swan Street, at the butcher's." Everywhere he is politely, but firmly, rejected. Kafka deals more openly with the indefensibility of the Jewish position in his story *Josephine the Songstress, or the Mice Nation.* The "Mice Nation" is, of course, the Jews.

The absence of "fixed abode" which accounted for the alienation of Kafka and other Jewish writers was probably responsible, too, for the importance Jewish intellectuals attached to the ideal of international community. Without fixed roots in their native lands, they shared few of the local prejudices against neighboring peoples and neighboring cultures. In the international community of intellect, for example, it was surely no accident that in nearly every instance the literary, art, and drama critics who did most to introduce foreign talent to local audiences were Jews. Georg Brandes, a Danish Jew, was the recognized father of modern European criticism and the first critic to introduce Polish and Russian literature to Western Europe. Alfred Kerr, a Berlin drama critic, led the journalistic campaign to call German attention to the significant contemporary playwrights of other countries. Jewish art collectors were almost invariably the first to purchase the latest works of foreign painters. Jews were also among the first to encourage foreign writers and musicians. "Whoever wished to put something through in Vienna," recalled Stefan Zweig, "or came to Vienna as a guest from abroad and sought appreciation as well as an audience, was dependent on the Jewish bourgeoisie."

On the political scene not all Jewish intellectuals were internationalists by any means. Quite the contrary: the urge to belong which drove them into a passionate mastery of their vernaculars made ardent nationalists of most of them, often more ardent than their non-Jewish neighbors. But there were others, a much larger minority than among Christian intellectuals, who were able, like the Jewish bankers before them, to emancipate themselves from the parochialism of their fellow citizens. It is worth noting that not a few of them fulfilled this internationalist role self-consciously as Jews. Whatever they may have felt about Judaism as a religion, they frequently expressed open admiration for the historic role of the Jew as an extranational influence. Bernhard Berenson, the distinguished art historian—and convert to Christianity—stated a common view when he observed:

> The Jew still has a mission. . . . In the future he should cultivate the qualities that anti-Dreyfusards and other anti-Semites have reproached him with. He should not identify himself with the rest of the nation in its chauvinism, in its overweening self-satisfaction, self-adulation, and self-worship. He should be in every land the element that keeps up standards of human value and cultivates a feeling for proportion and relations. He should be supernational as the Roman Church claims to be.

During the first World War Stefan Zweig took the initiative, together with Leonhard Frank, Franz Werfel, Emile Verhaeren, and a number of eminent non-Jews, in establishing an international community of intellectuals. The governments of Europe, too, were not slow to sense that Jews, whether intellectuals or businessmen, were valuable intermediaries for peacemaking. On the very eve of the first World War the governments of England and Germany sent their most eminent Jews, Sir Ernest Cassel and Albert Ballin, into conference, entertaining the hope that the two "blood brothers" would perhaps find a basis for a last-minute agreement to keep the peace. During the war the German government made its first peace overtures to the Allies through the medium of the Zionist Organization. Of course these negotiations failed: but they were not without significance in anti-Semitic propaganda during the Hitler era. Whenever the Nazis referred to the "international Jew," for that matter, they referred as much to the Jewish intellectual, "the debaser of European culture," as to the Jewish banker.

JEWISH INTELLECTUALS AND JUDAISM

As late as the twentieth century, the old problem of a "passport to European culture," which had bedeviled Western European Jews during the salon era, had not yet been altogether resolved. There were still a few Jewish intellectuals who moved into Christianity primarily for opportunistic reasons. It is probable that Gustav Mahler, for example, was motivated by careerist considerations. As a Viennese Jew, he was still excluded from the highest directorial positions in the Vienna State Opera; for, in Austria, civil service status attached to all cultural posts, and the civil service remained immune to emancipation. This presented a serious dilemma for a man like Mahler, an artist who wished desperately to escape the confines of *petit-bourgeois* life. It happened, however, that in Mahler's day Catholicism of an ascetic tendency had assumed a progressive appearance, as a kind of symbolic answer to the dogmatic yet lavish court of Emperor Franz Josef. The young nephew royal, Franz Ferdinand, was the spokesman for this ascetic reformist Catholicism, and gathered around him many writers, artists, and musicians who believed that his spiritual and political aspirations offered the most effective opposition to the *status quo.* Among those who accepted Franz Ferdinand's faith as their own were a number of gifted young Jews: Hugo von Hofmannsthal, Adolf Loos, Karl Kraus. Mahler, determined to maintain his connection with the world of the German spirit, followed them into conversion.

The need to maintain contact with the spirit of the non-Jewish world may have accounted, too, for Bernhard Berenson's conversion to Catholicism. Living in a richly illuminated world of Venetian and Florentine painting, steeped in the beauty and afterglow of the Catholic tradition, Berenson believed, with Santayana, that "there is no God and Mary is His mother," that the theology of Catholicism was less important than its pageantry. It was rather less for careerist reasons, and rather more for the purpose of transcending the limitations of a small "tribal" people, that Berenson sought to move into humanity at large—Christian humanity, of course. In his autobiography Berenson defends his conversion by laying continual emphasis upon the parochial character of Judaism:

> From Ezra down, this Jewish exclusiveness was due less and less to a feeling of superiority, certainly not in the ways of this world, but rather to a fear of contamination. Rabbinical Judaism is first and foremost an organization for keeping a small minority, scattered among the nations, from dissolving and disappearing. It was thus based on fear.

. . . Christianity is detribalized Judaism in nearly everything but its neo-platonic and Gnostic theology.

There were still Jews to be found, moreover, who fled from Judaism not for reasons of intellectual conviction, nor even for the sake of careerist advancement, but rather out of curiously twisted motives of shame and self-hatred. In the mid-1930's, for example, Dr. Karl Landsteiner, a Jewish-born Nobel prize winner and a refugee from Hitler's Germany, filed an injunction to restrain the publisher of *Who's Who in American Jewry* from including his biography in a new edition.

> It will be detrimental to me [declared Landsteiner in his legal petition] to emphasize publicly the religion of my ancestors; first, as a matter of convenience; and, secondly, I want nothing that may in the slightest degree cause any mental anguish, pain or suffering to any members of my family. . . . My son is now nineteen years of age and he has no suspicion that any of his ancestors were Jewish. I know as a positive fact that if my son were to see the book that is about to be published it would be a shock to him and might subject him to humiliation.

This *Selbsthass,* not at all typical of the majority of Jewish intellectuals, was expressed even more forcibly by the rather erratic young French-Jewish poetess and philosopher, Simone Weil. Not content merely to reject identification with the Jews, Simone Weil went so far as to identify the spirit of Nazism with the spirit of Judaism; Hitler, she insisted, was seeking only to revive under another name and for his own benefit the God of Israel, "earthly, cruel, and exclusive." It was devotion to such a God, she argued, that transformed the Jews into "a nation of fugitive slaves. . . . No wonder such a people was able to give scarcely anything good to the world." Her evaluation of Jewish history was phrased in terms reminiscent of Houston Stewart Chamberlain. Of course, Simone Weil's attitude toward the Jews revealed much more than shame; it revealed, as well, a furious rejection of the accident of Jewish birth, a fury all the more corrosive for its impotence. The career of this curiously talented, but tragically warped personality represented the final, the most desperate, and self-defeating of Jewish efforts to escape, not from Judaism, but from the condition of Jewishness itself.

But these examples of overt renunciation of Judaism in favor of Christianity, or near-Christianity, as in the case of Simone Weil, were increasingly rare, even for the most self-debasing of Jewish intellectuals. For one thing, Jewish emancipation had virtually been completed by 1870; the certificate of baptism was no longer an indispensable passport to intellectual or even to social position. Moreover, the rise of modern anti-Semitism was rapidly outdating the religious rationale for discrimination; race, the inescapable accident of birth, was now the key. Most important of all, however, was the fact that European culture was no longer exclusively religious: Christianity was becoming as intellectually unfashionable as Judaism. Scientific discovery, Biblical criticism, Darwinism, nationalism, and Marxism

—all were responsible for widening even further the gap between "faith and reason" which had originally opened in the Enlightenment era. During the "age of materialism" an antireligious point of view, anti-Christian as well as anti-Jewish, virtually became the proof of one's intellectuality. It was, in short, the impact of modern secular materialism, more than any other factor, which undermined the religious convictions of the Jewish and Christian intellectual alike.

Thus, whatever the circumstances of Jewishness that influenced their careers, few of the intellectuals we have discussed evinced more than a nominal interest in the Jewish religion. Most of them may have remained within the Jewish group, accepting the fact of their Jewish birth and their Jewish social status; but they ceased almost entirely to be practicing Jews. One of the most interesting examples of this ambivalence was provided by Sigmund Freud. Freud's friends were almost exclusively Jewish. He admired the drive and creativity of Jews and had a corresponding contempt for the ambitionless *goyim*. He was astonished that a non-Jew, George Eliot, could write about Jews and understand things "we speak of only among ourselves." Forever bubbling over with Jewish stories, Freud took pleasure in identifying himself with the Maccabees of Jewish history, and professed a feeling of kinship with the Messiahs of Jewish folklore. "I have often felt," he once wrote, "as if I had inherited all the passion of our ancestors when they defended their Temple."

And yet Freud stripped bare the "foibles" and archaisms of Judaism more thoroughly than the most acerbic of Biblical critics. There was hardly one Jewish, or Christian, ritual that he did not relegate to the junk heap of sexual totemism. In 1938 Freud expressed the notion, in his celebrated essay, *Moses and Monotheism*, that Moses was the illegitimate son of the Egyptian princess who rescued him from the bullrushes. He insisted, too, that monotheism derived not from the Jews, but from the personal religion of an Egyptian Pharaoh. Freud concluded his essay with the gratuitous and wholly specious theory that the Jews, revolting against the father image, eventually did Moses to death. At the very moment that European Jewry was facing destruction, Freud, the loyal "ethnic Jew," sought to deprive his people of their proudest accomplishments: their supreme lawgiver, and their claim to the parenthood of Western religion. But for all the literary and scientific skill with which he attacked the integrity of the ancestral religion in this and other books, Freud was a symptom, much more than a motivating influence, of the irreligiosity which characterized the majority of Jewish intellectuals.

There were some Jewish intellectuals, on the other hand, who were not willing, like Freud, to reject Judaism altogether. Franz Kafka, for example, represented a not insignificant group of Jewish writers and thinkers in Central Europe who were embarked on a serious quest for spiritual belonging, but who recognized instinctively that belonging could not be found in the inhospitable Christian world about them. Each thinker, each writer, has his own intimate loneliness, his own need for acceptance and anchorage. Kafka's loneliness as a Jew was probably compounded by his estrangement from his father. In the oft-repeated Jewish father-son estrangement, the father frequently was a traditional Jew, and the son, by reaction, usually broke from Judaism altogether. But Kafka *père* was himself an extreme example of the assimilated Jew, with little but contempt, openly expressed, for traditional Judaism and for Kafka's Jewish friends. "I don't deny," Kafka wrote later in his celebrated *Letter to His Father* (which his father never read), "that if you had shown any interest in [Jewish religious and cultural values] these things would immediately have become suspect in my eyes for that reason." Unable to find anchorage in the tradition of his father, he searched for it instead in the tradition of his fathers.

For most Jewish intellectuals—men like Freud, for example—Jewishness was a matter of social, rather than of intellectual or theological significance; their "involvement" was with Jews rather than with Judaism. Kafka's involvement, however, was deep enough to be a source of continual wonderment even to himself. "What have I in common with Jews?" he once blurted out to his friend, Max Brod. "I have almost nothing in common with myself, and should hide myself quietly in a corner satisfied with the fact that I can breathe." Such was the intensity of his loneliness, however, that he found himself drawn, almost independently of his own volition, into a warm, even impassioned communion with his fellow Jews. Thus, in 1910, Kafka took an active interest in a visiting group of Yiddish actors from Eastern Europe. He spent hours analyzing their idioms and mannerisms, and methodically jotted down his observations in his "Jewish" journal. He began to take up the study of Jewish history and literature, and later discussed these subjects with clarity and originality in his essay, *The Literature of Small Peoples*. From these Eastern European Jews, too, Kafka derived his sympathy for cultural Zionism; although his friend Brod could never persuade him to accept the political implications of the movement.

It was as a consequence of this immersion in Jewish history and folklore that Kafka began at last to experience a sense of spiritual belonging— although that belonging was never complete, by any means. In short, he acquired his interest in Judaism as a religion from a revived awareness of his Jewish "peoplehood." In the last years of his life, during his love affair with Dora Dymant, a Jewish girl from Poland, Kafka went so far as to attend classes in Hebrew and Talmud at the Institute for Jewish Studies in Berlin. His literary notebooks and diaries during this period were filled with Hebrew words. Long before this formal return to religious study, however, Kafka was able to transform his sense of alienation from non-Jews into an affirmatively Jewish interpretation of man's "distance from God." Both in *The Castle* and *The Penal Colony,* Kafka made the point that while God did what seemed absurd and unjust to man, it was to man alone that this appeared to be the case; a human being's life and deeds could not be measured by his own yardstick, but only by the yardstick of God. It was with this conclusion, expressed with an intensity all the more visceral for the studied economy of its prose, that Kafka reformulated the fundamental conclusion of the Book of Job.

While Kafka approached his Jewish identification because of his inherited membership in the Jewish people, Einstein's approach came from the opposite direction. Originally, in fact, Einstein's attachment to Judaism was the result of his intellectualized conception of God—not the God of Abraham, Isaac, and Jacob, the tribal God of the Jewish people—but rather the rational *élan* of Maimonides, Spinoza, and, perhaps, of Hermann Cohen (see p. 411). In his search for a unified field theory which would link all dimensions of the universe to one basic force, Einstein wrote to the quantum physicist Max Born, in 1944: "In our scientific expectation we have grown antipodes. You believe in God casting dice and I in perfect laws in the world of things existing as real objects, which I try to grasp in a wildly speculative way." The basis of this search was Einstein's oft-stated belief that a rational truth lay concealed behind the phenomena of nature. "To the sphere of religion," he wrote, "belongs the faith that the regulations valid for the world of existence are rational. . . ."

By itself this purely cerebral approach to Judaism was quite arid. Flesh and blood contact with his people, however, came to Einstein much more slowly. The son of assimilated German-Jewish parents, he received only the most perfunctory education in Jewish ethics and ceremonial. Later, as a young man living in Milan with his family, Einstein renounced both his German citizenship and his membership in the Jewish community. In this fashion he hoped to express his contempt for the "idols of the tribe." It was only later, as a Visiting Professor of Physics at the German University in Prague, that Einstein found himself drawn into corporate Jewish life. In Prague nearly half the German-speaking population was Jewish; it happened, too, that the city was undergoing a Jewish intellectual renaissance at the time, led by Martin Buber, Hugo Bergmann, and Max Brod. In 1921, after eleven years of residence in the Czech capital, Einstein issued a statement to the local Jewish press in which he declared himself to be a Zionist. Although it was known that he had been friendly with Buber and Bergmann, his announcement still came as a shock to those Jewish intellectuals who had admired him for his rejection of nationalism as "an excrescence of the herd mentality."

The revival of European anti-Semitism provided a partial explanation for Einstein's sudden conversion to Zionism. He gave little indication, in fact, that he had taken his Jewishness seriously until race prejudice touched him personally. "When I first came to Germany fifteen years ago," he wrote to State Minister Hellpach in 1925, "I discovered for the first time that I was a Jew, and I owe this discovery more to Gentiles than to Jews . . . If we did not have to live among intolerant, narrow-minded and violent people, I should be the first to throw over all nationalism in favor of universal humanity." An equally likely clue to his return, however, would probably be found in Einstein's statement that "the best in man can only flourish when he loses himself in a community." It was a confession of his inability to sustain indefinitely the ecstasy of pure reason, his inability to live in an icy universe of formulas and equations, and even, perhaps, of cold theology, which had formulas of its own. Irving Kristol has shrewdly suggested that Einstein's admiration of Zionism as "the embodiment of the reawakening corporate spirit of the Jewish nation," reflected his own re-awakening to the existence of people, particularly of the Jewish people, and of his own need for "the flesh-and-blood Jew born of woman." One senses this reawakening in his evaluation of Judaism's humanism; his reverence for a religious tradition which emphasized the "ideal solidarity of all living things." Einstein's nostalgia for humankind was evident, too, in the tone and inflection with which he wrote of his ancestors, the ghetto Jews: ". . . These obscure humble people had one great advantage over us; each of them belonged in every fiber of his being to a community in which he was completely absorbed . . ."

For thirty-four years after his entrance into Zionism, Einstein identified himself wholeheartedly not only with the Zionist movement, but with a wide variety of Jewish communal and philanthropic ventures. When he died, in 1955, he bequeathed his brain to science; few eulogies failed to point out, however, that his heart had long since belonged to his people.

THE INTELLECTUAL REFORMULATION OF JUDAISM

If the apostasy of the Mahlers and the Berensons, the self-hatred of the Landsteiners and the Weils, were not typical of the majority of the Jewish intellectuals, neither was the spiritual identification of the Kafkas and the Einsteins. Far more characteristic was the matter-of-fact Jewishness of Sigmund Freud, and his equally matter-of-fact rejection of functional Judaism as a meaningful experience in daily living. Yet if modern science, Darwinism, Biblical criticism, psychiatry, et al., were making serious inroads on the religious loyalties of Jewish and Christian intellectuals, they had their effect, as well, on the religious convictions of nonintellectuals. In the face of these new developments, many Western Europeans repudiated or profoundly modified their traditional religious beliefs and practices. There were others, perhaps even a majority, who remained nominally within their churches and synagogues, who continued to profess Christianity and Judaism, but who sought somehow to reconcile their inherited doctrines of faith and morals with the modern spirit of science and materialism. But even within this group the effort to salvage the spirit of true religious feeling was failing rapidly.

It was to meet the challenge of modern materialism that a group of Christian philosophers set about the task of reconciling science with traditional Christianity. In the early twentieth century the Italian thinker, Benedetto Croce, fashioned a "philosophy of the spirit" which interpreted the entire content of human history in terms not of its factual data, but of its guiding "spirits." The most creative of these spirits, according to Croce, was the religious; and from then on his proof was drawn not from logic or metaphysics, but from the accumulation of historical evidence. The French scholar, Jacques Maritain, formulated a kind of twentieth-century neo-Scholasticism which succeeded notably in reconciling some of the important differences between science and Catholicism.

This reconciliation of religion and modern scientific scholarship was attempted within the framework of Judaism by Hermann Cohen, the most justly noteworthy Jewish thinker of the early twentieth century. Cohen, a German Jew, was trained originally for the rabbinate, but he early abandoned his theological studies for the realm of pure philosophy. In 1897, after many years of university teaching, he became Professor of Philosophy at the University of Marburg. Even before his appointment to this professorship, however, Cohen had acquired a reputation as the leading neo-Kantian of Central Europe, and for many decades his philosophic articles were widely acclaimed in scholarly circles.

Undergoing a vaguely assimilationist period during the 1880's and 1890's, Cohen did not really return to his original religious interests until the opening of the twentieth century. Then, in 1912—in his old age—he produced *The Religion of Reason from the Sources of Judaism,* one of the truly massive contributions to the modern philosophy of religion. The volume was strongly Kantian in its orientation, for it stressed the importance of the "ought," the categorical imperative—or, in religious terminology, the idea of right and wrong. Ethics, law, moral behavior—these were crucial in Cohen's thinking, as in Kant's; and religion, so it seemed to him, was valid and purposeful insofar as it encouraged a rigid adherence to ethical law. Indeed, a rational and austere religious creed was capable of sustaining the ideal of ethics far more effectively than a mere "ethical philosophy"; for religion laid emphasis on the idea of God, thus sanctifying ethics as the will of God. Moreover, religion trained the individual for the ethical task by imposing upon him a regimen of conduct and observance. Judaism, Cohen argued, was a supremely effective religion, precisely because it nurtured the ethical ideal with both tenacity and rationality. In fact, Judaism was a kind of "Religion of Reason," a religion which encouraged its adherents not to attain communion with God or to find personal salvation—pagan ideas, according to Cohen—but rather to strive for the ideal society, the society of moral perfection. Cohen rejected the notion of a sudden revelation of the Law at Sinai; but he did endorse Judaism's central insight that piety must be molded through law. Judaism, in short, encouraged the individual to ask, not "How do I speak to God?" or, "How do I achieve salvation?" but rather, "How am I to fulfill God's mandate by living the good life? How may I create the kingdom of heaven on earth?"

It was a sound, airtight, thoroughly rational and modern philosophy of religion. Few Jews could argue with Cohen's emphasis on the primacy of ethics, or with Judaism's historic strength in that field. Ironically, Cohen's philosophy of religion appealed least of all to the Jewish intellectual, to whom Cohen was principally addressing himself. Quite frequently, the intellectual seemed to be less willing even than the typical bourgeois businessman to accept a "Religion of Reason." An intellectual, after all, was perfectly capable of formulating his own utilitarian ethic on rational grounds. What he really wanted, more often than not, was to relax from pure reason, to be able to communicate more directly with the throbbing living presence of God, without, at the same time, sacrificing his intellectual integrity.

One transition to a warmer kind of religious experience was provided by the philosophy of Leo Baeck, the outstanding and most beloved rabbi in Germany in the period preceding the second World War. Baeck distilled his philosophy of "moral perfection" in several books, a wide number of articles, as well as in the eloquent sermons and innumerable acts of kindness that made him one of the most deeply revered Jews of the twentieth century. So imposing was Baeck's reputation, in fact, that even the Nazis at first dealt cautiously with him; as late as 1938 they offered him the opportunity to leave Germany. He rejected the offer and chose instead to remain with his captive people. It was then, and during the five years of his imprisonment in the Theresienstadt concentration camp, that Baeck became a living incarnation of the affirmative faith he preached. Indeed, the commanding influence of his personality kept alive decency and compassion, as well as law and order, among prisoners who would otherwise have been thoroughly brutalized. Ministering to the ill and despondent, conducting clandestine religious services at the risk of his life, Baeck infused thousands of his fellow inmates with his own unshakable conviction that survival was a moral obligation, even in the depths of the Nazi hell. When the war ended and the danger of annihilation for the remnants of his people had passed, he yielded at last to the importunities of Jewish leaders in the United States and accepted the Professorship of Theology at the Hebrew Union College-Jewish Institute of Religion.

Both before and after the war, Baeck formulated a philosophy of ethics largely akin to Cohen's "Religion of Reason." The idea of God for Baeck, however, was not merely a philosophic postulate, but also a vital fact of personal experience. While the "thou shalt" of God imposed upon man the obligation of creating perfection on earth, it also imposed upon man the obligation of having faith in the very real possibility of that perfection. Baeck stated the obligation of faith most persuasively in his best-known volume, *The Essence of Judaism*:

> Judaism first experienced that great unconditional "thou shalt" which the one God speaks. This "thou shalt" arises from the very foundations of reality, and it presents reality to man, the full and fundamental reality. . . . And because the great "thou shalt" contains the reality, it also contains the great hope; thus hope itself becomes a commandment; hope, too, becomes an unconditional, categorical postulation. Thou shalt hope!

Unlike Kant's categorical imperative, which was envisaged as a generalized social law, the "thou shalt" of Judaism was felt by Baeck to be an immediate, compelling summons to personal action, leading toward a definite goal of perfection. It mattered not that perfection could be realized only in the "end of days"; in the love and devotion with which man sought to create social perfection, he created personal perfection, and, thereby, man reached God. Although, like Cohen, Baeck laid his greatest emphasis on ethics, and phrased his ideas in rationalist terminology, his philosophy also represented the transition between the Judaism of historic destiny and tradition, and the inward Judaism of personal faith, the "existentialist" Judaism of Franz Rosenzweig and Martin Buber.

It was Franz Rosenzweig who first made plain that the ancient faith of prophet and rabbi was not merely compatible with the externals of modern culture, as Cohen and Baeck had insisted, but that Judaism was in fact the answer to the deepest problems of the Jew's existence in the contemporary world. This was a truth Rosenzweig discovered only after undergoing a rather severe spiritual crisis in his own life. A German Jew, he was raised by typically middle-class parents, people for whom Judaism was merely a matter of formal observance. When Rosenzweig took up the study of philosophy at the University of Freiburg, and later at the University of Berlin—at both of which institutions he acquired a reputation for near-genius—Judaism rarely figured seriously in his many discussions on theology. Judaism might have fulfilled an important role in emphasizing the historic importance of ethics; but Rosenzweig and his friends were determined to break with the Hegelian "religious intellectualism" that was then all the vogue in Germany. They believed that God must redeem man not indirectly, through history, but that the redemption must come individually, through personal conviction. Rosenzweig yearned for a religion of personal belonging, but he did not look for it in a Judaism which he imagined to be merely an arid system of moral rules and regulations. In 1913 he reached the decision to convert to Protestantism.

Determined to enter Christianity as did its founders, as a Jew, not as a pagan, Rosenzweig attended synagogue services in the period immediately preceding his intended baptism. It happened to be the eve of Yom Kippur, the High Holy Day of Atonement, and the services were particularly solemn and awe-inspiring. Rosenzweig was more than moved; he was shaken to the depths of his soul. By the time he walked out of the synagogue he had discarded all notions of conversion, and was resolved, instead, to work out his theology within the framework of his ancestral religion. He traveled to Berlin to meet Hermann Cohen, and to learn the Hebrew language. Before Rosenzweig could seriously embark upon a program of Judaic studies, however, the war broke; he enlisted in the Kaiser's army almost immediately.

It was during his service an an *Unteroffizier,* on a short assignment to the Eastern front, that Rosenzweig made his initial contact with Polish Jewry. The experience had important consequences in his thinking, for the image of the "integral" Jewish existence of the Polish Jew remained with him throughout his life as a kind of yardstick against which to measure the "fragmentary" existence of the Jew in the Western world. Returning to the Macedonian front in August of 1918, Rosenzweig began to formulate his *magnum opus, Der Stern der Erloesung*—"The Star of Redemption." The book was written between maneuvers and battles, in hospitals, and, after the collapse of the front line, on the road with the retreating army. He would jot down his writings hurriedly on post cards and scraps of paper, and send them on to his mother for transcription. Under any circumstances, the creation of such a scholarly and original volume would have been a formidable accomplishment; but to have completed it in the periods which were rescued from the sterility of military service, even combat, was nothing short of fantastic.

The Star of Redemption formed the basis of a religious philosophy which Rosenzweig refined later in a succession of essays. He argued that a satisfying religion required more than a legal system, more even than "ethical behavior." It required "life" thinking, or "existential" thinking, which was less concerned with the establishment of universal truths, than with "making sense" of one's own existence. Of course, it was far easier to make sense if we had faith in the divinity of the universe and in God's plan for human fulfillment. For Rosenzweig such faith could not be other than a divine-human encounter, a meeting, in which man made his total commitment to God and God offered His grace to man. The life of faith, the only true religious existence, Rosenzweig believed, was lived on a plane where God and man were linked by a bond of personal communion, by revelation. The "new thinking," therefore, was thinking which bore a closer similarity to speech, to dialogue, than to abstract thought. Rosenzweig's God was not a remote lawgiver, nor a mere synonym for ideals and sentiments. It was a God who actually entered into one's life at every point, and without whom no moment of life could have meaning.

Rosenzweig's theology drew deeply from classical Jewish sources; it encompassed the entire breadth and depth of Jewish culture, as that culture had existed before it was "fragmentized," as Rosenzweig put it, in the era of Emancipation. During the nineteenth century, a great many Jewish thinkers, in their attempt to Europeanize Judaism, were willing to accept historical and sociological norms as the measure of spiritual values. Rosenzweig chose instead to re-examine the classics of Hebrew literature in an effort to discover the principles and regulations that were still valid in the contemporary world—and that could be integrated into the modern Jew's intellectual and spiritual equipment. In the "liturgic year," the sequence of Sabbath and holidays, Rosenzweig was convinced that he divined the symbolic representation of the three basic ideas of Judaism: Creation, Revelation, and Redemption. By full-heartedly accepting these ideas—and their ritual as well as moral enactment—as an intimate regimen of one's behavior, one brought God into one's life, touched, communicated with His Divine Presence in the process of "proving" one's belief in Him. It was this communication which invested Judaism with meaning in one's daily existence, and prevented religious observance from becoming a lifeless routine.

After the war, Rosenzweig established the Free Jewish Academy at Frankfurt, a college of instruction for Jews, who, like himself, had moved away from their traditional faith and who now sought to return. There were, in fact, thousands of Jews who had strayed even further from Judaism than Rosenzweig. And because the emphasis of teaching in the *Lehrhaus* was not "outward" from the Torah, but "inward" from life, it exerted a major influence on the modern, semiassimilated German-Jewish community. Then, in 1922, at the very height of his career, Rosenzweig was stricken with an agonizing disease, creeping lateral sclerosis, which progressively paralyzed almost every part of his body. Such was the spirit of this remarkable man, however, that the eight years that remained to him were the years in which he completed the most original of his essays. He sat strapped in his chair, his neck supported by a pulley, using an especially constructed typewriter to indicate the letters he wanted for his words, the words for his sentences; all the while his wife served as his amanuensis. Visitors to his study were deeply moved by the experience even though they frequently did not understand the full impact of what he said. When he died in 1929, at the age of forty-three, he bequeathed a personal religion of faith and reason that could be accepted by the Jewish intellectual on its own theological terms, without reference to Jewish history, peoplehood, or sentimental loyalties.

It was, however, a Viennese contemporary of Rosenzweig's, Martin Buber, who carried this theology of inwardness and of personal communion to its completest formulation. Like Rosenzweig, Buber received the finest possible secular education; his doctorate, in the field of philosophy, came from the University of Vienna in 1904. In the succeeding decade he earned his livelihood as the editor of several German-Jewish philosophical journals; after the war he taught Jewish philosophy at the University of Frankfurt. A Zionist all his life, Buber left Germany in 1938 to make his home in Palestine, and from 1938 to 1951 served as Professor of Social Philosophy at the Hebrew University of Jerusalem. He was a prolific writer, and, despite the turbulence of the years, he produced a wide variety of books and essays covering religion, philosophy, sociology, psychology, and mythology. Each creative effort, whatever its topic, directly or indirectly reflected his carefully formulated personal philosophy of religion.

Borrowing from the new science of psychiatry, Buber perceived in the Jewish people an unconscious, or a national "soul." That soul, he maintained, would not be found in the ideas and norms of formal Judaism, but rather in the unconscious drives that came to the surface in the great folk-pietist movements of Jewish history. The national soul was a restless, surging stream, which threw off the dogmas and rituals of official Judaism, as rocks and boulders were thrown off by raging waters. From this fundamental premise Buber projected the three major ideas of his philosophy. First, that the unconscious spirit of the individual Jew was a faithful expression of the unconscious spirit of the Jewish people. Hence, to discover his own true being, the Jew must learn to embrace in his mind and heart the entire spirit, or soul, of his people. Secondly, that the clearest modern expression of the "subterranean" Jewish soul was to be found in the Hasidic movement of the eighteenth century. Like Rosenzweig, Buber had encountered contemporary examples of Hasidic revivalism during a youthful sojourn in Galicia. Without accepting all the dogmas and excrescences of Hasidism—which, in fact, he had a tendency to rationalize away—Buber insisted that the warm and spontaeous Jewish pietism of southern Poland reflected the authentic spirit of the Jewish people. He deeply admired the rapture with which the Hasidim worshiped God, the compulsion which drove the Hasidim to search for God in the recesses of emotion rather than through the processes of reason. The Hasidim had learned a wondrous truth: it was possible to confront God as a person, to enter into communion, indeed, into dialogue with God.

It was from this truth, as he and the Hasidim conceived it, that Buber professed to derive his third major idea, which students of Buber have since called neo-Hasidism, or neo-Mysticism. But it was also an idea reflecting the intellectual climate of postwar Germany, which was rife with all sorts of mystical and semimystical philosophies: from neo-Buddhism and New Thought to the tragic mystique of *Blut-und-Boden*. It was Buber's contention that man could discover his own personality, his own "I," by saying "Thou" to God, and by entering into a kind of partnership with God for the creation of the good society. The "I-Thou" relationship between man and God was fundamentally different from the "I-It" relationship between man and things. By addressing God as "Thou," by maintaining the "tension" of a conversational attitude with God, man could sense the actual projection of the Personality of the Supreme Being; and by encountering that Personality as an equal, man exalted himself to the full extent of his own divinity. Thus Buber's neo-Mysticism rejected the sublimation of man in God, the goal of so many mystics. In Buber's thinking, man and God belonged together in an "I-Thou" relationship between two beings, and there was no loss of personality on either side, for each needed the other. "You know already in your heart," he wrote, "that you need God more than everything; but do you know, too, that God needs you?—in the fullness of His eternity, needs you?" In the dialogue, tension was continual, because contact with God was a process of mutual creativity, a surging, all-absorbing, joint labor of love.

Buber's influence reached far beyond the Jewish world, and his correspondence with prominent Christian theologians was voluminous. The socialist theorist, Dr. Heinz-Joachim Heydorn, for example, observed of Buber:

> Outside of Albert Schweitzer I know no one who has realized in himself a similar great and genuine deep identity of truth and life. . . . This little old man with the penetrating, incorruptible eyes has already today begun to project into the broken-ness of our time like a legendary figure; he is a living proof of what this life is capable of when it wills to fulfill itself fearlessly and only in responsibility. . . . Buber has accomplished what one can only say of a very few; he has reached the limits of his own being . . . and through this has made the universal transparent.

A gentle modest man, with a disarming softness, Buber in conversation demonstrated to his listeners what it meant to ask "real" questions and to receive "real" answers. A conversation with him was often an exhausting experience, for he demanded the utmost clarity and precision in the formulation of ideas; his own theories were enriched with an abundance of quotations, allusions, and qualifications, drawn freely and easily from Hebrew, German, Yiddish, and English. Those who managed to follow him, however, were amply rewarded.

Men like Cohen, Baeck, Rosenzweig, and Buber were largely responsible for the climactic renaissance of Jewish activities in Central and Western Europe between the first World War and the rise of Hitler. In addition to Rosenzweig's *Lehrhaus* in Frankfurt, the Academy for the Science of Judaism, established in Berlin in 1919, published a number of scholarly volumes on Jewish literature and philosophy. The movement for adult Jewish education spread from city to city throughout Germany and Austria. The collation of Jewish community histories, genealogies, statistics, and demographic studies was diligently pursued. Thus, the Soncino Society of the Friends of the Jewish Book was founded in Berlin in 1924 to promote the publication of beautifully bound volumes of Jewish interest. In 1926 the Society of the Friends of Jewish Music, and, four years later, the Institute for Jewish Historical Studies, were established, both in Berlin. German yeshivot were provided with wider financial support, as were Jewish art museums and publishing houses. The major revival of interest in Jewish values was so widespread that it might ultimately have reversed Western European Jewry's trend toward assimilation.

CONCLUSION

Hardly more than a generation after the end of the first World War, Nazi Germany signed the death warrant for European Jewry. The end came with undiscriminating speed and violence for *petit-bourgeois* Jews in Central Europe and for proletarian Jews in Poland, for rich Jews and for poor Jews, for the gifted and the unendowed, for the good and the bad. Certainly, by any save the Nazi yardstick, there could be no hierarchy of value for Jewish life. Each Jew was a creature of vessels and nerves, memories and aspirations, each a creature of divine potentialities and animal weaknesses. From the point of view of the Jewish people, no one of its members was more expendable than another. But from the viewpoint of the people of Europe, the Christian people of Europe, it was the loss of the Jewish intelligentsia which was to be felt most keenly of all.

European culture on the eve of the second World War was thoroughly, indeed indissolubly, interpenetrated by Jewish intellect. The world of literature, art, science, music, and scholarship—the humane and civilized world which was the eternal pride and glory of the European, and his last refuge of superiority after political and economic strength had failed—could ill afford to lose the creative resources of its gifted Jews: the fundamental insights of an Albert Einstein, or the raw intellectual courage of a Sigmund Freud; the stylistic delicacy of an Arthur Schnitzler, or the gentle *Gemütlichkeit* of a Stefan Zweig. It needed the distinguished conductor and the amateur musician; the erudite philosopher and the urbane and civilized conversationalist; the imaginative scientist who dealt with theories in a classroom; and the skillful physician who dealt with emergencies in a sickroom. When the hour for the eradication of the Jewish intelligentsia finally arrived, no chancellor, as Bettauer had envisaged it, would ever again be able to legislate their return.

European culture will surely survive: buildings will be designed; operations will be performed; plays will be produced and directed; books will be written and read. One wonders, however, if the talents of artists in isolated corners of Europe will as rapidly find their audiences in other lands; if European intellectuals will as readily comprehend the extent of their capacities and limitations, their legacies from, their responsibilities to, other civilizations. One wonders too, in the world of European intellect, if tears of compassion will yet be shed. Those tears were the mortar of Europe's most enduring cultural monuments. Without compassion, the inheritance of an ancient people's sanctification of life, genius is little more than a weapon for the fulfillment of personal or national ambitions.

Notes

Page 397. I am indebted to Professor Irving Fine of Brandeis University for help in interpreting the work of Mahler and Schönberg.

Page 398. Quotation from Ernest Jones, *The Life and Works of Sigmund Freud,* II, 162.

Pages 409-10. Irving Kristol quotation from his article, "Einstein: The Passion of Pure Reason," *Commentary,* September, 1950.

Page 411. Excellent brief summaries of the philosophies of Cohen, Baeck, Rosenzweig, and Buber are provided by Jacob B. Agus, *Modern Philosophies of Judaism.*

XX

The Onslaught of Nazism

In the early light of dawn of November 11, 1918, a group of German military delegates arrived at the village of Compiègne, France, and were ushered into the private railway carriage of Ferdinand Foch, the Marshal of the French armies. There the delegates put their hands to the document that ended the first World War. It is said that within the hour a sound "like the noise of a light wind" could be heard from the Vosges to the sea; it was the cheering of millions of soldiers, including German soldiers, even in defeat. For over four years Germany had carried the burdens of war, not the least of which were three ineffectual allies, in an exhausting and sanguinary struggle against twenty-three nations. Outnumbered, overpowered, her citizens yellow with hunger and disease, Germany finally was compelled to turn revolutionary and to scuttle her monarchy. Surrender to the Allies was the final penalty of the Kaiser's calamitous miscalculations.

Without doubt, each of the belligerent powers was responsible for the war. None of them, not even England, could totally absolve themselves of blame. Yet of all the warring nations, Germany was most responsible for having allowed a local dispute in the Balkans to flare up into a world conflagration. World War I was not simply a product of rival economic imperialisms. We know now—indeed, World War II has helped to teach us— that Germany's foreign policy, her decision to resort to hostilities, were the ultimate result of the myth of German folk destiny, of militant pan-Germanism, and of the idealization of the Leviathan-State. Unfortunately, these traditions were not obliterated by the fact of military defeat.

If Germany was guilty of provoking World War I, the victorious Allies were responsible in no small measure for crippling the peace. The Germans had surrendered on the assumption that Woodrow Wilson's Fourteen Points would serve as the basis of a merciful peace treaty. Once the armistice was signed, however, the victors rejected that assumption out of hand. There may have been some justification for the excision of Germany's border provinces: Alsace-Lorraine, northern Schleswig, Memel, and Danzig. But there was little moral justification for maintaining a relentless economic blockade of the Central Powers during the sessions of the peace conference, killing hundreds of thousands of German noncombatants through starvation and exposure. Similarly, the economic conditions imposed on the defeated nation were unconscionable: the Germans were obliged to pay for all damages suffered by the civilian population of the Allies, to pay for Allied war pensions, to relinquish the mineral-rich Saar Valley and Upper Silesia, to provide millions of tons of coal and thousands of railroad carriages and locomotives. The war debt imposed on Germany was set at the unprecedented sum of thirty-two billion dollars, payable in gold! It was hardly surprising that Germany's economy collapsed under this staggering financial burden. Life insurance policies, pensions, homes, chattels, everything of monetary value vanished in the disastrous inflation of the 1920's. The German middle class was wiped out—and with it the crucial pillar of the democratic process.

It was with this tragic inheritance that the Weimar Republic came into existence in 1919. Although the new regime was created according to the blueprint of a rather bourgeois constitution, reasonably liberal by German standards, it was the party of socialism, the German Social Democratic party, which, in the early postwar years, became the most powerful political force in the state. This was the party that had inspired the November revolt and had made the armistice possible. It was Friedrich Ebert, the Social Democratic chairman of the Council of People's Representatives, who sternly suppressed a Communist (Spartacist) attempt to take over the government in 1919. But it was the Social Democratic party, too, which failed to woo the Independent Socialists and the Catholic Center party into a united front against the German Right, the forces of reaction that waited impatiently for an opportunity to return to power. The defenders of the old imperial regime —the nationalists, the Prussian Junkers, the ex-army officers, the great industrialists of the Ruhr—were men of prestige and distinguished reputation. The Social Democratic regime never quite mustered up enough courage, even in the darkest days of the inflation, to curtail their property rights, to arrange for more equitable distribution of their vast estates, or to neutralize their interlocking directorates.

The rightists, on the other hand, were never bothered by matters of scruple. In March 1920, General Wolfgang Kapp, General Walther von Lüttwitz, and several other disgruntled military notables led a malcontent army into Berlin with the announced intention of eradicating the infant republic. The uprising was crushed; nevertheless the Social Democratic government dealt far more gingerly with the eminent generals than it had with the Spartacists. Indeed, the resulting jail sentences were surprisingly light. Most of the offenders were quickly released, and returned almost immediately to their conspiratorial activities. Among those activities were the development of powerful paramilitary formations, most of them staffed and financed by the right. Parading as sporting or gymnastic associations, and totaling not less than three quarters of a million men in 1921, these subversive groups spread terror throughout the land. Brazenly marking down liberals and socialists for death, they assassinated, with impunity, Hugo Haase, the founder of the Independent Socialist party, Reichsminister Matthias Erzberger, Catholic supporter of the republic, and numerous other defenders of the Weimar regime.

The real power behind these predatory terrorist gangs was the small group of businessmen, no more than three hundred, who "ruled" Germany by 1919. After the war, the concentration of industry which had already been far advanced under imperial policies made further giant strides. With the inflation of the 1920's the German industrial oligarchy was presented with an unprecedented opportunity to sell its coal, iron, and manufactured goods abroad, and to keep all returns deposited in gold in foreign banks. In this fashion, for example, Hugo Stinnes was able to bank his first billion dollars by 1922. Before long the Stinnes group and a handful of other economic oligarchs owned or controlled most of the heavy industry of Germany.

The cartelists had a crucial interest in stamping out any threat to the *status quo,* especially the kind of threat presented by the rise of Communism during the inflationary 1920's. It was during the inflation, therefore, that the coal and steel barons began their search for a regime in which the forces of the right, the army chiefs, the Junker aristocrats, the unemployed veterans, the *Lumpen* proletariat, would be in a position to keep "order" in the realm. The Weimar Republic was no match for these men. The very concept of democracy had been robbed of its meaning by the soaring price cycle. The implacable hostility of the Allies, who ringed Germany with high tariffs and undermined her economy with reparations demands, further exacerbated the bitterness of the German people. Against the background of this domestic chaos and foreign levy, it was little wonder that Nazi nihilism was able ultimately to batter down the legal and political restraints of the Weimar Republic.

ADOLF HITLER AND THE RISE OF NATIONAL SOCIALISM

Many of the ingredients of National Socialism (Nazism) were to be found in the *Weltanschauung* of nineteenth-century Germany. We have already discussed (in Chapter XI) the vindictive Teutomania which emerged from early nineteenth-century German romanticism. We have seen, too, that the worship of the state went far back into German history, and was newly rationalized by Hegel, by Bismarck's *Blut und Eisen,* and by the tradition of the *Machtstaat* to which Bismarck's career gave rise. If Treitschke argued that "might makes right," that Germany could move outward as far as its driving power would permit, the Pan-Germans put this philosophy into action, borrowing, too, from the racist ideology of Dühring, Wagner, Gobineau, and Chamberlain. Moreover the "respectable" German politicians and thinkers of the postwar period, puzzling over the meaning of mighty Germany's defeat, were no less influential in laying the intellectual groundwork for Nazism. The German-Jewish statesman Walter Rathenau arrived at the conclusion that Germany's strength, its primeval barbaric energy, was somehow undermined by the "arid" rationalism of Western Europe. Thomas

Mann, the eminent novelist and essayist, was no less concerned about the debilitating effects on Germany of Western "overintellectualization." Count Hermann Keyserling frankly admired the Nietzschean conception of the superman; while the historian Oswald Spengler warned that democracy was the most enervating of modern political systems. Indeed, it has become apparent in retrospect that the ruthless and destructive nihilism of Nazism was merely a crude vulgarization of the original parent: German reactionary nationalism in the nineteenth and twentieth centuries. Yet the rise and triumph of National Socialism was no less the result of other, more immediate factors that grew out of the chaos of the 1920's.

In the year 1923 an unkempt, wild-eyed ex-corporal of the Kaiser's army leaped upon a table of the *Reichskommissar* in Munich, fired his pistol into the air, and announced that the "National Socialist party" had taken over the Bavarian government and was preparing to march forthwith on Berlin. There was no march on Berlin; for that matter there was only a tatterdemalion parade in Munich, led by General Erich Ludendorff and the ex-corporal. Within a matter of hours, soldiers of the republic dispersed the motley array of marchers and arrested its leaders, including the ex-corporal, one Adolf Hitler. What was the National Socialist party? It was hardly more, in fact, than one of a multitude of tiny nationalist political groups that sprang up in Germany immediately following the end of the first World War. The organization had been founded by Anton Drexler, an obscure woodcutter who preached a weird *mélange* of non-Marxian socialism, nationalism, and anti-Semitism. In some ways Drexler's ideas bore a vague similarity to those of ex-Chaplain Stöcker (see Chapter XI), except that Drexler added the notions of racism and Pan-German expansionism. He gathered around him malcontents, romantic and careerist adventurers, homosexuals like Ernst Röhm, and demobilized soldiers like Adolf Hitler.

Adolf Hitler himself was an Austrian, born in the small town of Braunau in 1889, the third son of his father's third marriage. Later his family moved to Linz, where he spent most of his childhood. Because there was little future in Linz, however, Hitler departed for Vienna, where he hoped to develop what proved to be a very slight artistic talent. Failing lamentably as an artist, he managed to keep body and soul together only by accepting the hospitality of a variety of charitable institutions. Lazy and shiftless, living from hand to mouth among the dregs of the Viennese proletariat, Hitler spent much of his time reading the turgid pamphlet literature of the Christian Socialists and the Pan-Germans. He was immensely impressed by Mayor Lueger's shrewd appeal to the frustrations of the lower middle class, and by von Schönerer's dynamic Pan-Germanism. It was in Vienna that Hitler also developed his detestation for his companions in misery: workmen, socialists, Jews. He despised the capital, and the polyglot Hapsburg monarchy that it governed. Moreover, he seemed to find a vicarious personal satisfaction in conjuring up visions of a Germany proud and glorious, a nation of Teutonic knights, capable of arousing the awe and respect of the world.

When the first World War began Hitler hastened to implement this vision by enlisting in the German army. He fought bravely, and was awarded the Iron Cross; later he was felled by an Allied gas attack and spent the last months of the war in a military hospital. By the time he was on his feet Germany, his one love, was broken. It was impossible for Hitler to accept the fact that the mighty German military machine was defeated on the field of battle. He preferred to believe that Germany was brought to its knees, not by the Allies, but by international banking, international socialism, and, above all, by the Jews. It was then that he joined the National Socialist party, swiftly pre-empted the leadership from Drexler—Hitler had a truly hypnotic power of oratory—organized the abortive march in Munich in 1923, and was arrested and imprisoned.

During the year he spent in Landsberg Prison, Hitler formulated his political "philosophy" in an autobiography which he called *Mein Kampf* ("My Battle"), a volume that ultimately became the bible of the Nazi faith. The book was a potpourri of semitruth and naked fabrication, combined with an uncanny insight into mob mentality. It was easier to tell big lies than little ones, the author wrote. The people were always gullible; they would believe anything if it were sufficiently repeated. Democracy was a bankrupt façade for Communism. The Jews brought about the ruin of Germany by stabbing the German people in the back during the war, and by corrupting the "pure" Aryan blood stream. The Fatherland must arouse itself, repudiate the Versailles *Diktat,* fight, expand, seize land in the "subhuman" Slavic hinterland of Eastern Europe. None of Hitler's ideas was original: racism, the idealization of "blood" and "soil," the concept of dynamic expansion—all had been voiced before. What was unique was Hitler's emphasis on action for its own sake, action that was nihilistic in its self-emphasis. Further, Hitler was convinced that the Nazi party was the heaven-sent vehicle for the realization of the ideals of *Mein Kampf.*

The decade following Hitler's release from prison was a nightmare of inflation, then of depression, and always of corrosive, embittered nationalism. It was during this period that Hitler's hysterical and hypnotic oratory convinced hundreds of thousands of distraught German lower *Mittelstand* white-collar workers, the class which was the principal victim of the economic crisis of the 1920's, that the Nazi party was the one dependable instrument of Germany's salvation. Massive Nazi torchlight parades, spectacular appeals to German nationalism, and status-satisfying assaults on Jews and socialists exerted a mesmerizing influence on the German mass mind. Nazi political strength grew steadily. Eventually Fritz Thyssen and Emil Kirdorf, two of Germany's wealthiest industrialists, determined to employ Hitler to throttle the Communists; the iron and coal barons of the Ruhr readily joined them in contributing to the Nazi cause. Soon the Junkers were won over; they hoped to use the fiery Austrian demagogue as a tool with which to re-establish the monarchy. With this kind of rightist support, Nazi political success was incredibly rapid. In 1930, when the world Depression forced hundreds of German banks and factories to close their doors, the Nazis won 107 seats in the Reichstag and became Germany's second largest political party.

Yet Hitler's assumption of power in 1933 was not the result of an irresistible revolutionary movement, nor even of a popular victory at the polls; the Nazi party lost two million votes in the 1932 election. Rather Hitler was "jobbed" into office by backstairs intrigue. In January 1933, Chancellor Franz von Papen, alarmed at the inability of Germany's "scrupulous" conservatives to deal with the "Red menace," persuaded the senile old president, Field Marshal von Hindenburg, to offer the chancellorship to Hitler. Von Papen and the "respectable" rightists were convinced that they could control this raucous Nazi ruffian, and could use him as an instrument with which to terrorize the Reds into submission. They did not doubt for a moment that Hitler would remain their pliable puppet. There were few more calamitous misjudgments in European history.

Because they constituted a decided minority in the government, the Nazis at once set about winning a more effective popular mandate. Within five weeks after becoming chancellor, Hitler announced his plan for new elections. During the ensuing political campaign the Communists, Social Democrats, and Centrists were subjected to systematic terrorization; their headquarters were raided, their leaders arrested, their newspapers and mass meetings forbidden altogether. Then, on the eve of election, a fire broke out "mysteriously" in the Reichstag, and the Nazi government skillfully identified the Communists as the arsonists. The ruse worked. In the election of March 5, 1933, fear of "Bolshevist incendiarism" gave the Nazis the majority they needed to implement their program. Wearing his Nazi brown shirt and jackboots, Chancellor Hitler appeared before the Reichstag at its first postelection session and, borrowing from Mussolini's example of eleven years earlier, demanded dictatorial power for a period of four years. The Reichstag promptly acquiesced, and rushed through an enabling act which concentrated all political authority in the Chancellor's hands. The Nazis dissolved all other parties; and the Reichstag was transformed into a rubber stamp. In 1934 President Hindenburg died, and thereafter no other president was elected. Hitler assumed dictatorial control as *Der Führer*.

Never in the history of Western party politics had a candidate for public office unfolded his program with such brutal frankness; and never did an elected leader come so near to carrying out his campaign platform. By himself Hitler could never have been so sensationally successful. His Nazi supporters, after all, were the scum of Germany's streets, hardly the kind of people to inspire the confidence of a nation of eighty million. But he received support not only from the industrialists, large numbers of army officers, and the lower middle class; he was able to count, too, on the friendship and sympathy of a remarkably large number of intellectuals and religious leaders. With their help, the Nazis proceeded systematically to destroy all traces of a labor organization in Germany, and to create a cartelized economy in which power was concentrated almost exclusively in the hands of the industrial oligarchy. Priests and pastors were terrorized into rewriting their liturgy in such a way that Hitler was enshrined as a new deity. Education, too, was revolutionized, as racist and totalitarian ideals were drummed endlessly into the minds of children. One by one, the Nazis cast off the restrictions of the Versailles Treaty: by announcing Germany's right to *Lebensraum*—an ominous term that suggested no geographic limits; by rearming to the teeth, by seizing the Rhineland, Austria, and the Sudetenland. And then the Nazi State made ready for its final act of aggression: the violent explosion into Eastern Europe which was to begin the second World War.

NAZI ANTI-SEMITISM

Hitler's anti-Semitism, the single most valuable ingredient in his program, bore no resemblance to the "respectable" conservative movements of the nineteenth century; it was raw, naked Jew-hatred, wild, undisciplined, nihilistic. The crucial difference was not quickly apparent. Indeed, anti-Semitism in the early 1920's seemed at first to be merely the reaction of disgruntled conservatives to the triumph of the Weimar Republic. Junker diatribes against the Republic, nationalist and militarist accusations that the Jews had "stabbed" the imperial regime in the back, appeared to be little more than the conventional identification of Jews with liberalism. Even the brutal assassination of Walter Rathenau by Nazi hooligans in June 1922 appeared to be simply a savage and futile manifestation of nationalist frustration. The widespread circulation of the *Protocols of the Elders of Zion,* the physical assaults upon Jews in universities and secondary schools were not taken too seriously, even by the Jews themselves. Many of the leaders of the German-Jewish community actually preferred to lay the onus of this Jew-hatred on some eighty thousand Eastern European Jews who had entered Germany between 1917 and 1920 as refugees from Ukrainian nationalism. "The Oriental horde camped on the Brandenburg sands," Walter Rathenau had called them. *"Die Ostjuden sind unser unglück,"* "the Jews of Eastern Europe are our misfortune," was a frequent German-Jewish exclamation. Had not 100,-000 Jews, one in every six of the population, served in the German armies, they asked? Had not 10,000 Jews died for the Fatherland? Had not 35,000 Jews been decorated for bravery? Surely the revival of Jew-hatred could be no more than a passing phase. As soon as the *Ostjuden* became acculturated, as soon as the Weimar Republic proved its viability, anti-Semitism was bound to disappear.

They were blissfully ignorant of the social disintegration that was everywhere at work in the German world. The traditional religious and moral values of the countryside seemed innocuous and meaningless to many distraught and lonely German shopkeepers, fighting for survival in the modern industrial jungle. Philosophers like Nietzsche and Treitschke had long since urged the abandonment of conventional morality; their disciples gathered now in small political or cultural groups, and shrilled their contempt for the values of orderly government, law, or social restraint. The leaders of these splinter groups—men like Henrici, Förster, Böckel, Ahlwardt, even von Schönerer—were the true predecessors of Nazi nihilism. The Jews were their natural targets, for the Jews were identified with the state. After all, the Jews were the bankers who had traditionally supplied credit to the staid conservative regimes of Europe; it was comparatively simple to identify them as the powers behind the thrones, people who degraded all visible governments into mere fantasies. By attacking the Jews, the splinter groups were able openly to attack the state and state processes.

Even more important, the Jews could be depicted now as menaces to Pan-German internationalist ideals. Were not Jews "international" bankers: the Rothschilds, Oppenheimers, Seligmanns, and others? Were not Jews like Bleichröder, Ballin, and Cassel international go-betweens for diplomatic negotiations? Were they not employed, through their Zionist organization, for German peace overtures during the World War? The Jews—whether as bankers, peacemakers, or intellectuals—were a symbol of the common interest of European peoples. It was a symbol that Pan-German expansionism, a driving international movement under purely German control, could not possibly tolerate. Moreover, if the Pan-Germans, whether of the von Schönerer or of the Nazi variety, made claims to the status of an elite, they were obliged to project for themselves an international enemy making similar claims to "chosenness." The eradication of this foe provided the perfect excuse for Nazi movement outward. It was surely no accident that Nazi diatribes were not directed simply at "the Jew," but rather at the "international Jew." By identifying the Jew as their supranational enemy, the Pan-Germans—the Nazis—lent justification to their own supranational ambitions. All these nineteenth-century ingredients, then, the Nazis were prepared to use: they would stigmatize liberalism and Communism as "Jewish"; they would attack the structure of orderly government by identifying bourgeois governmental processes with sinister Jewish machinations behind the scenes; they would wage war on Germany's neighbors under the guise of rooting out "international Jewry."

One additional ingredient lent Nazi anti-Semitism its unprecedented virulence: it was the maniacal Jew-hatred of Adolf Hitler himself. The fact that Hitler disliked Jews was hardly surprising, for anti-Semitism was endemic in Vienna when he was living there. It was the consuming intensity of his hatred which was unusual. In his home town of Linz there had been very few Jews—"I do not remember having heard the word at home during my father's lifetime," he wrote in *Mein Kampf*. He saw his first Jews in Vienna, and only then developed his phobia. This embittered, frustrated young man asked,

> Was there any shady undertaking, any form of foulness, especially in cultural life, in which at least one Jew did not participate? On putting the probing knife carefully to that kind of abscess one immediately discovered, like a maggot in a putrescent body, a little Jew who was often blinded by the sudden light.

As Hitler brooded over the matter he decided that the Jew was not really a human being. In his writings and later in his speeches, the Jew became a mythical figure, the incarnation of evil into which Hitler projected all that he hated and feared: modernism in art, capitalism, socialism, pornography, prostitution, democracy. "There can be little doubt," writes Hitler's distinguished biographer Alan Bullock, "that Hitler believed what he said about the Jews; from first to last his anti-Semitism is one of the most consistent themes in his career, the master idea which embraces the whole span of his thought."

Nor could there be serious doubt that Hitler's anti-Semitism was sexual in its origin. "For hours," wrote Hitler in *Mein Kampf,* "the black-haired Jew boy, diabolic joy in his face, waits in ambush for the unsuspecting girl whom he defiles with his blood. . . ." Elsewhere he wrote of the "nightmare vision of the seduction of hundreds of thousands of girls by repulsive, crooked-legged Jew bastards." Most of Hitler's biographers have come to feel that the key to Hitler's racial bias lies hidden in these notorious passages. Later in *Mein Kampf,* for example, he referred to the Jews repeatedly as "the seducers of our people," and equated *Rassenschande,* racial shame, with venereal disease: both led to "blood poisoning." The concern with "blood poisoning," with "racial pollution," or—more directly—with incest, occupied a central position in Hitler's thoughts. Relations in the Hitler family were so restricted, according to Konrad Heiden, as to border on incest. Since Hitler's father had himself been an illegitimate child, one is in doubt as to his paternity, and it was therefore uncertain whether Hitler's mother was the father's second cousin or niece. In any case, the blood relation between Hitler's father and mother was so close that an episcopal dispensation was required for marriage.

There existed moreover an almost identical "incestuous" relationship between Adolf Hitler himself and his niece, Geli Raubal, the daughter of his then widowed half sister Angela. The love affair took place in the late 1920's when Hitler had settled down to a bourgeois life in Munich. Later Geli died of a bullet wound, and it has remained a mystery whether her death was suicide or murder. Whatever the cause of death, Hitler was driven into deep depression. The entire period of his early manhood was obsessed with incestuous guilt feelings. And by a kind of frantic desperation he projected his unconscious guilt—or his self-hatred—upon the Jew. Voigt, of the Manchester *Guardian,* after studying Hitler closely, reported:

> He is soft-featured, narrow-shouldered, wide-hipped. The dark eyes shift in timid fashion—until he begins to speak. Then they are fixed in a penetrating stare, the soft features harden, the effeminate form is rigidly bent as though by some iron stress, the deep voice booms and rages until it becomes half a roar and half a shriek, and the demoniac creature with the black hair and the little black moustache seems like the incarnation of all that is sinister and terrible in man, of all that it has ever brooded in moody silence on the Jew and against the Jew. And all the time it has meant "Hitler, Hitler," and has given the name "Jew" to the dreadful projection of itself.

Thus in Hitler's ideology anti-Semitism was employed with personal fury, as well as with Machiavellian cunning. The Jew became the "November criminal" and the traitor, the Marxist and the international banker, the Freemason and the ally of the clericals. The Jew was all things to all men. Above all, the Jew was linked with the traditional legal order of the state, with the international balance of power, with the conventional ebb and flow of European life. Of the twenty-five points adopted by the Nazi party in its comprehensive political program of February 20, 1925, no less than seven dealt with the Jews. Article Five would apply the status of aliens to Jews, would allow them to live in the country only by sufferance of special laws. Article Six would prohibit any but "pure Germans" from holding public office. Article Seven demanded the expulsion of all "aliens" from the country in periods of economic distress. Other articles demanded that the German press, Christian doctrine, German culture as a whole be "purified" of the Jewish "materialistic" spirit.

But over and above everything else the Nazi program demanded that Germany "Aryanize" itself, guard itself from "blood poisoning" by the "Jewish race." The doctrines of the nineteenth-century racists were swallowed whole and reasserted with unprecedented intensity. The lewd, lascivious, and pornographic anti-Semitism which pictured the Jew lying in wait to ravish the naive, blonde Aryan maiden became one of the most effective images in the Nazi racist arsenal. It was propagandized by Hitler and his colleagues, provided with pseudoscientific rationale by Goebbels, theorized by Rosenberg and Darré, and depicted graphically in cartoons, drawings, and public posters (the Jew was invariably the bogyman with a great hooked nose) by Julius Streicher, Hitler's specialist in incendiary journalism.

The assault upon the republic, liberalism, peace, and Christianity was launched originally upon, and through, the Jew. When Hitler took office he confirmed the worst suspicions of his enemies; every sacred institution of the Western state system was to be bludgeoned to death with this fearsomely effective weapon of Jew-hatred.

THE ANTI-SEMITIC PROGRAM IN ACTION

After the Nazis came to power they waited only three months before putting their program of anti-Semitism into action. On April 1, 1933, the government sponsored a nation-wide anti-Jewish boycott; every Jewish store and shop throughout Germany was blocked to customers by husky Storm Troopers stationed at the doors. The purpose of the boycott, the Nazis frankly declared, was to serve as an opening wedge in destroying Jewish economic life. Thus, on April 4 the new Civil Service Law barred Jews from all areas of public service: from administrative posts, all posts in the courts, the railroad system, and educational institutions. It was the Nazi practice to compel officeholders to produce certificates "proving" Aryan ancestry at least three generations back. The purge of "non-Aryans" in the educational institutions eliminated from German cultural life some of the world's most distinguished personalities, including five Nobel Prize winners; among them Dr. Albert Einstein, now labeled a "cultural Bolshevik." All books written by Jewish authors were burned by Storm Troopers in midnight ceremonies frighteningly reminiscent of Gothic paganism. Jewish children were removed from German schools and confined to classes provided by the Jewish community. Jews were not permitted to enroll in the universities, to belong to German sports clubs, learned societies, or art circles; to practice medicine or dentistry in any public service or hospital; to work in any capacity on a newspaper, in the theater, on the concert stage, in the movies, or on radio. No Jew, "half-Jew," or "quarter-Jew" was permitted to advertise on the radio or in the general press, to own, control, or act in any directive capacity in a department or chain store, to belong to any professional or trade association. No Jew, or "fraction thereof," could receive a government contract; and government contracts, under Nazi co-ordination, comprised a huge share of the nation's business.

Then on September 15, 1935, responding to a resolution passed by the Nazi national convention at Nuremberg, the Reichstag placed all German Jews beyond the pale of citizenship. The architect of this measure was Dr. Achim Gercke, the racial expert of the Ministry of the Interior (and later an official in the postwar Adenauer Government). Gercke devised a cunning apparatus of "racial prophylaxis" by which intermarriage between "Aryans" and "non-Aryans" was strictly forbidden. The definition of Jewishness was shaded with genealogical fractions and hairsplitting marital distinctions by which even half-Jews were banned from citizenship, by which quarter-Jews could be accepted as Germans but forbidden to marry other quarter-Jews. Moreover all persons of more than 25 per cent Jewish blood were forbidden to play the music of Bach, Beethoven, Mozart, and other "Aryan" composers, whose reputations presumably would be defiled by the tribute of Jewish appreciation.

By 1938, after five years of political, economic, and physical maltreatment, some 350,000 Jews still remained in Germany. They were broken, demoralized, hysterical, frequently suicidal (a hundred suicides a month by 1938); but many of them somehow still eked out a livelihood; a few even maintained a tolerable standard of living. In spite of boycott, oppressive taxes, economic restrictions, terror, some Jews still possessed a few financial assets, and these were eyed hungrily by the Nazi leaders and their impatient followers. In April 1938, therefore, the Nazi government formally announced the sequestration of all remaining Jewish wealth above 5,000 reichsmarks ($2,000) per person. To complete the ruin of Jewish life, it was also decreed that those Jews who left the country would not be permitted to retrieve any of their holdings. Until 1938 at least a fraction of Jewish capital could be redeemed; now those who gave up the hopeless struggle and left the country were compelled to depart as paupers.

Every little while there were special acts of barbarism. In October, twelve thousand Polish Jews residing in Germany were suddenly rounded up, packed into vans and trains, and dumped at the German-Polish frontier. There they found themselves stranded in a no man's land, forced to find shelter in stables and barns. Many died of hunger and illness while waiting for an unfriendly Polish government to permit them entrance. One such couple was an old pair who had lived in Hanover for thirty years. They sent a tearful post card to their seventeen-year-old son, Herschel Grynszpan, an exile from Germany who was living in Paris. The news that his aged parents were living in a boxcar drove the boy berserk. "I could bear it no longer," he said later, "I am not a dog." He determined to call the attention of the world to the outrage by killing a Nazi official. There is some evidence, too, that German agents, who got wind of the boy's plans, encouraged Grynszpan into his act of provocation. He bought a cheap revolver, entered the German Embassy, and shot Ernst vom Rath, the Embassy's Third Secretary. Then he gave himself up to the French police.

When vom Rath died on November 9, the Nazis were provided with the excuse they needed for a massive physical assault on the German-Jewish community. Indeed the date, November 9, 1938, represented the transition from legal disability to physical violence. Joseph Paul Goebbels, the Nazi Propaganda Minister, announced that vom Rath's assassination was part of an international Jewish plot, and that the Jews had to be punished for their "conspiracy." Accordingly, on November 9 and 10, the Nazis conducted a nation-wide pogrom. Nearly every Jewish home was smashed, while Jewish men, women, and children were savagely beaten. Some fifty thousand Jews were arrested and flung into concentration camps. On that same Black Thursday the five hundred synagogues of Germany were burned and gutted with bombs and kerosene. Reichsmarshal Goering added one final touch of German thoroughness. He fined the German-Jewish community the sum of one billion reichsmarks ($400,000,000) to cover the cost of the damage—"for which, after all, the Jews are responsible." In addition, Goering stipulated that on January 1, 1939, all Jewish businesses would be completely liquidated, and the necessary steps taken for the final "Aryanization" of German industry and commerce.

The Nazis brazened out the shocked protest of the world: for them the stakes went beyond the annihilation of Jewish life. The steady stream of anti-Jewish measures—especially the physical assaults—served to stimulate the dynamism of the Nazi movement until the day that it could be turned outward to Europe. The mounting violence moreover conditioned the German people to condone brutality; it prepared them to shed any lingering scruples toward "subhumans." Besides, it was expected that as the Jews were systematically reduced to beggary, they would inevitably sink into criminality. "At such a stage of development," wrote the *Schwarze Korps,* organ of the SS troops, "we would be faced with the harsh necessity of rooting out the Jewish underworld in the same manner in which our State, founded on law, extirpates criminals: with fire and sword."

At all times, the Nazis were careful to provide their anti-Semitic campaign with a rationale. If anti-Semitism was to be a technique for world conquest, it would have to be polished and refined to avoid the stigma of aimless brutality. The "intellectual" campaign was conducted on two levels. The first involved "raw" public propaganda for the masses, and it was placed under the direction of Dr. Joseph Paul Goebbels, whose twisted outlook made him an appropriate confidant for his beloved *Führer*. Born club-footed, embittered by his physical deformity, yet well-educated, and abundantly endowed with the keen "Jesuit" logic of his native Rhineland, he was a pathological character. "A Jew is for me an object of physical disgust," he wrote, "I vomit when I see one. . . . Christ cannot possibly have been a

Jew. I don't have to prove that scientifically. It is a fact. . . . I treasure an ordinary prostitute above a married Jewess." This feverish little man, with his deceptive smile and charming manner, was a propagandist of diabolical cleverness. He was able to idealize street brawls as thrilling epics; it was Goebbels, for example, who gave Horst Wessel the stature of a national hero, although the man was hardly more than a procurer killed in a scuffle over a prostitute. Goebbels utilized posters, inflammatory cartoons, film clips, radio programs, placards, even bus advertisements, to make Jew-hatred basic pabulum for every German family. His truly amazing propaganda skill played a large role in building Nazi power.

The anti-Semitic campaign was also conducted on a "scientific" level. Nazi anti-intellectualism notwithstanding, the semimagical slogan of "science" could not be ignored. It was necessary to mobilize the respectable academic world to give a scholarly coating to the anti-Semitic diatribes of the Nazi leadership. The man responsible for enlisting Germany's professors in this campaign was a handsome Baltic German with the unlikely name of Alfred Rosenberg. Rosenberg was a suave speaker, somewhat of an intellectual, and the author of a fairly popular volume entitled *Der Mythos des 20. Jahrhunderts,* "The Myth of the Twentieth Century"; it was the first pseudoscientific statement under Nazi auspices of the Aryan thesis. Bearing the imposing title of "Commissioner of the *Führer* for the Supervision of the Total Intellectual and Philosophical Schooling and Training of the National Socialist Party," Rosenberg set about recruiting Germany's leading academic personalities to help create the elaborate new "Science of Racism."

He had little difficulty in winning over these intellectuals. German scholars and scientists, who needed so little convincing before Hitler's assumption of power, who, indeed, had done their best to foster imperialism and Pan-Germanism in the days of the Kaiser, now flocked to Hitler's bandwagon. The rapidity and brazenness with which the representatives of the world-renowned *Deutsche Kultur* prostituted themselves was one of the most disillusioning and lamentable phenomena of the Nazi epoch. Under Rosenberg's supervision, an Academy of German Law was established; directed by Dr. Hans Frank, it provided the "data" for most of the Nazi anti-Semitic legislation, including the Nuremberg Laws. The Reich Institute of History, staffed with famous scholars from German universities, sought to give historical validity to the racist doctrine. Courses in "Racial Science" were established in Germany's leading universities. The Institute for the Exploration of the Jewish Question became the central clearinghouse for racial problems; its library of anti-Semitica was the most complete of its kind. The biologists and anthropologists attached to these institutes ground out articles and volumes dealing with the "eternal war" between the "Aryan" and the "non-Aryan." The central argument of the books, the courses, and the frequently convened "scientific" conferences was always the same: the German people were the citadel of "Aryan" purity; the Jews were a corrupted and corrupting Semitic tribe battening on the lifeblood of the Western world. In some respects the systematization of the Nazi racial doctrine was even more ominous in its consequences than the physical measures later taken against European Jewry. By 1945 the elaborate apparatus of Nazi hooliganism would be gone; but an entire generation of European young people trained on the racial myth would endure, even beyond the second World War.

It was apparent to the Jews of Germany that they could not remain indefinitely on German soil in the face of this Nazi horror. Yet the idea of departure did not come easily to them, for they were a well-entrenched, prosperous community. During the first two years after Hitler's accession to power—from 1933 to 1935—emigration involved 60,000 Jews at most. But with the Nuremberg Laws of 1935 even the most complacent and assimilated *Kaiserjude* recognized that a secure existence was no longer possible in Germany. The flight to other countries increased rapidly, reaching the total of 215,000 by July of 1939. The emigrants were aided in no small measure by Jewish philanthropy: by the *Hilfsverein,* established originally, as we recall, for Russian-Jewish refugees by the American Joint Distribution Committee; by Zionist Hechalutz and Youth Aliyah training centers that channeled the refugees on to Palestine. Later, after the Nazi seizure of Austria and Czechoslovakia, the stream of emigration was swollen by 97,000 Austrian Jews and 17,000 Czech Jews, bringing the total of emigration up to 329,000 within a space of six years.

Large as this melancholy emigration was, it would have been even larger but for two inhibiting factors. The first was the decision made by the Nazis, as far back as 1934, to force the refugees to "buy" their way out of Germany. For a few years the Jewish emigrant who paid the blackmail, 25 per cent of his yearly income, usually salvaged some capital to take with him. But after the Grynszpan pogrom of November 1938, the obligation to pay his share of the collective fine imposed by Goering left the emigrant virtually penniless. By compelling the Jews to leave the Reich as paupers, the Nazis buttressed the legend of the Wandering Jew; by forcing the Jews into uncompromising hostility against them, the Nazis created the pretext for taking a "defensive" interest in the domestic policies of all nations.

Then, late in 1938, the Nazis resorted to a second and even more cunning technique for financing their plan of large-scale rearmament. They decided to hold the Jews as hostages. The German government dispatched its best salesman, the "respectable" banker, Dr. Hjalmar Horace Greeley Schacht, to London to work out the details of an unprecedented ransom. Schacht notified British and League of Nations representatives that the Nazis would release 150,000 Jews within a period of three years—actually, 400,000 Jews remained in Germany and Austria—but that the "cost" of "relocating" them would come to approximately a billion and a half reichsmarks. Schacht suggested discreetly that Jewish financiers should be willing to provide this sum; for until they did, the Jews would remain in Germany as "security." Outraged as they were, Jewish representatives and League of Nations officials had no choice but to devise some method for coming to terms with the blackmailers. They had hardly begun to formulate their plans, however, when Hitler seized Czechoslovakia. A few months later, he ordered his armies into Poland. From September 1939 on, the fate of European Jewry became the least of the free world's preoccupations.

THE LAST DAYS OF AUSTRIAN AND CZECH JEWRY

One of the first victims of Nazi Germany's relentless drive for *Lebensraum* was the neighboring republic of Austria. No other country in Europe was so vulnerable to German aggression; for ever since the Paris Peace Conference of 1919 Austria had hardly been more than an appendage of Germany. By the Treaty of St.-Germain, completed in October of 1919, the Hapsburg Empire of fifty-two million had been cut to pieces and parceled out among a new group of successor states. After the surgery all that remained was a hunchback republic of six and a half million people, one third of whom lived in Vienna. "What is Austria and who is she?" asked Mussolini contemptuously in 1928. "She is a miserable spittoon." Surrounded by hostile states with high tariffs, deprived of virtually all her prewar markets, Austria went through two decades following the end of the war of inflation, poverty, and continual food riots.

In this turbulent, tariff-imprisoned little state lived 200,000 Jews. Most of them, about 175,000, were centered in Vienna, comprising 6 per cent of the city's population. During the starvation horrors of the early 1920's, the Jews suffered cruelly along with the rest of the Austrian population, for most of them were members of the vulnerable lower middle class. But, in addition, because of the economic paralysis, unemployment, and the frustration of Pan-German nationalism, the Jews found themselves under attack by Austria's anti-Semitic parties. The immediate targets of this postwar assault were 100,000 Galician-Jewish refugees who had fled the Russian zone during the war. By 1921 a running nationalist barrage against these *Ostjuden* forced the expulsion of all but 26,000 of them, the aged and infirm. Hardly had these refugees been shipped out, however, than the drive on native Austrian Jewry began, led by both the Catholic and the Pan-German parties. Incendiary pamphlets and leaflets, circulating the usual rumors of Jewish treason and criminality, were distributed by the hundreds of thousands. Some twenty thousand marchers participated in an anti-Semitic parade in Vienna in January of 1923. When Jews appealed to the courts for protection against outrages, the laxness of juries became so notorious that the government was obliged to change the system to include three judges. The universities were as virulent in this Jew-hatred as the hooligan bands. The rector of the University of Vienna imposed a strict *numerus clausus* on Jewish students, remarking that "the progressive Levanticizing of Vienna must at least be stopped at the doors of the University." Student riots in other universities offered excuses for the authorities to restrict Jewish admissions until the entire Jewish student body in 1922 was less than a tenth of its prewar total.

Austria was destined, however, to experience a brief respite between disaster and annihilation. England, the League of Nations, and the United States floated loans for the little republic in 1922, and a moderate, if superficial, recovery began which lasted for six years. Vienna turned lighthearted once more. Only the Austrian Social Democratic party refused to be duped by appearances, and insisted upon drastic economic reform. Winning control of the municipal government of Vienna, they made significant and far-reaching improvements in workers' compensation and health insurance laws. They constructed large numbers of public buildings and leased them at reduced rentals to working-class families. But these ambitious public projects had to be financed by heavy taxes on property owners. The agricultural and industrial leaders of the country, in control of the federal diet, were frightened by the steady progress of municipal collectivism; the Catholic Church was alarmed by the deep inroads of what it characterized as the "secular spirit." As always, anti-Semitism was a convenient weapon for the reactionaries, especially since many of the leaders who planned and engineered the reforms were Jews. Otto Bauer, for example, was Labor's most brilliant mind, chiefly responsible for the elaborate program of municipal improvement in Vienna. The leading liberal newspapers in Vienna were published and edited by Jews. Anti-Semitic propaganda, identifying the Jews with "Godless" Socialism, continued therefore even during the comparatively peaceful period of the temporary boom.

In 1930 the Austrian Republic was struck by the world depression. The tens of thousands of unemployed men and women who roamed the streets were grist for the mill of every activist political movement. The Social Democratic party tripled and quadrupled in strength; but so, too, did the Christian Socialist party, the group which represented the rural, Catholic hinterland of Austria, and which was violently antisocialist and anti-Semitic. The Christian Socialists, who won control of the Austrian diet in the early 1930's, were led by Dr. Engelbert Dollfuss, the tiny, pious "duodecimo Chancellor" who dominated Austrian politics until 1934. Dollfuss was willing to employ any method, constitutional or otherwise, to deal effectively with the "Red menace." In 1933, after he persuaded the president to invest him with dictatorial powers, Dollfuss summarily dissolved the diet, suspended freedom of the press and the right of assembly, and outlawed all political parties except his own. When the workers of Vienna, the backbone of the Social Democratic party, protested and struck, Dollfuss instantly sent the rightist paramilitary formation, the *Heimwehr,* into action. The workers' section of Vienna was subjected to systematic bombardment: men, women, and children were slain indiscriminately. After four days of carnage Social Democratic resistance collapsed. Almost immediately Dollfuss set about rescinding much of the socialist legislation of the 1920's. At the same time he issued a series of fiats that systematically excluded the Jews from the professional and university life of the country. Nation-wide boycotts against Jewish stores and businesses were also tacitly encouraged by the government.

But if Dollfuss was a standard and conventional fascist he was also an ardent Austrian nationalist and a devout Catholic. He detested the Nazi brand of nihilism, and was determined to resist to the limit all Nazi efforts to incorporate Austria in a Greater Germany. Assured by Mussolini of Italian military support, Dollfuss did not hesitate to exile the Austrian Nazi leaders and to outlaw their party. This audacious act proved to be Dollfuss's undoing. In July 1934, a group of German agents, sent across the border on personal orders from Hitler, broke into Dollfuss's office, pumped the little Chancellor full of lead, and left him to bleed to death. The Nazis failed to capitalize on this assassination by seizing control of the Austrian government; but the new Austrian Chancellor, Kurt von Schuschnigg, a well-meaning nonentity, proved helpless to stop the rapid proliferation of Nazi cells throughout the country. Mussolini, traditional "protector" of the Austrian republic, was soon involved elsewhere, in a war with Ethiopia, and Schuschnigg's diplomatic isolation rendered him all the more vulnerable to Nazi pressure. The Chancellor's Jewish policy was marked by public pronouncements that guaranteed the constitutional rights of all citizens, and by private sabotage that made mockery of these pretensions. Jews were ousted completely from public hospitals, from welfare organizations, from the school system, and, eventually, from the key areas of business activity. In February of 1938, Schuschnigg was summoned to Hitler's retreat at Berchtesgaden. For eleven hours Hitler browbeat his unfortunate visitor, ordering him to turn over all Austrian cabinet posts to Austrian Nazis or face German invasion. Schuschnigg wavered, returned to Austria, and then—unaccountably—decided to hold firm for Austrian independence. Unfortunately for Schuschnigg and his countrymen, Hitler was not bluffing. On March 13, 1938, German armies suddenly poured into Austria and seized the country in a bloodless coup. The *Anschluss,* von Schönerer's dream and Hitler's, was now a reality.

It was the beginning of the end for 200,000 Austrian Jews. The terror that now followed surpassed the brutality of the purge of German Jewry; for the Nazis were now quite certain of the impotence of world opinion. The Nuremberg decrees were quickly implemented. All areas of public life were "cleansed" of Jews, and within a matter of months Austrian Jewry was reduced to beggary. It is worth noting that most of the commissars supervising the elimination of Jewish life were Austrians; they were well-represented among the killers, the torturers, and the executioners of Hitler's concentration camps. West of Poland, no people, not even the Germans, matched the Austrians in anti-Jewish brutality. The one lesson the Germans could teach the Austrians was thoroughness; in sheer maniacal Jew-hatred the Austrians needed no instruction. It was no accident that Adolf Hitler, the most rabid anti-Semite of all, came from their midst.

Flushed with victory, driven ever eastward by his self-imposed doctrine of *Lebensraum,* certain of the supineness of the democratic powers, Adolf Hitler next turned his attention to Czechoslovakia. This thriving little successor-state, one of the most successful creations of the Paris Peace Conference, was no Austria. Its base was the Czech people, steady, industrious, intelligent. After the war, Czechoslovakia inherited three fourths of the industries of the old Hapsburg Empire, together with most of its mineral resources. A steady stream of ceramics, glassware, toys, shoes, and munitions flowed from its busy factories. Czechoslovakia's government, under the direction of the astute statesmen Tomáš Masaryk and Eduard Beneš, was democratic; its army was well-disciplined and efficient. Within this thriving oasis of equality and opportunity lived 350,000 Jews, 130,000 of them in Bohemia and Moravia, comparatively prosperous *Mittelstand* business and professional people. Perhaps another 120,000 were scattered in the towns of Slovakia, for the most part small businessmen. The remaining 100,000 Jews earned a modest proletarian livelihood in the rugged mountains of Carpatho-Russia. All the Czechoslovakian Jews, whatever their economic status, enjoyed complete political and economic freedom. In Carpatho-Russia the more traditional Jewish community even enjoyed the right to list itself as a separate nationality, and it operated its own schools. Any basic threat to security seemed quite remote.

Hitler found an ideal "provocative cause" for moving in: the Sudetenland, the area of western Czechoslovakia in which lived some three million Germans. Although they were well treated by the Czech government and enjoyed virtual autonomy, their cultural loyalties lay with Germany. These loyalties were exploited to the utmost by Hitler and by Konrad Henlein, the leader of the Sudeten Nazi party. Every conceivable Sudeten-German grievance was magnified in Henlein's party newspapers. Eventually, in 1935, this propaganda produced results, as the Nazis polled enough votes in the Sudetenland to win 44 of the 75 German seats in the 300-member Czech Chamber of Deputies. Anti-Semitism was, of course, included in the Nazi program for the Sudetenland. Henlein organized a powerful anti-Jewish boycott and promised his followers that a Nazi victory would immediately end all Jewish participation in Sudeten life. Soon the Slovak Separatist movement, sponsored by the Catholic priest, Father Andrej Hlinka, was committed to the same principle. But the Czech government leaders refused to be intimidated by Nazi pressure. Beneš was firm in his determination to punish every attempt to stimulate race-hatred; he took stern action to prevent the subsidized German press from engaging in anti-Jewish propaganda. It became apparent to Hitler that indirect measures alone would not suffice for the seizure of Czechoslovakia. Direct action was needed.

In the spring of 1938, after the *Anschluss* of Austria, German armies moved up to the borders of the little Czech republic. Hitler now prepared for a showdown. His speeches grew more vehement, his demands for an end to Czech "persecution" of Sudeten Germans became more insistent. Within the Sudetenland itself Henlein provoked riots that soon reached the proportions of a civil war. After each bloody clash, Hitler was able to point to renewed "provocations," to President Beneš's inability to keep order. In September 1938, Hitler issued an ultimatum, threatening invasion if the Prague government did not give instant satisfaction by turning over the Sudetenland to Germany. Faced with this new threat to the European *status quo,* Chamberlain, Daladier, and Mussolini met with Hitler in Munich late in September to settle, once and for all, the dangerous problem of German minorities. The result of the conference was perhaps the most appalling diplomatic betrayal in moden European history. Assured that German ambitions "ended" with the Sudetenland, the British Prime Minister, with Daladier in tow, agreed to cede the Sudetenland to Germany for the sake of "peace in our time" (Chamberlain was sixty-nine). A few days later German armies moved into the Sudetenland. Then, in March of 1939, Hitler honored his promise at Munich by sending his troops into the remainder of Czechoslovakia and incorporated the entire country into the "Greater Reich." All roads were now open to Poland.

The Jews of Czechoslovakia had known since the dread days of Munich that they were in mortal danger. Now, indeed, all the horror of mass arrests and imprisonment, the expropriation of Jewish businesses, the waves of suicides, the beatings, the torture, the blackmail, were repeated with strict fidelity to the Nazi pattern. The one difference was that the Nazi technique had been perfected over years of experimentation in the rest of the Greater Reich. It was therefore a matter of weeks before Czechoslovakian Jewry was stripped of its last possessions. Only a tiny percentage, some 35,000, managed to gain admission to other countries. The rest were doomed. On the eve of the annihilation, a gifted poet poignantly described the one exit that was left.

> This was the one country you could get a visa for,
> This country of the cold,
> The one unguarded frontier of them all;
> The only one that had an open door,
> The only one with quota still unfilled,
> Where race and credo matter not at all.

CONCLUSION

The German-speaking Jews of Central Europe were the most thoroughly acculturated in the world; none had taken the obligations of emancipation to heart as devoutly as they. In every facet of their lives—in their vernacular, their patriotism, their religious expression—they were, or convinced themselves that they were, Germans, Austrians, or Czechs to the depths of their beings. It was no accident that Reform Judaism was born in Germany, that Zionism received its coldest reception there, that, until the very advent of Hitler, large numbers of German Jews identified themselves as Germans of the "Mosaic" or "Israelitish" persuasion. They would still echo the sentiment of Joel Jacoby who wrote, with pathetic abandon, a century earlier, "How I do love you, Germanic life, Germanic thought, Germanic history. You, my second fatherland—how I love your iron discipline, your moral seriousness, the world of your sages and the character of your peoples! As in my divine homeland do I feel myself amidst your old temples and a spirit of kinship wafts over me. . . ." Now, when it was too late the Jews of Central Europe recognized what many of their more prescient intellectuals had suspected for several decades: the truth of Theodor Herzl's warning—Europe did not, could not, would not, love them back.

On the eve of the second World War the Nazi government of Germany still had not fully developed its plans for the complete physical extermination of the Jewish people. In fact, the Jews were needed for propaganda purposes; they were more valuable alive, impoverished and embittered, than dead. And yet the prelude to extermination could already be heard. The sinister and nihilistic doctrines of *Lebensraum,* German "folk-destiny," hierarchies of peoples, "race-purity"—all had proved valuable beyond Hitler's fondest dreams as instruments with which to consolidate his power. It was time to move from slogans and theories to the final deeds. If Hitler believed, and he profoundly did believe, all that he had written and said about the Jews, and if now their life or death was literally in his hands, then his next step was predetermined. Alan Bullock, the author of a definitive biography of Hitler, described the German *Führer* on his fiftieth birthday:

> The fabulous dreams of a vast empire embracing all Europe and half Asia, the geopolitical fantasies of inter-continental wars and alliances; the plans for breeding an elite, biologically pre-selected, and founding a New Order to guard the Holy Grail of pure blood; the designs for reducing whole nations to slavery—all these are the fruits of a crude, disordered, but fertile imagination soaked in the German romanticism of the late nineteenth century, a caricature of Wagner, Nietzsche, and Schopenhauer. This was the mood in which Hitler indulged, talking far into the night, in his house on the Obersalzburg, surrounded by the remote peaks and silent forests of the Bavarian Alps; or in the Eyrie he had built six thousand feet up on the Kehlstein, above the Berghof, approached only by a mountain road blasted through the rock and a lift guarded by doors of bronze. It was also the mood in which he and Himmler drew up the blueprints and issued the orders for the construction of that New Order which was to replace the disintegrating liberal bourgeois world of the nineteenth century.

It was the mood, too, in which the decision was ultimately taken to murder the Jewish people.

Notes

Page 437. Poem by Reitza Dine Wirstschafter from *Jewish Frontier,* May 1939.

Page 438. Quotation from Alan Bullock, *Hitler, A Study in Tyranny,* p. 342.

XXI

Europe *Judenrein*

HITLER GOES TO WAR

In his autobiography, *Mein Kampf,* Adolf Hitler issued a solemn forewarning that Germany was determined to carve out *Lebensraum* for itself in the vast Slavic hinterland of Eastern Europe. Few Allied statesmen took his pronunciamento seriously, however, until March 1939, when German troops suddenly marched into Prague. Within six months of the rape of Czechoslovakia, the Nazi chieftain gave his armies the signal for yet another drive to the East: German panzer divisions were sent battering their way into Poland. Faced with this blatant and reckless contempt for the European balance of power, England and Frace had no choice but to declare war on Nazi Germany. By then the intervention of the democratic West was hopelessly ineffectual, and Poland was overrun in less than a month. During the next half year the German General Staff consolidated its gains, reconnoitered Allied positions, and lulled the Western military command into a sense of false security. Since there was no further aggressive action, perhaps the *Führer* would be satisfied with his not too unimpressive loot and his exultant emancipation from the restraints of Versailles. Allied complacency was rudely shattered, however, in April of 1940, when the Nazis unexpectedly launched a new massive drive, aimed at breaking the back of the French and British armies. In a campaign lasting no longer than ninety days, fast-moving German armored columns overran Norway, Denmark, Holland, Luxemburg, and Belgium. The French Maginot line was flanked, the French army encircled and trapped, and the British Expeditionary Force driven off the continent of Europe. On June 22, stunned and shaken by the fury of the Nazi blitzkrieg, the government of France surrendered to Germany and its Italian partner. England alone held out. But England, isolated and ill-armed, seemed no longer to offer a serious military threat to Germany's western flank.

Hitler now felt free at last to concentrate his efforts on "Operation Barbarossa," the invasion of Russia, and the expansion of the "Aryan" race

439

into the breadbasket of Europe. To the *Führer* the Slavic peoples who inhabited this seductive territory were hardly more than "subhumans," only a little higher than the Jews in the Nazi racial hierarchy. And like the Jews, the Slavs were expendable. Exactly one year after the Nazi triumph in the West, Hitler tore up the Molotov-Ribbentrop Pact of 1939, and, without warning, loosed his legions on Soviet Russia. His blitzkrieg tactics were again incredibly successful. The *Wehrmacht* covered two thirds of the distance to Moscow within twenty-six days, seizing the entire Ukraine, the mineral wealth of the Donets Basin, the rich oil fields of Bessarabia. The Russian capital and the Red armies held out over the winter; but with the spring thaw of 1942 Hitler began his second overwhelming drive, pushing on across the Crimea into the Don Basin. In the middle of August, 1942, German armored columns crashed into the outskirts of Stalingrad. The Russian northern and southern armies were separated. Hitler's empire was at its apogee, and extended over more of Europe than any other domain since the days of Julius Caesar.

THE FORMULATION OF THE "FINAL SOLUTION"

As Nazi Pan-Germanism extended outward to the rest of Europe, Hitler was presented with an unprecedented opportunity to put his concept of "Aryan Blood Theory" into practice. On the eve of the Russian invasion he ordered his General Staff to conduct war in the east with the utmost ruthlessness, and to abjure all outworn notions of military chivalry. Nor was this pitiless concentration on victory at all costs confined to *Schrecklichkeit* on the battlefield. Logistics required the seizure of all enemy supplies, foodstuffs, and equipment. "Many tens of millions of people in the industrial areas," Goering informed his subordinates, "will become redundant and will either die or have to emigrate to Siberia. . . . This must be clearly and absolutely understood." And, indeed, tens of millions of non-Germans did die of starvation. The Germans inaugurated a carefully conceived system by which vast prison-armies of Russians, Poles, Yugoslavs, even Frenchmen and Dutchmen, were transported to Germany to work, and eventually to die, as slave laborers.

More comprehensive and terrifying was the Nazi plan to enervate Germany's neighbors "biologically." Hitler's scheme for "breaking the resistance of the settled populations" frankly envisaged the physical extermination of many millions of Slavs (according to some testimony, 30,000,000), the enforced transplantation and annihilation of entire peoples by hunger, forced labor, sterilization, and other means. There was to be little squeamishness in the implementation of this plan and even less pretense to compassion. Himmler made the Nazi viewpoint perfectly clear in a speech to his SS group-leaders on October 4, 1943:

> What happens to a Russian or a Czech does not interest me in the slightest. What the nations can offer in the way of good blood of our type we will take, if necessary, by kidnapping their children and raising

them here with us. Whether nations live in prosperity or starve to death interests me only insofar as we need them as slaves for our *Kultur:* otherwise it is of no interest to me . . . It is a crime against our own blood to worry about them and give them ideals, thus causing our sons and grandsons to have a more difficult time with them.

Himmler kept his promise. Under the guise of antipartisan warfare, the Nazis slaughtered 15,000,000 Russians, 2,000,000 Poles, at least 2,000,000 Greeks and Yugoslavs, 200,000 Gypsies; while several million others of all races perished of hunger and disease. The Jews, too, were among the peoples of Europe who fell victim to the Nazi biologists.

Even before the war began, "The Jewish Question" had been handed over to Hitler's specialists in terror, the *Schutzstaffel,* the political police. The SS was the most powerful institution in the Nazi State; its tentacles extended into all corners of German life, even into the army. Heinrich Himmler, the chief of the SS, was a weak-chinned nonentity who owed his position less to his talent for petty organization than to his undisguised hero worship of Adolf Hitler. Himmler lacked the imagination, therefore, perhaps even the ruthlessness, to handle the Jewish question with any degree of finality: he preferred to turn the matter over to his subordinate, Reinhard Heydrich, chief of the Gestapo and the Reich Main Security Office (RSHA). When the war broke out he was in his mid-thirties, a tall willowy man, with a long razor-edged but strangely girlish face. By temperament he was an unashamed sadist, a specialist in bloody purges, the architect of the Grynszpan pogrom of November 1938. In 1939 Heydrich opened an inconspicuous office in Berlin, in the Reich Main Security Office building at 116 Kurfurstenstrasse, later referred to simply as Bureau IVA, 4b, RSHA. It was placed in charge of a comparatively unknown SS major, one Adolf Eichmann. This inconspicuous little room—IVA, 4b, RSHA—was the nerve center of Jewish extermination.

The Nazi plan for the liquidation of the Jews proceeded in stages. At the outbreak of war in September 1939, it called for deportations en masse. Thousands of Jewish families were rounded up and dumped at ports and frontiers; other thousands were put aboard German ships with bogus Latin-American visas or with British permits for Palestine; while others were left to roam the high seas for months on end. For a while the Nazis toyed with the idea of a mass deportation of Jews to Madagascar. But systematic mass murder was not yet projected as a solution to the Jewish problem.

The beginnings of change were first noticeable in March 1941, when plans were afoot for the invasion of Russia. Rumors began to circulate through the Reich Main Security Office that the *Führer* had entrusted Reinhard Heydrich with the preparation of a Final Solution of the Jewish question (the extermination of European Jewry was never referred to in any other way). French and Belgian Jews were suddenly denied permission to emigrate from German-occupied territory. After the opening of the war with Russia, Goering ordered Heydrich, on July 30, 1941, to "take all preparatory measures . . . required for the final solution of the Jewish question in the European territories under German influence." And finally Heydrich himself revealed the Final Solution to his top staff members when he convened the notorious conference of January 20, 1942, in the office of the International Criminal Police Commission in Berlin, "Am Grossen Wannsee No. 56-8." Fifteen people were present, including SS and Gestapo heads of all occupied territories. Heydrich explained that the war with Russia had made unfeasible the plan of deporting all Jews to Madagascar. The only alternative, he pointed out, was extermination. Those Jews who survived the physical hardships the Nazis had in store for them "must be given treatment accordingly, for these people, representing a natural selection, are to be regarded as the germ-cell of a new Jewish development, should they be allowed to go free." With these orders the fate of European Jewry was sealed.

"ANTIPARTISAN" WARFARE IN RUSSIA

Already Russian Jewry was being systematically liquidated. The executioners were the SS troops, the so-called *Einsatzgruppen,* who dogged the heels of the invading *Wehrmacht.* Under the protective cover of general war, of shot, shell, and bombardment, and under the further guise of "antipartisan" warfare, Heydrich's men slaughtered as many Russian Jews as they could lay their hands on. As it developed, the Final Solution proceeded from East to West, from Russia to Poland to Western Europe, with the Grossen Wannsee Conference representing a sort of watershed dividing military from civilian extermination. Heydrich sent four units of *Einsatzgruppen* into the Russian area, one for each military front, every unit under the command of an SS general. The officers who commanded these jackbooted thugs were invested with supreme authority over all civilian affairs behind the front lines; no military officer was permitted to interfere with their activities. Because none of the *Einsatzgruppen* units ever numbered more than 900 men, non-German militia, particularly Lithuanians and Ukrainians, were recruited to help in the dirty work of rounding up and executing Jews.

The technique of extermination varied little. The *Einsatzgruppen* moved into Russian towns, sought out the rabbi or Jewish Council, and obtained a complete list of all Jewish inhabitants. The Jews were then rounded up in the market places, herded into trains, buses, trucks, or sledge carts and taken to woods or moors where burial pits awaited them. There they were machinegunned to death, thousands at a time, by small squads of soldiers. At the Nuremberg trial of 1945 a German civilian works engineer, one Hermann Graebe, gave testimony on a typical "action" he witnessed at Volhynia:

> . . . An old woman with snow-white hair was holding this one-year-old child in her arms and singing and tickling it . . . The parents were looking on with tears in their eyes. The father was holding the hand of a boy about ten years old and speaking to him softly; the boy was fighting his tears. The father pointed towards the sky, stroked the boy's head, and seemed to explain something to him. At that moment the SS man at the

pit shouted something to his comrade. The latter counted off about twenty persons and instructed them to go behind the earth mound. The family I have described was among them. I well remember the girl, slim and with black hair, who, as she passed me, pointed to herself and said: "Twenty-three years old." I then walked around the mound and found myself confronted by a tremendous grave. People were closely wedged together and lying on top of each other so that only their heads were visible. Nearly all had blood running over their shoulders from their heads. Some of the people shot were still moving. Some lifted their arms and turned their heads to show that they were still alive. The pit was already two-thirds full. I estimated that it held a thousand people. I looked for the man who did the shooting. He was an SS man who sat at the edge of the narrow end of the pit, his feet dangling into it. He had a tommy gun on his knees and was smoking a cigarette. The people—they were completely naked—went down some steps which were cut in the clay wall of the pit and clambered over the heads of those who were lying there to the place where the SS man directed them. They lay down in front of the dead and wounded. Some caressed the living and spoke to them in a low voice. Then I heard a series of shots.

Although two thirds of Russian Jewry managed to escape into the interior with the Red Army, it is probable that fully 1,000,000 Jews were trapped in the German zone of occupation. It was not difficult to dispose of the hundreds of thousands of Jews who were concentrated in the large cities of White Russia and the Ukraine. In Minsk alone some 75,000 Jews fell into German hands and were systematically slaughtered. In Kiev 33,000 people were murdered within two days on September 29 and 30, 1941, in the single largest massacre of the war; they were shot and buried in the huge Babi Yar ravine, where, a few months later, their gas-bloated bodies literally exploded out of the earth. In October 1941, 30,000 Jews of Dnepropetrovsk were machine-gunned to death and buried in the antitank ditches outside the city, and there were further mass executions at the Jewish cemetery of Dnepropetrovsk at intervals until March 1942. Another 20,000 Jews were slaughtered at Poltava, 20,000 at Kharkov, many of them buried alive in their huts, 35,000 in Odessa, 10,000 in Simferopol. In Latvia some 170,000 Jews were killed, and in Lithuania no less than 250,000. By 1943 the SS had largely completed its assignment in occupied Russia. Fully 800,000 Jews had been executed by that time. Not even the Jews of Poland were destroyed with such relentless speed and organized fury.

Few officers of the *Wehrmacht* raised any protest; usually they stood by calmly and watched the mass executions. As members of a strictly professional military caste, they regarded the dirty business as something outside their professional duties, and passively permitted their subordinates to take orders from the SS officers, whom they regarded as beneath the rank of soldiers. But the *Wehrmacht,* too, had been influenced by the high-powered Nazi propaganda campaign, with its diabolization of Jews as subhumans. It was to a *Wehrmacht* general that an SS officer wrote from Kamenetz-Podolsk on June 21, 1942, apologizing for his squeamishness on the matter of Jewish extermination:

> Dear Lieutenant-General Querner, I am answering your letter of the tenth immediately . . . Thank you for your reprimand. You are right. We men of the new Germany must be stern with ourselves, even if it means long separation from our families. Because we have to finish matters once and for all and finally settle accounts with the war criminals, so as to create a better and eternal Germany for our descendants. We are not sleeping here. Three or four actions a week. . . . I do not know if the Lieutenant-General saw such frightful kinds of Jews in Poland. I thank my stars for having been allowed to see this bastard race close up. If destiny permits, I shall have something to tell my children. Syphilitics, cripples, and idiots were typical of the lot. . . . They weren't men, but monkeys in human form. Oh, well, there is only a small percentage left of the 24,000 Jews of Kamenetz-Podolsk. The kikes in the surrounding country are also clients of ours. We are ruthlessly making a clean sweep and then. . . . "The waves die down and the world is at peace."

And yet even the murder of 800,000 Russian Jews, in comparison with which the slaughter of Russian prisoners and civilians was much less systematic, and certainly far less thoroughgoing, was merely a prelude to the Final Solution in Poland.

THE LAST DAYS OF POLISH JEWRY

As early as September 21, 1939, anticipating the formulation of the Final Solution, Reinhard Heydrich ordered that all rural and small-town Jews in the newly established General Government of Poland be transported into the large Polish cities. There they could be quarantined off from the rest of the Polish population, and kept under strict Gestapo surveillance. By 1941 this mass movement of people into the squalid slums of Warsaw, Lublin, Cracow, and Kovno was largely accomplished. In Warsaw alone some 450,000 Jews were compressed into an area where 145,000 Jews had been crowded. Brick walls were constructed to prevent any contact with the Aryan population. The process of exterminating the ghetto inhabitants fell into two phases. In the first phase, the Nazi plan was to stop the Jews from trading, and thus to drive large numbers of them to starvation. This, in turn, would leave a smaller and more manageable group with which to deal during the second phase of physical execution.

The Nazis had calculated correctly; starvation and disease did much of the work for them. The Jewish middle class was completely wiped out. The huge population of proprietors and white-collar workers, swollen by deportees from the surrounding cities and towns, found it impossible to go on. The caloric limit for Jews was set at no more than 800 calories of food a day, and the food rations consisted primarily of potatoes and ersatz fat. Although penalties for smuggling were severe, usually death by firing squad, children occasionally made their way through tunnels under the ghetto walls to beg or steal grain from the Aryan sections of the city. But the amount of food that reached the Jewish captives in this way was negligible. People were gradually reduced to walking cadavers. Indeed, the SS conducted tours of the ghettos, from time to time, to offer visiting journalists examples of the submen. As early as 1941 the death rate by starvation and typhus reached a proportion of 30 per cent. Each day streets were lined with bodies of new victims; there were occasional incidents when the corpses were cannibalized.

Even as the Nazis were implementing their program of extermination, they were obliged to devise techniques for maintaining effective supervision and control over the Jewish community. Accordingly, they established a Jewish Council (*Judenrat*) in each of the important ghettos, which they placed under the direction of a Jewish president (*Judenaelteste*). The Jewish presidents were the intermediaries through whom the Nazis issued their decrees, and from whom they obtained their victims. While they were never more than Nazi puppets, these officials may have sincerely hoped to alleviate Jewish suffering through personal intervention. Indeed, some of them, such men as Dr. Adam Czerniakow of the Warsaw *Judenrat* and Dr. Rotfeld of the Lwów *Judenrat,* committed suicide rather than be associated with the Final Solution. Those who co-operated with the Nazis found that they ultimately gained very little for themselves. Dr. Chaim Rumkowski, for example, president of the Lódź *Judenrat,* was invested with extraordinary power by the SS: he was permitted to raise taxes, to print money, even to engrave postage stamps with his likeness. A megalomaniac, Rumkowski frequently appeared in public in a white cape and hat, and enjoyed surrounding himself with a coterie of admirers and lackeys. When the SS evacuated the Lódź ghetto in August of 1944, Rumkowski was hurled into one of the last departing freight cars, together with the most anonymous of his subjects.

Whenever possible, the Germans utilized the dregs of Jewish society, the outcasts and criminals, for their own purposes. In Warsaw they employed sizable numbers of Jewish policemen, the scum of Jewish life, many of them apostates, to keep order, and to inform on their fellow Jews. The police were given uniforms, armed with whips and clubs, and permitted to swagger menacingly about the ghetto streets. Many of them were assassinated by the Jewish underground; those who survived were eventually done to death by the Nazis, in grateful recognition of their services.

Remarkably enough, few Jews lost the instinct for life during the horror-laden months of 1941 and 1942; in this period suicides actually declined 65 per cent from their prewar level. Even though most Jews were reduced to little more than walking skeletons, they hurled themselves into intellectual and artistic activity with an enthusiasm that bordered on frenzy. In the larger Polish ghettos, dramas, lectures, concerts, and other forms of cultural expression flourished until the lights went out completely. Classes and seminars dealing with virtually every field of knowledge were widely attended, even though forbidden by the Nazis. The interest in history and religion was especially intense; even the nonreligious seemed to be casting about frantically in search of some explanation for the Nazi catastrophe. As the end approached for the ghetto world, the passion for life flared up with a kind of compensatory brilliance.

Perhaps the Nazis sensed this will to survive. Certainly starvation and disease were not operating quickly enough for them. The Jewish population of Poland at the beginning of the war had been about 3,200,000. In March 1942, even after massed flight to the east, after the *Einsatzgruppen* massacres in the former Russian sector of Poland, and the appalling starvation and disease rate, there were still 2,000,000 Polish Jews who, by all Nazi predictions, should not have been alive. In the spring of 1942, therefore, Himmler and Heydrich decided to resort to more systematic extermination measures. They delegated the project of eradicating Polish Jewry to an Austro-Croatian underling, Odilo Globocnik, the SS police leader for Lublin Province. "Globus" Globocnik, a drunken fanatic, with a moral record unsavory even by Nazi standards, set about the task of organizing death camps with sadistic enthusiasm. Several key extermination centers were set up: Maidanek in the Maidan-Tatarski suburb, Chelmo, Treblinka, Belzec, Sobibor—all in Central Poland. In April the SS began to round up hundreds of thousands of Jews in the ghettos of Lublin, Lódź, Vilna, and the other historic cities in the General Government of Poland, and sent them on to the death camps at the rate of 6,000 to 10,000 a day.

The technique of extermination was devised by Hitler himself. Having suffered the agony of a gas attack during the first World War, he was determined that the Jews, too, should know the taste of gas. He sent Germany's "euthanasia" expert, Philip Bouhler, to Poland with orders to work closely with Globocnik in planning a system of gas chambers. At first Bouhler and Globocnik decided on simple vans, large boxes built over the exhaust pipes of captured Russian tank engines. In the early months of 1942 tens of thousands of Jews were stripped, marched into these vans, and slowly asphyxiated. Then, in March of 1943, Lieutenant-General Heinz Kammler, the *Wehrmacht* engineer who had designed the huge rocket bases on the French coast, was sent to Poland to devise an even more efficient technique of asphyxiation. Kammler supervised the construction of an ingenious system of gas bunkers: on the upper levels he installed furnaces for the mass cremation of corpses; while the lower levels, where the actual gassing took place, were disguised as shower rooms. The ground over the gassing cellar was converted into a well-kept lawn. Flowers were planted there.

Each day trainloads of Jews arrived at Belzec or Maidanek or one of the other death centers. They were compelled to strip, to surrender all valuables at "checkrooms," and then were marched, men, women, and children together, into huge "shower rooms." Very often unsuspecting, they waited for the water to start. When the amethyst-blue crystals of Zyklon B were dropped, gas escaped from the perforations in the sheet-metal columns. As a rule, the victims were too tightly packed in to notice this at first; but at other times they were few enough to sit in comfort, gazing up at the shower-drainage runnels. When they felt the gas they crowded together away from the columns, and finally stampeded towards the huge metal door with its little window. There they piled up in a blood-spattered pyramid, clawing and mauling each other even in death. A half-hour later the exhauster electric pumps removed the poisoned air, the great metal door slid open, and SS men entered, wearing gas masks. They hosed the blood and feces from the victims, and then pulled the dead apart with nooses and hooks in order to search for gold or valuables hidden or impacted in teeth and genital orifices. The booty was usually stacked in separate boxes. Hair, too, was cut off, and used later in range finders for German naval artillery. Soon rail-wagons arrived to carry the corpses up the concrete levels to the furnaces. After the bodies were burned, a mill ground the remains to fine ash, and trucks arrived later to scatter the ash into neighboring streams.

The extermination of Polish Jewry reached its ghastliest momentum during the summer of 1942. In May of that year Reinhard Heydrich was attacked by a partisan as he drove from Prague to his new country residence at Panenski Brezany. His spine severed by the grenade blast, he lingered in agony for six days before he died. The SS determined to memorialize this most efficient of Nazi butchers by lending the title "Operation Heydrich" to the final, most intensive phase of annihilation. Over the summer of 1942 the majority of the Jews of Poland was done to death. Each day between 6,000 and 10,000 Jews were placed on the trains that ran continually from the Polish cities to the death camps. As in all other phases of the planned exterminations, the "resettlement" procedures were developed in secrecy; the destination of the convoys was elaborately concealed. The Germans employed every variety of stratagem to nourish Jewish hopes of survival: fake post cards from deportees to surviving relatives in the ghettos painted dithyrambic pictures of the good life in resettled areas; work certificates were continually checked, modified, canceled, or revalidated by the Nazis. For long months Jews were encouraged in the illusion that they would remain alive, and that there was nothing particularly sinister about the Nazi deportation trains. This docility proved their undoing. Had the Jews of Warsaw, for example, resisted in the early phase of the resettlement when there were still 300,000 of them left, it was not impossible that some delay or postponement in their extermination might have been effected. As it was, they allowed themselves to be rounded up by the Nazis, several thousand a day, as helpless and unsuspecting as sheep. By October 1942, only a tiny walled-off segment of the Warsaw ghetto remained.

In the whole of Poland, perhaps half a million Jews, including 310,000 from Warsaw, were resettled in those ten weeks of June and July. It was an average of 7,000 killings a day. Two thirds of the victims were gassed to death at Treblinka, the rest at Maidanek, Belzec, Sobibor, Chelmo, and Auschwitz. But eventually even these highly efficient death factories were glutted with clients, and by September 1942, the SS was compelled to resort to Russian-style execution-pit shootings. By the end of 1942 the number of resettled Polish Jews had reached 1,274,000. During the autumn and winter months of that year, even the most credulous and optimistic Jewish survivors realized that the resettlement trains were not taking them to other ghettos, but rather to certain death. In Cracow the Yiddish poet Mordecai Gebirtig described the ominous silence that had fallen over his ghetto:

We do not sleep. We listen.
Dreadful thoughts pass through our head.
Whose lot will it be tonight,
Who tomorrow will be dead?

We lie awake and shudder
At the sound of a creaking door.
And the heart goes cold when a hungry
mouse
Scurries across the floor.

Perhaps half a million Jews remained in Poland at the opening of 1943. Throughout the spring and autumn of that year the Nazis systematically reduced the remaining ghettos: Lódź, Bialystok, Sosnowiece-Bendzyn, Vilna, Kovno, Riga. In a hotel lounge in Posen, on October 4, 1943, Heinrich Himmler informed a gathering of SS officials that the Final Solution was reaching a climax. "This is a page of glory in our history," he explained, "which has never been written and is never to be written." There were now desperate reasons for hurrying the grisly butchery. The tide of battle was turning against the Nazis; the Russians were moving closer to Poland. It was essential that there be no witnesses left behind to offer testimony to the Allies. "The liberation of prisoners or Jews by the enemy," declared Schoengarth, the Security Police Commander for the Central Government, "be it the Polish underground or the Red Army, must be avoided. Under no circumstances must they fall into the enemy's hands alive." In February of 1944, the last 80,000 Jews remaining in the work camps of Lódź were sent to Auschwitz for gassing. By the time Russian troops bored their way into Poland, the destruction of Polish Jewry had been fairly well completed. For several months, even after Russian occupation, a thin haze, light as dust, hovered above the chimneys of the crematoria. That haze was virtually all that remained of the largest community in the history of European Jewry.

THE DESTRUCTION OF WESTERN EUROPEAN JEWRY

The eradication of the Jews of Western Europe was the private preserve of Adolf Eichmann, whom Heydrich had charged with the over-all implementation of the Final Solution. Eichmann was a small, timid Austrian, a devoted husband and father, who began his career in the Nazi party as a minor functionary in charge of the card file on the Freemasons. Later, when he was given the responsibility of setting up a police museum on Jewish ritual objects, Eichmann made a systematic study of Jewish history and folklore. He taught himself both the Hebrew and Yiddish languages, and made a flying trip to Palestine in 1937 to analyze the Zionist movement. Eichmann soon acquired a reputation as the SS specialist on Jewish affairs. In 1941 he was promoted to major and placed in charge of the Jewish Section of the Reich Main Security Office, and during the summer of 1941 he drew up for Heydrich the details of the Final Solution. Technically, Eichmann was invested with unlimited powers, "independent of geographic frontiers." For the most part, however, he left the extermination of Russian Jewry to the *Einsatzgruppen,* and the destruction of Polish Jewry to Globocnik. He preferred to concentrate on the 1,300,000 Jews west of Poland.

Eichmann moved cautiously with these Jews, waiting until the destruction of Polish Jewry was well under way. Unlike Eastern European Jewry, the Jews of the West were close to home, close to the seat of German political power. They were no strangers to the citizens of the Reich; they could not be identified as subhumans, or "monkeys in human form"; many of them were known to be quite cultivated. Even after the Grossen-Wannsee Conference of January 1942, Eichmann therefore felt hesitant about destroying them on Reich soil. During the course of 1942 he decided instead to send 100,000 Jews from the Greater Reich (Germany, Austria, and Czechoslovakia) to Poland. There they were unobtrusively gassed at Belzec and Maidanek. Even as late as 1943, however, there were some 40,000 Jews living at large in Germany, and 100,000 still barely managing to exist in the privileged concentration camp at Theresienstadt. It was not until the end of 1943 that the bulk of Jews from the Greater Reich was done to death. These included 180,000 from Germany, 60,000 from Austria, 243,000 from Czechoslovakia. The rest had long since emigrated or died of starvation.

Eichmann's plans for the Jews of other countries west and south of Poland were far less equivocal. He was dealing, after all, with conquered areas, where there was little need for delicacy or hesitation. Thus the destruction of Dutch Jewry was swift and merciless. Out of a Jewish population of 140,000, 110,000 Dutch Jews were deported to Auschwitz and Sobibor for extermination during 1941 and 1942. On October 9, 1942, Anne Frank, hidden with her family in an Amsterdam warehouse, wrote in her diary: "The British radio speaks of their being gassed." It is probable, indeed, that many of these people knew where they were going. Thus, too, perished 25,000 Belgian Jews, 50,000 Yugoslav Jews, 80,000 Greek Jews. The number from these countries would have been even larger had not some 50,000 Belgian Jews escaped to France, and at least 10,000 Yugoslav Jews escaped into Italy and Albania. In the case of Greece, moreover, virtually half the Jewish population of Salonika died of starvation and typhus before the SS accumulated enough rolling stock to resettle them.

Until the summer of 1942 the Jewish deportees of central and western Europe were divided equally between the Polish death camps and Auschwitz. But in August 1942, Himmler finally decided on Auschwitz as the principal extermination center for Western Jewry. He preferred Auschwitz because it was camouflaged—having been planned originally as the center for a huge synthetic oil and rubber industry. Moreover, it was well supplied with housing, for it had once been used as an Austrian cavalry barracks, and later as a detention camp for Polish officers. Auschwitz was located at the marsh-ridden juncture of the Vistula and Sola rivers in southern Poland (where it was known as Oswiecim), and extended, octopuslike, into some forty square kilometers of northern Moravia. At its full capacity, the camp could hold 140,000 prisoners at a time; its five crematoria were capable of burning 10,000 bodies a day.

Auschwitz was supervised by an ex-convict named Rudolf Hoess. A brutal and rather dull-witted man, Hoess was able to administer the daily gassings with some degree of efficiency only because his aides were unusually competent people, many of them scientists from German universities. The mentality of these educated Germans, as distinguished from the criminality of thugs like Hoess, was perhaps the most terrifying human aberration of modern times. One reads, for example, in the diary of a Dr. Kremer, a professor of Münster University who was charged with administering the gassing actions:

> September 6-7, 1942. Today, Sunday, an excellent lunch: tomato soup, half a chicken with potatoes and red cabbage, *petits fours,* a marvelous vanilla ice cream. After lunch I was introduced to . . . (illegible word). Left at eight in the evening for a special action, for the fourth time.
>
> September 23. Present last night at the sixth and special actions. In the morning, Obergruppenführer Pohl arrived with his staff at the Waffen SS house. The sentinel at the door was the first to salute me. In the evening, at eight o'clock, dinner in the commanding officer's house, with General Pohl, a real banquet. We had apple pie, as much as we wanted, good coffee, excellent beer, and cakes.
>
> October 7. Present at the ninth special action. Foreigners and women.
>
> October 11. Today, Sunday, rabbit, a good leg, for lunch, with red cabbage and pudding, all for 1.25 RM.

The majority of these actions took place in spring and summer. The purpose of warm weather executions, ostensibly, was to preclude typhus epidemics. But the real motivation of the camp administrators was to allow the freezing winter cold to decimate the prisoners, and preclude the necessity of extermination actions. Thus the work of bricklaying performed by the inmates was purely nominal, its routine only occasionally broken by idiotic and homicidal roll calls, and by human experiments conducted by German medical men. The typical inmate stayed on his feet bricklaying from twelve to fourteen hours a day, living on a watery turnip soup until he became a "Musselman," a living corpse, wrapped in a scrap of blanket and waiting his turn to die. In this manner, more prisoners perished of starvation, exhaustion, and disease in Auschwitz than in the gas chambers. Whether its prisoners died by gassing or natural causes, however, Auschwitz was the single greatest extermination center in Nazi Europe. Within its confines perished nearly 2,000,000 Jews.

It is likely that the number would have been larger but for the squeamishness of Hitler's allies in surrendering their Jews for extermination. As a direct consequence of Pierre Laval's intransigence in Vichy France, for example, less than 65,000 out of a possible 300,000 French Jews were turned over to the SS—in spite of the most horrendous threats and warnings. Mussolini, categorically refusing to have anything to do with the Final Solution, not merely protected his 50,000 Italian Jews, but tacitly offered sanctuary to those Jews of Greece, Croatia, and southern France who managed to make their way into Italian territory. Ultimately less than 10,000 Italian Jews fell into German hands, and this only after the Nazi occupation of Rome in 1943. The Bulgarian government refused to deliver up so much as one Jew to the Nazi extermination machine. Even the rabidly anti-Semitic Hlinka Guard regime in Slovakia stopped its Jewish deportations when Father Tiso learned of the death camps from the Papal nuncio, although by then some 56,000 Jews had already been deported. But when the Nazis occupied Slovakia, they finished the job.

Only Romania, with a Jewish population of 800,000, was willing to lend its co-operation to the Final Solution. On the orders of General Ion Antonescu Jews were sealed into freight cars and deported by the tens of thousands across the Bug River into Russian territory, where the Germans took them over. In this fashion perhaps 200,000 Romanian Jews were wiped out by the end of 1942. When the tide turned against the Axis in 1943, however, the Romanians, with their traditional devotion to principle, decided to curry favor with the Allies, and the deportations stopped. The half million Romanian Jews who survived were subject to the most nightmarish disabilities—but they survived. They were more fortunate than the 150,000 Transylvanian Jews of Hungary who, as "foreigners," unlike the Jews of "integral" Hungary, were turned over to the Nazis by Admiral Horthy's regime and put to death en masse at Auschwitz in 1944.

WHERE JEWS FOUGHT BACK

It was principally as a result of this puppet-state hesitation that a small minority of European Jews managed to survive the Nazi terror. Some efforts, however, both of resistance and of bargaining, were made by Jews themselves. The consequences of these efforts were less significant in terms of numbers saved than in terms of self-respect and historic example. Jewish resistance did not come easily: the tradition of passivity was deeply imbedded in European Jewish history. Moreover, the elaborate apparatus of Nazi secrecy and subterfuge prevented most Jews from learning of the existence of the death camps until it was too late. Even when they did discover, in the middle of 1943, what the resettlements really meant, there appeared to be little that they could do to save themselves. The possibility of staging a successful uprising against the monolithic German military machine seemed preposterous; the ceaseless blare of Nazi propaganda, exultantly announcing one massive military victory after another, had its effect on conquered peoples no less than on the Germans themselves. Besides, the Jews of Poland were surrounded not merely by armed thousands of German soldiers, but also by Polish and Ukrainian populations whose hostility to Jews was a matter of historic record. Both out of conviction and out of vested self-interest, the presidents of the *Judenraten* in the various Polish ghettos issued stern warnings that any attempt at revolt would result only in disaster. In view of these considerations, the emergence of any kind of Jewish resistance movement in Poland was little short of miraculous.

The idea of last-ditch resistance was born with the Zionists; they had learned well from their comrades in Palestine how much could be accomplished by activism. In the summer of 1942, a twenty-four-year-old Warsaw Zionist named Mordecai Anielewicz convinced the Jewish political leaders of the Warsaw ghetto that military resistance, fantastic as it seemed, offered the only conceivable hope of survival. Speed was of the essence, however; the resettlement action was at its peak, and by autumn only 40,000 Jews were left in Warsaw. Grimly, the Jews made their preparations. Underground shelters and bunkers were dug. Money was raised both by voluntary contributions and by strong-arm pressure on the few Jewish capitalists who remained in the ghetto. A limited number of revolvers and grenades was purchased, at exorbitant prices, from Italian army deserters and from the Polish Communist party, and smuggled into the ghetto. By the autumn of 1942, despite their small numbers and inadequate weapons, the Jewish underground had become a major force among the remnant Jewish community. Marc Lichtenbaum, president of the Warsaw *Judenrat,* was compelled to admit to the Germans that "I have no power in the ghetto; another government rules here." All activities were geared for the impending battle. The Germans were not entirely ignorant of what was afoot; but neither did they imagine that the Jews would put up a serious fight—now that less than a tenth of Warsaw's Jewish population remained alive.

In January of 1943 Himmler himself visited the Warsaw ghetto, and issued the order for a final and complete eradication of the remaining Jews. Accordingly, on April 17, SS Major-General Jürgen Stroop arrived in the Polish capital from the Balkans to execute Himmler's instructions. He had under his command 2,000 men, half of them Polish and Lithuanian policemen, the others a motley collection of panzer grenadiers and cavalry reserves. On April 19, at dawn, Stroop sent his men into the ghetto. Outside, in the Aryan section of the city, Polish holiday crowds were awakening for Easter Mass. Inside, presumably, the Jews were making ready for their daily Passover observances. Stroop did not expect the action to take more than three days. It was destined to last for thirty-three days.

No sooner had the SS detachments moved into position than they were greeted by a withering fusillade from the housetops. Stroop was stunned by this resistance, but recovered his composure quickly; he ordered up artillery, and then flame-throwers. Block by block, the Nazis bombarded buildings, systematically leveling all homes and factories in which Jews might still be hiding. "Over and over," Stroop noted in his battle report, "we observed that Jews and bandits, despite the danger of being burned alive, preferred to return to the flame, rather than be caught by us." Thousands of living torches hurled themselves from the windows of buildings. After virtually all of the buildings had been leveled or gutted, the battle changed its character and went completely underground.

Down in the sewers and shelters, packed with starving and suffocating women and children, the Jews continued their savage resistance. Each day Jewish patrols, disguised in German uniforms, ventured out of the depths to bring back captured German arms and rations. Grenades and "Molotov cocktails" were hurled at German troop concentrations and at the tanks that prowled the streets. The SS brought up mechanical drills, dynamite, and gas shells. Sewers were flooded. Police dogs were unleashed. Gradually the shelters were demolished, principally by fire. Yet Stroop, in his reports, frequently expressed amazement at the insane courage of women who came out with guns blazing rather than surrender. A ghetto fighter, Ziviah Lubetkin, described the nightmare of the last days of resistance:

> Our comrades entrenched themselves near the entrance and waited with their weapons ready for the Germans. Finally the Germans began to send gas into the bunker. They let in a small quantity of gas, then stopped, trying to break their spirit with a prolonged suffocation. A terrible death faced the 120. Aryeh Wilner was the first to cry out: "Come, let us destroy ourselves. Let's not fall into their hands alive!" The suicides began. Pistols jammed and the owners begged their friends to kill them. But no one dared take the life of a comrade. Lutek Rotblatt fired four shots at his mother, but, wounded and bleeding, she still moved. Then someone discovered a hidden exit, but only a few succeeded in getting out this way. The others slowly suffocated in the gas. Thus, the best of the Jewish fighters met death . . . among them was Mordecai Anielewicz, the handsome commander whom we all had loved.

While Jewish resistance yet continued, the news of the revolt reached the Polish underground, but it was all but powerless to help. The Polish government-in-exile, located in London, begged the Allied governments for aid; but there was little that the Allies could do. A Polish officer smuggled out of Warsaw met with Jewish representatives in London, and urged them to fast, pray, wire, even demonstrate in the streets, if necessary, to call attention to the plight of their coreligionists in the ghetto. On May 11, 1943, Szmul Zygelboim, a leader of the Polish-Jewish Bund living in London, committed suicide in his apartment. He left a note for the Polish president-in-exile, Wladyslaw Rackiewicz: "I wish to make my final protest," wrote Zygelboim, "against the passivity with which the world is looking on and permitting the extermination of the Jewish people." Five days after Zygelboim's suicide, Stroop's action in the ghetto was completed; German casualties were nominal—certainly not more than 150 men. In all, some 40,000 Jews had been killed—7,000 by shooting, 20,000 by deportation to Treblinka, and the rest simply buried under the debris and burned to cinders. A few dozen Jews at most succeeded in escaping through sewers and joining partisan groups; a few others continued for months to lead a ghostlike existence amidst the rubble and ruins of gutted buildings, surviving as filthy human skeletons until the day Warsaw was liberated by Soviet forces.

The significance of the ghetto uprising was not lost either on the Germans or the Jews. "Fierce fighting is in progress," Reichsminister Goebbels noted in a diary entry of May 1, 1943, "and the Jewish high command even published daily communiques. This joke isn't going to last long." Then Goebbels added: "But one sees what the Jews can do when they are armed." The Zionists saw it. So, too, did the Jewish partisans.

There were, in fact, several hundred Jews who escaped to the Polish forests to fight on as partisans; within the Soviet zone the number of Jewish guerrillas may have numbered as high as 15,000. In Western Europe the proportion of Jews in all echelons of the French Resistance movement reached 20 per cent, and even within this group a disproportionately large number of Jewish *Maquis* were decorated by General De Gaulle for extraordinary valor. Perhaps, however, the most dramatic episode in the history of Jewish partisan warfare was provided by Palestinian Jews. During the early months of 1943 news of the Nazi death camps began to reach the Yishuv. Together with the accounts of mass extermination, information arrived that perhaps a million and a quarter Jews still remained alive in Bulgaria, Romania, Hungary, and Slovakia. The Jewish Agency proposed, therefore, that a number of Palestinian Jews, people not easily demoralized by physical danger, be parachuted into the Balkans. There they would organize Jewish resistance, aid in the enlistment of Jews in the partisan armies and establish centers of rescue from which Jews could be smuggled out of Nazi-occupied territory. The British agreed to co-operate in the project: they needed intelligence reports from the Balkans, and they were convinced that these Jewish parachutists would make excellent undercover agents. Indeed, the Middle East Command agreed to drop the parachutists only on the understanding that intelligence work would take priority over rescue activities.

Some thirty-two Palestinians were parachuted into the Balkans during 1944. Eight were killed; some returned only after escaping the most fiendish Nazi torture. Among these parachutists was a twenty-three-year-old girl, Hannah Senesch, who had come to Palestine from Hungary at the age of eighteen, and volunteered now, five years later, to return to Hungary to help organize a Jewish underground railroad. She had no illusions about her fate if she fell into Nazi hands; but her mother was still living in Hungary, and she refused to be deterred. Together with two other Palestinians, Reuben Dafni and Joel Nussbacker, Hannah Senesch was dropped into Yugoslavia in March of 1944. According to plan, they made contact with the Titoists. Dafni remained in Yugoslavia, where he helped rescue twenty-three American fliers shot down in the Ploeşti raids; later he was decorated by the British for extraordinary gallantry. Nussbacker and Hannah Senesch were smuggled into Hungary, where they were met by Hungarian partisans. Upon learning, however, that the parachutists were Jews, the partisans promptly turned them over to the Hungarian police, who, in turn, surrendered them to the Gestapo. After thoroughly, and fruitlessly, grilling the two captives, the Gestapo allowed the Hungarian Arrow-Cross government to bring the parachutists to trial for espionage. Hannah Senesch was found guilty, and was executed on November 6, 1944. The story of her heroism has since become part of Israeli folklore.

Almost miraculously, Joel Nussbacker escaped trial by hiding in Budapest's French Legation. With the aid of several Hungarian Zionist youth groups, he set about creating a Jewish underground. Nussbacker's principal goal was to stiffen the morale of the 250,000 Hungarian Jews who yet remained alive: he was determined to prevent the kind of passive extermination which had taken place in other parts of Europe. In this endeavor, Nussbacker's underground proved to be remarkably effective. The young Hungarian Zionists who became his agents managed to secure Hungarian army uniforms, to take "official" custody of Jews seized by Hungarian mobs, to forge passports for neutral countries. And yet, while several thousand Jews were rescued as a result of this clandestine operation, it soon became apparent that Jewish courage or resourcefulness alone could not save Hungarian Jewry. Large-scale rescue work would depend primarily upon the corruptibility of the German extermination machine, or at least upon the willingness of the Nazis to strike a bargain.

THE SS MAKES OVERTURES

In the autumn of 1942 the Axis suffered a series of shattering military defeats. The British victory at El Alamein, the American landings in North Africa, the capture of twenty German divisions at ill-fated Stalingrad—all markedly turned the tide of war in favor of the Allies. From then on, indeed, the Germans were obliged to fight a prolonged holding action. By the first week of January 1944, the Red Army had crossed the Polish border of 1939; five months later the Americans and British launched their massive invasion of the European mainland. The leaders of the German *Wehrmacht* knew in their hearts that the war was lost. So, too, did the dictators of Germany's satellites, such men as Admiral Horthy of Hungary.

Until 1944, there were 700,000 Jews living in Hungary. 150,000 of them, recent Transylvanian captives, were turned over to the Nazis for liquidation. Yet, in spite of the most intensive Nazi pressure, Horthy was unwilling to turn the native Hungarian Jews over to the SS for extermination. In March of 1944, the Nazis suddenly sent their troops into Hungary, immobilized Horthy, and established a puppet Arrow-Cross government in charge of the country. Heading the Nazi functionaries who entered the Hungarian capital in the wake of the *Wehrmacht* was Adolf Eichmann, the master planner of the Final Solution. He had come to Budapest to supervise Jewish extermination personally; within three months after his arrival some 300,000 Hungarian Jews were gassed or shot at Auschwitz.

At the very moment that he was ordering this destruction, however, Eichmann took the initiative, probably at Himmler's instigation, in attempting to negotiate a deal with representatives of the Jewish community. In May he made contact with Joel Brandt, and later with Dr. Rudolf Kastner, both eminent Hungarian Zionists and members of the Rescue Committee of the Jewish Agency for Palestine. When Brandt was ushered into Eichmann's office the German dispensed with introductory niceties:

You know who I am. I'm the man who liquidated the Jews of Poland, Slovakia, and Austria, and now I have been appointed head of the Liquidation Commando in Hungary. I'm willing to do business with you: human lives for merchandise. What do you want—women who can bear children? Men who can make them? Children? Old people? What's left of the biological potential of your people? Speak up!

While Brandt remained speechless, Eichmann continued. In exchange for what was left of Hungarian Jewry he wanted 10,000 trucks, 1,000 tons of coffee or tea, and 1,000 tons of soap; as a first installment Eichmann demanded a 10 per cent delivery of these goods as quickly as possible. In return he was willing to let 100,000 Jews go to Spain or anywhere else— except to Palestine, for he had solemnly promised his friend, the Arab Mufti, not to permit that.

Although he shuddered at the ghoulish dispassion with which Eichmann presented the offer, Brandt recognized that this was a rescue opportunity which had to be exploited to its limits. Leaving his family behind as hostages, he flew to Istanbul on May 19, and transmitted Eichmann's offer to representatives of the Jewish Agency. The information was relayed to the Allies. Lord Moyne, the British Resident Minister in the Near East, is reported to have said: "What would I do with one million Jews?" (he was assassinated later by Jewish terrorists). Churchill, on the other hand, genuinely wanted to help; but he was convinced that the offer was specious. Even if it were not, the Allied war effort had to take priority; the materiel Eichmann demanded was too precious to be turned over to the Nazis.

While the negotiations were then abruptly terminated in Istanbul and London, Kastner continued to maintain contact with Eichmann. He visited the "bloodhound" (Eichmann's proud description of himself) repeatedly in May and June in a desperate attempt to work out an alternative arrangement with him. Eichmann's mood changed with every report from the crumbling Eastern front. He blustered. He warned. At times he threatened to send Kastner to Auschwitz on the next train. At other times he broached new proposals: for example, the sale of 100,000 Jews in return for 5,000,000 Swiss francs. But the Jews of Hungary no longer had any ransom money, and the Allies were unwilling to provide it. Each day new thousands of Hungarian Jews were sent on to Auschwitz. The upshot of months of negotiations was a token release by Eichmann of 1,685 Hungarian Jews at $200 a head; they were permitted to entrain for Switzerland. Of this pathetic little group it is worth noting that 388 came from Kluj, Kastner's home town, and that many of them were members of Kastner's family. (Years later, in Israel, much was to be made of this fact in a bitter libel trial in which Kastner was involved; eventually he was assassinated by an Israeli terrorist.) Further negotiations with Eichmann were fruitless. On November 2, 1944, a Russian army pounded its way into the suburbs of Budapest. Eichmann ordered the 200,000 Jews who remained in the capital to be removed at once to Strasshof concentration camp near Vienna. But by then it was too late for mass execution: most of these Jews, although in wretched physical condition, were saved by Russian advance patrols.

The protracted negotiations between Eichmann, Brandt, and Kastner failed to save any significant number of Jewish lives. Perhaps their greatest significance was the insight they provided into the German mind.

Extermination as a result of hatred was primitive vengeance, a reversion to the jungle. Extermination as a result of racial principle was mania, a flight from reason. But extermination as a bargaining pawn of coldly logical business calculations was neither; it was, rather, a mutation of pure rationality, the kind of aberration found astonishingly in the most educated, the most scientific nation in Europe. This mutation lingered in the backwash of Nazi nihilism as a warning to the generation of Europeans which had been raised to believe, with H. G. Wells, that civilization was a "race between education and catastrophe."

As Allied armies moved rapidly to the borders of integral Germany, Heinrich Himmler decided at last to defy the *"Führer* Order"; he abruptly called a halt to the execution of the 200,000 Jews who yet remained alive in a dozen German concentration camps, including Dachau, Buchenwald, and Bergen-Belsen. There was still time, Himmler believed, to sell these near-corpses to the Allies for a price. In this case, however, the price was not to be war material, but rather an Allied promise that he, Himmler, would go free. He entered into tentative negotiations with Count Folke Bernadotte, vice-president of the Swedish Red Cross. But Bernadotte was mysteriously, unforgivably circuitous in working out arrangements with Allied and Jewish representatives. The negotiations dragged on through April. While few Jews were gassed or shot during this period, another 80,000 prisoners died of starvation before Red Cross supplies could be brought into the charnel houses. Even as Himmler and Folke Bernadotte continued to negotiate, British and American troops were beginning to liberate the survivors. Himmler abruptly broke off discussions and made ready to flee. He disguised himself as a shabby SS private, put a patch over one eye—and then, with typical obtuseness, blundered into the headquarters of the British Second Army. He was instantly recognized. Before he could be searched, however, he bit the cyanide capsule which was concealed in his mouth. Eichmann, the brains of the Final Solution, was not found until 1960, in the Argentine, where he had been living.

CONCLUSION

During the Nazi hegemony between 4,200,000 and 4,600,000 Jews were done to death (the figure of 6,000,000, released at the end of the war, has since been discounted. Approximately a third died by starvation and disease, the rest by direct physical execution. The Nazi party, and its instrument, the SS, were primarily responsible for this unparalleled mass murder. But there were others who could not be absolved. At the bar of history, the *Wehrmacht* High Command were undeniable accomplices. They may have regarded the Nazis and SS officers as ungovernable brutes; there were a number of instances where *Wehrmacht* generals protested vigorously, and with occasional success, against the open-pit murders in Russia. But usually the commanding officers at the front willingly co-operated in the incredible liquidation. Similarly, while there were many touching episodes of German civilian protest—and sacrifice—on behalf of Jewish neighbors, there was even greater evidence of the profound indifference, both during and after the war, of the overwhelming majority of the German people. The attitude of the Polish and Ukrainian peoples toward the agony of the Jews was in the worst tradition of man's inhumanity to man.

The Vatican ostensibly protested the deportations. But at no time during the war, even when the death factories were operating at maximum capacity, did the Papacy issue a public statement of denunciation. The Allies, too, were far from blameless. Britain coldly turned back the few refugee ships that managed to make their way to Palestine; while the American state department studiously refrained from protesting to the British against this heartless, and, as it turned out, profitless, implementation of the White Paper. The Allied Air Forces were adamant in their refusal to bomb the death camps, even though such a bombardment would have thrown the entire machinery of extermination into confusion. Over-all strategy remained the key to Allied policy.

And yet, because the essential guilt lay with the Nazis, the question remains: why did they do it? Why was Jewish extermination so indispensable to them that they were willing to disrupt their military communications, even at the most crucial phase of the war, by placing all available rolling stock at the disposal of the SS? One answer, certainly, lies in the compelling obsessive Nazi need for total domination. Totalitarianism could not be proved merely in the laboratories of the concentration camps. Nazism could prove its final and utter invincibility only by eradicating its victims altogether. A second explanation for the Final Solution, a rather simple one, was provided by Goebbels in another of his innumerable diary entries. "We are so entangled in the Jewish question," he wrote on March 2, 1943, "that henceforth it is impossible to retreat. All the better. A movement and a people that have burned their bridges behind them fight with a great deal more energy—experience shows it—than those who are still able to retreat." When one considers Hitler's determination, toward the end of the war, to pull everything and everyone down with him in a last *Götter-dämmerung*—a decision aborted by Albert Speer at the peril of his life—this explanation gains plausibility. But there were even more basic reasons for the Final Solution. From beginning to end the *Führer* was intoxicated with his geopolitical view of racism. If it was important to wage ruthless biological warfare against Slavs and gypsies, why should the most odious people of all have been exempted? Especially if, as Hitler believed with every fiber of his being, the Jews were the one supranational force which seriously threatened the Nazi master plan for dominating Europe and Central Asia; indeed, until the very end of his life, the Nazi chieftain remained profoundly convinced that the Jew stood, all-powerful, in every corner of the world where the German must stand instead.

On April 30, 1945, when the last victims of the Final Solution were being starved or driven by forced marches into the shrinking pockets of the Reich and the Russians held most of Berlin, Hitler was dead. At four o'clock on the previous afternoon his secretary, Frau Junge, had typed out the concluding words of his political testament. It was the *Führer's* final and most terrible farewell to the European civilization which had spawned him: "Above all, I bind the leadership and its subordinates to the painful observance of the racial laws and to merciless resistance of the world-poisoner of all nations, international Jewry." Hitler need not have been concerned. The "world-poisoners" had long since made up their minds, nearly a century and a half after Napoleon Bonaparte had elicited the National Affirmation from them, that their destiny no longer lay with "all nations."

At the date of writing, fifteen years have passed since the most systematic mass extermination in human history. The details—indeed, they are hardly that—of this genocide have not been recounted for their narrative validity; nor even because the revelations of the death camps are growing dim in the memories of Western peoples. The murder of a peaceful and creative people is recalled because it suggests more than the collapse of European liberalism; it challenges the claims of European civilization itself. Only against the background of the concentration camps and the crematoria is it possible to understand the frantic, the obsessive, indeed, the irresistible determination of the surviving members of European Jewry to find a home of their own at last.

Notes

Pages 442-43. Quotation, in summary form, of Nuremberg trial testimony may be found in Gerald Reitlinger, *The Final Solution*, pp. 205-7.

Page 444. Quotation from Reitlinger, *op. cit.*, pp. 128-29.

Page 448. Mordecai Gebirtig poem, "In the Ghetto," translated by Joseph Leftwich in "Songs of the Death Camps," *Commentary*, September, 1951.

Page 450. Diary extracts of Dr. Kremer from Leon Poliakov, *Harvest of Hate*, p. 210.

Page 453. Quotation from Ziviah Lubetkin, "The Last Days of the Warsaw Ghetto," *Commentary*, May, 1947.

XXII

The Birth of Israel

THE WAR AND ITS CONSEQUENCES

The Jews of Palestine were still numb from the shock of the British White Paper of 1939 when the second World War began. They found themselves, as a result, in the unhappy position of having to choose between Britain, "the betrayer," and Hitler, the murderer. Of course, the choice was made without hesitation. "We shall fight the War as if there were no White Paper," declared David Ben-Gurion, Chairman of the Jewish Agency Executive, "and we shall fight the White Paper as if there were no War." One hundred nineteen thousand Palestinian Jews, out of a total Jewish population of 550,000, registered for military service within the first month of the war—although the British, themselves, did not mobilize until the invasion of the Netherlands nearly a year later. Still keenly sensitive to Arab nationalism, the British War Office was reluctant at first to accept a large number of Jewish recruits without an equivalent number of Arab volunteers. When, however, the Arabs evidenced a distinct hostility to the Allied cause, even in the spring of 1941 when Rommel's *Afrika Korps* was dug in at the gates of Alexandria, Britain decided to abandon the "parity" ratio, and to accept able-bodied recruits wherever they could be found.

By the end of 1942 some 19,000 Palestine Jews—nearly 10 per cent of them women—were on active service with the British armed forces; this number would increase to 32,000 by the end of the war. Jewish troops were part of the military operations in both the Italian and North African campaigns. Special Jewish commando units fought in Libya and Ethiopia, and were involved in the Allied occupation of Syria and Lebanon in 1941. By the spring of 1944, after holding out stubbornly for years against world-wide Jewish pressure, the British War Office finally gave its permission for the establishment of a Jewish Brigade group flying its own Zionist flag; it was a standard which bore as its emblem the yellow Star of David, the ghetto badge of the medieval and Nazi eras. This group fought in Italy and later saw occupation duty in Germany. The economic mobilization of the Yishuv was no less intensive. Large quantities of vital war goods were produced for the British armed services: tank engines, foodstuffs, uniforms, parachutes, precision instruments, hospital equipment, land mines, electrical cables, gasoline tanks—even guns and ships. These contributions—in troops and equipment—were made with the central purpose of crushing Nazi Germany. But the Jews expected, too, that their loyal participation would not be forgotten by the British when the war ended and the time came for re-evaluating the question of Jewish immigration.

Ultimately, however, it was not merely the Jewish war effort, but the pro-Axis record of the Arab states which provided the Zionists with their most telling argument against the White Paper. Palestine Arab recruits for the British army were less than nominal. Indeed, Brigadier John Bagot Glubb, commander of the Arab Legion of Trans-Jordan, later admitted that, with the exception of his own unit, "every Arab force previously organized by us mutinied and refused to fight for us, or faded away in desertions." As Rommel and the Germans drove deeper into Egypt, pro-Axis sentiment among the Arabs deepened ominously. In 1941 the Egyptian Minister of Defense handed over Egypt's defense plans to the Italian Military Intelligence; the Grand Mufti, Haj Amin al-Husseini, established offices in Bagdad to subsidize and direct a pro-Axis revolt against British military installations in Iraq. When the revolt failed the Mufti fled to Berlin; there he became a paid propaganda agent for the Nazis. In Syria the only pro-British public figure, Dr. Shabander, was murdered by pro-Nazi Syrians; while under the Vichy regime, Beirut became a center of Nazi activity in Arab lands. The contrast between Jewish and Arab military participation notwithstanding, the British stubbornly refused to amend the Palestine White Paper—for fear of driving the Arabs into the Axis camp in even greater numbers. There were several tragic instances in which Jewish refugee vessels, their passenger cargo exceeding White Paper quotas, were sunk with the loss of hundreds of lives outside Palestine ports.

But in 1945 the war ended, and hundreds of thousands of Allied troops in the Mediterranean area were no longer preoccupied with Axis military might. The time for a tougher policy in dealing with the Arabs surely had arrived—so thought the Jews—especially when measured against the refugees' dire need for asylum. In just the American and British occupied zones of Germany, one hundred thousand "walking dead" had been liberated. Whatever their ideological orientation before the war, these bitterly tried survivors were now convinced that Palestine alone offered them the opportunity to rebuild their broken lives. During the course of 1945 this conviction was reinforced by a huge influx of Polish and other Eastern European Jews into the Western displaced persons camps. Originally, upon returning to their homes in Poland, these *Ostjuden* had encountered the same venomous Polish anti-Semitism, not excluding physical pogroms, that bedeviled their lives in the prewar era. They were obsessed, therefore, with the need to clear out of the European charnel house altogether; and it was in answer to their obsession that Mossad, the relocation authority which had been established by the Jewish Agency of Palestine, directed the massive migration of Polish Jews to the great "collecting stations" in the American zone of Germany. By 1946 a quarter of a million Jewish refugees were packed into the displaced persons camps in the West.

Their speedy return to life and creativity, after enduring the unspeakable horrors of Nazi slavery, provided a dramatic example of the indestructibility of the human will. In each camp the DP's quickly formed committees for education, for the tasks of reconstruction, for Zionist study and indoctrination, for elections to the World Zionist Congress at Basel. In 1946 they sent representatives to a "Congress of Jewish Displaced Persons," and established a "Federation of Jewish Displaced Persons" which was actually granted quasi-governmental recognition by the American occupation authorities. 1946 was a year of back-straightening and soul-healing. In barns repaired by Jewish young men, six hundred teachers in sixty schools instructed twelve thousand Jewish children. Tens of thousands of adult DP's attended classes in "people's universities," and participated actively in festival parties and political meetings. Everywhere the signs of returning vitality were apparent. The spirit of these survivors was well represented in the DP newspaper, *Resurrection*:

> How few we are! Dispersed and separated during those terrible years, we learned one thing: tenacity! And we shall once again revive and cement, and with all our physical and spiritual powers, we will rebuild our lives and the world anew. We come in an Ark that has floated to the top of Mount Ararat on a flood of blood. Are we the last to drag ourselves out alive, or are there others who await our sign? Like the Biblical Noah we are sending out the first dove . . .

The reconstruction of Jewish life in the DP camps was very nearly as remarkable an achievement as the establishment of the State of Israel.

The unshakable determination of the DP's to clear out of Europe and to reach and settle in Palestine was not lost on the Allied leaders. Some of them, deeply affected by the revelations of the crematoria, were quite sympathetic. In the summer of 1945 President Harry Truman sent a personal emissary, Earl Harrison, to inquire into the living conditions and morale of the DP's. The Jews greeted Harrison with Zionist pleas, buttressed by impassioned demonstrations. It was Palestine or nothing for them, they insisted; they would not return to countries that had become morgues for their families. Harrison was overwhelmed by the tragic evidence of suffering and by the courage and hope which had conquered it. In his report to the President he strongly recommended that one hundred thousand Jewish survivors be sent to Palestine immediately. His view was endorsed, in February 1946, by the Anglo-American Committee of Inquiry, which urged, in addition, that a bi-national, Jewish-Arab government be set up in Palestine. But new strategic and diplomatic problems were arising to strain the unity of the Allied Powers. The new Labour government of Great Britain, despite earlier promises and pledges, was in no way prepared to implement the recommendations of the Commission.

THE BRITISH HOLD FIRM

During the war, a powerful British army in Palestine had succeeded in driving the Arab nationalist movement underground. Not until 1944, when the mandatory gradually began to relax a number of its wartime restrictions, did the spokesmen for the Arab cause come out into the open again. But they could not speak with the authority of unity. By the war's end there were two groups of Arab political leaders in Palestine: those allied with the Palestine Arab Party and those allied with the Arab National Fund, headed by the spokesmen of the old Istiqlal party. The Mufti was still the official leader of the Arab community; but as a war criminal he was unacceptable to the British. The Arabs found it impossible to agree upon a new executive for the national movement. In the absence of political leadership at home, they tended to look to near-by countries for guidance and support—even as they had done in 1938-39. After 1945, in fact, all major decisions on the organization of Arab anti-Zionist resistance were made not in Jerusalem but in Cairo; for it was in 1945 that the League of Arab States came into existence, with permanent headquarters in the Egyptian capital. The British themselves had originally sponsored this league as an anti-Soviet and, indeed, an anti-French federation; but now the Arab members were determined to convert the League primarily into an instrument to combat Zionism. The Grand Mufti, who was placed in charge of the League's Palestine Department, dispatched his agents to London and Washington, where they issued ominous warnings against any alteration of the Palestine White Paper of 1939. The British government was not unaffected by these warnings.

A month before the end of the war, the people of Great Britain had elected a Labour government; the new Foreign Secretary was Ernest Bevin, a heavy-set, self-educated, hard-driving man, with a propensity for blunt speech, which had served him well during his career as a trade-union leader and as Minister of Labour in the Churchill Coalition Government. In the area of foreign affairs in a period that required tact and sensitiveness as well as intimate knowledge, Bevin's choleric stubbornness was rather less valuable. The new Foreign Secretary, who was quite ignorant of the problems of the Near East, found himself increasingly dependent for guidance and advice upon career officials and Near East "experts." They included the erudite, and rather glib, Arnold Toynbee of the Royal Institute of International Affairs (who was soon, in his philosophy of history, to equate Israeli treatment of the Arab refugees with the Nazi destruction of millions of Jews), the icy and forbidding Mohammed Ali Jinnah of Moslem India, the meticulously correct Harold Beeley, a kind of *éminence grise*. They and their bureaucratic colleagues convinced Bevin that a "stable" Near East was vital for the safety of Britain's imperial life line, that military and naval installations in Palestine were an indispensable base as a consequence of the Allied retreat from Egypt, Iraq, and the Levant states. Thus, Arab-Axis collaboration notwithstanding, it was practical diplomacy to cultivate Arab friendship, especially in view of the additional significance of the Near East as a source of oil for Britain's foundering economy. The "good will" of five Arab states and forty million Arab citizens could not be jeopardized for the sake of "appeasing" the Zionists. Bevin was convinced. "Britain," he solemnly declared to the survivors of death camps, could not "accept the view that the Jews should be driven out of Europe."

The Labour party had a long record of sympathy for the Zionist cause. In 1939 its membership had passed a near-unanimous resolution condemning the Chamberlain White Paper as an "act of moral betrayal." Against this background of Labour friendship and of Jewish participation in the war effort, Bevin's determination to maintain the niggardly immigration quotas of the 1939 White Paper came as a severe shock to the Jews. When Zionist spokesmen, both in Palestine and in the United States, urged Bevin to reconsider, the Foreign Secretary issued a response tinctured with anti-Semitic overtones. "If the Jews, with all their sufferings, want to get too much at the head of the queue," he declared in the winter of 1946, "you have the danger of another anti-Semitic reaction through it all." At a Labour party conference in Bournemouth in June 1946, Bevin sneered that Americans favored the admission of one hundred thousand Jews into Palestine because they "did not want too many of them in New York." Anyway, Bevin added later, he was definitely opposed to a Jewish state because he "did not believe in the absolutely exclusively racial States." The first DP reaction to these remarks was a mixture of grief and disbelief. Among the Jews of Palestine, however, the typical reaction was one of cold rage.

As far back as 1942 rumors of the Nazi death camps had provoked the leaders of the Yishuv into a new statement of policy: if the terminology of the Balfour Declaration deprived the settlers of the right to control immigration, even at a moment when an open door meant life or death to hundreds of thousands of Jews, then the initial conception of the Jewish National Home would have to be scrapped for a sovereign Jewish commonwealth, nothing less. Only in this way would control of immigration remain in Jewish hands as a matter of law. Few Jews, Zionist or non-Zionist, failed to recognize the urgency of controlling immigration. Nevertheless, the notion of a sovereign Jewish commonwealth struck many of them as audacious. Indeed it seemed too audacious for such eminent Zionists as Judah Magnes, President of the Hebrew University, and Chaim Kalvaryski, Chairman of the Arab Bureau of the Jewish Agency. These men believed that the idea of a Jewish state was needlessly insensitive to legitimate Arab nationalist aspirations. But the attitude of Magnes and Kalvaryski was not typical. Most of the Jews of Palestine were done with temporizing. So, too, were the leading Zionist spokesmen of the United States. In May 1942, the American Emergency Committee for Zionist Affairs called an extraordinary political conference at the Biltmore Hotel in New York. The gathering, attended by six hundred Zionist leaders, took an unequivocal position:

> The Conference urges that the gates of Palestine be opened; that the Jewish Agency be vested with control of immigration into Palestine

and with the necessary authority for upbuilding the country, including the development of its unoccupied and uncultivated lands; and that Palestine be established as a Jewish Commonwealth integrated in the structure of the new democratic world . . .

This position was formally endorsed by the Inner General Council of the Jewish Agency Executive in Jerusalem on November 10, 1942, by a vote of 21 to 4.

This victory of the propartition faction stemmed in no small measure from a realistic appraisal of the Yishuv's strength and spirit. When Chaim Weizmann visited Palestine again in 1944, he was moved and impressed by the growth of the Jewish settlement there. He wrote:

The war years had knit the community into a powerful, self-conscious organism, and the great war effort, out of all proportion to the numerical strength of the Yishuv, had given the Jews of Palestine a heightened self-reliance, a justified sense of merit and achievement, a renewed claim on the democratic world, and a high degree of technical development. The productive capacity of the country had been given a powerful forward thrust. The National Home was in fact here—unrecognized, and by that lack of recognition frustrated in the fulfillment of its task. Here were over six hundred thousand Jews capable of a vast concerted action in behalf of the remnant of Jewry in Europe—to them no impersonal element but, in thousands of instances, composed of near and dear ones—capable of such action, frantically eager to undertake it, and forbidden to do so.

Weizmann called the first postwar Zionist Congress to order in December 1946. Looking about him at the delegates assembled in the hotel ballroom in Basel, he was painfully conscious of the absence of most of his old friends. Polish Jewry was missing. Central and Southeastern European Jewry were missing. The European reservoir that Weizmann had represented, and upon which he had depended for many decades of his moderate pro-British Zionist leadership, had now vanished. The principal groups represented were the Palestinians, led by the tenacious and militant David Ben-Gurion, Chairman of the Jewish Agency Executive, and the Americans, led by the fiery Cleveland rabbi, Abba Hillel Silver. Both groups unhesitatingly lent their support to the Biltmore Program, and insisted upon statehood for the Yishuv.

Weizmann himself pleaded for moderation and for a renewed effort to co-operate with the British; but the delegates had had enough of moderation, and repudiated Weizmann by refusing to re-elect him president of the Zionist Organization. Out of deference to the old man's prestige and past service, however, the post was left vacant. Few of the delegates, even among the extremists, could fail to appreciate Weizmann's value to the Zionist cause. He had been a superb diplomat in the days of the Balfour Declaration and in the 1920's and 1930's, when his tact and cultivation had insured a reasonable degree of British friendship. Had Ben-Gurion, blunt and obdurate, been in charge of Zionist diplomacy in the interwar period, the Yishuv would probably not have survived many of its pitfalls. There were losses through compromise but there were infinitely greater gains in the emerging strength of the Yishuv. Weizmann had won precious time for it to become a practical entity and to be considered worthy of statehood. But now the times had changed, and Weizmann's gradualism, compounded by old age and physical infirmity, apparently was no longer adequate for the desperate emergencies presented by the DP camps and the hostility of Ernest Bevin.

Yet the formal endorsement of the Biltmore Program at Basel in December 1946 did not necessarily signify that the Yishuv had come "of age" as a political organism, nor that the trappings of mandatory status were altogether superfluous. This was hardly the case. Most of the Jews of Palestine were still not native-born; the core of the population was composed of very recent immigrants from Europe. Although thousands of them were imbued with a deep sense of Jewish nationalism, they recognized their weaknesses in numbers and physical resources. They understood, too, the incalculable advantages, in trade and military protection, to be derived from British mandatory control. It was not nationalism that animated Zionist claims and aspirations at the Biltmore or at Basel. The control of immigration was the head and front of all planning and action. Even as late as 1946, if Whitehall had insisted upon maintaining a tight grip on every aspect of the Yishuv's diplomatic, domestic, and financial life, but had permitted immigration to remain in Jewish hands, Ben-Gurion would probably have approved. It was Bevin's refusal to disavow or even to amend the White Paper that forced Ben-Gurion to make his maximalist demands for Jewish statehood. In effect, the immigration issue ultimately determined the rise of the State of Israel.

JEWISH "ILLEGALISM"

Bevin's intransigence provoked more than extremist political demands from the distraught and embittered Yishuv. It provided a physical response as well. For one thing, it lent a measure of respectability to those desperate elements who expressed their protest against the White Paper in the form of terrorist activity. The Irgun Zvai Leumi was one such terrorist group. Ostensibly, the Irgun was the military arm of the dissident Revisionist party; but its membership, which rarely exceeded two thousand men and women, was composed primarily of fairly recent arrivals from Eastern Europe. Having seen their families led to slaughter by the Nazis, they were less concerned with the internal politics of the Yishuv than with bringing the surviving displaced persons into Palestine. Unhinged by the horrors of the death camps, they no longer responded to such words as "patience," "moderation," or "legality." Even less responsible than the Irgun was the "Stern Gang," a small band of youthful extremists from the Oriental slums of Palestine's larger towns. The Sternists were convinced, with the late Abraham Stern, who was killed in 1942, that the most direct solution to British obstructionism was political assassination.

During 1946 and 1947, as the British turned back one refugee ship after another, the Irgunists and the Sternists ran wild in Palestine: setting fire to British military installations, shooting down British soldiers, even, in June of 1946, blowing up the King David Hotel in Jerusalem, with heavy and indiscriminate loss of British, Arab, and Jewish life. Although the terrorists were repudiated by the overwhelming majority of Palestinian Jews, they continued to be active as long as the White Paper remained in force. And even those who, like Ben-Gurion, opposed them most adamantly, recognized that they were not really responsible for their actions. They were goaded to desperation by the fate of their people and the unconscionable impersonality with which diplomacy moved to influence it.

Yet the most significant resistance to the White Paper came not in the form of terrorism, but rather through a vast, ingeniously organized program of "illegal" Jewish immigration into Palestine. It was an enterprise which in sheer human drama has few parallels in modern history. Even before the beginning of the war, the Jewish Agency had dispatched agents to Europe to organize an "underground railroad" to Palestine. As late as 1939 this emigration received the active help of Nazi leaders who, in those days, were eager to deport their Jews. But with the formulation of the "Final Solution," the Nazis substituted murder for emigration and influx of European Jews into Palestine slowed to a trickle; by 1943 it came to a complete halt. When the war ended, the Jewish Agency sent back Haganah agents with a mandate to smuggle as many DP's as possible out of Europe and past the British blockade. The refugees, their spirits soaring at the prospect of reaching Palestine, promised to co-operate to the limit of their endurance. There was more behind the plan than simple humanitarianism, more even than the reinvigoration of DP morale. "In the coming struggle," Ben-Gurion told a gathering of Jews at Landsberg Displaced Persons Camp, "you will play a decisive role . . . You are not only needy persons, you are also a political force." The plan, in short, was to drown the White Paper in a flood of "illegal" immigration.

Mossad, the Haganah organization in Europe, established its headquarters in Paris, under the direction of an imaginative undercover agent who has chosen to this day to remain anonymous. Other emissaries were sent to Mediterranean and Dalmatian ports to hire vessels, ranging from small fishing schooners to reconverted icebreakers, and to arrange for clandestine sailings. As a rule, the French, Italian, and Yugoslav governments refused to interfere with these sailings; they had little sympathy with British colonial policy and even less with the White Paper. In fact there were frequent instances in which these governments actively co-operated with Mossad by providing navigators and tide tables. Each month several thousand Jewish DP's left the American and British zones of Germany, either walked or were transported to secret inlets on the Mediterranean, and, while harbor police deliberately looked the other way, were loaded onto the awaiting ships. Mossad operations in Italy were particularly ingenious, guided by a tough, resourceful Haganah veteran, Yehuda Arazi. During the chaotic months following the end of the war, Arazi, in the uniform of a British army sergeant, used the British Army of Occupation as a "front" for his activities. The Palestinian units in Italy were particularly helpful in this endeavor; since the Jewish transport company was stationed in Milan, it became an ideal base for refugee-running from the northern frontiers. The company's officers prepared false papers, "requisitioned" isolated farmhouses for the DP's, and provisioned them with food, clothing, and fuel. Later, in British army vehicles and under cover of darkness, they brought the refugees down to the embarkation areas.

By the spring of 1946 the actual operations had developed clockwork precision. At nightfall, selected DP's were assembled at a specified refugee check point, loaded silently into trucks, and driven to the assigned ports. Jon and David Kimche recall:

> As the convoy neared the point of departure, *Palmach* [commando] lookouts ringed the area for miles around . . . At the point of embarkation itself, normally in some dark spot, a black MG car would invariably be waiting; Arazi would be there to see that everything went according to plan . . . The actual embarkation of the ship would be carried out quickly and smoothly; sometimes the boat would be able to come in close enough for the refugees to board it over long planks; at other times a wire would be connected from the ship to shore, and the immigrants, in groups of forty, in large rubber rescue dinghies, would pull their boats to the ship with the aid of the wire. A motorboat would pull several dinghies to the ship at one go; in this manner a transport of 800 could be embarked in under two hours. By dawn, the ship would be on its way to the east . . . And back on shore, Arazi would start the cycle over again; negotiations for another ship would begin; the soldiers would set about replenishing the stock of provisions and of diesel oil; more refugees would come south and the whole story would again repeat itself.

At all times, moreover, radio contact was maintained with Mossad lookouts throughout the peninsula—and, too, throughout all Europe.

This elaborate apparatus had its counterpart at the reception end on the shores of Palestine. There, however, the problems were considerably more complex. If the illegals managed to make their way out of European ports, they still had to evade the British Mediterranean Fleet, the RAF Mediterranean Patrol, and the Palestine Coastal Water Blockade. In Palestine proper one hundred thousand British troops were on guard against their arrival. But here again years of underground experience served the Haganah in good stead; its agents in Palestine usually maintained radio contact with the refugee vessel and guided it to its point of disembarkation. The spot was picked only after British countermeasures and the position of British patrols had been carefully studied. Haganah Intelligence functioned with an efficiency that was truly uncanny; frequently copies of top-secret Army Movement Orders were in Jewish hands before they reached their intended destination. When vessels landed, the immigrants were quickly smuggled inland and provided with false papers. Guards, couriers, lookouts, doctors, nurses—all were mobilized in the full-scale war (it was nothing less) against the

White Paper. Thousands of illegal immigrants managed in this fashion to break the British blockade.

But the majority of the DP's failed to make it. Of sixty-three ships that sailed clandestinely for Palestine between April 1945 and January 1948, fifty-eight were intercepted by the British; of twenty-five thousand DP's who crowded into the ships, hardly more than five thousand gained entrance into Palestine. But every defeat and disappointment was a long-range victory. When, for example, the British blocked the sailing of a large refugee ship from the Italian port of La Spezia in April 1946, Arazi ordered the DP's to stay on board and engage in a hunger strike rather than disembark. The British military police were helpless to intervene; Italian dock-workers laid down their tools as a gesture of sympathy for the refugees, while Italian officials, from Prime Minister De Gasperi down, sent messages of encouragement. Pilloried before the world as "heartless monsters," the British grudgingly permitted the vessel to depart. Throughout the Western world millions of people were deeply moved by accounts of Jewish refugee ships, laden with women and children, ramming onto the beaches of Palestine in a desperate effort to evade British interception. The newspapers of America and Europe carried front-page pictures of the refugee vessel *Beauharnais* challenging British destroyers at Haifa with the banner: "We survived Hitler. Death is no stranger to us. Nothing can keep us from our Jewish homeland. The blood be on your head if you fire on this unarmed ship." Graphic accounts were circulated in the world press of the primitive Cyprus detention camps, surrounded by barbed wire, deliberately deprived of water in the expectation that the blazing equatorial sun would discourage further illegal crossings. But far from being discouraged, Mossad and the DP's intensified their efforts. They were well aware that the British, as decent, civilized people, were ultimately vulnerable to the pressure of world opinion.

Foreign Secretary Bevin, however, did not yield easily. He was not oblivious to the damage the Palestine blockade was inflicting on Britain's reputation, at a time when the British economy was desperately in need of American financial support. But he decided to make a determined final effort to choke off the illegal immigration permanently. Word reached him in July 1947 that a battered little American river steamer, packed with 4,500 refugees, had set sail for Palestine from the French port of Sète. The order went out to intercept the vessel at the first opportunity. Six British destroyers and one cruiser "escorted" the refugee ship, appropriately named *Exodus-1947*, across the Mediterranean. Once the *Exodus* approached Palestine territorial waters, the British armada closed in for boarding. A desperate hand-to-hand struggle ensued. The DP's fought off the boarding party for several hours; eventually the British were compelled to use machine guns and gas bombs, killing three Jews and wounding a hundred. All the while a running account of the battle was radioed to Haganah headquarters in Tel Aviv, and later rebroadcast throughout the world. The crew of the *Exodus* surrendered only after the British threatened to sink the vessel outright.

This time the infuriated Bevin was determined "to make an example of this ship" by sending the refugees not to Cyprus, but back to Europe. The passengers of the *Exodus* were resolved to set an example of their own, however. Returned to Marseilles in caged prison ships, the DP's refused to disembark; under strict Mossad discipline, they insisted that it was Palestine or nothing for them. At the end of three weeks the British prepared to return the refugees to the Displaced Persons camps in the British zone of Germany. The odyssey of the *Exodus* had already claimed the world's rapt and sympathetic attention for over two months; but now the return of these hapless survivors to German soil, soil that even yet steamed with hundreds of thousands of Jewish bodies, elicited a world-wide revulsion which even Bevin found it impossible to ignore. Later it was the Palestinian Jew, by his bravery and fighting ability, who successfully established the State of Israel. But it was the illegal immigrant who broke the British mandate, by destroying the international good will upon which the mandate had rested.

THE ATTITUDE OF THE UNITED STATES

Casting about frantically for diplomatic support in its Palestine predicament, the British government instinctively looked to the United States. With moral and financial backing of Britain's position in Palestine, the United States could have assured Bevin of ultimate success in excluding the DP's. The Foreign Secretary had every reason to believe that American strategic and financial interests in the Near East would require Washington to endorse Britain's pro-Arab policy. The United States, after all, had invested millions of dollars in air and military repair bases in Saudi Arabia. Several of its lucrative commercial air routes connected in Cairo. It possessed even more vital commercial oil interests in Iraq, Kuwait, Bahrein, and Saudi Arabia, and it was even then planning a huge pipe-line system from the Arabian Peninsula to the Mediterranean. (The plans were later abandoned.) The United States, moreover, could have been no less concerned than Britain at the threat of Soviet expansion into the Near East. It was in response to such danger that the American government had allocated $400,000,000 for the purpose of underwriting the economies of Greece and Turkey. These strategic considerations were well stated by key figures in Washington. The joint Chiefs of Staff, Secretary of Defense Forrestal, the Near Eastern experts in the State Department, all felt that American strategic and commercial interests would be placed in jeopardy by a pro-Zionist policy. Their sentiments were echoed, with rather less disinterest, by James Terry Duce, Vice-President of the Arabian American Oil Company, by the American Potestant missionaries stationed in Beirut and Cairo, and by the Anglophiles who dominated the Washington social scene.

But there were other factors that, in their turn, exercised a pro-Zionist influence on the American government, and particularly on the White House and Congress. Chief among these considerations was American public opinion, which was deeply and genuinely affected by the plight of the displaced persons. Another influence, unquestionably, was the value American political figures placed on the Jewish vote in New York, Illinois, Pennsylvania, and other states heavily populated by Jews. This power, of course, could not have been mobilized had not the American-Jewish community in turn been won over to the Zionist viewpoint as a result of decades of patient cultivation. America's great Russian-Jewish population had never been ill-disposed toward Zionism; but until Hitler's rise to power the cause of Palestine had been little more than another Jewish charity, worthy, to be sure, but hardly more worthy than other philanthropic endeavors. However, the rise of Nazism, the destruction of European Jewry, the plight of the DP's, soon transformed a vague feeling of solicitude into a passionaate Zionist activism. Membership in the American Zionist Organization shot up from 100,000 families in 1939 to 400,000 in 1945. Jews from all corners of the United States willingly followed the directives of their Zionist or Hadassah presidents in wiring, writing, or in other ways importuning their congressmen to support the Zionist cause. This pressure was effective enough to elicit pro-Zionist resolutions from the national conventions of both political parties during the 1944 elections—as well as annual letters of friendship and encouragement to the American Zionist Organization and Hadassah from Franklin Roosevelt.

When Harry Truman assumed the Presidency in April 1945, he was subjected instantly to the full force of the Zionist appeal; it was an appeal expressed with growing urgency and intensity after the revelations of the death camps. Whatever his annoyance at the pressure of some of the professional Zionist leaders, there was no doubt that Truman was deeply influenced by a number of liberal spokesmen whose integrity he trusted. One of these was Governor Herbert Lehman of New York, a loyal political friend and confidant of both Roosevelt and Truman. Another was Mrs. Eleanor Roosevelt, whose counsel he cherished both for herself and because of his respect for the humanitarianism and political acumen of her husband. Yet another was Colonel Jacob Arvey, the chairman of Cook County's (Chicago's) powerful Democratic Committee. Behind the scenes there was David K. Niles, Truman's Special Assistant for Minority Affairs; through the office of this inconspicuous, rather dour man the full fervor of American pro-Zionist sentiment was most effectively transmitted to the President. It was Niles, moreover, whom the President used as his most dependable intermediary in working out agreements with and commitments to Ben-Gurion and the other leaders of the Yishuv. Finally, among the pro-Zionists close to Truman, there was Edward Jacobson, an unobtrusive little haberdasher in Kansas City, a former companion-at-arms and business associate of the President. Through the years the two men had remained warm personal friends and Jacobson had never taken advantage of that friendship after Truman became President. But in the cause of the displaced persons and later of the Palestine partition plan, Jacobson begged the President not to close his heart. In truth, the President never deviated in his essential sympathy for Zionist aspirations. He wrote in his autobiography later:

I had carefully read the Balfour Declaration, in which Great Britain was committed to a homeland for the Jews. I had familiarized myself with the history of the question of a Jewish homeland and the position of the British and the Arabs. I was skeptical, as I read over the whole record up to date, about some of the views and attitudes assumed by the "striped-pants boys" in the State Department. It was my feeling that it would be possible for us to watch out for the long-range interests of our country while at the same time helping these unfortunate victims of persecution to find a home.

It was as a result of this conviction that Truman took the initiative, after the Harrison Report and during the Anglo-American Committee of Inquiry hearings, and urged Britain to admit one hundred thousand DP's into Palestine. He was furiously reproached both by the Arabs and by the British Foreign Secretary. Bevin, indeed, violated the accepted rules of diplomatic courtesy by suggesting publicly that the President's pro-Zionism was dictated by political considerations. Truman neither accepted nor forgave the remark; and in his own way he could be quite as stubborn as Bevin. In a letter to ibn-Saud on October 26, 1946, the President made it clear that the United States, which had acquiesced in the original Balfour Declaration, had an unavoidable stake in the disposition of Palestine and the fate of the Jewish people. Of all the factors Truman had to weigh—Arab friendship, the Anglo-American alliance, Jewish suffering—it was the latter which influenced him most deeply. Political considerations undoubtedly played their part; but it appears likely that humanitarian considerations determined his ultimate position. Truman proudly identified himself, during his tenure as President and afterward, as the champion of the "little man." The fate of the Jewish DP fell within the framework of his humanitarian concern. Bevin would find no help here.

THE UNITED NATIONS TAKES OVER: PARTITION

In the summer of 1946 British Colonial Secretary Arthur Creech-Jones, a pro-Zionist of long standing, finally persuaded Ernest Bevin that it was simply not possible to devise a solution for the DP problem without reference to Jewish aspirations for Palestine. With profound reluctance, Bevin asked Truman if he were willing to share with Britain the responsibility for revising the Palestine mandate. Truman agreed with alacrity, and dispatched a State Department official, Henry F. Grady, to meet with Bevin and his colleagues in London. On July 31, Grady and Herbert Morrison, Lord President of the Council, presented a plan for a new "disposition" of Palestine. When the details were published, however, it was apparent that Grady had been won over to the British point of view; for the plan envisaged converting the mandate into a trusteeship of Arab and Jewish provinces under the strict control of a British High Commissioner. The Jewish province would have the authority to admit a maximum of one hundred thousand refugees over a period of five years; after five years had passed, the ultimate decision on immigration would be left to the Commissioner. The Zionists were furious: control of immigration, the one provision that mattered most to them, was once again to be taken out of their hands.

It was hardly surprising, therefore, that Jewish Agency spokesmen flatly declined a British invitation to discuss the Morrison-Grady plan with Foreign Office and Arab officials. Ben-Gurion did fly to London, however, as an "observer." At the last minute, in January 1947, Creech-Jones drew Bevin and Ben-Gurion together privately. "Why don't you believe we are honest about our policy?" Bevin asked. "We have no selfish intentions. It's peace and stability we are looking for, no more." Ben-Gurion accepted the opening. "Tell me frankly what you want," he replied. "Perhaps we Jews would be willing to help. Perhaps our interests coincide." As it happened those interests did partially coincide. In return for Jewish control of immigration, Ben-Gurion suggested that the Jews would have no objection to British bases in the Negeb as an alternative to Suez. Bevin was favorably impressed by the idea, but warned that its implementation depended upon the "amicable agreement" of both Arabs and Jews. At his next meeting with the Arabs, Bevin advanced a large part of Ben-Gurion's argument as his own. Of course, the Arabs rejected it flatly, and the rejection doomed the conference. Bevin now recognized that a totally new approach was necessary. On February 14, 1947, Bevin terminated the conference proceedings with the announcement, the momentous announcement, as it turned out, that Britain had decided to refer the entire Palestine problem to the United Nations. The cost of supporting one hundred thousand British soldiers in Palestine, and the even more incalculable cost of a running battle with American and world opinion, could no longer be borne. It was Bevin's final admission of failure.

In April 1947, the General Assembly of the United Nations set up an eleven-nation board, the United Nations Special Committee on Palestine, UNSCOP, to deal with the Palestine impasse. Over strenuous Arab objections UNSCOP decided to link its investigation with a careful study of the situation of the displaced persons. Accordingly, in the summer of 1947 the group toured the DP camps and visited Palestine. The committeee members talked with all groups, Jewish, Arab, and British, except the official representatives of the Arab Higher Executive, who boycotted the hearings. Weizmann himself appeared before the board in Jerusalem, and his brilliance, his mellow perspective, and his impassioned eloquence apparently left a deep impression. The presentation, at a critical juncture in Jewish history, was not the least of Weizmann's contributions. On August 31 UNSCOP completed its report. It urged the termination of the British mandate and the partition of Palestine into separate and sovereign Arab and Jewish states. Jewish territory would consist of Eastern Galilee, the coastal plain, and the Negeb; the rest would belong to the Arabs. Jerusalem would be administered by the United Nations under permanent trusteeship. The Arab League issued furious warnings against the acceptance of these recommendations; the Zionists expressed quiet satisfaction; the General Assembly of the United Nations referred the report to a Special Committee on the Palestine Question consisting of all the member nations. The drama of the Return, begun half a century earlier, was reaching its climax.

From September 23 on, the Palestine Committee consumed fourteen meetings and twenty-four days in open discussion, in which the Arab Higher Executive and the Jewish Agency both participated. The Arab states formally joined the Higher Executive in unequivocally rejecting the partition plan. The Jewish Agency formally accepted UNSCOP's proposal as the "indispensable minimum." It was apparent that the attitude of the Great Powers would now be crucial in determining the issue. Britain's position reflected Bevin's determination to salvage as much good will as possible in the Arab world. While ostensibly "neutral" during the debates of the General Assembly's Palestine Committee, Britain's transparent hostility to the partition resolution made it apparent that her "neutrality" was hardly more than a technicality. Sir Alexander Cadogan, the senior British delegate to the United Nations, emphasized that Britain would not co-operate in implementing any plan "on which agreement is not reached between Arabs and Jews."

For almost a month and a half after the release of the UNSCOP report, the American government refused to commit itself. Then, on October 11, Herschel V. Johnson, the American representative on the Palestine Committee, tentatively endorsed the basic idea of partition. At no time, however, recalls the Guatemalan delegate, Jorge García-Granados, did the United States bring pressure to bear on other nations to follow her lead. At best, America's support of partition seemed lukewarm. The evident timidity with which Johnson backed partition suggested that Washington was still at cross-purposes on the issue. The joint Chiefs of Staff and the Near East specialists of the State Department advised against supporting the partition resolution. They took with the utmost seriousness the Arab warnings of retaliation against American oil investments and American air bases. On the other hand, American public opinion was clearly in sympathy with the Zionists, more than ever now that a neutral United Nations inquiry apparently had validated the Zionist position. The White House still seemed to be pro-Zionist; yet the Truman Administration was unwilling to create a situation in Palestine that might conceivably involve the use of American troops to maintain order; American public opinion would reject any such action.

The confusion of the American position during the autumn of 1947 was quite apparent to other United Nations delegates. Jorge García-Granados recalls having asked Herschel Johnson: "Do you really think it useful to propose that the British govern Palestine during the transitional period? They will not help to implement partition; on the contrary, they will destroy it." When Johnson disagreed, García-Granados went on: "Their statement is explicit. They loathe everything we are doing here." To which Johnson replied, rather desperately: "They will co-operate—you'll see. They must. It is their responsibility and they will have to assume it." By attempting however vainly to persuade the British to accept the major responsibility for implementing partition, the United States hoped to avoid either Arab retaliation against American interests, or the kind of Near Eastern chaos that the Soviet Union would be capable of exploiting.

The Soviet stand on partition could swing the decision and both sides eagerly and prayerfully awaited it. It was a stand which was of course purely opportunistic. Stalin had no sympathy with Zionism, and for years the Zionists in Russia had been ruthlessly persecuted and purged. But if Russia's agelong ambition to gain a foothold in the Near East was to be fulfilled, it was an immediate advantage to create a vacuum there by ousting the British. In the autumn of 1947, it seemed to the Soviet regime that the creation of a modern Jewish commonwealth, imbued with a fiery nationalist spirit, would lead more certainly to the elimination of the British than would the establishment of another backward and indolent Arab sheikdom in Palestine. But even if a Jewish state did not come into existence, and the Soviets were by no means convinced that it would happen quickly, there would almost certainly be bitter fighting between Arabs and Jews once the British had withdrawn. Stalin recognized that he had little to lose if there were months and perhaps years of struggle and chaos in an area which Russian coveted. He had, in fact, everything to gain, especially if British withdrawal from Palestine and the Near East were not attended by a corresponding increase of American influence there. These were undoubtedly the considerations that dictated Russia's position. To the dismay and consternation of the Arabs, the Soviet delegate, Semyon K. Tsarapkin, endorsed the partition plan.

Influenced by the decision of Russia and the United States, a majority of the members of the Palestine Committee decided to approve the idea of partition. The matter was submitted to the United Nations General Assembly for the final two-thirds vote. Both Arabs and Zionists fought a passionate propaganda battle, each side buttonholing the voting delegates and their diplomatic entourages. The Arabs issued ominous warnings of canceled oil leases. The Zionists countered these warnings with documented evidence of Arab wartime collaboration with the Axis, and with impassioned appeals to the humanitarian conscience of the world. In addition their cause was buttressed because of the favorable UNSCOP majority recommendations; they accordingly benefited from the findings of a neutral committee. Ultimately it was a combination of these factors—the support of the United States and Russia, Zionist propaganda, the UNSCOP report—which decided the issue in favor of partition.

On November 29, 1947, thirty years to the month after the issuance of the Balfour Declaration, the General Assembly of the United Nations voted in favor of partition by a vote of 33 to 14. The proposed Jewish state would embrace 5,500 square miles, roughly 55 per cent of the land area of Palestine. Jerusalem would be internationalized. A five-nation commission would cooperate with Great Britain in the gradual and orderly implementation of partition. The "transitional" period would in no case extend beyond October 1, 1948. After that two new sovereign states, for the Jews and for the Arabs, would come into being in Palestine.

BEN-GURION CREATES A STATE

It was an exalted moment for world Jewry, all the more thrilling by contrast with the recent horrors of the death camps. Indeed, it appeared as if Herzl had prophesied accurately: that first a frightful catastrophe must befall the Jewish people before the dream of a Jewish state would be fulfilled. But even now formidable obstacles stood in the way. For one thing, Bevin was determined not to co-operate in the "implementation" of partition. His delegate at the United Nations, Sir Alexander Cadogan, announced that so long as the mandate was in effect, Britain would not permit the exercise of authority by a United Nations Commission in any part of Palestine. Hence there would be no preparation for independence up to the very moment of withdrawal. Convinced as he was that no Jewish state could possibly endure in the face of Arab armed might, Bevin had apparently decided to facilitate Arab conquest by leaving Palestine in chaos. This was to be the Foreign Secretary's last gesture of friendship to the Arabs, and his most effective technique of maintaining Britain's contacts in the Arab world. It was, however, Bevin's way of returning to Palestine through the back door: he fully expected that Britain's puppet, Abdullah, of Trans-Jordan, would conquer Palestine within a matter of weeks; and he was determined that Abdullah should have little difficulty in this effort. "The United Kingdom's plan and behavior will lead only to bloodshed in Palestine," observed García-Granados, the Guatemalan delegate, to Sir Alexander Cadogan. "I warn you that there will be torrents of blood, and I tell you now . . . that the party responsible for the blood will be the United Kingdom." Thirty years of competent British administration in Palestine deserved a better monument.

For their part, the Arab states were prepared to take advantage of the vacuum to be created by the British decision. By the end of 1947 Arab irregular bands, staffed, financed, and equipped by the Arab League, intensified their attacks upon Jewish farm colonies, killing several hundred Jewish settlers. When the Jews fought back, they were systematically disarmed by the British. As the fighting spread through the Holy Land, the American government began to waver in its support of partition; for here was the war predicted by the joint Chiefs of Staff, the State Department, and the oil companies. On March 19, 1948, Warren Austin, the American Ambassador to the United Nations, suggested that perhaps partition ought to be "temporarily" suspended in favor of a United Nations trusteeship over Palestine. Once again tension gripped the Jewish community, particularly the inmates of the displaced persons camps. They wondered in dismay if their hopes were about to be dashed once again.

In Palestine itself, there was neither hesitation nor equivocation and David Ben-Gurion emerged on the world scene as a new personality to make the Jewish determination clear. We recall Ben-Gurion's early career in Palestine as a member of the second Aliyah, his Spartan existence as a Judean farm hand and as a trade-union organizer for the Labor Zionists. In 1920, after a wartime stint in the British army, he became Executive Secretary of the Histadrut. It was Ben-Gurion, in fact, who, under the inspiration of Berl Katznelson, transformed the Histadrut into the dominant force in the economic life of the Yishuv. In 1936 he was elected Chairman of the Executive of the Jewish Agency, and found himself thrown willy-nilly into the world of statecraft.

He was no suave diplomat in the Weizmann manner. At heart he remained the tough trade unionist, gruff, blunt, as blunt as Bevin but even more stubborn, for he was fighting for the life of his people. He looked the militant role he was to play: short, stocky, muscular, his hands still calloused, his face hard and weather-beaten, with a tight, thin mouth, a massive prow of a chin thrusting belligerently forward, his bald head surrounded by a corona of white hair that lent itself superbly—perhaps intentionally—to caricature. When he spoke, his voice rasped, his fists banged. One sensed instinctively that this unpretentious man, who wore an open shirt and disdained a necktie even at the most formal affairs, was the spokesman for a new generation of Jews, a generation that would not allow itself to be pushed around any longer.

Now, on March 25, 1948, Ben-Gurion formally notified the United Nations Palestine Commission that the Jews were proceeding with the establishment of a Provisional Government. On the same day a Provisional Council came into being in Tel Aviv. By agreement among the political leaders of the Yishuv, the Council included all the Palestinian members of the Executive of the Jewish Agency and all the members of the *Vaad Leumi*—the Executive of the Yishuv's National Assembly—together with representatives of Jewish Palestine's leading political parties. It was also proposed that representation be given to friendly Arabs living in the area of Palestine assigned to the Jews by partition; but no friendly Arabs could be found. The National Council numbered thirty-seven members; it was responsible, in turn, for electing a National Executive, or Cabinet, of thirteen. The Provisional Government was composed of able men and women; most of them had the advantage of years of experience as members of the administration of the Yishuv.

But their experience notwithstanding, they now found themselves nearly overwhelmed by the planned chaos left behind by the departing British. The railways had stopped running; the mail service had ceased to function; the assets of the Mandatary were auctioned off or shipped to England. Not a penny was left in the treasury for a successor-state. The single financial provision made for the period after the end of the mandate was a grant of £300,000 to the Supreme Moslem Council. Inasmuch as the Council and the Mufti's Arab Higher Committee were virtually one and the same, this was nothing less than an indirect subsidy to the Arab war effort. The Jews desperately needed money, men, and equipment. Almost immediately the National Council set about raising a national loan. Civil servants were feverishly recruited from the older Yishuv administration to staff vital public departments: health, transportation, police, agriculture, shipping. Haganah agents were sent out to Europe and North and South America to train DP's and to arrange for arms purchases. Ben-Gurion and his colleagues were certain of their ability to set up a smoothly running administration and economy capable of absorbing the full shock of Arab invasion. What they needed most was time. They knew however that if they asked for a postponement of British withdrawal, they might permanently forfeit their opportunity for sovereignty.

There were some Zionist leaders, Moshe Shertok, Nahum Goldmann, Stephen Wise, and others, who were frankly pessimistic about the Yishuv's ability to withstand an Arab attack. They urged Ben-Gurion to move cautiously, to temporize in creating the Jewish state, to accept the American proposal of a trusteeship on a temporary basis. Ben-Gurion was not a reckless man; but he devoutly believed that the time for temporizing had passed. Calling the Haganah High Command—Yakov Dori, Israel Galili, Yigal Yadin—to his home, Ben-Gurion asked them for a frank appraisal of the Yishuv's chances in the event of an all-out war. He was told that there was a fair likelihood of holding out against the Arab guerrilla armies, but not against a full-scale invasion of Arab states, certainly not until more adequate supplies of fighter planes and artillery pieces could be brought in. The most the Haganah leaders could reasonably hope for was the protection of the compact coastal settlement. Jerusalem, its population of one hundred thousand Jews even then under siege, probably would have to be abandoned.

Ben-Gurion listened soberly. He knew the cost of protecting Jerusalem; his daughter's fiancé had been killed in the siege of the city, and others were dying daily. Nevertheless, he urged that a desperate effort be made to hold the ancient capital of the Jewish people. Within the next two weeks Dori managed to wrest the key city of Castel from the guerrilla bands, and to force several convoys through to Jerusalem. Although the situation was still critical, at least a thin trickle of arms and supplies was beginning to reach the besieged city. The following month, as the British withdrew from Haifa, Jewish forces, moving with speed and precision, seized the crucial seaport from under the very noses of a poised Arab army. These successes gave Ben-Gurion the encouragement he needed. The time had come to announce the birth of a Jewish state.

On May 14, 1948, while Egyptian fighter-bombers roared overhead and the last remaining British troops made ready to depart, Ben-Gurion and his cabinet gathered in the art museum of the city of Tel Aviv. There they proclaimed the independence of the Republic of Israel. The Declaration of Independence notified the world that the land of Israel had been the historic birthplace of the Jewish people, that the Zionist movement was enduring testimony to the role this land had played in Jewish history and religion, that the Balfour Declaration, the United Nations Partition Resolution, the sacrifice of Zionist pioneers, the unendurable torments suffered by Jews in recent years—all had laid the legal and moral foundations for the new state. Israel, it was announced, would be open to all Jews who wished to enter, would extend full social and political equality to all its citizens without distinction of religion, race, or sex, and would guarantee freedom of religion, conscience, education, and culture to all. In the face of the critical military situation, the authors of the Declaration issued a final plea:

> We extend our hand in peace and neighborliness to all the neighboring States and their peoples, and invite them to co-operate with the independent Jewish nation for the common good of all. The State of Israel is prepared to make its contribution to the progress of the Middle East as a whole. Our call goes out to the Jewish people all over the world to rally to our side in the task of immigration and development, and to stand by us in the great struggle for the fulfillment of the dream of generations for the redemption of Israel. With trust in Almighty God, we set our hand to this Declaration, at this Session of the Provisional State Council, on the soil of the Homeland, in the city of Tel Aviv, on this Sabbath Eve, the fifth day of Iyar, 5708, the fourteenth day of May, 1948.

Back in the United States Harry Truman made a crucial decision. Since March he had remained committed to Austin's trusteeship proposal. In fact, in the days immediately preceding May 15, the American government intensified its pressure on the Zionists, urging them to withhold their proclamation of statehood. It was true that events in Palestine—the withdrawal of British forces, the preliminary victories of Jewish soldiers—appeared to have invalidated the notion of a trusteeship. But in view of the spread of hostilities in the Holy Land, Truman himself apparently was giving closer attention to the cautionary voices of the State Department. On May 13, a day before the establishment of the Republic of Israel (by the American time schedule), Chaim Weizmann wrote a gravely eloquent letter to the President, urging him to recognize the forthcoming state as an act of historic justice. The usual pro-Zionist pressures continued to play on the White House; but there is no indication that any startling new development occurred, not even a last-minute visit by Eddie Jacobson. And then, on May 14, at 6:11 P.M., Eastern Daylight Saving Time—and ten minutes after Israel's Declaration of Independence—the White House extended to the new state America's *de facto* recognition.

The recognition took the American delegates to the United Nations completely by surprise. It is likely that the decision of recognition, sudden, even quixotic, as it seemed, was less the result of the President's sense of *Realpolitik* than it was his human sympathy for an underdog people. Truman had lost patience with the war strategists, the "striped-pants" boys in the State Department, and the oil lobbyists, who felt that they had him safely in their camp. "Mr. President," later observed Undersecretary of State Lovett, "they almost put it over on you." But because they had not "put it over" on the President, other nations soon followed the lead of the United States. Military circumstances in Israel were grim; but in the wake of this diplomatic recognition, Jewish—Israeli—morale was immeasurably buoyed.

THE WAR OF LIBERATION

The half year between the Partition Resolution and the establishment of the State of Israel had been a period of bitter fighting, outright war in all but name. During those six months over fifteen thousand Arab irregulars, well-armed and led by Syrian and Lebanese "volunteers," poured into Palestine, ambushed Jewish convoys, commanded key heights and villages, and besieged Jerusalem. Jewish defense problems were complicated by the isolation of Jerusalem east of the compact coastal plain; the city was connected to Tel Aviv by a thin finger of settlements and by a single mountainous road that was made to order for Arab ambush. Then, too, there were forty communal settlements in the vulnerable hill country, thirty-five in the Plain of Esdraelon, forty-nine in the northern region of the Jordan Valley, seventeen in the northern Negeb, all connected to the more heavily populated coastal plain by roads that ran through preponderantly Arab areas. Almost from the moment of the Partition Resolution of November 29, 1947, Jerusalem and these isolated communities came under attack.

The Jews had solid manpower—nearly forty thousand trained soldiers—but most of these soldiers were obliged to earn their living at the same time; until May 15 only a small elite commando group, the Palmach, could be maintained on a standing basis. Moreover, British occupation authorities continued systematically to disarm Jewish defense forces wherever they found them. Until May 15, 1948, the Yishuv's total armament consisted of a few thousand rifles, perhaps ten thousand homemade Sten guns, a number of light machine guns, and two or three mortars. There was no artillery; the "air force" was composed of six or seven obsolete Auster biplanes from which the pilots dropped homemade bombs by hand.

The first three months of hostilities, from December 1947, to February 1948, were a period of purely defensive operations. The problem was to hold the hills and roads dominating the major cities of Tel Aviv, Haifa, and Jerusalem. This was successfully accomplished. Savage fighting, often hand-to-hand, resulted in the capture by the Jews of the abandoned British police posts that dominated the key heights overlooking the Jewish areas of Palestine. Ben-Gurion gave orders to hold fast to every settlement, to consider nothing expendable. This, too, was accomplished. By May 14, the Jews maintained possession of the entire coast in western Galilee; in eastern Galilee the thin line of posts strung from the Lebanese-Syrian frontier to the Sea of Tiberias had widened into a broad belt embracing all the important towns, Safad, Tiberias, Samakh. The neck from the Mediterranean across to the Jordan had been broadened slightly. And Jerusalem still held out, connected by the precarious mountain road from Tel Aviv. As the Haganah High Command had predicted, the Yishuv was able to defend itself against guerrillas.

The problem became more serious after May 15, with the invasion of Palestine by the organized armies of the neighboring Arab states. By Western standards they were not significant armies. Of the fifty thousand men with which Egypt, Trans-Jordan, Syria, Lebanon, and Iraq invaded Palestine, only Trans-Jordan's Arab Legion, consisting of seventy-five hundred troops, could have been considered an effective military force. Arab officers were notoriously bad; their soldiers were diseased, brutally treated, and illiterate. At no time was there an effective unified command. The Arab League was ridden with factional jealousies: King Abdullah of Trans-Jordan and King Faruk of Egypt each hoped to seize Palestine as a lever for more far-reaching personal ambitions, Hashemite unity in the case of Abdullah, the Sudan and Suez in the case of Faruk. The governments of Syria and Lebanon each hoped to seize the fertile lands of Galilee for themselves. Meanwhile, the Mufti, waiting to return as head of an independent Arab Palestine, pinned his hopes on an ill-organized bandit gang called the "Arab Liberation Army." Nevertheless, these armies were well equipped with tanks, heavy artillery, and bombing airplanes, and they could always obtain more equipment from Britain. The sheer weight of their numbers and equipment was not to be discounted. They had large reserve populations and organized governments behind them. They controlled the sea and had ports at their disposal.

Israel, conversely, was particularly vulnerable to an invasion in force. Its entire territory consisted of a few thousand miles spread in a thin belt between the sea and the hills. The skeletal Israeli government barely had time to organize a defense, to obtain food, fuel, materiel, and arms. On the other hand, the Jews possessed superb, highly trained manpower. The Haganah, the backbone of Jewish military strength, possessed years of experience in self-defense, extending back beyond the civil wars of the 1930's to the first *Shomrim,* the guards of the early Jewish settlements in Palestine. There were, in addition, some thirty-two thousand Jews who had been members of the British army during the war, and who combined with their Haganah experience in commando tactics a mastery of formal military procedure. Their officers were young, tough, dedicated, and disciplined. And they were fighting for their own soil, for their very lives. They knew every nook and cranny in Palestine, the strategic character of every village and the quality of its inhabitants. After May 15, too, weapons of heavy caliber and good quality began to come into the country, purchased principally with money supplied in abundant quantities by world Jewry.

The Jewish plan of defense was dictated by Ben-Gurion's order to hold on to every inch of Jewish soil, to yield up nothing under the guise of military expediency. This meant that the isolated men, women, and children of the collective settlements would be compelled to endure intensive pressure until the army could come to their rescue. Ben-Gurion's faith in their tenacity was not misplaced, however. In the northern Negeb Desert, for example, there were only six Jewish settlements, with a total population of twelve hundred. When the Egyptian army invaded, the road between Tel Aviv and the Negeb was cut. But, although poorly armed with homemade weapons, the defenders of these tiny garrisons held out against normally discouraging odds, against shelling, bombing, even the penetration of their farmyards by Egyptian tanks and armored cars. In this fashion the settlement of Negba survived the most intensive artillery bombardment of the war, and barred the Egyptian drive to Tel Aviv, which was only thirty miles away.

On the eastern front the Jews struggled no less desperately to capture the villages controlling the Tel Aviv-Jerusalem highway. Until this road could be opened for full-scale convoys, the siege of Jerusalem would continue. On May 28, after weeks of unceasing bombardment, the Arab Legion had forced the surrender of the Old City of Jerusalem, and tightened its pressure on the New City. The Arab grip on Latrun, the key town controlling the eastern half of the Tel Aviv-Jerusalem highway, was never broken. The Jews decided instead to blast through an alternative highway, a kind of "Burma Road," from Deir Muheisin to Bab-el-Waad. It was murderous, back-breaking, throat-parching work. But by June 6 this alternative route was opened; Latrun was immobilized; supplies poured into the New City, Jerusalem was saved. When the pathetic and ill-conceived Syrian-Lebanese "invasion" of northern Palestine was halted within four days after its beginning by the bristling Jewish settlements in eastern and western Galilee, the Arabs lost their best chance to throttle the Jewish state.

On June 11, stunned and shaken by the fury of Jewish resistance, the Arabs gratefully accepted a United Nations Security Council order for a one-month truce. During this breathing spell the United Nations Truce Administrator, Count Folke Bernadotte, the Swedish diplomat who had negotiated with Himmler during the last days of the second World War, made a determined effort to reach a territorial settlement between Arabs and Jews. He hoped to persuade Israel, for the sake of peace, to turn over Jerusalem, Haifa, and the Negeb to the Arabs. Israel, however, had actually won for itself territory not originally contemplated in the United Nations Partition Resolution; and since the Arabs, after all, had launched the invasion, the Jews were quite unwilling to give up the fruits of their victory. It was true that the largest area of the projected Jewish State, the Negeb desert, still remained in Arab hands; but the Israeli High Command was certain now that it could be regained. Planes and tanks were coming into Israel from Czechoslovakia and France. Men were coming in, too, from Cyprus and were being trained for battle. Of no less importance was the fact that the government of Israel was now in working order; communications were restored in areas under Jewish control; measures were taken for public hygiene, for housing, or tenting, of the new immigrants; Israeli currency was put into circulation; a diplomatic corps was set up abroad.

When the truce expired, therefore, on July 9, the Jews struck quickly, seizing the vital airfield at Lydda, capturing the towns of Lydda and Ramle, occupying Nazareth in central Galilee, and consolidating their position in southern Palestine for a final offensive against Egyptian forces in the Negeb. It took the Arabs less than a week to sue for another truce, which the United Nations promptly ordered, and to which the Israeli government agreed with reluctance. Passions ran high in Israel: the battle against the invaders was going well; the notion of surrendering Jewish territory for the sake of a truce was summarily rejected by all parties. When, therefore, Bernadotte suggested that Israel cede the Negeb to the Arabs as a basis for a peace settlement, he strained Jewish patience to the limit. On September 17 a terrorist, presumably a member of the Stern Gang, shot down Bernadotte as he was driving through Jerusalem. Ben-Gurion used the Bernadotte assassination as the occasion to crack down vigorously on all private armies and terrorist groups, but the damage done to Israel's prestige as a responsible state was nevertheless severe.

Ben-Gurion knew that it was now only a matter of time before a permanent truce would be imposed. A quick decision would have to be made: should Israel's armed forces concentrate their efforts on securing the Samarian massif, a huge Arab bulge all but dividing the country in two? The Haganah High Command was inclined to favor this action. Or should a final offensive be launched to wrest the arid Negeb desert from the Egyptians? Ben-Gurion himself inclined to this view. The United Nations was still mulling over the Bernadotte plan of awarding the Negeb to the Arabs. It was necessary, therefore, to present the world body with the *fait accompli* of Israeli possession. Besides, Ben-Gurion had studied the historic desert for years, and was intrigued by Biblical references to its wealth in copper and iron. He visualized the economic future of his country assured by the resources of the Negeb. (It has since produced oil.)

Ben-Gurion's decision determined the last phase of the war. When the Egyptians resumed their shelling of the Tel Aviv-Beersheba road late in September, the Israeli army made preparations to seize the Negeb. On October 15 Jewish ground and air forces struck. A week later, after bloody and savage fighting against a brave Egyptian defense, the Jews cleared the entire area surrounding Beersheba, captured Beersheba itself, and opened up the main road to the southern desert. On December 26 the signal was given for the final Israeli offensive in the south. Jewish armored units sealed off the Egyptian front, divided the principal Egyptian bases of Gaza, Khan Yunis, and Rafa from each other, and penetrated deep into the Sinai Peninsula. By early January 1949, the Egyptian front was broken; the following month the Egyptians asked for an armistice with Israel on the basis of existing military boundaries. On March 10, after overcoming innumerable obstacles of supply and terrain, an Israeli armored column completed a two-hundred-mile journey to the Gulf of Aqaba. The Negeb was in Israel's hands. Ben-Gurion then agreed to an armistice.

Throughout 1948 Israel had agreed to United Nations requests for negotiations with the Arabs. The Arabs had refused, and now were obliged to pay for that refusal. The partition boundaries, as envisaged by the United Nations Resolution of November 1947, obviously were superseded. Under duress of Arab invasion, Israel had blasted out its own borders, and was not constrained to withdraw from them. By July 1949, all the Arab states had grudgingly concluded armistice agreements on the basis of the military *status quo*. The new Jewish state controlled the Negeb, except for the narrow Gaza Strip, from the Mediterranean to the Red Sea; it had a secure grip on the New City of Jerusalem; it had possession of Lydda and Ramle, of all Galilee, and of the Vale of Jezreel through the Jordan

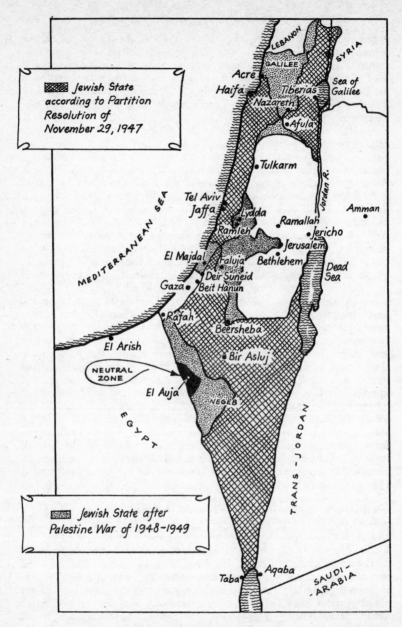

THE STATE OF ISRAEL BEFORE AND AFTER THE WAR OF 1948-1949

Valley, as well as of the coastal plain. The Arab armies, except perhaps for Trans-Jordan's Arab Legion, were broken and incapable of serious military efforts; and the Arab League itself, riddled by internal strife, was on the point of disruption. Arab Palestine, divided between Jordan in the east and Egypt in the west (the Gaza Strip), was in complete chaos.

The chaos was compounded by the presence of 650,000 Arab refugees from Israel. The plight of these pathetic, terrified creatures was the most heartbreaking tragedy of the Palestine war. It had been a needless tragedy. As the end of the Palestine mandate drew near, the Arab states bordering the Yishuv began to issue warnings to the Arabs of Palestine; they were told to clear out, to leave a clear field for Arab military operations, to seek temporary refuge in neighboring Arab lands. According to Arab League propaganda, there would be sufficient opportunity for all *émigrés* to return, once the Jews had been driven into the sea. The propaganda was effective. As early as October 1947, small groups of Arab villagers began to leave Palestine; in succeeding months the numbers of departing Arabs swelled rapidly. It was vitally important for Ben-Gurion and his colleagues to check this flight. For one thing, the Arabs played an important role in the economy of the Yishuv; their sudden departure would merely complicate the problems of survival for the Jews. In Haifa, for example, Arab stevedores were needed to unload the freightage, the arms and supplies, upon which the new state would depend for its security. And Arab agricultural produce was even more crucial for the Jewish city populations. But more serious than these economic considerations was the problem of world opinion. Israel was on trial before the world; the United Nations still had the power to attenuate Israel's boundaries, perhaps even to intervene with force. Every effort had to be made to keep the Palestinian Arabs at home, to give them equal rights and opportunities, if only to retain international good will.

In spite of the government's public and private assurance that they would not be harmed, the Arabs fled by the hundreds of thousands once the fighting broke out. They fled in answer to Arab League propaganda. They fled, too, as refugees have always fled, from the sound of shooting, the explosion of shells, the approach of soldiers. There were times when Israeli forces were obliged to bombard Arab towns to flush out military defenders. The news of these bombardments circulated throughout Arab Palestine and had their effect on Arab civilian morale. Additional thousands of Arabs fled, moreover, as a result of a particularly brutal and irresponsible act of the Irgun Zvai Leumi. On April 9, 1948, these terrorists occupied the Arab village of Deir Yassin, and slaughtered, without mercy, several hundred Arab men, women, and children. However much the Israeli government deplored this act, repudiating it publicly and imprisoning the Irgun leaders responsible for it, the effect on Arab morale was decisive. By the end of 1948 the majority of the Arabs of Palestine had fled the area under Israeli military control. They huddled now in squalid refugee camps, the unwelcome wards of their brethren in neighboring lands.

The United States, as we recall, had extended its *de facto* recognition two hours after the announcement of the formation of the Provisional

Government. Russia went further and granted *de jure* recognition within three days. Most other states followed suit. Britain alone held out, continuing to arm the Arabs until late 1948, backing to the limit the Bernadotte plan of amputating the Negeb from the Jewish state. The United States, too, had originally lent its support to the Bernadotte plan. For all Truman's original good will in extending recognition to Israel, he placed Ben-Gurion under continual pressure to be "moderate," to withdraw Israeli troops from Sinai, to allow the Egyptians to remain in the Gaza Strip (with calamitous consequences for the future). The President's support for the Bernadotte plan fitted into this campaign for "moderation." By the winter of 1948-49 however, Truman recognized that, for better or worse, Israel had carved out its own boundaries. Those boundaries appeared all the more realistic by virtue of the developing Arab-Israel armistice agreements. It is not unlikely, too, that the President was willing to listen more sympathetically now to his Jewish friends, for New York City had remained in the Democratic camp during the upset Presidential election of November 1948. Truman therefore instructed the American delegation in the United Nations to approve Israel's request to keep the Negeb. For all practical purposes the issue of Israel's borders was now closed. The election of Israel's first permanent government took place in January 1949; and in May 1949, the United Nations voted to admit Israel as its fifty-ninth member. The new state was riding the crest of its amazing birth and defense.

In the very first days of independence, the Israeli government knew what it had to do: it set about evacuating the refugee camps of Europe and Cyprus, and prepared to transport the long-suffering DP's to the shores of the ancient homeland. Priority was given to men and women of military age. Even before the end of May, the word *Geiyus*—mobilization—was on the lips of nearly every displaced person. Every camp, organization, and party carried on a vigorous campaign of recruitment. Thousands of DP's registered for military training, and within a few days of registration they were transported to predesignated collection points at Hochland, near Landsberg, and Geretsried. There, under the leadership of Haganah men, they were suitably outfitted, provided with new Israeli passports, and given basic training. Within a few weeks they were moved to ports of embarkation in France and Italy. There they received further training, and sailed for Haifa.

By June many of these young people, some of whom had received combat experience as partisans, or as regulars in the Allied armies, were fighting on the soil of Israel. By the winter of 1949 DP recruitment had added to the Israeli armed forces about eleven thousand men and women. Together with those who had emigrated earlier and enlisted or were drafted, they constituted a vital segment of the state's defenders. Soon a steady stream of DP's, recruits and otherwise, was leaving for Israel. By the autumn of 1949 the departure rate had reached ten thousand a month. By December 1949, only eighty thousand DP's were left in Germany. A year later most of them had been evacuated. On December 17, 1950, the Central Committee of Jewish DP's was formally terminated. Virtually all the refugees had reached the shores of Israel. There, at last, at Haifa Bay, their wandering had come to an end.

CONCLUSION

The establishment of independent statehood has always been an impressive achievement. It was a heroic feat in the nineteenth century, when Greeks, Serbs, Hungarians, Italians, and others were compelled to wage long and bitter battles against powerful overlords. It was no less heroic in the mid-twentieth century, in the era of the United Nations and "peaceful change," when the natives of Indonesia or Ghana demonstrated their ability to translate a sense of national destiny into sovereignty and viability. How much more formidable this achievement was, however, in the case of the Jews, who had not lived for generations on the soil they venerated, who had but recently lost two fifths of their people in the greatest genocide in history! They had no powerful allies, as did most of the other nations of the world in *their* early struggles for independence. They faced the hostility of a mighty empire and tens of thousands of well-armed Arab neighbors. And still they willed their state into existence.

It would be a mistake, even for the most scrupulously objective historian, to search too "scientifically" for the explanation of Israel's successful emergence, certainly to search for that explanation outside the Jewish people themselves. If the Jews had learned anything by 1948, it was the fact that no concession, no right, would come easily to them. For all the very real sympathy they had elicited from the democratic peoples of the West, the Jews received little in the way of tangible support. Even after the death camp revelations no government was willing to offer them asylum. Once the United Nations had voted for partition, no nation or group of nations was willing to implement this international resolution. And after Israel had fought for and secured its independence there was pressure upon the victors to be "reasonable" for the sake of peace and surrender hard-won territory and boundaries. Whatever the Jews gained, they gained by force of their own will, their own tenacity, their own toughness over a bargaining table, their own "illegal" refugee ships, their own bayonets. Their secret weapon was not the military valor with which they had destroyed forever the ghetto stereotype. It was rather the weapon of *ain breira*—"no alternative." More than any other people in the twentieth century, the Jews had learned the hard way that their ultimate security depended upon their own actions, and not upon abstract sympathy and good will. It was a lesson they would not easily forget.

Chaim Weizmann was in New York when the State of Israel was proclaimed on May 15, 1948. Two days later he received a cable from the Israel Council of State notifying him that he had been elected President of the Provisional Government of the Republic of Israel. In honor of its distinguished guest, the Waldorf-Astoria promptly raised the blue-and-white flag with the Star of David, an honor the hotel extended to all visiting chiefs of state. Crowds outside the Waldorf, tens of thousands of American Jews, felt for a moment as if they were witnessing the miracle as visibly as if they had been in Israel itself. A day later the old man was flown to Washington to be received by President Truman. Afterward, he departed for Switzerland and Israel.

Weizmann was seventy-four years old, half blind, and far from the impressive figure of a man he had been thirty-one years earlier when, by sheer force of genius and persistence, he had persuaded a group of English statesmen to lay the basis for the Jewish National Home in Palestine through the Balfour Declaration. Yet during his long life Weizmann embodied the modern odyssey of the Jewish people more fully and completely than any other personality of modern times. Here was the Russian Jew, steeped in the folk mores of the Pale of Settlement; educated in "emancipated" Western Europe, where he became a choice representative of the distinguished Jewish intellectual tradition; a man of means, a cultivated and respected dinner companion of statesmen and bankers, in the best tradition of the Western *shtadtlan*; yet continually sensitive and responsive to the needs and aspirations of anonymous millions of his fellow Jews. Departing now, in the twilight of his life, to accept the Presidency of a National Jewish State, he was the Jewish people, turning its back forever on that trancelike reliance on the National Affirmation which had nearly put an end to its collective existence.

Notes

Page 462. Newspaper editorial quoted in Leo W. Schwarz, *The Redeemers*, p. 56.

Page 468. Quotation from Jon and David Kimche, *The Secret Roads*, pp. 116-17.

Page 474. Quotation from Jorge García-Granados, *The Birth of Israel*, p. 251.

XXIII

A "Secondary Ring" of Jewish Communities

In the inventory of Jewish community survival in Western Europe after the second World War there was pathetically little to list. Hitler had done his work only too well. Only 35,000 Jews remained in Belgium, the majority in Brussels and Antwerp, and most of these were non-Belgian by birth, struggling to integrate themselves into the life of a strange land. Of the proud prewar Dutch-Jewish community of 140,000, only 24,000 Jews had survived the Nazi "resettlement." Switzerland's Jewry was intact, but numbered no more than 20,000. Twenty-three thousand Jews lived comfortable middle-class lives in Scandinavia, primarily in Stockholm and Copenhagen; but their intermarriage rate was the highest in the world, and their Jewish loyalties were fading rapidly. In Italy 33,000 Jews were still alive, as were 25,000 in West Germany and 10,000 in Austria. At best these were pathetic vestiges of once significant settlements. None of them was capable of making more than a nominal effort to continue the traditions of the past. A significant revival of Jewish cultural life seemed quite unlikely.

Only in France had the "Final Solution" failed altogether to achieve its ultimate goal of mass Jewish extermination. There the prewar population of 350,000 managed to survive with a comparatively minimal loss of 65,000. Even after the liquidation of these unfortunates, the surviving population still represented a significant increase since the end of the nineteenth century. As late as 1900 in fact, there had probably been no more than 90,000 Jews in all of France. The substantial population upswing began with the May Laws, when nearly 100,000 Jews arrived in France as refugees from czarist oppression. This number was further augmented in the years immediately following World War I, with the influx of perhaps another 50,000 Eastern European Jews, fugitives from Pilsudski's Ukrainian massacres. By the eve of the second World War, France possessed two distinct Jewish communities: the older, essentially Alsatian community, which, with a sprinkling of Sephardic Jews, represented approximately 180,000 people. Most of them, proud of their native status, had left the border provinces during the late 1800's to settle in Paris. The other community was the more recent Eastern European group who, by 1914, were very nearly as numerous as the Alsatians. Most of them settled in the slums of Paris, the Belleville section, which assumed a semighetto quality roughly akin to New York's East Side. And, as in New York, or London or Montreal or Buenos Aires, the majority of these newcomers, bearded Orthodox Jews and their families, began as peddlers, textile workers, tailors, seamstresses, hatters, and shoe-makers.

Working hard, saving their earnings, taking full advantage of the freedom of opportunity which France offered, without discrimination, to all its inhabitants, the immigrants managed to transform themselves into a *petit-bourgeois* community within the span of a generation. As rapidly as possible, too, they moved away from Belleville, into other Jewish middle-class neighborhoods in Paris. By the eve of the second World War France's Russian Jews were economically secure; and while they were not yet, perhaps, as thoroughly acculturated as the Alsatian community, neither did they constitute an "embarrassment" to the representatives of the older group.

In many instances political and cultural advancement was both rapid and extraordinarily far-reaching. Thus, in 1936, a Jew of Alsatian descent, Léon Blum, was elected premier by his colleagues in the Chamber of Deputies. Despite his own upper middle-class background, Blum was an ardent socialist during his entire political career. Far from being an inflexible ideologist, however, Blum was willing to take the initiative after assuming the premiership, in working out a coalition with the parties of the left, and forming a Popular Front designed to save France from the abyss of fascism. It was the first significant effort ever made by a modern French politician to subordinate party dogma to the needs of a national emergency. While the Popular Front itself failed to save France from eventual collapse, it did lay the basis for the policy of "coalitionism" which characterized the governments of the postwar era. In 1946, after the Nazi defeat, Blum was once again recalled to the premiership. So, too, in later years were two other Jewish political leaders: René Mayer and Pierre Mendès-France. In fact, Mendès-France was one of the most dynamic figures in French politics. His vigor and courage in ending the Indo-Chinese War in 1954, and concentrating on a widespread program of social and economic reform, provided France with one of its few moments of decisive and imaginative leadership in recent years. Jules Moch was the French representative in disarmament talks at the United Nations; Daniel Mayer served as Chairman of the Foreign Affairs Committee of the Chamber of Deputies. René Cassin presided over France's supreme court as president.

By the twentieth century Jewish participation and success in the intellectual life of France was no less notable. In literature, particularly, Jews played a leading role in nearly every one of the important *avant-garde* movements: Ephraim Mikaël was an influential spokesman for Parnassism; Marcel Schwob was a founder of the movement for the "purification" of Romanticism; for many years Gustave Kahn was the leading symbolist in France. In the world of scholarship, one of Renan's most creative disciples was James Darmesteter; Emile Durkheim was a leading spokesman for Comtian sociology; Taine's most influential follower was Lucien Lévy-Bruhl. A towering figure among the philosophers was Henri Bergson, the founder of vitalism; and Bergson's most gifted pupils—Frederick Rauh, Henri Franck, and Edmond Fleg—were all Jews. There was virtually no field in the intellectual life of France in which Jewish artists, essayists, musicians, and directors did not play a prominent role.

During the course of their economic, political, and cultural integration, French Jewry encountered little serious opposition in the way of anti-Semitism. But anti-Jewish agitation had been thoroughly discredited during the Dreyfus case, and Jewish settlement and adjustment proceeded without difficulty. Even during the depression years of the 1930's, when anti-Semitism was revived as a carefully cultivated instrument of modern French fascism, it did not attract more than the lunatic fringe. The fascist activist organizations, the *Action Française,* the *Croix de Feu,* the Cagoulards, drew their membership from the dregs of the French underworld. Yet because they were shunned by the "official" parties of the French right, and because they were fairly well recognized as semiofficial apologists for foreign ideologies, Nazism and Fascism, their impact was more noisy than serious.

Actually, the most ominous anti-Semitic movement in recent decades appeared well after the defeat of the Axis. It was spawned by the recurrent crises that bedeviled French economic and political life in the postwar era. The burden of supporting a vast program of public welfare measures at home, and an army of half a million men in Europe and North Africa, was draining the treasury of its crucial reserves. The Chamber of Deputies reacted to this crisis with shifts in policies and political coalitions, sending premiers in and out of office at the rate of two or three a year. Meanwhile, the bitter class hatreds of the prewar era still continued to fester during the late 1940's and 1950's.

As always, the members of the lower middle class were most vulnerable to rightist propaganda, for they feared that the inflation, together with the steadily mounting weight of taxation, would destroy their life savings. The reactionaries seized upon the "radical" leanings of the leading Jewish political leaders and used thinly disguised anti-Semitic propaganda, capitalizing on this *petit-bourgeois* discontent. Thus, even after his fall from the premiership in 1954, Pierre Mendès-France continued to be the favorite whipping boy for the rightist press. His principal journalistic supporters, Jean-Jacques Servan-Schreiber and Georges Boris, were attacked as sinister members of a "Jewish brain trust."

Lower-middle-class unrest boiled to a climax in 1954-55, when Pierre Poujade, a bookseller from the little town of Saint-Ceré in central France, initiated a revolt against the payment of taxes and sought to increase his following among the *petit bourgeoisie* by shrilly calling attention to the Jewish "conspiracy." He concentrated his attacks on Chamber members of Jewish origin and "all those Frenchmen of recent date, those Rosenkranzs and Rosenkopfs." One Poujadist speaker attributed the depression in the wine industry to the "combination of the little Levys and the little Dreyfuses," and similar themes were developed at other Poujadist rallies. Significantly the bylaws of the organization required members of its executive committee "to be of French nationality for at least three generations."

At its peak, in March of 1955, Poujadism claimed a membership of half a million Frenchmen. It was more of an aberration than a political force, however, and within a year or two it was generally assigned crackpot status. Two factors were responsible for the quick decline. One was a quiet, gradual, but none the less steady improvement in the French economic situation, the result of years of patient postwar industrialization, reclamation, and electrification. The franc still was far from stabilized, especially as the drain of the North African fighting continued; but at least the massive modernization of French industry was beginning to make itself felt in increasing exports, wider employment, and a steadily rising standard of living. The second factor ironically resulted from the intense nationalism that had been largely responsible for the original growth of such rightist movements as Poujadism. It was a nationalism inflamed and exacerbated by the struggle to subdue the insurrections in North Africa. Each week more French *colons* and soldiers were slain by Arab guerrilla bands who were more and more openly armed and provisioned by Egypt's ambitious President Nasser. Thus, Nasser soon became the Quai d'Orsay's *bête noire*; in the French press he was commonly referred to as the "Hitler of the Nile." Inevitably the French turned to Israel as a national ally. Israel, too, had reason enough to detest the Egyptian dictator, for he had publicly proclaimed his intention of destroying the Jewish state.

In 1955, sensing an opportunity to neutralize Nasser's influence in North Africa by immobilizing his heaviest equipment on the Egyptian-Israeli frontier, the French government began to supply the Israeli army with significant quantities of military vehicles and weapons. This Franco-Israeli "understanding" soon reached the stage of semiofficial collaboration during the Israeli invasion of Sinai, and the French assault on Suez in November 1956. In the months that followed, France continued to supply Israel with weapons and financial support; while Israel in turn remained useful to France as an effective potential military ally on Egypt's right flank. The French newspapers, even the rightist press, applauded this alliance, and devoted many articles, nearly all of them sympathetic, to descriptions of Jewish life in Israel. The Jews of France were indirect beneficiaries of this pro-Israel sentiment. Poujadist orators found it increasingly difficult to make distinctions between Jews in Israel and Jews in France, and anti-Semitism was soft-pedaled as a propaganda weapon.

The rise of Israel had a moderate rejuvenating effect on Jewish life itself. Some such invigoration was desperately needed, for until recently France possessed the least active, the least creative Jewish community, for its size, in the Western world. The Consistory, for example, the lay government of the French-Jewish synagogue federation, hardly represented more than an aristocratic group of wealthy Alsatians; as a rule, its members were quite unconcerned with the religious and cultural needs of the Eastern European immigrant group. Thus, the Consistorial synagogues, though strictly Orthodox in ritual, were much like the typical Reform German temples of pre-Hitler days: formal, rather cold, almost invariably poorly attended. The French rabbinate was quite uninfluential, preoccupied almost exclusively with matters of ritual and theology, rarely called upon for counsel in the critical social problems of the time.

The Russian- and Polish-Jewish newcomers added little to community vitality. Their desire to acculturate as rapidly as possible, to shake off the stigma of "foreignness," not infrequently led to outright assimilation. The older immigrants continued to attend their decrepit little *shuls* in the Belleville ghetto; but their children lost interest almost entirely in Jewish communal life. Thus the social intermingling between Alsatian and Eastern European Jews, which began in the late 1930's, resulted in no significant stimulus to Jewish religious and cultural activity in either group. During the interwar period there were a few Jewish intellectuals, the poets André Spire, Edmond Fleg, and Catulle Mendès, who took a vigorously affirmative approach to their Jewish inheritance. But the Jews who figured most prominently in French cultural life, such men as Henri Bergson and André Maurois, were scarcely ever identified as Jews.

After Vichy, strangely enough, French Jews began to convert to Roman Catholicism with increasing frequency. Apparently the horror of the Nazi epoch provoked a kind of negative Jewish psychosis; in their relative security before Hitler, there was no pressure to reject completely a Judaism that had long since ceased to be more than a vague family tradition. Hitler undermined this security. Some French Jews reacted by becoming ardent Zionists, others by consciously apostasizing. By midcentury the wave of Jewish conversions to Catholicism included many thousands, perhaps by some estimates, tens of thousands. Name-changing was even more common. Of France's 280,000-300,000 Jews, less than 10,000 had enrolled by 1957 in the registers of the Central Consistory of French Jews, still the only officially recognized community identification. The philanthropic activity of French Jewry, which had been quite notable in the days of Baron Maurice de Hirsch and the Rothschilds, dwindled markedly and never again resumed its earlier level. There were, after all, hardly any sizable Jewish fortunes left in France; nor did the French government permit philanthropic contributions to be written off against taxes. Basically, however, interest in the various causes themselves seemed to have lapsed.

But while assimilation took a heavy toll, perhaps a heavier toll than in any other major Jewish community in the West, there still existed in France a small hard core of men and women who, motivated by nostalgia, *noblesse oblige,* or deep conviction, remained closely and consciously identified with Jewish life. In a sense, these people were the caretakers of the French-Jewish community: the preservers of the skeletal structure of the Consistory, the *Alliance Israélite Universelle,* the Zionist Federation, and the Franco-Jewish press. During the late 1940's and 1950's this tenacious beachhead was strengthened at last by a gifted group of French-Jewish intellectuals, whose revived interest in Jewish affairs was largely the result of the impact of Zionism and the emergence of Israel. André Chouraqui, for example, one of the directors of the *Alliance,* produced a number of volumes on Jewish history that ranked with the best products of American-Jewish and Israeli scholarship. Manès Sperber, a Russian-Jewish immigrant, was the author of several excellent novels on Jewish themes. Vladimir Yankelevitch, Professor of Philosophy at the Sorbonne, wrote extensively and imaginatively on Jewish theological problems. Arnold Mandel was one of the leading Jewish journalists of Europe. In Strasbourg, the center of Alsatian-Jewish life, André Neher, a Hebraic scholar of international reputation, held the Chair of Hebrew Studies for several decades at the local university. At the same time, several new literary journals of excellent quality, *Arches* and *Evidences,* were attracting a widening constituency; by 1957 their paid circulation reached fifty thousand. In Paris four Jewish *lycées* were in operation, and their student body comprised the children of the older Alsatian community, as well as youngsters from the immigrant group.

Perhaps it was premature to identify this intellectual revival with the beginning of a major renaissance of Jewish culture in France. Certainly massive disinterest in Jewish life continued to characterize the majority of French Jews. Nevertheless it is worth noting that in the late 1950's this revival had a broader and deeper base than at any other time in modern French history. As the interrelationship between France and Israel tightens—and all evidence indicates that it will—it does not seem impossible, or even improbable, that the impact of Israeli civilization will make itself increasingly felt.

TO BRITAIN'S SHORES

When the May Laws of 1881 precipitated the massive migrations of Russian Jews, the settled community in the British Isles numbered scarcely sixty thousand. It was centered mainly in London, a typical middle-class group, the majority involved in shopkeeping and petty trade, but with a large minority of prosperous merchants, as well. It was, despite its size, politically and culturally quite secure. By the end of the nineteenth century several of its members—Sir George Jessel, Sir Julian Goldsmid, Baron Henry de Worms, Lionel L. Cohen—had won distinction for themselves in public affairs. Many English Jews were quite prominent, too, in the social life of the *haut monde;* for the Prince of Wales had set the standard by including a number of Rothschilds and Sassoons in his immediate entourage of close friends. By the turn of the century Jews mixed easily in English society at almost every level. There was little comparable strength, however, in Jewish communal loyalty or achievement. Scholars were few, and the handful of truly creative personalities—Israel Zangwill, Joseph Jacobs, Israel Abrahams, Lucien Wolf, Moses Gaster—were only at the beginning of their literary careers. The Jews of England, like the Jews of France, were at best lukewarm in their religious interest; in fact many of them, notably among the upper middle class, had already abandoned their Jewish identification altogether.

It was at this juncture that the Eastern European immigrants began to arrive. In transit to America, they passed through England by the hundreds of thousands. During the 1890's and the early years of the twentieth century, steamers left Europe weekly—four from Hamburg, three from Rotterdam and Bremen, and one from Libau—all made stops at London. During the thirty-three years of this migration, from 1881 to 1914, nearly a quarter of a million Jews decided to remain in England. The United States, after all, was still three thousand miles away; while England enjoyed a reputation as a tolerant and fair-minded democracy, a land which promised measurable if not unlimited economic opportunity. Those Jews who disembarked settled, for the most part, in the East End of London, the industrial slum area flanking both sides of Whitechapel Road, extending through the boroughs of Stepney, Bethnal Green, and Hackney. Other Jewish communities, too, sprang up during this period: in Leeds, Manchester, and Liverpool; by 1911, the "provincial" Jewish population had reached nearly one hundred thousand. Yet until the first World War 65 per cent remained in London, most of them in the vicinity of Whitechapel. Zangwill graphically described the "Judaization" of the East End:

> The dead walls and boardings were placarded with bills from which the life of the inhabitant could be constructed. Many were in Yiddish. . . . Even when the language was English, the letters were Hebrew. Whitechapel Public Meeting, Board School, Sermon, Police and other modern banalities, glared at the passerby in the sacred guise of the tongue associated with miracles and prophecies, palm trees and cedars and seraphs, lions and shepherds and harpists.

As a rule, the early immigrant neighborhoods were congested, dirty, even squalid. In Duke's Place, for example, the headquarters of the Jewish fruit trade, hens pecked about endlessly in the piles of refuse that strewed the streets. The neighborhood's black walls were chalked from end to end with orange-sellers' scores. Every corner was filled with sacks and boxes, while groups of people sat about the pavement washing their stock, or dandling and exhibiting their babies. The street and chamber trades met in Whitechapel to sell lemons from curbside or to stitch trousers in the tailor's shop. Perhaps two fifths of the East End's Jewish workers were tailors; the rest were peddlers, boot-and-shoe workers, furniture makers, cigar makers, produce dealers, and petty retailers. Before 1880 the Jews of England were merchants, shopkeepers, and financiers; they were superseded now by a community which, in the period between 1890 and 1914, was essentially proletarian.

Now the complaint was heard increasingly that "cheap" Jewish labor was depressing the employment market. "We sympathize with you," declared an English labor leader to a group of Jewish immigrants, "we have a feeling of solidarity with you, but we should have been thankful if you had never come." In 1902 Parliament responded to trade-union pressure by authorizing an official survey of working and living conditions in the East End. For six months a Parliamentary Commission toured the Whitechapel area, interviewing workers, analyzing work methods, studying home and family life. When at the end of the year the Commission issued its report, it observed that the Russian-Jewish newcomers were generally an honest and industrious group, and that most of the charges against them—cutthroat competition, immorality, and personal uncleanliness—were completely unfounded. The investigators recommended, however, that legislation be passed to deal with occasional "undesirable immigrants." Three years later Parliament passed its first restrictive Immigration Act: entrance was henceforth prohibited to aliens who were criminals, prostitutes, or persons likely to become a public charge. Most of the fugitives from Eastern Europe did not fall within these categories. But the fact that they were now suspect and subject to careful scrutiny, that officials were invested with the discretionary power of rejecting any "undesirables," ultimately exercised an inhibiting effect on further Jewish immigration into England. After 1905 the number of Jewish arrivals leveled off and declined.

In the years immediately preceding the first World War the newcomers succeeded gradually in winning economic security for themselves; they succeeded, too, although rather more gradually, in adjusting to the English way of life. Anglicization was largely the result of the splendid elementary education that Jewish children received from the nondenominational English schools. Partly responsible, too, were the clubs established by the older Jewish community for the purpose of teaching adult immigrants the English language and the "principles of English citizenship." The effects of this acculturation became most apparent in the period between the two World Wars. At first the East End was as typical a ghetto as New York's East Side or even Warsaw's Nalewki district. During the day Whitechapel Road abounded in petty salesmen, pushcart peddlers, fishmongers hawking their wares in Yiddish or broken English. In the evening thousands of Jewish families strolled through the streets greeting friends, gossiping, stopping occasionally to listen to Bundist or Zionist orators proclaim their doctrines from makeshift platforms. After the late 1920's the East End rapidly lost its ghetto characteristics: immigrants and their children moved into north and northwest London at the rate of twenty to thirty thousand a year. The pushcart peddlers and fishmongers all but disappeared; the "*shidduch* parade," the huge evening promenade, eventually vanished as a Whitechapel tradition. Those who remained in the East End, especially after the prolonged Nazi bombings of 1940, were primarily older people and derelicts whom the times had passed by.

After Hitler's rise to power 100,000 German and Austrian Jews came to England as refugees, raising the Anglo-Jewish population by mid-century to 450,000. The majority of the new immigrants came from a middle-class background, and only a few could bring any of their assets with them. But they were sympathetically received by the "older" Russian-Jewish community which provided them with living quarters, gave them employment, even set them up with loans. Thus encouraged and assisted, the newcomers were able to put their years of commercial and professional experience to good use. They managed to win back respected status within a surprisingly short period of time, in some instances within two or three years.

By the 1950's, therefore, Anglo-Jewry had largely resumed its nineteenth-century configuration as a middle-class community. Although Jews comprised less than 1 per cent of the total population, they founded and managed some of England's most prominent commercial enterprises: the Burton clothing shops, the Lyons restaurants and hotels, the Marks and Spencer department stores, each the largest chain of its kind in the country. The majority of Anglo-Jewish business leaders came from the Eastern European immigration. Sir Montague Burton, for example, began his career as an impoverished immigrant tailor in Leeds. Sir Simon Marks, and the owners of Lyons, Sir Isadore Salmon and Major M. Gluckstein, emerged out of equally modest immigrant beginnings. So, too, did Lord Bearsted (oil), Lord Melchett (chemicals), Lord Southwood (newspapers), Lord Swaythling (banking), Sir Samuel Instone (merchandising), Sir Louis Sterling (record-players), and countless other peers and baronets whose tradition-adorned titles usually superseded equally traditional Russian-Jewish birth names.

The measure of success and acceptance was no less apparent in the careers of Jews outside the field of business. Perhaps the three outstanding personalities to emerge from the Anglo-Jewish community in the twentieth century, and the most dramatic symbols of that community's "acceptance," were Rufus Isaacs, Herbert Samuel, and Harold Laski. Isaacs, the son of a fruit peddler, won distinction and fame as a queen's counsellor, and in 1904 was elected to the House of Commons as the Liberal candidate from Reading. Within the space of a decade, he was knighted, appointed attorney-general, and invited to a seat in the Cabinet. In 1913 he was named Lord Chief Justice of England, the highest position ever held in England by a professing Jew. Such was Isaacs' reputation for legal acumen and personal integrity that even opposition newspapers applauded his appointment. Elevated to the peerage as Lord Reading of Erleigh, he served as ambassador to the United States in 1918. Three years later he was honored with the most exalted appointive post in the British Empire: as His Majesty's Viceroy for India, the Whitechapel peddler's son presided over the destinies of hundreds of millions of Orientals. The Jews, and England, had come a long way in the half century since Lionel Rothschild pantomimed his way into Parliament.

Herbert Samuel, like Isaacs an active member of the Liberal party, was elected to Parliament in 1902, and embarked on a distinguished career of public service which led to a seat in the Cabinet in 1910. Unlike Isaacs, however, Samuel was quite active in Jewish affairs; during the war he was won over to Zionism by Moses Gaster and Nahum Sokolow. It was as a mark of special favor both to him and the Zionist movement, therefore, that the government appointed Samuel its first High Commissioner in Palestine, a post which he occupied from 1920 to 1925, and which he sought to administer with absolute fairness to Jews and Arabs alike. As it turned out, the Zionists were convinced that Samuel, as a Jew, leaned over backward to prove his impartiality; it was at his suggestion and under his administration, for example, that the largest part of Palestine was carved out of the mandate, and handed over to the Arabs as the Emirate of Trans-Jordan. Samuel was not forgiven for what his assailants called a gratuitous deference to ungrateful Arabs. But none could deny that the half-decade of his administration were years of unprecedented internal progress in the building of the Yishuv. It was truly the golden era of British-Zionist friendship. The friendship cooled rapidly after Samuel's departure.

Harold Laski, the son of a Russian-Jewish immigrant, first acquired his reputation as the author of several brilliant and original volumes on political theory and social planning. As Professor of Political Science at the London School of Economics during the 1930's and 1940's, he became England's leading intellectual spokesman for Fabian Socialism. Yet Laski was far from being a mere theoretician, for during the same period he served as the Labour party's Director of Economic Planning. He formulated the basic blueprint of the English welfare state, and lived to see the blueprint implemented, after World War II, by the Attlee Labour Government. The concept of complete cradle-to-grave security, quietly incorporated into law, assuredly represented one of the major social revolutions of modern times. It is doubtful, therefore, if any other theorist since David Ricardo or Jeremy Bentham, not excluding Sidney Webb himself, ever made so profound an impact on British economic and political thinking as this quiet, bespectacled, pipe-smoking English Jew.

There were, as well, many hundreds of other Jews who distinguished themselves in nearly every phase of English life: Professor Samuel Alexander of the Philosophy Department of the University of Manchester, until his death in 1939 the most beloved scholar of his day, and holder of the Order of Merit; Sir Leon Simon, the eminent Hebraist; brilliant young Lord Rothschild, war hero and Fellow of Trinity College, Cambridge; Dr. Redcliffe Salaman, distinguished agricultural scientist of Cambridge University and Fellow of the Royal Society, who served as Chairman of the Cambridge Board of Magistrates, and as a tireless worker for all Jewish and humanitarian causes. There were, in addition, countless Jews throughout England who, as tradesmen, doctors, schoolteachers, down to the humblest ranks of workers, became mayors of their towns, members of Parliament, officials or members of county and borough councils.

Until recently, however, the Anglo-Jewish community was still dominated by a small elite of "older" families: the Montefiores, the Mocattas, the Rothschilds, the Franklins, and five or six others. Not until mid-century did both groups—the Sephardic and the German on the one hand, the Russian on the other—mingle and occasionally intermarry. By then, too, the children of the Russian-Jewish immigration increasingly assumed the positions of leadership in Jewish communal life. Even in politics the domination of the "aristocrats" was beginning to break down. For many years it had been almost automatic for Jews to support the Liberal party; for until the post-World War I era, the Liberals represented the industrial middle class, and demonstrated a historic friendship for Jews and Nonconformists. In the 1900-14 period, as we have seen, the Jews who rose highest in politics, Lord Reading and Lord Samuel, belonged to this party. But with the Liberal collapse, industry and finance moved over largely into the Conservative party; many Jewish businessmen joined in this shift in political loyalties, and during the 1930's there were a number of Jewish M.P.'s sitting on the Conservative side of the House. Perhaps the most outstanding of these Jewish Conservatives was Alfred Mond, the first Lord Melchett. The Labour party, on the other hand, was slower to find Jewish adherents, since for many years the trade unions, in which the Jews did not play a significant role, were the dominant influence in Labour. But as the social background of the Labour party widened, increasing numbers of Jews enrolled, and in the 1945 election 28 Jews won Labour seats out of a total of 390 Labour M.P.'s. This increase in Jewish Labour membership hardly reflected a change in Anglo-Jewry's middle-class or lower middle-class economic status; it was rather that, after the demise of the Liberal party, Labour was viewed as the safest bulwark against political and economic reaction.

The danger of reactionary ascendancy was a matter of more than political partisanship to the Jewish minority; for the emergence of anti-Semitic regimes on the Continent revealed with frightening clarity the intimate connection between rightist politics and Jew-hatred. Actually fascism, or neo-fascism, had never made significant inroads among the British people. In the unemployment crisis of the early 1920's there was a brief gust of anti-Semitic agitation; it subsided rapidly, however, as economic conditions improved. During the mid-1930's a local admirer of Hitler, Sir Oswald Mosley, openly preached the Nazi doctrine; but his small band of followers made little serious impact on British public opinon. After the war the terrorism in Palestine in 1946-47 created among the English people a not inconsiderable revulsion against the Zionist cause, but even this ill feeling was not extended to the Jews of England. Whatever anti-Semitism did exist was usually much less crudely manifested than in the United States, and only rarely posed a barrier to educational, business, or professional opportunity. When the dangers of organized Jew-hatred were contemplated, it was less as a reaction to English anti-Semitism than it was to the horrors of Nazism and Fascism on the Continent. Only twenty miles of English Channel had separated the Anglo-Jewish community from the workings of the "Final Solution"; it was perhaps not surprising, therefore, that the menace of an anti-Semitic reaction loomed larger in the minds of Anglo-Jewry than domestic circumstances warranted.

While the Jews of England enjoyed virtually complete acceptance in political and social life, they remained, at the same time, quite cohesive in their religious and cultural identification. In the early years of the Russian-Jewish influx most of the new immigrants were Orthodox. The established leaders of the older settlement, represented by the Board of Deputies of British Jews, respected this Orthodoxy. Sincerely eager to help the newcomers preserve their traditional ritual and ceremonial, they established for them a completely new network of religious institutions: a federation of Orthodox synagogues. Henceforth, there existed in England two completely separate groups of synagogues. As in the United States, however, many of the immigrant children deserted the Orthodox Federation, usually for reasons of social status, and affiliated later with the older United Synagogue. Some of them even joined with Britain's one major Reform congregation, the West London synagogue, which had been established as far back as 1840 by a blue-blooded group of Sephardic and German Jews.

Notwithstanding these developments to the left and right, the principal institutions of Anglo-Jewry settled into a dignified conservatism by the 1950's. The level of synagogue attendance was remarkably high, much higher, certainly, than in France. For in France the Russian-Jewish immigrants had never been a majority; they were more susceptible, as a result, to the "nativizing" pressure of their predecessors. In England, on the other hand, the Russian-Jewish pride of ancestral tradition stimulated Jewish learning and literary expression and produced an impressive array of scholars and writers, men of the caliber of Cecil Roth, A. M. Hyamson, Louis Golding, Solomon Schechter, Harry Sacher, and Leopold Greenburg. Indeed, in terms of intellectual vitality, the Anglo-Jewish community was second only to German Jewry; after 1945 it was second to none. The Jews of England boasted many splendid synagogues, meeting halls, Jewish secondary schools on both the *Talmud Torah* and parochial, all-day levels. There was even a Jews' College, a rabbinical training school, in London. Anglo-Jewish journals strove for high standards; one of them, the *London Jewish Chronicle,* was read in the majority of Jewish homes in England, and was probably the finest newspaper of its kind in the world.

Long before the rise of Israel, Zionism, sustained by the Russian immigrants, had become a movement of compelling vigor in Anglo-Jewish life, despite the opposition of many of the older families. Later, the rapid growth of the Yishuv, and eventually of the State of Israel, made Zionists out of the most adamant of "aristocratic" English Jews. Perhaps the most dramatic example of this transformation was provided by the Marchioness of Reading, daughter of the first Lord Melchett. Educated as Christians or near-Christians, she and her brother, the second Lord Melchett, were "officially" reconverted to Judaism and became active Zionist leaders. The eminent Labourites, Harold Laski and Victor Gollancz, long adamantly socialist and "internationalist," began to reconcile their views with Zionism, as did many Jewish Labour members of Parliament. The reconciliation signified more than the acceptance of a *fait accompli;* it represented, too, the pride of rekindled peoplehood.

It was a pride which related also to a long record of creative achievements. Through the pages of Anglo-Jewish life moved some of the most influential figures in the modern annals of the Jewish people. The Rothschilds were there, financing Wellington's armies in a life-and-death struggle against Napoleon Bonaparte, wresting emancipation for the Jews of England by force of an immense prestige and an even more formidable tenacity. Moses Montefiore was there, defending the rights and liberties of his people in half a dozen lands with an assurance and authority vouchsafed only to the favorites of queens. Chaim Weizmann, too, moved through those pages, persuading a mighty empire to bestir itself on behalf of an incredible, barely formulated vision of a Jewish National Home. Others there were too, statesmen, philanthropists, scientists, scholars, industrialists, who moved through the pages in a dramatic and colorful procession. Like the island people of which it was a part, the Anglo-Jewish community drew its greatest strength from the tradition of *noblesse oblige* which animated its ablest sons.

TO THE COMMONWEALTH: CANADA

In the first frenzy of exodus from Slavophile reaction during the late nineteenth and early twentieth centuries, tens of thousands of Russian Jews flocked to the Dominions of the British Commonwealth. Some twenty thousand Jews managed to make their way to Australia and New Zealand; by 1950, their numbers grown to sixty thousand, they were among the leading merchants of Sydney, Melbourne, Wellington, and Christchurch. Others migrated to Cyprus, Malta, Gibraltar, even to India. Yet, aside from England itself, the Dominion of Canada was the most frequent catch basin for this swelling tide of emigration to the Commonwealth.

It was an immense stretch of land, more than twice the size of the United States, and with natural resources nearly as rich and extensive. Self-governing, democratic in political structure, Canada had attracted immigrants from northwestern Europe from the beginning of its corporate existence, and they were steadily augmented by hundreds of thousands of French and Scottish farmers and by peasants from Germany, Italy, Serbia, Poland, and Russia. Even before 1881 several thousands of newcomers were Jews, and they were to be found in the far reaches of British Columbia and Saskatchewan where a German Jew, Lumby Franklin, was elected Mayor of Victoria; while another German Jew, David Oppenheimer, was four times elected Mayor of Vancouver. By the late 1870's there were several synagogues in Canada, and a Jewish population of perhaps twenty-five hundred.

These were mainly outposts, however, and they attracted little immigration. Even the May Laws, which helped to people England and the United States, channeled few of the refugees into Canada. The Dominion was an unknown entity; reports of democratic government, unlimited resources, and proximity to the United States were counterbalanced by descriptions of the country's yawning immensity, its frigid temperatures, its sparse population and consequent loneliness and isolation. Many of the Russian refugees who arrived and settled in the two decades following the May Laws did so by accident, when British ships, offering cheap passage, happened to make their first ports of call in Canada.

After 1900, the immigration rate was accelerated. The process was a familiar one: those Jews who had settled in Canada and had found security there sent back remittances and tickets to their relatives in the Pale. At the same time the mounting immigration restrictions in the United States provided an added incentive for "temporary" residence, and between 1900 and 1931 another 120,000 Jews settled in Canada. Although they constituted a mere 2 per cent of the country's total immigration during the early twentieth century, the Jews eventually became the seventh largest ethnic group in the

Dominion. By 1950 natural increase brought their numbers up to 200,000 out of a total Canadian population of 15,000,000. Three fourths of these new-comers settled in the three main cities of Montreal, Toronto, and Winnipeg—43 per cent in Montreal, 22.5 per cent in Toronto, and 8.3 per cent in Winni-peg. Others scattered into the smaller communities of the interior, from fog-shrouded Cape Breton Island to snow-bound Dawson in the Klondike.

The earliest settlers had many picturesque and dramatic tales to match the adventures of the other intrepid ethnic groups, tales of the Sephardic river traders when Canada was a wilderness, and of the German banking and steamship entrepreneurs, as the commercial and industrial arts developed. For the massed thousands of Russian-Jewish textile workers who came in the twentieth century there were also astonishing sagas of adjustment and success. Out of the background of sweatshops and slum congestion emerged a powerful textile and clothing industry; as in the United States, it was the single most important Jewish contribution to the economic life of the coun-try. Of less ultimate significance, perhaps, but of historic interest in the growth of the Canadian hinterland, was the role played by hundreds of Jewish storekeepers in tiny railroad villages throughout the West. The typical Russian-Jewish trader of this type, only recently arrived from the belt of mixed populations of southeastern Europe, was able to make himself understood among the Germans, Ukrainians, Poles, Romanians, and Serbs who settled in the interior. Living in the isolated and wind-blown "bush" with these rough, uncouth workmen, housing his family in a reconverted railway car or in the back of his little store, the Jewish merchant served as provisioner, banker, translator, letter writer, and advisor for a growing and heterogeneous population. As the years passed, Jews moved, too, into urban retailing, into distilling, where the Jewish-owned firm of Seagram be-came one of the largest liquor empires in the world. They moved, as well, into the professions and occasionally into the government. By the 1950's the immigrant Jewish community had made the usual notable strides in self-improvement. By then it had become very largely a middle-class group.

Because Canada was a parliamentary democracy which guaranteed equal legal and political rights to all its citizens, the Jews never questioned their basic security in the country. Yet even this liberal Dominion posed a number of serious obstacles to Jewish self-adjustment. They were problems that arose primarily in French Canada, in the province of Quebec, where nearly half of Canada's Jews lived, most of them in the city of Montreal. Quebec maintained a rather complex educational system: each of the two major cultural-religious groups, the French-Catholic and the English-Protestant, supported its own parochial schools and paid for them out of special real estate taxes. The system worked reasonably well as long as the children of the province came exclusively from Catholic and Protestant homes. When the Jewish population of Montreal became large enough to comprise a homogeneous minority, they were faced with the urgent problem of finding a hospitable school system for their own children.

At first Jewish students attended the Protestant schools, and an agreement was reached in 1903, later legalized by the provincial legislature, by which they were to enjoy the full rights and privileges of the Protestants. In return the Jews paid their school tax into the Protestant "panel." In was at best an unsatisfactory compromise. For many years Jewish youngsters were segregated into separate classrooms, and were denied official permission to be absent during the Jewish holidays. Moreover, no Jew was permitted to sit on a school board or teach in the school system. After years of fruitless protest in the courts, the Jews finally reached the limit of their patience, and made preparations to establish their own parochial schools. Then, at the last moment, in 1931, the Protestant representatives agreed to a *modus vivendi:* they assured the Jewish community that henceforth Jewish children would attend the Protestant schools as of right, and that the segregation of Jews and Christians would be abolished. Jewish youngsters would be excused on the Jewish holidays, and from compulsory study of the New Testament. Control of the schools, however, was to remain exclusively in the hands of the Protestant Board.

The agreement did not work out as well in fact as it did in theory. As late as 1957 Jewish children were still frequently ghettoized in their own classes; while Jewish teachers were rarely hired except on a substitute basis. In addition, the Quebec legislature, controlled by the French-Canadian majority, rarely provided sufficient funds for schools with large numbers of Jewish students. It was this tax dispute which compelled Jewish families once again to consider the need for separate Jewish day schools. Before 1914 no such institutions existed in Montreal, except for a handful of ultra-Orthodox *yeshivot.* By mid-century, however, 18 per cent of Montreal's Jewish school children received all their education in parochial schools; while fully 50 per cent of all Jewish youngsters attended parochial classes in the afternoons and evenings. If this intensive program of Jewish education had developed voluntarily, rather than as a reaction to Christian exclusionism, it would probably have been heartily welcomed by Canadian-Jewish parents; but because the system represented a kind of obligatory ghettoization, few Jews sent their children to the parochial schools without intense unhappiness and frustration.

One of the sorriest features of the school controversy was the anti-Semitism it revealed. In the course of the long legal battle many of French Canada's newspapers stigmatized the Jewish community in libelous terms. Even after the settlement of 1931, anti-Jewish feeling simmered in Quebec. While there had been a few instances of anti-Semitic propaganda in the other provinces of the Dominion, they had been swiftly quashed by action of the provincial legislatures. But in Quebec, the situation was more serious. Wages and working standards were low among the French-Canadians: indeed, Quebec's backwardness and poverty were much worse than in any other province of Canada. For one thing, Quebec's Catholic Church hierarchy was among the most obscurantist in the world, and systematically drained the province of its savings. Then, too, the "normal" difficulties of poverty and clerical reaction were seriously compounded by the Depression of the 1930's. Fascist propaganda, the virtues of the corporative state were actively propagandized by many parish priests. The French-Catholic press was ardent and virtually unanimous in its support of Franco, and to a lesser extent of Mussolini.

The fascist campaign received official sanction in 1935 when Quebec's Minister of Labor, Adrien Arcand, supported by the provincial premier, Duplessis, openly encouraged an anti-Jewish boycott. Few of the Montreal Jewish leaders believed that even a provincial premier's bigotry would endanger the physical security of the Jews in French Canada. But the implications of a growing economic boycott was not lost upon them, and the four years following 1935 were overshadowed by their concern. Fortunately, the Catholic-fascist upsurge was more spectacular than effective; most of the industrial and commercial interests, shipping and the railroads, lumber and insurance, were in the hands of the English, who were completely out of sympathy with French-Canadian fascism. As a result, while the majority of French Canadians notably remained in full sympathy with the anti-Semitic campaign, the movement eventually stalled. Later the outbreak of war made the open display of fascist sympathy dangerous under the Treason Law. After 1945 Arcand emerged once again to reorganize a fascist group in Quebec, newly christened the *Front Corporatif Démocratique*. But his long association with the Nazis had hopelessly undermined his political influence and his attempt to stir up bigotry made no headway.

The failure of organized Jew-hatred had no appreciable impact on the tradition of exclusionism, as practiced both by French and English Canadians. As late as 1957 there were few Jews in government. No Jew sat as a judge until Harry Batshaw was named to the Superior Court Bench in 1950. No Jew served as a public prosecutor. The election of Nathan Phillips as mayor of Toronto in 1954 and in 1956 created astonishment as well as delight because it was so unexpected. The most capable Jewish doctors frequently enjoyed a lucrative practice; but it was difficult for them to secure adequate staff appointments in any but Jewish hospitals. Jewish lawyers were mainly limited to damage suits and small torts; they usually represented small businessmen and these were almost always Jews. Few Jews were hired by non-Jewish businesses. No Jew ever held a seat on the Montreal Stock Exchange or on the Curb Market; and, by a tacit but effective agreement, no Jew was ever a partner in an insurance company or a bank. Masonic lodges, the Canadian Legion, the Press Club admitted only a handful of Jews. Very rarely were Christian and Jewish families on visiting terms.

This policy of exclusion was not motivated principally by anti-Semitism, certainly not in the English provinces, nor was it applied only to Jews. It was the result rather of Canada's traditional *Kulturkampf* which divided the English and the French. The rivalry between these two civilizations established a tradition of separatism in Canada that was upheld, with only slightly less obduracy, vis-à-vis the other ethnic groups, the Italians, Russians, Poles, and Ukrainians. This separatism, in turn, encouraged the minorities to remain cohesive, even clannish. The Jews hardly needed this encouragement; most of them had brought with them the cultural and religious traditionalism of the Pale of Settlement. In Canada, too, no solidly established group of German-Jewish predecessors existed, as in the United States, to apply pressure to the newcomers, to rush them into "nativization." Hence, as late as 1957, the Jews of Toronto and Montreal and, to a lesser extent, of the smaller communities of the Canadian provinces, lived an "inner-directed" life of their own. They frankly preferred the company of their fellow Jews; even when vacationing outside of Canada they made a point of patronizing resorts where there were plenty of *"haimishe menshen"*—i.e., plenty of "home folks," gregarious fellow Jews. Few Montreal Jews evidenced any real desire to imitate their non-Jewish neighbors. One's social prestige rested upon honored participation in the philanthropic and religious activities of the Jewish community.

Russian-Jewish religious and cultural traditions, as a result, endured with much more vitality in Canada than in the United States. Virtually all Jewish houses of worship were Conservative or Orthodox in their orientation; Reform synagogues were extremely rare. While most Jews did not attend religious services with regularity, their nostalgia for old-country ways ensured that the ritual and ceremonial remained by their lights "authentic." Until the late 1940's the Yiddish language was still widely used. This ethnic cohesiveness was evidenced, too, in the remarkable longevity in Canada of *landsmannschaften,* associations of Jews who had been neighbors in the Pale; they had long since disappeared in the United States. It was apparent, as well, in the passionate devotion to Zionism demonstrated by nearly every adult Canadian Jew, in the rapid growth of B'nai B'rith, and in the strength and activity of the Canadian Jewish Congress.

Because of the comparative youth of the Jewish community in Canada and its limited numbers, it remained quite dependent upon the cultural and administrative resources of Jewish life in the United States. Nearly all of Canada's rabbis were imported from American theological seminaries or American pulpits and the executive directors of synagogues and Jewish centers came almost invariably from American cities. The organizational apparatus of B'nai B'rith, Hadassah, the United Jewish Appeal, and innumerable religious, cultural, and philanthropic associations extended into Canada. Tens of thousands of Canadian Jews took advantage of America's "administrative" leadership by joining these organizations. In years to come, the Jewish community of this Dominion, less than one twenty-fifth the size of the Jewish population of the United States, would probably remain dependent upon its southern neighbor for administrative "direction." Yet few communities matched the religious loyalty and the Zionist activism of the Canadian Jews. Their contributions to the United Jewish Appeal and to other basic philanthropies were the highest, per capita, in the world. It therefore seemed likely that as population grew the dependency on the United States would be counterbalanced by the creative intensity of the Canadian-Jewish spirit. Then Canadian Jewry would cease to be a kind of communal appendage of the American-Jewish community, and would become an active partner in the significant cultural and philanthropic projects of Western Jewish life.

SOUTH AFRICA

One of the popular areas of colonization during the Victorian period was the dark and mysterious subcontinent of South Africa. Alternating between long stretches of veld, cultivable farm land, and endless tracts of dust-blown semidesert, between brooding mountains and roaring cascades of waters, this rich and fascinating wilderness was less a sanctuary for the fugitive than a challenge to the adventurous and stouthearted. At first it appealed primarily to the Dutch; tens of thousands of tough, God-fearing agricultural families arrived in South Africa, and carved out farms and plantations for themselves in the interior. By mid-nineteenth century they were joined by equal numbers of English cattle ranchers and industrialists, German exporters and trappers, Indian and Burmese shopkeepers, Greek and Arab restaurateurs and brothel-keepers.

Among the earliest, too, of South Africa's settlers, long before 1881, were Jews from Central and Western Europe. In truth, they were pioneers in the most literal and authentic sense of the word. In the late 1820's, for example, an English Jew, Captain Joshua Norden, served as commander of the Grahamstown Yeomanry, and died by Kaffir bullets. His brother, Benjamin Norden, led the expedition to Matabeleland, opening the Namaqualand copper mines. In 1824 a Dutch Jew, Joseph Lima de Suasso, wrote the first Cape history published in South Africa. Aaron de Paas sailed for South Africa from England in 1846, and founded the Cape's fishing, sealing, and whaling industry; later he was elected Justice of the Peace for Capetown. Jonas Bergtheil, a member of the Natal Parliament several years before Jews were permitted to sit in Parliament in England, established South Africa's first cotton plantations. Three German-Jewish brothers, Joseph, Adolf, and Julius Mosenthal, founded the mohair industry, as well as the largest import-export house in the Transvaal. Together with the enterprising financier and empire-builder, Cecil Rhodes, a Whitechapel Jew, Barney Barnato, and a German Jew, Alfred Beit, opened up the huge Kimberley diamond mines. It was Barnato who, with the British-Jewish firm of Lewis and Marks, erected Johannesburg's first waterworks, its first collieries and breweries, its first glass, steel, brick, tile, and tube works. It was Beit who imported the machinery which opened up the gold mines of the Rand, the world's largest. Nowhere else did Jewish initiative and investment play so crucial a role in a nation's development.

Perhaps the most important, if least known, of South Africa's Jewish pioneers was Ernest Oppenheimer, a diminutive German immigrant who arrived in South Africa in 1902 as a buyer for a British jewelry chain. Shrewdly anticipating the enormous potential value of the Rand gold fields, he persuaded a group of English and American banking houses to back him in investing a million pounds sterling in a joint Anglo-American mining company. Within a decade the investment was repaid several times over, and Oppenheimer's personal fortune grew large enough to be applied to his first love: diamonds.

At the end of the first World War, the Union of South Africa assumed the ownership of Germany's adjacent colonies, and Oppenheimer quickly sensed the possibility of important diamond reserves in the new territories. He invested every shilling of his fortune in an extensive prospecting project in Southwest Africa, and was rewarded when his crews opened up for him hitherto undreamed-of riches in gems. By 1930 this quiet, modest Jew had become the wealthiest man in all Africa. Buying up large quantities of stock in the powerful firm of De Beers, Oppenheimer was soon elected a director, and then later chairman of Africa's greatest diamond cartel. He managed the firm with amazing astuteness; indeed, by carefully apportioning and restricting De Beers' diamond distribution to dealers throughout the world, he assured his adopted land of vital quantities of foreign currency for many decades to come. At the time of his death, in 1957, Oppenheimer was the master of 95 per cent of the world's production of precious stones, and had won for himself the undisputed title of "king of diamonds."

The rumors of South Africa's wealth and economic opportunity circulated throughout Europe and they had a powerful effect upon the distraught and demoralized Jewish communities in the Pale of Settlement. By the late 1890's the first significant numbers of Eastern European immigrants began to arrive in Capetown. Most of them came from Lithuania, where a skein of family connections provided mutual encouragement and financial support. By 1900 the Jewish population had reached 30,000; fifty years later their numbers had grown to 120,000, out of a white population of 2,500,000, and a total population of 13,500,000.

These newcomers were no less pioneers than their earlier predecessors, for they were not content merely to open shops and stores, or to work as tailors and seamstresses in the larger cities. Pushing into the interior of the Transvaal with wagons and oxen, they peddled goods, saddles, patent medicines, and agricultural implements, opened general stores where there was as yet no significant population, and depended upon payment whenever the rains provided their customers with a good crop. Some of these bearded Lithuanian Jews were only a year or two away from the musty *yeshivah* study rooms of Volozhin and Mir, and the Talmudical-dialectical intonation was still fresh on their lips in every business dealing. They must have asked themselves now what stroke of fate it was that had suddenly transported them to this exotic black wilderness, and surrounded them on every side with sullen and warlike tribes of Bantus and Zulus. Few of the newcomers paused long enough, however, to bemoan the circumstances that had wrested them from the familiar scenes of their childhood. Through fierce ambition and driving energy they transformed themselves into a secure middle-class community within two decades of their arrival. By 1950, represented primarily in retailing and importing but also heavily concentrated in the professions, fully two fifths of South Africa's Jews lived in the small cities and towns of the interior. The rest were mainly divided between Johannesburg and Capetown. Not infrequently, they were among the leading citizens of their communities.

Following the pattern laid down by Barnato, Beit, and other Jewish pathfinders before them, the Lithuanian immigrants and their children participated widely in the public life of South Africa, although nearly always in areas of British, rather than of Dutch settlement. Jews sat in the legislatures both of the Union and of the provinces. The citizens of Johannesburg twice elected Jewish mayors, Harry Graumann in 1910 and M. J. Harris in 1924; and there were other Jewish mayors in Capetown, Nigel, Kimberley, and Port Elizabeth. Most of these Jewish political figures were liberal in their party affiliations, and some of them, as in the case of "Solly" Sachs, a prominent trade-union leader, were closer to socialism. This liberalism and, to a lesser extent, socialism reflected more than Jewish economic self-interest; it reflected, as well, Jewish insecurity in the face of rising Boer nationalism. The Dutch farmers, who formed the largest part of the Union's white population, had never been reconciled to the "invasion" of the *uitlanders* (outsiders), the British, and the Jews who were the economic allies of the British. This resentment was exacerbated by jealousy: the British controlled virtually all the country's industry and finance. The Jews, far less influential in their "control" of commerce, were nevertheless disproportionately represented in the business world as members of the Johannesburg Stock Exchange and as middle-class shopkeepers and professional men. In 1930 General Hertzog's Dutch Nationalist Government "retaliated" against the Jewish *uitlanders* by closing off all further immigration from Eastern Europe; later, when Hitler's persecutions drove Jews out of Central Europe, the Boers maneuvered the passage of a bill severely restricting immigration from Germany and Austria.

In the period preceding the second World War, ominous changes in the political climate caught the Jewish minority in a very dangerous dilemma. South Africa's huge Negro and "colored" (mulatto and Indian) populations were emboldened to demand equal political and economic opportunity for themselves. The Boers, who had pre-empted most of the original Zulu and Kaffir lands, and who depended upon the Negroes and "colored" peoples for their cheap labor, reacted to these demands with terror and fury. The more ardent of the Dutch nationalists openly advocated a more stringent policy of apartheid—i.e., separation of the races. Daniel Malan and Johannes Strijdom, the leading spokesmen for this program, borrowed freely from Nazi jargon for their racist rationale. So long as the tough old war horse, Jan Christiaan Smuts, remained the most respected political figure in the Boer community, there was little danger that an extremist policy of apartheid would be implemented. But when his premiership ended in 1948, the Boers elected Daniel Malan, an ardent separatist, as his successor. Almost immediately thereafter the Dutch Nationalist Government embarked upon a savage policy of racist exclusionism. In a succession of brutally unequivocal measures, the South African Parliament quarantined the Union's Negro population into slum "suburbs," the most verminous areas in the country, and denied the franchise to all natives of "mixed blood," i.e., white and Negro, or white and Indian, or both. Later when the Union's Supreme

Court declared these measures unconstitutional, the Parliament transformed itself into a higher appellate tribunal and overrode the judgment of the Court.

No specifically anti-Semitic legislation was passed by the South African Parliament after Malan assumed authority. Both Malan and his successor, Strijdom, went to great lengths to assure all their white subjects of full equality, and in 1955 Strijdom officially reaffirmed this promise. Both men were scrupulous in maintaining correct diplomatic relations with the State of Israel. But the Jews of South Africa were not blind to the dangers of renegade racism; they sensed the threat to their security in the increasingly vicious propaganda of a number of Dutch nationalist politicians, who referred to the Jews as "international Communists and white niggers." They anticipated a very real danger, too, in the arbitrary denial of passports to some of the Union's leading Jews, on the specious grounds of "Communist" affiliation; in the Orange Free State's Education Ordinance of 1954, which made it obligatory for teachers in the provincial schools to foster "Christian Nationalism"; and in the recurrent introduction of bills to abolish *shehitah*, Jewish ritual slaughter. The most perceptive leaders of South African Jewry cautioned their people to avoid panic, but they were realistic enough to recognize that the racist mouthings of the Dutch nationalists carried familiar echoes of the Nazi oratory of the 1930's.

Because most of South Africa's Jews were of Eastern European origin, and of comparatively recent vintage at that, they managed to preserve much of the warmth and flavor of Russian-Jewish life. They were a strongly traditional community. Nearly all their synagogues were Orthodox. Jewish primary and secondary schools were attended by the majority of Jewish children, although rarely on an all-day basis. Similarly, South African Jewry supported an extensive network of community centers, brotherhoods and sisterhoods, benevolent and welfare societies, *hevras,* and loan associations, Anglo-Jewish and Yiddish journals. As in Canada, however, the tenacity of Jewish loyalties was only partly due to the European inheritance; it reflected the established tradition of separatism between civilizations: the English from the Afrikander, and both from the Negro and the "colored." Each group was thrust back upon its own resources, and South African Jewry, too, fitted its cultural and communal activity into this pattern.

Notwithstanding their economic strength and their official legal and political equality, the Jews of South Africa were far from psychologically secure in a land riddled with innumerable racial tensions. It was this insecurity, more than any other factor, that accounted for the zeal, even the fanaticism, with which they supported the Zionist cause; outside of Israel the South African Jewish community was without question the most ardently Zionist community in the world. In contributions to Zionist institutions it rivaled the generosity of the Jewish community of Canada. It contributed people, too: several hundred young men and women who fought in Israel's war of liberation; several thousand who settled in Israel after 1948. In their identifications they expressed the unspoken belief of perhaps the majority of their coreligionists in the "beloved country": Zion was more than a cultural center for world Jewry; for the threatened Jews of South Africa it was nothing less than a reserve homeland.

SETTLEMENT IN LATIN AMERICA

In nearly all instances the flight of Russian Jews to foreign sanctuaries was a completely spontaneous process. The single exception to this pattern of exodus was the large and, as it turned out, rather significant migration to South America. In its early stages the transplantation was planned, implemented, and subsidized by a wealthy Central European Jew, Baron Maurice de Hirsch. The son and grandson of Bavarian Court bankers, de Hirsch augmented his vast inheritance by marrying into the Bischoffsheim fortune; later, by financing most of the railroads of southeastern Europe, he carved out an enormous economic empire of his own. The mere accumulation of money had never been the principal motivation of his life however, and wealth meant even less to him after the shock of his only son's death. De Hirsch had been a loyal Jew and a generous philanthropist all his life; he decided now to devote his remaining years to the cause of his people, and to make them the heir his son had once been.

As he turned his attention to the plight of his less fortunate coreligionists, de Hirsch was determined to rise beyond compassion, and to meet their needs with "scientific" efficiency. His analysis of conditions in the Pale of Settlement had convinced him that mere philanthropy would never solve one of the most persistent problems of Jewish economic life: the problem of "marginalism," of petty retailing, peddling, small-scale tailoring, of earning a hand-to-mouth livelihood at the mercy of the slightest fluctuation of the business cycle. What was needed, de Hirsch believed, was a root-and-branch relocation of Jews in a new land, where they would have an opportunity to "make men" of themselves, returning to the rugged but "ennobling" life of the soil. The idea had been voiced before of course by the protagonists of *Haskalah,* and was even then being expressed, with variations, by the Zionists. In this case, however, de Hirsch was prepared to implement his theory by personally underwriting a massive transmigration.

Patient and unemotional study persuaded him that the Argentine Republic provided precisely the environment, in spirit, space, and soil, for the re-creation of a nation of agriculturists. A huge, sparsely settled land, the Argentine offered unquestioned economic opportunity to those Jews who were willing to forsake the dubious advantages of an urban existence. In 1891 de Hirsch founded the Jewish Colonization Association (ICA), capitalized it as a British stock company with $10,000,000, and later added an additional $40,000,000 to its assets. His agents purchased vast tracts of Argentine land in the provinces of Santa Fe, Buenos Aires, and Entre Ríos, encompassing hundreds of thousands of acres of virgin soil. When the czarist government in Russia officially approved the plan of transplanting Russian Jewry en masse, de Hirsch triumphantly announced that he was prepared to settle three hundred Jews a week in the Argentine, until 3,500,000 should have been relocated within the next twenty-five years.

De Hirsch's grandiose expectations were destined to be disappointed. Most of Russia's fugitive Jews were determined to go to the United States; desperate as they were for asylum, they were not willing to be hustled off to the Argentine pampas so long as the opportunities of a modern, established, and "civilized" nation awaited them. The few thousand Jews who were brought to the Argentine by the ICA's chartered vessels were swiftly disillusioned. They had not anticipated the severity of the heat, the isolation from urban surroundings, and the overt hostility of the hard-eyed *gauchos* who hovered about their farm colonies. Although de Hirsch provided the settlers with well-built frame houses and barns, and provisioned the farms with abundant quantities of agricultural implements and seed, the first few years, from 1892 to 1895, were a disaster. The newcomers were totally inexperienced in the techniques of farming, and, as a consequence, one bad harvest followed another. Of the original eight thousand colonists who had arrived under de Hirsch's sponsorship, only twenty-five hundred remained on the soil by 1895; most of the others had dispiritedly drifted off to the cities.

De Hirsch died in 1896, brokenhearted at the apparent frustration of his vision. Ironically, if he had lived but a few years longer he would have witnessed the ultimate, if qualified, success of his agricultural project. A hard core of pioneers remained on the farms; eventually, developing experience with the soil brought improved results. After 1900 the number of settlers in the Jewish agricultural colonies increased by several thousand; by mid-century, in fact, there were some 40,000 Jews in the ICA colonies. Their acreage annually produced thousands of bushels of wheat and vegetables; their cattle won coveted prizes in national and provincial fairs. Although their numbers were not large, certainly not large in terms of any mass relocation, they did at least vindicate de Hirsch's conviction that it was possible for Jews to live and thrive on the soil.

De Hirsch also succeeded in ultimately priming the pump of Jewish emigration to Latin America. After the turn of the century, as Jewish disabilities in Eastern Europe increased, more thousands of Russian Jews began to arrive in the Argentine, which became a tempting alternative to the congestion of New York and London. They now came by their own devices, and most of them shunned the ICA farm colonies; they preferred to settle instead in the capital city of Buenos Aires. The yearly average of 7,000 immigrants continued between 1921 and 1930, and by 1957 the Jewish population numbered 360,000 in a nation of 19,000,000. Three quarters of the Jewish community was located in Buenos Aires, and the rest was fairly well divided among the smaller cities: Rosário, La Plata, Córdoba, and Santa Fe.

For the most part, the first years of Jewish settlement in Buenos Aires were merely a Latin variation of early immigrant life in London, Montreal, or even New York. The ghetto neighborhoods, Lavalle, Corrientes, and Junin streets, the slums of the capital, might have been Whitechapel, Belleville, or the East Side. And, as in other large cities of the West, the immigrants began their careers as tailors and peddlers, as street hawkers and tiny shopkeepers. The single distinguishing characteristic in this pattern was the flourishing white-slave trade, which battened on penniless and forlorn Jewish immigrant girls, and which, for a decade and a half, made the words "Jewess" and "harlot" virtually synonymous in the Argentine. The traffic in prostitutes was directed by a few unscrupulous Jews, the most notorious of whom were the Migdal brothers, originally of Lithuania. In the 1930's, however, the Jewish community itself took the initiative in driving these procurers out of business. The Migdals and their associates were placed under a *herem*; no Jew was permitted to consort with them or with any other Jew who had dealings with them. Eventually, groups of Jewish workers, incensed by the presence of brothels only a few streets away from their families and children, stormed the red-light district with clubs and bricks, and drove the white slavers out of the city. They never returned.

Meanwhile there was the usual metamorphosis in Jewish status, the emergence of a moderately secure Jewish middle-class community, the exodus from the ghetto, the growth of more comfortable and aesthetic Jewish neighborhoods. By 1957 60 per cent of Argentine Jews were involved in commerce, as entrepreneurs and white-collar workers. Indeed, by that year there were nearly thirty thousand Jewish business firms in the Argentine, from tiny haberdashery shops to the powerful *Bunge-Born* of Alfred Hirsch, a vast holding company that purchased and operated farm lands, ranches, grain mills, banks, and the largest grocery chain in the country.

In their successful adjustment to Argentine life, few Jews were conscious of any serious danger to their physical or legal security until the Depression decade. The collapse of the European beef market all but destroyed the nation's crucial cattle industry, and completey paralyzed its economy. By the mid-1930's fully a third of the Argentine population was unemployed, living perilously close to the starvation level, an easy prey for the stimulation of racial hatreds. Yet even with the economic hardships of the time it is possible that anti-Semitism would not have assumed major proportions had it not been for the intervention of the sprawling Fascist and Nazi parties. The Argentine possessed large Italian and German populations, most of them postwar immigrants with strong cultural and emotional ties to the lands of their birth. Many of them willingly became tools of Axis penetration; when the Italian and German embassies launched a large-scale propaganda drive in the Argentine, urging the native population to boycott Jewish enterprises, the usual fifth column technique of undermining the solidarity of the country and of weakening its foreign policy, the country's German and Italian settlers co-operated by organizing mass meetings against "Jewish influence." Yet the Argentine people as a whole did not respond to the campaign of organized Jew-hatred. President Hipólito Irigoyen, and his successor, President Roberto Ortiz, took strenuous measures to contain the more overt forms of Fascist penetration. The German school system, which had become a major center of Nazi influence, was placed under government supervision. The arrogant machinations of the Fascists and the Nazis were angrily identified with anti-Catholic activity after Hitler and Mussolini had dealt roughly with the Catholic Church and the Vatican. The Argentine's devoutly Catholic peasant population treated with suspicion the propaganda claims of the Nazi stooges. In 1938 President Ortiz personally assured the Jewish community that his nation would never succumb to racist hysteria.

But while the Argentine people may have feared and resisted foreign dictatorship, they were too politically unsophisticated to withstand a native man on horseback when he shrewdly offered the usual promises of economic reform, and was colorful and flamboyant enough to appeal to the Latin imagination. In 1942, under the leadership of Juan Perón, a handsome, dashing cavalry colonel, a group of army officers suddenly overthrew the legitimate Argentine government. During the war years and for a decade thereafter, Perón governed in the Caesarian manner, first as Minister of Defense, and later as President. Seeking military and financial support, he had no hesitation about flirting with Nazism for the first two years of his incumbency, although he carefully avoided any intimation of Nazi domination. He modeled his army on the German style. His private bodyguard, the *Alianza Libertadora Nacionalista,* was a fascist cabal consisting principally of European quislings. From 1942 to 1944 anti-Semitic demonstrations and newspaper campaigns, this time ostensibly nativist-inspired, but in reality Axis-financed, were conducted with increasing frequency and increasing vituperation. Jews were forbidden membership in many cultural and social organizations, and occasional boycotts were conducted against Jewish business firms. Fortunately the more overt manifestations of race-hatred vanished when the war ended, for the Nazi power in the Argentine quickly collapsed. Bereft of German funds and now eager for the good will of the Western democracies, Perón performed an abrupt about-face, and began issuing genial assurances of friendship to the Argentine-Jewish community; from time to time he attended Jewish banquets and welfare drives, and willingly flashed his toothy smile for photographers from the Jewish press.

It turned out, nevertheless, that the immediate postwar years were in many ways the most dangerous of all for Argentine Jewry. The danger did not lie in anti-Semitism, which declined radically after the Nazi defeat, but rather in Perón's disastrous economic policies. To a large extent, the President's program was dictated by his wife, Evita. The beautiful and ambitious daughter of an Indian camp follower, Evita exercised an almost hypnotic influence over her husband. Thus it was at Evita's suggestion that the President increasingly turned for support to the Argentine's huge General Confederation of Labor and the hundreds of thousands of *descamisados* ("shirtless ones") who were its members. The government cultivated this support by granting wholesale wage raises to the industrial working population. Inasmuch as these wage raises were not linked to increased exports, the result was a runaway inflation that robbed the Argentine peso of three quarters of its prewar value. The inflation was ruinous, particularly for small businessmen; thousands of Jewish shopkeepers went bankrupt, and many others survived only by consuming their life savings.

Then, in September 1955, at the very moment when it appeared as if the country were to be swallowed up in irretrievable inflation, a combined naval and army revolt suddenly ousted Perón from office and sent him fleeing for asylum. The uprising was supported by the majority of the Argentine's liberals; but its success was assured primarily because of clerical endorsement. The Church, and the Argentine people in general, had been deeply offended by Perón's aggressive assault on the Catholic hierarchy as an "international menace." This implacable hostility proved as decisive in the Argentine as it did in nearly every other land where Catholics formed a major segment of the population. It was this Catholic resentment, too, that was responsible for renewed anti-Semitic agitation after the revolution. For Perón had secularized the public school system. Inasmuch as the Jews were the only considerable religious minority in the country, they benefited most directly from the elimination of Catholic religious instruction during school hours. Many clerics and clerical partisans suspected, erroneously of course, that Perón's secularization policy was somehow the result of Jewish advice. Although the leaders of the Jewish community were confident that the gravest threat to security had passed, they could not discount the danger of a "white" reaction and they remained vigilant.

For all their economic integration into Argentine life, their fluent use of the Spanish language, their mastery of the Argentine genre, the Jews of the Argentine remained as separatistic and "inner-directed" as the communities of South Africa and Canada. Their social life was almost exclusively Jewish. Their religious life, while not notably active, remained outwardly quite traditional, even Orthodox: as late as 1957 there was not one Reform synagogue in the entire Argentine. The emphasis on Jewish education was particularly strong; in 1956 some eleven thousand Jewish children were attending all-day Jewish parochial schools, and the number increased monthly as the post-Perón government reintroduced Catholic education into the public schools. Argentine Jewry sponsored a wide variety of institutions and activities: Jewish community centers, B'nai B'rith lodges, Zionist and Hadassah chapters, Yiddish and Ladino (Spanish-Hebrew dialect) newspapers. Similarly, the Jewish community made every effort to maintain close ties with the wealthy and resourceful Jewish population of the United States. The ties were strengthened by the extremely effective Buenos Aires branch of the World Jewish Congress, and by many flying visits of American representatives of the Joint Distribution Committee and the United Jewish Appeal. As in Canada, the Jews of Argentina were largely dependent upon the American-Jewish community for their religious and intellectual resources, and for nearly all their rabbis and professional leadership. But, again as in Canada, Argentine Jewry was by no means a mere appendage of its counterpart in the United States. Borrowing heavily from its northern neighbor, it, too, was growing steadily, if with typically Latin deliberativeness, into cultural and communal maturity.

In 1923 the Argentine's labor unions succeeded in closing the country's doors to Eastern European immigration. As a result, many thousands of distraught Polish Jews, denied entrance as well to the United States and Canada, turned for asylum to Brazil, the largest republic in South America. The vast majority of the Jewish newcomers, some fifty thousand of them, arrived during the mid-1920's as refugees from postwar Polish anti-Semitism. Settling in the two major cities, Rio de Janeiro and São Paulo, the immigrant group performed a miracle in economic adjustment. Within a decade they were a fairly prosperous section of the middle class, with little anxiety about either their political or economic security. The country was wealthy, with vast natural resources; its population was growing even more rapidly than that of the United States. It boasted one of the oldest constitutions in the Western Hemisphere. Unfortunately it was a country with undue reliance upon one product, the coffee crop. In 1930, with the advent of the world Depression, the world market collapsed, and with it the security of every planter, exporter, shipper, and businessman in the land. As bread lines formed in Brazilian cities, as unemployment riots grew more ominous in size and violence, a powerful fascist party, financed very largely by Mussolini, emerged, and it exploited the loyalty of Brazil's large Italian population, and the widespread unrest of the Brazilian people. The president, Getulio Vargas, fought back. Assailing the fascist party as an instrument of a foreign power, he withdrew legal recognition and drove it underground.

Getulio Vargas dominated the political scene of the country from 1930 to 1954. He was president of Brazil from 1934 to 1945 and again from 1951 to 1954. A ruthless, completely inflexible man, he ruled Brazil with a firm but heavy hand. Thus, when he stamped out the fascist party his action was motivated not by dislike of fascist methods, which he largely emulated; but rather by fear of fascism as the spearhead of another country's foreign policy—and Vargas was a militant nationalist. In fact, it was this nationalism that accounted for his intolerance of minority cultures within his own realm. Jews were given every political and economic opportunity, but Vargas had no sympathy with the concept or the techniques of cultural autonomy. He was suspicious of immigrants as representatives of an "alien" way of life. He halted many Jewish communal activities as a threat to Brazil's national integrity. The Zionist Organization was forbidden to conduct any public functions, and the two Yiddish dailies were closed down, along with the foreign language publications of other ethnic groups. Jewish representatives frequently remonstrated and he kept his door open to them, for he liked Jews personally. But he would not budge in his policy, even during the war years when Brazil's soldiers fought at the side of the Allies. He relaxed his restrictions somewhat when the war ended, but Jewish communal life recovered only slowly.

In 1954, faced with a demand by his generals that he resign as president, Vargas committed suicide. His successor, João Café Filho, proved himself to be much more tolerant of Brazil's minority cultures. In the case of the Jews, Filho was exceptionally friendly; he was a frequent guest at Jewish affairs and banquets, and openly encouraged the revival of Jewish community activities. Accordingly, Jewish primary and secondary schools took root in Rio de Janeiro and São Paulo, and by 1955 included about 20 per cent of Brazil's Jewish school children. Still close to their immigrant traditions,

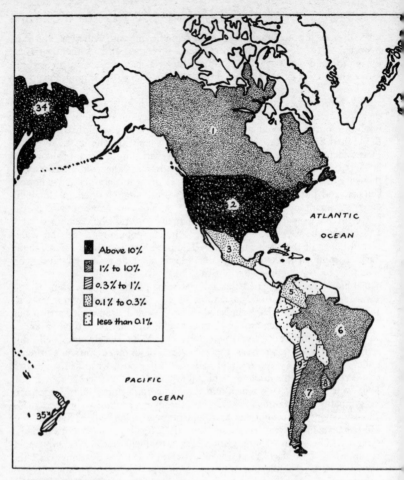

WORLD JEWISH POPULATION, 1956

Shading indicates percentage, in terms of total world Jewish population, of Jews living in each country (based on statistics from *American Jewish Yearbook, 1957*)

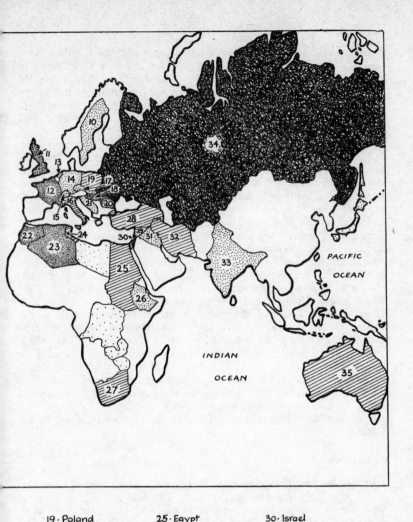

19 · Poland
20 · Romania
21 · Yugoslavia

AFRICA:
22 · Morocco
23 · Algeria
24 · Tunisia

25 · Egypt
26 · Ethiopia
27 · Union of
    South Africa

ASIA:
28 · Turkey
29 · Syria-Lebanon

30 · Israel
31 · Iraq
32 · Iran
33 · India
34 · USSR

35 · AUSTRALIA &
NEW ZEALAND

BY CONTINENTS: North and South America, 51%; Europe, 29%; Asia, 14.5%; Africa, 5%; Australia and New Zealand, 0.5%

intensely tenacious in their religious and cultural loyalties, Brazilian Jewry participated enthusiastically in Zionist activities, and in a wide variety of communal and philanthropic endeavors. But over everything hung the remembrance of the fascist assaults and of the chauvinism of the Vargas era. The Jews realized fully how vulnerable they were, 160,000 in a population of 52,000,000, and they entertained few illusions that their security was permanently or automatically guaranteed.

There were other enclaves of Jewish population, mainly middle-class businessmen, scattered through the countries of Latin America. Some forty thousand Jews lived in Uruguay's capital city of Montevideo. Most of them were refugees, not from Eastern Europe but from Hitler's Germany. Thirty thousand Jews were comfortably settled in Mexico, primarily in Mexico City, and another fifteen thousand lived in Havana, Cuba. A few families here, a few there, isolated, with little community life, were to be found in Chile, Colombia, Venezuela, Panama, and Peru. The Central European Jews of Uruguay and Cuba were not as active in their religious observance as the Eastern European Jews of the Argentine and Brazil; their cultural and social loyalties, on the other hand, remained steadfastly Jewish. B'nai B'rith lodges, Yiddish- and German-language newspapers appeared in Havana, Mexico City, and Montevideo. In Mexico two thirds of the Jewish children received their education in Jewish parochial schools, and very nearly that many attended Jewish parochial schools in Montevideo. Nearly everywhere in Latin America, Zionist activity was intensive, especially since the rise of Israel. But, as in the case of the Jews of the Argentine and Brazil, the Jewish communities of Mexico, Uruguay, and Cuba looked primarily to the United States for the resources, the manpower—the rabbis, scholars, and social workers—with which to consolidate their own Jewish institutions and to maintain their communication with the vital forces of the Jewish world.

CONCLUSION

By 1957 the Jewish populations of France, England, the British Commonwealth, and Latin America totaled nearly a million and a half. None of these communities could compare, in influence on the matrix of Jewish civilization, with the powerhouses of Israel and the United States; neither, on the other hand, were they "worlds passed by" in the tragic category with the broken relics of Eastern Europe, or the debilitated survivals of Morocco and Tunisia. In the case of Anglo-Jewry, the gravest problem was a continuing attenuation of financial resources. England was the most heavily taxed democracy in the world, and the expense of maintaining a welfare state and a defense apparatus left few of its Jewish citizens with sufficient funds for the endowment of Chairs of Jewish Studies at universities, or for the erection of Jewish community centers or libraries in the principal areas of Jewish settlement. In the case of France, financial problems were compounded by psychological hazards; it was hard to build for a long-range future in a land where, within living memory, the product of virtually every collective enterprise had been ground to bits under the heels of an invading army. In South Africa and Latin America uncertain political circumstances, the growing menace of Boer racism in the former, the endemic Latin vulnerability to flamboyant strong men in the latter, cast a shadow—at times dark, at times virtually imperceptible—over every creative joint effort. Even in Canada, the rigid separatism between civilizations, which was so largely responsible for intensifying Jewish loyalties in the first place, accounted, too, in large measure, for a steadily mounting exodus of young Canadians to the United States.

Yet even these difficulties did not preclude significant opportunities for modified service. Anglo-Jewry each year trained increasing numbers of learned and eloquent diplomats for Israel's foreign ministry and its civil service. It seemed likely, in fact, that the most significant contribution out of England might well be in the direction charted by Weizmann, Harry Sacher, and Herbert Bentwich: the disciplined training in international affairs through England's great universities, which has been the chief asset of the Foreign Office and the diplomatic corps. In the Commonwealth South African Jewry served the Zionist cause in very much the same capacity, by providing Israel with an extraordinarily large proportion of trained diplomats, civil servants, lawyers, doctors, and scientists. Canadian Jewry's principal role has been that of a spiritual conscience for the Jews of the Western Hemisphere: infusing the organizational network of North American Jewish life with the love of religious tradition and the Messianic ardor which, in the United States, has been seriously weakened after the passing of the first generation of Russian-Jewish immigrants.

The future of the Jews of France and Latin America is less certain. As late as 1957 the most that could be hoped for in France was a revival of Jewish community cohesion as a direct consequence of the larger Franco-Israeli *rapprochement*. Latin-American Jewry may be described as a sleeping giant, awaiting more direct contact with Israel and the United States to be galvanized into life and fecundity. In an age of phenomenally improving communications, such contact is bound to come; and with it intellectual and cultural revival seems hardly less probable. In fact there is every reason to expect that the second half of the twentieth century may witness an emergent three-way partnership among the so-called "secondary" communities and Israel and the Jewish population of the United States. The pattern of Jewish history in Alexandria, Babylon, Spain, Germany, and Poland offers dramatic and compelling evidence of this likelihood.

XXIV

The Growth of the American-Jewish Community

GERMAN JEWRY MAINTAINS ITS DOMINATION

Within less than a decade after the massive Russian-Jewish immigration began, precipitated by the May Laws of 1881, America's nativized German Jews found themselves outnumbered by "greenhorns"; within two decades they were inundated altogether. The fact, however, that German Jews were transformed into a numerical minority did not mean that their influence in the American-Jewish community automatically declined. Far from it. The Germans had lived in the United States for several decades. They had integrated themselves into American life. Most of them had won a solid measure of economic security. It was precisely because tens of thousands of the new immigrants were dependent upon their predecessors for financial aid that a group of eminent German-Jewish merchant princes—Oscar and Nathan Straus, Julius Rosenwald, Jacob Schiff, Felix M. Warburg, Paul Baerwald—managed to maintain a firm grasp on the leadership of America's principal Jewish philanthropies. Moreover, until well into the twentieth century distinguished German-Jewish attorneys, such men as Mayer Sulzberger and Alfred M. Cohen, guided the destinies of Jewish cultural agencies and the religious and fraternal orders that had become quite common. It was to the credit of these influential German Jews that in virtually all instances they demonstrated the highest degree of good will and concern for their less fortunate Eastern brethren.

The ideal of *noblesse oblige* was most effectively implemented in February 1906, when sixty leading Jews of German descent gathered in New York to create a central communal organization. Similar attempts had foundered in the nineteenth century (see Chapter VIII); but now the Russian pogroms, the refusal of the czarist government to issue visas to American Jews, the problem of creating job opportunities for the immigrating millions of *Ostjuden*—all seemed to compel a renewed effort to create an effective representative body. Of course the prosperous and well-motivated

520

men who convened the meeting had their own ideas of what "representative" meant. They had no intention of creating an organization based on democratic elections; a mass franchise, after all, would inevitably return a number of Russian-Jewish delegates, and would perhaps result in the use of undisciplined and irresponsible mass pressures. The issue was clearly stated in a letter from Simon Wolf, Adolf Kraus, and others to Mayer Sulzberger, the chairman of the February conference:

> The danger must be clear to any unbiased observer of the situation that unless this proposed new corporation . . . be composed of the most conservative men, the standing of the Jews in the American nation will be seriously affected for the worse. With the machinery for election as outlined, the probabilities are that conservative elements . . . will be crowded to the rear, and the new organization will fall into the hands of radical theorists whose vagaries [i.e., socialism and Zionism] will then be accepted by the American nation as expressive of the views and intentions of the whole Jewish community.

The transparent antiliberalism of these men—Wolf, Kraus, and Sulzberger—must not be judged too harshly. Children of the "gilded age," they lived in a period when labor unions and radicalism were still synonymous terms, and "Americanism" meant the renunciation of Old World loyalties, cultural as well as political. What emerged from their proceedings, therefore, was an American Jewish Committee, dominated by a small group of wealthy German Jews, self-appointed, co-opting all new members, and dedicated to the quiet, discreet, intercessory approach of the *Shtadtlan*.

The Committee was unrepresentative, but its leadership was most effective in mobilizing the friendship and support of the American government on behalf of Jews in the United States and in Europe. For seventeen crucial years, from 1912 to 1929, the president was the soft-spoken and erudite Louis Marshall. A stocky little man with a small round face and Franz Schubert glasses, Marshall was the son of German-Jewish immigrants, and lived most of his life in Syracuse, New York. As a distinguished practicing attorney, and a member of the New York State legislature, he commanded the widest respect of Christians and Jews. During his tenure of office as president of the Committee, he demonstrated a highly developed talent for shrewd and tactful negotiation. In 1912, for example, after his eloquent and closely reasoned presentation, the Taft Administration rejected the extension of the Russo-American Trade Treaty, in protest against Russia's refusal to grant entry visas to American Jews. Six years later he won over the Wilson Administration to the support of Jewish minority rights in Eastern Europe. It was Marshall, too, who persuaded the gullible and uninformed industrialist, Henry Ford, to cease publication of the *Dearborn Independent,* and to repudiate its anti-Semitic editorials. These were achievements which gave Marshall extraordinary standing and prestige among his fellow Jews. Israel Zangwill once jestingly remarked that American Jewry lived under Marshall Law; someone else called Marshall, Louis XIX.

Yet, though Marshall was conservative by temperament and political belief, he was steadfast in his devotion to democratic principles. Both in his political and in his Jewish activity, he demonstrated an abiding concern for the plight of "little people." He went so far as to study the Yiddish language in order to understand the needs and aspirations of the Russian-Jewish immigrants; and in the last year of his life, 1929, he swallowed his anti-Zionist convictions in order to join the Jewish Agency for Palestine. Marshall's successor, the distinguished philologist Dr. Cyrus Adler, was a man of very much the same mold, meticulous in scholarship, widely ranged in his communal interests. At different times he was acting president of the Jewish Theological Seminary, and president of the Dropsie College for Hebrew and Cognate Learning, the American Jewish Historical Society, and the American Jewish Committee. Like Marshall, Adler, too, preferred the *Shtadtlan's* approach to the solution of Jewish problems: the well-groomed interview, the dignified letter, the restrained memorandum. He was convinced that the mass-action techniques of Eastern European Jews were neither in good taste nor ultimately effective.

Because these pillars of American Jewry were of German origin, their personal brand of religion, Reform Judaism—in all cases save that of Adler—remained as powerfully entrenched as the German Jews themselves in most of the major communities of the United States. As we recall, Reform Judaism served as citadel of respectable Americanism for the majority native-born Jews. It had been "modernized," "de-Orientalized" by the Pittsburgh Platform of 1885; the liturgy had been Anglicized and purged of all "legalisms." Both in 1897 and in 1917 the Central Conference of American Rabbis had sternly repudiated all manifestations of Jewish nationalism, and had insisted that Judaism's true genius was embodied exclusively in "Prophetic ethics." No longer painfully preoccupied with problems of doctrine and liturgy, the Reform Jew felt free, even obliged, to concern himself primarily with the general issues of social justice.

Thus Reform rabbis such as the beloved Henry Cohen of Galveston and the eloquent Stephen Wise of New York City were mainly effective and best known as champions of humanitarian causes. Wise, the son of Hungarian Jews, tall, handsome, with piercing eyes and a granite jaw, and a powerful oratorical style, used the pulpit of his Free Synagogue of New York as a sounding board for his controversial convictions on a wide range of social issues: labor legislation, the single tax, municipal reform, transit unification, pacifism, the repeal of Prohibition, the League of Nations. He was one of the decisive factors in driving the venal Mayor Jimmy Walker out of office and into hiding in Europe. Fiorello La Guardia once remarked of Wise that whenever he attacked a politician, steamship business to Europe improved immediately. Wise founded a theological seminary, the Jewish Institute of Religion, which trained its rabbinical students to transcend narrow denominationalism, and to accept, instead, their prophetic responsibilities as social reformers.

Anchored in financial security, enjoying the respectability of nativism, cultivating the friendship and support of leading political figures in American life, and represented in community activities by eloquent rabbis whose principal theology seemed to emphasize the importance of good citizenship, German Jews in the United States maintained their leadership until well into the twentieth century, long after they had become a minority within the American-Jewish community.

CONFUSION AND WEAKNESS IN THE IMMIGRANT COMMUNITY

When three million Russian Jews arrived in the United States between 1881 and 1924, they sought to create for themselves a cultural and religious framework which would preserve the cherished values of the world they had left behind. One of the first institutions the newcomers devised for this purpose was the purely secular *landsmannschaft,* a mutual insurance or burial society for the families who hailed from the same town or region in the Pale of Settlement. As late as 1908 these *landsmannschaften* still had an enrollment of approximately 125,000 immigrants. As the years passed, however, large-scale commercial insurance superseded the mutual benefit societies, and later the social legislation of the New Deal displaced the *landsmannschaften* altogether.

In the early years of settlement, the Yiddish press served the immigrants as an instrument of cultural stimulation, and flourished for several decades with a range and exuberance unequaled by the press of any other minority group in America. Similarly, the Yiddish stage provided the newcomers with a uniquely Jewish cultural outlet. New York's Second Avenue Yiddish Theater, for example, managed to present a wide variety of excellent plays, by such able literary figures as Sholem Asch, Perez Hirshbein, David Pinski, Ossip Dymov, Zalman Libin. Moreover, the Yiddish Theater developed its own stars: Boris Thomashefsky, Jacob and Stella Adler, David Kessler, Menashe Skulnik, Muni Weisenfreund (Paul Muni), Rudolf Schildkraut, Molly Picon, and Maurice Schwartz. But in the case of both the Yiddish press and the Yiddish stage, interest could be maintained only as long as the first generation of Yiddish-speaking newcomers remained numerically significant. In time, the first immigrants passed on, and there were few Jews among the second or third generations with quite the same nostalgia for the Yiddish genre. In 1945 the Second Avenue Yiddish Theater closed its doors for the last time; by 1952, the circulation of the Yiddish press had fallen to 37 per cent of its 1916 mark of half a million.

But it was Orthodox practice and belief that suffered the most extensive attrition. As late as 1942 there were well over a thousand Orthodox synagogues in New York City alone, far outnumbering the Reform congregations, in which few Russian Jews felt at ease. Yet these numbers in no way reflected authentic strength. The Orthodox rabbinate never found it possible to unite into a cohesive and authoritative national organization, as the Reform rabbinate had done. Even the most distinguished of Orthodox rabbis—Bernard Louis Levinthal of Philadelphia, Aaron Mordecai Ashinsky in Pittsburgh, Bernard David Abramovitz in St. Louis—

conducted services in synagogues that were hardly more than abandoned little stores or halls, and they depended almost entirely upon rabbinical perquisites for their income.

Contact with a virile and attractive civilization, far more attractive, certainly, than the civilizations of Poland and Russia, rapidly dissipated old religious loyalties. Life in the big city, too, was much freer from religious supervision than it had been in the little *shtetl* of the Pale. Indeed, the very speed with which Eastern European Jews abandoned all but nominal loyalty to Orthodox Judaism cast doubt upon the original genuineness of their personal piety; most of them probably were simply following the conventional mores of the society in which they lived.

The impact of American secularism was largely responsible, too, for the decline of religious observance among the second generation of Russian-Jewish immigrants. After the first World War organized religion in general suffered a perceptible diminution of strength in the United States. The churches were gradually abandoned for a variety of Sunday morning recreational activities. Agnosticism was common enough to go largely unnoticed. People who attended devotional services regularly did so more in response to social convention than out of religious conviction. In the case of immigrant Jewish children, Judaism brought reminders of the ugliness of the Old World. Alfred Kazin, an incisive literary critic, recalled in his autobiographical volume, *A Walker in the City:*

> Secretly, I thought the synagogue a mean place, and went only because I was expected to. Whenever I crossed the splinted and creaking porch into the stale air of snuff, of old men and old books, and saw the dusty gilt brocade on the prayer shawls, I felt I was being pulled into some mysterious and ancient clan that claimed me as its own simply because I had been born a block away. . . .

Gradually, for Kazin and his generation, the Sabbath, and all its religio-historical associations, ceased to exercise its former influence, and other religious practices were also discarded.

The effort to transplant the institutions of the Old World was perhaps least successful of all in the area of religious education. As a rule, the local schools established by German Jews met only once a week, on Sunday, and the amount of instruction they provided in Hebrew and Bible was quite minimal. When the Russian-Jewish immigrants sought to introduce the traditional daily school, they encountered frustrating resistance, for Jewish education was not obligatory as it had been in the Pale, while secular education in the American public school system was. Most Jewish children were able to give the *heder* only the fringe moments of their time; they much preferred to play stickball in the streets. The typical *melamed* sensed the hopelessness of his task in America. Again, Alfred Kazin recalled:

> For several months before my confirmation at thirteen, I appeared every Wednesday afternoon before a choleric old *melamed* . . . who would sit across the table eating peas, and with an incredulous scowl on his face

listen to me go over and over the necessary prayers and invocations, slapping me sharply on the hands whenever I stammered on a syllable. I had to learn my passages by heart, but never understood most of them, nor was I particularly expected to understand them; it was as if some contract in secret cipher had been drawn up between the Lord of Hosts and Gita Fayge's son Alfred which the *Amerikaner idiot,* as the *melamed* called me, could sign with an X. In the "old country" the *melamed* might possibly have encouraged me to understand the text, might even have discussed it with me. Here it was understood that I would go through the lessons simply for form's sake, because my mother wished to see me confirmed; the *melamed* expected nothing more of me.

The children of the immigrants were zealous in their determination to Americanize themselves as quickly as possible, and to reject those mores of their ethnic group which they associated with the Old World. This passion for Americanization was eloquently expressed in Mary Antin's *The Promised Land,* published in 1912. Written in a lyric, ecstatic vein, it described the rhapsody of the persecuted immigrant child from Polotzk who found in America the golden dream come true. But she added to her paean of praise to America a desire for divorce from her past:

> All the processes of uprooting, transportation, replanting, acclimatization, and development took place in my own soul. . . . I think I have thoroughly assimilated my past. . . . I have done its bidding. . . . I want now to be of today. It is painful to be conscious of two worlds. The Wandering Jew in me seeks forgetfulness.

It should be added that this compulsion to escape the stigma of foreignness was no less characteristic of the children of other immigrant groups, the Italians, Croats, Slavs, and others. With the severe curtailment of immigration, the memories of transatlantic antecedents began to fade as the activities of the ethnic group, as a result, appeared increasingly unintelligible and irrelevant to the children of the foreign-born. Jewish youngsters were well aware that countless famous American Jews had successfully moved outside the tight culture of the ancestral group and established themselves without reliance upon specifically Jewish traditions or qualities.

The melting-pot concept of American life was given further, and perhaps unwitting, encouragement by the German Jews who established Young Men's Hebrew Associations and Educational Alliances. They were resolved to help Americanize and humanize the immigrant groups. But the children of the newcomers needed little further encouragement to shed their immigrant inheritance; they were aware that this legacy brought with it not merely the stigma of foreignness, but also the stigma of membership in an unpopular race. "My dominant childhood memory," recalls the novelist Meyer Levin, in his autobiographical *In Search,* "is of fear and shame at being a Jew." The most common means of expressing this shame, according to the psychologist Kurt Lewin, was the avoidance of the company of other Jews. Another technique was to "let the children decide their religious loyalty for themselves." Yet another variety of self-consciousness, perhaps even of self-hatred, was demonstrated by Jewish philanthropists who contributed exclusively to non-Jewish causes. Less pathological, but most typical of all, was the swift adoption of non-Jewish names. During the 1920's and early 1930's Weinstein became Winston, Schoenberg became Belmont, Ginsberg became Gaines, Horwitz became Orwitt, and Cohen became Priest.

In a climate where group affiliation, religious education, and synagogue attendance were entirely voluntary matters, Orthodox Jews floundered hopelessly in search of solid cultural and religious expression. The impact of American secular life, the preoccupation with economic advancement, the opportunities offered by an attractive and friendly non-Jewish civilization, made it progressively inconvenient to maintain intact the full spectrum of Jewish traditions and observances.

AMERICAN SECULARISM REDIRECTS JEWISH CREATIVITY: THE RISE OF
AMERICAN-JEWISH PHILANTHROPY

Although large numbers of the newcomers and their children were unenthusiastic about participation in Jewish cultural and religious activities, many of them were equally unwilling to abandon their Jewish identification; they still possessed a hard core of ancestral loyalty. They strove, however, for a loyalty to be manifested in an abstract, secular, efficient, clean, indeed, in an "American" manner. Such manifestations might prove expensive; but the cost would be inconsequential if it helped to exorcise the guilt of flight from personal contact with the old way of life. Here were the roots of a unique form of philanthropy. Because America represented a pragmatic civilization in which the doer was more important than the thinker, the American Jew envisaged his contribution to the Jewish community in practical terms. In generosity and efficiency American Jewish philanthropy had no parallel.

In 1902 Russian Jews established the Hebrew Immigrant Aid Society to provide for the emergency needs of the East European greenhorns. They created settlement houses in Jewish neighborhoods to Americanize the newcomers and to combat the dangers of juvenile delinquency. As Russian Jewry began to share the philanthropic responsibility, the range of service widened: by 1950, in nearly every large city there were Jewish hospitals and clinics, an old folks' home, and agencies to assist the needy and the underprivileged—Jewish-managed institutions were most often models of efficiency and advanced social thinking. As early as 1895 the Jews of Boston combined their local charities into a federation of Jewish philanthropies, and the resultant advantage in curtailing expense and augmenting income stimulated other Jewish communities to follow Boston's example. By 1952 well over $100,000,000 was raised by such federations.

After the first World War, when the situation of European Jewry grew increasingly precarious, the emphasis in American-Jewish philanthropy shifted from local to overseas needs. News of the horrors in the Eastern war zone convinced Jewish leaders in America that only the most strenuous effort would bring relief. At first individual organizations, the Union of Orthodox Congregations, the American Jewish Relief Committee, the People's Relief Committee, raised funds independently of each other. In 1915, under pressure of the mounting crisis abroad, all groups subordinated their ideological differences, and joined forces in the American Jewish Joint Distribution Committee. It is doubtful if any philanthropic agency in history was ever more efficient in its operation or more far-reaching in its influence. During the first World War the Joint distributed some $15,000,000 in food, clothing, and medical supplies among the uprooted Jewish populations of Eastern Europe. When the war ended a group of Joint doctors, nurses, social workers, sanitation and economic experts, headed by Dr. Boris Bogen and Dr. Julius Goldman, accomplished near-miracles in reconstructing Jewish life in Poland and the Ukraine. As catastrophes followed each other in horrifying succession—Hitler, the new World War, the Nazi annihilation routine—the Joint was the strongest link with humanity, often the only remaining hope. It requested and received vastly increased sums of money: $350,000,000 between 1945 and 1954 alone. The money was used to feed, house, and relocate displaced persons and refugees from Europe and Arab lands. Many of these DP's were trained for new vocations by ORT, the Organization for Rehabilitation through Training, an agency closely associated with the Joint.

Meantime each community was called upon to support a variety of Palestine causes. The federation movement grew, for the resources in campaign leadership were ultimately as severely taxed as the resources in contributions. The United Jewish Appeal emerged in 1939 as a union of the Joint and the United Palestine Appeal and, in many communities, the campaign for local causes was also merged for one over-all annual effort in what was usually the Combined Jewish Appeal. Within the span of the decade following the second World War, the Combined Jewish Appeal raised and expended no less than a billion dollars. No other ethnic group in the United States even approached this level of giving or of organization.

It was in this way that philanthropy came to occupy a central position in American-Jewish community life. The folklore of its fund-raising achievements can hardly be communicated in terms of statistics. It involved an endless series of complicated human relationships, ranging from a phone call to a business acquaintance, asking for a contribution to a pet Jewish charity for friendship's sake, to a high-pressure emotional assault at a public banquet. It was virtually impossible to resist the appeals; and, in truth, few Jews really wanted to resist them. The funds, after all, were not raised for strangers but rather for families and friends still in Europe. Few Russian-Jewish immigrants remembered the families they had left behind without experiencing a sense of guilt. They wondered, from time to time, if they had not abandoned their dear ones; or if they were not remiss in their obligations by failing to contribute enough for those who had remained behind. The second generation recognized that, but for the accident of a father catching a boat, they, comfortable American Jews, would still be in Europe, living in the Valley of the Shadow. It was a self-consciousness peculiar to people whose immigrant origins were still recent, and whose traditions of charitable giving had been assiduously cultivated for centuries. Besides, philanthropy became the one common denominator of participation in Jewish life, requiring little time, even less understanding of Jewish lore or prayers, and no personal contact whatever with the recipients; it proved, at the same time, an excellent communal and social outlet for those who were active in campaigns. Philanthropy became one of the outstanding contributions of the American Jewish community. For all its materialistic emphasis on budgets and publicity, it was as uniquely American, and as providentially generous and timely, as the Marshall Plan.

RUSSIAN JEWS TAKE OVER: THE RISE OF COMMUNITY DEMOCRACY

The fusion and federation of a wide variety of philanthropic campaigns was one of the factors which enabled the Russian newcomers to share the privileges and responsibilities of leadership with nativized German Jews. While most of the individual communal institutions retained their autonomy, the broadened scope of their operations required that funds be solicited from every group. Immigrants and children of immigrants had now won strong economic positions. If they were to be approached for substantial contributions they could not very well be denied seats on boards; nor was it possible to ignore their wishes, in the determination of budget. Moreover, the impact of American democracy, which frequently opened the doors of Christian groups to German Jews, now induced German Jews, in turn, to open their circles to their Eastern European brethren. Later, when the children of the two groups went off to college, romance often broke down the remaining barriers, and intermarriage between all strains of immigration became increasingly common.

The first major breakthrough of the Russian-Jewish immigrant community took place during World War I, as the American Jewish Committee made preparations to represent both American and European Jewry at the postwar Peace Conference. For all their good will, the members of the Committee had little understanding of the aspirations and needs, both Zionist and Autonomist, of the Jews who lived in the Eastern War zone, and little comprehension of the degree to which Polish and Russian Jewry had been stirred by the Wilsonian doctrine of self-determination. Yet it was precisely these *Ostjuden* whose problems would have to be solved at the Peace Conference. Many of their friends and relatives in America had long been unhappy at the domination of the American Jewish Committee, and of German Jews in general (whom the immigrants called "the Grand Dukes," or simply "the *Deitcher*"). The issue of representation at the Peace Conference now gave them the opportunity to vent their grievances openly, and to complain frankly that the Committee was antidemocratic.

Under the leadership of Stephen Wise, who was not a Russian Jew, a campaign was inaugurated to elect an American Jewish Congress. Such an assembly, presumably, would represent the will of the entire Jewish community at the Peace Conference, and would endorse the programs of

Autonomism and Zionism. Wise enjoyed the support of the Yiddish press, and of virtually all the lay and religious leaders of Russian Jewry in the United States. In December of 1918, therefore, after an election in which no less than 133,000 men and women cast ballots, the American Jewish Congress officially convened in Philadelphia. An imposing colloquium of 400 delegates endorsed a program of national rights and Zionism for their coreligionists in Eastern Europe, and voted to send a delegation to Paris. The Committee, many of whose members grumbled at Wise's "Zionist steam-roller" tactics, had no choice but to agree to co-operate with the Congress, and to co-operate in a united front at the Peace Conference. Symbolic and actual co-operation brought some gratifying diplomatic results.

The Congress did not go out of existence after the fulfillment of its mission in Europe. Convinced that it had a mandate from the masses, it set itself up on a permanent basis as the democratic organ of American-Jewish life. While it was far from the monolithic, all-inclusive organization it claimed to be, it did speak for the large Zionist center of the American-Jewish community. Under the dynamic and eloquent leadership of Stephen Wise, who was the organization's president from 1924 to 1939, the Congress worked unremittingly to expose and combat anti-Semitism, and in support of Zionism; it endorsed, as well, a wide variety of liberal causes: public housing, the Fair Employment Practices Commission, the United Nations and UNESCO. Wise deliberately rejected the *Shtadtlan's* approach; he preferred to organize mass meetings and parades, public boycotts of German-made goods, large-scale letter-writing campaigns to promote liberal legislation. The Congress was especially effective in New York where the Assembly was sensitive to Jewish pressure. After the second World War it lost some of its momentum and a measure of its significance. Financial difficulty compelled the curtailment of program. Its prewar antifascist activities were now subjected to severe criticism from the ardent nationalists who controlled the Congressional investigating committees. Stephen Wise himself began to suffer from diminished vitality and the old electrifying power went out of his oratory. While his name was still the best known throughout the world and drew the most voluminous correspondence of any Jewish leader, the old man was tired, broken, and unable to fight the battles of the new world. He died in 1949. Moreover, there were other agencies that had become prominent since those early days, during the first World War, when Wise had hammered away at the "oligarchic" control of Jewish life. One of those agencies was B'nai B'rith, whose membership had grown to 85,000 by 1930. It was no longer a conventional fraternal order, having long since abandoned the mutual insurance and pseudo-Masonic ritualism that had characterized its origins; by the end of the nineteenth century its emphasis had shifted to public service. The Order now was beginning to reflect the preponderance of Eastern European participation. The last president of German origin, Alfred M. Cohen, completed his incumbency in 1939; his successors, Henry Monsky, Frank Goldman, and Philip Klutznick, were all sons of Russian-Jewish immigrants. It was Monsky, particularly, whose imagination and force of personality elevated the B'nai B'rith program far above its rather pedestrian nineteenth-century standards. He was an Omaha lawyer with a long and distinguished record in public life. When he became the first Jew of Russian descent to be elected to the presidency of B'nai B'rith, he served notice that he intended to "Judaize" the Order, to infuse it with the Messianic traditions of the Old World, and to correct the old imbalance which had weighted it with "pure" secularism. Monsky was the man for the task. While not a stentorian orator in the manner of Wise, he spoke with a crystalline simplicity and sincerity that appealed equally to the logic and emotions of his followers. As an administrator, Monsky's mind worked like a steel drill, cutting directly to the core of a problem, solving it with imagination and common sense. As a judge of men, Monsky was realistic to the point of cynicism; but he knew, too, how to inspire his colleagues to efforts that they would not have anticipated of themselves.

Under Monsky's leadership, America's largest and oldest Jewish service organization quadrupled its membership and moved forthrightly into central areas of Jewish activity. It was with his encouragement that two gifted Chicago communal leaders, Sigmund Livingston and Richard Gutstadt, were able to nurture the Order's Anti-Defamation League into a first-rate agency of public defense. ADL representatives ferreted out demagogues, and combated prejudice by issuing effective and carefully prepared posters, circulars, film strips, and pamphlets to schools and civic groups. B'nai B'rith provided vocational, educational, and recreational guidance for tens of thousands of Jewish teen-agers, through its Vocational Guidance Bureau and its Youth Organization. One of Monsky's most cherished projects was the Hillel Foundations. Founded originally in 1923 by Rabbi Benjamin Frankel, the Foundations were established on American college campuses to provide training for Jewish students in the meaningful values of the Jewish tradition. After Frankel's death in 1927 the leadership passed to Abram L. Sachar, a young historian at the University of Illinois, and in the next twenty years virtually every campus in the United States and Canada, with substantial Jewish enrollment, came into the Hillel orbit. The Order's emphasis upon culture and education and a continuing relationship with Israel remained after Monsky's death in 1947, and was noticeably intensified by Philip M. Klutznick, one of Monsky's successors as president. Klutznick, a brilliant lawyer who had proved his administrative skills while serving as the Federal Housing Commissioner during the second World War, broadened the scope of B'nai B'rith. Skillful in negotiation and buttressed by a powerful mass membership which now reached beyond 300,000, Klutznick brought B'nai B'rith more integrally into the field of international diplomacy, vis-à-vis Israel, the State Department, and the United Nations. His unusual abilities were drafted by the American government when he was named in 1957 as one of its representatives in the United Nations.

Meantime democratization had its inevitable effect on the "aristocratic" old American Jewish Committee. It changed slowly, but it changed. For many years its leadership was in the hands of a needle-witted, sharp-tongued veteran of legal and political wars, Judge Joseph M. Proskauer. During his long tenure as president until 1948, he still firmly rejected the mass-action techniques of the Congress and B'nai B'rith, and he remained opposed to Jewish national or international "superbodies" which threatened the autonomy and the freedom of action of individual groups and their diversified historic roots. But he softened considerably on the structure of the Committee; before his term was over the membership base was substantially broadened and it became an open organization, claiming representative character. The Committee's emphasis in the battles against discrimination shifted steadily from discreet intercession to incisive and scholarly research projects that explored the nature of anti-Semitism and group friction. Under his successors, Jacob Blaustein and Irving Engel, the trend was broadened. The Committee became a helpful buffer in blunting the disastrous impact on American public opinion of the more violent anti-Zionist groups. The change in the Committee was perhaps best reflected in the columns of its monthly literary journal, the ably edited *Commentary*. Its articles were generally friendly to Israel and they dealt sympathetically and without condescension with the East European flavor of American-Jewish life.

Despite all the organic changes in the major national agencies, the attempts to bring about more effective co-ordination were not successful. Costs had grown astronomically. Before 1933 the fraternal and defense organizations were spending an average of $100,000 annually on their programs. By 1950 the budgets had grown to six million. Duplication of activity, unseemly competition for support, the continuous denigration of the programs of others—these internecine quarrels troubled the more sensitive leaders of the American-Jewish community. Besides, the duplication was as expensive as it was confusing and distracting; when resources for relief were desperately needed the luxury of internal warfare was no longer defensible. Agreement was therefore reached in 1951 to explore areas of possible co-ordination.

Dr. Robert MacIver, a professor of sociology at Columbia University, was called in to analyze the structure of the American-Jewish community and to make recommendations for its improvement. In 1952, after a year's study, MacIver presented his Report. As anticipated, he urged a redistribution of functions among the B'nai B'rith Anti-Defamation League, the American Jewish Committee, the American Jewish Congress, the Jewish War Veterans, and other national agencies. In some instances he recommended that functions be merged to avoid waste or duplication; in other instances, he urged that projects be dropped. Yet, as MacIver himself recognized, the separate national agencies were not merely stubbornly defended vested interests; they reflected, as well, irreconcilable social and economic differences. The Committee still represented the wealthier and more conservative element of the Jewish population; the Congress drew its constituents primarily from the East European lower middle class; B'nai B'rith's membership was essentially an Americanized middle class. Each of these economic and cultural groups buttressed their pride of sponsorship with a historic ideological compulsion which could not be easily abandoned. After several national conclaves and many weeks of heated debates, the MacIver Report was rejected; and with its rejection the hope of organizational unity was again abandoned, at least for the time being.

Some of the more thoughtful students of Jewish life, while regretting its waste and duplication, were not altogether unhappy. The divisions, even the factiousness and the angry clamor, were not entirely an unhealthy phenomenon. In many ways the fragmentation and open disputes were a wholesome contrast to the autocratic *kahal* tradition of Eastern Europe and the tightly knit *Gemeinde* tradition of Germany; for, in the name of discipline, such traditions had too often stifled healthy Jewish self-expression. One of the hallmarks of American democracy was the multiplicity of its functions and organizations, its checks and balances, the diversity it permitted among its minorities. In a sense, the Jews were secure in the United States because there was so much freedom to protest, and, if need be, to go one's own way. The democratic process could be irritating and costly but, by contrast with the stultifying precedents of the past, perhaps it had its compensations.

THE RESURGENCE OF DEEPER JEWISH LOYALTIES

During the period of "second generation indifference," during the 1920's and early 1930's, there was little diminution in general community identification. Jews continued to marry primarily within their own group, to socialize primarily with their fellow Jews, to hold membership in a synagogue or temple, in a B'nai B'rith lodge or a local YMHA. Meantime there was a steady rise of East Europen Jews to leadership and this shift in the fulcrum accounted for a new dynamism in the third generation. Their minimal activity was usually more affirmatively Jewish than the maximal commitments of their predecessors. The dynamism was affected by, and in turn effected, major changes in the techniques of Jewish education. In 1910 Dr. Samson Benderly founded the Bureau of Jewish Education in New York; in succeeding decades similar bureaus were organized in most of the country's major communities. Directed nationally by the American Association for Jewish Education, under the dedicated guidance of Israel Chipkin, Alexander Dushkin, Emanuel Gamoran, and others, these bureaus instituted modern teachers' training colleges and equally modern religious and Sunday schools. The texts they prepared were, as a rule, colorful and absorbing; the teachers whom they trained infinitely better equipped for more challenging service. By 1956 over 400,000 Jewish children were attending schools supervised and staffed by these bureaus. On the college level, too, the B'nai B'rith Hillel Foundations made an equally notable contribution: the Foundation directors, most of them trained rabbis and scholars, taught courses and seminars which, in many universities, were attended by an impressive minority of Jewish students. By the 1950's, in fact, the leadership in Jewish communal life was being assumed increasingly by Hillel graduates. The problem of Jewish education was far from solved, even as late as mid-century; but the improvement was marked.

In the very depth of second-generation indifference there were indications, too, of a reawakening of Jewish loyalties among the intellectuals. For one thing, the upsurge of nativist anti-Semitism after the first World War convinced many perceptive Jews that divorce from the Jewish past was not quite as simple a matter as it had first appeared. For another, the influential American philosopher William James, together with his Jewish disciple Horace Kallen, evaluated the melting-pot concept more critically. America, they suggested, ought rather to be viewed as an orchestra of diverse cultures, each of which might appropriately preserve its uniqueness in order to give tonal quality to the total harmony. "Cultural pluralism" was the term James and Kallen applied to this concept, and it appealed to a number of gifted writers.

One of those was Ludwig Lewisohn. In the immediate postwar period he had attained a rather wide reputation as a novelist and literary critic. During his lifetime, in fact, he was the author of more than thirty volumes of criticism, fiction, and philosophic exposition. As a teacher at Wisconsin and Ohio State Universities, and later as Professor of Comparative Literature at Brandeis University, this stocky little man, with his domelike forehead, inevitable pince-nez, and splenetic temper, proved to be one of the country's most penetrating commentators on the literary scene. Lewisohn's impact on the American-Jewish community began with his autobiographical novel *Upstream,* written in 1922. It represented a kind of watershed in his own life, for until he wrote it he had been a self-confessed "cosmopolite," or, in more realistic terms, an assimilationist. *Upstream* traced his odyssey of assimilation as a German Jew in the South, and then later his progressive awakening to the treasures of the Jewish heritage. The ideal of cultural pluralism loomed increasingly larger in Lewisohn's mind, until he decided at last that it was impossible to fulfill his destiny as an American without identifying himself wholeheartedly and unequivocally with the Jewish community. "The friend of the Republic," he wrote, "the lover of those values which alone make life endurable, must bid the German and the Jew, the Latin and the Slav, preserve his cultural tradition and beware of the encroachments of Neo-Puritan barbarism; beware of becoming merely another dweller on an endless 'Main Street.'" Lewisohn embellished this theme in many subsequent novels and articles. Indeed, he clung to it with such single-minded tenacity that ultimately he repudiated the liberal "illusion" altogether. It was an indiscriminate repudiation, manifesting itself in Lewisohn's frequently articulated contempt for the German, the Slav, the American Negro, for the barbarism of the Anglo-Saxon. Near the end of his life he became a devout Fundamentalist, rejecting the theory of evolution on the one hand, and the public secular school system on the other.

Lewisohn veered off to the extreme of narrow ethnic chauvinism; but his writings nevertheless helped to rectify the imbalance of assimilation. So, too, did the writings of a number of Lewisohn's contemporaries—Irving Fineman, Charles Reznikoff, and Charles Angoff. These men wrote beautifully and sensitively of the Jewish heritage, and effectively counteracted the irresponsible caricature of the Jew produced by such novelists as Jerome Weidman,

Ben Hecht, and Budd Schulberg. Meyer Levin, Irwin Shaw, Myron Brinig, Herman Wouk, Delmore Schwartz, Norman Katkov, Leslie Fiedler, and others, most of whom represented a younger generation than Lewisohn's, worked more sympathetically with their materials, and they found enrichment and inspiration in the reservoir of Jewish folklore and folk mores. Even more significant, perhaps, than their artistry was their willingness to eschew the old chestnut of anti-Semitism, and their ability to deal with a Jewish theme naturally and affirmatively. During the 1920's and 1930's many of these writers had revolted against the provincial Jewish middle class, as Heine, for example, had revolted in the 1820's; but they learned from the horrors of totalitarianism that there were many things worse than provincial middle-class morality, Jewish or Christian. Some of these novelists to be sure, still evidenced a trace of the old ambivalence and raised the question of whether their resurgent Jewishness was merely a guilt reaction to an earlier escape into humanity at large. "Does the logic of it," asked Meyer Levin, "lead back to the prayer shawl and phylacteries?" Perhaps another generation of introspection and experimentation would have to pass before a reasonable equilibrium could be found between flight and chauvinism.

Unquestionably, too, one of the factors responsible for this forthrightness of Jewish identification was the rise and heroic establishment of the State of Israel. The impact of Zionism upon Jewish education in America was particularly noteworthy: for Zionists constituted the rank and file of Hebrew teachers, the directors of the bureaus of Jewish education, the principals of the Jewish schools. Most of the scholars in the Jewish field were Zionist or emerged from Zionist backgrounds. Zionism infused Reform Judaism with new warmth and ceremonial, while its influence on Conservatism and Reconstructionism was even more striking. Zionism was, in fact, the principal morale builder of American Jewry after the revelations of the death camps. It profoundly affected the college generation, for romantic nationalism exercised a natural appeal to young people during the impressionable years of their postadolescence. The timidity and self-consciousness with which students had viewed their Jewishness only a generation earlier dissipated rapidly in the age of Israeli courage and creativity. Jewish college youth saw in Israel proof that Jewish civilization was not a matter for old people in "musty synagogues." Rather, it was a virile, throbbing civilization, and it became a catalyst for the loyalty of vigorous, action-minded young people.

In the result, the third generation was literally worlds away from its unhappy, ill-adjusted, assimilated parents. For the older group Jewishness had been synonymous with the ghetto, the pushcart, the thick foreign accent, although this was hardly less true of the children of other immigrant groups. All this was now changed. Marcus Hanson, the leading historian of American immigration, put it well when he suggested that "what the son wishes to forget the grandson wishes to remember." The third generation of Jews had little reason to feel inferior: they were American-born and comparatively prosperous; their parents, too, were for the most part English-speaking and integrated into American life. Few of these grandchildren experienced a sense of alienation. If anything, they were rather curious about the folk mores and quaint old customs of their grandparents. Many of them felt the need of roots, and a sense of origin, if only because respectability had become a cherished value in American life. While the need for respectability had frequently led to a deliberate rejection of Jewish religious and cultural values a generation earlier, most Americans, the fate of German Jewry yet fresh in their minds, recognized that assimilation was not the answer. One's origins, whatever they were, would have to be re-examined and, if possible, invested with respectability. And this was exactly what many thousands of third-generation American Jews set about to do.

Because the third generation—whether of Jews, Irish, Italians, or Croats —could no longer, and would no longer, foist otherworldly ways and dialects upon themselves, they concentrated their attention upon the old family religion. Inasmuch as the tie to religion had never been completely broken, it was to religion that many third-generation Jews (not all of them—nor even a majority) began to turn in order to define their place in American society. In this way they found it possible to sustain their Americanism and yet confirm the relationship which bound them to the forebears whom they no longer wished to reject; whom, indeed, for the sake of a heritage or, in the case of America, for the sake of a "brand" name, they now wished to remember. Perhaps in the days of metropolitan ghettos, Judaism was an entity to be absorbed passively, by osmosis. But the genteel suburbs in which increasing numbers of third-generation Jews lived were hardly Jewish "oceans"; at least 50 per cent of their neighbors were likely to be Christians. Judaism had to be cultivated actively if it were to survive, especially if it were to have any meaning for children growing up, once more, as members of a minority.

VARIETIES OF RELIGIOUS EXPRESSION IN AMERICA

Thus it was that the synagogue began to resume much of its old centrality in communal life. In 1950 there were over four thousand congregations in the United States, embracing approximately 70 per cent of the Jewish families. Clearly, the majority of those who affiliated with synagogues were not yet devout believers; at the most they were vaguely religious-minded. Most Americans, after all, were pragmatists; they had little patience with ideologies, and preferred to stay close to the ground of common sense. American Jews, too, found it difficult to sustain the burning Messianism of the Pale of Settlement or the inflexible ideological consistency of Germany; like their American neighbors, they preferred to live "as if" their faith were already proved. As a result, American churches and synagogues were usually short on metaphysics and long on all forms of social service. They dealt with religion not as a static body of dogmas, but as the upward surge of the human personality in all its fullness.

Of the various religious groupings within American Judaism, Orthodoxy, once numerically the strongest, if financially the weakest, was now eroding rapidly, even in terms of numbers. At mid-century the majority of Orthodox congregations found it difficult to hold their adherents; and they possessed virtually none of the ancillary groups, the brotherhoods and sisterhoods, the social functions and social-service programs, of their Reform and Conservative counterparts. There were occasional revivals of Orthodox activity following the second World War, especially in the Williamsburg section of Brooklyn where some of the Hasidic survivors of Polish Jewry created enclaves of followers. With the possible exception of Ludwig Lewisohn, however, whose Orthodoxy was rather more of a protest against the failure of "modernism" than an affirmative ideology, Orthodox Judaism found few authoritative spokesmen. These included Rabbis Joseph Baer Soloveitchik, Joseph Lookstein, Leo Jung, and other faculty members of Yeshiva University. These were brilliant and persuasive interpreters and they wrote and taught with considerable inner consistency. They tried strenuously to project and sustain their teachings by developing several all-day schools in New York and other large cities. Yet the influence of Soloveitchik, Lookstein, Jung, and these schools notwithstanding, Orthodoxy continued to lose ground, its adherents a minority even within the diminishing segment which was not native-born.

Conservatism was the most recent major alignment on the American-Jewish religious scene. We recall that even before the influx of Eastern European Jews, the disciples of Isaac Leeser, recoiling in horror from the "heresy" of Reform Judaism, sought to create a Jewish Theological Seminary which would train rabbis in the Orthodox tradition. The effort did not meet with success until 1902, when a group of sensitive and broad-spirited German Jews decided to assist the Russian-Jewish immigrants to achieve their own synthesis of traditionalism and modernism. They invited Solomon Schechter, a distinguished Anglo-Jewish scholar, to come to America, to reorganize the Jewish Theological Seminary, and to build around it an association of traditional synagogues that would minister to the needs of the immigrants. Schechter was ideally suited to this role. He had established his reputation in the academic and theological world with his discovery of the vital apocryphal Book of Ecclesiasticus, and with his felicitously written *Studies in Judaism*. As a critic of Orthodoxy he paid his due to higher Biblical criticism; but as a Conservative he believed that the folklore in Judaism was not to be crowded out by theology. Like Zacharias Frankel in the nineteenth century, Schechter's concept of "Catholic Israel" took into account the totality of Jewish peoplehood, the importance of ritual and ceremonial in maintaining the cumulative organic traditions of Jewish life.

It was Schechter's eloquence in formulating his viewpoint, together with his unique ability to excite the enthusiasm and support of Jewish laymen, that enabled him to transform the Jewish Theological Seminary into a respected citadel of Conservatism. His winning personality, an impressive patriarchal appearance, a kindly, generous interest in his faculty and students, won him a loyalty which bordered on reverence. Not the least of his achievements was the caliber of faculty he was able to assemble. It included such men as Louis Finkelstein, Louis Ginzberg, Mordecai Kaplan, and Saul Liberman. Ginzberg, indeed, was one of the monumental Jewish intellects of the twentieth century. Born in Lithuania, thoroughly grounded there in Talmudical literature, he pursued his graduate studies in history and philosophy at the University of Heidelberg where he received his doctorate. In 1901 the Jewish Theological Seminary appointed him as Professor of Talmud and Rabbinics. It was during his incumbency at the Seminary that Ginzberg wrote his encyclopedic studies on rabbinic literature, and established his reputation as the foremost rabbinic interpreter in modern times. His most celebrated works were his seven-volume *Legends of the Jews* and his *Commentary on the Talmud of Jerusalem*. His scholarship was in every way as thorough as that of Zunz and Steinschneider, and even more modern in approach, in its understanding of sociological and economic forces, and in its imaginative use of Oriental and European folklore. At the time of his death, in 1953, few tributes failed to identify him as the most original and erudite Jewish scholar of his time.

Ginzberg's outstanding pupil, Louis Finkelstein, who became president of the Seminary in 1940, carried on the scholarly tradition of his mentor. *The Pharisees* was an original re-evaluation of the ancient Biblical interpreters as "constitutional liberals" rather than as hairsplitting legalists; his *Jewish Self-Government in the Middle Ages* illuminated some of the darkest yet most significant corners of medieval Jewish life. Schechter, Ginzberg, Finkelstein, and their colleagues became the definitive spokesmen for Conservative Judaism, while their students, the graduates of the Jewish Theological Seminary, became its active ambassadors. The Conservative movement came to encompass some four hundred and fifty rabbis (the Rabbinical Assembly of America), and five hundred synagogues (the United Synagogue Council). Schechter's concept of "Catholic Israel" provided the rationale for this organizational network. In his "Essay on Abraham Geiger" (in *Studies in Judaism,* III), he stated:

> In other words, is it not time that theology should consist in the best that all men of Israel, including Geiger, gave us, but should modify and qualify his views, dating from a rationalist age, by the loyalty to the law of Rabbi Akiba Eger and Rabbi Mordecai Baneth, by the deep insight into Jewish history of a Zunz and a Krochmal, by the mysticism of a Ba'al Shem and some of his best followers, and by the love for Israel's nationality and its perpetuation of Herzl and Ahad Ha'am?

Most of the constituents of Conservatism came from the ranks of the Orthodox, and it is doubtful if they appreciated the minutiae of Schechter's philosophy; many of the names he mentioned were probably unknown to them. But Conservatism, with its emphasis upon ritual, ceremonial, and the Hebrew language, and its simultaneous rejection of the archaisms of Orthodoxy, appealed to them as an acceptable compromise between the needs of the New World and the sentimental nostalgia for the Old.

The organic-historical framework of Conservatism also offered hospitality to some of the most vital new departures in Jewish religious philosophy. Martin Buber's neo-Mysticism found its most persuasive American exponent in the Conservative rabbi, Abraham Heschel. In a series of penetrating, gracefully written volumes, Heschel restated the idea of a partnership between Man and God. To Heschel, as to Buber, piety was not a reasoned attitude, but a "response" to a divine call. By transforming neo-Mysticism into a living experience, a communicable mood, Heschel and his followers sought to create within Conservatism a more effective brake upon the modernization of ritual. At the same time Franz Rosenzweig's Existentialism was interpreted for Americans by the distinguished historian Nahum Glatzer, who wrote with rare lucidity of the "leap of faith" by which finite and limited man could bridge the gap between himself and God, could finally come face to face with God. Once he made the leap he would find that he could not have done otherwise, that God had willed it thus to convince man of the divinity of the universe and of his own being.

The extraordinary growth of Conservative Judaism could not be attributed solely to the theological synthesis it provided for Eastern European Jewry, nor to the hospitality which it offered to the provocative doctrines of neo-Mysticism and Existentialism. Its wholehearted absorption of Zionism also fed its strength and popularity. Reform was late in coming to terms with Zionism. Conservatism raced to meet it when it was little more than a dream. The warmth and beauty of many Conservative services, incorporating Israeli themes in music and poetry, exercised a very real fascination for the impressionable younger generation. It was perhaps because of the romantic-Zionist tinge of the Conservative liturgy that the most sizable number of recruits to the movement no longer came from the older group, but from the American-oriented generation.

These influences—historical, mystical, romantic—had their effect, as well, on Reform Judaism. Indeed, the protagonists of the Reform movement came to recognize that the arid rationalism of the Pittsburgh Platform of 1885 would have to be radically revamped if Reform were to meet contemporary emotional and intellectual problems. The fact, too, that a growing number of Reform rabbis were the children of Russian-Jewish immigrants encouraged the Central Conference of American Rabbis to re-evaluate its theological position. In 1937 this group met in Columbus, Ohio, to approve a new set of guiding principles formulated by Rabbis Samuel Cohon and Felix Levy. The Columbus Platform identified Palestine "not only as a haven of refuge for the oppressed but also [as] a center of Jewish culture and spiritual life." Similarly, the Platform encouraged the restoration of a greater measure of ritual and ceremonial to the Reform service. Judaism, suggested Samuel Cohon, was less an ideological essence than "the growing spiritual experience of a people." Reform too was prepared at last to accept as central to its theology the concept of organic Jewish peoplehood.

By mid-century the change in Reform's orientation was quite apparent: services were conducted on Friday evenings and Saturday mornings rather than on Sunday mornings; the *bar mitzvah* was nearly as common as confirmation. Fasting became the norm again on the Day of Atonement.

In some temples, prayer shawls were reintroduced. The trend in Reform was noticeably toward the reacceptance of ceremonial observances. "The early builders of our Movement," frankly confessed the Ritual-Survey Committee of the Central Conference of American Rabbis in 1950, "failed to recognize that man cannot live by reason alone, that he needs to satisfy his emotional hunger for the poetry and beauty, for the mysticism and drama, that are to be found in meaningful symbolism and ceremonialism." Because Reform set itself to meet such needs, its congregations multiplied almost as quickly as those within the Conservative group. By mid-century Conservatism and Reform were virtually equal in numbers of congregations and constituents; spurred on by competition, each group continued to vie strenuously for the emergent religious loyalty of American Jewry.

A description of the varieties of religious experience in American Jewish life is not complete without reference to Reconstructionism, whose principal exponent was Mordecai Kaplan, an Orthodox New York rabbi. In a series of learned and tightly reasoned books, primarily *Judaism as a Civilization* (1934), and in a biweekly publication, *The Reconstructionist,* Kaplan expounded his concept and program. His basic thinking drew liberally from the French-Jewish sociologist Emile Durkheim. Durkheim's group theory, as adapted by Kaplan, suggested that an awareness of God came primarily to those people who possessed a strong group consciousness. Inasmuch as Judaism began as the folk religion of the Jewish people, it could best be revitalized through an intensification of Jewish national consciousness. In every phase of its organized life, Kaplan insisted, the American-Jewish community ought to emphasize its character as an ethnic cultural group, as an enduring and creative people. It was necessary to call in the resources of art, folk music, the dance, and literature, and not rely entirely upon formal religious observance. The civilization of Judaism could best be expressed, in all its facets, if community life were reconstructed along organic lines: that is to say, if the crazy-quilt jumble of Jewish organizations were combined again in an all-inclusive community organization, a kind of synagogue-community-center-school.

If Kaplan had simply adapted the sociological theory of a rather dull European theorist, Reconstructionism would not have made much of an impact. But he drew vitality for it from the basic pragmatism which characterized American life and thought. In an effort to check the decline in church membership, many religious leaders were widening the orbit of church activity to include social and recreational programs. Some churches provided their members with psychiatric assistance; others conducted classes in subjects ranging from the dance to the manual arts. Kaplan, as rabbi of *Kehillath Jeshurun* congregation in New York, had been applying this "organic" concept pragmatically long before he translated it into a systematic philosophy.

In 1908 he joined to the strictly ritualistic functions of his synagogue a wide variety of social and recreational activities. The house of worship was restored to its historic position as the focal point for the social and educational life of the community. The response of Kaplan's congregants was enthusiastic; membership became more than perfunctory identification, and young and old flocked to the synagogue for activities which now had considerable attractive relevance. Other synagogues began to emulate Kaplan's example, an example no longer unusual in the American churches. This organic approach to Jewish life, it should be noted, also encouraged the widespread growth of Jewish Community Centers. Offering an even broader program of educational, cultural, and communal activities than the synagogues, the Centers, by 1953, drew in a membership of more than half a million.

Few of the community leaders who built the Centers, few of the rabbis who transformed their synagogues into organic microcosms of Jewish life, considered themselves Reconstructionists. Most of them, in fact, were still suspicious of Kaplan's de-emphasis of religion. But while they were uneasy in the ponderousness of his theology, they did not hesitate to implement the attractiveness of his sociology. Kaplan himself, for that matter, did not innovate as much as he intellectualized an unfolding communal phenomenon in Jewish life. Optimistic and practical, most of them paid little heed to any of their philosophers—their Soloveitchiks, Cohons, Heschels, or Kaplans—except as these men proved that Judaism could fit into the framework of modern life. For as long as Judaism still had relevance, it could be accepted, manipulated, adapted, merged with other interests, as evidence of the basic vigor and creativity of the American-Jewish community.

CONCLUSION

In many ways Jewish life in America bore a close resemblance to Jewish life in Europe. Jews still associated primarily with other Jews, even in the leisure-time activities that had no specific Jewish cultural content. This social clannishness, however, was not synonymous with ethnocentrism, or ethnic self-absorption. The Jews participated fully and actively in the political, economic, and cultural life of America. Perhaps, if the choice were theirs, Jewish social life would also have been more all-inclusive. But, as one young suburbanite put it: "Our daytime friends are Gentile; but our afterday friends are Jewish."

There were other ways, however, in which American Jews departed significantly from their European inheritance. They were rarely pious; impatient with principles and concepts they concentrated on more elementary group satisfactions. They were criticized by newcomers, and by some acerbic native critics, for being shallow, materialistic, secular, nonintellectual. This was the criticism that was leveled at America itself by many Europeans and some of it was not without validity.

But the secularism and the pragmatism of American Jews had their affirmative side, as well. The superb philanthropic instrument which they produced was surely as effective as the cultural tradition in salvaging European Jewry and in sustaining the State of Israel. Under the impact of American democracy, moreover, the apparatus of Jewish community life was democratized far beyond the traditions of the disciplined, antiliberal Russian-Jewish *ḳahal* or the German-Jewish *Gemeinde*. Cultural pluralism, too, was practiced by American Jews in a much healthier way than it had been practiced by Jews in Western Europe, where assimilation had dissipated the reserves of Jewish civilization; and in a healthier way than in Eastern Europe, where, through no fault of their own, Jews had lived hermetically, with little concern for, or faith in, the Slavic world about them.

From the vantage point of 1957, the American Jewish community was sound and wholesome. It was protected by the American tradition of egalitarianism; it was solidly anchored in American prosperity, which was hardly less of a tradition. Above all, it was continuously strengthened by close and intimate ties with the State of Israel. The doughty and courageous little state was more than a source of pride to American Jews, more even than a source of status and self-respect. It was also an inspiration for uninhibited Jewish identification, for increased interest in Jewish history and folklore, for creativity in Jewish literature, music, and art. For the first time in many years, children were learning Hebrew as a living language rather than as a burdensome inheritance from antiquity. College youth in increasing numbers were visiting Israel, attending its university, working on its farms. There was little likelihood that many of them would remain; but there was a great likelihood that many of them would bring the Israeli spirit back with them. It was a spirit of complete, unselfconscious, thoroughly affirmative Jewishness. Without this spirit Jewish life in America with all its wealth, security, community democracy, and pragmatic realism, would hardly signify more than the dissipation of an unprecedented opportunity for corporate self-expression. With this spirit, the American-Jewish community bade fair to create a civilization of such enduring vitality as to pre-empt from medieval Spain the title of "Golden Age."

XXV

The State of Israel

The war for liberation had been a costly one. Six thousand Jews had fallen. Much of the land was laid waste. The crucial orange crop had been destroyed. The actual fighting had ended, but the tasks which followed were sufficiently staggering to challenge the courage and ingenuity which had been so proudly vindicated by the war itself. It was necessary now to create a workable State with an effective apparatus of government and a sound economy out of the confusions of the calculated abruptness of the British withdrawal and out of the chaos of war. The problem of viability was rendered more difficult by the unique philosophy of "ingathering the exiles" to which the little republic was committed. Hundreds of thousands of newcomers had somehow to be absorbed into the economy and society of Israel. All who were in jeopardy anywhere in the world were welcome and thoughts of absorptive capacity and of stability were completely subordinated. Fortunately, the citizens of the State were not aborigines; they were Jews. They were endowed not merely with a desperate will to live, and a burning zeal to create for themselves one ultimate, secure refuge on earth. They were endowed, too, with a rich native intelligence, and with skills acquired from the many civilizations of the Diaspora.

After successfully shepherding Israel through the crisis of warfare for nine months, the Provisional Council of State, in January 1949, turned over the responsibilities of government to a nationally elected Knesset, or Parliament, of one hundred and twenty men and women. The Knesset incorporated both Anglo-Saxon and Continental legislative techniques: bills went through three readings (British style), and were studied by one of nine committees (French style). In practice the initiative in legislation was left to the Administration; but the right of review and amendment, as well as of rejection, was jealously guarded by the Knesset. For a while the Administration considered the idea of formulating a written constitution as Israel's Organic Law. The idea was never altogether abandoned; but Ben-Gurion and the Mapai party decided to move slowly, and to allow a fundamental law to develop out of the peculiar and special requirements of the land and the time. Meantime, the government still operated according to the principles of the basic code taken over from the Mandatary. The intention seemed to be to do as the British did, "muddling through" on each issue as it arose, instead of imposing a neat but confining constitution on a rapidly expanding society.

Anglo-Saxon law remained the frame of reference (with occasional reference to Turkish and Arabic law) for the regulation of domestic problems—corporation and commercial matters, civil and criminal procedure, equity, bills of exchange, bankruptcy, torts, probate. Israeli judges and attorneys, speaking in Hebrew, continued to quote from English and American law reports and English textbooks. In 1953, however, a project was established at Harvard University through which the complexities and diverse origins of Israeli law were to be resolved into a more consistent law code. The Israeli Minister of Justice sent over the corpus juris his country had inherited from the Mandatary, and the staff at Harvard, using the resources of its library and the counsel of experts in each field, made suggestions for amendment and improvement. The drafts went back to Israel, to be adapted by the Ministry of Justice and the Knesset. In 1956 the project was joined by Brandeis University, which underwrote its financial requirements. When the task is completed, it is expected that Israel will possess a modern, efficient legal system, a model for many new states.

It was in the area of public administration that the experience of the Yishuv's quasi government proved invaluable. The new ministries of government were direct transformations of the bureaus of previously existing institutions. The Political Department of the Jewish Agency became the Foreign Ministry; the Social Welfare Department of the National Assembly became the Ministry of Social Welfare; the Haganah became the Israeli army. When the sovereignty of Israel was proclaimed, many officials simply moved their files from the Jewish Agency, the Histadrut, the Anglo-Palestine Bank, and other institutions, to their new desks. In some instances there was overlapping. For example, the Jewish Agency still shared with the government the responsibilities of immigration and housing, even as the Histadrut shared the responsibilities of public health and municipal transportation. Administrative overlapping was complicated by the *pakid*, the civil servant, who traditionally obtained his job, as in nearly every country, through party patronage, and who moved with agonizing deliberation through the maze of bureaucratic red tape. The structure of Israeli politics did not help to simplify the problems of government. The political system traced back to the days of the Jewish quasi government under the Mandate, when parties competed for control of the National Assembly and had their counterparts outside the Yishuv in the World Zionist Organization. Unlike political parties in America those of the Yishuv and Israel were rigid and doctrinaire in their approach. Indeed, Israeli citizens rarely voted for men; they vere pledged to strictly defined party lists. Most of the voters had migrated from Central and Eastern Europe and they brought with them their familiar political practices.

As in the days of the Mandate, Israel's dominant party was the Mapai which, led by Ben-Gurion, derived its strength from the agricultural and industrial workers, and was intimately linked with the all-embracing Federation of Labor, the Histadrut. Over the years, the Labor party had become cautiously Social-Democratic. On the counsel of Berl Katznelson, the party's founder, it rejected strict Marxism, envisaged co-operation between labor and capital, and favored a measure of private enterprise in a controlled economy. Much more doctrinaire was the Mapam party, an offshoot of Mapai. It was established in 1949 out of Hashomer Hatzair and the Poale Zion, the two groups whose original fusion, in 1930, had created the Mapai. Led by Dr. Moshe Sneh, a disciple of the late Ber Borochow, Mapam remained adamantly Marxist and advocated cordial co-operation with the Soviet Union. In fact, except on issues that concerned Israel directly or the fate of the Jews behind the iron curtain, Mapam swallowed the Communist line in its entirety.

One of the oldest political organizations in Palestine was the General Zionist party. Its members had come primarily from Central Europe and were bourgeois in economic outlook; thus they favored an essentially capitalist economy for Israel. The Progressive party, an offshoot of the General Zionists, advocated closer co-operation with organized labor, but remained essentially welfare capitalist in orientation. Herut was created in 1948 by Menahem Begin out of the old Revisionist party, the activist arm of which had been the outlawed Irgun. It was strongly rightist, demanding firm guarantees for private property rights, and a frankly irredentist policy to restore Trans-Jordan to the Jews. There existed, in addition, several political groups—the Mizrachi, the Labor Ha-Poel Ha-Mizrachi, and the Agudat Yisrael—that were determined to structure the new State in accordance with the religious precepts of Judaism. This "Religious Bloc" sought to legislate Jewish Orthodox practice into Israeli law, and to make such practice the basis for all civil and criminal statutes.

Out of the congeries of political groupings, Mapai consistently remained the strongest single party in Israel. Next in order of strength were the Herut and Mapam (the former pulling ahead of the latter in the late 1950's), the General Zionists, and, lastly, the Religious Bloc. No party, however, was strong enough to govern on its own. The continual jockeying for position to create workable political coalitions was one of the unhappiest inheritances of the European experience. It reflected, too, the insecurities of a small people surrounded by hostile neighbors, and burdened with grave economic problems.

THE GATES ARE OPENED: THE JEWS IN COMMUNIST AND ARAB LANDS

One of the first acts of the State of Israel when it came into existence on May 14, 1948, was to fling open its gates to all Jews who sought entry.

As a result, the country's population, 650,000 in 1949, doubled within three years and tripled within nine years. At one point, between 1949 and 1951, refugees were coming in at the rate of between 18,000 and 30,000 a month. The displaced persons camps of Europe were emptied; and then a deadline for Polish emigration, set by Polish authorities, had to be met. Suddenly Romania decided to permit mass departures; then an Arab land here, and another there, and so it went. This unrestricted, undiscriminating welcome was extended in defiance of every known law of economic absorptive capacity. It was explained partly by Israel's desperate need for military manpower. But even more compelling was the Zionist concept of Israel as a homeland for physically and spiritually insecure Jews everywhere. And for years after the fall of Hitler there were still Jews, hundreds of thousands of them, who lived in the most oppressive kind of bondage.

In Russia some 1,800,000 Jews remained alive after the defeat of the Axis. Together with half a million other Jews trapped behind the iron curtain, 60,000 in Czechoslovakia, 300,000 in Romania, and 150,000 in Hungary, they were a miserable and terrified lot. In 1949, the problem of economic marginalism was compounded by an ominous Soviet anti-Semitic campaign. The revived appeal to racial prejudice came as no surprise to students of Soviet affairs; for it was an ill-kept secret that Jew-hatred had remained alive and active in Russia, even during the intensive re-education campaign of the 1920's. Indeed, this anti-Semitism had become quite violent throughout the Soviet Union during the black days of Nazi invasion. The Communist regime, which appealed to the ethnic nationalism of all its peoples, sternly repressed any "separatistic" anti-Nazi demonstrations by the Jews. If the war went badly, the Jews, the only minority people which had no choice but to resist the Nazis, were used as convenient scapegoats. While many Jews were decorated for heroism, they were never identified as Jews in the Russian press, although other minority peoples received such recognition. On the other hand, Jews who were singled out as slackers were almost invariably identified by racial or religious origin. There were instances of Jewish massacres by Russian partisan detachments. The Kremlin was not constrained to interfere; even after the war, Stalin was convinced that a little uninhibited Jew-hatred provided a welcome safety valve for an exhausted and impoverished population.

In 1949 anti-Semitism assumed major proportions when it received official government sanction. Under the guise variously of anti-Zionism, anti-imperialism, or anti-cosmopolitanism, the Soviet regimes in Russia and the satellite states began to spotlight prominent Jews as "disloyal" elements. By 1952 virtually all Jews had been purged from the Communist party leadership; in Czechoslovakia eleven in high position were hanged. In 1953 Moscow announced that nine doctors, six of them Jewish, had "confessed" to the 1949 "murder" of top Soviet officials Andrei Zhdanov and Alexander Shcharbakov; both of them, significantly, had been well-known anti-Semites. The murder was committed, the doctors confessed, in collusion with Zionists and by order of American Intelligence. With these confessions, the Soviet propaganda machine moved into high gear. Lurid, hooknosed caricatures of Jews, as diabolical in every respect as those that had characterized czarist or Nazi journalism, appeared now in the leading newspapers of Russia. Nearly all Jewish doctors lost their state positions; Jewish factory supervisors and civil servants in the upper echelons of the administration were summarily dismissed from their posts. Although the campaign was associated primarily with Joseph Stalin and his secret police chief, Lavrenti Beria, at least several others were active in stimulating Jew-hatred: among them Malenkov, Khrushchev, and Bulganin, men who later climbed to power as "anti-Stalinists." While the "doctors' plot" itself was repudiated in April 1953, after Stalin's death, thinly disguised diatribes against the Jews continued well beyond Malenkov's accession to power, and tapered off only in the later months of 1954.

There were several factors behind this malevolent Soviet anti-Semitism. For one thing, the defection of Yugoslavia's Marshal Tito in 1949 severely shocked the Soviet leaders, and imbued them with dread of any ideology which was not strictly Russia-centered. Zionism was viewed as such an ideology, and was identified in the Soviet mind with Western imperialism. Also, Jew-hatred was a convenient safety valve for the diversion of peasant unrest in the satellite countries. The passive resistance of these captive peoples, their sullen restiveness and occasional wildcat strikes against the high cost of living and the scarcity of consumer goods, were deliberately ascribed to "cosmopolitan" corruption and sabotage. Perhaps the principal Soviet motivation, however, in reviving Jew-hatred, was in the pattern so successfully exploited in earlier decades by Pan-Germans and Nazis. Soviet expansionists felt obliged to project an international enemy whose "necessary" destruction would serve as justification for international conquest. It was hardly accidental that a decline in the more public forms of Soviet anti-Semitism coincided with the new Khrushchev-Bulganin peaceful co-existence line after 1954.

Even then, however, anti-Jewish sentiment remained alive and quite powerful. In a series of articles published in the autumn of 1956, a staff writer for the New York Yiddish daily, *The Day-Jewish Journal,* reported on a recent visit to Russia. Wherever he went in Russia, the journalist wrote, he encountered evidence of anti-Jewish discrimination. Jewish medical students found it impossible to obtain internships in the better hospitals. Jewish engineers were virtually frozen out of industry. In Kiev, a Jewish metal worker at a plant employing twenty thousand people confided: "How often have I heard the admonition: 'Jew, go to Palestine!'" A year earlier a Russian Jew smuggled out this observation to an Israeli correspondent:

> It is evident today that our hopes were self-deception. A discerning eye can see that the anti-Semitic policy that had become so pronounced in 1948 has not been abandoned. It is only applied with greater caution, and therein lies the danger. The new rulers realized that they could not, like Stalin, pursue openly a policy of deliberate injustice against a whole people. So they blame Beria for the past evil committed against the Jews but have continued it with more circumspection.

In view of the difficulties and uncertainties of life behind the iron curtain, the Jews of Eastern Europe were more than eager to emigrate to Israel. Ben-Gurion, for his part, exerted every effort to pry them loose from their Communist captors. After the initial migration of 100,000 Polish Jews, however, the process of liberating the Jews of the satellite countries had become interwoven with unabashed blackmail. Romania's Foreign Minister, Jewish-born Anna Pauker, cynically released 123,000 Romanian Jews in return for direct cash payments from Israel. On the same basis, some 19,000 Czech Jews, 7,000 Bulgarian Jews, and 45,000 Hungarian Jews, 30,000 of them after the abortive uprising of 1956, were released to Israel. The rest were held behind the iron curtain. To inhibit Israel from adopting too anti-Soviet a foreign policy, small handfuls of them were occasionally released as a reminder of the much larger numbers of hostages that still remained. By 1957, nonetheless, some 500,000 European Jews, the majority of them Eastern European, had managed to find asylum in Israel.

The fate of 800,000 Jews living in Arab lands—200,000 in the Near East, the rest in North Africa—was a matter of even graver urgency in Israeli thinking. A "world passed by" until Israel's War of Liberation, these Jews suddenly became scapegoats for awakening—and frustrated—Arab nationalism. In the case of the Near Eastern countries, it was a nationalism exacerbated by Israeli military victories. In the tiny despotism of Yemen in the southwestern corner of the Arabian peninsula, the plight of some 50,000 Jews became so precarious after 1948 that Israel urged them to accept the Imam's brutal terms and to leave en masse, sacrificing all their money and property. Within less than a year, a skylift of spectacular proportions, "Operation Magic Carpet," brought into Israel the entire historic Yemenite Jewish community. Two years later 120,000 terrorized Iraqi Jews, people who had once been the mercantile aristocrats of Bagdad and Basra, agreed to the same conditions of property confiscation and entered Israel. Even before 1948 half the Syrian Jewish community of 30,000 sought refuge in Palestine. After Israel's War of Liberation a systematic government campaign of plunder and terror drove another 7,000 Syrian Jews into illegal exodus for Israel; the rest were trapped, beggared, and kept under virtual house arrest.

The Arab lands of North Africa, with 600,000 Jews, 4.5 per cent of the world's Jewish population, was another potential reservoir for Jewish immigration to Israel. The 140,000 Jews of Algeria, living primarily in Oran, Algiers, and Constantine, were of Sephardic origin; they were literate, and actively and successfully involved in commerce and the liberal professions. With the exception of the inhabitants of the *Mellah* (ghetto) of Algiers, they formed the most prosperous and cultured community in North Africa. Many of them went into a panic in the early 1950's, with the eruption of an Algerian nationalist revolt. The uprising was aimed primarily at the French colonial regime, but bitter experience had taught that inflamed Algerian nationalism could as suddenly turn on other non-Arab peoples. Yet because Algeria was legally, if not geographically, part of metropolitan France, the nationalist rebellion failed to spark a widespread Jewish emigration to Israel. France, after all, continued to remain open to Jewish *émigrés* as a matter of law, and several thousand Jews took advantage of their French citizenship to migrate to Marseilles and Paris.

In Tunisia, however, which had but recently won its independence from France, the Jewish community of 105,000 people was unable to count on asylum in France, or even on French protection locally, and the direction of Tunisian Arab nationalism remained an unknown factor. Although this nationalism was kept within disciplined bounds by a responsible Prime Minister (later President), Habib Bourguiba, the Jewish minority was no longer certain when political circumstances would place the non-Arab peoples in jeopardy. In the mid-1950's several thousand Sephardic Jews of Tunis, the most prosperous and educated elements, began to sell their businesses, close out their bank accounts, and leave for Israel. In southern Tunisia lived a poorer group, most of them quite devout; for them Israel was not only a political asylum but also the fulfillment of a Messianic dream. By 1957 perhaps 50,000 of them had made their way to Israel, and each month hundreds of others followed.

In Morocco lived a quarter of a million Jews, 90,000 in Casablanca, 56,000 in Marrakech, the rest equally divided between Fez, Meknès, and Rabat. They were all thoroughly assimilated Orientals, tracing their settlement back to the first Arab conquests in the Middle Ages. Most of them were petty traders and street hawkers, with standards much lower than those of the Jewish bourgeoisie of Algeria and Tunisia. Their economic stake in Morocco consequently was quite negligible. Moreover, they viewed with serious misgivings the religious fanaticism and xenophobia of the newly liberated Moroccan theocracy. They placed little faith in the promises of moderate Moslem leaders that the new State would be democratically constituted. Within a few years some 70,000 departed for Israel, and they continued to arrive at Haifa harbor at the rate of 3,000 to 5,000 a month.

As a consequence of this steady influx from European and Arab lands, Israel's Jewish population reached 1,620,000 by May 1957. Nearly all the new arrivals, European and Oriental Jews alike, were penniless, and at least half of them were entirely unskilled. The problem of adjusting hundreds of thousands of newcomers occupationally was a staggering one. So, too, was the problem of housing them. Until 1952 nearly 150,000 immigrants were at one time or another living in the huts and tents of *maabarot*—primitive and squalid reception centers. The government, chronically short of funds, was unable to build sufficient prefabricated housing units to relieve this *maabarot* congestion. Living in such tent cities for months on end, many of the immigrants, particularly the Orientals, became unruly and unmanageable. There were frequent disorders, crimes, even killings. From time to time epidemics broke out, and they were contained only by the most strenuous emergency measures. Many parents frankly feared that their children would be contaminated by diseases brought in by the Orientals. Worst of all, many of the immigrants lost confidence in the possibility of self-improvement and became chronic indigents, even after being resettled in more decent quarters. It was a desperately trying period, both for immigrant and native. At intervals, some of the older settlers petitioned the government to call a halt to the unsystematic, chaotic immigration, lest Israel's economy break under the strain.

But most of the newcomers, and most of the older citizens, bore the difficulties of resettlement without serious complaint. The immigrants were realistic enough to understand that the *maabarot* represented a transition, however painful, to new security. The Israelis, in their turn, were not blind to the very tangible advantages to be derived from widespread immigration. The new arrivals were a significant source of additional manpower for the army. Tens of thousands of them could be settled in the sparsely inhabited, and hence vulnerable, parts of the country. As an example: in 1948 only 6,000 Jews lived in southern Israel and the Negeb Desert; ten years later there were 100,000, nearly all newcomers. Moreover, the immigrants gave Israel the youngest population in the world. As late as 1957 50 per cent of the country's inhabitants were under nineteen years of age. These advantages, in numbers, in youth, in population distribution, were of incalculable benefit to a tiny country completely hemmed in by large and hostile neighbors. However much the influx of refugees complicated Israel's economic and cultural problems, it guaranteed the new state physical security, and it saved Jewish lives: all other considerations were secondary.

THE BATTLE FOR ECONOMIC SURVIVAL

When the War of Liberation ended Israel was all but bankrupt. The country was flooded with refugees long before the damage of war could be repaired, or before the expenditures for defense could be significantly scaled down. The need to feed, house, and employ the D.P.s involved the government in a frantically extended program of construction which included housing, factories, highways, and public buildings. Financing the network of projects and the soaring costs of government called for continuous sacrifice through a vast increase in taxation and through public bond issues. In 1952, however, when these resources proved insufficient, the government was compelled to resort to a forced loan of 10 per cent on all bank deposits, in essence a capital levy. The effect on public morale was quite grievous; combined with the unrestricted government issue of currency, it resulted in a disastrous inflation which siphoned out four fifths of the purchasing power of the Israeli pound.

To anchor its currency and to create a solid national income for public revenues it was necessary to achieve a favorable balance of trade. But this proved to be virtually impossible. It required several years simply to restore Israel's orange groves to their prewar condition, and no less than five years to rebuild the potash refineries on the shores of the Dead Sea. Gone for good was the vast spending power of the British army of occupation; seriously curtailed was the tourist trade after many world-famous shrines passed into the jurisdiction of Jordan. Moreover, a tight economic boycott maintained by the Arab countries closed off Israel's natural markets. A new range of products was assiduously planned for European export: cement, motor cars, tires, plastics. But such expansion required modern plant for optimum production; and this, in turn, required investment capital. Unfortunately, investment capital from abroad was tortuously slow in coming, much slower than had been anticipated. Even the most sympathetic American-Jewish industrialist had misgivings about investments in a country which was vulnerable to renewed Arab attack at any time while it took imaginative persuasion to overcome the natural reluctance of a typical capitalist to do business with a "Socialist" government. Besides, labor costs seemed too high, and the red tape of Israeli bureaucratic procedure too complicated. In spite of every conceivable inducement offered by the Ben-Gurion Administration, foreign investors hesitated to commit themselves.

By 1951 the shortage of exports, the increasing pressure of immigrants, the failure to attract investment capital resulted in a serious decline of Israeli living standards. Ben-Gurion was then persuaded by his Finance Minister, Eliezer Kaplan, to support a drastic and comprehensive scheme for borrowing from American Jewry although, in all probability, the plan would have been adopted even in less serious circumstances. The Prime Minister flew to the United States to launch a Bonds-for-Israel drive designed to raise half a billion dollars. American response was spontaneous, warm, and generous. A skillfully planned program of public relations, together with devoted leadership within the American-Jewish community, resulted in the purchase of $250,000,000 of Israel bonds within the first six years of the campaign.

Assistance now came from other sources as well. For several years spokesmen for the West German Federal Republic had indicated a willingness, even an eagerness, to compensate the Jews, in some small measure, for the horrors of the Nazi epoch. Within Israel, however, there existed a powerful sentiment against any dealings with Germany, for whatever purpose. The very process of sitting down with Germans, some Israelis argued, would imply forgiveness; it would also imply that it was possible to compensate for the murder of millions of Jews by the mere payment of money. Others reasoned that the acceptance of money in no sense implied forgiveness; it simply implied recognition of responsibility. The Germans had committed atrocities; were they to be permitted to turn their backs on Israel's problems, which were so largely of Germany's making? Eventually the viewpoint prevailed which favored an exploratory conference. In 1952 the Israel government and twenty-two world Jewish organizations entered into financial negotiations with the Bonn Republic. The talks resulted in a West German agreement to pay Israel $822,000,000, in the form of goods, over a span of twelve to fourteen years. During the period that followed the Germans honored their agreement in every respect, often providing the goods ahead of schedule. They were mainly heavy capital equipment carefully selected by Israeli economic experts, consisting of such items as passenger and merchant vessels, harbor supplies, tractors, heavy machinery, and concrete mixers. The combination of German reparations, the contributions of American Jews, and substantial loans from the American government and the World Bank, at last began to stem the tide of Israeli inflation.

The pump of Israel's economy was primed. Factories were erected: chemical and optical works, textile mills, iron-and-steel works, armament plants, cement and plywood factories, potash, phosphate and sulfate refineries. Many of Israel's products were exported; while Israeli imports, especially in the field of foodstuffs, declined notably as a result of improvements in cattle breeding, and in sugar, cotton, and vegetable cultivation. The economic problem was far from solved. A wide gap still existed between imports and exports. The young State was still dependent upon grants-in-aid, loans, reparations, bonds, contributions, and these could not be counted upon indefinitely. Most Israelis recognized that they would probably be living a Spartan life for many years to come. Yet, while sobered by the thought of continued austerity, few of them were unnerved. They had good reason for optimism. Scientific and engineering progress in Israel was opening up new avenues to ultimate economic security. Soil under irrigation, 230,000 dunams in 1948, had reached 1,000,000 dunams in 1955; and plans were underway to utilize the waters of the Dan, Yarkon, and Jordan Rivers for a wide-scale irrigation network. Moreover, new discoveries in hydrology—the technique of purifying the sewage of Tel Aviv, and of freezing and purifying the salt water of the Mediterranean itself—were already suggesting methods by which much of the tortuous rechanneling of rivers could be avoided. Indeed, in the area of pure research, Israel possessed unparalleled natural assets: the brain power of her citizens, the brilliant scientists and technicians who had come from the laboratories and universities of Europe, and whose papers were read annually at the various scientific conferences of the world. Many of these scientists had made significant progress in developing radioactive isotopes and enriching heavy water. In 1957 plans were under way to set up a nuclear reactor. It was this factor—the factor of unfailing Jewish ingenuity —which, more than any other, gave the little republic quiet confidence in its future.

CULTURAL, EDUCATIONAL, AND RELIGIOUS PROBLEMS

Not all of Israel's difficulties were military or economic. The influx of hundreds of thousands of Jews from Arab lands presented the Jewish State with a serious cultural and social dilemma. Most of the Orientals were desperately poor; many of them were illiterate and diseased, a walking museum of clinical exhibits in trachoma, body sores, ulcers, and tuberculosis. Thousands of Moroccan-Jewish immigrants were totally ill-equipped, psychologically and temperamentally, for the pioneering experiment that was being undertaken in Israel. Like the Moroccans among whom they had lived, they frequently were given to the kind of passive, contemplative pietism which did not encourage normal physical or secular activity. Indeed, the Oriental Jews viewed Zion in religio-romantic terms, and were willing to entrust the fate of the Holy Land to God's infinite mercy. It was an attractive viewpoint in some respects, but hardly consonant with the Zionist ideal of *halutziot:* physical labor, return to the soil, military defense.

One could sympathize with the newcomers who were fearful that the pace of Israeli life would destroy such cherished ancestral values as religious faith, economic contentment, and emotional detachment. But one could sympathize, too, with the reaction of Israelis of European background as they watched the flood of Arabized Jews pour into the land. Having worked diligently for years to create a model society in Israel, the European Israelis saw their social experiment in danger of foundering. They were repelled by the primitiveness, the disease and illiteracy of the Orientals, their initial inability to integrate into the pioneering hopes of Israeli life. Not infrequently, it must be added, the reaction of the Westerners was old-fashioned snobbery, the contempt of white people for those who were dark. They were certain that, with no protective restrictions, the Europeans would ultimately be completely inundated by the Orientals. It was a very real likelihood. By reproduction as well as immigration, the Oriental population was growing at a rate the Europeans could not begin to match. By 1957 Israel was already equally divided between the two. In spite of a sudden influx of iron-curtain refugees in 1957-58, it was estimated that by 1975 the country would become at least two-thirds Oriental. It was a serious question whether the Oriental Jews could be successfully acculturated along Western lines before they completely outnumbered the Europeans.

The older settlers made a vigorous attempt to modernize or Westernize the Orientals by teaching them the Hebrew language and the basic principles of Western hygiene. Many thousands of the new arrivals were sent, as well, to vocational and agricultural training schools. These educational efforts were not always effective. Second-generation Oriental immigrants found adjustment difficult; home environment counteracted change elsewhere; the schools were a most powerful assimilatory force, but school facilities were often inadequate. Some progress was made, however, by locating the newcomers in agricultural settlements alongside the European Jews, exposing them to the pioneering tradition which brought Israel into being. Many of these settlements conducted classes in citizenship which the immigrants attended between work hours. The army, too, worked its integration magic; every Israeli, native and immigrant alike, gave two years of service and these years had remarkable transforming power. Moreover, in the race between Westernization and Orientalization the Europeans possessed other advantages which offset mere numbers. They controlled not only the schools and the army but most of the instruments of public life: the Knesset, the newspapers, the movies. Accordingly, it was the European cultural influence which made itself felt in all public areas. Above all, the second generation of Orientals aspired to Westernization; they co-operated wholeheartedly in all educational efforts. These were the factors which made it likely that the Oriental immigrants would be Westernized before they became the majority, and that Israel's civilization would continue to grow essentially in the patterns established by the European pioneers.

There was one group, however, with whose cultural and sociological traditions the Israeli government refused to tamper. This was the Arab minority. By 1957 there were 192,000 Arabs in Israel—approximately 10 per cent of the population. After the War of Liberation, the government made a determined effort to fulfill its pledge of equal treatment for all of Israel's inhabitants. The Arabs were encouraged to participate in elections; Arab women, too, were permitted to vote, for the first time in their history. Arabs sat in the Knesset, and were assigned large representation in their local councils, townships, and public services. Several thousand Arabs were employed as civil servants. They were extended complete freedom of religious worship, and the government paid the salaries of all Moslem religious functionaries, even as it covered the salaries of the teachers who instructed, in Arabic, in the schools. It was hoped that such scrupulous respect for Moslem religious and cultural susceptibilities would insure the normal functioning of Arab life in Israel. But it did not. The Arab leadership simply could not bring itself to accept Israeli sovereignty; the imams fled from the mosques, the cadis from the courts; joining them in departure were the doctors, the teachers, and virtually all the intellectuals. Only workers and peasants stayed on and the cultural level of the existing Arab community, as a result, remained abysmally low. This was true, as well, of Arab economic life; it was shattered by the loss of their former market, the indispensable hinterland of Arab consumers. Psychologically, they found it almost impossible to adjust to their minority status. Recognizing that they were under continual suspicion as a fifth column, they went about their business sullenly, assuming hangdog expressions whenever Jews were in the vicinity. Normality in the relations between Arabs and Jews in Israel still awaited an Arab-Israel peace treaty. For the while, therefore, Israel concentrated most intensively on absorbing and training its Jewish inhabitants.

The problem of educating the Oriental newcomers, of welding the disparate immigrant groups into something approaching homogeneity, on the Western pattern, was complicated by the system of education inherited from Mandatary days; for the majority of public elementary schools remained under the direct supervision of one or another of Israel's political and economic groupings. The schools sponsored by Histadrut, for example, educated their youngsters along socialist lines; the schools of the Religious Bloc trained their students on strictly religious premises; those of the Agudat Yisrael according to ultra-Orthodox traditions. In recent years, the Mapai party, which dominated the government coalition, decided to fuse its Histadrut schools with the secular State schools; they established a network of institutions which ultimately provided education for three quarters of Israel's school children. But the religious groups tenaciously maintained their own school system, demanding, and receiving, national subsidies, and agreeing only to very nominal supervision by the Ministry of Education. Actually the struggle for control of the minds of school children was merely part of the larger Kulturkampf which had convulsed Israel since the State was born. It was a battle led by the Religious Bloc—the Mizrachi and Agudat Yisrael parties—to require the government to accept traditional Jewish law as the foundation of Israeli public life. With profound reluctance,

Prime Minister Ben-Gurion was compelled to make serious compromises with Orthodox demands so long as he depended upon the Religious Bloc for support in his Coalition Government.

As a result of these compromises the Religious Bloc, which failed to win more than 13 per cent of the public ballot in any Knesset election, managed to exercise a disproportionate influence over the public services of the State. Under the scrutiny of the Orthodox rabbinate, it became illegal during the Passover period to sell bread to any but non-Jews. On Saturday no restaurant or theater remained open; railways and bus lines were at a halt from Friday night to Saturday night; citizens in the interior, most of whom could afford neither automobiles nor the price of a taxi, were thus unable to reach the seashore on their one day of rest. The importation of nonkosher food into Israel became a statutory offense. Every synagogue in Israel was Orthodox; women who wished to worship were screened off in galleries. In marriage, divorce, and other intimate matters of personal status, a woman according to Israeli statute was technically as much a chattel as in Biblical times. A Jewish wife could not divorce her husband or make a will without his consent; a divorced Jewess might not marry a *cohen*. The rabbinate justified this rigidity by stating that an imposed Orthodoxy was a safeguard, in a Jewish State, against the sensation of alienism which had been the age-old burden of the Jews in a non-Jewish society. Now that Judaism had roots of its own, they argued, after so many centuries of flight and persecution, traditional religious practice took on the habiliments of solemn obligation. On the other hand, the critics of Orthodoxy—a majority of the Israeli population—wondered how one could respect a religion which required police enforcement.

In the late 1950's there was some evidence that the Orthodox group was moving toward moderation. Perhaps the inclusion of Orthodox representatives in the Cabinet tempered their religious convictions with a sense of national responsibility. At any rate, they demonstrated a willingness to compromise in the area of national defense—e.g., military maneuvers on the Sabbath, and in agricultural areas where milking and other basic chores continued during the Sabbath and holiday periods. Moreover, the growing strength of the Labor group after the military victory of 1956 enabled Ben-Gurion to resist the more extreme Orthodox demands.

The battle between the religious and the nonreligious parties over schools, dietary practice, public transportation, and other issues, often obscured the vigor and the creative integrity of the cultural life of the young country. In 1952 the Ministry of Culture and Education published statistics indicating that there were no less than 25 daily newspapers in Israel with a total daily circulation of 335,000; 211,000 radio sets; museums in three major cities attracting 130,000 visitors during the course of the year to view exhibits by some 350 artists, including the works of such world-renowned personalities as Reuben Rubin, Mordecai Ardon, Marcel Janco, Nahum Gutmann, and Joseph Zaritsky. Hundreds of thousands of Israelis attended performances by justly famous repertory drama groups, Habima, Ohel, and the Chamber Theater, and by the Israel Philharmonic Orchestra; each of these groups frequently performed works by native playwrights and composers. Israel's interest in the arts extended to the remotest farm settlements, where chamber-music groups and folk-dance teams practiced and performed before keenly appreciative audiences. Indeed, much of Israel's life was attuned to music and song, in the fields, in the factories, in the army.

It was literature, however, which remained the strongest area of creativity. Virtually from the outset of Jewish settlement, the Yishuv produced an exceptionally large group of talented writers. They were never at a loss for an audience, for the Jewish population was perhaps the most literate in the world. Even during the tension-racked years of World War II no less than fifteen hundred volumes were published in Palestine. In addition to a wide variety of books ranging from fiction to scientific dissertations, there were substantial monthly and quarterly journals, *Moznayim* and *Gilynot,* whose every issue compared favorably in intellectual and artistic quality with the best of America's university quarterlies. In addition, there were scores of scholarly journals in specialized areas. In 1953-54 Israel produced 1,000 articles (on all subjects); in that same year the United States, with a population 120 times larger than Israel's, produced 12,000 articles.

The novelists and poets of the new State ranked among the finest in the world. Bialik, Brenner, and Tchernichovsky, the giants of the Mandatary period, had long since passed on. But S. Y. Agnon was still alive and creative, as were Zalmon Schneur, Yitzhak Lamdan, and Uri Zvi Greenberg. There were others, too, whose prose and poetry were highly regarded by Israeli readers: Sh. Shalom, whose "mysticism" bespoke his Hasidic origins; Yitzhak Shenberg, a wonderfully gifted short-story writer, who described the spiritual trauma of relocation in Israel with sensitivity and sympathy; Jacob Fichman, distinguished critic and anthologist, and many others. One of Israel's most striking characteristics was the extraordinary range of its cultural expression: its books and its journals were supplemented by a profusion of lectures and recitals, festivals, displays, demonstrations, and conferences.

It was a culture in which, until recently, the values of the Diaspora were violently rejected. The pioneers were primarily socialist-secularists with a scorn for the merchant and for the *yeshivah bocher* which at times bordered on anti-Semitism. Their children, the tough, *kibbutz*-reared, army-hardened youth of Israel, believed that they had learned an additional lesson during the 1948-49 fighting: namely that in wartime the old leaders, the talkers, the dreamers, the rabbis, the intellectuals, did not win battles. The successful fighters were men like Alexander Yannai, hero of Shamir's thrilling historical novel, *King of Flesh and Blood,* or Raskin, hero of Meged's play, *Far Down in the Desert,* hard, tough, even unscrupulous men. The emphasis was no longer on the saint or the martyr; not even, as in the days of the *Haskalah,* on the religionist who was also the virile modernist. It was on the man of action and the hero.

Yet withal, an abiding consciousness of God was deeply embedded in the *halutziot* tradition. This sense of divine purpose may have been overshadowed by secular images; but it was rarely absent at any time. Even during the rugged pick-and-shovel days of the second and third Aliyot, endless numbers of lyrics, ballads, and dramatic poems managed to mingle religious idealism with an adulation of nature and physical labor. Uri Zvi Greenberg expressed this synthesis well:

> Like chapters of prophecy my days burn in all
>   their revelation,
> And my body in their midst is like the thick lump
>   of metal intended for smelting.
> And over me stands my God, the blacksmith, and
>   strikes with all His might:
> Each wound cut in me by time opens a lesion,
> And casts forth the imprisoned flame in sparks of
>   moments.
>
> This is my sentence and destiny till evening on the
>   road.
> And when I return to thrust the smitten lump of my
>   body upon the bed,
> My mouth is an open wound.
> All naked I then speak with my God: You have worked
>   hard,
> Now night has come; desist—let us both rest.

Several years after the death camps and the bloodletting of the War of Liberation, a growing number of Israeli poets and novelists felt that they had discerned a divine purpose in the agony of their country's birth. This was apparent, for example, in Y. D. Kamzan's epic poem, *On the Wing of Eagles*; Kamzan projected an image of the Jewish people as a charioteer hurtling across the horizons of the world, across space and history, across the Pale of Settlement, across the Nazi charnel houses, coming to rest at last in the devoutly Mizrachi community of Kfar Hasidim, outside of Haifa, there to revive the ancient spiritual heritage of the Jewish nation. The propaganda of the Religious Bloc obscured the fact that many of the country's leading intellectuals were embarking on a serious quest for faith and were sharply questioning whether Israel's future lay with pure secularism. They had seen their faith in socialism and international brotherhood shattered by the wars of the twentieth century, and were awakening, as a result, to the simple, undialectical humanism of the ancient Jewish tradition. This feeling was becoming so widespread that *sabras*—young, native-born Israelis—who once scorned religion as a symbol of Diaspora passivity, began to demonstrate a friendly interest in the theological viewpoint. Judd Teller describes this phenomenon in his conversations with Israeli students:

A few days later I ran into a Hebrew university student . . . "The Orthodox politicians make our life miserable," he said. "But one mustn't confuse religion in its pure meaning with the legalistic rigors of Orthodoxy. All great civilizations are based on religious faith. Western civilization is Christian, Rome is Catholic; America is Protestant. Gandhi's mind was steeped in Indian religious philosophy. Even the dissolute Arab students of the Levant, cynical as they are, speak the truth when they protest their reverence for the Koran. Only Israeli society served as a kind of substitute faith. But the Basel Program is hardly a *Weltanschauung,* and besides, it has already been realized." You find a lot of this sort of thing in the Israeli magazines.

Some of the young *sabras* frankly expressed doubt that the doctrines of their parties could serve as a substitute for a religious faith, as it had for their parents. Now that the State had come into being, it was no longer necessary to depend on the party for hospitalization, education, employment, old-age pensions; these functions were transferred to the government. The party, as a result, began to lose its old aura of omniscience.

What was emerging appeared to be a synthesis of the secular and religious viewpoints. Even for the nondevout, Jewish history, interwoven with ancient Hebrew rites and customs, exerted a compelling attraction. At the very least, the majority of Israelis seemed willing to regard the Bible as a majestic distillation of national literature. They respected and observed the holy days as popular festivals and celebrations. Even in the socialist settlements a more mellow attitude toward the religio-patriotic tradition was increasingly apparent; the ceremonials of Judaism were cherished now as the custom and folklore of a historic people. Waldo Frank, the world traveler and journalist, described a Seder at a collective settlement he visited in Israel in 1956:

> The feast was staged in a large, crude, unheated shed dedicated to sports and spectacles. Bare tables lined with backless benches filled it. In the center of a raised dais was a small orchestra of about twenty players, all of them Kibbutz members. And to one side was a larger platform for the dancers. The orchestra began with an introductory piece composed by a member; a very modern work influenced by the latest idioms of music, and yet redolent of the hard soil of Palestine, of the hard flesh of the Israelis. Then the leader (in work clothes) gave a slight sign with his hand and the two thousand seated at the tables poured forth the traditional music. The timing, the transition, the control were perfect, and without effort. This collective act could not possibly have been without an inward structure. And so the complex show proceeded, children sang, youth danced, the crowd was the chorus. No professional group could have achieved such smooth performance without weeks of rehearsal. And this community was not religious.

Perhaps it all depended upon one's definiton of religion. Such a community was assuredly not areligious.

ISRAEL AND HER NEIGHBORS

When the new State set about organizing its affairs after the War of Liberation, it staffed its Foreign Ministry, the largest Ministry in the government, with no less than a thousand civil servants. Israel needed them all, for its foreign relations were particularly entangled. For one thing, the complex problem of Jerusalem still remained. The United Nations reiterated its demands for Jerusalem's internationalization long after the war had ended and the city had been partitioned between Israeli and Jordanian forces. Ben-Gurion, however, was determined to ignore the pressure of the United Nations and the Catholic Church. Jerusalem had been isolated during the War of Independence; if the city's 100,000 Jews had depended upon the United Nations for protection they would unquestionably have fallen victim to Jordan's King Abdullah. Because it was apparent that the United Nations was unwilling and unable to ensure Jerusalem's safety, Israel itself assumed the responsibility. Equally decisive in the thinking of Israeli government officials was the fact that the Holy City had long been a spiritual lodestone of the Jewish people. Its excision from Israel would have been a severe moral shock to millions of Jews both within and outside the new State. Thus Ben-Gurion held firm, guaranteeing the sanctity of the Holy Places, and eventually winning the tacit agreement of the Great Powers to the maintenance of the *status quo*.

Much more complicated was the problem of the 650,000 Arabs who had fled Israel during the course of the Palestine War. Since 1948 these pathetic creatures, their numbers swollen by a huge birth rate and by innumerable thousands of drifters and hangers-on, had been living in refugee camps maintained by the United Nations in Arab towns and villages along Israel's borders. From 1948 to 1957 the United Nations Relief and Works Agency spent nearly $300,000,000 providing these refugees with food, housing, and medical care. The United Nations missions that visited the camps recommended that they be resettled in neighboring Arab lands, and that they be recompensed by Israel for the loss of their homes and farms. The American government endorsed this plan, and offered to provide Israel with a loan to help underwrite the cost of compensation. The Arab states, however, rejected the plan outright, determined to block all rehabilitation and resettlement schemes that might lead to a peace treaty with Israel. Exasperated with the intransigance of the Arab governments, the UNRWA representative in Jordan, J. R. Galloway, stated bluntly that "the [Arab States] don't care a damn whether the refugees live or die." It was true, but not in the sense Galloway meant. So long as the refugees remained alive, poverty-stricken and embittered, they provided a specious political issue for unscrupulous Arab nationalist politicians.

Israel's position on the refugee problem remained equally firm. Ben-Gurion was determined, as we have seen, to guarantee complete equality to the Arabs who remained in Israel, offering them every political and cultural opportunity that was open to the Jewish inhabitants of the State. But the idea of repatriating hundreds of thousands of Arab refugees was quite a different matter. The neighboring Arab governments repeatedly expressed their intention of obliterating the Jewish State. For years following the 1949 armistice Arab irregulars continued their incursions into Israeli territory, burning, marauding, stealing, and killing. Faced with this hostility, the Israeli government was convinced that the return of a large Arab refugee population—and who could say any longer how many were really refugees?—would be little less than suicidal. The probable increase in fifth-column activities could well paralyze Israel's economy, and undermine fatally Israel's military security. Since 1949, too, hundreds of thousands of Jewish immigrants had settled on abandoned Arab land; to these people, the idea of taking back any significant number of Arabs was not a subject for calm conversation. The Israeli government expressed a willingness to discuss compensation for the refugees, but only as an integral part of a general peace treaty. So long as the Arab states rejected the idea of such a treaty, it appeared as if the refugees were doomed to squalid and indefinite vegetation.

The plain truth was that the passage of years had failed to erase the sting of Arab defeat: the Arab rulers remained obdurate in their refusal to accept the fact of Israel's existence. There were several reasons for this inflexible hostility. One was the resentment of the *émigré* Palestine Arabs, their unwillingness to become a minority in a land inhabited for centuries by their ancestors. Secondly, hatred of the Jewish State was a stable and durable ingredient in intra-Arab politics: if Egypt were to destroy Israel she would assume the moral leadership of the Arab League, with all of its attendant prestige for penetration into the Sudan and North Africa. On the other hand, a victory over Israel would afford Syria or Jordan the distinction necessary for leadership in the Hashemite Levant. In terms of domestic Arab politics, certainly, anti-Israel propaganda, together with propaganda against Western imperialism, served as a convenient diversion from local economic and social discontent. But beyond these factors was the incontrovertible existence of a festering Arab nationalism, indeed, of Asian and African self-determination in its larger dimensions. It was a sense of collective destiny aimed primarily at the elimination of the last vestiges of European rule and influence. As far as the Arab world was concerned, the existence of Israel was merely an extension of British and Western imperialism into the Near East, and as such had to be resisted unto the death.

In the first generation after the Balfour Declaration, many Zionists tried to persuade themselves and the rest of the world that Arab nationalism was a myth, that it was artificially stimulated by the British, or by predatory Arab feudal landlords. The refusal of the Jews to recognize both the authenticity and the intensity of Arab national feeling was not only a political mistake of the first magnitude, but also an affront to Arab self-esteem which most of their leaders found intolerable. Ben-Gurion did not repeat this error after the successful conclusion of the Palestine War. He exerted himself to the utmost to placate Arab sensibilities; repeatedly he broached the possibility of economic and diplomatic co-operation between Arabs and Jews, of Arab-Jewish partnership in a Near Eastern federation of states. Only one Arab ruler, Abdullah of Jordan, expressed interest in "peaceful co-existence" and he was assassinated by a nationalist gunman in July 1951. After Abdullah's death, no Arab politician dared resume negotiations with Ben-Gurion. The endemic border warfare continued, while in Egypt the Suez Canal remained closed to all Israeli shipping.

The preservation of peace in the Near East was of supreme concern to the European nations. The West had long since learned that little wars could be the sparks that set off international conflagrations. In 1950 Britain, France, and the United States issued a Tripartite Declaration in the hope of reducing the possibility of further warfare. The Declaration guaranteed the borders of Israel and her Arab neighbors, and warned that any violation of frontiers would meet with swift punitive action by the Big Three. It was an impressive gesture, for it committed three great powers to unprecedented responsibility. Yet even this brought no peace. Night after night Arab marauders continued their raids on Israeli settlements, killing and maiming without respite. The occasional protests of the United Nations Truce Administration were completely ineffectual. The West refused to invoke the Tripartite Agreement against the Arabs. Indeed, as the months went by, it became apparent that the Tripartite Agreement could no longer guarantee Israel's security, even in the event of full-scale Arab invasion. By 1955 British soldiers had moved out of the Suez; Abdullah, Britain's reliable puppet, was dead; Cyprus, a key British military and naval base, was the scene of bitter revolt which made its dependability as a staging area problematical; France had suffered a grievous defeat in Indo-China and was deeply engaged in North Africa. It seemed increasingly unlikely, therefore, that the West would be able to move decisively in the event of an Arab attack upon Israel.

It appeared equally uncertain that the Big Three would be able to block Soviet expansion into the Near East, although the construction of an effective anti-Soviet barrier had been the principal goal of Western policy in the Mediterranean, and the principal reason for the Allied effort to preclude an Arab-Israeli war. By the early 1950's the danger of such expansion was growing steadily more acute. At no time since the end of the second World War had the Soviet leaders lost sight of Russia's traditional need for warm-water ports in the eastern Mediterranean. Moscow's first postwar effort to expand into the Near East had been virtually simultaneous attempts to move through the "hard-core" countries of Iran, Turkey, and Communist Yugoslavia. All three efforts had failed, and the Soviets decided to concentrate on Israel as a possible avenue into the Near East. It may be that the Kremlin's early pro-Jewish policy was followed in the hope that Israel's hatred for Britain and gratitude to Russia would make her a willing cat's-paw for Soviet penetration. Russia's opportunism backfired. It became apparent that Israel was determined to become a Western-style democracy and Soviet cordiality cooled rapidly. For his part, Ben-Gurion sought desperately to retain Soviet friendship: by announcing a policy of neutrality in the cold war; by avoiding any criticism of Soviet anti-Jewish policy in Russia and the satellite states. It was a losing effort. As the tensions of the cold war mounted, the Kremlin leaders increasingly viewed Israel as irredeemably hostile. They stepped up the attacks on their Jews at home and on the supporters of Israel abroad. Then, in 1954, Khrushchev and Bulganin launched an intensive drive to win the friendship and allegiance of the Afro-Asian bloc of nations, particularly the nations of the fluid and amorphous Arab world. It seemed at first to be an impossible gamble. Who among the feudal lords of the Arab lands could be intrigued by Communist blandishments? Late that year, however, an extraordinary figure erupted in the Near East whom the Russians felt they could use as an *agent provocateur*. He was a tall, muscular, hawk-faced Egyptian colonel named Gamal Abd al-Nasser.

ISRAEL AND NASSERISM

A wounded veteran of the Palestine War, Nasser belonged to the cabal of disgruntled officers which, in 1952, overthrew and exiled Faruk, Egypt's corrupt and enervated playboy king. Two years later Nasser emerged from the military junta as Prime Minister and *de facto* ruler. He governed dictatorially, to be sure, and breathed a fiery nationalism; but for a year and a half after he assumed control of his country, Nasser's well-advertised plans for economic rehabilitation, the Potëmkin village he built on the Nile, convinced top Western diplomats that he was a kind of Egyptian Mustafa Kemal, a strong man with enlightened aspirations for his land. American Ambassador Henry Byroade devoutly believed that Nasser was the last best hope for the Arab world, and convinced his chief, Secretary of State John Foster Dulles, that Nasser's friendship was worth cultivating.

Apparently neither Byroade nor Dulles had given serious attention to Nasser's autobiographical *Philosophy of Revolution,* a turgid mishmash of Caesarism, xenophobia, national socialism, anti-Zionism, and anti-Westernism. There was little in this political testament to suggest that Nasser would be governed by any principle save that of personal opportunism. Indeed, the Soviet Union sensed this fact far more readily than the West. In the summer of 1955 Russia brilliantly outflanked the Western Powers' series of alliances in the Near East (NATO, the Bagdad Pact) by negotiating a far-reaching arms deal with the Egyptian government. In return for a substantial share of Egypt's cotton crop for a decade to come, the Russians provided Nasser with large quantities of military weapons: 250 jet fighter and bomber planes, 300 heavy tanks, 2 submarines, 2 heavy cruisers, 2 destroyers. Simultaneously, a retinue of Soviet technicians and military advisors arrived in Egypt to train Nasser's armed forces in the use of the new material.

Nasser's limitless personal ambition exceeded Russia's fondest expectations. In 1955-56 he decided to exploit his vastly bolstered new prestige in the Arab world by bringing pressure to bear on four key areas: on North Africa, where he transshipped Soviet weapons to the rebel forces in Algeria and Morocco, and where he undoubtedly expected that Egyptian hegemony would ultimately replace French domination; on the Arab Near East, where Egyptian (i.e., Soviet) money and weapons bribed pro-Nasser regimes into office; on the Sudan and Suez, where Nasser hoped to destroy the last vestige of British control; and on Israel, which Nasser openly announced he intended to obliterate from the face of the earth.

In nearly every direction Nasser made astonishing headway. French strength and prestige in Algeria eroded rapidly. The Syrian government was replaced by a crypto-Communist regime openly friendly to Nasser; while Jordan's young King Hussein, in deference to Nasser's wishes, ousted his British military advisor, General John Bagot Glubb, on twenty-four hours' notice. In August 1956, in a sensationally audacious move, Nasser seized the Suez Canal, and announced that henceforth Egypt would exercise sole and exclusive sovereignty over the international waterway.

Of all Nasser's intended victims, Israel seemed to be the most vulnerable. To be sure, Israel's army was large, tough, and well-trained; every Israeli man and woman was conscripted for two years of military service, and was subject to annual recall. The staff headquarters and officers corps received superb specialized training both within Israel and in the military academies of Western Europe. Israel possessed an adequate quantity of small arms, and was receiving from France a fair supply of armored vehicles and artillery pieces. The typical Israeli soldier understood the importance of mechanical maintenance far better than his Arab counterpart. Morale in all branches of the Israeli armed services was excellent. But these advantages were counterbalanced by a serious shortage of jet airplanes and antiaircraft weapons. The harassed little state had virtually no funds with which to purchase expensive new weapons and to maintain an adequate standing army.

Across the border in Egypt, moreover, new shiploads of Russian jet planes and tanks were unloaded at Alexandria each week and rushed to key airstrips and military depots. Each day Nasser poured larger numbers of troops and equipment into the Egyptian-occupied Gaza Strip; each night he sent into Israel murderous bands of *fedayeen,* suicide raiders, to terrorize Israeli farm settlements. And all the while Cairo radio and Egyptian officials took turns in candidly announcing Nasser's plans for a full-scale assault on Israel. During the summer and autumn of 1956 the Israel government was keenly aware that every passing moment improved the Egyptian opportunity to master the new Soviet equipment; every passing day further tipped the military balance in Egypt's favor. Then, in early October, Nasser made the ominous announcement that Egypt, Syria, and Jordan had joined together in a united military command "in the event" of war with Israel. As Ben-Gurion watched the vise tightening, he agreed with his military advisors that Israel had no alternative but to "attack or die."

There is no authenticated account of the complicated military and diplomatic preparations that followed this decision. According to the information of several Paris newsmen, however (not denied by the French government), France was given advance warning of Israel's intention to smash the Egyptian military build-up in Sinai. The Israeli ambassador in Paris is alleged to have asked French Defense Minister Bourgès-Manoury for additional quantities of armored vehicles and jet planes. After consulting with French Premier Guy Mollet, Bourgès-Manoury notified the Israeli ambassador that France would not merely provide Israel with supplies, but would station a French jet squadron on Israeli airstrips as protection against Egyptian bombing attacks. Israel did not know, however, that in September the British and

French governments, exasperated beyond endurance by Nasser's Pan-Arabist policies, had come to a secret understanding for a joint military attack on Suez. The news that Israel was preparing a drive of its own against Egypt convinced Prime Ministers Eden and Mollet that they had found the perfect excuse to intervene at Suez for the sake of "separating the belligerents."

On October 28, Israel's citizen-army was suddenly mobilized. The following day, taking the Egyptian military high command completely by surprise, powerful Israeli armored columns and paratroop brigades speared deep into the Sinai Peninsula. Under the direction of Moshe Dayan, Israel's imaginative, one-eyed Chief of Staff, the advancing columns swiftly outflanked Egypt's key military bases in Sinai and the Gaza Strip. Within four days, the back of Egypt's army was broken; Israeli armed forces had captured intact 100 tanks, 200 artillery pieces, and vast quantities of ammunition and fuel, together with 5,000 demoralized Egyptian prisoners. Israeli troops quickly invested Gaza and the coastal areas controlling the entrance to the Gulf of Aqaba.

Within twenty-four hours of the Israeli invasion, Anglo-French air forces began a systematic bombardment of the Egyptian airfields adjacent to the Suez Canal. The excuse offered by Prime Minister Eden, that the Allies were acting to "separate" Israeli and Egyptian forces, was a fiction which singularly failed to impress world opinion. Even less impressive was the Allied plan of attack. By a slow and deliberate bombardment, instead of a swift and audacious paratroop drop, the Allied military command lost its opportunity to present the United Nations with a *fait accompli*. When paratroops were eventually dropped, their landing came too late to register the proper impact either on Nasser or the United Nations. Russia was infuriated at the beating its Egyptian puppet was taking, and made ominous references to "rocket attacks" on Britain. American Secretary of State Dulles, though he was certainly no longer an admirer of Nasser, insisted that the threat of force could not be used as an instrument of foreign policy; he was determined to give the Russians no precedent for military intervention. Two days after the Anglo-French attack began, the United States and Russia engineered a United Nations General Assembly resolution demanding the immediate withdrawal of Anglo-French-Israeli forces from Egyptian territory.

Under this kind of combined pressure, Eden and Mollet reluctantly decided to withdraw their forces, although they were within twenty-four hours of complete control of the Canal. The ineptitude of the Anglo-French campaign, militarily and politically, the failure of the Allies to complete the seizure of the Suez once they had begun, resulted in the forced resignation of Prime Minister Eden. It resulted, too, in minimizing the effect of the Israeli military victory in Sinai; for Anglo-French intervention gave Nasser an opportunity to save face both among his own people and among the Arabs of the Near East. There was no disgrace in losing to powerful Western forces; a clear-cut defeat at the hands of Israel, however, would have ruined Nasser. In fact the Israeli victory was clear-cut; but the Allied landing at Suez obscured that fact, and enabled Nasser to claim that he had beaten back the onslaught of three great powers. Of course, in the Arab mind, Israel was indelibly branded as a puppet of French and English imperial designs. Unhappily, by forcing Israeli forces out of Sinai without compelling Nasser to sign an Egyptian-Israeli peace treaty, the United States and the United Nations forfeited a superb opportunity to end the state of war between Israel and its most powerful Arab neighbor.

In the aftermath of hostilities, Ben-Gurion proved to be much more resolute than Eden or Mollet. He agreed to withdraw Israeli troops from Sinai, but not from the Gaza Strip or the coastal area abutting the Gulf of Aqaba. He insisted on assurances that these areas would never again be used as launching points for Egyptian attacks. The American government sympathized with Israel's position, but insisted that complete Israeli withdrawal behind the 1949 Palestine armistice lines was necessary before any kind of guarantee could be given. Ben-Gurion knew his Egyptian adversaries; he remembered how much more they respected force than legal agreements. He held out. Secretary of State Dulles was driven almost frantic by Ben-Gurion's obstinacy, for King Saud of Saudi Arabia was making Israeli withdrawal from Gaza a *sine qua non* for renewing the lease on American airfields. Hence, Dulles exerted the full force of American diplomatic pressure on the Israeli government, even threatening to impose crippling economic sanctions. Still Ben-Gurion held firm. Not until March, when President Eisenhower gave Ben-Gurion his personal assurance that United Nations forces would remain in Gaza indefinitely, and that the United States would guarantee the safety of Israeli shipping in the Gulf of Aqaba, did Ben-Gurion finally agree to withdraw his troops.

The doughty old Prime Minister had not won everything he wanted; but his gains were measurable. He had ruined the morale of the Egyptian armed forces, and had seriously, but not fatally, reduced Nasser's prestige among Egypt's Arab neighbors, especially in Jordan and Saudi Arabia. For a while, at least, he had immobilized the Gaza Strip as the vantage point for terrorist attacks. Finally, by winning from the United States the commitment to help prevent any interference with Israeli shipping in the Gulf of Aqaba, he had opened for Israel the commerce of Asia. For the first time since it had won independence in 1948, the Jewish State could entertain practical hopes of becoming a land bridge between the Mediterranean Sea and the Indian Ocean.

But while Israel had won an impressive victory, she had failed to insure her security by obtaining permanent peace with her Arab neighbors. Until peace could be won Israel remained in a state of isolation. Alone of the nations of the world Israel was unable to draw upon a regional community of allies. The little republic was surrounded by a hostile ring of Arab powers, a ring to which the North African states of Morocco, Tunisia, Algeria, and Libya, and the non-Arab Moslem countries of Pakistan, Iran, Afghanistan, and Indonesia, lent their diplomatic and economic support. Against the sleeping giant of Afro-Asian nationalism even the most highly disciplined and well-equipped military machine could not ultimately be successful. Israel would somehow have to find a way of dispelling the image of her which existed in the minds of Afro-Asian peoples: the image of an advance guard for Western imperialism. Unless and until this could be accomplished, Israel would live in continual danger. It was not the danger of annihilation; even Israel's bitterest enemies now conceded that point. It was the danger of living in continual tension, with gun in hand, with the children growing up as Spartans, sacrificing the civilized pleasures of peace and security.

CONCLUSION

As Israel moved into its second decade of independence, its citizens and its friends in other lands expressed ambitious hopes for its future. They hoped, of course, for peace with the Arab states, and for an end to the cold war between East and West, without which an Arab-Israeli peace treaty would be little more than a transitory truce. But there were other hopes, realistic hopes, that depended less on the resolution of the world's larger antagonisms. There was the hope of a reasonably improved standard of living, of an upsurge of prosperity resulting from trade with the Orient as well as with the Western world; resulting, too, from the rechanneling of the Jordan's waters, the draining of the Huleh marshes, the purification of salt water, from the unlocking of new mineral wealth in the Negev desert, and even, perhaps, from the exploitation of atomic energy.

Israel's friends anticipated, moreover, that the Jewish State would succeed in working out a proper and mutually enriching relationship with the rest of the world. Some Israelis, and many Jews elsewhere, believed that Zionist aspirations had been fulfilled when Israel became a sovereign, secular State. They expected now that Israel would carefully avoid "entangling alliances" with world Jewry; in this fashion, presumably, Israel would destroy the stereotype of the "international Jew," Pinsker's disembodied "phantom" people. But there were others who viewed Israel as more, not less, than a sovereign State, and who envisaged Israel as the single, authentic homeland of all Jews wherever they lived. Jews living elsewhere, they believed, were still in *Galut,* in the featureless limbo of exile. They argued that Israel must be more than a homeland for its own citizens; it must become the homeland for Jews everywhere. In fact, they insisted, there could be no ultimate security or purpose for Jews anywhere, until they returned at last to the ancestral soil.

Both viewpoints were extreme; and both viewpoints could claim the support of only a minority of Jews inside or outside Israel, Zionist or non-Zionist. The relationship for which the vast majority of Jews ventured to hope was much more moderate, if considerably more subtle, than either of these radical positions. Most Jews expected, by all means, that Israel would remain sovereign and independent. But Jews who lived in the free, democratic lands of the West were virtually unanimous in rejecting the notion that they were living in *Galut,* in exile. They were free and secure; their lives were to be lived as Frenchmen, Englishmen, Americans, and Canadians. On the other hand, they recognized that Israel as a State was performing for the less fortunate Jews of the world, behind the iron curtain, in the Arab lands, a service that could not be performed by the Jews of the United States or of

Western Europe. Israel was an "openly recognized, legally secured" home-land: it was the one dependable sanctuary for Jewish refugees. As a member, too, of the United Nations, Israel was in a position, whenever necessary, to focus world opinion on the plight of persecuted Jews in Russia or Egypt. Israel was, indeed, for better or worse, the moral spokesman for suffering Jewry everywhere. Not least of all, the Jews of Western lands recognized that their lives as Jews would gain in status and dignity if Israel, the corporate representation of Jewish civilization, endured and prospered. And they were willing, as a result, to lend Israel the full measure of their financial and moral support.

Finally, increasing numbers of Jews expected to find in Israel the source and inspiration of a revived and rejuvenated Jewish culture. Like Ahad Ha'am, they believed that Zionism had always envisaged much more than the mere normality of political sovereignty or of occupational diversity. The true, the enduring significance of a Jewish state lay in its role as a national touchstone from which Jews throughout the world could recreate the austere ethical grandeur of Hebrew civilization. Of course, much would depend upon the example set by the citizens of Israel, by those Jews who now lived closest to the hills and valleys, the flowing waters, and blazing deserts of sacred and historic memory. The words with which Chaim Weizmann completed his autobiography expressed the most deeply rooted of all Zionist hopes:

> Whether prophets will once more arise among the Jews in the near future it is difficult to say. But if they choose the way of honest and hard and clean living, on the land in settlements built on the old principles, and in cities cleansed of the dross which has been sometimes mistaken for civilization; if they center their activities on genuine values, whether in industry, agriculture, science, literature or art, then God will look down benignly on His children who after a long wandering have come home to serve Him with a psalm on their lips and a spade in their hands, reviving their old country and making it a center of human civilization.

To these words men of good will everywhere could say amen.

Notes

Page 546. Quotation from Judd L. Teller, *The Jews, the Kremlin, and the Middle East*, p. 133.

Page 556. Greenberg's poem translated by Simon Halkin, *Modern Hebrew Literature*, pp. 195-96.

Pages 556-57. Quotation from Judd L. Teller, "Religious Modernism Stirs Israel," *Commentary*, June, 1953.

Page 557. Quotation from Waldo Frank, "Journey to Israel," *Jewish Frontier*, July, 1956.

XXVI

The Growth of the Israeli Nation

Until the Sinai Campaign, Israel had been regarded, in many diplomatic circles, less as a state than as a kind of besieged refugee camp, frantically seeking to organize and defend itself in the midst of awesome economic, social, and military difficulties. After 1956, the corner was turned. The little nation was able at last to move from the challenges of sheer survival to those of integration and economic growth. One of the most palpable consequences of victory was a dramatic upsurge of immigration. Within the next decade 382,000 newcomers poured into Israel. Some two-thirds of them were refugees from nationalist xenophobia in Egypt, the Maghreb, and Iran, the rest fugitives from revived anti-Semitism in Communist Hungary, Romania, and Poland. Between 1956 and 1967, as a result, Israel's Jewish population grew from 1,667,000 to 2,384,000. By 1965, too, the numbers of Oriental and European Jews were equal for the first time in Israel's history, and three years later the Orientals comprised a slight majority. The ethnic trend would continue in future years.

Even as the Zionist republic "fleshed out" its demographic lineaments, the Jews broadened their grip on the soil. By 1967 they inhabited fully 729 of the country's 834 agricultural settlements and comprised a rural population of 340,000. Indeed, by then the land was meeting virtually all of Israel's staple food needs. The completion of a nation-wide irrigation project was surely a major factor in the new agricultural prosperity, for it included the massive Jordan Valley Project, transferring the Galilee's water surpluses to the more arid central and southern parts of the country. Moreover, the industrial as well as agricultural opportunities provided by enlarged water supplies opened out assurance of employment for an intended population of at least 5 million.

The anticipated site of much of this habitation was the Negeb Desert. By 1967 some 140,000 acres of the great former wasteland were under cultivation, supporting a rural community of 55,000 people. Yet it was assumed

567

from the beginning that minerals and industry offered the key to regional development in the south, particularly with the opening of the Gulf of Aqaba's export routes following the Sinai Campaign. To be sure, the desert's resources included not unimpressive quantities of copper ore, potash, brome, kaolite, quartz and gypsum, and these were imaginatively exploited by a score of recently constructed Negeb plants and factories. But essentially the Negeb's usefulness was augmented in other ways. One was as a land canal for the transshipment of Iranian oil through a series of large-diameter pipelines to Ashkelon and Haifa. Similarly, the Negeb provided space for the transplantation of industry from the north and for the settlement of a quarter-million immigrants in a score of new development communities, including Beersheba, Kiryat Gat, Ashdod, Arad, and the southern port of Eilat.

With the growth of agriculture and industry, of its southern hinterland, and of an impressive new merchant marine, Israel moved out of its earlier austerity to a condition of relative prosperity by the early 1960's. By 1965, in fact, it ranked midway among the world's thirty most affluent states. Much of this growth was accomplished by increased sophistication in government planning, by an enlarged work force, and by new trading opportunities overseas. But of equal importance were substantial infusions of foreign capital that helped cover the nation's still formidable import-export gap. Of the $6 billion import surplus between 1949 and 1965, for example, world Jewry made up not less than 59 per cent, largely through United Israel Appeal contributions and State of Israel Bond sales. West German reparation and restitution payments to Israel covered another 30 per cent of the balance of payments deficit, with United States government aid compensating for the rest. The little nation's continued dependence upon these overseas transfers revealed how tentative and vulnerable its economic circumstances still remained.

The truth was that living conditions in Israel were far from luxurious. The work week stood at forty-seven hours. Clothes remained a heavy investment. Furniture, even of the poorest quality, was very expensive. Lack of air conditioning lent a harassed, nerve-frazzled quality to the daily routine. If the amenities of life were improving, moreover, they were no longer as evenly distributed as in the pre-state period. In 1948 Israel was still largely an egalitarian society. Not so by the 1960's, as the gap between the poor (largely the Orientals) and the more comfortable (essentially the Ashkenazin) widened markedly.

The Arabs were a case in point. By 1966, as a consequence of natural reproduction, of improved medical care, and of declining infant mortality, Israel's Arab community reached 301,000, approximately 12 per cent of the state's population. The largest numbers of Arabs remained dispersed in some 100 rural villages in Galilee, the Carmel range, and the "Little Triangle," close by the Jordanian frontier. The rest lived in towns and cities. As the nation's military and economic prospects improved following the Sinai Campaign, the government could afford to deal more generously with this Arab minority. Equitable compensation was paid at last to Arabs who had been expropriated in border "security" zones. Lands confiscated from Arab refugees were leased back in substantial numbers to remaining Arab farmers. Throughout the 1960's, too, the government enlarged its efforts to improve the living standards of Arab towns and villages, to introduce progressive, mechanized farming techniques. Some I£ 120 million in public investments financed irrigation and land reclamation schemes. By 1967, as a result, Arab agricultural productivity had climbed sixfold over 1949 and was by far the highest in the Arab Middle East. Arab educational opportunities similarly were broadened beyond comparison elsewhere in the Arab world. Not least of all, military government in the Arab areas, which had been progressively relaxed over the preceding decade, was finally abolished altogether in 1966.

Notwithstanding these quite dramatic improvements, the lot of Israel's Arab minority was hardly enviable. The growing number of Arab high school and university graduates produced an educational elite that was unable to find its place either in the traditional Arab village or in the Israeli economy at large. Indeed, the new generation of Arab intelligentsia, tantalized by the revolution of rising expectations in Israel itself, and exposed to propaganda broadcasts from Amman, Ramallah, Damascus, and Cairo, tended to respond with increasing emotion to the charisma and grandiose declarations of Gamal Abd al-Nasser. As a result, the members of this educated bourgeoisie gravitated increasingly into Israel's Rakah (Communist) party. Here they found their best opportunity, under the guise of communism, to identify with the Arab nationalist cause and to repudiate Israel's very right to exist. Their mounting disaffection, together with their growing demographic proportion in a Jewish republic, signified a possibly serious threat to the nation's future domestic tranquility.

If Israel had other stepchildren, however, they were to be found less among its minority than among its majority. By the early 1960's, the nation's Oriental Jews comprised 55 per cent of the state's Jewish population. Like the Arabs, the Orientals were becoming noticeably impatient with their marginal living conditions, their inadequate housing, educational, and employment opportunities. Again, like the Arabs, these Jews of Eastern background were not unaware of the significant progress they had made in Israel, of the quite remarkable increase in their standard of living during a period of growing Israeli affluence. Yet they measured their improvements against the far more impressive progress of the Ashkenazic "establishment." Thus, by 1961, the bottom 20 per cent of the Jewish population (Oriental) was earning 5 per cent of the national income, and the upper 20 per cent (Ashkenazic) was earning more than 40 per cent. The government was fully aware of this discrepancy, of course, and to its credit launched a strenuous effort to remedy it. Among the measures undertaken during the Eshkol administration (p. 571) was a far-reaching "crash" program to improve the quality of education in Oriental Jewish neighborhoods, to underwrite special tutoring facilities, and to broaden vocational and high school opportunities for youngsters of North African and Middle Eastern background. At the government's initiative, jobs were made available, even artificially created, for unskilled Orientals in public projects, especially in development areas.

Yet if the gulf between the communities was stabilized, even narrowed, in certain areas, it was by no means eliminated. Neither were the Orientals prepared any longer to accept their second-class status. Increasingly they managed to exert their influence in the nation's political life, particularly in the development towns where the sheer weight of their numbers proved decisive to the party lists. Thus, by 1970 there were Oriental mayors in 30 per cent of the country's Jewish municipalities, and Oriental deputy mayors in 39 per cent. It appeared certain that this mounting political strength eventually would make itself felt in the national government. There was evidence of a rectified "balance" in another sphere as well, that of intermarriage. By 1969 the ratio of marriages between Orientals and Europeans rose to 17 per cent of all Jewish marriages in Israel. In this "mingling of the tribes" lay conceivably the most promising likelihood for single Jewish nationhood within a multinational Israeli republic.

A DECADE OF POLITICAL AND DIPLOMATIC ACHIEVEMENT

The dominance of Mapai in the nation's political configuration, meanwhile, remained unchanged in the aftermath of the Sinai victory. Indeed, the 1959 Knesset elections confirmed Mapai's mandate, and with it the leadership of the aging and iron-willed Ben-Gurion. As it happened, the prime minister for some years had cherished the ambition of effecting major changes in Israel's society, of introducing a more efficiency-oriented, technocratic approach to the nation's economic problems, including a transfer of health insurance from the Histadrut to the national government, and a freeze on living standards in order to develop competitiveness for the export market. These were proposals, nevertheless, that were distasteful to the Histadrut leadership. Additionally, the secretary-general of the labor federation, Pinhas Lavon, had long nurtured a personal grievance against Ben-Gurion and the latter's protégés, Moshe Dayan and Shimon Peres. Years before, in 1954, Lavon had served as minister of defense at the time Dayan was military chief of staff and Peres secretary-general of the defense ministry. During that period a spy-mission was launched in Egypt. Israeli agents and a group of Egyptian Jews were recruited for sabotage efforts against Western embassies, violence that hopefully would be attributed to Egyptian nationalists. The plot was clumsily executed; the conspirators were seized and tried, many imprisoned, and two hanged. During the inquiries secretly conducted in Israel afterward, Lavon denied advance knowledge of the plot. Yet, under pressure from Dayan and Peres, he resigned from office, his political future apparently destroyed.

In 1960, however, new intelligence information appeared to vindicate Lavon's original disclaimers of responsibility for the "security mishap." Sensing a political rehabilitation, the former defense minister demanded a new official inquiry. Ben-Gurion complied, and subsequent investigations appeared to confirm Lavon's account. On the other hand, Ben-Gurion rejected the legal finality of the exoneration, fearing that a new lease on Lavon's political future might threaten his, the prime minister's, program of "state technocracy." As the Mapai leadership remained deadlocked on the issue, Ben-Gurion threatened to resign and thus precipitated new Knesset elections. Although Mapai subsequently retained its working plurality, Ben-Gurion himself returned to office with his personal prestige seriously undermined. In 1963, exhausted by internecine fighting, the old man gave up the reins of office and retired to his desert kibbutz of Sde Boker.

The right-center parties, meanwhile, were not slow in exploiting Mapai's disarray. During the next year, Herut, the General Zionists, and important elements in the Liberal party reached agreement to join forces in a parliamentary bloc known as Gahal. Whereupon, determined to enlarge the base of his own political support, Levi Eshkol, Ben-Gurion's hand-picked successor as prime minister, initiated efforts to win over the left-wing Ahdut HaAvodah and Mapam parties into a new Labor "alignment." By 1968, with his prestige enhanced by the spectacular victory of the Six-Day War (p. 576), Eshkol overcame all lingering opposition and welded the leadership of Mapai, Ahdut HaAvodah, and many of Ben-Gurion's former adherents, into a combined Israel Labor party. Within the space of five years, therefore, a congeries of hair-splitting Zionist parties had been transformed into two or three major parliamentary blocs, a giant step forward toward the goal of political modernization.

The 1960's witnessed other important achievements by the Jewish state. On May 23, 1960, Prime Minister Ben-Gurion electrified his nation by announcing in the Knesset that "a short while ago the Israeli Security Services captured one of the greatest Nazi criminals, Adolf Eichmann, who together with the Nazi leaders was responsible for . . . 'the Final Solution to the Jewish problem.' . . ." The description of Eichmann was apt, of course. It is recalled (pp. 448–9) that the former SS officer had indeed presided over much of Hitler's liquidation of European Jewry. Although others of the leading Nazi war criminals were captured and tried by the victorious Allied powers, Eichmann had managed to escape, and ultimately made his way to Buenos Aires, where he resumed his life as "Ricardo Klement." It was not until 1960 that Israeli intelligence learned of his location. Aware that the Argentine government, with its long record of protecting Nazis, was unlikely to agree to extradition, Ben-Gurion authorized his security agents to move on their own. This they did, with spectacular success. On May 11, 1960, Israeli secret service men abducted Eichmann near his home and a few days later spirited him to Israel on an El Al plane.

The capture, and the announcement of Israel's intention to try Eichmann, precipitated a crisis in diplomatic relations with Argentina that was resolved only after an official apology from Jerusalem. And while no European government pressed for Eichmann's extradition from Israel, Western jurists and liberal journalists alike expressed reservations on the legality of the Israeli coup. Much of this criticism was dissipated, however, after the trial began in Jerusalem in April 1961. The proceedings were scrupulously fair; the legal precedents for Israel, as the successor of the British mandate and the acknowledged voice of Jewish martyrs in Europe, were carefully buttressed. The prosecution had accumulated an overwhelming repository of evidence proving Eichmann's crucial role in the Final Solution. When, on December 15, 1961, Eichmann was sentenced to death for "Crimes Against the Jewish People," few doubts remained any longer that justice had been done. The defendant's subsequent appeal to the supreme court was rejected. He was hanged on May 31, 1962.

The capture and trial of Eichmann had served Ben-Gurion's purpose of reminding the Israelis of Jewish vulnerability outside a land of their own. But the lesson also was for the nations that had allowed catastrophe to befall the Jews. Germany itself was preeminent among these, of course, and indeed the Eichmann trial proved a revelation to the younger generation of Germans, who first learned of the guilt incurred by their parents. The Adenauer government was not less sensitive to the unique moral obligation West Germany had incurred for Israel's survival and welfare. While concern for retaliation by the Arab states inhibited Bonn from establishing diplomatic relations with Jerusalem, Adenauer was prepared to supplement the original "Shilumim" payments (p. 550) by authorizing a massive $370 million development loan to Israel and by encouraging individual German companies to invest heavily in Israeli bonds.

From 1957 on, morever, Bonn similarly provided Israel with important quantities of military equipment, including jet planes, tanks, and rocket ammunition. This matériel was supplied gratis, and was delivered without the knowledge either of the German people or, most importantly, of the Arab states. Then, in October 1964, news of the clandestine arms deal suddenly broke in two German newspapers. Chagrined at having been kept in the dark on the arrangement, the West German parliament voted to end all further military aid to Israel. On the other hand, Bonn recognized that if it terminated its weapons deliveries, it was morally obligated somehow to compensate Israel. The Eshkol government promptly made it clear that the only acceptable compensation would be the establishment of diplomatic relations between the two countries. It was a condition the West Germans were prepared to accept. Thus, with the exchange of ambassadors in August 1965, a long and bitter chapter in Jewish and German history was closed at last.

Between Israel and France, conversely, a more equivocal chapter was opening. In the early aftermath of the Sinai Campaign, the two nations remained linked in a tight and mutually supportive friendship. Yet even as the sale of French military equipment to Israel continued into the mid-1960's, the award of independence to Algeria, and President Charles de Gaulle's determination to extend new political overtures to the Islamic world, produced a gradual "normalization" of Franco-Israeli relations. Joint naval and air maneuvers ceased. French diplomatic support in the United Nations became increasingly uneven. French economic relations with Israel remained quite minimal. Of graver concern, the French proved increasingly obstructionist to Israel's efforts to seek an associate relationship with the European Common Market. By the second half of the decade, leaders in both nations admitted that the once ardent relationship of the Sinai period was over.

Nevertheless, in the 1950's and 1960's, a new force was surfacing in the council of nations, one that appeared to offer Israel a major opportunity for diplomatic defense in depth. It was the "Third World" of recently liberated African and Asian countries. The opening of the Gulf of Aqaba after 1956 provided Israel with a maritime outlet to many of these nations, and facilitated new trade contacts with them. Simultaneously, not a few of these countries discerned in Israel a model for their own future development. This was especially true of the African states, with their suspicion of the colonial powers and their shared history of racial suffering with the Jews. If Israel had succeeded in overcoming the burdens of limited resources, a backward Oriental immigrant population, and military vulnerability, then conceivably African and other deprived nations could borrow from the Israeli example.

To that end, during the 1960's, many hundreds and eventually several thousand Africans, Asians, and Latin Americans visited Israel to attend government- and Histadrut-organized seminars on agricultural and educational development. Other Third World visitors participated in medical and engineering courses at Israeli universities. Still others received military training at the hands of Israel's army and air force. At the same time Israeli missions were dispatched to Third World countries, especially in Africa, to provide instruction on the spot, to establish model collectives, agricultural research stations, *nahal* (soldier-farmer) units, weather stations, departments of universities, clinics, and hospitals. The rewards of this extraordinary Israeli-African honeymoon were less economic than political. On a bilateral basis, African-Israeli friendship became warm enough to enable the Jewish state to surmount the Arab quarantine in the world's second-largest continent. And by 1967, indeed, Jerusalem's growing network of ties altogether in Africa, in Western Europe, and in North and South America, bespoke the remarkable degree to which the Jewish republic had become an abiding star in the international firmament.

NASSER PROVOKES A RENEWED CRISIS

Yet if Israel's growth and strength were increasingly a fact of Middle Eastern life, so, by the same token, was Arab hatred. On numerous occasions Gamal Abd al-Nasser gave vent to that animus. Thus, in an address before the United Nations in September 1960, the Egyptian leader declared that "the only solution to Palestine . . . is the annulment of Israel's existence." Again, in March 1965, Nasser warned that "[W]e shall not enter Palestine with its soil covered in sand. We shall enter it with its soil saturated in blood." Sanguinary declarations were less easily translated into meaningful plans, however. The jerry-built United Arab Republic had collapsed upon Syrian withdrawal. In Iraq, the revolutionary government of Abd al-Karim al-Qasim was engaged in open ideological battle with Cairo.

At the same time, Nasser's impulsive decision to ship troops to the Yemeni battlefield seriously drained Egypt's foreign currency reserves.

By 1965, nevertheless, border crises between Israel and Syria were developing a lethal momentum that ultimately affected the rest of the Arab world. All along the main demilitarized area Syrian guns in the Golan Heights disrupted the efforts of Israeli farmers to cultivate the Huleh stretch of the frontier. Repeated exchanges of fire caused numerous Israeli deaths. Soon the confrontation escalated into prolonged Syrian-Israeli artillery duels and even aerial dogfights. Much of this Arab belligerence reflected the unique nature of the Syrian Ba'ath government, a junta of officers that had come to power in 1962 and that soon revealed itself as the most grimly leftist, anti-Western, and chauvinistic regime in the Middle East. In its anti-Israel campaign, the Syrians now made active use of a radical Palestinian refugee group known as al-Fatah. Armed and trained by the Syrian army, Fatah guerrillas began striking into Israel, attacking Jewish settlements, ambushing Israeli army patrols, and inflicting numerous casualties. When Syrian artillery protected these incursions, the Israelis responded in kind, and on April 7, 1967, a major air battle erupted in which Israeli jets downed six Syrian MiGs.

For his part, Nasser had still hoped to avoid involvement in the Isreali-Syrian crisis. It was Soviet intercession that forced his hand. With Syria evidently in the process of becoming the first Communist state in the Arab world, the Soviets were certain that they had access to a Mediterranean base even more dependable than Egypt. Determined to protect their Middle Eastern foothold, the Russians began loosing a tough series of warnings to Israel on the "possible consequences" of further military action against Syria. Unfazed, on May 11, 1967, Prime Minister Levi Eshkol notified the UN Security Council that unless Syrian provocations ended, Israel would act in self-defense. At that point, alarmed by the possible vulnerability of their favored Arab protégé, the Russians made a calamitous misstep. They accused Israel of preparing an attack across its northern frontier. In fact, the charge was false, but the very accusation could fulfill a useful purpose for Moscow. If the Jews subsequently failed to move, their inaction could be attributed to Russian support for the Syrian Ba'ath regime. On May 12, therefore, the Soviet ambassador in Cairo passed on to Nasser "information" concerning the massing of Israeli troops for an attack on Syria, and asked the Egyptian leader to "take the necessary steps."

Nasser in turn agreed to dispatch a military mission to Syria. The latter found no evidence of Israeli border concentrations. Even so, Nasser now deliberately allowed the crisis to escalate. Several factors influenced his decision. One was his nation's desperate financial plight and Egypt's seething domestic unrest; a confrontation with Israel would serve as an outlet for this discontent. Moreover, Nasser was being systematically taunted by the Hashemite and Saudi governments for his "cowardice" in reducing border friction with Israel, and in tolerating United Nations forces on his soil. Somehow the wind had to be taken out of his rivals' sails. Dependent upon his Soviet patrons, too, the Egyptian president could hardly ignore their request that he make a gesture to shore up the Ba'athist cabal in Damascus.

On May 15, therefore, Nasser ordered the bulk of his army deep into the Sinai. At first the Israeli leadership, celebrating their independence day, regarded the Egyptian maneuver as a bluff. But on the afternoon of May 17 Nasser suddenly ordered the 3,400-man UNEF contingent out of the Gaza Strip. At this point the UN secretary-general, U Thant, inexplicably failed to call an emergency meeting of the General Assembly to debate the Egyptian order. Instead, the little Burmese compliantly ordered the international units removed from the Gaza buffer. Unwittingly, the secretary-general thereby dislodged the stone that loosed the avalanche in the Middle East. Egyptian forces promptly entered Gaza. Heartened, too, by the supineness of the world body, Nasser went further, and on May 18 ordered the evacuation of the UNEF contingent at Sharm es-Sheikh, which was guarding the Strait of Tiran. Again, U Thant acquiesced, permitting the return of Egyptian troops to this crucial waterway. At that point, regaining his former status as the decisive leader of the Arab world, and intoxicated by assurances of support from other Arab nations, which hurriedly began mobilizing in preparation for a *jihad* against Israel, Nasser proceeded to overstep the last bounds of restraint. On May 21 he made a chilling announcement: "The Strait of Tiran is part of our territorial waters. No Israeli ship will ever navigate it again."

With the declaration of this blockade, Abba Eban, Israel's foreign minister, urgently began seeking reassurance from Western capitals that freedom of navigation in the Gulf of Aqaba would be protected, if necessary by an international naval flotilla. Eban's efforts proved unavailing. The United States was mired in Vietnam, and President Lyndon Johnson, for all his personal goodwill, was unable to secure Congressional approval for American participation in such a naval armada. Without an American commitment, Britain's Labour Government was unprepared to move on its own. De Gaulle, meanwhile, refused to countenance the notion of military action —either by the Great Powers or by Israel—and now went so far in his quest for Arab friendship as to terminate all military shipments to Israel. The United Nations similarly proved a dead end. Faced with the threat of a Soviet veto, the Security Council meetings on the blockade devolved into an exercise in windy irresolution.

As diplomative alternatives for resolving the crisis failed, the Israelis prepared for war. All available reserves were called up. By the end of May the nation's streets were empty, the towns silent at night. Parks were consigned as military cemeteries. Responding to public pressure, Prime Minister Eshkol invited the opposition Herut into a government of national unity and subsequently turned over the ministry of defense to Moshe Dayan, the hero of the 1956 Sinai Campaign. The threat facing the nation was unquestionably as grim as any in its short history. Jordan's King Hussein flew to Cairo to accept Egyptian military leadership of a combined command. Syria and Iraq also adhered to the mutual "defense" pact, as did Saudi Arabia and even the Republic of Yemen. As mass demonstrations throughout the Arab world exhorted their peoples to holy war against the Jews, all these various states then dispatched men and matériel toward the Israeli frontiers. Gathered along Israel's southern border alone were seven highly trained Egyptian divisions, 120,000 troops, supported by 1,000 guns and 2,000 tanks. The Syrians, Iraqis, and Jordanians together disposed of nearly half this quantity of men and equipment—an array that outnumbered the Israelis by 3 to 1. It was a somber picture for the little Jewish republic.

It was not the entire picture, however. Israeli intelligence had proved its mettle over the years by infiltrating agents into enemy camps and acquiring vital data on Egyptian and Syrian defense installations. Learning, too, that the Russians were reorganizing the Egyptian army according to classical Soviet methods—large troop concentrations and heavy fortifications—the Israeli general staff developed its own techniques for coping with the "Russian doctrine." Vast maneuvers were carried out periodically in the Negeb against models of Egyptian positions. Additionally, under Chief of Staff Yitzhak Rabin, Israel's defense forces were significantly augmented during the 1960's with modern equipment secured from France, West Germany, and the United States. Yet the most decisive factor in the efficiency of Israel's armed forces was the quality of the nation's manpower. Training was intensive, initiative and imagination were endlessly stressed—precisely the characteristics of a nation that had been schooled in the quick-motion methods of social and economic development.

On June 3, aware that no possibility existed any longer of resolving the crisis through diplomacy, the government made the decision to attack preemptively. At 7:10 A.M. of June 5, therefore, the Israeli air force went into action. Thanks to near-perfect intelligence, the location of virtually all Egyptian planes had been pinpointed. Thus, within 170 minutes, Israel's pilots smashed Egypt's major air bases and turned 300 of Nasser's 340 combat planes into flaming wrecks. Thereafter Israel's fliers roamed at will over Sinai, destroying entire convoys of Egyptian armor and other vehicles. During the first day, too, as Egypt's allies began probing offensives (p. 577), Israeli planes all but annihilated the Jordanian, Syrian, and Iraqi air forces.

Meanwhile, at 8:15 A.M. of the same day, Israeli ground forces attacked. The offensive moved with clockwork precision. General Yisrael Tal's northern armored brigades smashed through the Rafa-al-Arish defense complex, the first of Egypt's "locks" to the northern Sinai; even as General Ariel Sharon's infantry and armored units brilliantly infiltrated, then overran, Um Cataf, the linchpin of the Abu Agheila network of defenses across the Nitzana-Ismailia axis. With the forcing of this second "lock," all central Sinai lay open by late afternoon of June 6. At the same time yet another Israeli brigade, commanded by Brigadier Avraham Yoffe, moved through the wasteland between Egypt's two key defense areas, and after a thirteen-hour battle against Egyptian armor, managed to reach the Mitla Pass, blocking the enemy line of retreat. The entire Egyptian army in Sinai was now trapped between a massive Israeli pincers.

Throughout the first day of this pulverizing offensive, meanwhile, the only official communiqués were from Cairo, and they spoke of devastating Egyptian victories, of Egyptian columns driving on Tel Aviv. The "news" was accepted unquestioningly elsewhere in the Arab world, and it influenced the decisions of Syria, Jordan, and Iraq to enter the fighting. But again, as in two earlier wars, the Syrians forfeited their best opportunity for an offensive. On June 5 their gunners simply bombarded Israel's Galilee settlements, but held back on a major attack. At first this was also Hussein's strategy, as his artillerists began shelling from the Jerusalem promontory, striking not only at the Israeli New City but at towns and installations in the interior. But then, at 1:00 P.M. on June 5, the Jordanians crossed the Jerusalem armistice lines and occupied United Nations headquarters on the Hill of Evil Counsel. The shift to ground attack, with its threat to the Israeli garrison on Mount Scopus, was a misstep that produced disastrous consequences for the Hashemite monarch.

Hussein was by no means alone in his miscalculations. It was not until late afternoon of June 5 that Nasser was first informed of the liquidation of his air force, and of the crushing Israeli offensive in Sinai. The Soviets learned of these events at approximately the same time. Alarmed, Prime Minister Alexei Kosygin telephoned Lyndon Johnson on the "hot line," demanding that the Americans press Israel to withdraw. But the American president, gratified that the Israelis themselves were successfully liquidating an agonizing world crisis, held firm. As a warning to the Soviets, Johnson ordered the United States Sixth Fleet toward the fighting zone. By nightfall of June 7, therefore, the Israeli spearheads reached their objective. With Tal and Yoffe's brigades cutting off the Gidi and Mitla exits, Sharon's armor drove the fleeing Egyptians into the trap. What ensued was a slaughter, with more than 800 Egyptian tanks destroyed or captured. By morning of June 8, Israel's columns were ensconced along the eastern shore of the Suez Canal. As Rabin had anticipated, too, the rout of the Egyptian army in northern Sinai allowed Sharm es-Sheikh to drop like a ripe plum into the hands of Israeli amphibious units. At 8:00 P.M. of June 8 Nasser accepted Israel's demand for an unconditional cease-fire.

A RECONSTRUCTION OF FRONTIERS

Meanwhile, on the afternoon of June 5, responding to the threat posed to New Jerusalem by the Jordanian occupation of the Hill of Evil Counsel, Dayan ordered the Israeli central command to assume the offensive. The occupied terrain was recaptured forthwith. Soon afterward, at 2:20 A.M. of June 6, a paratroop brigade commanded by Colonel Mordecai Gur attacked Jordanian fortifications along the perimeter of the Arab City, then successfully moved against the Arab Legionnaires atop the heights near Mount Scopus. Soon afterward a major armored attack was launched on June 6 for control of the entire Jerusalem promontory, including Ramallah and Bethlehem. With close air support, the Israelis succeeded by mid-morning of June 7 not only in capturing this high ground, but in investing the entire Hashemite West Bank, down to the Jordan River. The capture of the Jerusalem—and Palestinian—hinterland sealed the fate of the Jewish Old City (in Arab hands since 1948). That same morning Gur's men blasted through the Lion's Gate, rolled up the narrow Via Dolorosa, then dashed for the Western Wall, the revered site of the ancient Temple. By noon the Wall and its neighboring Arab mosques were in Jewish hands. Arab resistance in Jerusalem ceased. The Jews had returned to the cradle of their peoplehood.

The final decision awaiting the government was the action to be taken against Syria, the nation whose endless border ambushes and shelling of Galilee settlements had initially provoked the crisis. The Galilee farmers themselves pressed Eshkol for an offensive against this most implacable of Arab enemies. The premier and the cabinet were convinced, and on the morning of June 9 ordered the attack against the Golan emplacements. It was an awesome assignment. Syrian troops were emplaced in powerfully fortified redoubts hundreds of feet above the Israeli valley floor. Nevertheless, General David Elazar, the northern front commander, decided to crack these lethal defense positions by ascending the boulder-strewn Golan ridges in a direct frontal assault. Thus, at high noon of June 9, the Israelis set out, with bulldozers clearing the rocks, followed by tanks, and infantrymen bringing up the rear. They took heavy casualties. Confounded by the Israeli route of attack, however, and deprived of reinforcements by a murderous air bombardment, the Syrians failed to stop the Jews from reaching the escarpment. By early June 10 Israeli heliborne commandos were leapfrogging Arab positions, capturing village after village on the plateau, including Quneitra, "capital" of the Golan. By noon Syrian troops were fleeing toward Damascus, and with them nearly all of the Golan's civilian population. At 6:30 P.M. the Syrians agreed to a cease-fire. The entire Golan was in Israel's hands; the long nightmare of Syrian bombardment was over. So, almost at the very moment, was the last Arab pretension to a blockade of Israel's waterways. At Sharm es-Sheikh, Israeli troops welcomed a Zim freighter that had steamed uneventfully through the Strait of Tiran en route to Eilat.

Israel's losses were astonishingly light considering the magnitude of its victory: 759 troops killed, about three times that many wounded. More important, a new military-geographic reality had been created in the Middle East. Before the war, Israel's population centers had lain within four minutes' flying time of the nearest Arab air base. Much of Israel's narrow waistline had fallen within Arab artillery range, as had Jewish Jerusalem and the northern Galilee settlements. Now the situation was reversed. It was Israeli planes and troops that were within striking distance of Amman, Damascus and Cairo. In the south, the 200-mile frontier between the Sinai and Negeb deserts, with its threatening spike of the Gaza Strip into Israel, was replaced by the 110-mile barrier of the Suez Canal. In the east, Israel had pushed the long and involuted Israeli-Hashemite border to the straight

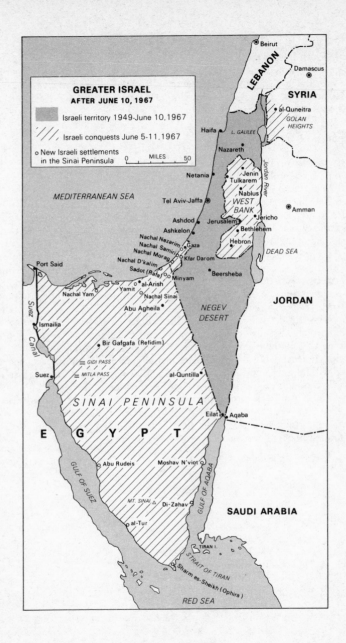

GREATER ISRAEL
(after June 10, 1967)

north–south line of the River Jordan and the Dead Sea. It was an astounding military achievement, and one widely heralded throughout the entire free world. The discipline and gallantry of Israeli soldiers and civilians, who had shattered a seemingly overwhelming threat to their survival, touched the hearts of common men everywhere.

CONCLUSION

It was specifically this international goodwill that protected Israel from the diplomatic isolation it had encountered in the Sinai War of 1956. Soviet and Arab demands for unconditional Israeli withdrawal received short shrift both in the UN Security Council and General Assembly. The United States joined Israel now in urging direct Arab-Israeli negotiations, and a peace treaty based on secure and mutually recognized boundaries. But in a world body fractured by competing political interests, neither the Soviet nor the American resolution was able to achieve the necessary two-thirds majority. It was not until mid-November 1973 that a compromise formula eventually was hammered out. Entitled Security Council Resolution 242, the statement on the one hand placated the Arabs by urging the withdrawal of Israeli armed forces from "territories occupied" in the recent conflict, and asking for a "just settlement of the refugee problem." On the other, it conciliated the Israelis by demanding an end to belligerency in the Middle East and "acknowledgment of the sovereignty, territorial integrity, and political independence of every State in the area and their right to live in peace within secure and recognized boundaries free from threats or acts of force." Although each side put its own interpretation on the resolution, the Israelis saw it as a promising augury at last for their long-cherished dream of peace and security among their Arab neighbors. Surely the future that was opening out now before the little Jewish country was radiant beyond the fondest hopes of even its most utopianist visionaries.

XXVII

Greater Israel

The impact of the June victory was to be discerned not alone in the euphoria of the Israelis, but in the stunned bewilderment of the captured Arab population. Nearly a million of these instant "subjects" remained in the 28,000 miles of terrain overrun by the Israeli army, including 670,000 on the West Bank and East Jerusalem, 356,000 in the Gaza Strip, 33,000 in Sinai, and 6,000 on the Golan. Those with first claim on Israel's attention logically were the Arabs nearest at hand, the 67,000 who lived on the east side of the barriers that had divided Jerusalem for nineteen years. Israel promptly coped with these Arab Jerusalemites as fellow townsmen, repairing the debris of war in their sector, then linking their public services into a newly combined municipal administration. In this fashion the Israelis made it clear that they had entered the reunited city to stay. Thus, on June 27, 1967, the Knesset formally placed East Jerusalem under Israeli "law, jurisdiction and administration." Although the Arab inhabitants officially maintained their Jordanian citizenship, their city for all practical purposes was now incorporated into the State of Israel. Moreover, if Jewish rule was less than a psychological comfort, it soon proved to be an economic bonanza for Jerusalem's Arab population.

Neither was Israeli conquest the hell of brutality that had been anticipated by Arabs in the West Bank and in the Gaza Strip. It was Dayan, as minister of defense, who laid down the guidelines for the military government in these occupied sectors. His approach was both compassionate and imaginative. Determined that Israeli occupation should be as unobtrusive as possible, he kept his troops out of the main population areas and ensured that public services continued to be administered largely by the prewar Arab civil service. In the West Bank, Jordanian law remained operative. Local citizens were free to conduct their affairs, to teach, to publish, to criticize the Israeli presence without restraint or censorship—insofar as they did not incite to violence. To revive the flow of goods and services, moreover, Dayan eliminated all road barriers and curfews within days after the fighting ended, then allowed free crossing from Jewish territory to the "administered" areas. The response was a wave of Israeli tourism and purchases in Arab cities and towns. More significantly, the defense minister soon afterward authorized the free movement of the Arab population—not only to integral Israel, but across the Jordan River to the Hashemite East Bank. The consequence of this audacious decision was an almost immediate revival of West Bank agriculture, which once again found its natural market in Jordan proper. If Hussein allowed this traffic, it was exclusively for the political purpose of maintaining his connections with his former subjects. Similarly, Israel's reasons were political no less than humanitarian. Dayan and others appreciated that the conduit of the West Bank offered Israel its first tangible hope of wider communication with the surrounding enemy nations.

Indeed, the Israelis regarded the June victory as an unprecedented opportunity for concluding a final, negotiated settlement with the Arabs. The benignity of Israeli rule scarcely concealed the hard evidence, which the Arab governments presumably would recognize, of the Jewish state's unchallengeable military strength and new defensibility in depth. On this assumption, Prime Minister Eshkol outlined his peace terms to Dr. Gunnar Jarring, the United Nations emissary who had been dispatched to the Middle East under the terms of Security Council Resolution 242. They were: that peace should be achieved through direct negotiations and a formal treaty; that Israeli ships should be allowed free passage through the Suez Canal; and that the refugee problem should similarly be resolved within the framework of peace. Yet when Jarring conveyed these terms to the Arab governments, he elicited only a negative response.

To be sure, Hussein, who had lost half his kingdom to Israel, was the likeliest prospect for a settlement. Yet as a transplanted dynast facing the perennial threat of civil war, the Jordanian monarch was too insecure on his throne to move without approval from Cairo or Damascus. That approval was emphatically not forthcoming. In truth, the Syrians were less interested in a settlement than were any of Israel's foes. Intensely nationalistic, they did not regard the economically marginal Golan as sufficient an inducement to come to terms with the Zionists; while the ruling Ba'ath party, a suspect minority junta, dared not risk public outrage by acknowledging so much as Israel's right to exist. Even Nasser, whose personal prestige had been most critically undermined, reacted to his Sinai disaster with stiffened truculence. He, too, sensed that compromise with the Israelis might risk civil upheaval in his own country. By late summer, moreover, Egypt's financial losses in Suez revenues were being partially made good by subsidies from the oil-rich Persian Gulf nations; even as the Soviets shipped and airlifted to Egypt vast quantities of heavy military equipment as compensation for the recent battlefield losses. Regaining a measure of his self-confidence, therefore, Nasser in late August led a conference of Arab leaders at Khartoum in pledging refusal to countenance peace with Israel under any circumstances. By 1968 it was becoming painfully clear to the Israelis that their expectation of a "phone call" from the Arab world was a pipe dream.

The consequence of this Arab intransigence was to harden Israel's own political stance. At first, to be sure, Eshkol turned to communal leaders on the West Bank itself, in the hope of developing a possibly autonomous regime in the "administered" territories. Yet, fearful of alienating Hussein or Nasser, the various sheikhs and mukhtars declined to commit themselves. The Israeli government thereupon quietly began establishing *nahal* settlements throughout the Golan Heights, in the West Bank, even in the eastern Sinai Peninsula. This new defense belt represented what Dayan termed the creation of "facts." "If the Arabs refuse to make peace," the defense minister explained, "we cannot stand still. If we are denied their cooperation, let us act on our own." The settlements reflected not only security needs, however, but also the pressure of Israel's militant religious bloc. It was this belligerent Orthodox minority that was chiefly responsible for evacuating several hundred Arab householders from the area adjacent to Jerusalem's Western Wall, and for establishing a Jewish settlement, Kiryat Arba, near Hebron, a town revered by devout Jews as the burial place of the Patriarchs.

Some outraged Palestinian Arabs devised their own response to these "facts." Before the war, it is recalled, a growing campaign of border violence had been mounted by the al-Fatah guerrilla organization. Now, after the June debacle, it was again this network of irregulars that revived its activities. The initiative for the renewed guerrilla upsurge was provided by a veteran Fatah leader, Yasser Arafat, a short, heavyset man in his late thirties, a distant relative of the ex-Mufti Haj Muhammad Amin al-Husseini. Convinced now that large Arab population centers under Israeli rule offered the combustible ingredients for a major insurrection, Arafat began to recruit members from the West Bank and Gaza, and in these same territories to attack Israeli patrols and kill Arab "collaborators." The guerrilla campaign in Palestine endured less than a year. Israeli countermeasures were forceful and effective. Indeed, they were helped substantially by the tacit cooperation of the West Bank population, which regarded Fatah violence as suicidal in the face of overwhelming Israeli military preponderance. By the end of 1968, as a result, some 1,400 Fatah members had been captured in the West Bank alone, and most of their cells rooted out.

Arafat's followers had no choice then but to move to the Hashemite East Bank, from whence they launched occasional forays across the river. But again, powerful Israeli counter-strikes wreaked a heavy toll on the Fatah, and the guerrillas pulled back deeper yet into integral Jordan. There they posed a graver threat to Hussein than to the Israelis, for they soon established a virtual substate of their own, flouted Hashemite laws, and eventually exercised near-veto power on the operation of Hussein's government. The Jordanian king swallowed this indignity for more than a year. But in September 1970, exploiting Egypt's momentary withdrawal of support for Arafat following the end of the War of Attrition (p. 584), Hussein loosed his Bedouin army against the Fatah and other guerrilla elements. Within ten days some two thousand *fedayeen* were slaughtered, and in the ensuing months their surviving remnants were driven from Jordan altogether.

If absence of local cooperation was one of the factors undermining Arafat's efforts in the occupied territories, it was no less the result of material prosperity under Israeli rule. Thus, in the Gaza Strip, which formerly comprised little more than a seething ant-heap of unemployed and embittered Arab refugees, the Israelis established factories, provided thousands of new jobs both on the spot and in Israel itself, and ultimately eradicated unemployment altogether in this once-volatile zone. Similarly, in the West Bank, Arab farmers were given access not only to the markets of the East Bank but also to Israeli markets. They received loans and subsidies as well, and extensive technological advice for their agriculture. Local industry similarly was augmented by Israeli investment funds and Israeli managerial expertise. Not least of all, some 100,000 West Bank Arabs found employment in Israel proper. The sum of these opportunities wiped out unemployment in the West Bank and raised the area's per capita income by 80 per cent between 1967 and 1973. Little wonder that the "administered" Arab population should have evinced meager interest in subversion of any kind.

THE WAR OF ATTRITION AND A MUTATION OF ARAB VIOLENCE

The Egyptian government was inhibited by no similar concern for the welfare of the occupied areas. Except for scattered Bedouin tribes, none of its citizens was under Israeli rule, and none therefore faced retaliation in the event of renewed warfare. Faced with domestic unrest, Nasser now regarded vindication on the battlefield as the one sure method of strengthening his hand within his own country. Indeed, his hand was already being strengthened by the Russians, who continued to pour vast quantities of weaponry into Egypt. As early as October 1968, therefore, the Egyptians launched into a "War of Attrition," using their superior manpower and artillery strength to mount a rising crescendo of bombardment on Israeli positions east of the Suez Canal. In April 1969, Nasser went so far as to declare the 1967 cease-fire void. His goal, clearly, was to prevent the transformation of the Canal into a *de facto* border, and to achieve this by inflicting such heavy casualties that the Israelis would be forced back deeper into the Sinai.

The weight of Egyptian manpower and artillery took its toll. The Israeli casualty rate had climbed to seventy a month by July 1969. To reverse the heavy losses, then, the Jews began digging into hardened concrete and steel-reinforced bunkers and fortifications. These positions were known subsequently as the Bar-Lev Line, after Israel's then chief of staff, General Chaim Bar-Lev. Simultaneously, Israeli planes battered away at enemy emplacements west of the Canal, then attacked Egyptian targets deep in the Nile Valley. By 1970 the countermeasures had forced the evacuation of some half million Egyptian civilians from the Canal Zone and destroyed a third of the Egyptian air fighter force. Not least of all, they inflicted a political humiliation on Nasser himself. In response to an urgent appeal from the Egyptian leader, finally, the Soviets agreed to enlarge even further the scale of their support. By spring of 1970 the Russians had dispatched not less than 14,000 military "advisers" to Egypt, together with a naval armada of sixty vessels off the Egyptian coast. More ominously yet, Soviet pilots assumed responsibility for the protection of the Egyptian interior, and even began flying combat patrols only fifty miles from the Canal. In June and July of 1970, too, Soviet-manned SAM antiaircraft rockets proved effective in shooting down a number of Israeli jets. Moscow clearly was laying its own prestige on the line, and the battle on the Canal's west bank had become almost overnight a Soviet-Israeli confrontation. By the end of July 1970, Israel had suffered 3,000 casualties since the 1967 war. In the event the Russians intervened directly, those losses would mount catastrophically.

There was another side to the picture. The Egyptians had taken a fearful pounding of their own, some 10,000 casualties to Israeli air and artillery action in 1970 alone. Then, on July 30, four Soviet planes were shot down over the Gulf of Suez by Israeli fighters. It was Jerusalem's warning that it was prepared to create a Vietnam for the Russians, if the latter were prepared to risk it. The Soviets were not. On July 23, Nasser won Moscow's approval for accepting an American-sponsored cease-fire, which thereupon came into effect on August 7. By then the United States had become as alarmed as Israel by the astonishing enlargement of the Soviet presence in the Mediterranean. This sense of joint anxiety, in turn, laid the basis for a much closer American-Israeli understanding, and in future months ensured the shipment of substantial quantities of American planes and other advanced weaponry to the Israelis. With the balance of power restored in the Middle East, the likelihood of renewed Arab-Israeli warfare apparently diminished for the near future.

The collapse, almost simultaneously, of the War of Attrition and of the guerrilla movement on Hashemite soil had the effect meanwhile of driving the *fedayeen* into Lebanon, the only remaining nation possessing a border contiguous with Israel. In the spring of 1970 the Arab guerrillas were sufficiently ensconced in this peaceful little trading nation to begin rocket firings and marauding attacks against Israeli border communities. Again the response was vigorous. Israel promptly launched an army sweep into "Fatahland," the Palestinian refugee and guerrilla enclaves along the Lebanese base of Mount Hermon, and then established an unofficial standing military presence in the hilly Lebanese border region. Very soon, as a result, *fedayun* penetration of Israeli territory was choked off.

Whatever their ideological divergences, the various guerrilla factions soon recognized that if traditional methods of assault against Israel had failed, they would have to strike at Israelis elsewhere—outside 'the Jewish state or even outside the Middle East itself. Accordingly, the *fedayeen* as early as 1968 developed the technique of aerial hijacking. In July of that year several (disguised) Arab passengers forced an El Al transport en route from Rome to Tel Aviv to land in Algeria, where it was immediately interned. The Algerian incident triggered a chain-reaction of *fedayun* assaults on El Al planes, and in 1969 and 1970 on those of other airlines maintaining scheduled service to Israel. Meanwhile, Israelis in a number of Western cities were killed or wounded by imported *fedayun* gunmen. The most sensational assault occurred at the Munich Olympic Games in the summer of 1972, when eleven Israeli athletes were captured and shot dead by Arab guerrillas.

Yet the magnitude both of Arab governmental hostility and of guerrilla violence remained in striking contrast to the quiescence of the "administered" territories themselves. By 1972, Israel, Gaza, and the West Bank were linked together economically in a kind of Palestinian "Common Market." Some 150,000 West Bank and Gaza Arabs were commuting to jobs in Israel, and almost as many Arabs from the Jordanian East Bank were visiting their kinsmen west of the river. Everywhere in the occupied areas the traditional pattern of mutual quarantine slowly was being eroded by daily contacts. During the West Bank local elections of 1972, some 82 per cent of the registered voters cast ballots, voting by and large for moderate representatives, those who favored a tacit accommodation with the Israeli presence. It was in turn the congeniality of these Arab-Jewish relations in the territories, as much as the unlikelihood of peace negotiations with neighboring Arab states, that dissuaded the Israeli government from making a serious effort to introduce an autonomous regime in the West Bank and Gaza.

Rather, Prime Minister Golda Meir, the 71-year-old Mapai veteran who had succeeded Eshkol upon the latter's death in 1969, quietly let it be known that she endorsed a formula proposed by Yigal Allon, Ahdut HaAvodah leader and now deputy prime minister. The "Allon Plan" envisaged *nahal* settlements on the hilly terrain overlooking the Jordan River, as a kind of permanent Israeli crescent encircling the occupied West Bank and guarding Israel's security along a "natural" defense frontier—without intruding flagrantly upon the more densely inhabited areas of the West Bank. Mrs. Meir went so far, however, as to encourage additional Jewish settlement not only in the Jordan Valley but also on the Golan Heights, even in the northern Sinai Peninsula and along the Red Sea littoral between Eilat and Sharm es-Sheikh. The economy and manpower of the territories continued gradually to be integrated with those of Israel. In this manner, the *faits accomplis* of the post-1967 years were emerging, bold and incontrovertible.

OVERTURE TO AN EARTHQUAKE

It was upon the basis of these "facts," an apparent military impregnability combined with a soaring postwar economic boom, that Israel's Labor party confidently began its campaign for the Eighth Knesset elections, scheduled for October 31, 1973. By then, indeed, the government's self-assurance influenced not only its political stance but its military posture as well. The nation luxuriated in the defense in depth afforded by the captured territories. Admittedly, the new defense lines created their own problems; for in the south, Egyptian and Israeli forces were "eyeball to eyeball" along the Canal, and Israel as a result had lost its crucial early warning time. Yet the Bar-Lev Line was intended at least partially to resolve this problem. During the War of Attrition the defense barrier had been strengthened by additional layers of concrete and by elaborate underground facilities, until its thirty major strongholds along the waterway came to resemble a miniature Maginot Line. To be sure, discipline in the armed forces had slipped in the early 1970's, and even weapons-maintenance had occasionally been neglected. Yet, for the while, little danger was perceived in a certain "relaxation." The Arabs surely would not be so foolhardly as to risk full-scale war again.

Neither was Israeli self-assurance weakened by the death of Nasser in September 1970, and his succession by Anwar al-Sadat, an apparent moderate. But, in fact, Sadat's moderation was deceptive. For all his apparent indifference to the late Nasser's doctrinaire socialism and Pan-Arabist adventurism, the new president was less the pacifist than he seemed. The truth was that Sadat was politically susceptible to domestic and army pressures for liberating the Canal. Failing to win American support in achieving a unilateral Israeli withdrawal, Sadat accordingly embarked on building a common strategy within the Arab camp. By 1973 he had won over President Hafez al-Assad in Syria to the notion of a joint military offensive against Israel early the following year. This common strategy, in turn, was profoundly influenced by Moscow's assurance of an accelerated flow of modern weaponry. Infuriated by the groundswell of Soviet Jewish demonstrations for emigration to Israel, the Kremlin envisaged a renewed Arab-Israeli war as an opportunity at the least to cripple the Zionist state economically, and reduce its ability to absorb large quantities of Soviet Jews.

After several postponements in 1973, Sadat and Assad eventually settled on the date of October 6 for their joint offensive. The water table of the Canal would be low then, the moon high for night crossings. The Israelis would be preoccupied with their won election campaign, they would be worshipping on their holy day of Yom Kippur, and in any case would hardly expect an attack during the Moslem festival of Ramadan. In the interval, Egypt's military staff shrewdly limited its objective to a crossing of Suez and the emplacement of forces on the east bank, without an immediate attempt to launch sweeping envelopments in Sinai beyond Egyptian missile protection. To that end, the Egyptians and Syrians now embarked upon a simple but thorough training program under Soviet guidance. Detailed models of Israeli fortifications were built, and endless rehearsals conducted for storming them. Both Arab forces counted heavily this time on SAM rockets to neutralize the superior Israeli air force, upon shorter interior lines than in previous wars, and upon an overwhelming superiority in manpower and weaponry.

Not least of all, the Arabs counted on surprise. Throughout September of 1973, even as the Egyptians and Syrians massively augmented their forces close to the cease-fire lines, they periodically withdrew selected units in the daylight hours to foster the illusion of large-scale training maneuvers.

At the same time, Sadat dispatched his emissaries to various Western capitals, including Washington, in what appeared to be renewed efforts to activate negotiations on the Middle East. As late as October 3 the Egyptian cabinet held its weekly meeting to discuss essentially domestic issues. The Israeli general staff was not oblivious to the magnitude of enemy troop concentrations, and indeed had responded vigorously to earlier threatened crises in December 1972 and April 1973. But the cost of mobilization each time had been heavy, and in October 1973 the Meir government regarded the latest Arab maneuvers simply as the continuation of a war of nerves. This assumption was not rebutted by Israeli military intelligence, which operated on the assumption that Sadat and Assad understood that a far-reaching offensive operation was unthinkable without dominant air power —which the Arabs did not have.

It was not until October 5, the eve of Yom Kippur, that the evidence of large-scale Arab preparations became too overwhelming to ignore. Early the next morning, therefore, Dayan and General David Elazar, the chief of staff, held an emergency meeting with Prime Minister Meir. Elazar requested a full, immediate mobilization and a preemptive air strike. For political reasons, Mrs. Meir rejected preemptive action. Instead, at Dayan's suggestion, she agreed simply to a limited, partial mobilization of 100,000 armored corps troops. Yet this qualified mobilization was executed in a slipshod fashion, with many trained regulars allowed to remain on leave, and with reserve personnel ordered on the alert for an attack that was anticipated at 6:00 P.M. that day.

THE YOM KIPPUR WAR

In fact, the assault began at 2:00 P.M. with thousands of shells and bombs exploding among Israeli positions on the eastern bank of the Canal and on the cease-fire line of the Golan Heights. In the north, heliborne Syrian commandos swept out of the mist to capture Israel's "eyes," the radar-surveillance station atop Mount Hermon. Simultaneously, not less than 800 Syrian tanks and three infantry divisions blasted through the lightly-defended Israeli picket and swept headlong through the Golan Plateau. By dawn of the seventh, advance Syrian columns had all but inundated the remnants of Israeli armor and were within gunnery range of the Jordan River. At the foot of the Golan, in the Huleh and Jordan valleys, kibbutzim began hastily evacuating wives and children. With Israeli reserves arriving at the front belatedly, in ill-organized units, the shadow of a new holocaust descended upon the Jewish state.

To the southwest, during those same grim hours of October 6–7, the Israelis were tasting the power of one of the largest standing armies in the world. Covered by a murderous shelling of the Bar-Lev Line, waves of Egyptian infantry crossed the Canal in fiberglass boats. Flooding on between and behind the Israeli positions, the Egyptians by nightfall had ensconced fully 30,000 troops throughout the eastern length of the waterway. That night, pontoon bridges went up across the Canal and tanks began moving over. The Israeli air force, decimated by SAM missiles, was unable to stem the avalanche. Neither was Israeli armor. Under cover of darkness, Egyptian infantrymen used Sagger rockets to destroy scores of counterattacking tanks. The Israeli command hurriedly attempted to reinforce its defenses at the Gidi and Mitla passes; but if the mobilization effort lagged on the Golan front, much closer to Israel, it was even more gravely obstructed in the distant Sinai. Days passed before reserve armored units could arrive. During the interval, the Egyptians completed their encirclement and capture of the Bar-Lev fortifications. News of these reverses at the Canal and on the Golan shocked the Israeli nation to its depths.

By noon of October 9, Israel's general staff reached a critical decision: to shift most of the reserves originally allocated for Sinai to the Golan front, where a Syrian breakthrough appeared imminent into the Galilee. News had arrived, too, that an Iraqi division was approaching Syria, and that Hussein was about to open a third front. Israel's air force consequently turned its full strength against the Syrian civilian economy, bombing key power stations and fuel reservoirs. Although suffering heavy losses, the fliers managed in this fashion to lever the Syrian missile system back from the Golan. Throughout the ninth, too, Israeli armored reinforcements were arriving on the Golan in larger numbers, inflicting heavy casualties on the enemy. By nightfall the initial Syrian drive was shattered. Within hours, a makeshift Israeli force began counterattacking, and by late afternoon of the tenth actually succeeded in recapturing most of the lost terrain. It was a remarkable comeback.

The struggle on the Suez and Golan battlefields was critical enough in its international implications, meanwhile, to require decisive Great Power action. Within hours of the Arab attack Washington was calling for a ceasefire and a return to the original pre-October 6 lines. It was a proposal that Sadat and Assad, in the exhilaration of their initial victories, rejected with contempt. Rather, in the United Nations, the Soviet delegate vehemently supported Arab demands for a total Israeli withdrawal to the pre-1967 frontiers. And outside the United Nations, Moscow openly called upon other Arab nations to supply troops and transport facilities to Egypt and Syria. By October 9, in fact, the Soviets augmented their massive arms shipments to the Arabs by inaugurating a round-the-clock airlift of tanks, guns, and ammunition to Egyptian and Syrian fields.

Both the flagrancy and the magnitude of this Soviet intercession were a grave shock to the Nixon administration in Washington, and particularly to Secretary of State Kissinger, the author of "detente" with the Russians. Although a Jew himself, and thus inclined to circumspection on Middle Eastern issues, Kissinger recognized that a Soviet-engineered victory in the Middle East would critically alter the Mediterranean balance of power. After initial hesitation, therefore, the United States government finally responded to Israel's anguished appeal for planes, tanks, and other matériel, to compensate for the disastrous early losses of the war. On October 13, giant American air force cargo planes, loaded with crucial ordnance, began an emergency airlift to Israel. Between October 13 and November 14, the

United States transported 22,000 tons of equipment in 566 flights. As it turned out, the timely infusion literally saved Israel's war effort.

A REVERSAL OF MILITARY FORTUNES

Even earlier, on October 11, the day Israel's armor cracked the Syrian defenses, Elazar and his colleagues agreed that the principal military effort now could safely be transferred to the Egyptian front. By then fully 70,000 enemy troops had crossed the Canal and had established an unbroken front six miles in depth. In fact, this represented the apogee of Egypt's offensive. Spending the next few days consolidating their positions, Sadat's forces inadvertently allowed Israel time to shift its armor to the protection of the vital Gidi and Mitla passes, gateways to the eastern Sinai. When finally, at dawn of October 14, some 650 Egyptian tanks moved forward toward the passes, they were awaited by 430 Israeli tanks. The battle lasted half a day, and it was a slaughter; over 250 Egyptian tanks were destroyed within the first two hours of combat. Sadat's generals then attempted to bring infantry forward, but hundreds of their personnel carriers were similarly knocked out. By the time the Egyptians retreated in disarray after midnight, Israel had won an armored victory that exceeded even Montgomery's triumph over Rommel in 1942.

Immediately, then, the Israelis made the decision to move to the offensive. Plans were laid for crossing the waterway on the evening of October 15. In the deepening twilight of the fifteenth, General Ariel Sharon's armor pushed through sand dunes toward the Canal's east bank. Only a few thousand yards from its intended staging area, however, this task force was struck by heavy Egyptian fire. A furious battle erupted, and was destined to continue for the next two days. Undaunted, Sharon decided not to await his portable bridge. Under cover of darkness, a small advance force of his men crossed over on rafts. They went undetected. Even as merciless enemy fire on the east bank continued, Israeli engineers managed to lash tanks onto barges and send them floating across the water. By evening of the sixteenth, 30 tanks and 2,000 soldiers had reached the west bank. During the next day, Israeli armor finally succeeded in rumbling over hastily erected pontoon bridges in some strength.

Although Cairo awakened now to the fact that the Israeli crossing was more than a raid, the discovery came too late. Throughout the eighteenth, growing columns of Israeli tanks were systematically destroying Egyptian missile batteries, tearing great holes in enemy air defenses. Israeli planes now supplied cover for the unfolding offensive. Soon Israeli armor was pushing south through the agricultural terrain of the west bank and threatening to outflank Egyptian forces in Sinai. The brilliant and audacious maneuver completely reversed the course of the war.

Watching this new development with mounting concern, the Soviet government on October 18 quickly shifted its own diplomatic course and persuaded Sadat to agree to a cease-fire in place—an action the Egyptian president had scorned until that moment. It was the Israelis, however, who appeared likely to reject the offer, now that they had turned the tide of battle. Thus, to ensure their compliance, the Soviets requested an immediate emergency meeting with Kissinger. The American secretary of state flew to Moscow on October 20, and there reached agreement with the Russians on a cease-fire formula. As inducement for stopping in place, the Israelis would be assured not only a stronger bargaining position, with their forces established at last on the Canal's west bank, but joint Soviet-American endorsement of direct peace negotiations between Israel and Egypt. Under American pressure, then, the Golda Meir cabinet reluctantly accepted this formula, which was immediately incorporated in a new Security Council Resolution on October 22.

For the Israeli general staff, time now became vital, to close the trap on the Canal's west bank before the cease-fire came into effect at 6:50 that evening. Their best opportunity was in the south, where Egyptian resistance was crumbling. Thus, while Israel's armored columns did not quite reach the Gulf of Suez, the cease-fire deadline found the Egyptian Third Army with its supply lines cut, 8,000 of its troops already prisoners in Israel's hands, and its main force of 20,000 men on the east bank in mortal danger. Under these circumstances, the Egyptians ignored the cease-fire and launched a frenzied effort to break the Israeli vise. Thereupon the Jews renewed their offensive on the twenty-third, battering southward until they reached the Gulf. By then the Egyptian Third Army was entirely trapped.

Facing this disaster, Sadat on October 23 issued a panic-stricken appeal for Soviet help. Moscow responded by issuing a dire warning to Washington that, unless the Israelis withdrew immediately to the October 22 cease-fire line, the Soviets would intercede unilaterally to save their Egyptian client. Kissinger's and Nixon's response to this threat, in turn, was to order a world-wide alert of American armed forces. The Russians backed down. Yet once again, as in 1956 and 1967, the Arab-Israeli conflict had threatened a Great Power confrontation. The implications for the future were ominous. At American insistence, meanwhile, the Israelis accepted a second United Nations cease-fire resolution on November 24. Indeed, at that point, they had accomplished more than simply cutting their enemy's supply lines. The cost of war with Israel, even under the most favorable circumstances to the Arabs, had well registered on the Sadat government. Like the Syrians, the Egyptians had lost many thousands of casualties and the bulk of their equipment. Their capital, too, had been threatened.

However much the Israelis would have cherished letting Sadat savor the full flavor of his defeat, they were constrained by Washington to allow a Red Cross convoy to pass across the Canal with food and medicines for the beleaguered Egyptian Third Army. This gesture reflected not alone concern for the fate of over 200 Israeli prisoners in Egyptian hands, but a sober appraisal of what renewed fighting would entail. In its purely military terms, the Yom Kippur War had ended with the most impressive victory in the Jewish state's history. But the price had been exceptionally high: 2,552 dead and over 3,000 wounded in the eighteen days of fighting, painful attrition for a small nation. The expenditure of equipment and damaged property, the cost of manpower mobilization, and the decline in production, totaled $7 billion, the equivalent of Israel's Gross National Product for an entire year. Four brutal wars had taken place within a single generation. How much longer, the Israelis wondered, could this endless hemorrhage in lives and material resources be sustained?

AFTERMATH OF AN EARTHQUAKE

There were other costs, too, in international isolation, that affected Israel's subsequent negotiating position. Within days after the outbreak of war, the full complement of African nations, with which Israel had maintained uniquely cordial relations over the previous decade and a half (p. 573), closed ranks with their Arab partners in the Organization of African Unity and severed diplomatic relations with Jerusalem. In part the decision reflected Arab economic pressure, in part a reactive spasm to Israel's invasion of African Egypt. The political setback was shattering for Israel. Yet it was the erosion of European support that proved even more traumatic for the Israelis—and the Americans. Fearful of being sucked into a confrontation with the Soviets, America's NATO allies all but unanimously refused to provide the United States with refueling bases during the wartime airlift to Israel. Nor could this European temerity be attributed to detente politics alone. The Arab oil embargo proved a decisive weapon. In the midst of the war, on October 17, the various Arab petroleum ministers gathered in Kuwait to vote a total oil cutoff to the United States and a selective cutback in oil shipments to the NATO powers—America's (and, by implication, Israel's) allies. Accompanying this orchestrated embargo was a massive and indiscriminate oil price-rise that threatened seriously to cripple the Western economies. Quite frantic by then under Arab pressure, the Common Market nations on November 6 issued a declaration urging Israel to restore all captured Arab territories and to take into account "the rights of the Palestinians."

As the Israeli government faced this diplomatic quarantine, it sensed that its last best hope was the United States. But Kissinger in turn was keenly aware that the United States was in a unique position to exert its influence on both exhausted parties to achieve a Middle East settlement. Sadat, who had regained face by crossing the Canal, but whose army had been spared a murderous beating only at the last moment by American intercession, had intimated that he was in no mood to prolong an indefinite war. Neither, surely, were the Israelis. As a result, the secretary of state persuaded the Meir cabinet to allow a permanent supply corridor to the trapped Egyptian Third Army, in return for Egyptian agreement both to an exchange of prisoners and to the principle of an early peace conference with the Israelis at Geneva. Following this understanding, on November 15, 1973, the first scheduled convoys began rolling across the waterway to the Third Army. Egypt released 238 Israeli war prisoners, and Israel returned some 8,000 Egyptians.

Thereupon, during a series of personal visits to Middle Eastern capitals,

Kissinger succeeded in pinning down the Israelis, Egyptians, and Jordanians (but not the Syrians) to the widely heralded "peace conference." Held nominally under United Nations auspices, but in practical fact under the joint chairmanship of the United States and the Soviet Union, the conference of foreign ministers began in Geneva on December 22, 1973. Although the formal gathering devolved into little more than an exchange of propaganda broadsides, the conference by prearrangement was "temporarily" adjourned to give Israeli and Egyptian military teams an opportunity to negotiate a disengagement of forces. These lower-level discussions similarly proved unproductive. It was left then to Kissinger to begin a new round of personal shuttle diplomacy between Cairo and Jerusalem.

Again, the secretary's efforts were successful. By January 17, 1974, he had managed to persuade both sides to accept a disengagement arrangement that embraced an Israeli withdrawal from the west bank of the Canal and from advance positions on the east bank some 15 miles into integral Egypt. The *quid pro quo* was Sadat's agreement to reduce the Egyptian military presence on the east bank to a nominal 7,000 troops and a few score guns and tanks. A buffer zone would separate both sides on the east bank. If Israel had unilaterally abandoned the territorial advantage gained in the recent war, as well as the promised diplomatic breakthrough of face-to-face negotiations with the enemy, it was by no means left empty-handed under the disengagement agreement. Through Kissinger, Sadat promised not only to reopen the Canal and repopulate the Canal cities—thereby in effect making them hostages to peace—but also to allow Israeli (nonmilitary) cargoes to pass through the waterway in third-party vessels. In their satisfaction with this disengagement, the Arab nations simultaneously agreed to end their oil embargo.

By then Kissinger's reputation as a "miracle man of peace" was sufficiently enhanced for him to be asked by Syria and Israel to negotiate a similar disengagement on the Golan front. The task consumed most of the spring of 1974, but after endless shuttling between Damascus and Tel Aviv, the secretary finally refined an acceptable compromise formula on May 31. The Israelis pulled back from the territory occupied in the recent war, even from Quneitra, the Golan capital taken in the 1967 conflict. Little of strategic value was abandoned on the plateau, however. Troops and equipment were limited on both sides of the new disengagement line, and separated by a buffer zone occupied by a 1,250-man UN "observer" force. Most important of all to Israel, sixty-five of its prisoners of war, those who had survived a particularly harrowing Syrian captivity, were now repatriated. For the near future, the likelihood faded of renewed hostilities in the north.

POLITICAL UPHEAVAL, DIPLOMATIC ISOLATION

Yet the impact of the recent war remained a palpable fact of life in Israel itself. Although the December 31, 1973 Knesset elections (they had been postponed from October 31) allowed the Labor coalition to retain a working, if attenuated, majority, the new government survived only three weeks.

It was torpedoed by an official commission report, issued on April 12, 1974, dealing with Israel's lack of preparedness for the Yom Kippur hostilities. The document severely indicted senior officials of the military intelligence branch, and even Chief of Staff Elazar. At the commission's recommendation, therefore, the cabinet accepted the resignations of the impugned officers. Yet if the report abstained from commenting explicitly upon Dayan's responsibility for Israel's unpreparedness, the public at large was unwilling to exonerate the defense minister, nor by implication Prime Minister Meir. Public demonstrations, editorial criticism, and finally a revolt within the Labor party itself, had their cumulative effect. On April 10, 1974, Mrs. Meir submitted her resignation, thus causing the fall of her cabinet.

Labor's task at this point was to find a successor to the redoubtable old woman. Eventually the party's central committee reached agreement on an essentially apolitical choice. This was Yitzhak Rabin, who had served as chief of staff during Israel's spectacular 1967 victory. Although Rabin was currently minister of labor in the Meir cabinet, he was untainted by the setbacks of the recent war. Rather, as an authentic popular hero, and as a former ambassador to Washington, he was seen as the man best capable of exploiting Israel's special relationship with the United States and of achieving a negotiated peace with the Arabs. At the least, as Israel's first native-born prime minister, heading a cabinet of men in their early middle age, Rabin inaugurated a new era in the nation's political life: a transfer from the generation of Ben-Gurion, Sharett, Eshkol, and Golda Meir to a younger *sabra*, or near-*sabra*, generation.

Rabin inherited problems, however, that would have overwhelmed even a political veteran. The cost of the war, the vastly heavier defense budget required by withdrawal from the Suez barrier, and the leap in import prices world-wide caused by escalating Arab oil charges, all had the effect of touching off a skyrocketing Israeli inflation. The price level jumped 56 per cent in 1974 alone. Under the circumstances, the Rabin government was obliged to impose drastic new taxes and to curtail public subsidies for food and transportation. These measures were not only unbearably rigorous for the Israeli population; they had the effect, as well, of inhibiting immigration from other countries, and not least of all from the Soviet Union, which in the years before the Yom Kippur War had allowed as many as 30,000 Jews to depart annually for Israel. Indeed, the postwar austerity, the dangers of renewed hostilities on the scale of 1973, intensified a serious outflow of Israelis to affluent and presumably safer Western countries. By 1977 fully 300,000 Israelis were settled in the United States alone.

The impact of Israel's initial defeats in the recent war was no less evident among Palestinian Arabs. Thus, in the Knesset elections of December 1973, the Arabs of Israel cast an unprecedented 32 per cent of their vote for Rakah, the Communist (in effect, Arab nationalist) faction. In the West Bank and Gaza, there was a sudden upsurge of bombing attacks against Israeli installations. To the younger Arab inhabitants of the occupied territories, meanwhile, the recent struggle appeared to confirm the belief that

Israel was militarily vulnerable after all, and that force, not Jordanian-Israeli negotiations, was the one practicable method of terminating Israeli rule. As the nationalists saw it, too, only Yasser Arafat and the PLO once again embodied that alternative.

In fact, Arafat and the other guerrilla leaders envisaged more than the liquidation of Israel's presence in the West Bank. They anticipated the liquidation of Israel altogether. The Israelis understood this with perfect clarity as, after the October war, *fedayun* infiltrators slipped across the Lebanese border, renewing their attacks on Jewish frontier villages, indiscriminately killing men, women, and children. Israel did not hesitate to retaliate, sending its army units again into southern Lebanon, scouring "Fatahland," blowing up houses, abducting suspected guerrilla collaborators. These preemptive measures did nothing for Israel's image in the West, and surely not among spokesmen for the "Third World" and the "New Left," who increasingly embraced the *fedayun* cause. Indeed, defying the provisions of the United Nations Charter itself, in October 1974 the Communist-Afro-Asian majority in the General Assembly voted to invite Arafat to address the world body (whereupon the Fatah leader promptly demanded a "secular" state for all of Palestine). In the summer of 1975 the General Assembly came within a hair's breadth of expelling Israel from the United Nations altogether, and the following November isolated Israel diplomatically by endorsing a resolution that described the Jewish state as "the racist regime in occupied Palestine."

In its state of near-quarantine, therefore, Israel concentrated its hopes upon the United States. Yet by then Washington was committed to maintaining its leverage in both camps in the hope of achieving a negotiated settlement, and with it a possible reduction of Arab oil prices. To that end, Kissinger proposed to bypass a resumed Geneva conference in favor of shuttle diplomacy between Israel and Egypt. The proposal was gratefully accepted. Like Sadat, Rabin was prepared to go the indirect route again, sure that it offered more tangible possibilities than an exchange of propaganda charges in "direct" negotiations. In any case, Rabin had devised a formula under which Israel would gauge the extent of its additional Sinai withdrawal by the extent of meaningful Egyptian political concessions: in short, "a piece of territory for a piece of peace."

Kissinger discovered, however, as he resumed his shuttle diplomacy in March 1975, that Rabin's formula was one the Egyptians were not prepared initially to accept. Rather, Sadat insisted that the Israelis withdraw from some two-thirds of the Sinai, including the Mitla and Gidi passes, the two defiles that represented Israel's last natural protective barrier in the south; while in return the Egyptian leader was unwilling to offer meaningful assurances of nonbelligerency. The Israelis for their part held firm, and negotiations soon broke down. It was not until several weeks later that Sadat intimated finally that he might be willing to compromise for the sake of reviving his nation's moribund economy. As triangular diplomacy was quietly resumed, Kissinger's intercession at last bore fruit. In September 1975 an agreement was initialed by Sadat and Rabin. Under its terms,

Israel agreed to withdraw its forces to the eastern entrances of the Gidi and Mitla passes. The Egyptians would move closer to the western entrances. In neither of these critical zones, however, would the parties be allowed more than a minimal number of troops and heavy weapons; while in the "buffer" area of the defiles themselves, a United Nations occupation force would be supplemented by some two hundred American technicians, who would monitor electronic listening stations as warning against unauthorized military movement. The accord did not significantly weaken Israel's strategic posture in the Sinai.

What was ominous in the agreement, on the other hand, was Sadat's unwillingness to provide Israel with the latter's most coveted desideratum, a public Egyptian statement of nonbelligerency. Instead, the document's most important assurances were embodied in an Egyptian commitment not to Israel, but rather to the United States, as the third party in the curious triangular negotiations. It was of some consolation to the Israelis, admittedly, that Washington buttressed these assurances with promises of its own to Jerusalem: of an open-ended supply of weapons in the years ahead; of support for Israel's insistence on face-to-face negotiations in any future Syrian or Jordanian disengagements; and of close consultations with Israel in the event of a direct Soviet military threat to the Jewish state. Even so, recalling Washington's open hostility in 1956, its paralysis in the weeks before the 1967 war, and its "evenhandedness" following the Yom Kippur conflict, large numbers of Israelis were skeptical of placing full value on American guarantees. Although the Knesset eventually ratified the second disengagement agreement in September 1975, it did so only as an agonized gamble that peace somehow might be wrested from the abyss of endless bloodshed and mutual suspicion.

CONCLUSION

If Israel faced the seemingly implacable hostility of its Arab neighbors as it approached the fourth decade of its independence, it wrestled with the no less invidious danger of moral erosion from within. Following the spectacular victory of the Six-Day War, life in the Jewish state had experienced an attrition of its cherished Yishuv characteristics of straightforwardness and camaraderie. Respect for plain and simple hard work, for the dedicated self-sacrifice of the original Zionist redemptive effort, had been threatened by the post-1967 boom, with its reservoir of cheap labor from the "administered" Arab territories. Yet if self-indulgence had become the mood during the seven ensuing "fat years," the Yom Kippur War may well have represented the moment of truth for the nation's political and intellectual leadership; for it was now evident that public complacency had gone so far as to affect even the nation's military discipline—indeed, had threatened its very survival.

The lesson was not lost. By the late 1970's, as a result, the outlines of an embryonic moral awakening were becoming faintly visible. The topics discussed in schools, the letters written to newspapers, the articles published in journals, the questions raised in public lectures, appeared to erase any doubt that the country's most sentient elements were obsessed by the need to find their way back to the causeway of an "authentic" and idealistic Zionism. Indeed, one of the most intriguing consequences of that search was the emergence in late 1976 of a new political party, the Democratic Movement for Change. The DMC's leader was Professor Yigael Yadin, commander of Israel's army during the 1948 War of Liberation, and subsequently a distinguished archaeologist at the Hebrew University. One of the country's most respected figures, his reputation untainted by earlier involvement in the tub-thumping of conventional politics, Yadin called for a moral regeneration, a revamping of the desiccated party-list system, a renewed concentration upon the social needs of the "other" Israel—that is, of the Oriental majority.

Yadin's impact was destined to be far-reaching. By the early months of 1977, the public was shocked by exposures of corruption among the ruling Labor party. Government ministers and other eminent party officials were revealed to have been guilty of influence-peddling, of bribery and profiteering. It was ironic that Yitzhak Rabin himself, who had come to the prime ministry less than three years before as a "new broom," and who in fact had effected numerous improvements in Israel's diplomatic and military posture, should have been found guilty with his wife of illegal currency transactions stemming from his earlier tenure as ambassador to the United States. Faced with impending national elections, Rabin chose to resign as Labor's candidate; in April 1977 he was replaced by Shimon Peres—long a contender for his party's top post. Yet the last-minute substitution proved insufficient to rescue Labor's cause. The May 18 elections allowed the voters to express their revulsion at the Left's flaccidity, its inability to check the rampant political nepotism, the soaring inflation and chronic industrial strikes that had all but paralyzed Israel's ability to achieve economic growth, or even stability.

Thus, in a political upheaval of unprecedented magnitude, Labor's representation in the Knesset dropped from 51 seats to 32, a collapse that deprived the Socialists of their control of the government for the first time in the twenty-nine years of Israeli independence. No less astonishing was the emergence of the Likud party as the major beneficiary of the political revolution. This coalition of the former Herut and Liberal parties increased its representation in the Knesset from 39 to 43 seats, and accordingly Likud's spokesman, Menahem Begin, was charged with organizing Israel's first right-wing cabinet. However, if the nation was stunned at the prospect of a fire-eater like Begin as its next prime minister, it nevertheless re-evaluated the full import of the election during the subsequent postmortems. Plainly, the electorate had not registered its approbation of Begin as its future leader, and still less had it intended to give a mandate to Begin's avowedly annexationist designs on the West Bank. In truth, Likud had picked up a mere four seats over its 1973 showing.

Rather, the vote had signified a repudiation of corruption and complacency, and a gesture of support for the Democratic Movement for Change.

For it was Yadin's meteoric new group, winning an astonishing fifteen seats in the forthcoming Knesset, that had spelled the margin of Labor's defeat. And it was the "moral" protest represented by the DMC, as a result, that portended the most far-reaching changes in Israel's social and political configuration. It bespoke the nation's obsession with renewal and regeneration. Indeed, whatever the immediate composition of the new government, that obsession was the nation's best hope of meaningful and creative survival. For within it lay the seeds of renewed dedication: to the kind of morally-infused civilization that Herzl and Weizmann alike, and the ensuing generations of their spiritual followers, had envisaged as Israel's—the People of Israel's—unique and abiding mission to the contemporary world.

The Jews had come a long way since those early days when our traveler-friend had first encountered them as harassed and obsequious peddlers locked in the squalid *Judengasse* of Frankfurt. In the second half of the twentieth century one had only to survey the principal centers of Jewish life to realize how far the road extended. In London it led to the House of Lords, where Jewish peers shared their Parliamentary responsibilities with the scions of England's oldest baronial families. In Paris the road led to the Cour de Cassation, the Supreme Court, where a Jewish Chief Justice presided with calm authority over France's most far-reaching litigation. In the United States the road led to the Governor's Mansion in Connecticut, to the Senate chambers in Washington, to innumerable city halls and state legislatures, where Jewish political figures occasionally cast the decisive votes. The road of Jewish progress led from the backward little *heder* of a nineteenth-century *shtetl* to the renowned libraries of the twentieth century, where Jewish names appeared on thousands of volumes dealing variously with physics, philosophy, literature, politics, indeed with virtually all the sciences and the arts.

The road led to faculty clubs at Harvard and Oxford, where Jewish professors shared classroom experiences with their Christian colleagues; it led to hospitals in Rio de Janeiro and Buenos Aires where Jewish surgeons performed delicate operations on the leading citizens of Latin America; to courtrooms in Melbourne and Johannesburg, where Jewish barristers pleaded the causes of the Commonwealth's most powerful corporations. The road led from the wealthy Jewish *shtadtlan*, the banker-intercessor of the early nineteenth century, who stood, hat in hand, waiting to petition a Council of Ministers on behalf of his rightless people, to the General Assembly of the United Nations, where an Israeli delegate cast his vote on issues affecting not only the Jews of Israel, but the Catholics of Latin America and Hungary, and the Protestants of East Germany.

The road which traversed a century and a half of Jewish history was riddled with pitfalls, as well, and was barred at every juncture by new obstacles. For long decades its course passed through dark tunnels of oppression—in Metternichian Europe, in czarist Russia, in the postwar Ukraine—and the casualties of those agonies of darkness numbered in the hundreds of thousands. When, at last, the road seemed to open for permanent and unimpeded progress, it was inundated once again, this time by the avalanche of the "Final Solution." Thus, while the squalid ghetto of Frankfurt no longer existed, neither did the Jews of Frankfurt; nor the historic Jewish populations of Berlin, Warsaw, Amsterdam, Budapest, or Bucharest. Between the Vistula and the Seine only a tiny remnant of the vital and creative Jewry of 1939 still remained alive. In Russia three million Jews still survived; their bondage under the soviets, however, was hardly less oppressive than it had been under the czars.

But while the tragedy of the Nazi and Soviet eras cannot be overestimated, it is clear that the road is in the open again, that humiliations and disabilities are no longer the rule in Jewish life. Virtually all Jews who today live outside the Iron Curtain—and they are the great majority—are free people. They are free in their legal and political security, but also in their opportunities for intellectual self-expression; and in most instances, too, they are steadily emancipating themselves from their ancestral legacy of psychological insecurity. Each year of their journey the Jews have moved closer to equality, to opportunity, and, in the case of Israel, to the dignity of national sovereignty. There are those who now look back in complacency and indifference, who accept the fruits of the long journey but ignore the bitter cost of liberation and its lessons in tenacity and endurance. They are the strangers and the road passes them by. There are others who look back with gratitude and humility, who remember that few present blessings have been won without the sacrifices of the past, who continually re-evaluate the spiritual and cultural treasures which the travail of the journey has produced. These are the true heirs of the generations, and for them the long and agonizing journey has been worth while.

BIBLIOGRAPHY

BIBLIOGRAPHICAL NOTE

The bibliography of each chapter has been dealt with as a self-contained unit. Thus, the reader will note that listings of volumes and articles have been repeated in their entirety as they reappear in new chapters. Whenever possible, too, foreign works are referred to in their English translations. For example, although Theodor Herzl's writings are available in their original nineteenth-century German editions, they have been listed here according to their date and place of publication in translation.

While many journals have been of value in the preparation of this volume, the author wishes to express his particular gratitude to those two splendid organizations, the Conference on Jewish Social Studies and the Yiddish Scientific Institute (YIVO); their publications, *Jewish Social Studies, YIVO Bletter,* and the *YIVO Annuals of Jewish Social Science,* have been literally indispensable as sources both of textual material and of bibliographical reference.

Bibliography

I. THE JEW AS NON-EUROPEAN

BARON, SALO W. *The Jewish Community*, 3 vols. (Vol. II.) Philadelphia, 1942.
ENGELMAN, URIAH ZEVI. *The Rise of the Jew in the Western World*. New York, 1944.
FINKELSTEIN, LOUIS. *Jewish Self-Government in the Middle Ages*. New York, 1924.
FRISCH, E. *Historical Survey of Jewish Philanthropy*. New York, 1924.
LOWENTHAL, MARVIN. *The Jews of Germany*. Philadelphia, 1944.
——. *A World Passed By*. New York, 1933.
MARCUS, JACOB. *The Jew in the Medieval World*. Cincinnati, 1939.
PHILIPSON, DAVID. *Old European Jewries*. Philadelphia, 1894.

FOR FURTHER RESEARCH

ALTMANN, BERTHOLD. "The Autonomous Federation of Jewish Communities in Paderhorn," *Jewish Social Studies*, April, 1941.
BARON, SALO W. *A Social and Religious History of the Jews*. 3 vols. (Vol. II.) New York, 1937.
BER OF BOLECHOW. *Memoirs*, ed. M. Vishnitzer. London, 1922.
CRONBACH, A. *Religion and Its Social Setting*. Cincinnati, 1933.
DUBNOW, SIMON M. *History of the Jews in Russia and Poland*. 3 vols. (Vol. I.) Philadelphia, 1946.
——. *Pinkas ha-Medinah*. (Minutes of the Lithuanian Council of Provinces.) Berlin, 1925.
——. *Weltgeschichte des jüdischen Volkes*. 3 vols. (Vol. II.) Jerusalem, 1938.
ELBOGEN, I. *Geschichte der Juden in Deutschland*. Berlin, 1935.
FINKELSTEIN, LOUIS (ed.). *The Jews: Their History, Culture, and Religion*. 4 vols. Philadelphia, 1949.
GLÜCKEL OF HAMELN. *Memoirs*, ed. Marvin Lowenthal. New York, 1932.
GRAETZ, HEINRICH. *History of the Jews*. 6 vols. (Vols. IV, V.) Philadelphia, 1894.
HALPERIN, ISRAEL. "Accounts of the Council of Four Lands in Poland" (Hebrew), *Tarbiz*, VI, 1934-35.
——. "The Council of Four Lands and the Hebrew Book" (Hebrew), *Kirjath Sepher*, IX, 1932.
——. "Zur Frage der Zusammensetzung der Vierländersynode in Polen," *Monatsschrift für Geschichte und Wissenschaft des Judentums*, LXXVI, 1932.
LESTSCHINSKY, JACOB. "The Pauperization of the Jewish Masses in Poland" (Yiddish), *YIVO Bletter*, March-April, 1934.
OELSNER, TONI. "The Jewish Ghetto of the Past," *YIVO Annual of Jewish Social Science*, I, 1946.
PARKES, JAMES. *The Jew in the Medieval Community*. London, 1938.
POSENER, S. "The Social Life of the Jewish Communities in France in the Eighteenth Century," *Jewish Social Studies*, July, 1945.

ROTH, CECIL. "Memoirs of a Siennese Jew," *Hebrew Union College Annual,* V, 1928.

——. "Origin of the Ghetto: A Final Word," *Romania,* LX, 1934.

SCHIPPER, I. "Polish Regesta for the History of the Council of Four Lands" (Yiddish), (*Historische Schriften.* 3 vols. Vol. I. YIVO.) Warsaw, 1929.

SHOHET, D. M. *The Jewish Court in the Middle Ages.* New York, 1931.

SOSIS, I. "The Jewish Diet in Lithuania and White Russia in Its Legislative Activity" (Yiddish), *Zeitschrift* (Minsk), II-III, 1928.

STARR, JOSHUA. "The Ghetto." (*Universal Jewish Encyclopedia.* Vol. IV.) New York, 1948.

TEIMANAS, D. B. *L'Autonomie des communautés juives en Pologne aux XVIe et XVIIe siècles.* Paris, 1933.

II. THE GLIMMERING OF DAWN IN THE WEST

ALTMANN, BERTHOLD. "Jews and the Rise of Capitalism," *Jewish Social Studies,* April, 1943.

ARENDT, HANNAH. "Privileged Jews," *Jewish Social Studies,* January, 1946.

BARON, SALO W. "Ghetto and Emancipation," *Menorah Journal,* June, 1928.

BARZILAY, ISAAC E. "The Jew in the Literature of the Enlightenment," *Jewish Social Studies,* October, 1956.

FEUCHTWANGER, LION. *The Jew Süss.* London, 1927.

LESSING, GOTTHOLD. *Nathan the Wise.* New York, 1917.

MAIMON, SOLOMON. *An Autobiography,* ed. Moses Hadas. New York, 1947.

ROTHMAN, WALTER. "Mendelssohn's Character and Philosophy of Religion," *Yearbook of the Central Conference of American Rabbis,* XXIX, 1929.

STERN, SELMA. *The Court Jew.* Philadelphia, 1950.

WALTER, HERMANN. *Moses Mendelssohn.* New York, 1930.

FOR FURTHER RESEARCH

ANDRÉADÈS, A. M. *History of the Bank of England.* London, 1924.

ANSCHEL, R. "Les juifs à Paris au XVIIIe siècle," *Bulletin de la Société de l'histoire de Paris,* XIX, 1932.

BARON, SALO W. *The Jewish Community.* 3 vols. (Vol. II.) Philadelphia, 1942.

——. *A Social and Religious History of the Jews.* 3 vols. (Notes on Italian and Dutch Haskalah, Vol. III.) New York, 1937.

BLOOM, HERBERT. *The Economic Activities of the Jews of Amsterdam in the Seventeenth and Eighteenth Centuries.* Williamsport (Pennsylvania), 1937.

BOURGIN, G. "Le Problème de fonction économique de juifs," *Souvenir et Science,* III, 1932.

DUBNOW, SIMON M. *An Outline of Jewish History.* 5 vols. (Vol. II.) New York, 1925.

ELBOGEN, I. *Geschichte der Juden in Deutschland.* Berlin, 1935.

EMMERICH, H. *Das Judentum bei Voltaire.* Breslau, 1930.

ENGELMAN, URIAH ZEVI. *The Rise of the Jew in the Western World.* New York, 1944.

FREUDENTHAL, MAX, and KAUFMANN, DAVID. *Die Familie Gomperz.* Frankfurt, 1907.

GERSHOY, LEO. *From Despotism to Revolution, 1763-1789.* New York, 1944.

GLÜCKEL OF HAMELN. *Memoirs,* ed. Marvin Lowenthal. New York, 1932.

GRAETZ, HEINRICH. *History of the Jews.* 6 vols. (Vol. 5.) Philadelphia, 1894.

HAGANI, B. "Coup d'oeil sur l'évolution économique du peuple juif," *La Grande Revue*, CXXX, 1929.

KOPALD, LOUIS J. "The Friendship of Lessing and Mendelssohn in Relation to the Good-Will Movement Between Christian and Jew," *Yearbook of the Central Conference of American Rabbis*, XXXIX, 1929.

KUHN, ARTHUR. "Hugo Grotius and the Emancipation of the Jews in Holland," *Publications of the American Jewish Historical Society*, XXXI, 1928.

LEVY, FELIX A. "Moses Mendelssohn's Ideals of Religion and Their Relation to Reform Judaism," *Yearbook of the Central Conference of American Rabbis*, XXXIX, 1929.

LEWKOWITZ, A. "Das Judentum und die geistigen Strömungen der Neuzeit: Die Aufklärung," *Festschrift Breslau*, I, 1929.

LIEBEN, S. H. "David Oppenheim," *Jahrbuch der Jüdischen Literaturgesellschaft*, XIX, 1928.

LOWENTHAL, MARVIN. *The Jews of Germany*. Philadelphia, 1944.

MENDELSSOHN, MOSES. *Gesammelte Schriften*. 7 vols. Leipzig, 1843-45.

———. *Jerusalem: A Treatise on Ecclesiastical Authority and Judaism*. London, 1838.

PATINKIN, DON. "Mercantilism and the Readmission of the Jews to England," *Jewish Social Studies*, July, 1946.

RACHEL, H. "Die Juden im Berliner Wirtschaftsleben zur Zeit des Merkantilismus," *Zeitschrift für die Geschichte der Juden in Deutschland*, II, 1930.

REICH, NATHAN. "Capitalism and the Jews," *Menorah Journal*, January, 1930.

ROTH, CECIL. *A History of the Jews in England*. Oxford, 1941.

SAENGER, H. *Juden und Altes Testament bei Diderot*. Wertheim, 1933.

SAYOUS, A. E. "Les Juifs ont-ils été les fondateurs du capitalisme moderne?" *Revue économique internationale*, XXIX, 1932.

SÉE, HENRI. "Dans quelle mesure puritains et juifs ont-ils contribué au progrès du capitalisme moderne?" *Revue économique internationale*, XXIV, 1927.

SOMBART, WERNER. *The Jews and Modern Capitalism*. London, 1913.

SPIEGEL, SHALOM. *Hebrew Reborn*. New York, 1930.

STERN, SELMA. "The Jews in the Economic Policy of Frederick the Great," *Jewish Social Studies*, April, 1949.

———. *Jud Suess*. Berlin, 1929.

SUNDHEIMER, P. "Die jüdische Hochfinanz und der bayerische Staat im 18. Jahrhundert," *Finanzarchiv*, XLI, 1924.

TAWNEY, R. H. *Religion and the Rise of Capitalism*. New York, 1926.

WIENER, M. *Jüdische Religion im Zeitalter der Emanzipation*. Berlin, 1933.

III. EMANCIPATION IN THE WEST

BERMAN, LÉON. *Histoire des juifs de France*. Paris, 1937.

FREUND, I. *Die Emanzipation der Juden in Preussen*. 2 vols. Berlin, 1912.

LEMOINE, A. *Napoléon I et les juifs*. Paris, 1900.

LOWENTHAL, MARVIN. *The Jews of Germany*. Philadelphia, 1944.

LUCIEN-BRUN, HENRI. *La Condition des juifs en France depuis 1789*. Paris, 1907.

OELSNER, TONI. "Three Jewish Families in Modern Germany," *Jewish Social Studies*, July, 1942.

POSENER, S. "The Immediate Economic and Social Effects of the Emancipation of the Jews in France," *Jewish Social Studies*, July, 1939.

SZYSTER, B. *La Révolution française et les juifs*. Toulouse, 1929.

FOR FURTHER RESEARCH

ADLER, ELKAN (ed.). *Jewish Travellers*. New York, 1930.
ANCHEL, R. "Les Juifs à Paris au XVIIIe siècle," *Bulletin de la Société de l'histoire de Paris*, LIX, 1932.
———. "Les Lettres patentes du 10 juillet 1784," *Revue des études juives*, XCIII, 1932.
ARENDT, HANNAH. *The Origins of Totalitarianism*. New York, 1951.
BARON, SALO W. "The Modern Age." (*Great Ages and Ideas of the Jewish People*, ed. Leo W. Schwarz.) New York, 1956.
BRINTON, CRANE. *A Decade of Revolution*. New York, 1934.
CRÉMIEUX, A. "Pour contribuer à l'histoire de l'accession des juifs à la qualité de citoyen français," *Revue des études juives*, XCV, 1933.
DELAHACHE, GEORGES. "Les Juifs d'Alsace," *Souvenir et Science*, I, 1930.
ECKSTEIN, A. *Der Kampf der Juden um ihre Emanzipation in Bayern*. Fürth, 1905.
ELBOGEN, I. *Geschichte der Juden in Deutschland*. Berlin, 1935.
GRAETZ, HEINRICH. *History of the Jews*. 6 vols. (Vol. 5.) Philadelphia, 1894.
KOBER, ADOLF. "The French Revolution and the Jews in Germany," *Jewish Social Studies*, October, 1945.
MORGENSTERN, FRIEDRICH. "Hardenberg and the Emancipation of Franconian Jewry," *Jewish Social Studies*, July-October, 1953.
MOSSÉ, B. *La Révolution française et le rabbinat français*. Avignon, 1890.
OFFENBURG, B. *Das Erwachen des deutschen Nationalbewusstseins in der preussischen Judenheit*. Hamburg, 1933.
PHILIPPSON, MARTIN. *Neueste Geschichte des jüdischen Volkes*. 3 vols. (Vols. I, II.) Leipzig, 1907, 1910.
PIPE, SAMUEL ZANVEL. "Napoleon in Jewish Folklore," *YIVO Annual of Jewish Social Science*, I, 1946.
POSENER, S. "Les Juifs sous le Premier Empire," *Revue des études juives*, XC, 1931, XCIII, 1932.
REISSNER, H. "Mirabeau's Judenpolitik," *Der Morgen*, VIII, 1932.
ROUBIK, F. "Zur Geschichte der Juden in Böhmen in der ersten Hälfte des 19. Jahrhunderts," *Jahrbuch für Geschichte der Juden in der tschechoslovakischen Republik*, VI, 1934.
SAGNAC, PHILIPPE. "Les Juifs et Napoléon (1806-1808)," *Revue d'histoire moderne et contemporaine*, II, 1900-1901, III, 1901-2.
SHULIM, JOSEPH. "Napoleon I as the Jewish Messiah: Some Contemporary Conceptions in Virginia," *Jewish Social Studies*, July, 1945.
SRAER, E. *Les Juifs en France et l'égalité des droits civiques*. Paris, 1933.
SZAJKOWSKI, ZOSA. *The Economic Status of the Jews in Alsace, Metz, and Lorraine, 1648-1789*. New York, 1954.
———. "Jewish Participation in the Sale of National Property During the French Revolution," *Jewish Social Studies*, October, 1952.
TAYLOR, A. J. P. *The Course of German History*. New York, 1946.
THOMPSON, J. M. *Napoleon Bonaparte*, Oxford, 1952.
———. *The French Revolution*. New York, 1945.
WALDMAN, M. *Goethe and the Jews*. New York, 1934.

IV. INCARCERATION: THE JEWS OF EASTERN EUROPE

BUBER, MARTIN. *The Legend of the Baal Shem.* New York, 1955.
——. *Tales of the Hasidim.* 2 vols. New York, 1947.
COHEN, ISRAEL. *History of the Jews of Vilna.* Philadelphia, 1943.
DUBNOW, SIMON M. *History of the Jews in Russia and Poland.* 3 vols. (Vols. I, II.) Philadelphia, 1946.
FLORINSKY, MICHAEL T. *Russia: A History and an Interpretation.* 2 vols. New York, 1953.
GINSBURG, SAUL M. "Max Lilienthal's Activities in Russia: New Documents," *Publications of the American Jewish Historical Society,* XXXV, 1939.
GREENBERG, LOUIS. *The Jews in Russia.* 2 vols. (Vol. I.) New Haven, 1944.
LEVITATS, ISAAC. *The Jewish Community in Russia, 1772-1844.* New York, 1943.
LILIENTHAL, MAX. "My Travels in Russia." (*Max Lilienthal,* ed. David Philipson.) New York, 1915.
MINKIN, J. S. *Romance of Hassidism.* New York, 1935.

FOR FURTHER RESEARCH

BOYARSKY, JOSEPH. *Life and Suffering of the Jews in Russia.* Los Angeles, 1912.
The Cambridge History of Poland. Cambridge, 1941.
DUBNOW, SIMON M. *Geschichte des Chassidismus.* 2 vols. Berlin, 1931, 1932.
——. *Weltgeschichte des jüdischen Volkes.* 3 vols. (Vol. III.) Jerusalem, 1938.
DYBOSKI, ROMAN. *Outlines of Polish History.* New York, 1931.
FRANCK, A. *Kabbalah, or the Religious Philosophy of the Hebrews.* New York, 1926.
GELBER, N. M. *Aus zwei Jahrhunderten.* Vienna, 1924.
—— (ed.). *The Jews and the Polish Insurrection* (Hebrew). Jerusalem, 1953.
GINSBURG, SAUL M. *Historische Werke.* 3 vols. New York, 1937.
GINZBERG, LOUIS, and KOHLER, KAUFMAN. "Cabbala." (*Jewish Encyclopedia.* Vol. III.) New York, 1903.
Historische Schriften. 3 vols. (YIVO.) Warsaw, 1929, Vilna, 1937, Vilna, Paris, 1939.
The Jews in Poland From Earliest Times up to the Second World War (Yiddish). (Committee for the Publication.) New York, 1946.
KAZIS, ISRAEL J. *Hasidism.* Unpublished Ph.D. dissertation, Harvard University, 1939.
KLAUSNER, ISRAEL. *A History of the Jewish Community in Vilna* (Yiddish). Vilna, 1938.
LORD, R. H. *The Second Partition of Poland.* Cambridge, 1915.
——. "The Third Partition of Poland," *Slavonic Review,* III, 1925.
LOURIE, ANTON. "The Testament of a Pinsk Jew of the Early Nineteenth Century" (Yiddish), *YIVO Bletter,* September-October, 1939.
MONTEFIORE, MOSES, and MONTEFIORE, JUDITH. *Diaries,* ed. Louis Loewe. 2 vols. Chicago, 1890.
NEWMAN, LOUIS I. *Hasidic Anthology.* New York, 1934.
RAISIN, JACOB S. *The Haskalah Movement in Russia.* Philadelphia, 1915.
RAPHAEL, P. "Les Rapports polono-israélites et l'insurrection de 1830-31," *Révolution 1848,* XXIII, 1926-27.
RINGELBLUM, EMANUEL. *Polish Jewry in the Kosciusko Revolt of 1794* (Yiddish). Warsaw, 1937.
SAN-DONATO, PRINCE DEMIDOFF. *The Jewish Question in Russia.* London, 1884.

SCHECHTER, SOLOMON. *Studies in Judaism.* 3 vols. (Vol. I.) New York, 1924.

SCHOLEM, G. *Major Trends in Jewish Mysticism.* Jerusalem, 1941.

SHATZKY, JACOB (ed.). *History of the Jews of Warsaw* (Yiddish). 2 vols. New York, 1947, 1948.

SOSIS, I. *The History of the Jewish Social Currents in Russia During the Nineteenth Century* (Yiddish). Minsk, 1929.

TCHERIKOWER, E. "Jewish Revolts Against the Discriminatory Legislation of Nicholas I" (Yiddish), *Di Zukunft,* March, 1939.

WEINRYB, S. B. *Neueste Wirtschaftsgeschichte der Juden in Russland und Polen, 1772-1881.* Breslau, 1934.

YACHINSON, J. *Social and Economic Life of the Jews of Russia in the Nineteenth Century* (Yiddish). Kharkov, 1929.

YUDITZKY, A. *Jewish Bourgeoisie and Jewish Proletariat in the First Half of the Nineteenth Century* (Yiddish). Kiev, 1931.

V. THE TRIUMPH OF LIBERALISM

BARON, SALO W. "The Impact of the Revolution of 1848 on Jewish Emancipation," *Jewish Social Studies,* July, 1949.

———. "The Jewish Question in the Nineteenth Century," *Journal of Modern History,* March, 1938.

———. "The Modern Age." (*Great Ages and Ideas of the Jewish People,* ed. Leo W. Schwarz.) New York, 1956.

ELBOGEN, I. *A Century of Jewish Life.* Philadelphia, 1944.

KOBER, ADOLF. "Jews in the Revolution of 1848 in Germany," *Jewish Social Studies,* April, 1948.

KOHLER, MAX. "Jewish Rights at the Congresses of Vienna (1814-1815) and Aix-la-Chapelle (1818)," *Publications of the American Jewish Historical Society,* XXI, 1918.

LOWENTHAL, MARVIN. *The Jews of Germany.* Philadelphia, 1944.

LUCIEN-BRUN, HENRI. *La Condition des juifs en France depuis 1789.* Paris, 1907.

PINSKER, POLLY. "English Opinion and Jewish Emancipation," *Jewish Social Studies,* January, 1952.

ROSSI, MARIO. "Emancipation of Jews in Italy," *Jewish Social Studies,* April, 1953.

SACHER, H. *Jewish Emancipation—The Contract Myth.* London, 1917.

VALLENTIN, ANTONINA. *Poet in Exile: The Life of Heinrich Heine.* New York, 1934.

FOR FURTHER RESEARCH

BARON, SALO W., and KOBLER, F. *Die Judenfrage auf dem Wiener Kongress.* Vienna, 1920.

BERLINER, A. *Geschichte der Juden in Rom.* 2 vols. Frankfurt, 1893.

BERMAN, LÉON. *Histoire des juifs de France.* Paris, 1937.

BIEBER, HUGO (ed.). *Confessio Judaica.* Berlin, 1925.

CAHN, WILHELM. *Aus Eduard Laskers Nachlass.* Berlin, 1902.

CESARE, RAFFAELE DE. *The Last Days of Papal Rome.* London, 1909.

CHARMATZ, H. *Adolf Fischhof.* Vienna, 1910.

ELBOGEN, I. *Geschichte der Juden in Deutschland.* Berlin, 1935.

———. "Ein Jahrhundert Wissenschaft des Judentums." (*Festschrift zum 50-jährigen Bestehen der Hochschule für die Wissenschaft des Judentums.*) Berlin, 1922.

ELIA, R. "Gli Ebrei e lo statuto pontifico del '48," *Israel,* X, 1935-36.

FREUND, I. *Die Emanzipation der Juden in Preussen.* 2 vols. (Vol. 2.) Berlin, 1912.

———. *Die Rechtsstellung der Juden in preussischen Volksschulrecht.* Berlin, 1908.

FRIEDLANDER, FRITZ. *Das Leben Gabriel Riessers.* Berlin, 1927.

GOLDMARK, JOSEPHINE CLARA. *Pilgrims of '48: One Man's Part in the Austrian Revolution and a Family Migration to America.* New Haven, 1930.

GRILLI, MARCEL. "The Role of the Jews in Modern Italy," *Menorah Journal,* Fall, 1939.

GRUNWALD, MAX. *History of the Jews of Vienna.* Philadelphia, 1936.

HEINE, HEINRICH. *Germany, A Winter's Tale.* New York, 1944.

———. *Sämtliche Werke,* ed. Georg Müller. 11 vols. Munich, 1925.

———. *Travel Pictures.* New York, 1904.

LOEVINSON, E. "Gli Israeliti dello Stato Pontifico nel periodo del Risorgimento," *Rassegna storica del Risorgimento,* XVI, 1929.

MACCOBY, S. "The Emancipation of British Jewry," *Contemporary Review,* May, 1934.

MASUR, G. *Friedrich Julius Stahl, Geschichte seines Lebens.* 2 vols. (Vol. I.) Berlin, 1930.

MAYER, GUSTAV. "Early German Socialism and Jewish Emancipation," *Jewish Social Studies,* October, 1939.

MAYER, SIGMUND. *Die Wiener Juden, 1700-1900.* Vienna, 1918.

OELSNER, TONI. "Three Jewish Families in Modern Germany," *Jewish Social Studies,* July, October, 1942.

PHILIPPSON, MARTIN. *Neueste Geschichte des jüdischen Volkes.* 3 vols. (Vols. II, III.) Leipzig, 1910, 1911.

POSENER, S. *Adolphe Crémieux.* 2 vols. Philadelphia, 1940.

RANDALL, J. H., JR. *The Making of the Modern Mind.* Boston, 1940.

RIESSER, GABRIEL. *Gesammelte Schriften.* 4 vols. Frankfurt, 1867-68.

ROLLINS, HAROLD. "The Jews' Role in the Early British Railways," *Jewish Social Studies,* January, 1953.

ROTH, CECIL. *A History of the Jews in England.* Oxford, 1941.

———. *The History of the Jews of Italy.* Philadelphia, 1946.

SACHAR, A. L. "The Jew Enters Parliament," *Menorah Journal,* September-October, 1924.

SRAER, E. *Les Juifs en France et l'égalité des droits civiques.* Paris, 1933.

TAYLOR, A. J. P. *The Course of German History.* New York, 1946.

———. *The Habsburg Monarchy.* London, 1951.

UNTERMEYER, LOUIS. *Heinrich Heine, Paradox and Poet.* 2 vols. New York, 1937.

VALENTIN, VEIT. *The German People,* New York, 1946.

VI. JEWISH ECONOMIC LIFE AND THE FRANKFURT TRADITION

CORTI, COUNT EGON. *The Reign of the House of Rothschild.* New York, 1927.

———. *The Rise of the House of Rothschild.* New York, 1928.

EINZIG, PAUL. "The Jews and German Finance," *The Jewish Review,* June-September, 1933.

FREIMANN, A., and KRACAUER, F. *Frankfort.* Philadelphia, 1929.

GOODMAN, PAUL. *Moses Montefiore.* Philadelphia, 1925.

KOBER, ADOLF. "Emancipation's Impact on the Education and Vocational Training of German Jewry," *Jewish Social Studies,* January, April, 1954.

LESTSCHINSKY, JACOB. "The Economic and Social Development of the Jewish People." (*The Jewish People, Past and Present.* 4 vols. Vol. I.) New York, 1946.

————. "Finance." (*Universal Jewish Encyclopedia.* Vol. IV.) New York, 1948.

POSENER, S. *Adolphe Crémieux.* 2 vols. Philadelphia, 1940.

ROTH, CECIL. *The Magnificent Rothschilds.* London, 1939.

STRAUS, RAPHAEL. "The Jews in the Economic Evolution of Central Europe," *Jewish Social Studies,* January, 1941.

FOR FURTHER RESEARCH

ANDRÉADÈS, A. M. *History of the Bank of England.* London, 1924.

ARENDT, HANNAH. *The Origins of Totalitarianism.* New York, 1951.

BARON, SALO W. "The Modern Age." (*Great Ages and Ideas of the Jewish People,* ed. Leo W. Schwarz.) New York, 1956.

DELAHACHE, GEORGES. "Les Juifs d'Alsace," *Souvenir et Science,* I, 1930.

EDWARDS, G. W. *The Evolution of Finance Capitalism.* New York, 1938.

EINZIG, PAUL. "Jews in International Banking," *The Banker* (London), XXVIII, 1933.

ELBOGEN, I. *A Century of Jewish Life.* Philadelphia, 1944.

EMDEN, PAUL H. "The Brothers Goldsmid and the Financing of the Napoleonic Wars," *Transactions of the Jewish Historical Society of England,* XIV, 1940.

————. *Money Powers of Europe.* New York, 1938.

ENGELMAN, URIAH ZEVI. "Decline of Jewish Population Density in Europe," *Social Forces,* XII, 1933.

————. *The Rise of the Jew in the Western World.* New York, 1944.

FRANKLIN, E. L. "International Finance Jew," *Contemporary Review,* July, 1933.

HEINE, HEINRICH. "The Stamp of My Being." (*Memoirs of My People,* ed. Leo W. Schwarz.) Philadelphia, 1943.

IORGA, N. "Histoire des juifs en Roumanie," *Académie roumaine: Bulletin de la section historique,* January, 1914.

"Die Juden im deutschen Reich, 1916 bis 1933," *Wirtschaft und Statistik,* XV, 1935.

LESTSCHINSKY, JACOB. *Das wirtschaftliche Schicksal des deutschen Judentums.* Berlin, 1933.

MARCUS, A. *Die wirtschaftliche Krise der deutschen Juden.* Berlin, 1931.

MARCUS, JACOB. *Rise and Destiny of the German Jew.* Cincinnati, 1934.

MONTEFIORE, MOSES, and MONTEFIORE, JUDITH. *Diaries,* ed. Louis Loewe. 2 vols. Chicago, 1890.

PHILIPSTAL, W. "Bevölkerungsvorgänge bei den Juden in Deutschland," *Archiv für soziale Hygiene und Demographie,* N. S., VIII, 1933.

RIESSER, J. *The German Great Banks and Their Concentration.* (61st Cong.; Senate Doc. 593.) Washington, D. C., 1911.

RUPPIN, ARTHUR. *The Jews in the Modern World.* London, 1934.

SAYOUS, A. E. "Les Juifs," *Revue économique internationale,* March, 1932.

SILBERGLEIT, H. *Die Bevölkerungs- und Berufsverhältnisse der Juden im deutschen Reich.* Berlin, 1930.

SOMBART, WERNER. *The Jews and Modern Capitalism.* London, 1913.

STEEFL, LAWRENCE D. "The Rothschilds and the Austrian Loan of 1865," *Journal of Modern History,* March, 1936.

UNNA, S. *Statistik der Frankfurter Juden bis zum Jahre 1866.* Frankfurt, 1931.

ZANGWILL, ISRAEL. *Selected Works.* Philadelphia, 1939.

VII. THE IMPACT OF WESTERN CULTURE ON JEWISH LIFE

BAMBERGER, FRITZ. "Zunz's Conception of History," *Publications of the American Academy for Jewish Research*, XII, 1941.

BARUCH, S. "Leopold Zunz, Humanist," *Menorah Journal*, February, June, August, 1923.

DEUTSCH, GOTTHARD. "Heinrich Graetz," *Yearbook of the Central Conference of American Rabbis*, XXVII, 1917.

GREENBERG, MARTIN. "Heinrich Heine: Flight and Return," *Commentary*, March, 1949.

KOHN, HANS. "The Jew Enters Western Culture," *Menorah Journal*, April, 1930.

LANDSBERG, MAX. "The Reform Movement After Abraham Geiger," *Yearbook of the Central Conference of American Rabbis*, XX, 1910.

LIPTZIN, SOL. *Germany's Stepchildren*. Philadelphia, 1944.

MARCUS, JACOB. *Rise and Destiny of the German Jew*. Cincinnati, 1934.

MARX, ALEXANDER. "Zunz and Steinschneider." *(Studies in Jewish History and Folklore.)* New York, 1944.

MEYER, BERTHA. *Salon Sketches*. New York, 1938.

PHILIPSON, DAVID. *The Reform Movement in Judaism*. New York, 1907.

RAISIN, JACOB S. "The Reform Movement Before Geiger," *Yearbook of the Central Conference of American Rabbis*, XX, 1910.

VALLENTIN, ANTONINA. *Poet in Exile: The Life of Heinrich Heine*. New York, 1934.

WALLECH, L. "The Beginnings of the Science of Judaism in the Nineteenth Century," *Historia Judaica*, April, 1946.

FOR FURTHER RESEARCH

AGUS, JACOB B. "Abraham Geiger." *(Modern Philosophies of Judaism.)* New York, 1941.

ARENDT, HANNAH. *The Origins of Totalitarianism*. New York, 1951.

———. "Privileged Jews," *Jewish Social Studies*, January, 1946.

ARTZ, FREDERICK B. *Reaction and Revolution*. New York, 1934.

BAMBERGER, BERNARD. "Beginnings of Modern Jewish Scholarship," *Yearbook of the Central Conference of American Rabbis*, XLII, 1932.

BARON, SALO W. "I. M. Jost, the Historian," *Publications of the American Academy for Jewish Research*, I, 1930.

BIEBER, HUGO (ed.). *Confessio Judaica*. Berlin, 1925.

BIEBER, HUGO, and HADAS, MOSES (edd.). *Heinrich Heine*. New York, 1957.

BRANN, MARCUS. *Zacharias Frankel: Gedenkblätter*. Berlin, 1901.

DISRAELI, BENJAMIN. *The Wondrous Tale of Alroy*. London, 1948.

———. *Coningsby*. London, 1948.

ELBOGEN, I. *A Century of Jewish Life*. Philadelphia, 1944.

———. "Ein Jahrhundert Wissenschaft des Judentums." *(Festschrift zum 50-jährigen Bestehen der Hochschule für die Wissenschaft des Judentums.)* Berlin, 1922.

———. "Leopold Zunz zum Gedächtnis." *(Bericht der Lehranstalt für die Wissenschaft des Judentums.)* Berlin, 1936.

FREEHOF, S. B. "Moritz Steinschneider," *Yearbook of the Central Conference of American Rabbis*, XXVI, 1916.

GEIGER, L. *Abraham Geiger*. Berlin, 1910.

GINZBERG, LOUIS. "Zecharia Frankel." *(Students, Scholars, and Saints.)* Philadelphia, 1943.

GRAETZ, HEINRICH. *History of the Jews.* 6 vols. (Vol. 5.) Philadelphia, 1894.

GRUBWIESER, V. "The Jewish Contribution to Modern German Literature," *The Jewish Review*, June-September, 1933.

HEINE, HEINRICH. *Works,* ed. C. G. Leland, 12 vols. New York, 1924.

HELLER, MAX. "Samson Raphael Hirsch," *Yearbook of the Central Conference of American Rabbis,* XVIII, 1908.

HERZ, HENRIETTA. "A Salonist Remembers." *(Memoirs of My People,* ed. Leo W. Schwarz.) Philadelphia, 1943.

KARPELES, G. *Jewish Literature and Other Essays.* Philadelphia, 1895.

KEY, ELLEN. *Rahel Varnhagen.* New York, 1913.

KOBER, ADOLF. "Jewish Communities in Germany from the Age of Enlightenment to Their Destruction by the Nazis," *Jewish Social Studies,* July, 1947.

KOHLER, KAUFMAN. *Studies, Addresses, and Papers.* Cincinnati, 1948.

LOWENTHAL, LEO. "Heine's Religion," *Commentary,* August, 1947.

LOWENTHAL, MARVIN. *The Jews of Germany.* Philadelphia, 1944.

MARX, ALEXANDER. *Essays in Jewish Biography.* Philadelphia, 1947.

MEISL, JOSEF. *Heinrich Graetz.* Berlin, 1917.

MODDER, MONTAGU F. "The Jew in English Literature of the Nineteenth Century," *Menorah Journal,* Spring, 1935.

MORGENSTERN, JULIAN. *As a Mighty Stream: The Story of Reform Judaism.* Philadelphia, 1949.

PETITPIERRE, JACQUES. *The Romance of the Mendelssohns.* New York, 1950.

POLITZER, HEINZ. "From Mendelssohn to Kafka," *Commentary,* April, 1947.

RABINOWITZ, S. P. *R. Yom Tob Lippman Zunz* (Hebrew). Warsaw, 1898.

RANDALL, J. H., JR. *The Making of the Modern Mind.* Boston, 1940.

ROTH, CECIL. *Benjamin Disraeli.* New York, 1952.

SACHER, H. *Jewish Emancipation—The Contract Myth.* London, 1917.

SCHECHTER, SOLOMON. *Studies in Judaism.* Philadelphia, 1924.

SLOCHOWER, HARRY. "Attitudes Towards Heine in German Literary Criticism," *Jewish Social Studies,* October, 1941.

TABAK, ISRAEL. *Judaic Lore in Heine.* Baltimore, 1948.

UNTERMEYER, LOUIS. *Heinrich Heine, Paradox and Poet.* 2 vols. New York, 1937.

WIENER, M. *Jüdische Religion im Zeitalter der Emanzipation.* Berlin, 1933.

ZANGWILL, ISRAEL. "The Sabbath Question in Sudminster." *(Selected Works.)* Philadelphia, 1939.

VIII. THE RISE OF JEWISH LIFE IN THE NEW WORLD

GOODMAN, ABRAM VOSSEN. *American Overture.* Philadelphia, 1947.

GRINSTEIN, HYMAN B. *The Rise of the Jewish Community of New York, 1654–1860.* Philadelphia, 1945.

GUTSTEIN, MORRIS A. *The Story of the Jews of Newport.* New York, 1936.

HANDLIN, OSCAR. *Adventure in Freedom.* New York, 1954.

HIRSHLER, ERIC E. (ed.). *Jews from Germany in the United States.* New York, 1955.

JANOWSKY, OSCAR (ed.). *The American Jew.* New York, 1942.

KOHLER, MAX. "The German Jewish Migration to America," *Publications of the American Jewish Historical Society,* IX, 1901.

————. "Phases in the History of Religious Liberty in America With Particular Reference to the Jews," *ibid.*, XIII, 1905.

KORN, BERTRAM W. *American Jewry and the Civil War.* Philadelphia, 1951.

LEARSI, RUFUS. *The Jews in America: A History.* Cleveland, 1954.

LEBESON, ANITA. *Jewish Pioneers in America, 1492–1848.* New York, 1931.

LEVY, B. H. *Reform Judaism in America.* New York, 1933.

MARCUS, JACOB. *The Americanization of Isaac Mayer Wise.* Cincinnati, 1931.

FOR FURTHER RESEARCH

BARON, SALO W. *The Jewish Community.* 3 vols. (Vol. III.) Philadelphia, 1942.

BENJAMIN, I. J. *Drei Jahre in Amerika, 1859–62.* 3 vols. Hanover, 1862.

BLUM, ISIDOR. *The Jews of Baltimore.* Baltimore, 1910.

BOGEN, BORIS. *Jewish Philanthropy.* New York, 1917.

BROCHES, S. *Jews in New England.* (Parts 1, 2.) New York, 1942.

CARMAN, HARRY J., and SYRETT, HAROLD C. *A History of the American People.* 2 vols. (Vol. I.) New York, 1952.

COHEN, HENRY. "A Brave Frontiersman," *Publications of the American Jewish Historical Society,* VIII, 1900.

DALY, CHARLES P. *The Settlement of the Jews in North America.* New York, 1893.

DA SOLA POOL, DAVID. "Religious and Cultural Phases of American Jewish History," *Publications of the American Jewish Historical Society,* XL, 1950.

ELIASHOV, H. *German-American Jews.* Chicago, 1915.

ELZAS, B. A. *The Jews of South Carolina.* Philadelphia, 1905.

ENGELMAN, URIAH ZEVI. "Jewish Statistics in the United States Census of Religious Bodies (1850–1936)," *Jewish Social Studies,* April, 1947.

FONER, PHILIP S. *The Jews in American History,* New York, 1945.

FREUND, MIRIAM K. *Jewish Merchants in Colonial America.* New York, 1939.

FRIEDENBERG, ALBERT M. "American Jewish Journalism to the Close of the Civil War," *Publications of the American Jewish Historical Society,* XXII, 1914.

FRIEDMAN, LEE M. *Early American Jews.* Cambridge (Massachusetts), 1934.

————. *Pilgrims in a New Land.* Philadelphia, 1948.

GLANZ, RUDOLF. "Jews in Early German-American Literature," *Jewish Social Studies,* April, 1942.

————. *Jews in Relation to the Cultural Milieu of the Germans in America.* New York, 1947.

GOLDMARK, JOSEPHINE CLARA. *Pilgrims of '48: One Man's Part in the Austrian Revolution and a Family Migration to America.* New Haven, 1930.

GOLDSTEIN, ISRAEL. *A Century of Judaism in New York: B'nai Jeshurun, 1825–1925.* New York, 1930.

GOTTHEIL, RICHARD. *The Life of Gustav Gottheil.* Williamsport (Pennsylvania), 1936.

GRINSTEIN, HYMAN B. "Communal and Social Aspects of American Jewish History," *Publications of the American Jewish Historical Society,* XL, 1950.

HANSEN, MARCUS. *The Atlantic Migration.* Cambridge (Massachusetts), 1940.

————. "German Schemes of Colonization Before 1860," *Smith College Studies in History,* October-January, 1923–24.

————. *The Immigrant in America.* Cambridge (Massachusetts), 1948.

KISCH, GUIDO. *In Search of Freedom.* London, 1949.

————. "A Voyage to America Ninety Years Ago," *Publications of the American Jewish Historial Society,* XXXV, 1939.

KOHLER, MAX. *Haym Salomon.* New York, 1931.

————. "Jews in the Anti-Slavery Movement," *Publications of the American Jewish Historical Society*, V-VI, 1897.

LEBESON, ANITA. *Pilgrim People*. New York, 1950.

LEESER, ISAAC (ed.). *Occident and American Jewish Advocate*. 26 vols. Philadelphia, 1843-69.

MARCUS, JACOB. *Early American Jewry*. 2 vols. Philadelphia, 1951, 1953.

PACKMAN, HENRY E., and SCHULTZ, ARTHUR R. (edd.). *Bibliography of German Culture in America to 1940*. Madison (Wisconsin), 1953.

PHILIPSON, DAVID. "The Jewish Pioneers of the Ohio Valley," *Publications of the American Jewish Historical Society*, VIII, 1900.

————. *The Reform Movement in Judaism*. New York, 1907.

RABINOWITZ, BENJAMIN. *The Young Men's Hebrew Associations (1854-1913)*. New York, 1948.

SCHAPPES, MORRIS U. *A Documentary Story of the Jews in the United States*. New York, 1950.

TARSHISH, A. *The Rise of American Judaism*. Cincinnati, 1938.

TREPP, L. "Of German Jewry," *Conservative Judaism*, III, No. 1, 1947.

WATTERS, LEON L. *The Pioneer Jews of Utah*. New York, 1952.

WISCHNITZER, MARK. *To Dwell in Safety*. Philadelphia, 1949.

WISE, ISAAC M. *Reminiscences*. Cincinnati, 1901.

WOLF, SIMON. *The American Jew as Patriot, Soldier, and Citizen*. Philadelphia, 1895.

IX. FALSE DAWN IN THE EAST

BROV, STANLEY R. *Jewish Family Solidarity: Myth or Fact?* Vicksburg (Mississippi), 1940.

DUBNOW, SIMON M. *History of the Jews in Russia and Poland*. 3 vols. (Vol. III.) Philadelphia, 1946.

GAMORAN, EMANUEL. *Changing Conceptions in Jewish Education*. New York, 1924.

HERZOG, ELIZABETH, and ZBOROWSKI, MARK. *Life Is With People, The Jewish Little-Town of Eastern Europe*. New York, 1952.

LEVIN, SHMARYA. *Childhood in Exile*. New York, 1929.

PALÉOLOGUE, MAURICE. *The Enigmatic Czar*. New York, 1938.

SACHS, A. S. *Worlds That Passed*. Philadelphia, 1943.

SAMUEL, MAURICE. *The World of Sholom Aleichem*. New York, 1943.

FOR FURTHER RESEARCH

BRAFMAN, JACOB. *Das Buch vom Kahal*. 2 vols. Leipzig, 1928.

COHEN, ISRAEL. *Jewish Life in Modern Times*. New York, 1914.

DUBNOW, SIMON M. *Weltgeschichte des jüdischen Volkes*. 3 vols. (Vol. III.) Jerusalem, 1938.

DYBOSKI, ROMAN. *Outlines of Polish History*. New York, 1931.

————. *Poland*. London, 1933.

ELBOGEN, I. *A Century of Jewish Life*. Philadelphia, 1944.

FLORINSKY, MICHAEL T. *Russia: A History and an Interpretation*. 2 vols. (Vol. II.) New York, 1953.

FRIEDLANDER, ISRAEL. *The Jews of Russia and Poland*. New York, 1915.

GINZBERG, LOUIS. *Students, Scholars, and Saints*. Philadelphia, 1928.

GRAHAM, S. *Tsar of Freedom: The Life and Reign of Alexander II.* New Haven, 1935.

GREENBERG, LOUIS. *The Jews in Russia.* 2 vols. (Vol. I.) New Haven, 1944.

HALL, WALTER PHELPS, and DAVIS, WILLIAM STEARNS. *The Course of Europe Since Waterloo.* New York, 1951.

Historische Schriften. 3 vols. (YIVO.) Warsaw, 1929, Vilna, 1937, Vilna, Paris, 1939.

The Jews in Poland From Earliest Times up to the Second World War (Yiddish). (Committee for the Publication.) New York, 1946.

KOHN, HANS. *Pan-Slavism.* South Bend (Indiana), 1953.

KON, PINKAS. "The Attitude of the Czarist Authorities to Maimonides" (Yiddish), *YIVO Bletter,* November-December, 1938.

KORNILOV, A. *Modern Russian History.* New York, 1948.

LESTSCHINSKY, JACOB. "The Anti-Jewish Program: Tsarist Russia, the Third Reich, and Independent Poland," *Jewish Social Studies,* April, 1941.

LEVITATS, ISAAC. *The Jewish Community in Russia, 1772–1844.* New York, 1943.

MAYBAUM, IGNATZ. *The Jewish Home.* London, 1945.

MENDELE MOCHER SEFORIM. *Collected Works* (Yiddish). Warsaw, 1928.

MONTEFIORE, MOSES, and MONTEFIORE, JUDITH. *Diaries,* ed. Louis Loewe. 2 vols. Chicago, 1890.

PHILIPSON, DAVID. "Max Lilienthal." *(Centenary Papers and Others.)* Cincinnati, 1919.

RUPPIN, ARTHUR. "The Jewish Population of the World." *(The Jewish People, Past and Present.* 4 vols. Vol. I.) New York, 1946.

SCHWARZ, SOLOMON M. "The Historical Legacy." *(The Jews in the Soviet Union.)* Syracuse (New York), 1951.

SOSIS, I. *The History of the Jewish Social Currents in Russia During the Nineteenth Century* (Yiddish). Minsk, 1929.

STEINBERG, I. N. "Jewish Colonization in Russia." *(The Jewish People, Past and Present.* 4 vols. Vol. II.) New York, 1948.

SZAJKOWSKI, ZOSA. "The Alliance Israélite Universelle and East-European Jewry in the 1860's," *Jewish Social Studies,* April, 1942.

WEINRYB, S. B. *Neueste Wirtschaftgeschichte der Juden in Russland und Polen, 1772–1881.* Breslau, 1934.

WENGEROFF, PAULINE. *Memoiren einer Grossmutter.* 2 vols. Berlin, 1908, 1910.

YACHINSON, J. *Social and Economic Life of the Jews of Russia in the Nineteenth Century* (Yiddish). Kharkov, 1929.

YUDITSKY, A. *Jewish Bourgeoisie and Jewish Proletariat in the First Half of the Nineteenth Century.* Kiev, 1931.

X. JEWISH HUMANISM IN EASTERN EUROPE

GREENBERG, LOUIS. *The Jews in Russia.* 2 vols. (Vol. I.) New Haven, 1944.

HALKIN, SIMON. *Modern Hebrew Literature.* New York, 1950.

HOWE, IRVING, and GREENBERG, ELIEZER (edd.). *A Treasury of Yiddish Stories.* New York, 1954.

KLAUSNER, JOSEPH. *A History of Modern Hebrew Literature.* London, 1932.

MENDELE MOCHER SEFORIM. *The Travels and Adventures of Benjamin the Third.* New York, 1949.

PERETZ, ISAAC LOEB. *Stories and Pictures.* Philadelphia, 1936.

RAISIN, JACOB S. *The Haskalah Movement in Russia.* Philadelphia, 1913.
SAMUEL, MAURICE. *Prince of the Ghetto.* New York, 1948.
———. *The World of Sholom Aleichem.* New York, 1944.
SHOLOM ALEICHEM. *The Adventures of Mottel.* New York, 1953.
———. *Inside Kasrilevke.* New York, 1948.
SLOUSCHZ, NAHUM. *The Renascence of Hebrew Literature, 1743–1885.* Philadelphia, 1909.

FOR FURTHER RESEARCH

BERNFELD, S. *A Wise Generation* (Hebrew). Warsaw, 1896.
BRAININ, REUBEN. *Abraham Mapu* (Hebrew). Warsaw, 1900.
———. *Perez Smolenskin* (Hebrew). Warsaw, 1886.
DUBNOW, SIMON M. *History of the Jews in Russia and Poland.* 3 vols. (Vol. III.) Philadelphia, 1946.
ERTER, ISAAC. *The Guardian of Israel: The Life of Meir Letteris,* with an introduction by Reuben Brainin. Warsaw, 1908.
FLORINSKY, MICHAEL T. *Russia: A History and an Interpretation.* 2 vols. New York, 1953.
FRANK, HELEN (ed.). *Yiddish Tales.* Philadelphia, 1945.
GINZBURG, S. *The Life and Works of Moses Hayyim Luzzatto.* Philadelphia, 1931.
GORDON, JUDAH LOEB. *Complete Poetic Works* (Hebrew). 3 vols. Warsaw, 1905.
GOTLOBER, ABRAHAM BAER. *Poems* (Hebrew). Warsaw, 1890.
GREENBERG, S. *Isaac Baer Levinsohn.* New York, 1927.
GUNZBERG, MORDECAI AARON. *The French Invasion of Russia* (Hebrew). Vilna, 1884.
———. *The Inner Temple* (Hebrew). Warsaw, 1883.
———. *Letters* (Hebrew). Warsaw, 1883.
KATSCH, ABRAHAM I. "Nachman Krochmal and the German Idealists," *Jewish Social Studies,* April, 1946.
KROCHMAL, NACHMAN. *Werke,* ed. Simon Rawidowicz, Berlin, 1924.
KUNITZ, JOSHUA. *Russian Literature and the Jew.* New York, 1929.
LACHOWER, F. *Essays on Hebrew Writers from Mendelssohn to the Present* (Hebrew). Tel Aviv, 1934.
———. *A History of Modern Hebrew Literature* (Hebrew). 4 vols. Tel Aviv, 1928–33.
LEBENSOHN, ABRAHAM BAER, and LEBENSOHN, MICAH JOSEPH. *Complete Works* (Hebrew). Vilna, 1895.
LEBENSOHN, MICAH JOSEPH. *Gesammelte Schriften,* edited and with an introduction by J. Fichman. Berlin, 1924.
LEFTWICH, JOSEPH (ed.). *The Golden Peacock: An Anthology of Yiddish Poetry.* Cambridge (Massachusetts), 1939.
LEVINSOHN, ISAAC BAER. *The Mission of Israel* (Hebrew). Warsaw, 1901.
———. *The Myth of the Blood Libel* (Hebrew). Warsaw, 1894.
———. *Poems* (Hebrew). Warsaw, 1890.
LILIENBLUM, MOSHE LEIB. *The Way of the Wanderer* (Hebrew). Warsaw, 1899.
LIPTZIN, SOL (ed.). *Peretz.* New York, 1947.
MAHLER, RAPHAEL. "The Social and Political Aspects of the Haskalah in Galicia," *YIVO Annual of Jewish Social Science,* I, 1946.
MARK, YUDEL. "Yiddish Literature." (*The Jews: Their History, Culture, and Religion,* ed. Louis Finkelstein. 4 vols. Vol. IV.) Philadelphia, 1949.
MEISEL, J. *Haskalah.* Berlin, 1919.
MENDELE MOCHER SEFORIM. *The Nag.* New York, 1955.
———. *The Parasite.* New York, 1936.

MIRSKY, D. S. *Contemporary Russian Literature*. New York, 1926.
NIGER, S. "The Gift of Sholom Aleichem," *Commentary*, August, 1946.
PERETZ, ISAAC LOEB. *One Act Plays from the Yiddish*. Cincinnati, 1923.
———. *The Three Canopies*. New York, 1948.
POLISH, DAVID. "Perez Smolenskin's Contribution to Jewish Thought," *Reconstructionist*, June 11, 1943.
RAWIDOWICZ, SIMON. "Nachman Krochmal als Historiker." (*Dubnow Festschrift*.) Berlin, 1930.
———. "War Nachman Krochmal ein Hegelianer?" *Hebrew Union College Annual*, V, 1926.
REISEN, Z. *From Mendelssohn to Mendele* (Yiddish). Warsaw, 1923.
———. "On the History of the Haskalah Literature" (Yiddish), *YIVO Bletter*, April, 1931.
ROBACK, A. A. *The Story of Yiddish Literature*. New York, 1940.
SCHULMAN, KALMAN. *Land of the Orient* (Hebrew). Vilna, 1890.
SHATZKY, JACOB. "Alexander Kraushar and His Road to Total Assimilation," *YIVO Annual of Jewish Social Science*, VII, 1952.
———. "Warsaw Jews in the Polish Cultural Life of the Early Nineteenth Century," *ibid.*, V, 1950.
SHOLOM ALEICHEM. *The Great Fair*. New York, 1915.
———. *Jewish Children*. New York, 1929.
———. *The Old Country*. New York, 1946.
———. *Tevye's Daughters*. New York, 1949.
SMOLENSKIN, PEREZ. *Complete Works* (Hebrew). 6 vols. Warsaw, 1910.
———. *Selected Works* (Hebrew), ed. Sholom Kramer. Tel Aviv, 1947.
SPIEGEL, SHALOM. *Hebrew Reborn*. New York, 1930.
TCHERNOWITZ, CHAIM. "Grandfather Mendele As I Remember Him," *Commentary*, November, 1948.
WALDSTEIN, A. S. *The Evolution of Modern Hebrew Literature*. New York, 1916.
WAXMAN, MEYER. *A History of Jewish Literature*. 4 vols. (Vols. III, IV.) New York, 1929.
———. "Modern Hebrew Literature." (*The Jewish People, Past and Present.* 4 vols. Vol. III.) New York, 1952.
WEINREICH, URIEL (ed.). *The Field of Yiddish*. New York, 1954.
WIENER, L. *A History of Yiddish Literature in the Nineteenth Century*. New York, 1899.

XI. THE EMERGENCE OF ANTI-SEMITISM

ACKERMAN, NATHAN W., and JAHODA, MARIE. *Anti-Semitism and Emotional Disorder*. New York, 1950.
ARENDT, HANNAH. *The Origins of Totalitarianism*. New York, 1951.
BARZUN, JACQUES. *Race—A Study in Modern Superstition*. New York, 1946.
BIENENFELD, F. R. *The Germans and the Jews*. New York, 1939.
BUTLER, ROHAN D'OR. *The Roots of National Socialism*. New York, 1942.
BYRNES, ROBERT F. *Anti-Semitism in Modern France*. New Brunswick (New Jersey), 1950.
FENICHEL, OTTO. "A Psychoanalytic Approach to Anti-Semitism," *Commentary*, July, 1946.
HALASZ, NICHOLAS. *Captain Dreyfus*. New York, 1955.
KARBACH, OSCAR. "The Founder of Political Anti-Semitism: Georg von Schoenerer," *Jewish Social Studies*, January, 1945.

LOEWENSTEIN, RUDOLPH M. "The Historical and Cultural Roots of Anti-Semitism," *Psychoanalysis and the Social Sciences,* I, 1947.

LOWENTHAL, MARVIN. *The Jews of Germany.* Philadelphia, 1944.

MASSING, PAUL. *Rehearsal for Destruction.* New York, 1949.

PARKES, JAMES. *Emergence of the Jewish Problem, 1878–1939.* London, 1946.

SAMUEL, MAURICE. *The Great Hatred.* New York, 1940.

TRACHTENBERG, JOSHUA. *The Devil and the Jews.* New Haven, 1943.

FOR FURTHER RESEARCH

AHLWARDT, HERMANN. *Der Verzweiflungskampf der arischen Völker mit dem Judentum.* Berlin, 1890.

BEARD, MIRIAM. "Anti-Semitism—Product of Economic Myths." (*Jews in a Gentile World,* edd. Isaque Graeber and S. H. Britt.) New York, 1942.

BENDA, GEORGE. *La Trahison des Clercs.* Paris, 1928.

BENNS, F. LEE. *European History Since 1870.* New York, 1943.

BERGMAN, SHLOMO. "Some Methodological Errors in the Study of Anti-Semitism," *Jewish Social Studies,* January, 1943.

BOECKEL, OTTO. *Die Juden—die Könige unserer Zeit.* Berlin, 1887.

BROGAN, D. W. *France Under the Republic.* New York, 1940.

CHAMBERLAIN, HOUSTON STEWART. *Foundations of the Nineteenth Century.* New York, 1913.

CHAPMAN, GUY. *The Dreyfus Case.* London, 1955.

DRUMONT, E. *La France juive.* 2 vols. Paris, 1886.

DÜHRING, E. *Die Judenfrage als Rassen-, Sitten- und Kulturfrage.* Berlin, 1881.

ELBOGEN, I. *A Century of Jewish Life.* Philadelphia, 1944.

FRANK, WALTER. *Hofprediger Adolf Stoecker und die Christlichsoziale Bewegung.* Hamburg, 1935.

GOBINEAU, COUNT J. ARTHUR DE. *Essai sur l'inégalité des races humaines.* 4 vols. Paris, 1953–55.

GRUNWALD, MAX. *History of the Jews in Vienna.* Philadelphia, 1936.

HAYES, CARLTON J. H. *Essays on Nationalism.* New York, 1925.

HERZOG, WILHELM. *From Dreyfus to Petain.* New York, 1947.

HIRSCHFIELD, MAGNUS. *Racism.* London, 1938.

JÖHLINGER, OTTO. *Bismarck und die Juden.* Berlin, 1921.

KAUFMANN, WALTER. *Nietzsche.* Princeton, 1950.

KOHN, HANS. "Germany: Treitschke." (*Prophets and Peoples.*) New York, 1946.

KÜRENBERG, JOACHIM VON. *The Kaiser.* New York, 1955.

LAZARE, BERNARD. *Antisémitisme.* Paris, 1903.

LEBLOIS, L. *L'Affaire Dreyfus.* Paris, 1929.

MARR, WILHELM. *Der Judenspiegel.* Hamburg, 1863.

———. *Der Sieg des Judentums über das Germanentum.* Bern, 1879.

PALÉOLOGUE, MAURICE. *An Intimate Journal of the Dreyfus Case, 1894–1899.* New York, 1957.

PARKES, JAMES. *Enemy of the People: Anti-Semitism.* New York, 1946.

PINSON, KOPPEL. *Modern Germany.* New York, 1954.

ROHLING, AUGUST. *Der Talmudjude.* Münster, 1872.

ROSENBERG, ARTHUR. "Trieitschke und die Juden," *Die Gesellschaft* (Berlin), II, 1930.

SOLTAU, ROGER. *French Parties and Politics.* London, 1930.

SPEIER, HANS. *The Salaried Employee in German Society.* New York, 1939.

STEIN, LEO. *The Racial Thinking of Richard Wagner.* New York, 1950.

STOLPER, GUSTAV. *German Economy, 1870–1940.* New York, 1940.

STRACK, H. S. *The Jew and Human Sacrifice.* London, 1909.

TREITSCHKE, HEINRICH VON. "Ein Wort über unser Judentum," *Preussische Jahrbücher,* Vols. 44, 45, 1879.

VALENTIN, HUGO. *Anti-Semitism.* New York, 1936.

WAWRZINEK, KURT. *Die Entstehung der deutschen Antisemitenparteien.* Berlin, 1927.

WEINRYB, BERYL. "The Economic and Social Background of Modern Anti-Semitism." (*Essays on Anti-Semitism,* ed. Koppel Pinson.) New York, 1942.

WERTHEIMER, MILDRED S. *The Pan-German League, 1890–1914.* New York, 1924.

XII. BEGINNING OF THE END FOR RUSSIAN JEWRY

ARENDT, HANNAH. *The Origins of Totalitarianism.* New York, 1951.

BARON, SALO W. *Modern Nationalism and Religion.* New York, 1947.

DUBNOW, SIMON M. *History of the Jews in Russia and Poland.* 3 vols. (Vol. III.) Philadelphia, 1946.

GREENBERG, LOUIS. *The Jews in Russia.* 2 vols. (Vol. II, ed. Mark Wischnitzer.) New Haven, 1951.

HARGRAVE, SIDNEY S. "The Jewish Question in the First Russian Duma," *Jewish Social Studies,* April, 1944.

KOHN, HANS. *Pan-Slavism.* South Bend (Indiana), 1953.

KOHLER, MAX, and WOLF, SIMON. *Jewish Disabilities in the Balkan States.* New York, 1916.

LESTSCHINSKY, JACOB. "The Anti-Jewish Program: Tsarist Russia, the Third Reich, and Independent Poland," *Jewish Social Studies,* April, 1941.

STARR, JOSHUA. "Jewish Citizenship in Rumania, 1878–1940," *Jewish Social Studies,* January, 1941.

TAGER, ALEXANDER B. *The Decay of Czarism.* Philadelphia, 1935.

VISHNIAK, MARK. "Anti-Semitism in Tsarist Russia." (*Essays on Anti-Semitism,* ed. Koppel Pinson.) New York, 1942.

FOR FURTHER RESEARCH

ASCH, SHOLEM. *Three Cities.* New York, 1933.

BASKERVILLE, BEATRICE. *The Polish Jew.* New York, 1906.

BERKOWITZ, J. *La Question des israélites en Roumanie.* Paris, 1923.

COHEN, ISRAEL. *Jewish Life in Modern Times.* New York, 1914.

ELBOGEN, I. *A Century of Jewish Life.* Philadelphia, 1944.

FLORINSKY, MICHAEL T. *Russia: A History and an Interpretation.* 2 vols. (Vol. II.) New York, 1953.

FREDERIC, HAROLD. *The New Exodus.* London, 1892.

HALL, WALTER PHELPS, and DAVIS, WILLIAM STEARNS. *The Course of Europe Since Waterloo.* New York, 1951.

JACOBS, JOSEPH. "The Jewish Question, 1875–1883," *Trübner's American, European, and Oriental Literary Record,* IV, 1893.

JANOWSKY, OSCAR. *The Jews and Minority Rights, 1898–1919.* New York, 1933.

The Jews in Poland From Earliest Times up to the Second World War (Yiddish). (Committee for the Publication.) New York, 1946.

KISSMAN, JOSEPH. *Studies in the History of Roumanian Jews in the Nineteenth and the Beginning of the Twentieth Centuries* (Yiddish). New York, 1944.

KOHN, HANS. "Russia: Dostoevsky." *(Prophets and Peoples.)* New York, 1946.
LABIN, DANIEL. "Roumania." *(Universal Jewish Encyclopedia.* Vol. IX.) New York, 1943.
LEROY-BEAULIEU, ANATOLE. *The Empire of the Tsars.* 3 vols. (Vol. III.) New York, 1896.
LEVIN, SHMARYA. *The Arena.* New York, 1932.
MAHLER, RAPHAEL. "Anti-Semitism in Poland." *(Essays on Anti-Semitism,* ed. Koppel Pinson.) New York, 1942.
MARGOLIN, ARNOLD D. *The Jews of Eastern Europe.* New York, 1926.
MARRIOTT, J. A. R. *The Eastern Question.* Oxford, 1940.
NETCHVOLODOW, A. *L'Empereur Nicolas II et les juifs.* Paris, 1924.
POBEDONOSTSEV, K. P. *Mémoires politiques.* Paris, 1927.
"POBEDONOSTSEV AND ALEXANDER III," *Slavonic Review,* June, 1928.
ROUCEK, J. S. *Contemporary Roumania.* Palo Alto, 1932.
RUBINOW, I. M. "Economic Condition of the Jews in Russia," *United States Bureau of Labor Bulletin,* No. 72, 1907.
SAVICKIJ, N. "P. A. Stolypin," *Le Monde slav,* November-December, 1933, December, 1934, March, 1936.
SCHWARZFELD, E. "The Situation of the Jews in Roumania Since the Treaty of Berlin," *American Jewish Yearbook,* III, 1901-2.
SEMENOFF, E. *The Russian Government and the Massacres.* London, 1907.
SETON-WATSON, HUGH. *The Decline of Imperial Russia.* London, 1952.
SETON-WATSON, R. W. *A History of the Roumanians.* Cambridge, 1934.
SINGER, ISIDORE (ed.). *Russia at the Bar of the American People.* New York, 1904.
URUSSOV, SERGE DMITRIYEVICH. *Memoirs of a Russian Governor.* New York, 1908.
WITTE, COUNT SERGE DE. *Memoirs,* ed. Avrahm Yarmolinsky. London, 1921.
WOLF, LUCIEN. *Notes on the Diplomatic History of the Jewish Question.* London, 1919.

XIII. THE RISE OF ZIONISM

AHAD HA'AM. *Selected Essays.* Philadelphia, 1912.
BEIN, ALEX. *Theodor Herzl.* Philadelphia, 1940.
GREENBERG, LOUIS. *The Jews in Russia.* 2 vols. New Haven, 1944, 1951.
HALKIN, SIMON. *Modern Hebrew Literature.* New York, 1950.
HERZL, THEODOR. *The Jewish State.* New York, 1946.
LEARSI, RUFUS. *Fulfillment: The Epic Story of Zionism.* Cleveland, 1951.
LITVINOFF, BARNET. *Ben-Gurion of Israel.* New York, 1954.
LOWENTHAL, MARVIN (ed.). *The Diaries of Theodor Herzl.* New York, 1956.
PARKES, JAMES. *A History of Palestine.* London, 1949.
SYRKIN, NACHMAN. *Essays on Socialist Zionism.* New York, 1935.
WEIZMANN, CHAIM. *Trial and Error.* New York, 1949.

FOR FURTHER RESEARCH

AHAD HA'AM. *Memoirs and Letters* (Hebrew). Tel Aviv, 1931.
———. *Ten Essays on Zionism and Judaism.* London, 1922.
BARDIN, SHLOMO. *Pioneer Youth in Palestine.* New York, 1932.
BARON, SALO W. *Modern Nationalism and Religion.* New York, 1947.
BIALIK, CHAIM. *Complete Poetic Works,* ed. Israel Efros. New York, 1948.
BOROCHOV, DOV BER. *Nationalism and the Class Struggle.* New York, 1937.
———. *Poale Zion Shriften.* 2 vols. New York, 1920-28.

CITRON, S. L. *History of the "Love of Zion" Movement* (Hebrew). Odessa, 1914.
DE HAAS, JACOB. *A History of Palestine.* New York, 1934.
DRUCK, D. *Baron Edmond Rothschild.* New York, 1928.
DRUYANOV, A. *Documents for the History of the "Love of Zion" and the Colonization of Palestine* (Hebrew). 3 vols. Odessa, Tel Aviv, 1910–32.
GALANTÉ, A. *Turcs et juifs: étude historique politique.* Istanbul, 1933.
GOODMAN, P., and SIMON, SIR LEON. *Zionist Thinkers and Leaders.* London, 1929.
GORDON, A. D. *Collected Writings* (Hebrew). 5 vols. Tel Aviv, 1925–29.
GOTTHEIL, RICHARD. *The Life of Gustav Gottheil.* Williamsport (Pennsylvania), 1936.
HAYES, CARLTON J. H. *Essays on Nationalism,* New York, 1925.
HERZL, THEODOR. *Old New Land.* New York, 1941.
HESS, MOSES. *Rome and Jerusalem.* New York, 1943.
KIRK, G. *A Short History of the Near East.* New York, 1949.
KLAUSNER, JOSEPH. *Menahem Ussishkin.* New York, 1942.
KOHN, HANS. "Italy: Mazzini." *(Prophets and Peoples.)* New York, 1946.
———. *Nationalism, Its History and Meaning.* Princeton, 1955.
LEWISOHN, LUDWIG (ed.). *Theodor Herzl: A Portrait for This Age.* Cleveland, 1955.
LIPSCHITZ, J. *Zichron Yacob.* 3 vols. (Vol. III.) Frankfurt, 1881.
MARRIOTT, J. A. R. *The Eastern Question.* Oxford, 1915.
MONTEFIORE, MOSES. *Narrative of a Forty Days' Sojourn in the Holy Land.* London, 1877.
NORDAU, ANNA, and NORDAU, MAXA. *Max Nordau.* New York, 1943.
OLIPHANT, LAURENCE. *The Land of Gilead.* London, 1881.
PINSKER, LEON. *Self-Emancipation.* London, 1891.
RABINOWICZ, OSKAR K. "Herzl and England," *Jewish Social Studies,* January, 1951.
ROUCEK, J. S. (ed.). *Central-Eastern Europe.* New York, 1946.
SAMUEL, MAURICE. *Harvest in the Desert.* New York, 1944.
SETON-WATSON, HUGH. *The Rise of Nationality in the Balkans.* New York, 1918.
SIMON, ERNST. *Chajim Nachman Bialik.* Berlin, 1925.
SIMON, SIR LEON. *Studies in Jewish Nationalism.* London, 1920.
SMOLENSKIN, PEREZ. *Essays* (Hebrew). 4 vols. Jerusalem, 1925–26.
SOKOLOW, NAHUM. *History of Zionism.* 2 vols. London, 1919.
SOUSA, NASIM. *The Capitulatory Regime of Turkey.* Baltimore, 1933.
SPIEGEL, SHALOM. *Hebrew Reborn.* New York, 1930.
ZANGWILL, ISRAEL. *Voice of Jerusalem.* New York, 1921.
ZLOCISTI, THEODOR. *Moses Hess.* Berlin, 1921.

XIV. THE GROWTH OF JEWISH SOCIALISM

BABEL, ISAAC. *Collected Stories.* New York, 1955.
BERNSTEIN, EDUARD. "Jews and German Social Democracy" (Yiddish), *Di Zukunft,* March, 1921.
DENNEN, LEON. "The Jew in the Russian Revolution," *Menorah Journal,* Summer, 1932.
GREENBERG, LOUIS. *The Jews in Russia.* 2 vols. (Vol. II. ed. Mark Wischnitzer.) New Haven, 1951.
The Jews in the Eastern War Zone. (American Jewish Committee.) New York, 1916.

MENES, ABRAHAM. "The Jewish Socialist Movement in Russia and Poland." (*The Jewish People, Past and Present.* 4 vols. Vol. II.) New York, 1948.

PATKIN, A. L. *The Origins of the Russian-Jewish Labour Movement.* Melbourne, 1947.

PINSON, KOPPEL. "Arkady Kremer, Vladimir Medem, and the Ideology of the Jewish Bund," *Jewish Social Studies,* July, 1945.

———. "The National Theories of Simon Dubnow," *ibid.,* October, 1948.

SINGER, I. J. *The Brothers Ashkenazi.* New York, 1936.

FOR FURTHER RESEARCH

ASCH, SHOLEM. *Three Cities.* New York, 1933.

BARON, SALO W. *Die politische Theorie Ferdinand Lassalles.* Leipzig, 1923.

BEER, M. *Fifty Years of International Socialism.* New York, 1935.

BENNS, F. LEE. *European History Since 1870.* New York, 1943.

BROSS, JACOB. "The Beginning of the Jewish Labor Movement in Galicia," *YIVO Annual of Jewish Social Science,* V, 1950.

BUCHBINDER, N. A. *History of the Jewish Labor Movement in Russia* (Yiddish). Vilna, 1931.

BULASCHOW, D. *Bolschewismus und Judentum.* Berlin, 1923.

DIMENSHTEIN, S. *The Revolutionary Movement Among the Jewish Masses in 1905* (Yiddish). Moscow, 1929.

ELBOGEN, I. *A Century of Jewish Life.* Philadelphia, 1944.

FLORINSKY, MICHAEL T. *Russia: A History and an Interpretation.* 2 vols. (Vol. II.) New York, 1953.

FRUMKIN, ABRAHAM. *In the Springtime of Jewish Socialism* (Yiddish). New York, 1940.

GERGEL, N. "Jews in the Russian Communist Party and in the Communist Youth Organization" (Yiddish), *YIVO Bletter,* January, 1931.

———. *The Pogroms in the Ukraine, 1919–21* (Yiddish). Vilna, 1928.

HALL, WALTER PHELPS, and DAVIS, WILLIAM STEARNS. *The Course of Europe Since Waterloo.* New York, 1951.

JASZI, OSCAR. "Socialism." (*Encyclopaedia of the Social Sciences.* Vol. XIII.) New York, 1934.

KAUTSKY, KARL. *Rasse und Judentum.* Stuttgart, 1921.

LESTSCHINSKY, JACOB. *The Jewish Worker* (Yiddish). Vilna, 1905.

LEW, SYMCHA. *Chapters in Jewish History: Social and National Movements Among the Jews of Poland and Russia During the Years 1897–1914* (Yiddish). Brooklyn, 1941.

MARCUS, JACOB. *Rise and Destiny of the German Jew.* Cincinnati, 1934.

MARX, KARL. "On the Jewish Question." (*Selected Essays.*) London, 1926.

MASSING, PAUL. *Rehearsal for Destruction.* New York, 1949.

MAURACH, REINHART. "Liberalismus und Judenpolitik im Zarenreich," *Zeitschrift für Politik,* October, 1939.

MEHRING, FRANZ (ed.). *Aus dem literarischen Nachlass von Karl Marx, Friedrich Engels, und Ferdinand Lasalle.* Stuttgart, 1902.

ONCKEN, HERMANN. *Lassalle, eine politische Biographie.* Stuttgart, 1904.

RAPPAPORT, CHARLES. "The Life of a Revolutionary Emigré," *YIVO Annual of Jewish Social Science,* VI, 1951.

ROSENBERG, ARTHUR. "Socialist Parties." (*Encyclopaedia of the Social Sciences.* Vol. XIII.) New York, 1934.

SILBERNER, EDMUND. "Friedrich Engels and the Jews," *Jewish Social Studies,* July, 1949.

———. *Western Socialism and the Jewish Question* (Hebrew). Jerusalem, 1955.

SINTOWSKI, ELY. "The Bristle Workers Alliance: Contribution to the History of the Jewish Revolutionary Movement in Russia" (Yiddish), *Di Zukunft,* October, 1938.

The Socialist Movement Among the Jews up to 1897 (Yiddish). (*YIVO Studies in History.* Vol. III.) Vilna, 1939.

TARTAKOWER, A. *A History of the Jewish Labor Movement* (Hebrew). 3 vols. Warsaw, 1929–31.

TCHERIKOWER, E. "Peter Lavrov and the Jewish Socialist Emigrés," *YIVO Annual of Jewish Social Science,* VII, 1952.

TROTSKY, LEON. *The History of the Russian Revolution.* New York, 1932.

YARMOLINSKY, AVRAHM. *The Jews and Other Minorities Under the Soviets.* New York, 1928.

XV. THE GREAT MIGRATION AND SETTLEMENT IN AMERICA

HANDLIN, OSCAR. *The Uprooted.* Boston, 1951.

HIGHAM, JOHN. *Strangers in the Land.* New Brunswick (New Jersey), 1955.

JOSEPH, SAMUEL. *Jewish Immigration to the United States.* New York, 1914.

RIIS, JACOB. *How the Other Half Lives.* New York, 1890.

STOLBERG, BENJAMIN. *Tailor's Progress.* New York, 1944.

SZAJKOWSKI, ZOSA. "How the Mass Migration to America Began," *Jewish Social Studies,* October, 1942.

WIRTH, LOUIS. *The Ghetto.* Chicago, 1928.

WISCHNITZER, MARK. *To Dwell in Safety.* Philadelphia, 1948.

FOR FURTHER RESEARCH

ANTIN, MARY. *The Promised Land.* Boston, 1912.

BERNHEIMER, CHARLES S. (ed.). *The Russian Jew in the United States.* Philadelphia, 1905.

BOGEN, BORIS D. *Jewish Philanthropy.* New York, 1917.

CAHAN, ABRAHAM. *Pages Out of My Life* (Yiddish). 5 vols. New York, 1926–31.

——. *The Rise of David Levinsky.* New York, 1917.

CANTOR, EDDIE. *Take My Life.* New York, 1957.

CORSI, EDWARD. *In the Shadow of Liberty.* New York, 1935.

DAVIE, MAURICE R. *World Immigration.* New York, 1917.

ENGELMAN, URIAH ZEVI. *The Rise of the Jew in the Western World.* New York, 1944.

FREDERIC, HAROLD. *The New Exodus.* London, 1892.

GRAHAM, STEPHEN. *With Poor Immigrants to America.* New York, 1914.

GUTSTEIN, MORRIS A. *Priceless Heritage: The Epic Growth of Nineteenth Century Chicago Jewry.* New York, 1939.

HOURWICH, ISAAC. *Immigration and Labor.* New York, 1922.

KOHLER, MAX. *Immigration and Aliens in the United States.* New York, 1936.

LESTSCHINSKY, JACOB. "Economic and Social Development of American Jewry." (*The Jewish People, Past and Present.* 4 vols. Vol. IV.) New York, 1955.

LEVINE, LOUIS. *The Women's Garment Workers.* New York, 1924.

LINFELD, H. S. *Jewish Migration as a Part of World Migration Movements, 1920–30.* New York, 1933.

MAHLER, RAPHAEL. "The Economic Background of Jewish Emigration from Galicia to the United States," *YIVO Annual of Jewish Social Science,* VII, 1952.

ROBISON, SOPHIA M. *Jewish Population Studies.* New York, 1943.

RUPPIN, ARTHUR. *The Jews in the Modern World.* London, 1934.

SCHULMAN, ELIAS. *A History of Yiddish Literature in the United States, 1870–1900* (Yiddish). New York, 1943.

SZAJKOWSKI, ZOSA. "The European Attitude to East European Jewish Immigration, 1881-1893," *Publications of the American Jewish Historical Society,* XLI, 1951, 1952.

————. "Jewish Emigration Policy in the Period of the Rumanian 'Exodus,' 1899–1903," *Jewish Social Studies,* January, 1951.

TCHERIKOWER, E. "Jewish Immigrants to the United States, 1881–1900," *YIVO Annual of Jewish Social Science,* VI, 1951.

WALD, LILLIAN. *The House on Henry Street.* New York, 1915.

WITTKE, CARL. *We Who Built America.* New York, 1940.

XVI. RUSSIAN JEWRY'S "LIBERAL" TRADITION IN AMERICA

EPSTEIN, MELECH. *Jewish Labor in the United States.* 2 vols. New York, 1950.

FUCHS, LAWRENCE. *The Political Behavior of American Jews.* Glencoe (Illinois), 1956.

HANDLIN, OSCAR. *Adventure in Freedom.* New York, 1954.

JANOWSKY, OSCAR (ed.). *The American Jew.* New York, 1942.

LEARSI, RUFUS. *The Jews in America: A History.* Cleveland, 1954.

McWILLIAMS, CARY. *A Mask for Privilege.* Boston, 1948.

MASON, ALPHEUS T. *Brandeis the Man.* New York, 1946.

MENES, ABRAHAM. "The Jewish Labor Movement." (*The Jewish People, Past and Present.* 4 vols. Vol. IV.) New York, 1955.

RICH, J. C. "Sixty Years of the 'Jewish Daily Forward,'" *New Leader,* June 3, 1957.

SOLTES, MORDECAI. *The Yiddish Press.* New York, 1925.

STOLBERG, BENJAMIN. *Tailor's Progress.* New York, 1944.

FOR FURTHER RESEARCH

American Jewish Yearbook, years from 1922 seriatim.

BERNSTEIN, HERMAN. *The History of a Lie.* New York, 1921.

BETTELHEIM, B., and JANOWITZ, M. *Dynamics of Prejudice.* New York, 1950.

BLOOM, SOLOMON F. "The Liberalism of Louis D. Brandeis," *Commentary,* October, 1948.

BOOKBINDER, HYMAN H. *To Promote the General Welfare: The Story of the Amalgamated Clothing Workers.* New York, 1950.

BROUN, HEYWOOD, and BRITT, GEORGE. *Christians Only.* New York, 1931.

CAHAN, ABRAHAM. *Pages Out of My Life* (Yiddish). 5 vols. New York, 1926–31.

————. *The Rise of David Levinsky.* New York, 1917.

CARLSON, JOHN ROY. *The Plotters.* New York, 1945.

————. *Undercover.* New York, 1943.

COHEN, ELLIOT E. (ed.). *Commentary on the American Scene.* New York, 1953.

COHEN, GEORGE. *The Jews in the Making of America.* Boston, 1924.

COHEN, MORRIS R. *Reflections of a Wondering Jew.* Boston, 1950.

DAVIS-DUBOIS, RACHEL, and SCHWEPPE, EMMA. *The Jew in American Life.* New York, 1935.

DRACHSLER, JULIUS. *Democracy and Assimilation.* New York, 1920.

DRINKWATER, JOHN. *The Life and Adventures of Carl Laemmle*. New York, 1931.
FINEBERG, SOLOMON. *Overcoming Anti-Semitism*. New York, 1943.
FORSTER, ARNOLD, and EPSTEIN, BENJAMIN. *The Trouble Makers*. New York, 1952.
GERSH, HARRY. "The New Suburbanites of the 50's," *Commentary*, March, 1954.
GOLDWYN, SAMUEL. *Behind the Screen*. New York, 1923.
GOMPERS, SAMUEL. *Seventy Years of Life and Labor*. New York, 1925.
Jews in America. (edd. of *Fortune*.) New York, 1936.
JOSEPHSON, MATTHEW. *Sidney Hillman*. New York, 1952.
KAGAN, SOLOMON R. *Jewish Contributions to Medicine in America*. Boston, 1934.
KAUFMAN, I., and KOHS, SAMUEL C. (edd.). *American Jews in World War II*. 2 vols. New York, 1947.
LANG, HARRY. *"62," Biography of a Union*. New York, 1940.
LESTSCHINSKY, JACOB. "Economic and Social Development of American Jewry." (*The Jewish People, Past and Present*. 4 vols. Vol. IV.) New York, 1955.
LEVINE, LOUIS. *The Women's Garment Workers*. New York, 1924.
LEVINGER, LEE J. "The Disappearing Small-Town Jew," *Commentary*, August, 1952.
LIVINGSTON, SIGMUND. *Must Men Hate?* Cleveland, 1944.
MEYER, HENRY J. "The Economic Structure of the Jewish Community in Detroit," *Jewish Social Studies*, April, 1940.
MORRISON, S., and COMMAGER, H. S. *The Growth of the American Republic*. 2 vols. (Vol. II.) New York, 1950.
ROBISON, SOPHIA M. *Jewish Population Studies*. New York, 1943.
SCHLESINGER, ARTHUR, JR. *Crisis of the Old Order*. New York, 1957.
SHATZKY, JACOB. *Studies in the History of the Yiddish Press in America* (Yiddish). New York, 1934.
SHERWOOD, ROBERT. *Roosevelt and Hopkins*. 2 vols. New York, 1948.
STRONG, DONALD S. *Organized Anti-Semitism in America*. Washington, D. C., 1941.
VALENTIN, HUGO. *Anti-Semitism*. New York, 1936.
WATKINS, GORDON S. (ed.). *The Motion Picture Industry*. Philadelphia, 1947.

XVII. THE JEWS OF EASTERN EUROPE BETWEEN THE WARS

BARON, SALO W. *The Jews in Roumania*. New York, 1930.
COHEN, ISRAEL. "The Jews in Hungary," *Contemporary Review*, November, 1939.
GOODHART, ARTHUR L. *Poland and the Minority Races*. London, 1920.
LESTSCHINSKY, JACOB. "The Anti-Jewish Program: Tsarist Russia, the Third Reich, and Independent Poland," *Jewish Social Studies*, April, 1941.
———. "Economic Aspects of Jewish Community Organization in Independent Poland," *ibid.*, October, 1947.
———. "The Economic Struggle of the Jews in Independent Lithuania," *ibid.*, October, 1946.
ROBINSON, JACOB, KARBACH, OSCAR, *et al*. *Were the Minority Treaties a Failure?* New York, 1943.
SACHAR, A. L. *Sufferance Is the Badge*. New York, 1940.
SCHWARZ, SOLOMON M. *The Jews in the Soviet Union*. Syracuse (New York), 1951.
TELLER, JUDD L. *The Kremlin, the Jews, and the Middle East*. Syracuse (New York), 1957.

FOR FURTHER RESEARCH

BENNS, F. LEE. *European History Since 1870.* New York, 1941.

BERKOWITZ, J. *La question des israélites en Roumanie.* Paris, 1923.

BOGEN, BORIS D. *Jewish Philanthropy.* New York, 1917.

BUELL, RAYMOND. *Poland: Key to Europe.* New York, 1939.

CANG, JOEL. "The Opposition Parties in Poland and Their Attitude Toward the Jews and the Jewish Problem," *Jewish Social Studies,* April, 1939.

COHEN, ISRAEL. "The Jewish Plight in Poland," *The Nineteenth Century and After,* March, 1938.

————. *Journal of a Jewish Traveler.* New York, 1925.

DENNEN, LEON. *Where the Ghetto Ends.* New York, 1934.

DROHOJOWSKI, JAN. *A Brief Outline of the Jewish Problem in Poland.* Brooklyn, 1938.

DUKER, A. G. *The Situation of the Jews in Poland.* New York, 1936.

ECK, NATHAN. "The Educational Institutions of Polish Jewry," *Jewish Social Studies,* January, 1947.

ELBOGEN, I. *A Century of Jewish Life.* Philadelphia, 1944.

FODOR, M. W. *Plot and Counterplot in Central Europe.* Boston, 1937.

GELBER, N. M. "Jewish Life in Bulgaria," *Jewish Social Studies,* April, 1946.

GLIKSMAN, G. *L'aspect économique et la question juive en Pologne.* Paris, 1929.

GOLDELMAN, SOLOMON. "The Jews in Czechoslovakia Before the Crisis," *Contemporary Jewish Record,* October, 1938.

JANOWSKY, OSCAR. *The Jews and Minority Rights, 1898–1919.* New York, 1933.

————. *A People at Bay.* London, 1938.

The Jews in Poland From Earliest Times up to the Second World War (Yiddish). (Committee for the Publication.) New York, 1946.

LEHMAN, FRITZ KARL. "Die Juden in der Karpathen-Ukraine," *Weltkampf,* March, 1939.

LESTSCHINSKY, JACOB. *The Economic Status of the Jews in Poland* (Yiddish). Berlin, 1931.

————. *Der wirtschaftliche Zusammenbruch der Juden in Deutschland und Polen.* Paris, 1936.

LIPSHITZ, EZEKIEL. "Jews and Germans in the Baltic Countries" (Yiddish), *Di Zukunft,* December, 1939.

LUZZATTI, LUIGI. *God in Freedom.* New York, 1930.

MAHLER, RAPHAEL. "Jews in the Liberal Professions in Poland, 1920–39," *Jewish Social Studies,* October, 1944.

MENES, ABRAHAM. "The Yeshivots in Eastern Europe." (*The Jewish People, Past and Present.* 4 vols. Vol. I.) New York, 1946.

MEYER, H. *Das Recht der religiösen Minderheiten in Polen.* Breslau, 1932.

MOSKOWITZ, MOSES. "Polish Public Opinion on the Ghetto Benches," *Menorah Journal,* Winter, 1938.

————. "Totalitarianism and Anti-Semitism in Poland," *Contemporary Jewish Record,* January, 1939.

REICH, NATHAN. "Towards a Solution of the Jewish Problem in Poland," *Menorah Journal,* Spring, 1938.

ROBINSON, JACOB. *Das Minoritätenproblem und seine Literatur.* Berlin, 1935.

ROUCEK, J. S. (ed.). *Central-Eastern Europe.* New York, 1946.

SCHUSTER, HANS. *Die Judenfrage in Rumänien.* Leipzig, 1939.

SEGAL, SIMON. *The New Poland and the Jews.* New York, 1938.

SINGER, I. J. *The Brothers Ashkenazi.* New York, 1936.

————. *East of Eden.* New York, 1939.

La Situation des juifs en Roumanie. (World Jewish Congress.) Geneva, 1938.
STARR, JOSHUA. "Jewish Citizenship in Rumania," *Jewish Social Studies,* January, 1941.
TIMASHEFF, N. S. *Religion in Soviet Russia, 1917–1942.* New York, 1942.

XVIII. THE PALESTINE MANDATE

ANTONIUS, GEORGE. *The Arab Awakening.* Philadelphia, 1934.
ASSAF, MICHAEL. *The Arab Movement in Palestine.* New York, 1937.
BEIN, ALEX. *Agricultural Settlement of the Jews in Palestine* (Hebrew). Jerusalem, 1944.
BURSTEIN, MOSHE. *Self-Government of the Jews in Palestine Since 1900.* Tel Aviv, 1934.
Great Britain and Palestine, 1915–1945. (Royal Institute of International Affairs.) London, 1946.
HYAMSON, A. M. *Palestine Under the Mandate, 1920–1948.* London, 1950.
KURLAND, SAMUEL. *Cooperative Palestine: The Story of Histadrut.* New York, 1947.
Palestine: A Study of Jewish, Arab, and British Policies. 2 vols. (Esco Foundation for Palestine.) New Haven, 1947.
PERLMANN, MOSHE. "Chapters of Arab-Jewish Diplomacy, 1918–1922," *Jewish Social Studies,* April, 1944.
RUPPIN, ARTHUR. *Three Decades of Palestine.* Jerusalem, 1936.
SAMUEL, MAURICE. *Harvest in the Desert.* New York, 1944.
SPIRO, MELFORD E. *Kibbutz.* Cambridge, 1956.
WEIZMANN, CHAIM. *Trial and Error.* New York, 1949.

FOR FURTHER RESEARCH

AARONSOHN, AARON. *With the Turks in Palestine.* Boston, 1916.
ADLER, SELIG. "The Palestine Question in the Wilson Era," *Jewish Social Studies,* October, 1948.
ANKORIAN, A. *The Government of Palestine.* Jerusalem, 1945.
ASHERY, R. E., and SERENI, ENZO. *Jews and Arabs in Palestine.* New York, 1936.
ATIYAH, EDWARD. *An Arab Tells His Story.* London, 1946.
ATTIAS, MOSHE. *The Community of Israel in Palestine: Its Foundation and Its Organization* (Hebrew). Jerusalem, 1944.
BENTWICH, NORMAN. *The Mandates System.* London, 1930.
BIN-NUN, AARON (ed.). *Jew and Arab on the Border.* New York, 1940.
BOEHM, ADOLF, and POLLAK, ADOLF. *The Jewish National Fund.* Jerusalem, 1929.
CHAZAN, Y. *Thirty Years of Hashomer Hatzail.* Tel Aviv, 1944.
DE HAAS, JACOB. *Louis D. Brandeis.* New York, 1926.
DJEMAL PASHA. *Memories of a Turkish Statesman, 1913–1919.* London, 1922.
DUGDALE, BLANCHE E. *Arthur James Balfour.* 2 vols. New York, 1937.
EDIDEN, BEN. *Rebuilding Palestine.* New York, 1939.
FINK, REUBEN. *America and Palestine.* New York, 1944.
GARNETT, DAVID (ed.). *The Letters of T. E. Lawrence.* New York, 1939.
General Federation of Jewish Labor in Eretz-Israel. Tel Aviv, 1946.
GOLDMAN, SOLOMON (ed.). *Brandeis on Zionism.* Washington, D. C., 1942.
GRAVES, R. M. *Experiment in Anarchy.* New York, 1949.
HALKIN, SIMON. *Modern Hebrew Literature.* New York, 1950.
HANNA, PAUL L. *British Policy in Palestine.* Washington, D. C., 1942.
HITTI, PHILIP K. *History of the Arabs.* London, 1940.

Horowitz, David. *The Development of the Palestine Economy* (Hebrew). Tel Aviv, 1948.
Hourani, Albert. *Syria and Lebanon.* London, 1946.
Howard, Harry N. *The Partition of Turkey.* Norman (Oklahoma), 1931.
Hurewitz, J. C. *The Struggle for Palestine.* New York, 1950.
Infield, Henrik F. *Cooperative Living in Palestine.* New York, 1944.
Katznelson, Berl. *Revolutionary Constructivism: Essays on the Jewish Labor Movement in Palestine.* New York, 1937.
Lawrence, T. E. *Secret Despatches from Arabia.* London, 1939.
Learsi, Rufus. *Fulfillment: The Epic Story of Zionism.* Cleveland, 1951.
Levenberg, S. *The Jews and Palestine: A Study in Labour Zionism.* London, 1945.
Levinger, E. E. *Fighting Angel: The Story of Henrietta Szold.* New York, 1946.
Litvinoff, Barnet. *Ben-Gurion of Israel.* New York, 1954.
Manuel, Frank E. *The Realities of American-Palestine Relations.* Washington, D. C., 1949.
Morgenthau, Henry. *All in a Lifetime.* New York, 1922.
———. *Ambassador Morgenthau's Story.* New York, 1918.
Nardi, Noach. *Zionism and Education in Palestine.* New York, 1934.
Palestine Royal Commission Report. London, 1937.
Pearlman, Maurice. *Mufti of Jerusalem.* London, 1947.
Revusky, Abraham. *Jews in Palestine.* New York, 1935.
Sokolow, Nahum. *History of Zionism.* 2 vols. London, 1919.
Storrs, Ronald. *Orientations.* London, 1937.
Twenty Years of Medical Service to Palestine, 1919–1938. (Hadassah Medical Organization.) Jerusalem, 1939.
Ulitzur, A. *Two Decades of Keren Hayesod.* Jerusalem, 1940.
Yale, William. "Ambassador Morgenthau's Special Mission of 1917," *World Politics,* April, 1947.

XIX. THE IMPACT OF THE JEWS ON WESTERN CULTURE

Agus, Jacob B. *Guideposts in Modern Judaism.* New York, 1954.
———. *Modern Philosophies of Judaism.* New York, 1941.
Bevan, E. R., and Singer, Charles. *The Legacy of Israel.* Oxford, 1928.
Brod, Max. *Franz Kafka.* New York, 1947.
Buber, Martin. *I and Thou.* Edinburgh, 1950.
Fiedler, Leslie. "Simone Weil: Prophet Out of Israel," *Commentary,* January, 1951.
Frank, Philipp. *Einstein, His Life and Times.* New York. 1947.
Friedman, Morris. *Martin Buber: The Life of Dialogue.* Chicago, 1955.
Glatzer, Nahum. *Franz Rosenzweig.* New York, 1953.
Jones, Ernest. *The Life and Work of Sigmund Freud.* 3 vols. New York, 1953, 1956, 1957.
Kristol, Irving. "Einstein: The Passion of Pure Reason," *Commentary,* September, 1950.
Politzer, Heinz. "From Mendelssohn to Kafka," *Commentary,* April, 1947.
Rosenzweig, Franz. *Der Stern der Erlösung.* Breslau, 1933.
Sachs, Joseph. *Beauty and the Jew.* London, 1937.
Wassermann, Jacob. *My Life as German and Jew.* New York, 1933.
Zweig, Stefan. *The World of Yesterday.* New York, 1943.

FOR FURTHER RESEARCH

AGUS, JACOB B. *Banner of Jerusalem: The Life, Times, and Thought of Abraham Isaak Kuk, Late Chief Rabbi of Palestine.* New York, 1946.

ARENDT, HANNAH. *The Origins of Totalitarianism.* New York, 1951.

BAECK, LEO. *The Essence of Judaism.* New York, 1948.

——. *The Pharisees and Other Essays.* New York, 1947.

BERENSON, BERNARD. *Rumor and Reflection.* New York, 1952.

BETTAUER, HUGO. *The City Without Jews.* New York, 1929.

BUBER, MARTIN. *At the Turning.* New York, 1952.

——. *Between Man and Man.* London, 1947.

——. *Hasidism.* New York, 1948.

——. *Israel and the World.* New York, 1948.

——. *The Legend of the Baal Shem.* New York, 1955.

——. *Mamre, Essays in Religion.* London, 1946.

——. *Tales of the Hasidim.* 2 vols. New York, 1947, 1948.

COHEN, MORRIS R. *Reflections of a Wondering Jew.* Boston, 1950.

DAVIDSOHN, JOSEPH. "The Problem of Georg Brandes' Jewishness," *YIVO Annual of Jewish Social Science,* II, 1947.

FARBRIDGE, M. *Judaism and the Modern Mind.* New York, 1927.

FRIEDENWALD, L. *The Jews and Medicine.* Baltimore, 1944.

FREUD, SIGMUND. *Moses and Monotheism.* New York, 1939.

GERSHENFELD, L. *The Jew in Science.* Philadelphia, 1934.

GOLDSCHMIDT, HERMANN L. "The Key to Kafka," *Commentary,* August, 1949.

GREENBERG, CLEMENT. "The Jewishness of Franz Kafka," *Commentary,* April, 1955.

HAYES, CARLTON J. H. *A Political and Cultural History of Modern Europe.* 2 vols. (Vol. II.) New York, 1936.

HYMAN, STANLEY EDGAR. "Freud and Boas: Secular Rabbis?" *Commentary,* March, 1954.

JACOBS, JOSEPH. *Jewish Contributions to Civilization.* Philadelphia, 1919.

KAFKA, FRANZ. *The Castle.* New York, 1941.

——. *Diaries,* ed. Max Brod. 2 vols. New York, 1948.

——. *The Penal Colony.* New York, 1948.

——. *Selected Short Stories.* New York, 1952.

——. *The Trial.* New York, 1937.

KROJANKER, G. (ed.). *Juden in der deutschen Literatur.* Berlin, 1922.

LEWISOHN, LUDWIG (ed.). *Among the Nations.* Philadelphia, 1948.

LIST, KURT. "Mahler: Father of Modern Music," *Commentary,* July, 1950.

McCALL, LILLIAN BLUMBERG. "The Hidden Springs of Sigmund Freud," *Commentary,* August, 1954.

MARCH, HAROLD. *The Two Worlds of Marcel Proust.* Philadelphia, 1948.

MARCUS, JACOB. *Rise and Destiny of the German Jew.* Cincinnati, 1934.

NATHANSEN, HENRI. *Jude oder Europäer: Porträt von Georg Brandes.* Frankfurt, 1931.

NEIDER, CHARLES. *The Frozen Sea.* New York, 1948.

PUNER, HELEN WALKER. *Freud: His Life and His Mind.* New York, 1947.

ROBACK, A. A. *Jewish Influence on Modern Thought.* Cambridge (Massachusetts), 1929.

ROSENZWEIG, FRANZ. *On Jewish Learning.* New York, 1955.

ROTH, CECIL. *The Jewish Contribution to Civilization.* New York, 1940.

ROTH, S. *Juden im ungarischen Kulturleben in der zweiten Hälfte des 19. Jahrhunderts*. Berlin, 1934.
RUNES, DAGOBERT D. (ed.). *The Hebrew Impact on Western Civilization*. New York, 1951.
SALESKI, G. *Famous Musicians of a Wandering Race*. New York, 1927.
SENDREY, ALFRED. *Bibliography of Jewish Music*. New York, 1951.
STERLING, ADA. *The Jew and Civilization*. New York, 1924.
VEBLEN, THORSTEIN. "The Intellectual Preeminence of Jews in Modern Europe," *Political Science Quarterly*, March, 1919.
WEIL, SIMONE. "Factory Work," *Politics*, December, 1946.
———. "The Iliad: Or the Poem of Force," *ibid.*, November, 1945.
———. "Reflections on War," *ibid.*, February, 1945.
———. "Words and War," *ibid.*, March, 1946.
ZWEIG, ARNOLD. *Insulted and Exiled*. London, 1937.

XX. THE ONSLAUGHT OF NAZISM

ARENDT, HANNAH. *The Origins of Totalitarianism*. New York, 1951.
BULLOCK, ALAN. *Hitler, A Study in Tyranny*. New York, 1952.
BUTLER, ROHAN D'OR. *The Roots of National Socialism*. New York, 1942.
FODOR, M. W. "The Austrian Roots of Hitlerism," *Foreign Affairs*, July, 1935.
Hitler's Ten Year War on the Jews. (Institute of Jewish Affairs.) New York, 1943.
KRIEGER, SEYMOUR (ed.). *Nazi Germany's War Against the Jews*. New York, 1947.
KURTH, GERTRUDE M. "The Complex Behind Hitler's Anti-Semitism," *Commentary*, January, 1948.
REICHMANN, EVA. *Hostages of Civilization*. Boston, 1951.
SNYDER, LOUIS L. *German Conservatism*. Harrisburg (Pennsylvania), 1952.
TENENBAUM, JOSEPH. *Race and Reich*. New York, 1955.

FOR FURTHER RESEARCH

BAUMONT, M., FRIED, J. H. E., and VERMEIL, E. (edd.). *The Third Reich*. New York, 1955.
BENEDICT, RUTH. *Race: Science and Politics*. New York, 1940.
BLOCH, JOSHUA. *Nazi Germany and the Jews: An Annotated Bibliography*. New York, 1936.
BLUME, FRIEDRICH. *Das Rassenproblem in der Musik*. Berlin, 1939.
BRADY, ROBERT A. *The Spirit and Structure of German Fascism*. New York, 1937.
BRAMSTEDT, E. K. *Dictatorship and Political Police*. London, 1945.
BRENNECKE, FRITZ. *A Nazi Primer*. New York, 1938.
CRANKSHAW, EDWARD. *Gestapo*. London, 1956.
DARRÉ, R. W. *Um Blut und Boden*. Munich, 1940.
DREXLER, ANTON. *Mein politisches Erwachen*. Munich, 1923.
EBELING, H. *The Caste: The Political Role of the German General Staff Between 1918 and 1938*. London, 1945.
FRASER, LINDLEY. *Germany Between Two Wars*. London, 1944.
FRISCHAUER, WILLI. *Himmler*. Boston, 1953.
FRITSCH, THEODOR (ed.). *Handbuch der Judenfrage*. Leipzig, 1938.
GOEBBELS, JOSEPH PAUL. *Diaries*. London, 1948.
GOLDEN, G. M. *Murder of a Nation*. London, 1943.
GRAU, WILHELM. *Die Judenfrage in der deutschen Geschichte*. Berlin, 1942.
GROSS, WALTER. *Der deutsche Rassengedanke und die Welt*. Berlin, 1939.

GUENTHER, HANS F. K. *Rassenkunde des deutschen Volkes.* Munich, 1923.
GUTTMANN, T. *Dokumentwerk über die jüdische Geschichte in der Zeit des Nazismus.* 2 vols. Jerusalem, 1943, 1945.
HALL, WALTER PHELPS, and DAVIS, WILLIAM STEARNS. *The Course of Europe Since Waterloo.* New York, 1951.
HEDENQUIST, GOETE (ed.). *The Church and the Jewish People.* London, 1954.
HEIDEN, KONRAD. *History of National Socialism.* New York, 1935.
HITLER, ADOLF. *My Battle (Mein Kampf).* Boston, 1938.
JACOBY, GERHARD. *Racial State.* New York, 1944.
The Jews in Nazi Europe. (Institute of Jewish Affairs.) New York, 1941.
KESSLER, HERMANN. *Walter Rathenau.* New York, 1930.
LANG, SERGE, and SCHENCK, ERNST VON (edd.). *Rosenberg's Memoirs.* New York, 1949.
LOWENTHAL, MARVIN. *The Jews of Germany.* Philadelphia, 1944.
LUDECKE, KARL. *I Knew Hitler.* New York, 1937.
MICKLEM, NATHANIEL. *National Socialism and the Roman Catholic Church.* London, 1939.
NEUMANN, FRANZ. *Behemoth: The Structure and Practice of National Socialism.* London, 1944.
PINSON, KOPPEL. *Modern Germany.* New York, 1954.
RAUSCHNING, HERMANN. *Germany's Revolution of Destruction.* London, 1939.
ROSENBERG, ALFRED. *Blut und Ehre.* Munich, 1939.
———. *Der Mythus des 20. Jahrhunderts.* Munich, 1930.
ROSENTHAL, ERICH. "Trends of the Jewish Population in Germany, 1910–1939," *Jewish Social Studies,* March, 1944.
SACHAR, A. L. *Sufferance Is the Badge.* New York, 1940.
SCHEELE, GODFREY. *The Weimar Republic.* London, 1946.
SCHUSCHNIGG, KURT. *My Austria.* New York, 1935.
TENENBAUM, JOSEPH. *In Search of a Lost People.* New York, 1948.
THOMPSON, DOROTHY. *Refugees: Anarchy or Organization?* New York, 1938.
WEINREICH, MAX. *Hitler's Professors.* New York, 1946.
WEISER, BENNO. "Unsentimental Journey to Vienna," *Commentary,* July, 1955.
WHEELER-BENNET, JOHN W. *Prologue to Tragedy.* New York, 1948.
WISCHNITZER, MARK. "Jewish Emigration from Germany, 1933–1938," *Jewish Social Studies,* January, 1940.
———. *To Dwell in Safety.* Philadelphia, 1948.
WOLFE, HENRY C. *The German Octopus.* New York, 1938.

XXI. EUROPE *JUDENREIN*

BERG, MARY. *Warsaw Diary.* New York, 1945.
BULLOCK, ALAN. *Hitler, A Study in Tyranny.* New York, 1952.
FRIEDMAN, PHILIP. *Martyrs and Fighters.* New York, 1954.
KERSTEN, FELIX. *Memoirs.* New York, 1947.
KOGON, EUGEN. *The Theory and Practice of Hell.* London, 1951.
POLIAKOV, LÉON. *Harvest of Hate.* Syracuse (New York), 1954.
REITLINGER, GERALD. *The Final Solution.* London, 1953.
SCHWARZ, SOLOMAN M. *The Jews in the Soviet Union.* Syracuse (New York), 1951.
TENENBAUM, JOSEPH. "The *Einsatzgruppen,*" *Jewish Social Studies,* January, 1955.
———. *Race and Reich.* New York, 1956.
WIERNIK, YANKEL. *A Year in Treblinka.* New York, 1945.

FOR FURTHER RESEARCH

BAECK, LEO. *We Survived.* New Haven, 1949.

BERNADOTTE, COUNT FOLKE. *The Curtain Falls.* New York, 1945.

BERNSTEIN, VICTOR H. *Final Judgment: The Story of Nuremberg.* New York, 1947.

The Black Book. (Jewish Black Book Committee.) New York, 1946.

The Black Book of Polish Jewry. (American Federation for Polish Jews.) New York, 1943.

BLOOM, SOLOMON F. "Dictator of the Lodz Ghetto," *Commentary,* February, 1949.

CARP, MATATIAS. *The Sufferings of the Jews of Rumania, 1940–1944.* Bucharest, 1945.

CIANFARRA, CAMILLE M. *The Vatican and the War.* New York, 1944.

DUFOURNIER, DENISE. *Ravensbrueck: The Women's Camp of Death.* London, 1948.

DVORJETSKI, MARC. *Ghetto à l'est.* Paris. 1950.

FRANK, ANNE. *The Diary of a Young Girl.* New York, 1953.

FRIEDMAN, PHILIP. "The Jewish Ghettos of the Nazi Era," *Jewish Social Studies,* January, 1954.

———. *This was Oswiecim.* London, 1946.

FRUMKIN, GREGORY. *Population Changes in Europe Since 1939.* New York, 1951.

GOEBBELS, JOSEPH PAUL. *Diaries.* London, 1948.

GOLDSTEIN, BERNARD. *The Stars Bear Witness.* New York, 1949.

GRINGAUZ, SAMUEL. "The Ghetto as an Experiment of Jewish Social Organization," *Jewish Social Studies,* January, 1949.

HERSEY, JOHN. *The Wall.* New York, 1951.

HERSHKOVITCH, BENDET. "The Ghetto in Litzmannstadt (Lodz)," *YIVO Annual of Jewish Social Science,* V, 1950.

Les Juifs en Europe, 1939–1945. (Conférence des commissions historiques et des centres de documentation juifs.) Paris, 1947.

KISCH, E. E. *Tales from Seven Ghettos.* London, 1948.

KULISCHER, EUGENE. *The Displacement of Population in Europe.* Montreal, 1943.

LAQUEUR, W. Z. "The Kastner Case," *Commentary,* December, 1955.

LAZARUS, JACQUES. *Juifs au combat.* Paris, 1947.

LEFTWICH, JOSEPH. "Songs of the Death Camps," *Commentary,* September, 1951.

LEVAI, EUGENE. *The Black Book of the Martyrdom of Hungarian Jewry.* Munich, 1948.

LINGENS-REINER, ELLA. *Prisoners of Fear.* London, 1948.

LUBETKIN, ZIVIAH. "The Last Days of the Warsaw Ghetto," *Commentary,* May, 1947.

MELEZIN, ABRAHAM. *Demographic Processes Among the Jewish Population of Poland, 1939–1945.* Lodz, 1948.

MENASCHE, ALBERT. *Birkenau, Auschwitz II.* New York, 1947.

MONNERAY, HENRI. *La Persécution des juifs en France et dans les autres pays de l'ouest.* Paris, 1947.

Nazi Conspiracy and Aggression. 11 vols. (United States Department of State.) Washington, D. C., 1946–48.

PERL, GISELLA. *I Was a Doctor in Auschwitz.* New York, 1948.

POLIAKOV, LÉON. *La condition des juifs en France sous l'occupation italienne.* Paris, 1950.

SACHAR, EDWARD J. "Goods for Blood": A Case Study in Twentieth Century Diplomacy.* Unpublished thesis. Harvard University, 1952.

SCHWARZ, LEO W. (ed.). *The Root and the Bough.* New York, 1949.
STARR, JOSHUA, and SHAPIRO, LEON. "Recent Population Data: Articles on Statistics of Jewish Survival in Germany, Poland, the Balkans, etc.," *Jewish Social Studies,* January, April, June, 1946.
STEINER, FREDERIC. *The Tragedy of Slovak Jewry.* Bratislava, 1949.
SYRKIN, MARIE. *Blessed Is the Match.* New York, 1947.
SZAJKOWSKI, ZOSA. "The Organization of UGIF in Nazi-Occupied France," *Jewish Social Studies,* July, 1947.
SZALET, LEON. *Experiment "E".* New York, 1945.
TENENBAUM, JOSEPH. "Auschwitz in Retrospect," *Jewish Social Studies,* July, October, 1953.
———. *In Search of a Lost People.* New York, 1948.
———. *Underground: The Story of a People.* New York, 1952.
TREVOR-ROPER, H. E. *The Last Days of Hitler.* London, 1947.

XXII. THE BIRTH OF ISRAEL

CUNNINGHAM, SIR ALAN. "Palestine—The Last Days of the Mandate," *International Affairs,* October, 1948.
FRYE, R. (ed.). *The Near East and the Great Powers.* Cambridge (Massachusetts), 1951.
HUREWITZ, J. C. *The Struggle for Palestine.* New York, 1950.
KIMCHE, JON, and KIMCHE, DAVID. *The Secret Roads.* New York, 1955.
LITVINOFF, BARNET. *Ben-Gurion of Israel.* New York, 1954.
McKAY, VERNON. "The Arab League in World Politics," *Foreign Policy Reports,* November, 1946.
SACHER, HARRY. *Israel: The Establishment of a State.* New York, 1952.
SETON-WILLIAMS, M. V. *Britain and the Arab States.* London, 1948.
WEIZMANN, CHAIM. *Trial and Error.* New York, 1949.
WILLIAMS, FRANCIS. *Ernest Bevin.* London, 1952.
ZANDER, W. *Soviet Jewry, Palestine, and the West.* London, 1947.

FOR FURTHER RESEARCH

The Arab War Effort. (American Christian Palestine Committee.) New York, 1947.
ARSENIAN, SETH. "Wartime Propaganda in the Middle East," *Middle East Journal,* October, 1948.
BEIGIN, MENAHIM. *The Revolt: Story of the Irgun.* New York, 1951.
BERNADOTTE, COUNT FOLKE. "Report on Palestine," *Current History,* November, 1948.
"Bevin Concedes Arab Rights," *Bulletin of the Institute of Arab-American Affairs,* March 15, 1947.
BILBY, KENNETH. *New Star in the Near East.* New York, 1950.
BRODIE, BERNARD. "American Security and Foreign Oil," *Foreign Policy Reports,* March, 1948.
CADETT, THOMAS. "The Exodus 1947: The British Case," *New York Herald Tribune,* September 17, 1947.
CARLSON, JOHN ROY. *Cairo to Damascus.* New York, 1951.
CASPER, B. M. *With the Jewish Brigade.* London, 1947.
CHENERY, HOLLIS B., and MIKESELL, RAYMOND F. *Arabian Oil: America's Stake in the Middle East.* Chapel Hill (North Carolina), 1949.

CROSSMAN, RICHARD. *Palestine Mission: A Personal Record.* New York, 1947.

CRUM, BARTLEY C. *Behind the Silken Curtain.* New York, 1947.

EILON, A. *Jerusalem Did Not Fall: The Siege of 1948* (Hebrew). Tel Aviv, 1949.

FANNING, LEONARD M. *American Oil Operations Abroad.* New York, 1947.

FEIS, HERBERT. *Petroleum and American Foreign Policy.* Palo Alto, 1944.

GARCÍA-GRANADOS, JORGE. *The Birth of Israel.* New York, 1948.

GLUBB, JOHN BAGOT. *The Story of the Arab Legion.* London, 1948.

GRUBER, RUTH. *Destination Palestine.* New York, 1948.

HIRSCHMANN, IRA. *Lifeline to a Promised Land.* New York, 1946.

KOESTLER, A. *Promise and Fulfilment: Palestine, 1917–1949.* New York, 1949.

LEVIN, H. *I Saw the Battle of Jerusalem.* New York, 1950.

LOWDERMILK, WALTER C. *Palestine, Land of Promise.* New York, 1944.

McDONALD, J. G. *My Mission in Israel.* New York, 1951.

MANUEL, FRANK E. *The Realities of American-Palestine Relations.* Washington, D.C., 1949.

MONROE, ELIZABETH. "British Interests in the Middle East," *Middle East Journal,* April, 1948.

PERLMANN, MOSHE. *The Army of Israel.* New York, 1950.

Police State, Nazi Model: Palestine Under British Rule. (Nation Associates.) New York, 1947.

REITZEL, W. *The Mediterranean, Its Role in America's Foreign Policy.* New York, 1948.

REVUSKY, ABRAHAM. *Jews in Palestine.* New York, 1935.

ROBINSON, JACOB. *Palestine and the United Nations.* Washington, D. C., 1947.

ROOSEVELT, KERMIT. *Partition of Palestine, A Lesson in Pressure Politics.* New York, 1948.

SCHWARZ, LEO W. *The Redeemers.* New York, 1953.

STONE, I. F. *Underground to Palestine.* New York, 1946.

SULZBERGER, CYRUS L. "German Preparations in the Middle East," *Foreign Affairs,* July, 1942.

Summary of Middle East Oil Developments. (Arabian-American Oil Company.) New York, 1947.

SYRKIN, MARIE. *Blessed is the Match.* New York, 1947.

TARTAKOWER, A. "Making of Jewish Statehood in Palestine," *Jewish Social Studies,* July, 1948.

TELLER, JUDD L. "What Did U. S. Recognition Really Mean?" *New Palestine,* June 11, 1948.

TREVOR, DAPHNE. *Under the White Paper.* Jerusalem, 1948.

TRUMAN, HARRY S. *Memoirs.* 2 vols. New York, 1955, 1956.

VAN PAASEN, PIERRE. *The Forgotten Ally.* New York, 1943.

VILNAY, Z. *Battles for the Liberation of Israel* (Hebrew). Jerusalem, 1949.

WATERS, M. P. *Haganah: Jewish Self-Defence in Palestine.* London, 1946.

WILSON, R. D. *Cordon and Search: With the 6th Airborne Division in Palestine.* Aldershot (England), 1949.

XXIII. A "SECONDARY RING" OF JEWISH COMMUNITIES

COHEN, J. X. *Jewish Life in South America.* New York, 1947.

HOTZ, LOUIS, and SARON, GUSTAV (edd.). *The Jews in South Africa.* London, 1956.

JOSEPH, SAMUEL. *History of the Baron de Hirsch Fund.* Philadelphia, 1935.

LIPMAN, V. D. *Social History of the Jews in England, 1850–1950.* London, 1954.

SACK, BENJAMIN. *History of the Jews in Canada.* 2 vols. Montreal, 1945.
SIGLER, BETTY. "Montreal: The Bonds of Community," *Commentary,* April, 1950.
ZANGWILL, ISRAEL. *Children of the Ghetto.* Philadelphia, 1938.

FOR FURTHER RESEARCH

ADLER, ELKAN. *London.* Philadelphia, 1930.
ALPERSOHN, MORDECAI. *Thirty Years in Argentina* (Yiddish). 2 vols. Berlin, 1923, 1928.
ANCHEL, R. *Les Juifs de France.* Paris, 1946.
BENTWICH, NORMAN. "Jewish Life in South Africa," *Jewish Social Studies,* January, 1942.
CATANE, MOSHE. *Les Juifs de France des Croisades à nos jours.* Paris, 1957.
COWEN, PHILIP. *Memories of an American Jew.* New York, 1932.
DEUTSCH, BABETTE. "André Spire," *Menorah Journal,* February, 1922.
ELBOGEN, I. *A Century of Jewish Life.* Philadelphia, 1944.
EMDEN, PAUL H. "Pioneers of South Africa," *Menorah Journal,* Spring, 1937.
EVANS-GORDON, W. *The Alien Immigration.* London, 1904.
HART, A. D. *The Jew in Canada.* Toronto, 1926.
HERRMAN, LOUIS. *A History of the Jews in South Africa.* London, 1930.
HERTZ, J. H. *The Jews in South Africa.* London, 1905.
LEVEN, NARCISSE. *Cinquante ans d'histoire: l'alliance israélite universelle.* 2 vols. Paris, 1911, 1920.
———. *Cinquente años de colonización Judia en la Argentina.* Buenos Aires, 1939.
LITVINOFF, BARNET. "Zangwill's Ghetto is No More," *Commentary,* October, 1950.
MANDEL, ARNOLD. "French Jewry in a Time of Decision," *Commentary,* December, 1954.
MONTAGU, LILY. "Liberal Judaism in Great Britain," *Hebrew Union College Quarterly,* Third Quarter, 1949.
ROSE, MILLICENT. *The East End of London.* London, 1951.
ROSENBERG, LOUIS. *Canada's Jews.* Montreal, 1939.
———. "Jewish Agriculture in Canada," *YIVO Annual of Jewish Social Science,* V, 1950.
———. "The Jews of Canada," *Jewish Review,* July-October, 1945.
ROTH, CECIL. *A History of the Jews in England.* Oxford, 1941.
SACHAR, A. L. *Sufferance Is the Badge.* New York, 1940.
SAPIR, BORIS. "Jews in Cuba," *Jewish Review,* April, 1946, January, 1947.
SPIRE, ANDRÉ. "The Jews in French Literature," *Menorah Journal,* April, 1924.
WEIL, SIMON. "Argentina." (*Universal Jewish Encyclopedia.* Vol. I.) New York, 1948.
WOLF, ARNOLD. *The Modern Jew.* London, 1899.
WOLF, LUCIEN. *Essays in Jewish History.* London, 1934.

XXIV. THE GROWTH OF THE AMERICAN-JEWISH COMMUNITY

AGUS, JACOB B. "Current Movements in the Religious Life of American Jewry." (*The Jewish People, Past and Present.* 4 vols. Vol. IV.) New York, 1955.
FRIEDMAN, THEODORE, and GORDIS, ROBERT (edd.). *Jewish Life in America.* New York, 1955.
GLAZER, NATHAN. "The Jewish Revival in America," *Commentary,* December, 1955, January, 1956.

JANOWSKY, OSCAR (ed.). *The American Jew.* New York, 1942.
KAPLAN, MORDECAI. *Judaism as a Civilization.* New York, 1934.
KARPF, MAURICE J. *Jewish Community Organization in the United States.* New York, 1938.
LEARSI, RUFUS. *The Jews in America: A History.* Cleveland, 1954.
LEWISOHN, LUDWIG. *Upstream.* New York, 1922.
MERSAND, JOSEPH. *Traditions in American Literature: A Study of Jewish Characters and Authors.* New York, 1939.
MORGENSTERN, JULIAN. *As a Mighty Stream: The Story of Reform Judaism.* Philadelphia, 1949.
RIBALOW, HAROLD U. (ed.). *This Land, These People.* New York, 1950.
SKLARE, MARSHALL. *Conservative Judaism.* Glencoe (Illinois), 1955.
WISE, STEPHEN. *Challenging Years.* New York, 1949.

FOR FURTHER RESEARCH

ADLER, CYRUS. *I Have Considered the Days.* Philadelphia, 1941.
———. *Jacob Henry Schiff.* New York, 1921.
BERKSON, ISAAC B. *Theories of Americanization.* New York, 1920.
BLAU, JOSEPH L. "The Spiritual Life of American Jewry, 1654–1954," *American Jewish Yearbook,* Vol. 56, 1955.
BOGEN, BORIS D. *Jewish Philanthropy.* New York, 1917.
CAHNMAN, WERNER J. "The Cultural Consciousness of Jewish Youth," *Jewish Social Studies,* July, 1952.
CAMPBELL, MONROE, JR., and WIRTZ, WILLIAM (edd.). *The First Fifty Years: A History of the National Council of Jewish Women, 1893–1943.* New York, 1943.
CHIPKIN, ISRAEL. *A Decade of Progress in Jewish Education, 1939–1949.* New York, 1949.
COHEN, ELLIOT E. (ed.). *Commentary on the American Scene.* New York, 1953.
COHEN, MORRIS R. *A Dreamer's Journey.* New York, 1949.
———. *Reflections of a Wondering Jew.* Boston, 1950.
DAVIS, MOSHE. *Jewish Religious Life and Institutions in America.* Tel Aviv, 1953.
———. *The Shaping of American Judaism: The Historical School of the Nineteenth Century.* New York, 1951.
DUSHKIN, ALEXANDER M. *Jewish Education in New York City.* New York, 1918.
EDIDEN, BEN. *Jewish Community Life in America.* New York, 1947.
FREEHOF, S. B. *Reform Jewish Practice.* 2 vols. Cincinnati, 1944, 1952.
FRIEDMAN, PHILIP. "Political and Social Movements and Organizations." (*The Jewish People, Past and Present.* 4 vols. Vol. IV.) New York, 1955.
GLAZER, NATHAN. "America's Ethnic Pattern," *Commentary,* April, 1953.
GOODMAN, PHILIP (ed.). *A Documentary Story of the Jewish Community Center.* New York, 1953.
GORDON, ALBERT I. *Jews in Transition.* Minneapolis, 1949.
HANDLIN, OSCAR. *Adventure in Freedom.* New York, 1954.
HERBERG, WILL. *Catholic, Protestant, Jew.* New York, 1956.
———. *Judaism and Modern Man.* New York, 1951.
———. "The 'Triple Melting Pot,'" *Commentary,* August, 1955.
HESCHEL, ABRAHAM. *God in Search of Man.* Philadelphia, 1951.
———. *Man Is Not Alone.* Philadelphia, 1951.
HINDUS, MILTON. "Ludwig Lewisohn," *Jewish Frontier,* May, 1956.
Jewish Landsmannschaften of New York (Yiddish). (Yiddish Writers' Group.) New York, 1938.

KALLEN, HORACE. *Of Them Which Say They Are Jews.* New York, 1954.

KAPLAN, MORDECAI. *The Future of the American Jew.* New York, 1948.

KATSCH, ABRAHAM I. *Hebrew in American Higher Education.* New York, 1941.

KAZIN, ALFRED. *A Walker in the City.* New York, 1951.

KRAFT, LOUIS. *A Century of the Jewish Community Center Movement.* New York, 1953.

LEVIN, MEYER. *In Search.* New York, 1950.

LEWISOHN, LUDWIG. *The American Jew.* New York, 1950.

———. *The Island Within.* New York, 1928.

LEWIN, KURT. "Self-Hatred Among Jews." (*Resolving Social Conflicts,* ed. Gertrude Weiss-Lewin.) New York, 1948.

LURIE, H. L. "Jewish Communal Life in the United States." (*The Jewish People, Past and Present.* 4 vols. Vol. IV.) New York, 1955.

MacIVER, ROBERT M. *Report on the Jewish Community Relations Agencies.* New York, 1951.

MONSKY, DAISY, and BISGYER, MAURICE. *Henry Monsky: The Man and His Work.* New York, 1947.

NIGER, SAMUEL. "Yiddish Culture." (*The Jewish People, Past and Present.* 4 vols. Vol. IV.) New York, 1955.

RAWIDOWICZ, SIMON (ed.). *The Chicago Pinkas.* New York, 1952.

REZNIKOFF, CHARLES (ed.). *Louis Marshall: Selected Papers and Addresses.* 2 vols. Philadelphia, 1957.

ROBACK, A. A. *The Story of Yiddish Literature.* New York, 1940.

SROLE, L., and WARNER, W. L. *The Social Systems of American Ethnic Groups.* New Haven, 1945.

TRACHTENBERG, JOSHUA. "American Jewish Scholarship." (*The Jewish People, Past and Present.* 4 vols. Vol. IV.) New York, 1955.

XXV. THE STATE OF ISRAEL

BARATZ, G., et al. *New Way of Life: The Collective Settlements of Israel.* London, 1949.

DAVIS, MOSHE (ed.). *Israel: Its Role in Civilization.* New York, 1956.

HALKIN, SIMON. *Modern Hebrew Literature.* New York, 1950.

HOROWITZ, DAVID. "The Economic Problems of Israel," *Middle Eastern Affairs,* November, 1956.

IZZEDIN, N. M. *The Arab World: Past, Present, and Future.* Chicago, 1953.

LEHRMAN, HAL. *Israel: The Beginning and Tomorrow.* New York, 1951.

LONDON, ISAAC. "Evolution of the U.S.S.R.'s Policy in the Middle East, 1950–1956," *Middle Eastern Affairs,* May, 1956.

MEYER, PETER, WEINRYB, BERNARD, DUSCHINSKY, E., and SYLVAIN, N. *The Jews in the Soviet Satellites.* Syracuse (New York), 1953.

RESNER, LAWRENCE. *Eternal Stranger: The Plight of the Modern Jew from Baghdad to Casablanca.* New York, 1951.

ROBINSON, NEHEMIAH. *The Arab Countries of the Near East and Their Jewish Communities.* New York, 1951.

SAMUEL, EDWIN. *Problems of Government in the State of Israel.* Jerusalem, 1956.

SCHWARZ, SOLOMON M. *The Jews in the Soviet Union.* Syracuse (New York), 1951.

TELLER, JUDD L. *The Jews, the Kremlin, and the Middle East.* Syracuse (New York), 1957.

WALLENROD, REUBEN. *The Literature of Modern Israel.* New York, 1956.

FOR FURTHER RESEARCH

"About the New Literature in Israel," *Youth and Nation*, May, 1950.

ALEXANDER, MARK. "Israel's Communists and Fellow-Travelers," *Commentary*, August, 1952.

BEN-GURION, D. *Rebirth and Destiny of Israel.* New York, 1954.

BORKENAU, FRANZ. "Was Malenkov Behind the Anti-Semitic Plot?" *Commentary*, May, 1953.

COHEN, ISRAEL. *Contemporary Jewry.* London, 1950.

DALLIN, DAVID J. "Soviet Policy in the Middle East," *Middle Eastern Affairs*, November, 1955.

"Documents: Sinai-Suez Issues," *Middle Eastern Affairs*, January, 1957.

DORON, P. H. "Irrigation Blueprint for Israel," *Israel and the Middle East*, June, 1950.

EBAN, ABBA. *Voice of Israel.* New York, 1957.

FEUER, LEWIS S. "The Quality of Life in Israel's Collectives," *Commentary*, May, 1950.

FRANK, WALDO. "Journey to Israel," *Jewish Frontier*, July, 1956.

GOITEN, E. DAVID. "The Worship of the Strong Man," *Jewish Horizon*, January, 1956.

GRUBER, RUTH. *Israel Without Tears.* New York, 1950.

HENRIQUES, R. *One Hundred Hours to Suez.* New York, 1957.

HOWARD, H. N. *United States Policy in the Near East, South Asia, and Africa.* Washington, D. C., 1954.

HOWARTH, HERBERT. "Israel's Modern Poetry," *Commentary*, August, 1950.

HUDSON, G. F. "America, Britain, and the Middle East," *Commentary*, June, 1956.

HUREWITZ, J. C. *Diplomacy in the Near and Middle East.* 2 vols. (Vol. II.) Princeton, 1956.

Israel Yearbook, 1950–57.

KHAN, MIZRA. "The Arab Refugees," *Midstream*, Spring, 1956.

KLINGER, R. *Art and Artists in Eretz Israel.* Tel Aviv, 1946.

LAQUEUR, W. Z. "Israel," *American Jewish Yearbook*, Vol. 57, 1956.

———. "The Moscow-Cairo Axis," *Commentary*, May, 1956.

LAWRENCE, E. V. *Egypt and the West.* New York, 1956.

LICHTENBAUM, J. *Our Authors* (Hebrew). Jerusalem, 1950.

LICHTHEIM, GEORGE. "Soviet Expansion into the Middle East," *Commentary*, November, 1955.

MEYER, PETER. "The Jewish Purge in the Satellite Countries," *Commentary*, September, 1952.

MOWSHOWITZ, ISRAEL. "Warsaw to Prague," *National Jewish Monthly*, September, 1956.

NASSER, GAMAL ABDEL. *Egypt's Liberation: The Philosophy of the Revolution.* Washington, D. C., 1955.

PARKES, JAMES. *End of an Exile: The Jews and the Gentile World.* New York, 1954.

PATAI, RAPHAEL. *Israel Between East and West.* Philadelphia, 1953.

PATAI, RAPHAEL, and WOHLMUTH, ZVI (edd.). *Palestinian Stories: A Prose Anthology From Forty Palestinian Authors* (Hebrew). Jerusalem, 1947.

RACKMAN, EMANUEL. *Israel's Emerging Constitution.* New York, 1955.

RAFAEL, Y. "Our Spiritual Positives," *Igeret Lagolah*, December, 1950.

RAYMIST, MALKAH. "How Thin the Border," *Jewish Horizon*, March, 1955.

SACHS, J. "Towards an Israeli Culture," *Jewish Chronicle*, Rosh Hashona Annual, 1954.

SAMUEL, MAURICE. *Level Sunlight.* New York, 1953.
SAMUELS, G. "Reading and Writing in Israel," *New York Times Book Review,* October 9, 1949.
SHAMIR, M. *He Walked Through the Fields* (Hebrew). Merhavia, 1947.
———. *The King of Flesh and Blood* (Hebrew). Merhavia, 1954.
SILBERNER, EDMUND. "Libraries in Israel," *Middle Eastern Affairs,* March, 1955.
SIMON, ERNST. "Are We Israelis Still Jews?" *Commentary,* April, 1953.
STOCK, ERNEST. "The New Climate in Israel," *Commentary,* May, 1954.
SWET, G. H. "Israel Philharmonic Orchestra," *Israel Life and Letters,* January, 1951.
TAYLOR, EDMUND. *The Real Case Against Nasser.* Washington, D. C., 1957.
TELLER, JUDD L. "Religious Modernism Stirs in Israel," *Commentary,* June, 1953.
———. "The Spartan Youth of Israel," *ibid.,* July, 1950.
"Themes in Modern Israeli Literature," *Leader,* Spring, 1950.
WEINER, HERBERT. "The Liberal Religious Impulse in Israel," *Commentary,* July, 1955.
WEISBERGER, R. M. "Religious Freedom in Israel—Fact and Fiction," *Reconstructionist,* June 24, 1949.
WHARTMAN, E. "What Israel is Reading," *Jewish Chronicle,* February 4, 1949.
What of Their Future? (American Jewish Committee.) New York, 1956.
WILSON, EDMUND. *Red, Black, Blond, and Olive.* New York, 1956.
ZANDER, WALTER. "Arab Nationalism and Israel," *Commentary,* July, 1956.

XXVI. THE GROWTH OF THE ISRAELI NATION

BELL, W. BOWYER. *The Long War: Israel and the Arabs since 1940.* Englewood Cliffs, N.J., 1969.
BEN-GURION, DAVID. *Israel: A Personal History.* New York, 1971.
DEUTSCHKRON, INGE. *Bonn and Jerusalem: The Strange Coalition.* Philadelphia, 1970.
EISENSTADT, S. N. *Israeli Society.* London, 1967.
ELON, AMOS. *The Israelis: Fathers and Sons.* New York, 1971.
HALEVI, NADAV, and KLINOV-MALUL, RUTH. *The Economic Development of Israel.* New York, 1968.
HAUSNER, GIDEON. *Justice in Jerusalem.* New York, 1966.
KIMCHE, DAVID, and BAVLY, DAN. *The Sandstorm.* London, 1968.
LANDAU, JACOB. *The Arabs in Israel.* London, 1969.
LAUFER, LEOPOLD. *Israel and the Developing Countries.* New York, 1967.
LUTTWAK, EDWARD, and HOROWITZ, DON. *The Israeli Army.* London, 1975.
PRITTIE, TERENCE. *Eshkol: The Man and the Nation.* New York, 1969.
SACHAR, HOWARD M. *A History of Israel.* New York, 1976.
SAFRAN, NADAV. *From War to War: The Arab-Israeli Confrontation, 1948–1967.* New York, 1969.
SEGRE, V. D. *Israel: A Society in Transition.* London, 1971.

FOR FURTHER RESEARCH

AKZIN, BENJAMIN, and DROR, YEHEZKAL. *Israel: High-Pressure Planning.* Syracuse, N.Y., 1966.
ANTONOVSKY, AARON, and ARIAN, ALAN. *Hopes and Fears of Israelis.* Jerusalem, 1972.
ARIAN, ALAN. *The Choosing People: Voting Behavior in Israel.* Cleveland, 1973.
AVI-HAI, AVRAHAM. *Ben-Gurion: State Builder.* New York, 1974.

BAR-ZOHAR, MICHAEL. *Embassies in Crisis: Diplomats and Demagogues Behind the Six-Day War.* Englewood Cliffs, N. J., 1970.

BRECHER, MICHAEL. *Decisions in Israel's Foreign Policy.* New Haven, Conn., 1974.

———. *The Foreign Policy System of Israel.* London, 1972.

CAIDEN, GERALD E. *Israel's Administrative Culture.* Berkeley, 1970.

CHURCHILL, WINSTON and RANDOLPH. *The Six Day War.* Boston, 1967.

CROSBIE, SYLVIA K. *A Tacit Alliance: France and Israel from Suez to the Six Day War.* Princeton, 1974.

CURTIS, MICHAEL, and CHERTOFF, MORDECAI S. (edd.). *Israel: Social Structure and Change.* New Brunswick, N.J., 1973.

DAN, URI. *De Gaulle contre Israël.* Paris, 1969.

———, and BEN-PORAT, Y. *The Secret War: The Spy Game in the Middle East.* New York, 1970.

DODD, C. H., and SALES, MARY (edd.). *Israel and the Arab World.* London, 1970.

EISENSTADT, S. N., BAR-YOSEF, RIVKA, and ADLER, CHAIM (edd.). *Integration and Development in Israel.* London, 1970.

ELIACHAR, E. *Israeli Jews and Palestinian Arabs.* Jerusalem, 1970.

FEINBERG, NATHAN. *The Arab-Israel Conflict in International Relations.* Jerusalem, 1970.

GILBERT, MARTIN. *The Arab-Israeli Conflict: Its History in Maps.* London, 1974.

HAREL, ISSER. *The House on Garibaldi Street.* Boston, 1975.

HARKABI, YEHOSHAFAT. *Arab Attitudes to Israel.* Jerusalem, 1972.

HENRIETTA SZOLD INSTITUTE. *Children and Families in Israel.* New York, 1970.

HOROWITZ, DAVID. *The Enigma of Economic Growth: A Case Study of Israel.* New York, 1970.

KLEINBERGER, AHARON F. *Society, Schools and Progress in Israel.* London, 1969.

KREININ, MORDECAI. *Israel and Africa.* New York, 1974.

LALL, ARTHUR. *The United Nations and the Middle East Crisis, 1967.* New York, 1968.

LAQUEUR, WALTER (ed.). *The Israel-Arab Reader.* New York, 1969.

MARSHALL, S. L. A. *Swift Sword.* New York, 1967.

MEDDING, PETER Y. *Mapai in Israel: Political Organization and Government in a New Society.* London, 1972.

PERES, SHIMON. *David's Sling.* New York, 1970.

PERLMUTTER, AMOS. "Assessing the Six-Day War," *Commentary,* L, Jan., 1970.

RABINOVICH, ABRAHAM. *The Battle for Jerusalem, June 5–7, 1967.* Philadelphia, 1972.

SACHAR, HOWARD M. *From the Ends of the Earth: The Peoples of Israel.* New York, 1970.

SANDERS, RONALD. *Israel: The View from Masada.* New York, 1966.

SEGEV, SHMUEL. *Israel, les arabes et les grandes puissances, 1967–1968.* Paris, 1968.

SPIEGEL, ERIKA. *New Towns in Israel: Urban and Regional Planning and Development.* New York, 1967.

TEVETH, SHABTAI. *The Tanks of Tammuz.* London, 1969.

WEINGROD, ALEX. *Israel: Group Relations in a New Society.* New York, 1965.

———. *Reluctant Pioneers.* Ithaca, N.Y., 1966.

YAARI, EHUD. *Strike Terror: The Story of Fatah.* New York, 1970.

XXVII. GREATER ISRAEL

BAVLY, DAN, and FARHI, DAVID. *Israel and the Palestinians.* London, 1970.

DAYAN, MOSHE. *My Life.* London, 1976.

ELIAV, ARIEH. *Land of the Hart.* Tel Aviv, 1972.
GITELSON, SUSAN A. "Africa's Rupture with Israel," *Midstream*, XX, Feb. 1974.
HEIKAL, MOHAMED. *The Road to Ramadan.* New York, 1975.
HERZOG, CHAIM. *The War of Atonement.* London, 1975.
KALB, MARVIN and BERNARD. *Kissinger.* New York, 1974.
KANOVSKY, ELIAHU. *The Economic Impact of the Six-Day War.* New York, 1970.
MEIR, GOLDA. *My Life.* London, 1976.
REMBA, ODED. "Israel and the Occupied Areas: Common Market in the Making," *New Middle East*, Nov. 1970.
SACHAR, HOWARD M. *A History of Israel.* New York, 1976.
SCHIFF, ZE'EV. *October Earthquake: Yom Kippur 1973.* Tel Aviv, 1974.
———, and ROTHSTEIN, RAPHAEL. *Fedayeen.* London, 1972.
TEVETH, SHABTAI. *The Cursed Blessing.* London, 1969.
WEIGERT, GIDEON. *Arabs and Israelis: Life Together.* Jerusalem, 1973.

FOR FURTHER RESEARCH

ABRAMOV, S. Z. "The Agranat Report and its Aftermath," *Midstream*, XX, June–July 1974.
ARON, RAYMOND. *De Gaulle, Israel, and the Jews.* New York, 1968.
AVINERI, SHLOMO. "The Palestinians and Israel," *Commentary*, L, June 1970.
BENVENISTI, MERON. "Reunion without Reconciliation: Jews and Arabs in Jerusalem," *New Middle East*, March 1973.
DAN, URI. *L'embargo.* Paris, 1970.
ECKMAN, LESTER S. *Soviet Policy Towards Jews and Israel, 1917–1974.* New York, 1974.
The Economy of the Occupied Territories (Bank of Israel.). Jerusalem, 1970.
Facts About the Administered Areas. (Israel. Information Center.) Jerusalem, 1975.
Four Years of Military Administration, 1967–71. (Israel. Ministry of Defense.) Tel Aviv, 1972.
GOTTHELF, YEHUDA (ed.). *Israel and the New Left.* Tel Aviv, 1969.
HARKABI, YEHOSHAFAT. *Fedayeen Action and Arab Strategy.* London, 1968.
HORELICK, ARNOLD L. "Soviet Involvement in the Midddle East and the Western Response," *Middle East Information Series*, June 1972.
The Impact of the October Middle East War. (United States. Congress: House Committee on Foreign Affairs.) Washington, D.C., 1973.
Insight on the Middle East War. (*Sunday Times* Correspondents.) London, 1974.
KIMCHE, JON. "The Riddle of Sadat," *Midstream*, XX, April 1974.
KOLLEK, TEDDY. "Undivided But Still Diverse: The Mosaic That Is Jerusalem," *New Middle East*, Jan.–Feb. 1973.
LAQUEUR, WALTER. *Confrontation: The Middle East War and World Politics.* London, 1974.
MEDZINI, MERON. "Israel and Africa—What Went Wrong?" *Midstream*, XX, Jan. 1974.
The October War. (*An-Nahar.* Arab Report.) Beirut, 1974.
OFRY, DAN. *The Yom Kippur War.* Tel Aviv, 1974.
PRYCE-JONES, DAVID. *The Face of Defeat: Palestinian Refugees and Guerrillas.* New York, 1972.
RABINOVICH, ITAMAR. "The Limitations of Power: Syria under al-Asad," *New Middle East*, March 1973.

REICH, BERNARD. *Israel and the Occupied Territories.* Washington, D.C., 1973.

REJWAN, NISSIM. "Palestinians under Israeli Occupation: The Search for Identity," *Midstream*, XVII, Feb. 1971.

RODINSON, MAXINE. *Israel: A Colonialist Settler State?* New York, 1974.

ROTH, STANLEY. *Middle East Balance of Power after the Yom Kippur War.* Cambridge, Mass., 1974.

SCHROETER, LEONARD. *The Last Exodus.* New York, 1974.

———. "The Status of East Jerusalem," *Midstream*, XVIII, Aug.–Sept. 1972.

SEGAL, RONALD. *Whose Jerusalem? The Conflicts of Israel.* London, 1973.

SHEEHAN, EDWARD R. F. "How Kissinger Did It: Step by Step in the Middle East," *Foreign Policy*, No. 22, Spring 1976.

TAHTINEN, DALE R. *The Arab-Israeli Military Balance since October, 1973.*

URI, PIERRE. "Israel and the European Economic Community: The Prospects for Integration," *Middle East Information Series*, Dec. 1972.

WHETTON, LAWRENCE L. "June 1967 to June 1971: Four Years of Canal War Reconsidered," *New Middle East*, June 1971.

INDEX

Index